W9-CZM-244

"This book is truly amazing! I've been involved in hockey all my life and I didn't realize all of the history behind it. A great read for all hockey fans and anyone wanting to learn more about a sport that speaks to people in all corners of the world."

—**KARYN BYE DIETZ,** 1998 Olympic Gold Medalist

"This book captures the sport of hockey from its beginnings throughout the world and how it has evolved into the great international sport that we have today. A must-read for anyone with a passion for hockey."

—**BILL CLEARY,** 1960 Olympic gold medalist

"Hardy and Holman have produced a classic world overview of our sport. It will unquestionably stand for years to come."

—**ROGER A. GODIN,** former executive director, United States Hockey Hall of Fame

"Founded on scholarly research and several years in the making, it should be on the bookshelf of every student of hockey. In four sections it tracks the origins of the sport from pre-1877 folk games to the beginnings of 'corporate hockey' in the 1970s. Based on themes such as 'convergence and divergence,' the two authors are to be congratulated for such an in-depth analysis of key moments in the story of hockey both in North America and internationally."

—**MARTIN C. HARRIS,** author of *The British Ice Hockey Hall of Fame*

"This study of hockey is an exhaustive history of the nearly 150-year trajectory of Canada's great contribution to the world. But it is more than that. Hardy and Holman provide a fascinating tour of hockey's development over time as it became a truly global sport. In the process, they take the reader to times and places as varied as the old Soviet Union, Finland, and Israel. *Hockey: A Global History* is full of insights on the politics, economics, and culture of this great game. It's a fascinating read for players, fans, experts, and novices alike."

—**JEFF FRIEDEN,** Harvard University

HOCKEY

SPORT AND SOCIETY

Series Editors
Aram Goudsouzian
Jaime Schultz

Founding Editors
Benjamin G. Rader
Randy Roberts

A list of books in the series appears at the end of this book.

OCKEY

A GLOBAL HISTORY

STEPHEN HARDY AND ANDREW C. HOLMAN

UNIVERSITY OF ILLINOIS PRESS
Urbana, Chicago, and Springfield

Manufactured in the United States of America
1 2 3 4 5 C P 5 4 3 2 1
♾ This book is printed on acid-free paper.

Library of Congress Cataloging-in-Publication Data
Names: Hardy, Stephen, 1948– author. | Holman, Andrew C. (Andrew Carl), 1965– author.
Title: Hockey : a global history / Stephen Hardy and Andrew C. Holman.
Description: [Champaign, Illinois] : UIP, [2018] | Series: Sport and society | Includes bibliographical references and index.
Identifiers: LCCN 2018025159| ISBN 9780252042201 (hardcover : alk. paper) | ISBN 9780252083976 (paperback : alk. paper)
Subjects: LCSH: Hockey—History.
Classification: LCC GV846.5 .H37 2018 | DDC 796.962—dc23
LC record available at https://lccn.loc.gov/2018025159

E-book ISBN 978-0-252-05094-7

CONTENTS

PART THREE: THE DIVERGING WORLD OF CANADA'S GAME, 1920–1971

PART FOUR: THE RISE OF CORPORATE HOCKEY, 1972–2010

ACKNOWLEDGMENTS

Our story owes much to the work of others, whose efforts the reader can find listed in the endnotes. We especially salute members of the Society for International Hockey Research. At the same time, we have been digging through our own choices of primary source material that others have not yet used. We trust that our synthesis will present a lively and interesting story. In the end, hockey is a game of joy as well as conflict and angst. And if nothing else, its history is filled with lively and interesting characters. We hope to bring some of them to life.

In the last two decades especially, a number of historians have combed through old newspapers, magazines, league records, memoirs, and scrapbooks; interviewed players, coaches, and administrators; walked along the banks of old ponds, canals, lakes—all carefully prying out material to use in reconstructing chapters of hockey's history. At the same time, a number of libraries, halls of fame, and museums have begun to build collections of materials organized and maintained for researchers like us. One of those places is the University of New Hampshire, where Director of Special Collections Bill Ross and his staff have helped build the Charles Holt Archives of American Hockey. Joe Bertagna, commissioner of Hockey East and executive director of the ACHA, donated several boxes of important materials, as did Dan Doyle, Bill Rothwell, Bill Cleary, Sean Pickett, Sid Watson, Jim Finke, Roger Godin, Tom Burke, Dave O'Connor, Lynn Burke, Steve Bamford and the Eastern College Athletic Conference, Kristin Markovich, and the Holt family. Cleary and Watson also provided interviews, now cataloged in a collection of oral history. Readers will see many notes citing the Holt Archives.

We benefited from many other collections, including: the Hockey Hall of Fame in Toronto, where Phil Pritchard, Craig Campbell and Jeff Davis opened their vaults of material; the Library of Congress, where Dave Kelly facilitated our research in old hockey guidebooks; St. Paul's School, where Matt Soule, Bill Matthews, and Dave Levesque and his fellow librarians helped us unravel a key case study; the 1932 and 1980 Lake Placid Winter Olympics Museum, where Liz DeFazio and Steve Vasser helped us find important hockey materials; the US Hockey Hall of Fame, where Tom Sersha kindly opened his archives; USA Hockey, where Dave Ogrean, Art Berglund, Lou Vairo, Dave Fischer, and Kim Folsom provided endless resources and hospitality; the Minnesota Historical Society, where Steve Nielsen helped us with several small but important collections; and the Dartmouth Heritage Museum, whose Collections Assistant Shannon Baxter gave us timely and skilled help in securing two Starr skate advertisements. We also traveled to and benefited greatly from the Library and Archives of Canada, the Bibliothèque et archives nationales du Québec, Archives of Ontario, and other regional repositories in Canada, where the richness of the history of "Canada's Game" is treasured and well preserved.

Many other people provided information, images, and support. These include: Tom Burke; Tom and Rosalie Brown, who provided important material on the lives of George V. and Walter A. Brown—one of the great father-son manager duos in the history of sport; Rich Johnson at the Sports Museum of New England, whose knowledge is challenged only by his generosity; the late Jack Grinold at Northeastern University, a friend for decades, who provided documents and a detailed walking tour of Matthews Arena—originally the Boston Arena (1910); Aaron Schmidt at the Boston Public Library; Jeff Mifflin at the MIT Archives; Patty Perez at the Lake Placid Public Library; Colin Howell and John Reid at St. Mary's University in Halifax; and Wayne Wilson at the LA Amateur Sports Foundation. Grant Jarvie and Wray Vamplew generously provided material on shinty and hurley, as did Michael Talbot and Martin Harris on British and European actors and events, Paul DeLoca on early skating rinks, Bill Fitsell on early hockey, Paul Patskou on hockey broadcasts, Mark Mowers on European hockey, Andrew Ross on Clarence Campbell, John Cross on Bowdoin College, and Tobias Stark on international coaching symposiums. Stark and Jyri Backman each shared some of their important unpublished work on Swedish and Finnish hockey. Roger Godin at the Minnesota Wild led a tour of rinks in the Twin Cities area and gave us copies of his important writing. Eddie Doyle found an obscure 1917 article on Hobey Baker and SPS. Walter Bush Jr. and Ken Johannson shared their personal histories in long telephone interviews, set up by Dave Ogrean. Wayne Burton, president of North Shore Community College, provided space for an important early planning meeting. Jillian Hartley gave us copies of material from the scrapbook of her grandfather, Dr. Charles G. Hartley. Bruce Kidd and Phyllis Berck of Toronto hosted the visit to the Hall of Fame in 1991 that kick-started this book.

At the University of New Hampshire, Laura Prisco, Jill Bevan, Ellen Weinberg, Samantha Holmes, Carrie Jokiel, Colleen Coyne, Kim Deane, and Mike Ayers did excellent research on a number of topics. Samantha Holmes provided copies of her correspondence promoting Olympic hockey for women. Dean Jim McCarthy provided timely and generous support at a crucial point in the research and writing, as did the Office of the Provost. Students in the UNH seminar "Coolest Game: Hockey and History" uncovered numerous primary sources that found their way into the book. Our thanks go to Bridgewater State University's Department of History (and especially its chair, Dr. Keith Lewinstein) for the supplementary funding it provided to help us acquire many of the book's images.

Many people listened patiently to our ideas, reviewed earlier chapter drafts, and/or gave us important feedback. These include: Joe Bertagna, Bill Cleary, Hart Cantelon, Iri Cermak, Dan Doyle, Bill Fitsell, Roger Godin, Rick Gruneau, Chris Hardy, Erl Hardy, Samantha Holmes, Colin Howell, D. J. Keating, Brian Kennedy, Jeff Klein, Chuck Korr, Daryl Leeworthy, Don Morrow, Mark Mowers, Dave Ogrean, Andrew Ross, Ed Saunders, Howard Shubert, John Soares, Mike Souza, Julie Stevens, Szymon Szemberg, Tobias Stark, Dick Umile, Michel Vigneault, Sean Withington, and John Wong. Drake McFeely and Ben Hardy read many of the chapters and gave us both encouragement and sage advice from their long experience as editors. Our colleagues in the History departments at UNH and Bridgewater State University have provided both inspiration and important feedback, as did our editors at the University of Illinois Press: Danny Nasset, Tad Ringo, and Julie Gay. They and the Press's anonymous reviewers all did their best to spare us from egregious errors. We hope we have held up our end of the bargain.

More than anyone, we thank our spouses/partners/best friends Donna Hardy and Andrea Doty. For too many years we have told them we expected to "finish the book by June." They have indulged us with support and love. We dedicate this book to them.

PART ONE

EARLY GAMES TO 1877

1

Searching for Hockey's History

In June 1998, Canadian writer Dave Bidini committed a cardinal sin. He abandoned *Hockey Night in Canada*'s Stanley Cup–final match between the Washington Capitals and the Detroit Red Wings. He was bored by the game's pace, bogged down by the latest team tactic—the "neutral-zone trap." He didn't know who was winning and he didn't care. He grabbed the remote control and clicked away until he found something more interesting. Martha Stewart baking cookies. After coming to his senses, he embarked on a journey to travel the world and rediscover hockey "as it was before it became complicated by economics, corporate lust, the ravages of progress; before the pro game had betrayed tradition for quick-buck teams and a style that relied more on chalkboard patterns than spontaneous, tongue-wagging, river play." The way it was "once played" in Canada: "a game of passion, of the people."[1]

Bidini's angst, if not his long journey, conveyed romantic attitudes common to most sports fans. There is a sense of something better somewhere. Bidini found his redemption in hockey's developing world: in China, Transylvania, and the United Arab Emirates. Most fans find it in history, where the game seems always purer. But there is a flaw in this logic, as this book will attempt to reveal. There was no golden age of hockey or of any other sport. For centuries, hockey has reinvented itself in countless ways, in countless places, shaped and sculpted by countless players, promoters, coaches, and fans. Since the most popular modern version arose in Montreal between 1875 and 1886, every hockey generation has endured Bidini's disenchantment.

But joy can displace despair. Bidini's fellow Canadian, Don Bell, found it in the 1980s, just eight hours north of Montreal, in the little town of Métabetchouan. "Sunday," he wrote, "would be boring in this tranquil Lac St-Jean community," if it weren't for the *SS Norfruit de Métabetchouan*, the junior team, "the fabulous young minstrels in the Pittsburgh Penguin colors." Two thousand locals crammed into space for only a thousand in the town's little rink, *Le centre sportif*, to see their heroes take on rivals like *les Marquis de Jonquière*. Bell described the scene: "Here they come now, charging on the ice, ready to fight to the last drop of blood and die in the rink for the honor of the team." For most fans, it was the week's highlight. "It's a sickness," said one, "worse than somebody with alcohol disease."[2]

Even the staid old National Hockey League, Bidini's punching bag, enjoyed a millennial resurrection in Minnesota, a state the league abandoned years before for greener pastures in Texas. The Minnesota Wild—the Gopher State's latest professional incarnation—seemed to have the best of all worlds in May 2003. Enlightened owners, a competitive team, a new arena, and America's No. 1 hockey market. As *Sports Illustrated* reported, hardcore fans began to queue in the early morning rain shortly after the Wild had won their second-round playoff series against Vancouver. A block of forty-five hundred tickets for the Western Conference championship series would go on sale twelve hours later. Kathy Spina and Susan Bakula were among the first hundred in line. "This is a cult," admitted Bakula. Spina, ironically a mental-health therapist, invoked an image of Jonestown: "We've drunk the Kool-Aid, symbolically." In truth, she went on, most people were swigging beer or Bloody Marys. Soon the Wild marketers wisely opened the doors to the Xcel Energy Center, where the faithful congregated in the lobby, communing with free hot dogs, soft drinks, or their own elixirs. Forty-five hundred tickets sold out in five minutes. Minnesota fans knew their hockey. Forty percent of season-ticket holders also played the game, not surprising in a state that supported 188 high school teams, sold out both the girls' and the boys' tournaments, and enjoyed a state university program that regularly won NCAA championships with a largely homegrown roster that consistently packed American Olympic teams, most notably during the 1980 "Miracle on Ice."[3]

Cultures and Nations

Minnesota hockey, like hockey in general, runs the gamut of experiences—from the backyard rinks that moms and dads scrape and flood nightly, to the lavish Xcel Energy Center, with its twelve broadcast booths, its Iron Range Grill on the main concourse, stocked with forty television sets to quench the thirst for highlights, and its home-team locker room that includes a sauna and a steam bath. As Bidini himself discovered, hockey is alive and well around the world. Europe in particular embraces a host of national professional leagues. While they do not get the broad media coverage of their world football counterparts, their fans are equally avid. As with other sports, today's hockey-lover can find depth of coverage on the internet, which was unthinkable only twenty-five years ago.

All hockey games and venues share some common elements, so lyrically captured by Bidini and a host of other writers. These include the sense of speed and power produced by humans on razor-sharp skates; the hand-eye coordination needed for stick handling, passing, and shooting; and the high levels of aggression and collision. No sport combines speed, skill, and violence quite like hockey does. Whether in fancy new arenas or backyard rinks, in fundamental ways the game is the same. NHL players have recently babbled like schoolboys when given the chance to play in the Winter Classic, a relatively new annual special event held on an outdoor professional football or baseball venue. Blistering cold and blizzard-like snow only increase the sense of return to frozen ponds of youthful memory.

At the same time, the sport dubbed the "Coolest Game" differs in rules, in levels of bureaucracy and commercialism, and in symbolism. American Karyn Bye may find the same joy in a pick-up game as she did competing for the gold-medal Olympic team in 1998. But training regimens and off-ice bureaucracies clearly recast the "big-time" experience. This book traces the history of convergence and divergence of a range of hockeys, via stories of people, organizations, events, venues, equipment, coaching strategies, marketing schemes, and political campaigns, to name just a few topics.

There is an abundance of literature on this sport, but most of it comes from Canada and revolves around professional stars and events, in particular the National Hockey League. This is understandable. Canada is the birthplace of the game, as we know it today. The NHL and the Stanley Cup are Canada's gifts to fans around the world. For young and old, from Vancouver to Halifax, in French or English, for players and spectators, hockey has long been a central component of being Canadian. But there are limits to the reality of this ownership. As Richard Gruneau and Dave Whitson explained in *Hockey Night in Canada*, "there is something to be said for the argument that hockey draws on and dramatizes the Canadian experience . . . the problem arises when Canadians' appreciation for hockey is mistaken for 'nature' rather than something that is socially and culturally produced."[4]

Part of this production is a belief that commercial interests, especially American ones, have tainted hockey's original "pureness." This sentiment has typically exploded among Canadians during periods of NHL expansion into the United States. The mother of all such eruptions occurred in August 1988. Wayne Gretzky's trade from Edmonton to Los Angeles tweaked Canada's ulna nerve, prompting popular and scholarly writers to whelp relentlessly with critical prose, lamenting and analyzing a deepening crisis, for hockey and for Canadian identity. The Maple Leaf was dripping dry—its sweet hockey sap diverted south. In the Canadian mind, American colleges, minor leagues, and NHL franchises had leveraged their stronger currency to lure talent. Gretzky's loss was symbolic of a larger threat: the "Americanization" of Canada. Gretzky's father, Walter, offered *Newsweek* a summary of the nation's indignation: "He's a Canadian institution and what's Canadian should remain Canadian. . . . You Americans think you can buy anything we have."[5]

These feelings are surely genuine. But as we hope to convey, they offer but one take on the story. Hockey's past is much more complex. Similar games aroused deep passion among some Americans, long before the NHL moved south in the 1920s. This was true for schoolboys at St. Paul's School in Concord, New Hampshire, more than 120 years ago. It was true in Michigan's Upper Peninsula, when the first openly professional players glided, slapped, and hacked their way to frozen legend in the early 1900s. It was also true across a wide swath of Europe. At the same time, hockey has continually struggled to find space on the world's sports calendar, despite the eternal optimism of entrepreneurs and boosters. While America's 1980 Olympic victory over the USSR ranks among the most important "national" victories of the twentieth century, it did not threaten baseball, football, or basketball as America's favorite sports. Across Europe, hockey is typically second fiddle to world football in terms of popular passion. And so, outside of Canada, the game has largely been a sport of subcultures, of hotbeds, and of mavericks vying for space, for air time, for a piece of a budget, for a little respect. But it has steadily grown, in many ways independent of Canadian interests.

This book presents a broader story of diffusion and development at amateur, school, college, and professional levels around the world. If Canadians felt threatened by American capitalism, they largely ignored Europe, except as an exotic alternative for positions as coaches and players. That view changed only momentarily when European teams defeated Canada in World or Olympic competition, in 1936, 1954, and 1956. Even Soviet domination beginning in 1963 did not drastically disrupt Canadian identity. After all, Canada's best players were barred from competition by quaint amateur rules that seemed to wink at a Soviet sports system that supported year-round training for its "amateurs." This changed for good in 1972, when the Soviets took Canada's measure in the Summit Series—Paul Henderson notwithstanding. The Maple Leaf was now forced to look east as well as south. Ten years later, Ken Dryden admitted what many had denied: "It is our fundamental dilemma. A game we treat as ours isn't ours. It is part of our national heritage, and pride, part of us; but we can't control it."[6]

Like America, Europe and the wider world have a history on ice. We offer glimpses of hockey's development in the Soviet Union, Sweden, England, China, Australia, Czechoslovakia, Switzerland, Germany, Finland, Israel, and other countries. In some places, it became a national sport. In others it did not. We don't claim the definitive answers as to why or why not. But we begin to tell the stories. We recognize that this book is limited by our inability to interrogate most hockey-playing cultures (particularly Russian, Swedish, Finnish, and Czech) in their own languages. As a result, North American bias constrains our work. Nonetheless, we try to move hockey history beyond the limits of one national bias, and we eagerly await responses from researchers throughout hockey's wide world.

We also examine several hockey-like alternatives that thrived one hundred years ago in North America and Europe, and which still exist today. These include bandy and polo (roller hockey), which preceded "Montreal" hockey in parts of Canada, America, and Europe. As *New York Times* hockey writer Jeff Klein wrote in 2005, bandy and polo are hardly extinct: "Bandy is a thriving sport in Sweden, Finland and Russia, drawing thousands of people to stadiums in minus-20-degree cold. Roller polo (or "roller hockey," or "hockey sobre patines") is the No. 3 game in many Iberian countries, and counts among its clubs no less a world sporting power than FC Barcelona."[7]

Themes on the Rise of Organized Sports

The history of bandy, polo, hockey, or any sport should include the analysis of two broad processes: production and distribution, and consumption and cultural significance. These are obviously interrelated; there is never one without the other. At its core, any sport is a performance, involving an array of athletes, coaches, officials, promoters, media, sponsors, and fans who merge at events where they simultaneously produce and consume an experience that is both tangible (in programs, equipment, scoreboards, playing surface, stands) and intangible (in atmosphere and memories). As one authority suggested thirty years ago, every contest, every season, and every era should be considered "not primarily as productions put on *for* spectators, but as ceremonies accomplished *with* them." This process is repeated at every event, at every level, from the simplest game of shinny on a frozen pond to the final game for the Stanley Cup or for Olympic gold. This vast arcade of experience is shared through conversation or media presentation, but it is shaped to individual and collective needs by the mysteries of human perception and memory. The pull of these images led Dave Bidini on his pilgrimage to find the game he loved.[8]

Our book traces the development of hockey over the past two hundred years, from an unorganized pastime to a commercial spectacle governed by transnational and international bureaucracies like the NHL and the International Ice Hockey Federation. This history in many ways parallels those of football and baseball. Each of these sports entered the nineteenth century without a dominant set of rules or a governing body. Villages, towns, and tribes around the world had for centuries played games that involved kicking, throwing, or hitting a ball with a stick—toward or through some form of goal. Many contests had ceremonial qualities and were tied to certain holidays. As early as 1500 BCE, Mesoamericans played a form of football that represented battles of good versus evil and life versus death. There is evidence of human sacrifice tied to the outcomes. Shrove Tuesday football matches were popular in some English villages, where one parish might compete against another, or bachelors might take on married men. While human sacrifice was not part of the mix, injury and occasional death were. The rules varied from place to place and even from year to year, dependent on oral tradition and misty memory. In America's early republic, different versions of base ball and town ball were popular in Boston, New York, and Philadelphia. Players from different areas might recognize the broad contours of the game: pitching, hitting, and running bases. But the field's configuration and the specific rules varied. The years from 1840 to 1880 brought a whole new ballgame to supremacy.[9]

In some cases, historians have established a moment in time when one form of a folk game emerged to become the dominant form, eventually sweeping alternatives to history's dustbin. In the decade before America's Civil War, the New York version of baseball began to spread in popularity, boosted by missionaries, team tours, and the reach of Gotham's magazines and newspapers. Football also spun off in several national directions during the nineteenth century. Australians fashioned their own game in 1859. Four years later, a collection of London-area clubs formed the Football Association and agreed to rules limiting the use of hands. Others who preferred more "manly" conventions like running with the ball, tackling and "hacking" (in other words, kicking) the runner, soon split off to organize the Rugby Football Union. Within decades, America and Canada had their own football rules. Each of these codes quickly became national in scope, but only the Football Association would enjoy the world's embrace. We will describe a similar process in hockey's past—from local pastime to national and international sport.[10]

Scholars have examined, among other sports, the international diffusion of British football and cricket and two American brands, the National Basketball Association and the National Football League. Across centuries, the process includes a similar cast of characters: missionaries who introduced the game; athletes, coaches, and fans who grabbed hold of a novel activity; promoters and their media partners who saw a chance for mutual profit. In all of these cases, there were clear links between the scope of a country's economic empire and the spread of its national sports brands. If soccer and cricket were carried abroad on British merchant ships, the NHL and the NBA benefited from television and the internet. For empire builders (and critics), there have been few better symbols of cultural influence than the champion athlete, whether that be the British cricketer W. G. Grace or the American hoopster Michael Jordan.[11]

This process of standardizing and circulating particular codes of sport depended on fundamental changes in communication. In one of those wonderful books that many cite but few actually read, Benedict Anderson theorized about the connections between the rise of a capitalistic printing industry, the attenuation of old religious and dynastic regimes, and the development of new "imagined communities" of nation-states. Anderson's central argument was that fifteenth-century developments in printing set up a nineteenth-century "lexographic revolution": a "golden age of vernacularizing lexicographers, grammarians, philologists, and litterateurs." This golden age of the vernacular included the development of monolingual and bilingual dictionaries (think Noah Webster and his American dictionary), new schools and universities teaching in the vernacular (rather than in Latin), music scores, literature, and other modes of language that were the fabric of nationalism. In Anderson's words, this lexographic revolution nurtured the power of language to be "the personal property of quite specific groups—their daily speakers and readers." Equally important, "these groups, imagined as communities, were entitled to their autonomous place in a fraternity of equals." Notions of being French, German, Swedish, American, or British date to this period.[12]

Among the lexographic specialists were people like Joseph Strutt, whose 1801 epic, *The Sports and Pastimes of the People of England*, attempted to catalog folk and children's games in ways that would also define what it meant to be English. Strutt's work was mimicked by others, including William Clarke, whose *Boy's Own Book* was reprinted almost annually after its first British (1828) and American (1829) publications. Their entries on various activities offered a synopsis of historical development and a general description of rules and playing styles. All were rather vague and (according to many later critics) often inaccurate. As the nineteenth century progressed, such manuals both reflected and nudged the process whereby a number of old folk games like football and hockey were recast into specific rules that served the interest of particular communities with access to printing and distribution. One such group lived in Montreal and enjoyed skating at the Victoria Rink. By 1900, baseball, football (in several national versions), basketball, hockey, and other sports circulated in very detailed rulebooks, written and endorsed by young governing bodies like the Amateur Hockey Association of Canada, and published for sale by international sporting-goods manufacturers like A. G. Spalding & Bros. In this way, Anderson's lexographic revolution was at the heart of Canada's hockey identity.[13]

Diffusion was a global process with a much longer, wider, and more complex history. Ancient sources such as Herodotus describe interactions and clashes of language, law, religion, and custom as empires rubbed into one another. Imperial success—Roman or Chinese, for example—sometimes meant widespread convergence toward uniformity in language, food, dress, and even sports. The age of European discovery and empire-building replicated this process.[14] But if countries and cultures have occasionally embraced or adopted the games of another country, they have just as often adapted and refashioned them to meet their own needs and desires. As one scholar argued, sports have frequently been contests where "the initially dominated have turned the tables on their erstwhile dominators." There are two aspects to this. One involves adapting styles of play, coaching, and administration. Even the casual fan of world football recognizes the *notion* of differences between "British," "Dutch," "Italian," and "Brazilian" versions of the game. Of more symbolic importance is the underdog's international victory—the act of "beating them at their own game." American basketball fans of middle age will never forget the Soviet basketball victory at the 1972 Olympics. Regardless of the controversy over the final few seconds of play—the disputed "extra time" given to the Soviets—it was America's first Olympic loss in "their game." It still stings American pride. But that Soviet victory probably boosted basketball enthusiasm in Yugoslavia, China, and other countries that have since become breeding grounds for NBA stars. This is precisely what Ken Dryden pondered when he wrote that the "game we treat as ours isn't ours." And, as we discuss, the issues of adaptation and control existed on dimensions beyond nationhood, particularly along lines of class, gender, and race.[15]

While crude, unorganized games on ice have existed for centuries among peoples in cold-weather climates, the fundamental innovation occurred in Montreal in the late 1870s and early 1880s. Over the next half-century in North America, this form of hockey slowly became THE form of hockey worth investing time, status, money, even whole careers, for men and women. During the twentieth century, the same process unfolded throughout Bidini's far-flung tropic of hockey. As Gruneau and Whitson argued, the process was not "natural" or "inevitable." Hockey grew in particular ways, through the efforts and struggles of entrepreneurs, reformers, bureaucrats, players, reporters, and everyday fans, who clashed over rules, technologies, representations, and meanings. Cold winters were no insurance or even a prerequisite. Sweden became a hockey power. Why not Norway? And artificial ice was no guarantee when that innovation took off at the turn of the last century. St. Louis and Baltimore enjoyed indoor arenas with the new technology before Toronto or Montreal. But brief exhibitions of the new game were not sustained in the former cities. Chicago and Detroit supported professional hockey as early as Boston and Minneapolis did; they also endured cold winters. But neither metropolis became a hotbed for the high school and college game at anything like the level of Boston or Minneapolis/St. Paul (and Minnesota generally).

Four Periods

Hockey's history may be divided into four periods during which various elements and forms of the game (we might say its culture and structure) converged, diverged, and then re-converged. Current shifts happened in rules, governance, and tactics, among other things. Part 1 of this book examines the folk versions of hockey that existed in Europe and North America until the emergence of the "Montreal" game in the last half of the 1870s. Part 2 describes the next four decades, during which the Montreal version gradually became the dominant form in North America, so that when players, writers, and fans used the term "hockey," they typically meant the Montreal game. We end this period in 1920, by which time Canadian entrepreneurs had established the National Hockey Association (1910), which later became the NHL (1917). A decade earlier, representatives from four European countries founded the Ligue International de Hockey sur Glace (1908), which grew into the International Ice Hockey Federation (1954). While the LIHG's founding did not yet reflect a broad victory for Montreal hockey in Europe (bandy was still more popular in many countries), it did provide impetus for conversion. International federations meant international recognition and glory—ultimately Olympic glory in 1920, when the Games at Antwerp included for the first time a team competition on ice, played under Canadian rules. It was a key moment.[16]

In many ways, the NHA and the LIHG secured the dominance of the Montreal game. But as we noted above, dominance did not mean lockstep uniformity. Even within the broad framework of THE game, there was room and opportunity for alternative and competing visions. We address these in part 3, covering the next six decades, which we call the "Diverging World of Canada's Game." The period from 1920 to 1972 saw a centrifugal pattern of development. Canada might be the center of the hockey universe, and the term "hockey" might more universally conjure images of pucks and broad-bladed sticks, boards, and blue lines. But within this standard framework were rules diverging on significant lines, with different patterns of play and different meanings across and within nations and continents. This process was akin to the splintering of a religion. The founding creed was subject to interpretation and attempts to find or retain the "true" path. In hockey's case, one sees clear cleaving among a few core denominations: professional leagues in North America; American schools and colleges; and international-amateur groups. The NHL may have secured the Chalice of the founders (the Stanley Cup), but other groups believed that they were equal guardians of the true faith. This was seen in multiple sets of playing rules, protective eligibility regulations, and bitter controversies. All of these sources are to some degree like interpretations of sacred text. If the game itself went global, its practice was divided among fiefdoms. This was, in short, a period of distinct divergence and brand building.

We title our final section the "Rise of Corporate Hockey," a centripetal period when the NHL's version of the game became more dominant worldwide. The year 1972 is a break point because, among other reasons, it was the year of the monumental series between Team Canada and the Soviet National Team. Canada won the series, but many analysts (including Team Canada's Ken Dryden) felt it had lost ownership of the game. Hockey would be forever changed by the Soviets' convincing demonstration of tactical genius and their disciplined, flowing game of puck control. When a crew of young American collegians skated to a miracle in the 1980 Olympics, they did so with their sense of Soviet training and tactics. The "Miracle on Ice" also cast a bright light on the American college game, stripped as it seemed to be of the mindless violence and the crassness of the NHL, or the obvious "shamateurism" of the Soviet program.

In fact, by the 1980s, both the American collegiate and the Soviet international brands were cracking apart and yielding to the NHL brand. This could be seen in rules changes, coaching tactics, and officiating that tolerated or encouraged greater levels of violence. It could be seen in heightened levels of commercialism and bigger arenas. It could be seen in league structure. And most tellingly, it could be seen in the slowly building stream of Swedish, Finnish, and Czech players leaving their national teams to play in the NHL; in the growth of minor leagues in the American midwest and south; and most visibly in the 1989 move of the NHL headquarters from Montreal to New York City. International television broadcasts of new "summit" competitions like the Canada Cup focused increased attention on the NHL and its highly paid stars. In 1967, Canadian players made up 98 percent of NHL rosters; by 2001 the number had shrunk to 53 percent. The first round of the 2004 NHL draft highlighted the centripetal pull. Fourteen players came from the traditional feeder, Canadian juniors. Three, including the top two picks, came from Russia; five from the Czech Republic and Slovakia; three from Finland; three from NCAA programs, and two from American prep schools. It was the era of "open" hockey, and the opening resulted in a convergence of the game back toward a single vision, style, and code. The following year, when the NHL locked out its players, many flew east to Europe, where leagues welcomed the NHL's cachet. As Pavel Barta, a Czech league official, told the *Boston Globe*, the big bonus was the return of Czech players from the NHL: "The fans will finally see the big names they otherwise see only on television." Meanwhile, Russian oligarchs refashioned their teams and league in the image of the NHL—only they added National Football League–style cheerleaders.[17]

These are the broad lines of our argument: innovation, standardization, divergence, and convergence. We also consider some themes that cross all four periods, including the effects of technological innovation (for example, rinks and equipment); the battles for power among competing governing bodies, including fights for control of communications, marketing, and branding, and conflicts over the truth about amateurism; the struggle among coaches, players, fans, and promoters to balance hockey's central elements of speed, skill, and violence; tensions at all levels between what can be crudely called capital and labor; and, finally, hockey's wider cultural and social connections to structures of class, race, and gender.

We hope to convey the exhilaration and sense of freedom that have driven hockey's development for 150 years. But that same grace has not been universally available. Hockey may provide physical freedom, but not social freedom. It has long been a white man's game. Native, black, and female enthusiasts have had to venture into hostile territory. For instance, Dave Bidini found the spirit of hockey in the United Arab Emirates. Not long afterward, Samantha Holmes had a different experience in Saudi Arabia. Holmes grew up in Mississauga, Ontario, helped the University of New Hampshire win the first women's collegiate US national championship in 1998, and trained with the Canadian National Team. In 2001 she was in Saudi Arabia visiting her mother. Like any rink rat, she couldn't resist the lure of indoor ice. As she recalled, "I tried to skate with all these Canadian guys over in Saudi, I had to dress up like a man and I still got busted. I had to leave the rink (which was in a small strip mall) and I was only allowed to watch from outside through glass windows. The 'matawa' (like the Taliban but not as severe) was sent in to sit in front of me and watch to make sure I didn't commit another 'sin.' It would have been cool to skate over there but not in return for losing a hand or imprisonment." The story says as much about hockey's long history as it does about contemporary Saudi culture. The ice has never been completely open.[18]

Our book does not claim to be a comprehensive account of hockey's total history. We make no effort to cover every big game or every big star. There are plenty of excellent books filled with those topics. Instead, we offer more detailed glimpses of exemplary case studies. Old hockey hands will find some of it standard fare: the creative force of the Patrick brothers and the Pacific Coast Hockey Association; Anatoli Tarasov and the rise of the Soviet machine; Boston's collegiate Beanpot Tournament. But we also open windows on lesser-known episodes such as polo in the 1880s, the "big-bang" year of 1895–96, the inherent corruption of amateurism, the power struggle at the 1948 Winter Olympics, the international influence of an Irish-born travel agent named John "Bunny" Ahearne, and the rise, fall, and resurrection of organized hockey for girls and women over the last century. We hope our book is worthy of its fascinating subject.

2

Folk and Field Games

Foster Hewitt, the young and already-prominent voice of *Hockey Night in Canada*, opened his 1934 memoir/history with a whimsical comment: "Games, like family trees, have origins that lose themselves in the mists of ages." He might have added that families feud over origins—and none more so than Canadians over hockey. Seven years after Hewitt's remark, the *Montreal Gazette* published a set of stories about an eighty-four-year-old resident named John Knox, who claimed that his father had played in Canada's first "ice-hurling" or "hockey" match, in 1837 in Montreal. The old-timer spun a vivid tale based on a hundred-page manuscript. He offered, among other "facts," that a local wood-turner had made the "first stick" and the first goal poles, which had iron tips at their base and red flags at their tops. The rules called for eight men per side, three goals to win, with game time limits, such as two hours. Within two months, Knox insisted, teams had "sprung up all over Montreal." Challenge matches between neighborhoods were played at a "rink" near the intersection of Bleury and Dorchester Streets. The contests prompted chaotic intrusions by crowds of fans, and widespread interest "in every home and schoolyard." Knox's manuscript even recorded the times of important goals. Conveniently, one of the early championship teams was a group of Francophones who called themselves the "Canadians" [*sic*].[1]

The story was a frieze of fraud and fantasy. The seams of the hoax unravel when the reader notes the casual reference to a rubber puck (not invented for decades) and the description of a distinct line-up, complete with set positions like "point," "cover point," "goal," and "rover." There are no contemporary accounts, anywhere, of any hockey-like game in North

America that employed such precise notions of position. In most sports (and certainly in hockey) these developments came decades later. There may have been games like hockey played on Montreal ice in 1837, but they weren't on rinks as we know them, and they would have been rather disorganized shinny-like contests. Sadly, journalists—and even some historians—were and still are quick to jump on a good story, even if it bears no resemblance to historical reality.[2]

Battles over Birthplaces

This 1941 Montreal claim appeared during an increasingly heated debate about hockey's birthplace. Ontario powers, led by Capt. James Sutherland, longtime mogul in the Canadian Amateur Hockey Association, had claimed for years that Kingston was the sport's true home. Nova Scotians scoffed at this notion, and for good reason, since hockey-like games had been popular in their province since at least the early 1800s. Four years before the Montreal hoax, the *Halifax Herald* published a story claiming that local players developed a set of "Halifax Rules" decades before Confederation. Of course, the *Herald* had no tangible evidence of these rules, only someone's memory.[3]

Promising to end such disputes, the CAHA appointed a committee in 1941 to investigate origins. Not surprisingly, James Sutherland was on the committee. So was his pal, W. A. Hewitt (Foster's father and Ontario Hockey Association secretary), who had previously supported the Kingston claim. Montrealers had never accepted Sutherland's stories. After all, their teams were at the center of hockey championships as long as anyone could remember. They must have smelled a rat with the appointment of a clearly biased blue-ribbon committee. If Sutherland had "evidence" of hockey in Kingston as early as the 1860s, it is not surprising that someone in Montreal (in other words, Knox) would easily discover "eyewitness" accounts dating to 1837, just as Haligonians did with the so-called "Halifax rules." Sutherland and company were not impressed. When the CAHA committee published its official account in 1942, it placed Kingston at history's epicenter.

This was not the end of the bickering. It has continued into the present, fueled in the 1980s when Nova Scotians mounted a public campaign that included press conferences, books, a museum, and eventually a website, all stating emphatically that hockey "originated around 1800" in Windsor on Nova Scotia's northwest shore, where boys at King's College School adapted an Irish folk game to frozen ponds. In 2006 the Northwest Territories leaped into the fray. A hockey historian discovered separate "hockey," "skating," and "games" references in the journals and correspondence of Sir John Franklin, a British explorer whose 1825 expedition had wintered at Fort Franklin (now Deline) NWT. Deline's territorial representative jumped on the prospects: "Let's bring the community of Deline and the original birthplace of ice hockey on the map."[4]

A passing reference in Windsor or Deline, however, does not support claims to a "birthplace." Finding one means tracing lineage backward and forward, as a good genealogist would. It requires paying close attention to the structure of a game, its rules, its administration, and its administrators. To that extent, most historians agree with the 2002 report of the *Society for International Hockey Research*: the game of hockey, *as we know it today*, first developed in Montreal between 1875 and 1886.[5]

This Montreal product, however, was hardly original. It was born in a confluence of peculiar circumstances, which brought together certain people, ideas, and material conditions necessary to concoct a particular game. Researchers have documented hockey-like games on fields and ice across Europe and North America over several centuries before the Montreal "birth." The Montreal inventors in effect grabbed bits and pieces from many older, existing games that had been played for centuries by the Irish, Scots, and English, by the French and First Nations, in Halifax and other places. That has been the nature of sports for as long as we have recorded their history: borrow from others, then shamelessly beat them at their own game. The next few chapters describe the broad background of this invention. Then we examine how the Montreal Game swept alternatives into the frozen backwaters of Canada, America, Europe, and beyond. In the course of five decades, one new version of hockey became THE version of hockey. There was more at stake than just rules. If the older versions had been tied closely to local, regional, tribal, or national identities, whose identity would count in the new game? Contemporary fights over origins suggest the weightiness of the question and its answers.[6]

Foster Hewitt understood that hockey had misty origins in ancient games of sticks and balls. Yet he also claimed in his 1934 book that "the thought of chasing a puck across an icy surface is purely Canadian and comparatively recent." Of course, he was wrong. When Hewitt wrote his book, Europeans had been holding hockey championships for more than two decades. Some American promoters believed their collegiate game was superior to the NHL's. The Japanese national team was training for its first Olympic competition. In 1934 the thought of chasing a puck was not "purely Canadian." On the other hand, Hewitt's concern to control hockey's identity was very much Canadian.[7]

Ancient, Medieval, and Early Modern Ball Games

The young men who developed the Montreal Game did not design it from scratch. They borrowed from several sports with published sets of rules, including field hockey and lacrosse. These formal games, in turn, had long lineages. Historical and archeological evidence suggests that games with sticks and balls have an ancient past. Local customs might have slowly twisted the form of play in a number of directions based on how the ball was hit or propelled (from the ground, along the ground, above the ground) and the ball's objective or target (to cross a line, to go over an obstacle, to enter a confined space, to leave a confined space).[8]

Some evidence is slim, requiring imaginative leaps. For instance, an ancient Egyptian tomb at Beni Hassan contains a drawing of two people, each with a short stick touching a large ball. The International Hockey Federation refers to it on its web page: "Historical records show that a crude form of the game was played in Egypt 4,000 years ago." But what does a single tomb painting prove?[9] The Greeks have their own claims. Archeologists in 1922 unearthed an Athenian statue base, dating to the fifth century BCE, which contains several reliefs depicting ball games. One appears to show two men "facing off" in a way similar to how today's field hockey or lacrosse players start up play, and similar to the picture in the tomb at Beni Hassan. Each is bent over a small ball that lies between their crossed sticks, which look more like short crooks. Four other men look on, casually holding their sticks. Are they spectators watching a contest between individuals, or are they teammates loafing at a face-off? Unfortunately, we have no other evidence about this game.[10]

There is also a long Eastern tradition of ball and stick games. The Japanese game of Dakyū (so-named from the Chinese characters for "strike" and "ball") could be played on foot or on horse, the teams trying to hit or hurl a red or white ball into a goal. Introduced from Persia via China as early as the seventh century CE, Dakyū changed form over the centuries. As two modern historians concluded, "the game resembled modern lacrosse as well as modern polo." Dakyū may have spawned Gitchō, a street game employing a square-ended stick and a round disk that was whacked back and forth in an eerie proto-mix of modern hockey, golf, and "Guts" Frisbee.[11]

Dakyū and Gitchō both had seasonal significance, a trait common in many such ball games. The Ethiopian game of genna, which also resembles field hockey, is played during the Christmas season (*genna* being an Amharic word for Christmas). Its roots are, by various traditions, linked to King Solomon, John the Baptist, and the Nativity. As one reporter noted, teams of young men organize by village or neighborhood for competitions that demand stick-handling skill, endurance, and the courage to be "bopped on the head with a hard wooden stick." Algeria had its own game, explained to one 1921 traveler as "koora," played during the spring festival. It "very closely resembled hockey" and was apparently "of great antiquity."[12]

Europeans found similar games in the Americas. William Strachey, secretary to the Virginia Company, included descriptions of native festivals in his *The historie of travell into Virginia Britania* (1612). One pastime required a wooden ball and a curved stick, similar, he thought, to England's "auncyent game" of bandy. Spaniards described a hockey-like game played by the native Araucano. It was called *cheuca*—the "twisted one"—so named after the curved stick used to drive a leather-covered ball toward the opponent's goal, which was a black line drawn across the width of the field. The field size varied with the number of players but was usually one hundred paces by ten paces, with four to ten players in the scrum. Canadian Plains natives played something similar, using a hide-covered ball, stuffed with buffalo or antelope hair. Rubber-ball games were widespread in Mesoamerica. Modern anthropologists discovered a hockey-like game in Angáhuan, a remote Tarascan village in Mexico, played with short sticks of mango using a ball of rags or cord wound around a solid, rubbery core collected from worms of madzone trees.[13]

Europeans had their own folk games, which are the most immediate ancestors to modern hockey, carried with the cultural baggage they brought to North America. The French played "la soule" with a stuffed leather ball, which was driven by hand, foot, or stick as far into "enemy" territory as possible. The stick version was called "soule à la crosse." The available records show the game as a medium for traditional rivalries between special groups—married men versus bachelors or parish versus parish—played out on feast days such as Christmas, Candlemas, Shrovetide, or Lent. They were sometimes wild affairs, ranging over wide territories, with dozens on each side. Blood, injuries, ill feelings, and fights were doubtless regular parts of the game, as suggested by the occasional prohibitions from both Church and State. Such a game's name often derived from the implement, an etymology that can cause problems for today's casual interpreters of sport history. Take the case of *golf*, which appears to be based on the Middle Dutch word *Kolf* or *Kolve*, the name for a shepherd's crook. Early references to *Kolve* or *golf* in Dutch or Scottish texts, however, do not necessarily refer to anything resembling the modern game. In fact, some probably refer to a game closer to la soule.[14]

Ball-and-stick games had ancient roots in the British Isles. Hurling (Ireland) and shinty (Scotland) derive from the same core game of "driving" a ball (*iomáin* in Gaelic) with a curved stick (*camán* in Gaelic). Both the terms *camán* and *iomáin* appear in early legal records and in literary works such as the legend of Cu Chulainn. Irish missionaries brought the game to Scotland. The terms *hurling* and *shinty* may come from Gaelic, but they emerged as written descriptors only as Gaelic receded as the standard language in Ireland and Scotland.

As with all folk games, it is very difficult to tease out from the earliest records any clear outline of rules or tactics. Laws denouncing or prohibiting "horlinge" do not explain the game. Nor do the literary sources. Cu Chulainn earned his name (originally Sentana) by driving a ball through the foaming mouth of a dog, with disemboweling force and accuracy. This may have demonstrated great stick skill, but it doesn't describe how players interacted in a contest. Nineteenth-century publications provide more detail, such as a sketch and description of shinty in an 1835 edition of *The Penny Magazine*. Still, it would be difficult to prove that the game played in one district was the same as the game played in another. Both hurling and shinty, however, were slowly codified by organized clubs in Ireland and Scotland during the last three decades of the nineteenth century—the same period when ice hockey was codified in Canada.[15]

By that time, Irish and Scottish immigrants had brought their pastimes to North America, where they served among the prototypes for the Montreal game. For example, one Canadian authority reported that "organized shinty games began in Kingston, Ontario in 1839 on New Year's Day, and the following year a Camac Club was formed. In January 1843, a shinty match took place between Scotsmen born in the counties of Argyle and Ross, which lasted three hours."[16]

THE PENNY MAGAZINE

OF THE

Society for the Diffusion of Useful Knowledge.

181.] PUBLISHED EVERY SATURDAY. [JANUARY 31, 1835.

THE GAME OF SHINTY.

[Game of Shinty.]

IN the Highlands of Scotland it is customary for persons to amuse themselves, in the winter season, with a game which they call "shinty." This sport has a considerable resemblance to that which is denominated "hurling" in England, and which Strutt describes under that name. The shinty is played with a small hard ball, which is generally made of wood, and each player is furnished with a curved stick somewhat resembling that which is used by golf players. The object of each party of players is to send the ball beyond a given boundary on either side; and the skill of the game consists in striking the ball to the greatest distance towards the adversaries' boundary, or in manœuvring to keep it in advance of the opposing side. Large parties assemble during the Christmas holidays, one parish sometimes making a match against another. In the struggles between the contending players many hard blows are given, and frequently a shin is broken, or by a rarer chance some more serious accident may occur. The writer witnessed a match, in which one of the players, having gained possession of the ball, contrived to run a mile with it in his hand, pursued by both his own and the adverse party until he reached the appointed limit, when his victory was admitted. Many of the Highland farmers join with eagerness in the sport, and the laird frequently encourages by his presence this amusement of his labourers and tenants.

The game of shinty (*The Penny Magazine*, January 31, 1835)

The English versions were called *bandy* and *hockey*. The term *bandy* was used interchangeably for the stick and the game. It is mentioned in the late sixteenth century as a Devonshire favorite. Robert Forby's *The Vocabulary of East Anglia* (1830) described the bandy as made from "very tough wood, or shod with metal, or with the point of the horn or the hoof of some animal." The game's object was to "beat" a hard, wooden ball "with their bandies through one or other of the goals."[17]

The association of name with game implement is also likely in hockey. The *Oxford English Dictionary*, which was built on establishing historical precedent and etymology, is cautious about hockey: "Origin uncertain; but the analogy of many other games makes it likely that the name originally belonged to the hooked stick. OF [Old French] *hoquet* 'shepherd's staff crook' suits form and sense; but connecting links are wanting." Cautious indeed.[18]

What is clear is the recognized danger. One description of English schoolboys, titled *The Book of Games* (1811), provides a running exchange between a father and son as they travel about and chance to view boys at play. The action and energy of "hockey" especially rouses the son's attention, but his father returns a firm warning. He had a friend at school who lost an eye to an errant stick: "The eagerness with which boys are too apt to play at it has been the occasion of many accidents, and it is I believe forbidden at many schools."[19]

The English colonial record is less robust. One historian argued that American conditions were less favorable than those in the old country for activities like bandy or hockey, which required large numbers of players and flat, open space. The games did later appear on some school and college campuses, where they were sometimes prohibited. In 1787, for instance, the Princeton College faculty banned "shinny" because it was "low and unbecoming gentlemen and scholars." The 1851 Regulations of Chauncey-Hall School included among a list of prohibitions: "to bring bats, hockey sticks, bows and arrows, or other dangerous play-things to school."[20]

But play they did. Boston boys liked to "drive" on the Common, hitting a small ball back and forth with their "hawkies." The game is described in an 1839 book called *Caleb in Town*, written by Jacob Abbot, who gained fame with his Rollo series. While walking near his Boston home with his Cousin Dwight, young Caleb spots a large pile of sticks and logs of varying sizes. "O what real hawky wood," he shouts. When cousin Dwight expresses ignorance about "hawky," Caleb explains that "a hawky is a small, round stick, about as long as a man's cane, with a crook in the lower end, so that a boy can hit balls and little stones with it. A good hawky is a great prize to a Boston boy." It still is.[21]

Nathaniel Beverley Tucker's antebellum novel *The Partisan Leader* (1836) mentioned bandy as a game that helped to build the code of "fair play" and honor, so self-consciously trumpeted by Southerners, especially in accentuating the love that supposedly existed between slaves and their masters: "You have the equal friendship of those with whom you ran races, and played at bandy, and wrestled in your boyhood. If sometimes a dry blow passed between you, they love you none the less for that." Then as now, violence could be cloaked in righteousness.[22]

Or in health. In January 1831, the Philadelphia-based *Journal of Health* included an article on "Winter Sports," which discussed the benefits of exercise "to give present vigour, as to prevent future disease, and the languor and debility to be expected in the succeeding summer." The *Journal* hoped that "dyspeptic fathers" and "nervous mothers" would learn from their children the joys and benefits of "such games as that called by the English hockey, the Scotch shinty, and our boys, in school plainness, shinney." By the middle of the 1800s, hockey-like folk games with stick and ball were well established on fields across the Old World and the New.[23]

Field Games on Ice in Europe and North America

The *Journal of Health* clearly linked hockey to winter, but the author did not mention ice. So, when did these field games move to frozen waters? There is no clear answer in the historical record, but the transition seems likely wherever the climate allowed. And the climate was favorable, for these field games gained popularity during a period known as the Little Ice Age, roughly 1300 to 1850, one of eight or nine such episodes over the last 730 millennia.

The Little Ice Age was not an uninterrupted block of frozen tundra. It had repeated cycles of deep freeze and mild weather, droughts and rain. On balance, however, it was colder between 1150 and 1460 AD, and it was much colder between 1560 and 1850. The cycles had an impact on human life, including long stretches of poor crops, which led to mass starvation, as in the great hunger of 1315–1319. Famine was a regular and unwelcome guest among European peasants, who often rioted for grain and bread. But stretches of colder winter also aided in the development of skating and the movement of field games onto the ice. Fortunately for ice hockey, the warming period that began after 1850 came at the dawn of indoor rinks and artificial ice.[24]

One of the earliest English descriptions of an ice game is in William FitzStephen's famous *Description of London,* which was written in the late twelfth century. It provides clues about primitive skates and the ease with which a field contest, in this case the joust, could be transferred to the ice:

> When the great marsh that laps up against the northern walls of the city is frozen, large numbers of the younger crowd go there to play about on

the ice. Some, after building up speed with a run, facing sideways and their feet placed apart, slide along for a long distance. . . . Others are more skilled at frolicking on the ice: they equip each of their feet with an animal's shin-bone, attaching it to the underside of their footwear; using hand-held poles reinforced with metal tips, which they periodically thrust against the ice, they propel themselves along as swiftly as a bird in flight or a bolt shot from a crossbow. But sometimes two, by accord, beginning far apart, charge each other from opposite directions and, raising their poles, strike each other with them. One or both are knocked down, not without injury, since after falling their impetus carries them off some distance and any part of their head that touches the ice is badly scratched and scraped. Often someone breaks a leg or an arm, if he falls onto it.

Not hockey, to be sure, but a good example of the logical flow from field to ice.[25]

It would be just as simple to move "kolv," or "shinty" or "hockey." Artists left abundant evidence of this fact. Pieter Brueghel the Elder (1525–1569) painted numerous scenes of peasant life, among them *Hunters in the Snow* (1565), in which a small group returns to their Dutch village with a meager catch. In the distance, dozens of tiny figures frolic on two frozen surfaces. Some of them appear to play at a ball game on the ice. His *Winter Landscape with Bird Trap* (1565) provides a closer look at such peasant pastimes. One group handles something like curling stones. Several people carry curved sticks, and one looks to be snapping off a shot, to nowhere in particular. Hendrick Avercamp (1585–1634) was a specialist in winter landscapes. Many of his paintings include images of men addressing a ball with a "kolv" in their hand, steadying themselves as if they were on the first tee. In other paintings, skaters crouch low, trying to control the ball with their short sticks. Esaias van de Velde (1590–1630) and Aert van der Neer (1603–1677) painted similar vistas; so did the Irish-American John Toole, whose *Skating Scene* (ca. 1835) depicts a dozen skaters, including four men or boys in a hockey scrum, sticks a-flying as they fight for the ball.[26]

There is evidence that the Dutch, the Swedes, and the English brought their skates to America. A history of early Philadelphia noted that the Delaware River typically froze to thicknesses of two feet or more and supported large numbers of people who could skate for long stretches. Another chronicle stated that skating was "relatively common" in New York, Delaware, and Pennsylvania, where long winters brought "snow covered

John Toole, *Skating Scene* ca. 1835 (National Gallery of Art, https://www.nga.gov/Collection/art-object-page.45857.html)

hills and roads" and where "waterways froze, and travel became difficult without a pair of skates, a sled, or a sleigh." New Englanders were vexed by many sports and dissipations. And yet John Adams, who often worried about idleness, insisted that his grandchildren learn "pretty" amusements such as dancing, skating, and fencing.[27]

But where did they get the skates? As William FitzStephen suggested in his *Description of London*, the earliest skates were probably crafted from animal bone. The shift to metal blades took time, even though the materials and the skill were readily available. Almost four centuries after FitzStephen, Sweden's Olaus Magnus included a description of skates and skate races in his well-known *Historia de Gentibus Septentrionalibus* (1555). Among the tribes, he wrote, were men "who attach to the soles of their feet a piece of flat, polished iron, a foot long, or the flat bones of deer or oxen, the shin bones, that is." On these devices, skaters raced for valuable prizes that included copper pots, silver spoons, and (more often) "young horses." One might expect that, given an incentive, more skaters shifted to metal blades, but Magnus claimed that the "shin bones of deer thoroughly smoothed and greased with pork fat" actually worked better than the metal blades. Either way, the "northern people" had practical reasons for developing durable and effective skates for everyday travel during the long, frozen winters.[28]

In the same general period, the Chinese developed skates for their ice games, races, and contests, which were described in the *Seasonal Records of the Capital*: "Skating shoes are made of iron," wrote the scribe. "In the middle of each there is a leather lace, to fasten the iron shoe to the leather shoe." Although this does not sound very stable, the "skillful players" were described "like dragon flies touching the surface," or like "purple swallows flying over the waves."[29]

As late as the nineteenth century, skates were typically handcrafted, awkward, and uncomfortable amalgams of wooden blocks and iron runners—short or long. They were strapped onto a boot or shoe, hardly the instrument for speed or agility on the ice. The wooden blocks were prone to splitting, which had embarrassing or even dangerous consequences. It is not clear when European artisans first ventured into special methods and designs for skate production, but they were well ahead of their North American counterparts. One scholar of nineteenth-century American skating discovered an 1833 bill of sale between a Philadelphia merchant and the firm of C. W. Wirths and Bros., Remscheid, Germany. The American bought six hundred pairs of "English skates" and 354 pairs of "fine skates." Six years later, Frederick Stevens began manufacturing his versions in New York.[30]

Wider production upped the odds for games on ice. In fact, references to hurling, shinty (or shinny), and hockey on ice pick up in the early nineteenth century in England, Scotland, Canada, and America. Among other documents, English garrisons and Scots immigrants left written evidence in Kingston, Ontario. In January 1843, Arthur Freeling, an officer of the Royal Engineers, wrote in his diary about playing "hockey" in Kingston: "Began to skate this year, improved quickly and had great fun at hockey on ice." Around the same time, local Scots groups issued shinty challenges to one another, for contests on riverways or on frozen commons.[31]

Nova Scotia was an early center for such games. Local Mi'kmaqs had words for a ball stick (oochamkunutk) and a game (alchamadijik) that was doubtless played on fields and on ice. An old Dartmouth (Nova Scotia) speed skater later recalled playing with Natives who ran in moccasins or skated on wooden skates: "They could run like moose on the ice and were very rough in their style of play." The *Acadian Magazine*, published in Halifax in January 1827, included a poem with vivid images:

> Now at ricket with hurlies some dozens of boys
> Chase the ball o'er the ice, with a deafening noise.
> Now some play at curling, and some with great ease
> Cut circles or figures whichever you please
> On their skates, or else letters—the true lover's knot,
> And a dozen such things which I've really forgot.[32]

Schoolboy alums recalled playing "hurley" on ponds near King's College School, founded in 1788 in Windsor, some 50 kilometers northwest of Halifax. Windsor, at the junction of the Avon and St. Croix Rivers, had a history as a confluence of cultures, from Mi'kmaq to Acadian, English, Irish, and American Loyalists. Haligonians had strong connections with Windsor; many owned farmland in the fertile area and sent their boys to King's. The Halifax-Windsor Railway opened in 1853. With native traditions, a military garrison (Fort Edward), a school-college, and an active port, Windsor was a perfect spot for developing a game like hurley or hockey.[33]

Canadian novelist Thomas Chandler Haliburton, an 1810 King's graduate, included a passing description of a schoolboy scene in his 1844 novel, *The Attaché*—the boys "racin', yellin', hollerin', and whoopin' like mad" at their games that included "hurley on the long pond on the ice." This "Long Pond" still exists on the back end of the late Howard Dill's pumpkin farm, just down the hill from the school (now called King's Edgehill School). Thanks to a few Canadian Broadcasting Company television specials and a dedicated website, it has become something of a shrine to many Canadians. It is in fact a small pond, marked only by a sign designating it the "Cradle of Hockey," but on any day a modern pilgrim can still hear the echoes of boys yellin', hollerin', and whoopin' as they whacked away with their hurleys.[34]

The games, however, were never codified. They remained winter customs defined by oral tradition and not a set of rules. As one authority put it: Haligonians "could not decide on one game with a distinctive name." In fact, in 1867 the *Halifax Reporter* described a mass skating scene on Dartmouth's Oathill Lake, where some were playing ricket and hockey. The writer complained that "very little science was displayed in either game," but he also provided a clue to the ethnic and social-class bases of the games. At times the "aristocratic hockey ball" played by the British gar-

Long Pond in 2005 (authors' collection)

rison officers would fly into the ricket match, where the "plebian hurleys" would whack it around before returning it.[35]

Hockey was also played on English ice. In January 1864 the *London Times* reported on a skating excursion by the Prince and Princess of Wales and their entourage of "40 ladies and gentlemen." After coaching to a lake near Frogmore Lodge, the group chose sides for a "hockey game" in which the Prince's side was "distinguished by a white riband on the left arm." The *Times* shilled for the Prince, claiming he "proved himself a first-rate skater and player, being as active with his hockey stick as he was on his skates, puzzling many of the most expert players." Perhaps the experts simply got out of the way. The Princess was near term in pregnancy, and though "much interested in the game," watched from the sideline, "occasionally driven about in a sledge."[36]

In America, schoolboys played their own version at St. Paul's School, founded in Concord, New Hampshire, in 1855 by a prominent Boston physician. Their student newspaper included a description of the first, firm black ice of the 1860 season:

> Here, near the shore, is a group of teachers looking on and talking and joking with the boys around them. There a little further out is seen a party of boys in pursuit of a hockey ball. One boy swings his hockey and away

> goes the ball skimming over the ice. The party dashes off in pursuit. The head boy catches up with the ball, and takes aim at it, but misses it and sends himself sprawling over the ice on all fours with the force of the blow.

Amid the visions of steel blades cutting the ice surface, one dreamer could also imagine himself "hockey in hand, driving the ball into the midst of a crowd, and then emerging with it still safe." Less romantically, the description of one heroic ice rescue mentioned that a skater used his "hockey" to pull a friend from the frigid water.[37]

The Concordians were hardly alone. By the 1860s, hockey-like games thrived on frozen ponds, lakes, and rivers around the northern hemisphere. There were many common aspects. Someone from Halifax might well recognize the general contours of "bandy" as it was played in the English Fens district. But there was also great variation in specific rules, sticks, balls, and skates. Over the next forty years, uniformity began to press out variation.

3

The Montreal Birthing: 1875–77

On March 3, 1875, the following notice appeared in the *Montreal Gazette*:

> A game of Hockey will be played at the Victoria Rink this evening between two nines chosen from among the members. Good fun may be expected, as some of the players are reputed to be exceedingly expert at the game. Some fears have been expressed on the part of intending spectators that accidents were likely to occur through the ball flying about in a too lively manner, to the imminent danger of on lookers, but we understand that the game will be played with a flat, circular piece of wood, thus preventing all danger of its leaving the surface of the ice.

The next day's *Gazette* included a report on the match, describing it as "an interesting and well-contested affair," with the skaters "exciting much merriment as they wheeled and dodged each other."[1]

The story is filled with messy contradictions. For instance, the March 4 report indicated that a "very large audience" had gathered to watch "a novel contest on the ice." How could the game have been "novel" if (as the March 3 notice claimed) some of the players were "exceedingly expert" in playing? It is more likely that many of the players had enjoyed some form of hockey for years. More confusing, the March 4 report stated that "the game of hockey, though much in vogue on the ice in New England and other parts of the United States, is not much known here." If Canada, and more specifically Montreal, was the birthplace of hockey, why would a reporter admit that the founders stole the game from some Yankees? And if Canadians simply lifted the game from their neighbors, why is this date so important?

There are several good reasons. First, this Montreal bunch was not grabbing a New England game. They were settling on a name for a product they hoped to nurture. They might just as well have called it hurling or shinty, or even lacrosse, all of which (as we have seen) had been played on Canadian ice. In fact, the reporter also stated that "the game is like Lacrosse in one sense—the block having to go through flags placed about 8 feet apart in the same manner as the rubber ball—but in the main the old country game of shinty gives the best idea of hockey."

The players also appear to be promoters. The March 3 story was quite likely a notice prepared by the players and sent to the *Gazette* (and perhaps other papers) in hopes of attracting spectators. More crucial to their marketing plans, the fundamental innovation—replacing the ball with a flat "block"—was described not as a means to a more appealing game, but as a *protection for spectators*. The March 4 account repeated that of March 3: "Hockey is played usually with a ball, but last night, in order that no accident should happen, a flat block of wood was used, so that it should slide along the ice without rising, and thus going among the spectators to their discomfort." We may reasonably guess that earlier indoor hockey-like games had been hindered by errant balls, and that spectator danger was well understood by the patrons of the Victoria Rink. These player-promoters, then, had one eye on the game and one eye on the spectacle.

They could not control all the dangers or all the reports. The *Gazette* had the game ending at 9:30, with the spectators leaving "well satisfied with the evening's entertainment." The Montreal *Witness* and Kingston's *Daily British Whig* both had another take on the game's end, which the *Whig* described as a "disgraceful sight" where "shins and heads were battered, benches smashed and the lady spectators fled in confusion." Apparently, wrote the *Witness*, some boys had skated out on the ice during play and one was "struck across the head," leading to a larger altercation (perhaps with the boy's friends or family?), a "regular fight," the broken benches, and the fleeing ladies. Why the fight? Had the "boys" jumped on the ice to claim their own slot of rented time? If so, it would not be the last case of precious ice time triggering a donnybrook.[2]

The March 4 report contained a list of the players, the third point of importance: "The players last night were eighteen in number—nine on each side—and were as follows: Messrs. Torrance (captain), Meagher, Potter, Goff, Barnston, Gardner, Griffin, Jarvis and Whiting. Creighton (captain), Campbell, Campbell, Esdaile, Joseph, Henshaw, Chapman, Powell and

Clouston." If researchers hunt long and hard enough, they might well find a list of players in an earlier "hockey" match. But it is not the list that counts; it is the names on the list. Several of them did not simply disappear into the dustbin of history. They reappeared as they refined and spread the gospel of the game they fashioned and first took public on March 3, 1875.

Innovations in Skates and Rinks

A number of developments set the scene for this Montreal experiment. The 1860s saw a skating boom in Europe, America, and Canada. Perhaps cold weather provided longer, more certain skating seasons (weather databases do not extend that far back). One way or another, manufacturers recognized potential. Their numbers swelled. The Union Hardware Company in Torrington, Connecticut (1854), was joined by Seth C. Winslow in Worcester, Massachusetts (1857), Barney and Berry in nearby Springfield (1865), the Starr Manufacturing Company in Dartmouth, Nova Scotia (1864), and many others, all producing thousands and thousands of higher-quality skates. Imports from Europe added to the mix. Ottawa merchants in 1864 advertised shipments of "London Club," "Rocker," "Parisian Lady," and a model named after the famous skater Jackson Haines. Design innovation was rampant. In the United States, patents for skates increased from seventeen in the 1850s to 149 in the 1860s, many designs using springs and clamps for easier attachment to shoes or boots. The wooden block gave way to all-metal skates by the 1870s. And prices went down to as low as 25 cents for a cheap pair, with higher quality versions at $5 and upward.[3]

This produced what contemporaries called a "skating mania." George Beers, Canada's "father" of lacrosse and a premier sports promoter, recalled the winter of 1862:

> There was a skating mania from Gaspé to Sarnia, and I don't believe you could find four out of every twenty without one or more pair of skates in the house. . . . On the sides of the lakes and rivers, on brooks and ponds and wherever there is ice, you may see multitudes on the steel runners.

There were similar scenes in America, on New York's Central Park, Boston's Jamaica Pond, and the Detroit River, to name just a few. New York papers in the 1860s estimated upwards of twelve thousand skaters a day on the Central Park skating pond—probably an exaggeration, but a good indication of the craze.[4]

Skating took a crucial turn in the 1860s toward organized clubs, commercialized venues, and indoor rinks. This created the foundation for organized hockey. Edinburgh, Scotland, claimed a skating club as early as the middle of the eighteenth century, perhaps even earlier. London, England, and St. John, New Brunswick, had skating clubs by the early 1830s; Philadelphia in 1849; Montreal in 1850. The 1860s saw a spike in new clubs, such as the New York Skating Club, founded in 1863. Several years later, Russians in St. Petersburg opened a rink in Yusupov Garden for their Skating Club, and Swedes founded Stockholm's Royal Skating Club. Membership dues paid for rink development and maintenance.[5]

In September 1860, for instance, the *Detroit Free Press* announced the formation of a skating club to finance construction of a "pond" on an enclosed 2.5 acres near the junction of Grand River and Third Street. The project required extensive development, including leveling, creating embankments, and constructing "a fence nine feet high . . . around the ground, and a building containing reception-rooms, dressing rooms, etc. . . . in one corner." Estimated costs were about $1,200 for both the excavation and thirty thousand barrels of water to be used over the winter. Snow increased operating costs. One rink required the labor of thirty men to keep the ice clear. Even with cheap labor, this was no trifle of expense. And so the rinks, whether formally private or public, usually sold access by the day (25 cents) or the season ($3–5). The Montreal Skating Club collected subscription memberships of 10 shillings. Plenty of people were willing to pay. The *Detroit Post* described an 1867 scene as people streamed to yet another new rink: "The Woodward avenue street cars did a heavy business. . . . The Rink was the general destination . . . skates were to be seen everywhere on Monday . . . in the hands of pretty schoolgirls, slung over the shoulders of pale, sleek clerks, and in the windows of stores." Rink patrons were entertained by "Bohemian" bands, visits from "Christmas Santa Claus," and lots of fancy skaters.[6]

Hockey's future lay inside covered rinks, which insulated skaters and their activities from blizzards, thaws, and biting winds. Skaters in Quebec City enjoyed a covered rink—120 by 60 feet—in 1852. Within a decade, the Montreal Skating Club had upped the ante with a 200-by-40-foot structure that included gas lighting, dressing rooms, and a bandstand. One spectator described it in a letter to the *Spirit of the Times*: "On entering, I was very much struck with the brilliancy of the whole scene. The band of the Canadian Rifles was playing a tune to which ladies and gentlemen, grand-

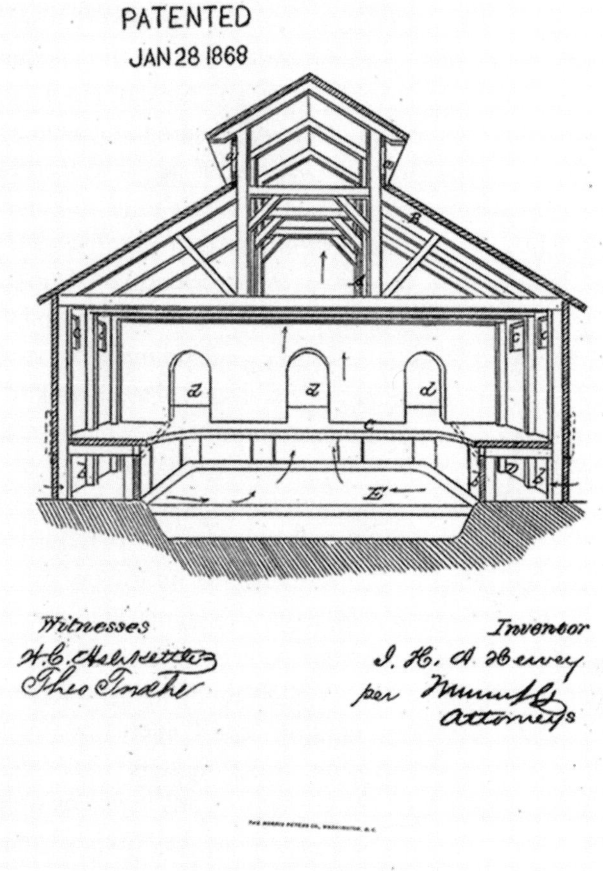

Hervey Brothers rink patent drawing, 1868 (U.S Patent and Trademark Office)

mothers and grandchildren were flying about, as if they were mad." Covered rinks might require greater initial investment, but they seemed to promise more consistent revenue streams. And so they spread. Haligonians opened a 180-by-60-foot rink in 1862. St. John, Hamilton, and Toronto followed suit in the next few years. Canada had some dozen covered rinks by the 1870s.[7]

Canada was not alone in this new business. In America, the skating boom of the late 1860s was fed by the construction of indoor natural ice rinks in cities around the country, including Chicago, Boston, New York, Brooklyn, Detroit, St. Louis, Pittsburgh, Cleveland, Springfield (Ill.), Indianapolis, Rochester, and Columbus. New York's Empire City Rink opened in 1868 with a huge ice bed—200 by 130 feet. A number of these buildings were built and operated by the Canadian-born Hervey brothers. Historian Paul DeLoca's exhaustive research indicates that the Herveys built and managed dozens of rinks "from Quebec to Chicago to New York to Philadelphia" using their patented design, engineered to pull in cold, outside air along the ice surface yet retain warmer air above. It was crude science that often resulted in slushy ice. But amenities could brighten the experience. The Boston Skating Rink (1868–69) on Tremont Street boasted of its ability to "accommodate 5000 persons, including skaters and spectators," and its "warm and comfortable rooms . . . where polite attendants will always be found to assist in putting on skates." The restaurant was a proto-skybox, with "a front entirely of glass" that offered a "fine view of the ice surface, and of the entire audience." It was a place to skate, to see, and to be seen.[8]

Why Montreal?

Indoor rinks transformed hockey from a loose, if intense, folk game into an organized, commercial spectacle. Entrepreneurs, organizers, and promoters could rely on ice time as well as ready-made skates and, in many cases, sticks and balls as the first three components to an enduring game. What was lacking was organization—rules, records, and bureaucracy. That transformation began in 1875 at the Victoria Rink in Montreal, a venue built in 1862–63 by local elites committed to healthy, fun-filled (and exclusive) forms of exercise.

Montreal was a logical place for the game's re-invention. It had been a center of the French fur trade, and after New France fell to the British in 1760, the city became a mecca for English merchants looking to carve out their own empires. While much of Quebec stayed Francophone, Montreal was ruled by English-speaking immigrants from England, Ireland, Scotland, and America. French-speaking Québécois remember it as "the Conquest." Fur yielded to other forms of commerce, driven by improved shipping (with the Lachine Canal) and eventually rail. From some nine thousand residents in 1800, Montreal grew to fifty-eight thousand in 1851 and a quarter-million by 1900. Immigrants accounted for much of the increase—from eastern and southern Europe, from Russia, and from the surrounding parts of French Canada—who came to work in the growing factories. Montreal was a swirling caldron of diverse cultures: native and European, trapper and soldier, farmer and industrialist. At the same time, as a cog in the machinery of British Empire, the city experienced a slow but steady circulation and convergence toward "uniformity" in language, food, dress, senses of time, and eventually sports.[9]

Anglophones controlled politics and economics, and they did not neglect social and cultural life, including sports. The Montreal Curling Club was organized by Anglophone elites in 1807. British garrison officers formed the Hunt Club and the Cricket Club in 1829. The Montreal Snow Shoe Club was born in 1843; in 1856 several members of the MSSC organized the Montreal Lacrosse Club. Over the next three decades, Montrealers founded new clubs around each new sport that swept in from England, including golf (Montreal Golf Club 1873) and bicycling (Montreal Bicycle Club 1878). By 1881, several of the clubs saw the wisdom in pooling resources to secure indoor facilities and equipment. This confederation became the Montreal Amateur Athletic Association, capitalized at $13,000 and symbolized by a winged wheel whose hub and spokes were expressions of strength through integration. The MAAA played a crucial role in hockey's early development; later, the winged wheel found a second home in Detroit.[10]

It is not surprising that hockey was codified in the 1870s; it was a decade of budding leagues, aspiring governing bodies, and hungry bureaucrats—both in Britain and in North America. England's Rugby Football Union formed in 1871, to classify and reinforce the differences between its game and that of the older Football Association (1863). Along similar lines, the Intercollegiate Football Association (1876) began the divorce of American football from rugby and soccer. That same year, American baseball embarked on a fundamentally different structure with the National League, an avowedly professional operation controlled by capitalists who saw as their first responsibility the need to control labor and markets. Canadians were part of this process; they had organized a National Lacrosse Association in 1867.

The sporting press in England, America, and Canada promoted these movements, which promised to elevate sports from allegedly haphazard organization and unsavory associations with gambling, intoxication, and violence. In most cases—baseball being an exception—the new, higher moral ground was staked out by emerging "amateur" clubs like those in

Montreal. Elite universities such as Harvard, Oxford, or Montreal's own McGill were also leaders in this quest for sporting order. All of these institutions represented the interests of educated bourgeoisie. Whereas shinty, hurling, bandy, and the original forms of hockey were largely folk traditions with agrarian roots, the new, reconfigured and re-invented game of hockey was, at conception, urban, urbane, and male. The Victoria Rink in Montreal was ground zero on March 3, 1875.

One of the most famous skating names of the nineteenth century appeared on that day's roster. Daniel Meagher (1845–1912) was one of nine boys and six girls born in Kingston to John Meagher, whose own father had migrated to Canada from Tipperary in 1814. The family later moved to Toronto and then Montreal, where Daniel blended hockey with a career as a physician. Daniel's younger brother George was born in 1866. Perhaps he was at the Victoria Rink the night of the first game (and brawl). The sights and sounds of crisp skating, dodging, passing, and stickhandling would have cemented his passion for the activity. In fact, George became a champion skater who traveled to Europe for some of the first world championships in what became known as figure skating. As we shall see in part 2, he claimed to have introduced at virtually every stop the new game of hockey.[11]

In the lore of early Canadian hockey, however, the most prominent roster name is James George Alwyn Creighton, who was born in 1850 in Nova Scotia. A graduate of Halifax's Dalhousie College, Creighton came to Montreal in 1872 to make his fortune as an engineer, lawyer, and journalist. He also fell into Montreal's sporting club scene, including the Victoria Skating Club. Henry Joseph, another of the March 3 players, later claimed that Creighton was the brains behind this new version of hockey. Among other things, Joseph said, Creighton drafted the rules and secured sticks from Halifax. Because of this, Creighton is one of the key anchors in the Halifax claim to being hockey's birthplace. Unfortunately, documentary evidence only supports the notion that Creighton had sufficient skills and knowledge to have been a leader in building the Montreal game. There is no evidence that James Creighton brought from Halifax a printed set of rules. And during his long life, Creighton never made any claims to being the "father of hockey."[12]

So where did Creighton and his colleagues get their ideas for this "novel" game? It appears that they simply drew from rules they knew in rugby, lacrosse, and field hockey. All of these sports had been codified and organized by 1875. The sporting press of the time circulated information about such matters, and it is likely that the Montreal men read the sporting press, either at their clubs or at home. This may also explain why they did not call their game hurling or shinty on ice. Neither folk game had yet spawned a club or association eager to publish the rules by which to propagate a "new" sport and control its destiny. Shinty games were still very local affairs in 1875; widely accepted rules did not appear until the founding of the Camanachd Association in 1893. Hurling waited until the Gaelic Athletic Association was formed in 1884.[13]

On the other hand, hockey rules were available. In November 1875, for instance, the boys at St. Paul's School in Concord, New Hampshire, had published "new rules for Hockey," the sport that rivaled football for fall popularity and ruled the winter ice. A year earlier, the student newspaper called for a published set of rules "just as we do in football." The new hockey code limited stick girth to five inches in diameter and prohibited the use of "blocks" or cricket balls: "Base-balls only, covered with thick leather." No sticks above the shoulder, except on a free lift. A player had to stay "on his own side" (behind the ball). Chronic violators risked expulsion. It was a rough game. As one commentator put it: "Unless you wish to get struck on the shins, hands or even head, you must be very quick." And it was a mass game. The St. Paul's rules limited the number of players to fifty in a game. The St. Paul's boys were aware of sporting developments in England, including the rules of the Football Association. We might reasonably consider that their hockey rules were informed by those of the Teddington Cricket Club, which had begun to codify a common set of field hockey rules in 1874–75. But St. Paul's was an isolated hotbed of its own brand of hockey, and the schoolboys would eventually adopt the Montreal code.[14]

Creighton and his Montreal mates continued to tinker, apparently drawing more and more on field hockey. Press accounts of games in 1876 and 1877 emphasized their embrace of the "onside" rules that distinguished the flow of rugby, football, and field hockey from that of shinty or hurling. In fact, the first list to appear in Canadian print, in the *Montreal Gazette*, February 27, 1877, was very closely modeled on that of field hockey—even using the term "ball." Some historians claim that the set was "identical" to existing field hockey rules except for the exchange of "field" for "ice." During these years, however, press accounts were inconsistent in describing the object of every player's attention. At times, it was a "block"; at others,

McGill University's first hockey team, Crystal Palace Skating Rink, 1881 (McCord Museum, Montreal, MP-0000.1589)

a ball; and in one account, a "puck." Either players were using whatever was available, or reporters were hopelessly inept (a common complaint by later coaches). On the other hand, onside play was the norm. Rule 2 of the 1877 Montreal rules stated, "A player must always be on his own side of the ball." It took almost forty years for revisions to this basic rule. Not so with the "bully," the means of starting play at the game's beginning, after goals, and at certain other times. The bully was essentially a face off without a referee. It was a field hockey standard. Two players lined up against the ball or puck, banged their sticks three times, then went after it. The *Gazette* concluded that "the 'bully' is indispensable, for without [it], hockey is a thing of naught." While the bully remained a field hockey fixture, the ice game soon adopted the referee-based face off.[15]

One game description captured what was probably a typical scene. Few players were adept skaters. The St. James team captain "turned a complete somersault" that "even a professional acrobat would have envied." A teammate fell "nobly" after entwining his stick "between another man's legs in the most extraordinary manner." While action started under certain restraints, the game could quickly blow the lid off tempers, as reflected in Rule 3, which prohibited high sticks above the shoulder, as well as "charging from behind, tripping, collaring, kicking or shinning." Over the next few years, hockey was a come-and-go proposition in Montreal. There is no way to tell if the February 1877 rules were always in force. Game reports appeared in the press from time to time, involving only a few teams—the Victorias, the Montreal Football Club, the Metropolitans, the St. James Club, and McGill University, whose team was organized in February 1877.[16]

Over the next several decades, McGill was a hockey laboratory, breeding players who would greatly influence the game. McGill's 1881 team provided the first photograph of uniforms and equipment on the ice. While players clearly posed for the camera, the picture reveals a rubber puck and short sticks with wide blades, more like "hurlies" than the "hockeys" found in New England. Several McGill contemporaries later claimed to have been the "inventors" of key rules or equipment innovations, such as the rubber puck. While historians generally dismiss these stories, they do reinforce the certainty that McGill University stood, along with the Victoria Rink, as the Montreal game's central institution. When hockey swept down from Canada to the United States in the mid-1890s, the terms "Montreal" and "McGill" rules were often interchangeable.[17]

Fusing Freedom and Restraint

By the 1880s, Montreal hockey was poised for export, to challenge and vanquish similar pastimes in Ottawa, Quebec, Halifax, western Canada, the United States, England, and Europe. The game continued to evolve. From the moment of conception, it contained tensions and contradictions that reflected both its characteristics as a centuries-old folk game and its incubation in a particular urban, industrial context. One of these tensions arose when an open, whirling, mass affair was moved into a fixed space, outdoor or indoor, which reduced team size and emphasized different skills. But if rinks moved hockey toward control and rationalization, they could never repress the players' desire to bust loose. Some of the pressure manifested itself in brutal assaults with sticks and fists.[18]

The residual urge for freedom also helps explain the retention of an old term—shinny. Even as hockey rose to be the dominant form and term, players and coaches continued to use the word "shinny" for unorganized scrums and contests, where players made up their own rules, played indoors or outdoors, with no limits on numbers. In some instances shinny might be nothing more than a game of keep-away. In others it might mean team against team, with no goaltenders, and no lifting. In all cases, however, shinny meant unrepressed fun as well as skill development.

Why the term "shinny"? The *Oxford English Dictionary* defined it as "a (north country and American) game similar to hockey." Its etymology is called "obscure," but the *OED* offered this: "the cry used in the game shin ye, shin you (also shin your side)" or "a dial[ect] name for shinty." Some histories have attempted to describe shinny as a more formal game in which players had to "shinny on" their "own side." Unfortunately, no one has clearly explained with primary-source evidence what "shinny on your own side" meant in the context of a North American ice game. It is more likely, as suggested by the *OED*, that "shinny" was a substitute name for "shinty" or any shinty-like game, which could also include hockey or bandy.[19]

It seems just as likely that players embraced a name that represented all that was lost when folk games turned into organized sports. As hockey became more organized and regimented, with tight-fisted bureaucrats and owners, with oppressive coaches, with stifling tactics and systems, old players sometimes yearned for the freedom they remembered in shinny. That lament started early. Walter Prichard Eaton wrote an ode to "Shinny" in the December 1913 issue of *Outing*, a magazine that championed the purest notions of amateurism (especially if it meant keeping control of sports in the hands of elites). "Hockey is fast becoming a major sport in American colleges," he said, "but it was always a major sport of boyhood. It was called shinny then, and the rules were not complicated." In Eaton's memory, shinny was a team game that focused on individual skill: "We knew nothing of passing in those days." Sides were chosen by two captains, themselves "elected by the rough democracy of boyhood." Many players used hand-hewn sticks, cut from ash or oak, good enough to control the hard rubber ball in the back-and-forth action that had "no periods" but only the "breathing spaces" that came with an errant ball—It was continuous action until "we were exhausted" or could see "the solemn green sunset up the pond to the west." Eaton concluded, "the boys are at it yet, though they all have 'store sticks' now, and call the game hockey." A piece of nostalgia for sure, but one with legs. For more than a century, pond hockey players have been just as likely to call their game shinny—an unacknowledged homage to their sport's early roots.[20]

"Shinny," *Outing*, 1913 (Walter Prichard Eaton, "Shinny," *Outing* 63 [December 1913]: 288)

Arthur Farrell, a famous hockey-playing relative of the Meaghers, captured the feel of shinny in an early guidebook:

> Boys swarmed to the lakes in battalions and rattled along on old iron or wooden skates tied to their feet with rope. A few broken bones, a few frozen fingers, but never mind, there were plenty of men to replace the dead. What a sight did a shinny match present! Hundreds on the same

> sheet of glare black ice, all eagerly engaged in one glorious game. What laughing, calling, cheering and chasing there was to be sure! With their bright eyes and rosy cheeks they dart now in one direction, now in another, till finally the vast struggling crowd surges toward the goals, surrounds them, and a fierce, lucky swipe knocks it through, while a hundred lusty voices cry their loudest: "Game! Game!"

While anyone who has played on ponds understands that the young, the weak, and the unskilled might not share this romantic vision, it has remained an important symbol of hockey's first internal tension. Shinny would carry the old spirit of freedom in a game later distinguished by collisions and caroms off the confining boards of indoor rinks.[21]

Turning Pucks into Bucks

Indoor rinks added another tension—commercialization. Enclosures protected skaters and spectators from nature's extreme elements. Investors dreamed of secure revenues; the rinks could return the capital investment, meet operating costs, perhaps even turn a profit. But a roof could not keep the spring and summer temperatures from melting the ice. A roof could not slow down the escalating taxes assessed on valuable urban space. And a roof could not protect investors from the public's fickleness or boredom. Very quickly then, even the most private of operations was forced to look for new ways to bring a paying public through their doors. Montreal's elite learned this quickly, after they had invested $20,000 to build the Victoria Skating Rink in 1862–63. The brick-and-truss-built structure had a large (200 by 85 feet) ice surface surrounded by a raised promenade a yard wide. A gallery big enough for seven hundred spectators wrapped around one end of the rink. Large windows offered daylight; six huge gas chandeliers offered a bright skating surface at night. And those nights were filled with gala masquerade balls and skating festivals.[22]

Within a few years, however, shareholders could see that the finances were much tighter than they had projected. By 1873, annual operating profits were under $1,000. An economic panic had swept Western capitalism. Were patrons pinching their pennies? Was the public getting bored with skating? Changing conditions required a change in strategy and policy. Perhaps this explains why the hockey players of 1875 were deliberate in their desire to cultivate spectators. Hockey offered the promise of new revenue streams. In fact, the Victoria Skating Club soon opened its doors to outside groups, to summer activities, and to a more commercial operation. In August 1878, for instance, the rink hosted a reception for Ned Hanlan, the famous Canadian oarsman. Hanlan drew a huge crowd; he was a celebrity. But he was also a professional, the sort of fellow whom elite club members might secretly admire but publicly disdain. In the end, however, the money talked. By 1883, a more commercial operation garnered the Victoria Rink a profit of $5,459; a year later the profit was $9,544.[23]

It soon became clear that hockey needed rinks and rinks needed hockey. This marriage spawned another fundamental tension. The elites who controlled the Victoria Rink were the same elites who controlled the young "amateur" governing bodies like the Montreal Amateur Athletic Association. Their central credo was that sport should be pursued for the sake of healthy and wholesome competition, not for money. This creed was part of an all-out assault on professionals like Hanlan. It was part of a struggle for control. The amateurs quickly discovered, however, that their own enterprise depended on attracting huge crowds of paying customers who would all be bringing their money in the front door. Their rinks and their clubs would become commercial operations. And so hockey's earliest formal organizations—like those of football, track and field, and lacrosse—were born with amateur skins but commercial souls. Aspiring entrepreneurs and promoters from the working class recognized the prospects and opened their own rinks with their own teams. Eventually they ripped off the amateur skin.

Like other sports of the era, hockey had great potential value—as a spectator attraction, as a cultural symbol, as an exciting form of exercise. In both Canada and the United States, immigrants from Ireland, Scotland, England, or Wales had brought their native games with them. Hurling, bandy, and shinty would yield to hockey as the term of choice. The Anglophones of Montreal saw to that. Within two decades of hockey's reinvention at McGill, however, Francophone and Irish workers in Quebec and New York, sporting goods entrepreneurs in Halifax and Boston, rink owners in Winnipeg and Washington, DC, and young female students in Edmonton and South Hadley, Massachusetts, grabbed a piece of the game on their own terms. By the early twentieth century, the struggles for control moved to Europe. The Montreal game eventually ruled the world of hockey, but quests for control of that game looked more like shinny.

PART TWO

A GAME BECOMES *THE* GAME, 1877–1920

Global Capitalism and the World of Sport: 1877–1920

In February 1901 the American Sports Publishing Company (ASPC) produced the fourth annual edition of Spalding's *Ice Hockey and Ice Polo Guide*. The 1901 *Guide* included advertising images and details on America's Spalding brand pucks, skates, and sticks, including one page on the "championship model" stick. This included a note to the firm from Harry Trihey, captain of Montreal's Shamrocks HC, holders of the Stanley Cup. Trihey's testimonial must have grated on Canadian readers. He boldly certified that the Spalding stick, "made from models furnished by our players" was "the only stick" for the Shamrocks. It was the "best stick" they had ever used, and a stick they would "strongly recommend to all hockey players." Trihey's treason was telling. Not yet three decades old, the Montreal game was now an international commodity. Canada's best players were selling their homegrown secrets south, in return for American-made equipment, delivered to the Spalding retail outlet on Craig Street in Montreal.[1]

Few readers knew or cared that the ASPC was a subsidiary of the Spalding sporting goods firm. But it was a potent parable for part 2 of our story. Fifteen years after its 1876 birth as a small Chicago retail store, Spalding & Bros. was a colossal conglomerate, with specialized manufacturing plants (making, for example, baseball bats in Chicago, leather products in Philadelphia) feeding finished goods in dozens of sports to retail outlets around North America and some of Europe, and directly to consumers via mail order. Part of the firm's expansion strategy was the ASPC's 10-cent booklets in *Spalding's Athletic Library* series. In 1901 there were fifty-three listed, on subjects ranging from archery, baseball, fencing, and ground tumbling to

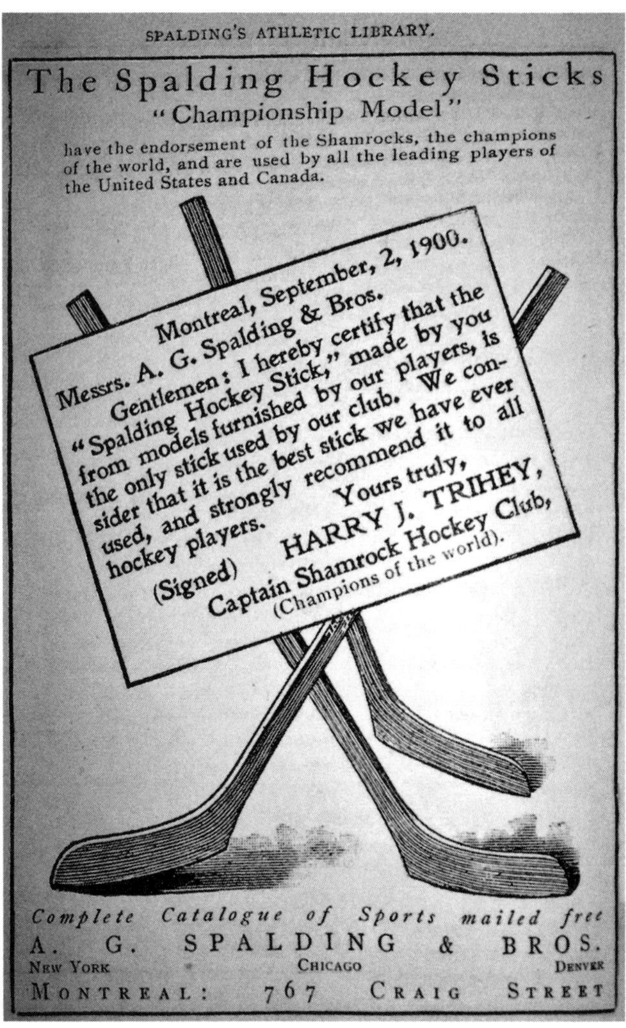
SPALDING'S ATHLETIC LIBRARY.

The Spalding Hockey Sticks
"Championship Model"
have the endorsement of the Shamrocks, the champions of the world, and are used by all the leading players of the United States and Canada.

Complete Catalogue of Sports mailed free
A. G. SPALDING & BROS.
NEW YORK CHICAGO DENVER
MONTREAL: 767 CRAIG STREET

Trihey note in Spalding 1901 *Guide* (*Spalding Ice Hockey and Ice Polo Guide* [New York: American Sports, 1901], 76)

rowing, water polo, and wrestling. Spalding's international vision showed in guidebooks for cricket, Gaelic football, soccer, and ice hockey.[2]

Most of the books included rules, history, skill instruction, player and team pictures, and abundant ads for Spalding equipment. A move into the hockey market required the purchase of Canadian expertise. Hence the deal with Trihey. But there was more. The 1901 *Guide* was "compiled" by Arthur Farrell, who began his hockey days at Montreal's Collège Sainte-

Marie, a bilingual institution. His next team was the Shamrocks, where he won Stanley Cups with Anglophones like Trihey and Francophones like Louis Belcourt, a friend from Sainte-Marie. A man of letters, Farrell edited Canada's first real hockey guidebook, *Hockey: Canada's Royal Winter Game* (1899), which appeared at least one year after Spalding's first hockey guide and included Farrell's ode to shinny. When he turned his coat to the Spalding colors, he brought his material, much of which was reprinted verbatim. This included a section titled "The Royal Game of Hockey" containing words that echoed across subsequent decades. "Canada no longer has a monopoly of the sport," he admitted. "The United States have the fever, and ice hockey is now a recognized winter sport where a few years ago it was unknown." Rinks were "springing up everywhere . . . even in distant Europe teams have been organized in Glasgow, London and Paris." It was a "regular occurrence for clubs to send their representatives thousands of miles to meet their adversaries in a friendly match." Better yet, he mused, it would "not be surprising if, some day, an enterprising team sails the broad Atlantic to cross sticks with an English or Parisian aggregation." That day was close at hand.[3]

The sport that Montreal athletes codified in the late 1870s was not yet the one we now play. Within ten years, however, they further tinkered with the rules, created a governing body in 1886 (the Amateur Hockey Association of Canada), and cemented their place as founders. By 1920, most North Americans and growing numbers of Europeans who saw or heard the term "ice hockey" conjured images of the Montreal game. Part 2 is the story of this convergence, through which *A* version of sticks and skates on ice became *THE* version.[4]

The "coolest" winter game was fashioned by humans like Farrell and Trihey, who lived and played amid the broader social and cultural conditions that they also built shift by shift, stick by stick, article by article. Montreal hockey was not the only sport to sweep across continents and oceans between 1877 and 1920. Baseball, association football, rugby, basketball, golf, and tennis enjoyed even wider circulation, all aided by particular economic conditions. As historian Jeffry Frieden showed in his masterful work on the long history of global capitalism, our current sense of open markets is nothing new. The same period that witnessed the spread of Montreal's game also witnessed an extraordinary expansion of capital. In 1870, for instance, the total railroad mileage in Canada, Russia, Latin America, India, South Africa, and Australia barely equaled that of Great Britain. By World

War I, their combined mileage was ten times greater. Frieden called the period between 1896 and 1914 the "Golden Age" of global capitalism. It rested on the gold standard, relatively open borders, and new technologies like the railroad, the steamship, and the telegraph, all of which moved money, labor, raw materials, and finished goods at speeds unimaginable a few decades before. In Frieden's words, "It would be a hundred years before the world returned to that level of globalization." Hockey was a beneficiary of these conditions. In a global (and still very much imperial) market, however, there were also many losers. Polish grain farmers could not compete easily with their competitors in Canada or the United States. Indian weavers lost their trade to British textile firms. But with prices and wages rising in much of the world, many were happy to play the game.[5]

In some ways, a newly codified sport like hockey (or football or baseball) simply took a ride on the global capital express. As Frieden put it, "Europe's free trade manufacturers and lenders found allies among the developing world's primary exporters and borrowers. British industrialists and investors had economic ties to Brazilian and Egyptian farmers, American bankers, and Australian miners. These ties were also often cultural and social, as demonstrated by the spread of English, of soccer football, and of British political economy and by the large and influential British and Anglophile communities from Buenos Aires to Shanghai." Hockey also circulated with the clerks, merchants, engineers, and missionaries who were the human faces of global capitalism. At the same time, local workers adopted the sport or not, depending on how easily they could learn the skills necessary to call it their own. Canada was an active participant in global capitalism, despite its status in these years as a self-governing but less-than-sovereign Dominion. As with its wheat, timber, fish, and fur, with the game of hockey, the young country was exporting a resource it had in abundance. Harry Trihey and Arthur Farrell represented a giant store ready to do business.[6]

New Technologies, New Markets, New Products, and New Meanings

Global capitalism grew and supported far-flung systems of harvest, production, and distribution. Many engines drove this enterprise of commodities like cotton or coal, raw materials like cloth or steel, and finished goods like dresses or bicycles. One of them was technology, which may be broadly considered as combinations of materials, knowledge, and labor that create new products and services. Technology has had a profound effect on hockey history. We have seen how ready-made, easy-on, steel skates and indoor rinks fueled a boom in skating, which nurtured more episodes of hurling, shinty, shinny, and other folk games on ice, which, in turn, spawned an experiment in Montreal in 1875. The period 1877–1920 witnessed even more developments, including new equipment, new processes of making and keeping ice indoors, new approaches to training and coaching players, new rules and new tactics developed to balance offense and defense, speed and skill, brute force and safety.[7]

Over the past century, historians and social theorists have argued that the rise of organized sport was in large part a reaction to technology's dark side. Humans increasingly embraced sports (as one theory has it) to overcome the mental and physical shackles of a machine age. The golden age of global capital certainly saw a rapid expansion of industrial technology. Russia, for instance, increased its steel production sixfold in the last decades of the nineteenth century, and doubled it again between 1905 and 1913. By World War I, Russia had two million industrial workers. In these same years, German ironworkers and steelworkers found themselves operating in larger and larger facilities, some containing more than one thousand hands. Factories and cities burgeoned with people jammed together in new forms of labor and social life. Was it not logical for workers to seek avenues for physical and mental recreation? At night and on weekends, they might find their way to a park or playground or YMCA to throw and catch, pass and shoot, punch and parry. Or, if they had the cash, they might hop a trolley downtown to a bigger venue to watch a star player do the same things. To some degree, sports became popular because they offered proof that individual, human skill still mattered, still stirred emotions. "Modern" life, it seemed, could be oppressive, and sports like hockey appeared as an antidote.[8]

Some sports, such as basketball and volleyball, were actually invented with an eye on meeting the physical and psychological needs of sedentary workers who had the discretionary income for a club membership or a ticket. In most respects, hockey was just another of these sports. What distinguished hockey, however, was its electric sense of speed and (by 1920) its clear bridge between the most advanced technology and the most primitive of human characteristics. As the sport moved outward from its Montreal stronghold and into new markets like Manitoba or Minnesota, New York or Boston, Stockholm or Berlin, what is striking is the uniform reaction in the press. The action was remarkably fast. A skilled skater was a thing to behold! At the same time, the matches seemed to trigger bloody violence, especially stick-swinging and brawling.

Hockey appealed in ways similar to hiking or bicycling. It offered a moment of physical and mental freedom. As much as coaches and managers imposed order on play, the great uncertainties caused by slick ice, round pucks, and surrounding boards meant that the players still ruled in ways that were far less evident in baseball or American football. Any athlete who plays multiple sports today will still trumpet this sense of freedom and control on the ice. It is not surprising, then, that hockey quickly attracted participants beyond the narrow social band of white, Anglophone, bourgeois males who fashioned the Montreal rules in the 1870s and 1880s. Unlike today's market, filled with hard and high economic barriers to entry, ice time and equipment were not so outrageously expensive. Historian Tobias Stark noted that in Sweden, hockey was promoted as a cheaper and more practical game than bandy because the ice surface was much smaller. And so the emerging enterprise quickly saw the tentative entries of women, blacks, Francophones, First Nations, workers, and others from backgrounds that would have quickly excluded them from the social clubs frequented by a James Creighton. But what happened to them? How did they influence the sport's development? Their story begins in the following chapters.[9]

The grinding monotony of "modern" work in factories, offices, or mines may have prompted interest in hockey as a temporary experience in freedom. But the same iron cages of innovative technology produced the infrastructure that expanded its popularity. This included the production of standardized (and often cheaper) equipment—skates, pucks, sticks, and pads—and indoor artificial ice rinks, which were essential to success in the United States and much of Europe in the 1890s and early 1900s. Many of the new rinks were heated with steam. If steam power energized the stultifying factories, it likewise moved the railroads that created regional and national markets for sports competition as much as for wheat and textiles.[10]

By the 1900s, new indoor rinks were running day and night, thanks to the expansion of electric power and electric lights. We take this all for granted now, but at the time it was a marvel to behold and report. So were new media. The telegraph, the penny press, and the camera combined to convey rich descriptions and images of sporting events to wide-

Outing magazine illustrates a "Face" for its American audience, 1893 ("Ice Hockey," *Outing* 21 [January 1893]: 254)

spread audiences. Michael Oriard skillfully argued that daily newspapers like Joseph Pulitzer's *New York World* "created" American college football in the 1880s and 1890s as part of building circulation with sensational accounts of any topic that might sell. Celebrity writers produced formulaic narratives about football's heroes, strategies, and the surrounding festival—all matched with evocative illustrations. The daily and weekly doses reached a much wider audience than any live event. As Oriard concluded, "the overwhelming majority of football's emerging audience discovered football not from the grandstand but from the daily press." It was hardly different for hockey in Montreal, Winnipeg, London, Prague, Melbourne, or Boston. New technologies of communication helped to establish new identities based on affiliation with a particular sport.[11]

The Hockey Industry and Profession

By the 1890s, the Montreal game was poised to sweep alternatives to the margins of frozen rinks, ponds, and rivers across North America. Equally important, its missionaries were set to carry the sport back across the Atlantic, where it would compete against its ancestors. Hockey would become the winter sport in Canada and parts of the United States. It would challenge for that status in several European countries. But this was not a foregone conclusion. As part 2 of our book suggests, global capitalism may have set the table, but it did not guarantee the success. It was one thing to create a set of rules that appealed to fifty or one hundred local players, as cohorts in Quebec, New Hampshire, or Cambridgeshire did in the 1880s; it was quite another to convince a wider region, a nation, or a continent. This required marketing. In the words of the period's master economic theorist, it was "not enough to produce satisfactory soap, it was also necessary to induce people to wash."[12]

Over the next four decades, hockey followed (sometimes quite deliberately) baseball's path, as entrepreneurs interacted with consumers in the marketplace to introduce and develop ready-made products designed for sale and consumption with a minimum of adaptation. These included rulebooks, "how-to" guidebooks, skates, sticks, pucks, balls, goals, and gloves. Consumers could learn by following the text and pictures in *Henley's Official Polo Guide* (1885) or Spalding's first *Ice Hockey and Ice Polo Guide* (1897). Successful commodities require systems of production and distribution. Like their counterparts in baseball, then, hockey promoters developed industry models that addressed three key elements: developing, organizing, and disciplining labor; financing the enterprise; and governing and regulating member organizations and events.[13]

As John Wong argued in his thorough account of the National Hockey League's ascent to prominence, the years between 1877 and 1920 witnessed the rise and fall of many alliances of entrepreneurs, journalists, rink owners, politicians, and assorted moguls-on-the-make, all of whom saw promise in this new product. Some lasted and others died quickly; some people were predators, some were prey. Who but the most committed historian or trivia maven remembers the Intercollegiate Hockey Association or the Federal Amateur Hockey League? And yet, they all played a role in hockey's development. In Wong's words, they "all left their imprints."[14]

In any case, the basic unit of organization was the club. Nineteenth-century sporting cultures were club cultures, built around memberships and boards of directors. They had basic purposes: circulating rules and information; raising collective capital for equipment and fields; insuring a regular supply of players; and, equally important, providing emotional support to adults playing children's games. Sports clubs were part of a wider cultural movement. Alexis de Tocqueville, the brilliant French analyst of the young American Republic, wrote that "Americans of all ages, all stations in life, and all types of disposition are forever forming associations. There are not only commercial and industrial associations in which all take part, but others of a thousand different types." It was a similar scene in Canada and England, where individuals regularly exercised their right to assemble and organize as associations, without prior approval from state authority.[15]

Continental Europe was more complex, with great variation from state to state. On the whole, however, the environment was less friendly to the development of such organizations. This was a vestige of longstanding imperial fears of rebellion and revolution. During the nineteenth century, European states had mixed and changing relationships with militaristic exercise societies and schools such as the German Turner clubs, the Spanish Pestalozzi, the Danish shooting associations, or the French gymnastic societies. Team sports like football or bandy or hockey came in the 1880s and 1890s with British or North American apostles, happy to spread their new rules, new equipment, and new games. By then, France, Germany, Switzerland, Belgium, Norway, Sweden, and others were slowly, unevenly, but palpably opening their voting rights and politics to a wider range of male citizens. Sports clubs grew in this milieu. But there was still more government oversight than in North America or Great Britain. As one history of leisure in late czarist Russia noted, the new athletic societies of the 1890s had to be "fully chartered by the Ministry of Internal Affairs." Nevertheless, in the major cities they "virtually exploded after the 1905 Revolution, when many Russians felt newly empowered."[16]

In any country, clubs provided more than funding and organization. They also built or reinforced status and identity. Some clubs grew out of occupational interests, such as New York baseball's Knickerbockers (bourgeois clerks) or Mutuals (volunteer firefighters), or factory owner interests, such as West Ham United, which started as the Thames Ironworks Football Club. Still other clubs grew within schools and universities (Eton or

McGill). Some clubs and some sports provided opportunities for women and ethnic or racial minorities to break old molds. Club membership, leadership, purposes, finances, and outcomes ranged widely in sometimes complex patterns.[17]

Part 2 traces the early years of hockey's organization, years that also saw the rise of amateurism as a new concept, a protective sphere for certain bourgeois men. Unfettered capitalism (and very little personal taxation) produced quick fortunes for those with a keen eye for the latest commodity, the newest technology, and the means to finance them. Old ruling families saw the parvenus build their own gaudy mansions, arrive at the theater in the finest new clothes, and dine at the finest restaurants. It wasn't just the new rich who were bothersome. Business needed cheap labor, which was filled by immigrants from rural areas and from overseas. Open immigration policies might be wrapped in a white robe of freedom and democracy, and they might be good for business, but they couldn't make the immigrants look "respectable" or make them speak intelligibly or worship the right God. Democracy had other negative features. As broader voting rights opened the ballot box, the corrupt political machines grew proportionately. And nothing could stop the frequent economic recessions that stirred up organized labor.[18]

In many ways, amateurism and amateur sports clubs were constructed as bastions against this tide, as safe havens, and as weapons to control it. Old elites and their allies might not be able to control political, social, and economic life, but they could build a new world of sport. Organized hockey was part of that world. Its early guardians—McGill University, the Montreal Amateur Athletic Association, the Ontario Hockey Association in Canada, Brown University, Yale University, the Amateur Hockey Association in America—all had ready access to powerful networks in finance, politics, and media.

Similar to athletics (track and field), football, golf, and tennis, Montreal hockey was codified and organized during a brief interlude in the history of sport, one that may be called the age of amateurism. It was an interlude because in England, North America, and parts of Europe, amateurism was built on top of an existing structure of commercialized and professionalized spectacles, principally in boxing, rowing, horse racing, and rudimentary forms of track and field. In the late eighteenth and early nineteenth centuries, tavern owners and assorted urban promoters had transformed older, folk amusements into spectacles, with admission fees, prize money, specialized venues, and slick advertising. England, America, and Canada all had strong, if small and sometimes outlaw, sporting crowds, which writers called the "fancy:" a term for those who followed the latest challenge matches in the sporting newspapers, who crowded the omnibuses, the special trains, and the boats that whisked them to the (often clandestine) venues where the betting was fierce, the whiskey and gin flowed freely, and pistols or knives might be drawn at the slightest affront. In this hardscrabble underworld, the patrons who put up stakes might be rich gentlemen, but the champion boxers, rowers, and runners were almost always from the working class: butchers, farmers, barkeeps—men who knew how to work with their powerful hands, arms, and legs.[19]

Respectable newspapers and magazines, and those who wrote in them, had no use for what they deemed a corrupt and corrupting subculture. But they did have a strong interest in wholesome exercise and recreation, especially in the burgeoning cities where sensational exposés and scientific, statistical studies seemed to prove that life was not healthy. When new sports like baseball, lacrosse, English football, and hockey were codified and organized by clubs between 1840 and 1890, their promoters (like James Creighton and his Montreal mates) tried to position them within the broader movement of health reform. Among other things, they promised three important elements: health, morality, and manliness.[20]

But how to prevent the butchers, the barkeeps, and the wheelwrights from taking the spotlight, as they had done early in English boxing, American baseball, or Canadian lacrosse? How to protect the spectacle from the specters of hard liquor, gambling, and crowd violence? The answer lay in the notion of amateurism. As one scholar has cogently argued, amateurism was a "strictly modern concept" that began "as the ideological means to justify an elitist system that sought to bar the working class from competition." Tight rules against prize money or other compensation might squeeze out the riffraff who could not afford the time to train and compete unless they saw the prospect of a prize for winning or (better yet) just for competing. But there was more to the proscriptions. William Curtis, a central figure in America's Amateur Athletic Union (est. 1888), put it this way:

> It should be remembered that the amateur definition, strict though it may be, is not sufficient by itself to properly protect a respectable contest. Many corner-loafers and bullies from the slum have never transgressed the amateur definition. Thieves, murderers . . . even cigarette smokers are frequently amateurs under the strictest rules.

Caspar Whitney, the influential writer for *Outing* magazine, the movement's national voice in America, was gentler but no less clear: "Let us have our own sport among the more refined elements." And so amateurism and amateur codes grew around the world in the last half of the nineteenth century, creating a separate sphere for the "respectable" classes.[21]

But herein lay the rub. If amateurism intended gentlemanly conduct for the love of the game, amateurism never intended to be free from a cash nexus. Every amateur club wanted to win. It took money to support ice time, equipment, and assorted other expenses. This meant charging admission as well as harvesting membership dues, hiring managers and coaches, and, often, making surreptitious payments to the best players. The top talent in any sport quickly recognized the leverage that came with market scarcity. Team managers quickly learned that some of the best amateurs expected to play for more than the love of the game. Some were satisfied with a sinecure job in the firm of a club booster. Others wanted cash, under the table. From the very beginning in the 1860s, then, the people who ran the amateur show had an interest in maximizing revenue. By the time avowedly professional hockey teams emerged early in the twentieth century, the struggle was less about generating cash and more about who got to keep the cash.

Every sport had its own evolution amid the turmoil of endless decision-making on how to organize competition, how to grab talent, where to play, how to control the gate and extract revenue. In broad brush, however, the entrepreneurs, promoters, and club directors who groped for more than survival recognized several alternatives to purist amateur models of clubs run *by* members *for* members. One was American baseball, which in the 1860s and 1870s fragmented over questions of amateurism. Following the successful 1869 tour of an openly professional team (Cincinnati Red Stockings), a like-minded cohort formed the National Association of Professional Base Ball Players in 1870. This group promised a fixed schedule to determine a champion, rather than a loose barnstorming or challenge system. It was a major step, but not enough for some players and directors who fumed at weak-market teams that forfeited games and failed to make payroll or to control their players or their fans. And so came the coup of 1876, when William Hulbert, Albert Spalding, and others formed the National League, where individual franchises were ruled by owners who limited the number of league franchises, controlled player movement, and plotted their way to domination. While the National League faced challengers and challenges, in 1903 it allied with its only serious rival (the American League) to form one giant cartel that stood atop a hierarchy of "minor" leagues whose teams lived in perpetual relegation. In the American baseball model, there was no way for small-market, small-venue Binghamton, New York, to be in the major league.[22]

British football experienced a similar evolution in the decades after a group of London-based clubs formed the Football Association (FA) in 1863. The FA may have begun with more upper-crust participants, but its membership quickly expanded across classes and across Britain. By the 1880s, it had swept the Midlands and on to Lancashire, where railroad workers formed the Newton Heath LYR Football Club in 1878. Clubs like Newton Heath competed according to their own schedule, except for the FA Cup Challenge (begun in 1871), at least until regional leagues took hold. With championships came squabbles over amateur purity, just as in baseball. In 1885 the FA finally legalized professionalism. But paying players required steadier revenue streams, so twelve clubs formed the Football League (FL) in 1888 with a schedule and a point system. Newton Heath joined this league in 1892, a decade before changing its name to Manchester United. Like the National League (NL) of American baseball, the FL had rivals. Unlike the NL, however, the FL did not simply crush or absorb or merge with its rivals to maintain its cartel. The British model incorporated divisions within the same league, with elevation and relegation between divisions each season. In the British football model, unlike in baseball, the small-market, small-venue Blackpool FC could play its way up and down all divisions after its founding in 1887. While slower to acknowledge and embrace outright professionalism, European hockey evolved toward the British football model of governance. America and Canada moved toward the baseball model.[23]

Part 2 of this history includes the gradual development of hockey as a profession, an avenue to fame and fortune. Professions are more than just jobs that pay. They are defined as collections of individuals recognized by their commitment to service, supported by specialized research and training, bolstered by academic credentials and codes of ethics, and often protected from competition by state licensure. The decades between 1877 and 1920 saw the rise of many professions, with significant social consequences. The "professionalization" of medicine and law, for instance, shifted and concentrated power into the hands of fewer and fewer people.[24]

Sports such as hockey, however, represented a different but equally important form of profession. What hockey shared with medicine, law, or engineering was specialized knowledge and skill that the public craved and for which they would pay. In this regard, the most important hockey "professionals" were not the players, whose shelf life was typically five to ten years. The real professionals were the growing body of coaches, administrators, officials, and journalists who enjoyed long careers in the game, shaped the playing rules, and spun the tales that captivated readers (and later listeners and viewers). In many ways hockey was a more attractive professional vehicle for these characters than it was for players. Any notions of hockey's shift from amateur to professional must encompass this body of compelling expertise and the people who wielded it.

Looking Ahead

As with all historical phenomena, circumstance and character acted in concert to create and codify hockey into one, soon-to-be dominant version, the Montreal game. Beyond this contingency, the spread of Montreal hockey can be explained historically in rational, orderly, and systematic ways. The diffusion followed traceable geographic, economic, and social patterns in the five decades after 1877. The "big push," a popular impulse to spread the game widely in these years, was remarkable for the pace of its progress, the depth of the inroads it made into North American culture, and the foothold it gained in Europe. To comprehend and map hockey's organic growth in these years, we need to understand both *soil* and *seed*, and, as important, how that seed was cast.

Chapter 5 discusses developments in Canada from 1877 to 1895, beginning with the importance of Montreal's Winter Carnival, 1883–89. History often moves via contingencies, and this was one of them. It is no stretch to suggest "no Montreal Carnival, no Stanley Cup, no NHL, no Canada Cup." But the Carnival did occur, and hockey benefited. At the same time, there was no guarantee that the game would succeed beyond its little beachhead on the St. Lawrence River. Skaters had already developed organized alternatives in America and in Europe. Chapter 6 describes the history of three such competitors: hockey at St. Paul's School in Concord, New Hampshire; the wildly popular game of "polo," played indoors on roller skates and outdoors on ice; and the European game of bandy. The last two sports still exist, in organized, popular forms. Yet by 1920 all of these competitors yielded center stage to the Montreal game. Chapter 7 describes how that happened in America. Chapters 8 and 9 consider two fundamental questions: *What game?* and *Whose game?* If the shape of hockey converged, its social base expanded. By 1920, it enjoyed rabid followings among female clerks, black factory workers, students, Icelandic immigrants, Francophone and First Nations peoples, and more. They all played by the same rules, but in many important ways they were all making the game their own. Chapter 10 examines the European experience. Only a series of contingencies, culminating at the 1920 Antwerp Olympics, gave James Creighton's game the nod over bandy.

5

Breakout in Canada: 1877–1900

"Canada," one American recalled of her visit to the Montreal Winter Carnival, "is the land where King Winter holds high court." Fannie Coe wasn't the first to equate winter with the essence of Canada, and she would be far from the last. But there was something special about Montreal's weeklong frozen festivals of 1883–89 that drew the connection forcefully to thousands of visitors like Coe. Aimed to boost a sagging local economy, the carnival was a series of special events that *staged* winter within the city. To create a spectacle of the season, organizers constructed elaborate "sets," such as the Living Arch, the Ice Lion, and the Ice Palace, a veritable castle made of five-hundred-pound ice blocks piled 130 feet high. In addition to fancy dress balls and masquerade skating parties, there were other performances of winter: snowshoeing "tramps," tobogganing competitions, and an ice hockey tournament. For the finale, the carnival featured the Attack of the Ice Palace, where members of local snowshoe clubs, each holding roman candles, "defended" their terrain against an onslaught of locals and visitors, who "stormed" the castle amid an impressive display of fireworks. It all reads like the event script for a twenty-first-century First Night celebration. But this was the Montreal Winter Carnival in the 1880s. It proved to be a crucial lever in the expansion of the still-infant game conceived in the Victoria Rink.[1]

Hockey's diffusion from Montreal to parts east and west is a story about the movement of men, goods, and capital to such swift and wide embrace that by the late 1890s player-author Arthur Farrell would dub it "Canada's Royal Winter Game," and a respected writer James Macdonald Oxley would call it "a distinctly home product."[2] Between 1875 and 1895, the Montreal game experienced what economists call extensive and intensive growth. That is, it spread quantitatively and changed qualitatively. Increasingly more Canadians played it in increasingly more places, as it was altered and improved, and codified. These years constitute a critical moment, for it was not inevitable that Montreal hockey would take root anywhere outside of that city. Indeed, it was not guaranteed that it would appeal beyond the small circle of elite Anglo-amateur sportsmen who published the rules. But something important happened. Hockey "took off," just as did industrialization in 1780s Britain, revivalist Christianity in 1820s America, or separatism in 1960s Quebec. Like all historical patterns, this mushrooming was remarkable, but nonetheless explicable. A Montreal game became Canada's national game in two short decades because of familiar historical forces: contingency, individual interests, and luck.

In the past thirty years, historians and geographers have begun to examine the ways that games tend to spread among people—"ludic diffusion," they call it. Before the mid-1980s, one authority wrote, the "growth and international spread of sport . . . tended to be interpreted as a somewhat random series of events, lacking in any historical order of predictability."[3] Sports somehow popped up in various places at various times. Since then, scholars have come to see sport diffusion as a more orderly form of cultural transfer, as innovations not unlike business inventions that left persistent, consequential and measurable wakes. Research has pointed to several vectors for the spread of international sport, including such things as imperial connection (for sports such as cricket and soccer), hierarchical diffusion, geographical proximity or "neighborhood," and common climate.[4] Within countries, sports spread by logical means: along main transportation routes such as rivers, roads, and railways; among those of common racial, ethnic, and class backgrounds; individually, by single human "carriers"; and through facilities—designated playing fields and stadiums—created for the purpose.[5] These vectors worked in concert, producing complex patterns of diffusion.

Hockey's particular case has received limited attention, with debates focused more on origins—where and when the modern version actually began—than on how it spread.[6] Any serious study must acknowledge the varying claims for "genesis," those of Halifax, Dartmouth, Kingston, and Montreal. But birth details would matter little (beyond antiquarian interest) if the game and its followers, players, and promoters had never grown, if they had never become fruitful and multiplied. In fact, the game

TABLE 5.1. Hockey's Diaspora: Montreal Rules Hockey in Canada, 1875–1895

1875	Montreal, QC
1878	Quebec City, QC
1884	Ottawa, ON
1886	Kingston, ON; Winnipeg, MB
1888	Toronto, ON
1889	Halifax/Dartmouth, NS
1890	Lindsay, ON; Hamilton, ON
1891	Cornwall, ON; Peterborough, ON
1891–93	London, ON; Niagara Falls, ON
1892	Saint John, NB; Portage la Prairie, MB
1893	Carberry, MB; Brandon, MB; Calgary, NWT
1894	Regina, NWT; Moose Jaw, NWT; Edmonton and Strathcona, NWT; Fort Saskatchewan, NWT; Rat Portage (Kenora), ON; Moncton, NB
1895	Moosomin, NWT; Medicine Hat, NWT; Fredericton, NB; Revelstoke, BC

grew quickly—but not randomly. There was an order and a direction to its early diffusion.

Montreal rules spread quickly eastward and westward within Canada. Table 5.1 provides dates and places of first débuts, compiled from references in the scholarly and antiquarian literature.[7] The list is not comprehensive; there is still too little research on early local hockey in Canada. Still, it provides a strong and promising indication of the scale of growth and its direction. It also begs explanation.

At the Hub of Empire: Montreal and the Carnival, 1877–1890

As we have seen, the affair on the Victoria Skating Rink in March 1875 was a clever hybrid that borrowed heavily from hurling, shinty, rugby, lacrosse, and especially field hockey. Like rugby football, early hockey was an onside game that outlawed forward passing. More conspicuously, but for their skates and sticks, early hockeyists *looked* like rugby players, with distinctive costumes: striped sweaters, high stockings, and calf-length padded pants. From lacrosse came the goals: two six-foot poles placed six feet apart and sometimes adorned with flags on top. Lacrosse's one referee and two goal judges (one for each goal) recommended to hockey men the same system of policing. At the same time, the matches in the Victoria Rink possessed at least two unborrowed traits: nine men a side and a wooden disc as the object of players' pursuits—not a vulcanized rubber "puck" until 1876. The first written rules, then, were hardly a comprehensive delineation of the game; they were grafted onto the sport as it was being played. But things changed quickly. According to newspaper reports in 1880, Montreal teams had, by convention, reduced the number of players to eight per side and settled on the appropriate span for a contest's duration: two thirty-minute periods with a ten-minute intermission. This was the sport, an improved version, which entered the 1880s.[8]

And here is a historical contingency. The new game was hatched and nurtured just before the Montreal business community and city leaders decided to sell their city and its attractions to wealthy visitors through an annual pageant, the Montreal Winter Carnival. The idea was simple. By hosting a carnival, a seasonally depressed local economy could pitch its industry, its modern buildings, its transportation facilities and its unique cultural character though a celebration of its *nordicity*. The plan worked. "Upwards of 50,000 visitors attended the Carnival Week festivities held in Montreal in 1883, 1884, 1885, 1887, and 1889," one observer noted. "They came from other Canadian cities, from across the US, and from as far afield as England, Germany, and Havana. . . . Montreal became a 'winter resort,' so that international visitors might see for themselves how Canadians had mastered the climate and, far from suffering in the winter, could relish its health-giving benefits."[9]

Though hockey was included from the start among the panoply of winter doings, one point is clear: hockey needed the Montreal Winter Carnival more than the carnival needed hockey. When Montreal AAA member R. D. McGibbon first aired his idea of a winter fair in 1882, hockey was not at the top of the list of intended activities. Instead, snowshoeing and tobogganing—Anglo-Canadian Montrealers' inventions of Canadian tradition—were to be the backbone of carnival activity.[10] But hockey was not inconspicuous. Adorning the carnival's monumental arch (constructed at the corner of St. James Street and McGill College in the city's financial district) at the 1887 fair were all the meaningful symbols of the winter city: royal emblems, snowshoes, conifer branches, toboggans, *and hockey sticks*.[11]

Venues changed over the years. The first carnival tournament was played on the St. Lawrence River in February 1883 among three teams: McGill, the Montreal Victorias, and a side from Quebec City. Since the latter could only field a seven-man team, the other two teams followed suit. The tournament was first organized by the Victoria Hockey Club and, after 1884, the Montreal Hockey Club. Representatives from these clubs "determined the direction of the carnival's programs [and] subscribed the money."[12] Teams competed for a coveted prize, the silver Birks (or "Bedouin") Cup donated, presumably, by the Montreal silver merchant. The 1884 tournament moved to an outdoor rink on the campus of McGill University, but by the following year, the event had moved indoors, to the Crystal Ice Rink.

The competitors changed, too, slightly but significantly. In 1884 four Montreal teams—Crystals, Wanderers, Victorias (the winners), and McGill (the hosts)—were joined by the Ottawa Hockey Club, where the sport had only recently started. In 1885 Ottawa faced off against five Montreal teams, losing to the MAAA in the championship game.[13] When the carnival returned in 1887 and 1889 after brief absences in 1886 (due to a smallpox epidemic) and 1888 (due to finances), hockey returned with it. By 1889, however, the Carnival had become "dehydrated . . . overdrawn . . . [and] tedious." For hockey, the free ride was over.[14]

But in a broader, historical context, the carnival survived long enough to provide an important platform to showcase a new sport's worth. The carnival shaped and spread the Montreal game in its early years, for at least three reasons. The first involved *form*. Quebec's necessity was the mother of hockey invention: in 1884 the Carnival tournament committee confirmed the previous year's decision to play seven-man hockey, and it stuck. A seven-man game created space for skating and stickhandling, passing and shooting—a faster, more exciting version that lasted in eastern Canada until 1911 and longer in western Canada and the United States. For the (ill-fated) 1886 tournament, a clearer and augmented set of rules were set out, by which all invited teams were expected to abide. These changes were made by Sam Robertson of the Montreal Amateur Athletic Association and Jack Arnton of the Montreal Victorias along with representatives from the hockey clubs at McGill and the Montreal Crystals. By and large, the changes they proposed and codified were fine tuning, more additions than revisions. For example, among these amendments were stipulations that described stick length (any length) and width (no more than three inches wide) and the composition of the "puck" (vulcanized rubber), that forbade goaltenders from kneeling or lying on the ice, and that revised the height of the goal to four feet. The new rules, now fourteen in number, were published in the *Montreal Star* in 1886.[15]

Second, the carnival exposed this still-new pastime to an audience of visitors who had the potential to help it grow. Hockey did not have to rely solely on its early advocates—its "evangels"—to spread the word to the "unwashed" far afield: the carnival itself brought them to Montreal. A final point dovetails with the second. It was during the Montreal Winter Carnival that hockey found its most famous patron and potentially influential backer: Her Majesty's newly appointed representative to the Government of Canada, Frederick Arthur (Lord) Stanley, first baron of Preston. "In February 1889," archivist James Whalen wrote, "Lord Stanley witnessed his first hockey match at the Montreal Winter carnival when the Montreal Victorias defeated the Montreal AAA team by a score of 2–1. Expressing 'his great delight in the game of hockey and the expertness of the players,' Stanley became a regular and distinguished spectator." Three years later, he donated a challenge trophy for the amateur hockey champions of the Dominion.[16] Circumstance had intervened: the carnival was dying in 1889, but it still had the power to proclaim the game. The Montreal Winter Carnival happened at a critical time for ice hockey. It provided a popular national and international venue for a new sport and stamped it as a symbol of Canadian winter. It kept a fledgling game aloft. It ennobled and legitimated the sport, and set it up for widespread growth in the following decade.

Moving beyond Montreal

A notable feature of hockey's early geographic diffusion was a two-stage pattern of growth. Between 1875 and 1885, Montreal-rules hockey was concentrated in urban central Canada (Montreal, Quebec City, and Ottawa), about a 250-mile span. After 1885 the game spread like a swirling blizzard to old, established eastern centers such as Halifax, Saint John, Fredericton, and Moncton; to the urban industrial heartland of southern Ontario (Toronto and Hamilton) and to the urban frontier in Canada's west: Winnipeg, Calgary, Regina, and Edmonton. Moreover, hockey spread across the Canadian countryside as well: to railway boomtowns, transportation depots, and agricultural service centers. By 1895, it was played in six of Canada's (then) seven provinces and in its only territory (Northwest Territory). This "takeoff" in the late 1880s and early 1890s continued strongly into the early twentieth century. As historian Alan Metcalfe wrote: "By 1905 it had invaded all corners of Canada," urban and rural, English and French. "[B]y 1905, hockey leagues had become a permanent part of the Canadian winters. . . . Hockey pervaded the whole country."[17] And such explosive growth could hardly be contained by international borders; it leapt swiftly across the Canadian-American boundary, establishing itself in eastern, midwestern and West Coast American cities and towns.

Expansion was visible in its depth as much as in its breadth. In places such as Montreal and Winnipeg, hockey captured the public's fascination and following in profound ways. "In Winnipeg, by 1898–99," wrote historian Morris Mott, "there were well over one hundred teams. . . . Ten years later, by 1909, there were so many . . . that no person possibly could have counted them all." In Montreal, according to Michel Vigneault, by 1910 there were 1,082 hockey players in the city, of whom almost one-third were French-Canadian.[18] The Montreal game grew *vertically* as well as horizontally. Its promoters developed a pyramid structure in the 1880s and 1890s, which ranked rationalized play according to age and skill groups, crafted and enforced rules of play, and rewarded the best teams with honors. Hockey was institutionalized. The game's governors made sense of the sport and sorted out its players and teams. Growth beckoned control.

The proliferation of players and teams triggered the mushrooming of intra- and intercity leagues and the need for governing bodies. By 1895, Montreal, Toronto, Kingston, Winnipeg, Halifax, Saint John, Quebec City, Peterborough, Ottawa, and other places boasted leagues made of teams composed by bankers and clerks, coreligionists and service club members, and other constituencies among urban and urbanizing populations. The universities, moreover, established intercollegiate competition. Town and city teams competing in intercity leagues (or "series") required stability and governance. The grandiose-sounding Amateur Hockey Association of Canada (AHAC) was formed in 1886 when the three teams from Montreal (the Victorias, Crystals, and Montrealers) joined with teams from Ottawa and Quebec in a series of scheduled competitions. The AHAC codified and kept the official rules—the gold standard of the game—later adopted by hockey players, teams, and leagues across Canada and into the United States. "From this date," Arthur Farrell wrote in 1899, "hockey made rapid strides in its advancement as a popular, scientific sport."[19] It was the AHAC teams that the Canadian Governor General, Lord Stanley, had in mind when he donated in 1892 the famous trophy bearing his name for the Dominion hockey championship. In an oft-quoted letter, he wrote of his intentions:

> I have for some time been thinking that it would be a good thing if there were a challenge cup which would be held, from year to year, by the leading hockey club in Canada. There does not appear to be any such

> outward or visible sign of the championship at present, and considering the interest that hockey matches now elicit, and the importance of having the games fairly played under rules generally recognized, I am willing to give a cup that shall be held from year to year by the winning club.[20]

Within two years the association held extensive discussions on the criteria for awarding the trophy, already known as the Stanley Cup. "So great," note the AHAC minutes, "was the importance attached to the possession of this trophy that every technicality was made use of to fix conditions so that there could be no possibility of any discussion as to title at a later date." The Cup was intended to elicit open competition among all teams in Canada, like England's Football Association Cup. In fact, the Cup's importance became so great within two decades that a few particular leagues schemed to wrestle sole jurisdiction.[21]

Lord Stanley's gesture raised the stakes of play among AHAC members, but it also highlighted their national aspirations. The AHAC did not last past 1898; it was replaced with the Canadian Amateur Hockey League in that year, a move that signaled the beginning of the end of amateur, gentlemanly hockey in Canada.[22] But as the Dominion's first elite league of senior hockey, the AHAC established the game's rules, and for most of this era showcased the highest standard of play. Of course, the AHAC was not alone. In Manitoba, senior teams began a series of challenge matches as early as 1890, and by 1892 the Manitoba and North-West Amateur Hockey Association had come into being.[23] Farther south and east, the Ontario Hockey Association was founded with thirteen teams in 1890, the central governing body and regulator for senior (and later junior [1893] and intermediate [1896]) play in Canada's most populous province.[24] By 1891, the OHA had established its own schedule of games and playoffs, and its own Championship Cup, donated by the league's first president, Lieutenant Colonel A. M. Crosby.[25] In only two decades, Canada's hockey world had become a busy place. It had not taken very long for this newly codified sport to become both broadly cast and thick on the ground.

The Four Vectors of Growth

By 1895, much of Canada had embraced this winter game, in some ways old, in some ways new. A hockey *flood* was about to sweep across the northern tier of the United States. Why the speed and passion of this diffusion both north and south of the 49th parallel? Cultural historians have begun to explain why the sport appealed to Canadians at a time when their identity as a nation was in an adolescent stage. Recently granted Dominion status by Britain in 1867, Canada was wrestling in the late nineteenth century with its place in the Empire and in the world. Even sport could be related to this cultural reckoning. Michael Robidoux has argued that ice hockey and lacrosse, Canada's national sports, appealed to late Victorian Canadians precisely because the contests seemed to reject imperial imperatives. Openly violent, simply played, and (in the case of the former) uniquely northern; they were colonial alternatives to staid and stolid English "garrison" games, such as cricket, and the emblematically American game of baseball. In this context, the growth of lacrosse and hockey in Canada was a subtle cultural declaration of difference. "[In] a disparate nation, divided in terms of language, region, and ethnicity—lacking in identity and national unity," Robidoux wrote, hockey became "a valuable vehicle for expressing national identity. . . . Hockey displayed men who were perceived to be stoic, courageous, and physically dominant: . . . an identifiable image outside of a British Victorian framework. . . . In essence, hockey became a vehicle of resistance against British and American hegemony."[26] Though intriguing, cultural theorizing goes only so far toward a full explanation. At a more demonstrable level, four identifiable vectors directed the game outward from Montreal, across much of Canada and beyond it, to the United States and Europe: individual carriers, social groupings, transportation routes (especially railways), and indoor rink development.

Canadian Evangels

The first vector involved individuals, hockey's Canadian evangels. The game spread across the Dominion and beyond because, in short, people took it there. Examples abound. Among the very first disciples was Albert Peter Low (1861–1942), captain and goaltender of the McGill University team that won the first Montreal Carnival tournament. Having graduated with first-class honors, Low became a trailblazing geologist and mapmaker, gaining success very early in his career. He joined the Canadian Geological Survey (CGS) in Ottawa in 1881 and impressed his superiors well enough that he was appointed director of the CGS in 1906 and deputy minister of mines by 1907. He authored exploration and geological texts. Curiously, Low's biographical entries mention nothing of his role in spreading the

Montreal game. Here, his accomplishments were important, too, but brief. Ottawa's "iron man" helped organize the very first Ottawa hockey sides and starred (along with fellow McGill alumnus T. D. Greene) on Ottawa's carnival team of 1884. It is likely he didn't play much after that. From 1885 to 1895, Low was in northern Quebec and Labrador, exploring and mapping the territory for the CGS. But he had opened a new hockey market in the nation's capital.[27]

In Kingston, the game was introduced on harbor ice by Royal Military College cadets, such as William Archibald Hastings Kerr, a native of Montreal. "Hockey skated up into Ontario from the Province of Quebec," Kerr recalled in a piece he wrote for *Dominion Illustrated* magazine.[28] In 1886 a team of RMC cadets took on a side from cross-town Queen's University—the first game in an annual series—which the latter won 1–0. A star of the 1887 RMC-Queen's game (he scored four goals), Cadet Kerr went on to enroll in law school in Ontario and served as vice-president of the Ontario Hockey Association. But Kerr was only one of several cadet evangels who brought the game to Kingston. RMC's early teams were made up of cadets from the Maritimes (where shinny and Halifax Rules hockey had long been played) and Quebec. "The three Queen's RMC matches, 1886 to 1888 . . . were of historic significance to the new ice sport," wrote Bill Fitsell.

> They brought together players from two areas of Canada . . . where hockey originated and developed, and also from the centres where it first spread, Quebec and Ottawa, and produced dedicated players who were dispersed to other non-playing centres throughout North America. . . . The cadets' captain, William Herchimer Rose, a native of Sorel, P.Q. . . . later settled in Morrisburg, Ont., and captained that town's early teams.[29]

Montreal hockey first appeared in Toronto in 1888, not out of any miraculous conception but because Thomas Paton brought it there. Paton was a goaltender for the Montreal Amateur Athletic Association's "Winged Wheelers." Like Low, he had played in the Montreal Winter Carnival tournament. Visiting friends in Toronto, he explained the game, sent for hockey sticks and a puck via telegraph and train, and assembled the first scrimmages at Toronto's Granite Curling Club in February 1888. Once demonstrated, the sport caught on well, even after Paton returned to Montreal to resume his play with the Winged Wheelers. A goaltender, Paton was a member of the first team ever awarded the Stanley Cup.[30]

In small-town Lindsay, Ontario, hockey was introduced by no less an authority than the community's member of Parliament, John Barron (1850–1936), a barrister (later county court judge) and legal scholar who practiced law in Lindsay but played hockey with a parliamentary team in Ottawa while the House of Commons was in session. After the town built a covered skating rink in 1889, Barron helped form the Lindsay Hockey Club in January 1890. The club had an auspicious beginning when, in February 1890, the Rideau Rebels (the Government House team featuring James Creighton and two of Lord Stanley's sons) visited Lindsay's new arena and narrowly trimmed the hosts, 4–3. Barron played goaltender in the game, but he must have known his playing days were numbered. He took on a new role in November of that year as chairman of the formative meeting of the Ontario Hockey Association.[31]

Montreal missionaries moved west as well. Hockey came to Winnipeg through the person of P. A. Macdonald, a lawyer born in Gananoque, Ontario, in 1857 who came to Winnipeg as a young man in 1880. "Sometime in the mid-80s, perhaps in the winter of 1885–86," noted Morris Mott, Macdonald "traveled to Montreal [returning] to Winnipeg with a few of the hockey sticks then in use in the 'home' of hockey. . . . He was a participant in the 'Bankers' vs. 'All-Comers' matches. . . . Soon he became one of Winnipeg's leading citizens and references to him over the years in the city's newspapers often mentioned that he had introduced hockey to Winnipeggers."[32] Though Macdonald conveyed the game, it was not until 1890 that Winnipeg had its first hockey club, fittingly called the "Victorias." Founded and bolstered by other hockey players from the east, the Victorias did not take long to master the game, finishing first in their league in each of their first twelve years of play. "The Vics played 'state of the art' hockey in the years from about 1890 to 1903," wrote Mott, and they introduced it to many westerners.[33] In 1896 they won the Stanley Cup. The same pattern of diffusion was repeated farther west. "Many of the first hockey players in Saskatchewan came from Ontario," wrote another historian. "Imports were often necessary since communities with American, central and eastern European and British immigrants had not been exposed to hockey. It was the children of the new immigrants that became the 'home grown' source of talent for later teams."[34]

Missionaries were not needed in Atlantic Canada. Sportsmen in Halifax and Dartmouth, Nova Scotia, had been playing their own brand of the sport—shinny, or "Halifax Rules" hockey. That game, with significantly different rules, thrived in Maritime Canada. But the two versions collided when a team from Dartmouth, the Chebucto Amateur Athletic Club, toured Montreal and Quebec City in 1889. The Chebuctos fared poorly against their central Canadian opponents, losing all four scheduled games (including those played under Halifax Rules) and being outscored 23 to 3. Whether or not the results were interpreted as an indictment of Halifax Rules, Maritime hockeyists began to abandon their traditions and play the game by Montreal rules in the early 1890s. Here, it seems, no one needed to say anything: the proof of the pudding was in the eating.[35]

Social Class—A First Look

Hockey in the 1880s and early 1890s was not indiscriminately contagious; it traveled in certain circles. At first, it was not a vehicle for social integration. The game spread initially among cliques and coteries of middle- and upper-class Anglo-Canadians, the scions of wealth and men on the road to respectability in new cities and towns. As one archivist wrote, the young sport was "restricted to the privileged segments of society." Only in the late 1890s and the 1900s did it begin to gain an unsure foothold among others in Canadian society: workers, Natives, blacks, French Canadians, and women.[36]

In mid-Victorian urban Canada, class mattered. Class shaped the economic, geographic, and social landscapes in which ordinary people lived. If social mobility was sometimes attained, Victorian Canada was no "best poor man's country," and three perennial classes—working, "middle," and upper—became entrenched during the Second Industrial Revolution (1870–1920).[37] Class was not merely an objective reality for Canadians in this era; it was a subjective and gendered experience. Respectable, "manly" men strove for gentility through a polished appearance, modest and tactful demeanor, and dignified carriage. And organized sport in nineteenth-century Canada was an important proving ground for those seeking manly character, a classroom for lessons in respectability, humility, hard work, and fair play. Canadian playing fields were reflections of the gentlemanly conduct first articulated in British boarding schools and didactic literature such as *Tom Brown's School Days*, codified in the innumerable constitutions and bylaws of amateur athletic associations and burned into the consciences of individual players. Even in the heat of athletic battle, Victorian Canadian sportsmen were expected to be gentlemen. Hockey was no exception, despite its violent tendencies. On the ice, character mattered. As Colin Howell noted, "the hockey gentleman . . . played with 'ginger' but also with respect for his opponents, the referee, and the game."[38] Hockey was a character builder as well as a vigorous form of manly exercise. Montreal Shamrock and author Arthur Farrell wrote in 1899: "The very adhering to the rules, the spirit of fair play that characterizes a manly game, the overcoming of all fears and all difficulties, the modest victory, the frank acknowledgement of defeat, all tend to build up, to educate, the mental faculties, just as the long practice, the swift race, and the hard check help to develope the physical man."[39] Hockey in the 1870s and 1880s was claimed by a bourgeois class culture in Canada. The reward for its players was not to be found in wins or in pay, but in playing well and honorably—cleanly, fairly, and unselfishly.

In Toronto, the sport first landed at the exclusive Granite Curling Club, a respectable social organization whose two hundred to three hundred members frequented a prominent downtown clubhouse and fenced complex on Church Street. Founded in 1875, its grounds featured lawn tennis and bowling courts; its edifice housed dining rooms, a reading room, and, after 1880, a large indoor rink, used in summer for lacrosse training, art fairs, and political gatherings, and in winter for curling matches and the Montreal game. "We have seen many a merry bout of hockey played within the walls of the 'old rink,'" club officer James Hedley reported in an article for *Outing* magazine published in the year after the sport's Toronto debut.[40]

When the Ontario Hockey Association (OHA) was formed in November 1890 (at the suggestion of Arthur Stanley), the league's thirteen founding members comprised six Toronto clubs that included private schools and universities, places where the bourgeois ideals of gentlemanly sport were rooted. In addition to the Granites, among the OHA's first Toronto members were the Victorias, St. George's, the Royal School of Infantry, and Osgoode Hall (the province's preeminent law school). The University of Toronto established a hockey club in 1891, and when the Toronto Junior Hockey League was formed in the city in 1893, its members included the Granite Club, the province's leading elite private school (Upper Canada College), and three university teams: Trinity, Varsity (University of Toronto), and Victoria.[41] With these origins, it is not difficult to see how the OHA became known as an elite-run bastion of old-style amateurism. It was born that way.[42]

Hockey moved in genteel circles when it spread to Ottawa as well. Some of the first generation of players in the national capital were members of Canada's growing civil service, professionals like Albert Low and like James Creighton, by the late 1880s a well-placed clerk in the Canadian Senate. They were respectable young men whose occupational authority spilled over into their athletic endeavors. One such man was Philip Danksen (P. D.) Ross, a former McGill player who laced up his skates for the Rideau Rebels and the Ottawa Hockey Club in the 1880s and 1890s, winning an OHA title with the OHC in 1891. Publisher of the *Ottawa Journal*, it was him (along with Sheriff John Sweetland) to whom the governor general turned in 1893 when he needed trustees to administer challenge matches for the Stanley Cup.[43]

This early elite phase could hardly last for very long. Fast and challenging, hockey was much too broadly appealing for that. Even by the mid-1890s, the game had begun to escape its bourgeois beginnings. In Ottawa and Toronto, Halifax and Saint John, it was taken up by urban bankers, mercantile clerks, and women. Moreover, in more peripheral areas such as the Canadian West, burgeoning frontier cities and towns were never large enough in these years to host a bourgeois *class*. The first clubs in mid-1890s Edmonton and Strathcona, for example, were "open to both patricians and plebeians": Hudson's Bay Company officers and manufacturers crossed sticks with simple farmers, ranchers, clerks and shopkeepers. "[C]lass lines were not yet fully established," historian Terence O'Riordan wrote. "The games, the parties, and even the clubs themselves were accessible to most of the citizens."[44]

Still, for at least a quarter-century after its founding, hockey was widely reputed to be a bourgeois game rooted in respectable educational institutions and the professions. Its genteel aura lingered. This cultural equation was expressed clearly in a saccharine but telling short story written by Gertrude Cundill for *Outing* magazine in 1899, titled "A Hockey Match." The piece traces the doings of "young Curwin," a gregarious petty bourgeois Montrealer. Popular, though unlucky in love, he was a "fair all-round athlete" and the recently elected captain of the Beavers, the city's most prominent hockey team. In the story, Curwin struggles through the winter—bored at the office, tired of dinners with his male friends at the "clubs," evenings at home alone with the book and pipe and "drinking tea . . . in somebody's drawing-room," and longing for a meaningful relationship with a woman—until he is smitten with the image of a young beauty he meets in the street as she is running after her stray dog. Curwin aids her, but in a case of mistaken identity he is informed by a neighbor that his crush is, in fact, a married woman. Himself crushed, Curwin resolves to focus his efforts on the Beavers' success and plans a trip to New York "to see what a round of theatres would do for him." On the strength of Curwin's final goal, the Beavers win the Canadian championship game, but in the process a broken stick (Curwin's) escapes the rink boundaries and injures a young woman spectator. Coincidentally, that woman turns out to be Curwin's belle. He delays his New York trip to visit her at home and apologizes to her with flowers. Here, he discovers the mistake: the young woman is not married at all (it was her sister to whom the neighbor had referred) and is, in fact, a big fan of Curwin's and the Beavers'. The title's pun is completed: Curwin does go to New York, but not alone. Despite its thinness and hokum, "A Hockey Match" is most interesting for its setting. The Beavers are lodged in *bourgeois* Montreal, where vigorous and desperate sport coexists comfortably with honor and old-style chivalry. For Cundill (herself a Westmount bourgeoise), it made perfect sense to use the Montreal game as a vehicle for her bourgeois love story.[45]

The Railway

The third, more practical vector of hockey's dissemination involved transportation routes, particularly the expanding national and international railways on which rested the hope and promise of late-nineteenth-century Canada. The era saw nothing less than a transportation revolution. "Before the Grand Trunk opened its first line between Montreal and Toronto in November 1856," historian Ken Cruikshank noted, "fewer than 900 miles of railway were in operation in Canada. By 1905, [Canada had] produced a network covering over 20,000 miles."[46] Central among these railways was the Canadian Pacific Railway (CPR), the first Canadian transcontinental line (completed in 1886), the economic spine of the new nation and a mythic symbol of national integration. Though a subject of political scandal and the cause of appreciable public debt, the CPR earned admiration from contemporaries because, as one early railway promoter declared, it "magically transformed a widely scattered Dominion into a prosperous and progressive nation."[47] Like the United States, Canada's railway age witnessed mergers and monopolization on a massive scale: hundreds of charters for railway construction were granted by Canadian governments in the 1850s, '60s, and '70s, but by the late 1880s most lines had become consolidated into a few large corporations, the CPR and the Grand Trunk

Pacific being unquestionably at the vanguard. The story of the railway has been a central theme for Canadian historians seeking to explain the growth of national spirit and iconography, or the development of a national economy.[48] For scholars, the railway was important as a conveyor of men, goods, capital, and ideas. Hockey was one of the many pieces of cultural freight that traveled on early Canadian rails.

It was, of course, the railway that carried Tom Paton from Montreal to Toronto in 1887, Royal Military College students from Montreal and Halifax to their studies and training in Kingston, Ontario, and P. A. Macdonald from Gananoque to Montreal to Winnipeg in 1886. It was the railway that carried the Chebucto Amateur Athletic Club from Halifax to Montreal and Quebec in 1889. It was the railway that bore the critical tour of the Rideau Rebels to play fledgling local clubs and demonstrate the sport in Lindsay, Toronto, and Kingston in 1890. And it was the railway that conveyed the eastern exhibition tours of the Winnipeg All-Stars in 1893 and the Winnipeg Victorias in 1895.

Railways moved countless others from one North American town to the next, carrying the game with them as they went. Railways spread the good news of this new sport and enabled its consolidation. Hockey followed the railway and the telegraph into Canada's western provinces. Together, these two technologies allowed for rapid organization. One writer in 1896 remembered the winter of 1892–93 as one "marked by a wave of hockey that rolled over the North-West like a flood."[49] Railways hauled most of this product. "Hockey began in southern Saskatchewan in towns and villages along the Canadian Pacific Railway (CPR) line," one local historian added. The same was true in Alberta. "Railway routes often determined which teams joined a league," Gary Zeman wrote in *Alberta on Ice*. "In the first Central Alberta Hockey League of 1903 Didsbury, Olds, Lacombe, Red Deer, Wetaskiwin and Leduc were all members because they were on the same line."[50] And Montreal-rules hockey appeared in the mining, lumbering, and smelting towns in the Kootenay region of British Columbia in the late 1890s because CPR and (the American) Great Northern branch lines connected them to the rest of eastern Canada.[51] Canada's railways had important psychological effect on Canadian sportsmen of the 1880s and 1890s. Though the country now sprawled across an unfathomable distance, railways consolidated Canada's hockey world, just as it did the economy and politics. Integrated transcontinental railways somehow made the idea of truly national sport and a national championship seem both practicable and promising.

Indoor Rinks

Rinks were the final piece. As we saw earlier, the Montreal game was hatched in Victoria Rink, built for the promotion of skating in general. Some of the most important hockey promoters, like the Meagher brothers, were figure skaters. Where there was skating, there was the prospect of hockey. But if skating or hockey were to be something beyond a sport for those who lived in frozen winters, indoor ice rinks—and, more important, artificial ice rinks—were a necessity. This breakthrough occurred in the mid-1890s. From that point on, the game would endure (and suffer) from prophesies repeated in markets around the world: "We have a rink, hockey has a bright future." It would not be so easy.

Commercially run, covered rinks were critical to hockey's expansion. If Canada had a dozen in the early 1870s, many more towns built outdoor and indoor rinks over the next two decades. By the mid-1890s, the citizens of Portage la Prairie, Manitoba, were willing and able to invest $3,000 in a rink, and Edmonton had one rink that boasted three waiting rooms. In 1894, when the Montreal game was moving south into America, a feature article in the *Philadelphia Inquirer* recognized this reality. "Hockey," wrote the author, "is perfected with a view to its being played in covered rinks."[52]

The proprietors of these rinks remain somewhat shadowy figures, but Ottawa's Dey family was probably representative of the period's entrepreneurs. Joseph Dey and his sons Edwin (Ted), William, and E. Frank opened and operated three "Dey" rinks in the capital city between 1884 and 1927. The facilities complemented the family's other business, boat building, a logical coupling since both enterprises required an eye for efficient design. Ottawa boasted an indoor natural ice rink as early as 1868, but in December 1884 the Deys opened a competitor on the east bank of the Rideau Canal, right near their boat works. Historian Paul Kitchen described the rink as a "striking building with a high curved roof, . . . some 200 feet long by 99 feet wide" with a natural ice surface roughly 150 by 90 feet. It featured steam-heated dressing rooms and electric lights. Like roller-rink proprietors throughout North America and Europe, the Dey brothers (father Joe quickly turned the rink business over to his sons) envisioned their prime revenue streams to come from open skating, festivals, and exhibitions. The average patron paid 15 cents (gentlemen) or 10 cents (ladies) to skate or watch. Hockey was a supplement in 1884. It would take time for it to displace skating as the core revenue source. Still, in 1887 the Deys worked a deal with the young Ottawa Hockey Club, which used the rink for meetings, practice, and games.[53]

Hockey expanded beyond its Montreal base hand in hand with new, indoor ice rinks. By 1905, in one account, "nearly every community contained a commercially operated ice arena where games were played from January until early March." It was not just the major cities. Digby, Nova Scotia (pop. 12,470), had the North End Rink; and High River, Alberta (pop. 1,182), had its own Victoria Rink. These were natural ice surfaces and often unheated, but they insured a regular schedule of matches in confines that certainly beat sitting, standing, or skating amid snow, sleet, or blasts of arctic air. In 1890s Ottawa, the Dey brothers lost the sites of their rink and their boat business to urban progress, in their case to the Canada Atlantic Railway. But if the steam rail bumped them out, the electric streetcar gave them a new home. Like streetcars everywhere, the Ottawa Electric Railway promised in its promotions to give Ottawans "access to every quarter of the city and to remote places." While time and cost limited the realities of this vision, there is no doubt that streetcar transit opened new horizons to urban dwellers. This allowed Ted and William Dey to buy a parcel of land on the corner of Ann and Bay Streets (along one of the trolley lines), where they built a bigger rink with an eye on hockey. The rink opened in December 1896 with a natural ice surface that measured 200 by 81 feet. It featured "spectator galleries" at both ends and a bandstand that housed musicians during public skating and the press during hockey games. Although the Ottawa Hockey Club had left the Dey brothers for cheaper ice when the Rideau Rink opened in 1890, the now-championship club saw the chance for bigger crowds at the Dey's new Ann Street (later Gladstone Street) venue, and they called it home all but one year of the next ten. The rink's capacity is not clear. In press accounts the crowds ranged from one thousand (a small turnout) to well over three thousand. Uncertainties in actual attendance doubtless caused tensions between the Dey brothers and the Ottawas since the rink owner normally shared gate receipts with both teams.[54]

By 1910, Arthur Farrell still described hockey as Canada's "national winter game," but he also noted a bipolar phenomenon, with eastern hotbeds in Montreal, Ottawa, and Quebec and western strongholds in Kenora and Winnipeg. In Farrell's opinion, Toronto had not yet produced the "same skilled aggregations which have fought the battles of east and west" because it lacked the "same steady winter weather." Wherever indoor natural ice could be more or less guaranteed from December until mid-March, hockey crowds buoyed the game "to the same relative position as base ball does in summer in the United States." A simple roof, however, would not get the job done in Toronto. Farrell concluded that Toronto had only one way to reach the same "eminent position" as its rivals in Quebec or Manitoba: build an "artificial ice plant." A year later, the Patrick brothers built artificial ice rinks in Vancouver and Victoria. Toronto followed in 1912. These rinks helped to spread "big-time" hockey across all of Canada. Farrell's east-west axis now ranged from Victoria to Quebec.[55]

The four vectors are critical for understanding how and why hockey arrived where it did in Canada and beyond the 1880s and 1890s. Individual and evangelical promotion, a bourgeois embrace by elite and middle-class sportsmen, emerging technologies in transportation, communication, and ice-making: these were the basic pathways by which the newly coded sport spread in its early and most critical years. Still, in describing it, there is a danger of oversimplification. Cultural diffusion of any sort is never an even or predetermined process. Several scholars have recently outlined grand theories to explain why certain sports (and not others) gained supremacy on Europe's and America's cultural calendars. Their works are provocative and valuable, but they also underestimate or ignore the role of contingency and chance. Maarten Van Bottenburg, for instance, explained the diffusion of "global games" largely on the basis of social class. "Which sports became popular in which areas depended on the social origins of its devotees and the social significance with which they invested their sports." He dismissed "ad-hoc explanations for the popularization of a particular sport in a particular location at a particular moment in time." While social class was important, it was hardly the only factor in determining why hockey developed as it did. As we have seen, there were other contingencies.[56]

It is important to note that these vectors—individual enthusiasm, social class, transportation, and indoor rinks—developed in a sort of dynamism or synergy. They relied on one another to spread the game as quickly and effectively as they did. Enthusiasm for Canada's game abounded during these late-nineteenth-century years. The sweep of Montreal hockey even inspired saccharine musings among the game's players and observers in this era. "Like the Klondyke gold fever, the love of hockey spreads," Farrell wrote in 1899. "A few years ago, the sport was known only in a few cities of the Dominion—now, from far east Halifax to frigid Winnipeg the glorious game is played. . . . It is a regular occurrence for clubs to send their representatives thousands of miles to meet their adversaries in a friendly match. Teams from Manitoba and Nova Scotia have repeatedly visited Montreal, and clubs from the latter place have returned the compliment."[57] But enthusiasm for the game alone would not suffice. It had to be placed in a social context and given the ability to travel quickly and plant itself in architectural nodes—ice arenas. Because of these vectors, hockey became a national rite of winter. The result was a permanent foothold in the Canadian imagination.

There is an important final point to make about the *direction* of Montreal hockey's growth in the 1870s, '80s, and '90s. It is perhaps ironic that Montreal's generosity begat its own decline as the prime locus. One product of the game's spread was the realization that hockey's best and brightest could play and live outside of the city that gave birth to the game—in Ottawa, Winnipeg, Toronto, Halifax, and in many other places, large and small. Montreal's moment as the sole, dominating hub of hockey was short lived. As historian Colin Howell noted, the observation that sport "radiates outward from the imperial centre to elites in colonial hinterlands and then downward through the social scale" leaves an unfortunate impression that, in the process, "the metropolis is acting upon, shaping, and asserting its control over the hinterland." Sport never travels so neatly. Howell added: "Sport history has always been made on the ground." In this way, the Montreal game, as it spread, was shared, not asserted; negotiated, not imposed. Players in the game's many and varied hinterlands, from British Columbia to Nova Scotia, adopted it not out of duty or direction but because it suited them. Hockey developed local resonance and following because it thrilled people and, over time, developed local meaning for players, promoters, managers, and spectators.[58] Once outside of Montreal, hockey's genie was out of the bottle. In 1896, when Winnipeg's Victorias won the Stanley Cup, the symbolism could not have been lost on the followers of the game. Not only had hockey "won the West" but "the West had won" at hockey.[59] If Winnipeg could own the game, why not anywhere else?

6

Alternative Games: 1880–1900

In the late 1990s, Dave Bidini's tropic of hockey swathed over a renaissance of global capitalism. He suited up and played in China, the Persian Gulf, and eastern Europe. A century earlier, he might have been equally at home with the easy international flow of goods, people, and their cultures. But he would have been surprised at the varying forms of hockey in North America and Europe alone. The Montreal game was only then emerging from its regional success in the province of Quebec. Canadians to the east and west quickly embraced the special, new sport. But America and Europe had their own games of sticks and skates on ice. It would take years of vigorous promotion to convert some of their markets to the version Bidini took for granted a century later.[1]

By 1890, the Montreal Winter Carnival had launched something special. From a fan's casual perspective a century later, events seem ordained. Within a few short decades, the Montreal game ruled as the world's coolest winter team sport. This triumphant perspective, however, overlooks the most interesting part of this history: the market struggles between 1890 and 1920, when this one version of the ice game competed against ancestors and close relatives. Montreal hockey was a latecomer wherever its missionaries advanced. It is not too far-fetched to suggest that, with a twist of fate here or there, the Stanley Cup might have been lost in someone's attic years ago, as Canada, the United States, and Europe embraced world and Olympic competition in a sport called bandy or polo.

In the same years the Montreal game was widening its winter grip, several alternative stick-and-ball games competed for popularity in North America and Europe—equally legitimate sports that might well have become *the* winter game. Each began as a local pastime whose foundation gradually shifted from collective memory to written rules. Each was soon embraced and promoted by governing bodies: some local, some national, and some international. Each played a role in preparing particular markets for organized and commercialized forms of Canada's new product. Two of them—polo (now called roller hockey) and bandy—have continued to the present day. One of them, at St. Paul's School, represented the way local skating games adapted and thrived in isolation, even if they eventually gave way to the Montreal version. It is important to recognize these alternatives, and there were doubtless *many* more, because their existence both qualifies the novelty of hockey as a sport in this era and belies the inevitability of Canadian supremacy. These games prepared the way for Montreal hockey even as it swept them aside. They provide pithy examples of the ways in which many sports experienced convergence—how one version became *the* version.[2]

St. Paul's School

Boys and masters at St. Paul's School in Concord, New Hampshire, played hockey as early as 1860. By the 1870s, they began to refine and codify their game, just as Creighton and his McGill associates were doing for their own in Montreal. A set of "Hockey" Rules appeared in 1875 in the St. Paul's student newspaper, the *Horae Scholasticae*—intended to organize and tame the popular, mass game played on fall fields. They outlined a maximum of fifty players, prescribed specifications on equipment, offside, and free hits, and made clear prohibitions on high sticks. School records, however, also indicate that the field game moved to ice in the winter. "Hockey," said the *Horae* in 1877, "has again been resumed on the playgrounds, and we are sure it will meet with its usual popularity when the skating is fine." As in Montreal, a set of published rules helped to nudge a pastime toward a standardized part of the local culture. Within four years, the school store was stocking skates and "hockeys" (sticks) to meet and expand demand. By 1881, the *Horae* reported that the game "claims the attention of the whole school."[3]

One of the leaders in this winter craze was James P. Conover, a popular master who was described as a "sinewy" athlete, possessed of "great strength, quickness, and versatility." At a time when school athletics were all intramural, Conover exemplified the playing master who was both mentor and teammate. He led a decade of developing athletic fields, tennis courts, skating rinks, even a toboggan slide. Since hockey was played outdoors on natural ice, shoveling and flooding were necessary labors. Conover exhorted the boys to organize shovel crews, who garnered fees for keeping the ice clear and smooth.[4]

In November 1883, the boys took their next step: they developed and published a set of ice-hockey rules. These are the first published American rules uncovered to date. A preface clearly indicates that the boys had read the Montreal rules, but the president of the St. Paul's Athletic Association, Robert L. Stevens, Conover's distant cousin, complained that he was "at a loss to understand the terms employed in the rules of the Montreal club." He concluded that "they would be of little value" to the local game, so he and his colleagues went their own way. Their rules suggest an amalgamation of field hockey and rugby. If the president could not appreciate some of the Canadian rules, he did recognize the value of a puck. In a nod to Montreal, this game featured a "block" (a wooden disc) knocked toward goals of ten-foot width. The teams played eleven a side, beginning with a "knock off," like a kickoff, at center ice. Two especially unusual features were "safeties" (awarded when a player moved the block behind his own goal line) and rugby-style "knock outs" (or line-outs) to put the block back into play from the sidelines. High-sticking above the hips was prohibited; the sole umpire was charged to disqualify repeat offenders.[5]

By 1885, Stevens, his younger brother Richard, Master Conover, and others formed a Hockey Association to organize teams, develop a schedule, and oversee play, which was closely followed in the school paper. To avoid lopsided matches of form versus form (class versus class) the boys organized interclass clubs with names like Delphian, Mohican, and Rugby. Competition was intense. Despite a school ethos that formally scorned *emulation*, a casual perusal of game stories suggests the emergence of some star players, including Conover, the Stevens brothers, and a young student named Malcolm Gordon, who would later teach at the school and coach Hobey Baker. The emergence of stars was a logical result of an 1885 rule outlawing "lagging" or offsides. Since teammates could not be ahead of the block carrier, solo rushes or "runs" were a standard form of attack.[6]

The 1880s were something of a golden age for the St. Paul's ice sport. A set of standard rules, published schedules, and articles that created heroes all wrapped the game in an aura of manliness and skill. A photo of the 1889 champion Mohicans depicts a hardened bunch of skaters.

Mohican (Isthmian) champion hockey team, 1889, St. Paul's School (Courtesy of St. Paul's School Archives)

The youthful Malcolm Gordon, with visible moustache, stands among his teammates, each clenching a short "hockey," which was probably wielded with one hand. Wool gloves, heavy sweater, and stocking hat were their only protective equipment. As one scribe announced, the game "requires as much quickness of eye and hand, and I may say foot, as [football or lacrosse], but at the same time a learner can enjoy it as well as an old hand." Cold winters, abundant nearby ponds, and organized groups of shovelers provided the ice. The school store stocked ready-made equipment: hockeys, skates, skate straps, and blocks. As to the last, the student newspaper recommended the "Canadian blocks, which are so made that they cannot rise from the ice, thereby freeing the players from the danger of being hit in the face or head."[7] In 1886, St. Paul's School had a base of hockey just as well organized as that in Montreal. Had the school been (or chosen to be) better linked to other schools and to public newspapers, it is possible that the St. Paul's game could have been a strong rival to the Montreal Game. That did not happen, in part because of other historical contingencies.

We have seen the importance of indoor rinks in shaping Canadian developments. A wall of boards around the ice helped turn a freewheeling affair into a precise, more uniform exploitation of space. More important, even in cold climates, *indoor* rinks rescued hockey from sleet, snow, and the rising azimuth of February's sun. St. Paul's boys played on ponds, which suffered the fickle New England weather. School records are filled with odes to clear, black, late November ice and curses to January or February snow, rain, or thaw.[8] Associations and clubs of shovelers could clear the snow, for fees. And by 1883, some genius had crafted a way to flood the low grounds between the Rectory and the Upper School, thus gaining an advantage over the sleets that could periodically rough up the ice.[9] But only a roof and refrigeration could combat high temperatures. St. Paul's had neither. Players did their best to tame nature, but it was not enough to save the new sport of 1883. And so, from 1888 to 1895, a stretch of unfavorable weather dissolved the hockey traditions. A recurring, ill-timed rhythm of snows, thaws, and rains cut ice-time to little or nothing. One entry in the 1890 *Rural Record* (the school journal) told all: "the lack of good skating" meant no scheduled matches. The next year's weather data included 6.7 inches of rain in the month of January, hardly the stuff for a brisk skate. By 1895, when they got back on the ice in earnest, players adopted a novelty called ice polo.[10]

Bandy

Things were slightly different in Europe, where one 1901 primer on ice sports included a chapter on "Bandy, Or Ice Hockey." The author clearly described bandy, a game played with a short stick and ball, much like field hockey. He had no reservations, however, using an array of names: "Bandy, otherwise known as Hockey on the ice, or Shinty." With equal ease, he linked bandy to ancient games in China and northwestern Europe, where he claimed the game "sprang spontaneously into life long generations ago, in East Anglia and the Netherlands," whose frozen winter waterways gave many workers a long "enforced holiday." Human imaginations alone, argued the author, insured the "discovery of primitive bone or horn runners," on which the "man of speed and accuracy of hand and eye" could wield stick on ball and thus enjoy "full scope for the display of his cunning."[11]

As we have seen, such a winter game may have been a logical development in many northern countries during the Little Ice Age. But the name bandy was distinctly English. And so was its home. North of London lies "The Wash," a large bay into which run the rivers Welland, Great Ouse, and Nene. They and their tributaries traverse a low-lying, marshy area known as the Fens of Lincolnshire, Cambridgeshire, and Norfolk. As one of bandy's best-known champions (C. G. Tebbutt) wrote in 1894, the Fen district was "specially suitable" for a game like bandy. "The uplands," he wrote, "send their water after heavy rains down into the Fen rivers, which overflow and flood the washes and low-lying meadows; then should a frost come, any quantity of ice is available." The nineteenth century provided ample frost, and places like Bury Fen became hotbeds of skating and bandy, particularly, wrote Tebbutt, among the "bargemen and fishermen." While local tradition claimed a long history of bandy, Tebbutt traced organized matches to the "great frost of 1813–14," when the Thames also froze over. In the decades that followed, locals like William Leeland and Joseph Tebbutt played for fun, for a leg of mutton, or for good cheer over a post-match "randy" at a local pub. They cut their bandies "from the lower branches of the pollard willow trees" that thrived in the Fens. A cricket ball, a bung of cork or wood, or later an India-rubber ball served them well. Fenmen brought their game to London in 1860 and 1868. The cold winters that nurtured St. Paul's School hockey in the late 1870s and 1880s also saw a bloom in Fen-district bandy. In Tebbutt's words, "matches and return matches were played with Swavesey, Chatteris, St. Ives, Huntingdon, and Godmanchester at Mare Fen, Hertford, Houghton, and on Bury Fen." But bandy also flourished around London, "in the neighbourhood of Hampton Court, on the Rick Pond, Home Pond, Virginia Water, Wimbledon Lake" and other waterways.[12]

By 1882, the Fenmen held a "general meeting" at St. Ives to discuss and adopt a code of rules. By that time, the National Skating Association (NSA) had published rules for "Hockey on the Ice: As Played in the Fens" and also "As Played in the Metropolitan District." The Fens rules used "bandy" and "hockey" interchangeably. Different rules in different places were no ingredient for expansion. Bandy's major breakthrough came in February 1891 with the formation of the Bandy Association, which provided a formal, autonomous structure for rules, records, and competition. Like St. Paul's and Montreal hockey, the bandy rules, whether NSA or Bandy Association, described a game much like field hockey, which had been codified in England in 1875. On a recommended ice surface of 100 by 50 yards, eleven players per side wielded short sticks (one handed) that were limited to a width of 2 inches and a length of 4 feet. The game began (and commenced after goals) with the referee throwing the ball (or bung) into the air at center ice. Teams advanced the ball with clever stickhandling or passing, but players had to stay onside (even or behind the ball) in the attacking half of the ice. Thus, unlike the Montreal game, forward passing was allowed in a team's defensive half. Goal posts were 11 feet apart, with a tape or lathe forming the crossbar 7 feet high. The 1895 Bandy Association rules (like those of field and ice hockey) prohibited "charging, kicking, collaring, shinning, tripping . . . and rough play." While the early rules were silent about goalkeepers, in later years they took the stick out of the keeper's hands. Balls crossing the sidelines or end lines were restarted with free hits or corners, as in field hockey.[13]

In January 1891 four Tebbutt boys led a Bury Fen team across the Channel for a match at a Haarlem rink against a team representing the Netherlands Football and Athletic Union. It was played "before a large number of spectators," recalled C. G. Tebbutt, and accompanied by "the strains of a large band." Two additional matches followed in Amsterdam. Organized bandy had gone international. Three years later, Tebbutt traveled to Sweden for an international skating championship. According to Swedish historian Bill Sund, he "brought along necessary equipment" for bandy and "offered instruction to members of the Stockholm Gymnastics Association." The response was "disappointing." In 1896, nonetheless, three Swedish nobles, "who had played bandy in England, founded the Stockholm Hockey Club." This interplay of names—bandy and hockey—was also reflected on the ice. According to Sund, "the game was played according to the English rules and at first with the stipulated rubber ball, but this was later exchanged for a wooden puck." In Sweden and in other countries, the terms bandy and hockey were often used interchangeably, a fact that makes the historian's job both frustrating and interesting. The Stockholm club attracted other members of the city's "upper crust" as well as "diplomatic staff from the British and American embassies" who competed, wrote Sund, "in the exclusive suburb of Saltsjöbaden."[14]

Sund's research reveals that bandy-hockey was soon embraced by Stockholm-area schools, and then by the "nearby university town of Uppsala, where well-to-do upper- and middle-class students pursued further studies." Some formed the Uppsala Students' Hockey Club and the Uppsala Secondary Pupil's Hockey Club (which evolved into IFK Uppsala). Often played on club grounds that were flooded in the winter, the game moved to a new level in 1901 with the start of the Nordic Games, a celebration of winter sports held intermittently from 1901 to 1926, which included ski jumping, curling, bandy-hockey, and skeleton. Largely a Swedish phenomenon, the Nordic Games inspired the growth of many bandy-hockey teams, including IFK Uppsala, the Royal Naval College Hockey Club, the Djursholm Hockey Club, and the Officers' Hockey Club. The Swedes held their first national bandy-hockey championships in 1907. The game was well suited to the country's long, frozen winters and its still largely rural economy. In Sund's words, players competed on "frozen-over football pitches or measured fields or natural ice on ponds, lakes, and the sea." It was often called "winter football."[15]

The Swedes soon formed a bandy-hockey alliance with their old enemies, the Russians. Global capitalism replaced war with trade. Peter the Great had built his capital on the Gulf of Finland, and St. Petersburg's famous lion faced west toward Sweden and Charles XII's armies in a symbolic gesture of defiance. By 1900, however, Russia was importing Swedish timber, iron ore, and various other agricultural products. As Sund put it, "Russia, and more particularly St. Petersburg became a primary foreign base for Swedish industry at the beginning of the century." Russia's bourgeoisie embraced western culture and western business models, especially those of the British and the Germans. The engineers, clerks, foremen, and managers who opened western businesses in Russia in the 1880s and 1890s also brought along soccer, cycling, track and field, and bandy-hockey—as well as the club model of organizing these various sports. Russian clubs organized around status, location, and business. According to historian Robert Edelman, bandy-hockey debuted in Russia alongside soccer-football. In his words, "English and some German residents played the game in Petersburg in an organized fashion in 1897, and by 1901, regularly scheduled games were taking place in the capital among teams representing many of the same clubs that had fielded soccer teams." By 1907, the capital supported fifteen clubs, including Yusopov Sad, which conducted a successful tour of Sweden, Norway, and Germany, winning six of eight matches. On the eve of the Great War, the All-Russia Ice Hockey Association boasted thirty-two member clubs. War and revolution would disrupt this line of evolution.[16]

Clearly, this was all bandy, but like the Swedes, the Russians called the game "hockey" (*khokkei*), adding to the confusion for historians and providing themselves with ammunition to make Cold War claims of "invention." If bandy-hockey migrated with global capital from west to east, the Russians were soon surpassing their earlier masters. According to Sund, when Yusopov Sad visited Stockholm and Uppsala in 1907, they taught the Swedes how to swat down high balls with a "tennis stroke," play better defense, strap skates onto boots more securely, and wrap pigskin around the stick. In his words, since 1907, "technical innovations in bandy have tended to come from Russia, whether it involved the skates, the sharpening of edges, club design, the crouching, very fast style of skating, the system of play or the introduction of sideboards along the long sides of the field."[17]

Russia and Sweden were not alone in adopting bandy before they took up the Montreal game. For instance, in January 1896, Vienna's *Allgemeine Sport-Zeitung* offered a story about seven-per-side "hockey." Apparently, the game was actually bandy, which within three years gained some traction in Vienna and spread from there to other cities. Hungary embraced bandy in 1905; by 1914, Budapest's BKE club was among Europe's elite teams, winning international contests in Prague and St. Moritz. Switzerland, Germany, Bohemia, and Austria all hosted organized bandy before they converted. In some cases (such as Switzerland) the conversion was swift. In others (such as Russia and Sweden), it took decades for the Canadian game to dominate. In either case, one cannot say that Montreal hockey summarily swept bandy away. Bandy's large ice surface (maximum 200 by 100 yards, minimum 100 by 50 yards) put a premium on speed and ball control. While some players brought their game to indoor rinks, bandy stayed largely outdoors, on big sheets. Montreal hockey, on the other hand, evolved more as an indoor game on a restricted ice surface. Ironically, it was this dependence on indoor rinks that gave hockey an advantage. Rink owners and rink managers were a powerful lobby, one that bandy lacked.[18]

Polo

While players in Montreal, in Concord, and in England's Fens District were slowly organizing local codes of rules, another hockey-like game bloomed on both sides of the Atlantic as a full-fledged commercial and (in America) professional sport, complete with its own rabid fan bases and strong media attention. In many ways, it was far more developed that its rivals. It was called polo. It was played on wood surfaces or on ice. The players wore roller skates or ice skates. In most other ways the game looked much like bandy. It was born of historical coincidence and commercial convenience, in the wake of a nineteenth-century invention—the roller skate. In

1863, American James L. Plimpton improved earlier European designs to create a patented roller skate that offered at once speed, maneuverability, and balance. Within a few years, private associations and entrepreneurs erected roller rinks on both sides of the Atlantic. Women and men from all walks of life flocked to these venues both to skate and to watch. But there was a clear problem to the business. Skating or watching lap after lap around a short track proved monotonous. Polo emerged as a way to attract and keep the customers.[19]

Why the name polo? It was probably another historical coincidence. About the time of this roller boom, British officers returned home from India with a new equestrian game that involved whacking a ball through goal posts. In 1876, James Gordon Bennett brought that version of polo to America, using the elite resort of Newport, Rhode Island, as a launching pad. Within a year or two, someone or some group in London or Newport rechristened this game of hockey-on-roller-skates, calling it by the fancier name of polo. *Henley's Official Polo Guide, 1885*, claimed that organized club play began in 1878 in Newport, where the well-heeled Roller Skating Association had converted a downtown building into a roller rink. South London's Lava Rink was also an early site for polo (the English called the game rink polo; North Americans often called it, simply, polo). The game was fast and fan-friendly. By 1885, it spread across America's northeast and Midwest, leading Henley's *Guide* to claim that "every good roller skating rink has a well organized club." As proof of its "great popularity," the *Guide* noted, "it is only necessary to call attention to the fact that on nights when Polo is played, the rinks are crowded, not only by skaters, but by people who go only to see the game."[20]

The Maine Polo League's 1884 rules offer the game's basics. Goals were 6 feet wide and from 3 to 4 feet high (polo developed goal cages years before they were adopted for hockey). In Maine, each team had seven players: a goalkeeper, two defenders (called goal-cover and point-cover), two midfielders (called backers) and two forwards (called rushers). Other leagues used six or five players per side. The ball was 3 inches in diameter. The stick was the basic "hockey" or "bandy," with a maximum 4-foot length and 1-inch diameter. The game started with a "rush" toward a ball placed at rink center, the players on each side having positioned themselves in an inverted wedge, with the rushers at the wide top of the wedge. At the referee's signal, they skated to the ball and the game was on. Players whacked or dribbled with one hand, there was no offside, and the ball

Polo at Newport (*Harper's Weekly* 27 [8 September 1883]: 561)

could bounce into the stands and back into play. So the action was fast and furious. Matches were best of three or best of five goals. There was no intentional striking, kicking, or tripping. The whirling sticks, however, often triggered fisticuffs. It was a game that promised speed, scoring, and violence.[21] Within a decade, polo clubs and leagues stretched from Saint John, New Brunswick, to Washington, DC; from Gloucester, Massachusetts, to Covington, Kentucky, and Marquette, Michigan. The English took another decade to organize in leagues. Some were one-year wonders. Others, like the Western League, were avowedly professional.[22]

Polo's growth in the 1880s linked closely to a boom in roller rink building, which in turn was driven by more improvements in skate design and more aggressive marketing campaigns by skate manufacturers. In 1885, for instance, a reporter for the *St. Paul Pioneer Press* listed eleven rinks in Minneapolis, four in St. Paul, and some three dozen sprinkled around other towns. Most of them were under two years old, built at costs from $1,000 to $10,000. That same year, the *Muncie (Ind.) Daily News* reported "numerous rumors of the erection of rinks until nearly every capitalist of Muncie was reported to have under construction plans and specifications tending in the direction of a rink." Some rinks were barely more than warehouses. Others reached palatial proportions. Boston's Institute Rink (1883) housed 50,000 square feet of Seyssel asphalt surrounded by a 30,000-square-foot birch track, where a thousand skaters could wander "without crowding" under the electric lights. There were also cloak, toilet, and smoking rooms. A restaurant sold popcorn balls and hot cider.[23]

In a crowded market, rink entrepreneurs needed to be creative to grow revenues, which came from four basic sources: admission, skate rental, lessons, and concessions. The rinks needed a range of products. Few patrons could abide skating in circles on a short track, hour after hour, night after night. And so the rink owners and managers scheduled costume balls, exhibitions, and demonstrations of all types. Historian Dwight Hoover found that one Muncie rink owner offered succeeding nights of "football, Peck's Bad Boy and his Pa, and three Mormon giants, all on skates." Contortionists and tight ropers—all on wheels—joined trapeze artists and bicycle acts to keep the crowds coming. But it was not enough. Roller polo was a logical addition. A typical rink program might include open skating from 7:00–9:00 P.M., followed by a one-hour polo match, followed by more "circuit skating." Boston's Institute Skating Rink billed polo, fancy skating, a one-mile race, and a "grand parade" among events for its grand opening on November 27, 1883.[24]

Rink owners joined hands with manufacturers and local newspapers to promote the new game. In Richmond, Indiana, M. C. Henley operated a skate factory where his three hundred workers turned out almost twenty-five hundred pairs of skates per day. He quickly began publishing a *Polo Guide* that offered tips on playing, rules from six different leagues, testimonials, and lots of advertisements for his equipment, including the balls, sticks, and goal posts that were "regulation" in the Western League. In Boston, sporting goods dealers George Wright and Henry Ditson became "official publishers" for the New England Polo League when it opened in 1883. Ditson served on the league's board of directors. The Wright and Ditson Company also sponsored a team in the league. Local newspapers jumped on the new sport as a source of juicy narrative. For instance, the *Brockton Enterprise* described an 1887 match between a local side and one from New Bedford: "The floor, which was permeated with wax for dancers' use, was as slippery as glass and the falls were numerous and so hard that you could hear the players' souls rattle when their bodies struck the floor." Many papers ran regular columns about polo and skating, under taglines such as "On Rollers" or "Polo at the Rinks." The *Boston Herald* promoted the leagues (and their readership) with pocket schedules that included pictures and lineups.[25]

Newspaper stories—often nothing more than press releases written by team and league officials—graphically described the slashing sticks, whirling fists, cracked bones, and bloodied heads. One 1895 promo conveyed the visceral attraction: "Roller polo can arouse the sluggish blood, make the businessman forget his troubles, and afford much food for heated argument." Newspapers cast players as heroes and villains, just as they did in baseball and football. The *Herald* targeted brawlers such as Stoneham's LeDuc and Woburn's McKay, who went at it in one game with hard checks and slashes; McKay reacted with a wild swing. "The hickory hit LeDuc on the right temple," the reporter wrote, "and he went down to the surface as if dead."[26]

In New England, in some parts of the Midwest, in England, and on the Continent, polo leagues continued well into the twentieth century. Children continued to play roller hockey on playgrounds in many towns and cities. The game was resurrected with every improvement in skate design. By the 1990s, roller hockey was back on a big-time stage. But the first boom ended in the 1890s, a victim of intense competition, speculation, changing consumer taste, and attacks by moralists, who viewed indoor and often dark rinks as nothing but dens for Satan's worst evils. Many of the rinks were converted into warehouses.[27]

In polo's cold-weather markets—particularly the Upper Midwest, New England, and the Maritimes—the game had another life, on ice. In Minnesota, Frank Barron and the St. Paul Polo Club (1883) were playing on ice almost as soon as they were playing on a wood floor. Several Twin Cities roller rinks flooded their surfaces in winter to provide for indoor ice versions of skating and polo. By 1886, the St. Paul Winter Carnival included ice polo in its lineup of competitions. "Up here in St. Paul," the local *Globe* announced in January 1887, "polo is played by enthusiasts on skates." Around the same time, the roller polo teams in Marquette, Calumet, Ishpeming, and Houghton, Michigan, also moved their indoor games to ice. So did teams from Saint John, New Brunswick. New England was a bit slower to organize ice polo clubs, but by the mid-1890s, students at Yale, Brown, Boston College, MIT, Tufts, and Harvard had organized teams, as did students in a dozen Greater Boston high schools. After the opening of three artificial ice rinks in 1896, ice polo was even more organized in metropolitan New York, with dozens of amateur, school, and college clubs. In most of these locations, the players first learned the game on roller rinks. As Brown University's Alexander Meiklejohn ('93) recalled some six decades later, he and others basically moved to the ice "the game which the professionals were playing on roller rinks." Meiklejohn added that he was an "ardent devotee to that game in both of its forms."[28]

Within a decade, ice polo yielded to ice hockey in most North American markets. At the same time, the sport of polo was much more than a passing craze. The roller version was gaining strength in Europe. By 1914, the English Amateur Rink Polo Association had dozens of teams organized in three regions: northern, midlands, and southern. On the Continent, the game thrived in Italy as *hockey su rotelle* and in Spain as *hockey sobre patines*. In parts of Canada and the United States, roller and ice polo were bridge sports that linked unorganized games like shinny to the Montreal game that swept across the Dominion in the 1880s and down into the Lower Forty-Eight in the next decade. Bill Fitsell found, for instance, that when Canada's Queen's College and the Royal Military College played the "first game of organized hockey in Kingston," the players borrowed polo sticks "from the new roller rink." In the mid-1890s, whole teams of ice polo players converted en masse to ice hockey. Polo had prepared them to take that step. In Vancouver, roller polo served as a backup for hockey when the weather did not allow outdoor ice. In January 1903 the *Vancouver Province* announced that the January thaw had prompted "nearly all the crack hockey players" to swell the ranks of the roller skaters. Moreover, they planned to organize a "roller hockey" league that would "no doubt soon be as popular here as it is in the East." Clearly, they were thinking of polo. If ice hockey was the "fastest sport," the *Province* was happy to mark polo as the "next fastest."[29]

Polo and hockey players were merging during these decades. So were fans. Polo contained the ingredients found later in hockey: lighted indoor rinks, skill and violence, heroes and villains, published schedules, and rabid fan followings. For workers, the sport replayed their everyday harsh, physical experience, where the tough hand ruled. For bourgeois fans, the game was a titillating window into that same world. This combination created loyal followings. When the Stillwater, Minnesota, team came to play Minneapolis in March 1885, their fans rode on a "special train." A *Boston Herald* game story that same year captured similar communities at work. The "Paris" team of East Boston played at Gloucester on January 9. At "Johnson's Central" billiard rooms in East Boston, fans could bet and "hear" the results via telephone, and the Eastern Railroad offered a special excursion for three hundred Paris supporters from East Boston and Chelsea. The match in Gloucester lasted almost forty minutes in front of fifteen hundred fans, who cheered and jumped so much, they "broke down the raised platform for reserved seats." The *Herald* mentioned "two or three rough and tumble fights among the fans." Roger Pout's research suggests that on the eve of World War I, English crowds typically averaged between fifteen hundred and twenty-five hundred people, with the occasional "big match" attracting more than six thousand raucous fans. A polo match was a chance to bust loose, for players and spectators alike.[30]

Montreal hockey eventually emerged as *the* championship team sport on the international winter calendar. But we must remember the historical alternatives. There was nothing that *guaranteed* ascendancy for the game that used a puck rather than a ball, favored a long, broad-bladed stick rather than the short, more traditional "hockey" or "bandy," and did not allow forward passing. The rise of hockey was in large part a conversion experience. For instance, the St. Paul's School game of the 1880s faded away, but several of that era's players led New York City's shift to hockey a decade later. Bandy and polo did not die off by 1914. In some areas, they continued to grow. In Russia and Sweden, bandy remained *the* game of choice for decades.

In the end, and with the benefit of historical hindsight, we may see a process of convergence, a process of choices leading to the adoption of

Montreal hockey. And part of this convergence involved hockey borrowing from its rivals. For instance, polo rules demarked a line around the goal cage to protect the goaltender—the forerunner of hockey's goal crease, which followed in Canada more than a decade later. Polo equipment manufacturers also devised goal cages well in advance of ice hockey. While Canadian officials have claimed eureka moments of innovation, it is just as likely that they recognized and borrowed these attractive elements from polo. Convergence on the ice was a two-way shift.[31]

Forecheck into America: 1890–1920

In January 1893, *Outing*—the mouthpiece of American amateurism—carried a long and laudatory article on "ice hockey." "[The] Canadian game requires truly skillful players," wrote Canadian-born, New York–based, banker-socialite Beverley Bogert. When "properly played," he added, it "combines science, fast skating, and grace. No game is stronger in fixing the attention of the onlookers." The attractions also included the "kaleidoscopic changes of formations" and the "varied colors" of the uniforms. In short, hockey combined the qualities essential to any successful sport. For players, it offered the chance to develop and demonstrate "pluck, strength, agility, and good judgment." For spectators, it displayed all the right "dash" while not requiring "a too great consumption of busy folks' time." Bogert outlined the basic rules, as dictated by the Amateur Hockey Association of Canada, guardian of the Montreal game. His vivid description of tactics and strategy would have made the game appealing to any athlete, male or female, for he emphasized that "ladies" had "proved themselves ardent admirers" and had on occasion "played the game and played it well." In Canada, he wrote, "every town of a size sufficient to maintain a skating-rink now possesses at least one club, while the larger cities and towns can number several." "It is quite safe to say," he predicted, "that if climatic conditions allowed, it would speedily become the leading winter pastime in New York." Technology soon proved him right.[1]

The Borderlands, 1890–1920

Canadian evangels brought their game south across the border even before it surfaced in Victoria and Vancouver. In February 1886, Burlington,

Vermont, hosted a winter carnival that included hockey, a gift passed from Montreal, whose own Winter Carnival was cancelled by an outbreak of smallpox. Importantly, the Burlington tournament was more than a spectacle for a passive American audience: Burlingtonians participated, too. In the three-team format played on Lake Champlain, two Montreal teams (the MAAA and Crystals HC) faced off against a local seven, Van Ness House. It was the sport's first-ever international tournament.[2]

This was no isolated beachhead. As in Canada, diffusion in the United States was uneven and sporadic, but not random or unexplainable. Before 1920, hockey thrived where climate and elevation permitted natural ice rinks (northern states and the Rocky Mountains) and in eastern cities that had artificial ice venues. It blossomed, moreover, where regular transportation routes connected American populations with Canada and delivered players, promoters, "know-how," and equipment. In these borderlands, the game developed a new meaning to local players, spectators, journalists, and organizers. Like water resources, fire services, fraternal organizations, and library facilities, it became part of a shared culture—another sort of "hand across the border" over which ordinary British subjects and American citizens had regular social intercourse.[3]

A few examples illustrate this phenomenon. The proximity of Plattsburgh, New York, to hockey's birthplace made it likely that local "hockeyists" there and in neighboring towns—Malone, Saranac Lake, and Rouse's Point—drew their training, experience, equipment, and, perhaps, inspiration from Montreal.[4] The formation of a competitive senior hockey team in Buffalo, New York, in December 1898 is best explained by its proximity to potential opponents across the Niagara River in southern Ontario and was welcomed, notably, by the *Toronto Evening News*.[5] In the upper Great Lakes region, the Portage Lakes Hockey Club of Houghton, Michigan, formed in 1900. "Initially," says one account, "the team's players were all locals," but by 1903 they were replaced with transplanted Canadian professionals who had skipped Ontario amateur teams for more profitable performance in what became the openly professional International Hockey League (1904–07) against teams from Sault Ste. Marie, Ontario, Calumet and Houghton, Michigan, and Pittsburgh. Local boosters built some of America's first indoor rinks, but the teams also drew most of their coaches from north of the border.[6] It is unclear how the Montreal game made its way to North Dakota, but by 1900, matches pitted the local, select Grand Forks "Flickertails" against teams from towns located along the Great Northern Railway. By 1906, challenges were formalized in regular cross-border league play, the Southern International League, with teams such as Pilot Mound, Deloraine, and Manitou in Manitoba, and Hannah (and by 1908, Langdon) in North Dakota. "The year or two before I arrived at Hannah," M. J. "Buzz" Dixon recounted, "Hannah played against South Manitoba teams. . . . When we went to Canada to play of course it took two days [and involved] horses, bobsled . . . straw and fur robes." The league thrived until war clouds and a "damaging" drought killed local senior hockey until the 1930s.[7]

We know even more about this cross-border phenomenon in the Rocky Mountain west, where it was shared between mining and smelter towns, capitalists and laborers, citizens and subjects in south-central British Columbia, northeastern Washington, northern Idaho, and northwestern Montana—people connected to one another by work, investments, "rough culture" and above all else, the Great Northern Railway. Americans in the western interior played on both sides of the line in the years before World War I. Some borderlanders played for Canadian teams, squads (such as those from Nelson, Greenwood, and Rossland) that competed in the mix of leagues in the Kootenay region. Others formed clubs of their own and played south of the boundary. Teams budded in Spokane, Washington, in Coeur d'Alene, Idaho, and in Anaconda, Butte, and Missoula, Montana. "Hockey Is Growing in Popular Favor," the *Anaconda Standard* proclaimed in January 1910.

The region's connective tissue included regular challenge matches and the transience of players, coaches, and managers across the border. In 1907 the Rossland Winter Carnival began to feature among its offerings an "International Tournament," awarding a sizeable trophy, the "International Cup," to the best team in the Kootenay region. Though American representatives in these years (Spokane, Missoula, Butte, and Anaconda) recorded little success on the scoreboard, this was not nearly as important as the fact that they were there at all. The "international" tournament distilled and gave form to a feeling that seems to have pervaded the western interior. Hockey was a medium for bringing Canadians and Americans together.[8] Nowhere was this sort of cultural transfer more salient than on a mid-February day in 1910 in the small borderland town of Moyie, British Columbia, where, according to the *Nelson Weekly News*, "a most interesting hockey match [was] played in the rink . . . between teams representing John Bull and Uncle Sam, the latter team was victorious by a score of 6–4. A large number of spectators were in attendance and the game was one of the most amusing ever played here, this fact being attributed . . . to the costumes of the different players and their antics."[9] Amusing, and perhaps for Canadian nationalists, ominous.

The Tours of 1894–95

This slow, borderlands diffusion was matched by a few swift thrusts south into major urban markets, where polo still ruled. One of the triggers was a tour of eastern Canada taken around the New Year of 1895 by a group of American ice polo players. *Harper's Weekly* ran a coincidental story about "Hockey in Canada," noting that "a new interest" in the game was awakened even in Canada "by the arrival of an American team." Scheduled matches were "eagerly" anticipated, since the American game differed "in many points from that accepted here." Many hoped for "new developments" arising "from a comparison of methods of play." Among the clear differences, the author mentioned polo's ball versus hockey's puck ("which for the greater part of the time is actually on the ice"), polo's mad opening rush versus hockey's face off, polo's lack of an offside rule, and polo's smaller, caged goal.[10]

A *New York Times* preview described the tour as a challenge from the previous summer, when a collegiate tennis team, led by Yale's Malcolm Chace and Arthur Foote, competed against Canadian counterparts in a tournament at Niagara Falls. As Brown's Alexander Meiklejohn recalled six decades later, when the tennis players began "discussing their winter sports," they recognized "that they were playing different games on the ice." And so the Canadians called for a tour. By December 19, Captain Chace (who first played polo at Brown, before his transfer to Yale) had picked his lineup, which included Foote, Meiklejohn, two from Harvard, two others from Brown, and one from Columbia. Matches were scheduled for Montreal, Toronto, Hamilton, Kingston, and Ottawa. The most important element, however, was that some of the games would be played in the "American style" and some "after the style in vogue in Canada." Toronto's *Globe* described "great excitement and interest in society and sporting circles." The *New York Times* added, "Canadians anticipate the result of the American visit will probably be the adoption of the Canadian game."[11]

The competition opened at the Victoria Rink. Playing each half under different rules, the Americans earned a 1–1 tie in polo but were drubbed in hockey 5–1. In a script that recurred in Toronto, Kingston, and Ottawa, each side had trouble adapting to the other's approach to offside (allowed in polo; not allowed in hockey). The Americans were lauded for their stick handling, the Canadians recognized for their superior skating. Counting each of the halves as a full contest, the Yanks managed two ties and two close wins in ice polo but were annihilated in all four Canadian versions, losing by a total goals margin of 34–1. In a telling comment after the first game, Toronto's *Globe* concluded that "the Canadian game seemed infinitely more scientific than that played in the United States." The polo ball bounced erratically, and the short stick offered less control than the long, broad-bladed hockey stick. The *Toronto Mail* added that the generally "open" play of polo also meant less "team work."[12] A month later, Chicago's Spalding Hockey and Polo Club—promoted as an all-star team—played eleven mixed matches in western Canada. They fared no better, earning only one win and one tie. There was a general sentiment after both tours that the Canadian game was more scientific. Most important, the American players seemed to concur. "[I]t was pretty well agreed among us," recalled Meiklejohn, "that the Canadian game was better than ours."[13]

Making the Ice

Across North America, in every town, school, or city ever bitten by the skating bug, stories in newspapers or diaries speak to the optimism of black ice in December and to the despair of a thaw or a blizzard in midwinter. Ralph Winsor, who played and coached at Harvard in the early twentieth century, recalled the challenges of outdoor ice. The players had to seek out nearby ponds, "part of the way by electric cars and part by walking," all the while carrying their sticks and bags. With luck they might find "some secluded spot" without a biting wind. Good ice was always a chancy proposition.[14]

Indoor, natural ice rinks, like their roller rink counterparts (some buildings converted from one to the other), opened and closed in America with some regularity during these years. None could support a "big-bang" moment for a new sport like hockey. The fundamental breakthrough was artificial ice, which first made its commercial appearance during this period. Attempts at mechanical refrigeration date back at least to 1746, but it took another century before inventors like Ferdinand Carré fashioned a machine that produced ice commercially. These early devices relied solely on a closed-circuit vapor system using gases such as ethyl ether or ammonia to cool air or water. In its simplest form, the vapor was condensed or compressed and then run through piping, where it naturally expanded by drawing in any surrounding heat. It was clear enough science, but the trick was to find the most efficient vapor and develop a leak-proof system. It was one thing to refrigerate a small area, quite another to freeze water over a large surface. But try they did. By one account, an inventor named William Newton built an artificial ice surface as early as 1870 in New York, using a refrigerant mix of ammonia gas, ether, and carbonic acid running through pipes. More successful was John Gamgee, who fashioned a very small (40 feet by 24 feet) ice rink in London six years later, using copper piping that circulated a refrigerant mix of "glycerine" and water chilled by steam-run condensers that moved sulfuric acid in constant circulation, from vapor to liquid to vapor. The building and rink operation cost £20,000, a handsome sum raised by subscription among "noblemen and gentlemen under certain conditions." The rink was referred to as the "Glaciarium," which became a standard name for British ice rinks.[15]

Condenser inefficiency, coolant ineffectiveness, and refrigerant leakage—these problems plagued designers who attempted to freeze large ice surfaces. Then came a technological breakthrough, described in the January 7, 1893, issue of the *Scientific American*. Many of the old artificial ice systems, such as Newton's in New York, used pipes under the ice that contained expanding (and hence cooling) vapors such as ammonia. These systems, wrote the author, were "evidently defective, because of the leakages inevitable in a system of piping several kilometers in length." The leakage was not just inefficient; it was hazardous to anyone on the rink surface. A new French design, however, took an old idea (like Professor Gamgee's) to new levels. Rather than have a single closed system, it used two closed systems of piping that passed through common "reservoirs or refrigeratories." The first system compressed and converted ammonia gas into liquid, then forced the liquid ammonia into large holding tanks where the ammonia reconverted to gas by grabbing all available heat and hence chilling the tank. The ammonia gas was then forced back into the condensers and recompressed to begin the cycle anew. The real trick, however, was using the refrigeratories to chill another line of piping full of "uncongealable liquid" (brine) which exited the refrigeratories at subzero temperature to move under the ice (to keep it frozen) and finally flow back to the refrigeratory, where it was rechilled. In this system there was no worry about leaking vapors under the ice surface (leaking brine was another matter). This is essentially the same system used today.[16]

The First Southern Strategy

When Montreal's new game first drove its way south of the borderlands, it landed in Baltimore, Pittsburgh, and Washington, DC—places hardly renowned for winter sport. The reason was simple. These cities had new artificial ice facilities. Among the first ventures was Baltimore's North Avenue Rink, which opened in 1895. Organized hockey followed closely, although there are competing claims about who first brought the sport. The *Spalding Ice Hockey and Ice Polo Guide* (1897) credited two people. One was Dr. W. A. Bisnaw, whom locals dubbed the "father of Baltimore hockey." The other was Alfred Mitchell, who had played for the Queen's University team in Kingston and was studying in Baltimore. In 1899, Canadian player/author Arthur Farrell emphasized a Montreal connection: "The game was first introduced into the United States some years ago by a Montrealer, Mr C. Shearer, who was studying in the Johns Hopkins University."[17]

There may be doubt about who fathered hockey in Baltimore, but there is no doubt about a Quebec team's exhibition on April 11, 1895, a match that ushered in a three-year hockey surge that converted most American ice polo players to ice hockey. One correspondent described the Quebec team in words that would echo: "Neatly dressed in ermine and white, with dark stockings, the tall, strong-limbed and handsome Canadians glided over the ice like masters of the subtle substance. They were active, graceful, and clever as they were big and strong and the home team appeared alongside them as so many children." Baltimore has other hockey claims. The Yale–Johns Hopkins game of February 1, 1896, has been called the "first intercollegiate" hockey game in the United States. But that is stretching the term. The "Yale" lineup included three names from the famous tour of 1894–95: Chace, Larned, and Jones. Only Malcolm Chace was a Yale student. Larned was from Columbia, Jones from Brown. The "Yale" team was more likely a group of ringers, a scenario common in intercollegiate contests of the day.[18]

Despite the North Avenue Rink's narrow width—"scarcely thirty feet"—by January 1897, it hosted four teams that formed the Baltimore Hockey League: the Maryland Athletic Club (MAC), the University of Maryland, the Northampton Hockey Club, and Johns Hopkins University. The combination of amateur-club and university teams was a model that supported most early leagues. Organization did not preclude bickering. The final match, between the University of Maryland and the MAC, ended with a disputed University of Maryland goal. The referee rebuffed MAC's challenge and, since the protested goal had forced a tie, he ordered the teams to play overtime. When the university won in overtime, the MAC brought their protest to the league's executive committee, which supported the original protest, negated the late, tying score, and awarded the victory (and league title) to the MAC. Not to be outdone, the university team secured three prominent lawyers, who convinced a judge that league rules (borrowed from the Amateur Hockey Association of Canada) did not allow appeals to an umpire's or referee's decision. Early on, American hockey reached the hallowed zone of litigation.[19]

The skating bug drifted south from Baltimore. On January 6, 1896, Washingtonians flocked to a new rink with a surface that measured 200 by 115 feet, about the size of today's Olympic sheets. The *Post* reported "one thousand on skates" inside the new "Convention Hall." *Scientific American* covered this engineering news, adding (with probable exaggeration) that "over 9000 people" attended the opening gala.[20] Within days, the *Post* announced an exhibition match between a local "all-Baltimore" team and Queen's University of Kingston, Ontario, described as Canada's intercollegiate champions. A "strong set of players" was on tour "in search of a championship here." Soon after that exhibition, a side of local residents (dubbed the "Washingtons") was ready to take on the "Baltimores." Rink manager Towers was amply impressed by the new sport, and he sent a request to the Secretary of the Amateur Hockey Association of Canada for a set of rules. Americans were converging on the Montreal game.[21]

Into Gotham

That same winter, hockey made its appearance in New York City, in two venues: the Ice Palace and the St. Nicholas Club rink. In late 1895 several Philadelphia capitalists converted an old armory on the corner of Lexington Avenue and 107th Street into the Ice Palace. The investors promised that "the rink will be used for hockey, polo, and curling, all of which sports it is expected will have a revival this winter, when good ice is assured [to] lovers of the games." *Scientific American* reported the grand opening on December 14, 1895, describing a refrigeration system much like the ones in Paris and Washington. The interior was "dazzling," its ceiling and walls "hung with artificial icicles, illuminated by 2000 electric lamps of various colors." The ice surface could hold eighteen hundred skaters and was surrounded by "two galleries, large enough to seat 5,000 spectators." These numbers were doubtless exaggerated, but there is no denying the rink's effect.[22]

The Ice Palace was home to rival sports, as conveyed in newspaper notices that announced "Sports on the Ice: Hockey and Polo Games at the Ice Palace this Week." The Palace sponsored an eponymous polo club that squared off in regular matches against the likes of the Jersey City Polo Club and the Passaic Polo Club. The New York Hockey Club (NYHC), stocked largely with transplanted Canadians, represented the Montreal game. These players, the American tour veterans, and other hockey enthusiasts may well have rented ice time in the Palace, and they played occasional matches, but there were not yet enough organized hockey teams to justify regularly scheduled and promoted games in the Palace. For a while at least, polo had the upper hand.[23]

Two heavily promoted events in early 1896 altered that balance. The first was an intercity match that pitted the NYHC against the Baltimore Athletic Club on March 6. The *Times* noted that while the Baltimore players were "experts," "most" of the New York team "have been trained at the sport in Canada." Confusion over terms still existed, however, as the game story, despite the use of Montreal rules, mentioned "Bandy, as the Englishmen call it, or hockey-on-ice." The author described the "flat, circular disk of rubber, called the bung, or puck" in one paragraph and in the next talked of the "ball in play." There was no confusion, however, over hockey's attraction. The players dazzled the crowd as they moved "forward, backward, and in eccentrics and circles in a fashion that a champion figure skater might envy, in driving the puck, over the glassy ice." The New Yorkers won, 3–2, thrilling the large crowd, which included "more than 1000 skaters" who "in less than a minute" after the game's conclusion "were skimming over the surface of the glare ice to the merry music of the steel runners."[24]

The quality of play improved four days later when the Ice Palace crowd saw Montreal's "Shamrocks" and "Montreals" square off as part of their first American tour, with stops in Washington, Baltimore, and New York. The *Montreal Daily Herald* announced the "Invasion of U.S." on February 29. A *Times* correspondent warned New Yorkers that in Canada, "the game is taken more in the way of serious labor than a light recreation." Apparently, a Canadian promoter had seen a recent New York match in which extended time and "tender care" was given to repair the lip of a "slightly wounded" Malcolm Chace. The story back in Montreal "created great amusement among the votaries of the game here," where such a trifle would have been deferred until halftime. New Yorkers could, in short, expect a rougher and faster game. "The match between the New York and Baltimore clubs will look like a pillow fight compared to a prize fight."[25]

The Shamrocks-Montreals matches in Washington and Baltimore heightened expectations, as the teams traded victories. New York hosted the rubber match, for a trophy sponsored by the Ice Palace. The *Times* promised "lightning rushes" down the ice, with the twenty-five hundred "ladies and gentlemen" in the stands responding "as baseball crowds do when a man at bat makes a three-base hit or a base run with the bases full." The skilled action lived up to its billing. The crowd "sat as if spellbound," as the forwards rushed "like an arrow, nursing, passing, lifting, or pucking the little rubber disc." The Shamrocks "point" (defender) Stevens showed particular expertise at lifting the puck "high over the heads" of the Montreal forwards and halfway down the rink to his own forwards. Although one player was struck in the eye with a stick, the play was judged to be "uniformly gentlemanly." The *Times* concluded that the deference to the referee and the general "absence of disputes" was a striking contrast to the "squabbling and disputations" and the "exhibitions of temper" that were common at football games. New York's first product sampling of grade "A" Montreal hockey was a success.[26]

The Ice Palace was hockey's first home in New York, but it soon faced stiff competition. In August 1895 the St. Nicholas Skating Club (which had earlier operated an outdoor natural ice rink) broke ground on 66th Street, between Central Park and Columbus Avenue, for a new artificial ice rink with an estimated cost of $300,000, raised by the likes of Cornelius Vanderbilt, Mr. and Mrs. John Jacob Astor, and Mr. and Mrs. J. P. Morgan. The club promised an ice surface of 80 by 200 feet, balcony seating for two thousand, clubrooms, a café, and public lockers.[27] The rink opened in mid-March 1896. For the next several years, the Ice Palace and the St. Nick's Rink, joined in 1896 by Brooklyn's Clermont Rink, were dueling venues, representing different brands of hockey, with 66th Street the home of a more gentlemanly game, played by the more elite collegians, private schools, and private athletic clubs. By 1920, however, the St. Nick's Rink was Gotham's principal hockey venue, in part because of its superior systems of temperature control and ventilation.[28]

A St. Nick's team hosted a number of games in March and April 1896 under the Canadian rules. One sign of the conversion is in the newspaper's printed lineups, which listed four forwards, a point, a cover point, and a goal—the standard seven-man lineup for the Montreal game. The team's schedule ended on April 4 against the New York Hockey Club, which the *Times* billed as a "championship" to decide the "strongest team in the United States." The match attracted eight hundred fans. While both sides were ostensibly amateur, the NYHC was a team of transplants who had "played the game in Canada, where it is the national Winter sport." They represented the commercial rink operation, the Ice Palace. The Nicks were elite sportsmen whose lineup included several St. Paul's School alums. This first "championship" went to the Canadian-born skaters, 4–2, as they showed a continual edge in puck control, passing, and shot blocking. Canadian transplants and visitors, who organized teams such as the NYHC and helped to schedule exhibitions on the new artificial ice rinks, were crucial to conversion. One *Outing* magazine article recognized their importance. "Canadian residents in our Eastern cities," said J. Parmly Paret, "are really our benefactors . . . and deserve the credit for introducing the game to us as well as for teaching us the fine points of the play."[29]

Into the Midwest

The import process was similar in the American Midwest. In one of the first games, the University of Minnesota squared off against a team from Winnipeg (the Victorias) in mid-February 1895 at Athletic Park, Minneapolis. The *St. Paul Pioneer Press* called it the "first hockey game ever played in the United States." In fact, about the same time, the *Press* ran another story on "early St. Paul hockey" that described how one local polo club had converted the year before. In any event, the Gophers were converts, described as "old football and ice polo players, all first-hand skaters" who had been practicing daily for two weeks. The Canadians were a formidable foe, stocked with virtually the same lineup that won the Stanley Cup the following year. It was no contest, as three hundred spectators watched the Victorias roll 11–3. Still, the *Press* predicted that "hockey promises to become as popular a sport at the university as football, baseball, and rowing." Such boosterism and exaggeration were commonplace in local media reports. Few were as prescient.[30]

In 1896 the St. Paul Winter Carnival included hockey among its scheduled sports. Two teams from the host city squared off against squads from Minneapolis and Winnipeg. Over the next few years, amateur and school teams played occasional games, but area players had to wait until January 1902 for a formal league to take shape—the Twin City Hockey League, which included the St. Paul Hockey Club, Mechanics Arts High School, the Mascots, the Virginias, and Minneapolis. A local curler named Robert Dunbar donated a trophy for the annual league champion. In 1904 the Twin City league champion began to play either Two Harbors or Duluth "to determine the state Senior Champion."[31]

Some of the locals skated inside Minneapolis's old Star Roller Rink, converted to a natural ice arena in 1900. It was one of several small, short-lived indoor facilities in the area. Twin City hockey got a boost in 1906, however, when the Minnesota State Fair Board built the Hippodrome for livestock displays and competition. In 1911 the building saw its first winter conversion to a natural ice arena, with a huge surface, 270 by 119 feet. Holding sixty-seven hundred seats, the Hippodrome had great spectacle potential. It was home from 1914 to 1926 for the era's best team, the St. Paul Athletic Club (SPAC), whose roster included Frank "Moose" Goheen, a graduate of nearby White Bear Lake High School. Goheen was a rugged, rushing defenseman, the second American (after Hobey Baker) inducted into the Hockey Hall of Fame. The "Hipp" rocked on many nights when the likes of Duluth, Portage Lakes, or the American Soo came to town. But the SPAC often struggled at the gate, in part because of location and in part because the Hippodrome lacked general heating. Only those in reserved seats (50 cents) or box seats (75 cents) had access to a "warming room." Then, as now, premium seats had what modern marketers call "value added."[32]

At the same time, Montreal hockey was sweeping through border towns like Roseau and Warroad, and into the Iron Range mining towns of Eveleth, Virginia, and Hibbing. Eveleth's first teams in 1903 had access to an enclosed natural ice rink with a surface of 75 by 150 feet. It lasted only a few years, but hockey took root among young and old alike, hardscrabble immigrant mining families looking for ways to beat the long, dark, cold winter days and nights. In 1919 town boosters built the Eveleth Recreation Building, which boasted indoor, natural ice sheets for both hockey and curling. Eveleth needed this new rink if it was to compete with its larger rival Duluth, whose Curling Club Arena had opened in 1913. When the Eveleth side played Two Harbors in January 1903, the local *Mining News* concluded, "Hockey is practically a new game on the Range. With proper support, Eveleth can put up a good team, and there is plenty of first class material here." Within two decades that prophecy was more than fulfilled as Eveleth began sending its sons to play on professional, senior amateur, and collegiate teams in numbers that are still staggering in relation to the town's size.[33]

Chicago sputtered for years in attempts to nurture the new game. In the pivotal winter of 1895–96, the Chicago Athletic Association's (CAA) team played other local clubs and even entertained a visiting Canadian contingent called "Spalding's Team" on short-lived artificial ice inside "Tattersall" auditorium. The CAA also traveled to matches in Minnesota's Twin Cities, Milwaukee, Detroit, and Buffalo. Pittsburgh and Cleveland enjoyed early powerhouse teams after developers built indoor artificial ice rinks: the Steel City's Schenley Park Casino (1894) and Duquesne Gardens (1896), and the Forest City's Elysium (1907).[34]

Boston and the Arena

The 1909 *Spalding Guide* included a story on "Hockey in Boston and Vicinity." The author lamented the Hub's place "behind" other cities, largely because it lacked an indoor rink. Greater Boston had plenty of local rivers, ponds, and lakes—Fresh Pond, Bullough's Pond, Spy Pond, Ell Pond, Hammond's Pond, the Charles and Mystic Rivers, Crystal Lake, and Lake Quonnapowitt—to provide natural ice when the weather cooperated. The area also had a strong sports tradition at the professional, collegiate, and schoolboy levels. The last two, especially, offered a guaranteed infrastructure for competition in any new hot sport. In the mid-1890s, Harvard, MIT, Boston College, and Tufts all had ice polo teams. Schoolboys organized the Suburban High School Ice Polo League. Within a few years, however, they all converted to ice hockey, impressed by the "science" of the new game. Long-time hockey writer Fred Hoey later described the reason for the quick conversion: "the hit-and-miss-slam-bang feature of polo had no place in the new game." Compared to New York, however, Boston limped along. Schoolboy schedules melted in January thaws. For a few winters, Harvard flooded its grand new football stadium, and its students skated when they could. It was no match, however, for the certainty of ice-time that Princeton and Yale enjoyed at the St. Nicholas Club.[35]

All of this changed in 1909–10 when a few investors from Chicopee and Boston built the Boston Arena (still in operation today as Northeastern University's Matthews Arena). The arena was designed by George C. Funk, a lifelong Brookline native and MIT graduate ('05), whose later rink proj-

Boston—Arena
Week of January 20, 1913
ST. BOTOLPH AND MASSACHUSETTS AVENUE

Boston Arena Grand Entrance (Boston Arena Program 1912–13; Collection of Richard A. Johnson)

ects included the Madison Square Garden, the Boston Garden, and the 1932 Lake Placid Olympic Rink. Funk planned the Arena as a multipurpose facility whose ice surface—90 by 244 feet—was the largest of its time and bigger than most rinks today. Maintaining cold ice in a warm rink was the work of the adjoining engineering building, where Funk used two 100-ton York refrigerating machines and a 400-horsepower Babcock and Wilcox boiler to push an ammonia/brine solution through some 55,000 feet of pipe under the ice surface. Funk's system, which he later revised and patented, was supposedly capable of maintaining a "skatable surface with a temperature as high as 110 degrees Fahrenheit."[36]

In many towns and cities, indoor rinks and their hockey teams became part of the fabric and identity of the local community. Like American baseball parks and European football grounds, hockey rinks could be strategically situated to maximize their importance to people's sense of place. The Boston Arena was a case in point, built in an ideal location, as its investors trumpeted in their prospectus: "From every viewpoint it is the most desirable in the city. It is in the midst of the new amusement centre of Boston—a district that is destined to be the very nub of the Hub. Near at hand are the new Museum of Fine Arts, the Boston Opera House, Symphony Hall, Horticultural Hall, Chickering Hall, The New England Conservatory of Music, Mechanics hall, etc. Situated practically at the corner of Massachusetts and Huntington avenues, it is the most central point in the whole city of Boston." Better yet, this area enjoyed trolley lines connecting the Arena to "every section of the city and its suburbs." During the years between 1877 and 1920, new venues like the Arena became more than places to play. In many cities and towns, they emerged as badges of identity, symbols of success or failure.[37]

Promoting an American Game

On December 30, 1900, the *Brooklyn Eagle* published an article with Nostradamus-like predictions, projecting the future of sport in twentieth-century America. The prophets expected baseball to decline, while football, hockey, and yachting gained participants and audiences. In American hockey's case, the future would "depend upon the artificial congealing of the skating surface—a process complicated and expensive." The *Eagle* also recognized a crucial reality for many of the newly codified sports being introduced to markets across the world, including football (in its various forms), hockey, and basketball. Long-term success depended on a synergy between playing and watching. And a truly popular sport would have many more spectators than players. In this regard, it appeared that hockey was on solid ground in the New York area. The core of avid, skilled players was attracting crowds of "several thousand" to the "bigger matches to see a game that has probably never been played by one out of every fifty of the spectators." The game's future in America, concluded the *Eagle*, rested on more artificial ice rinks, where more college teams could develop (college athletics being the gold standard for most team sports beyond baseball). These teams, in turn, would attract more spectators who would help to promote the game to more players and thereby build the crucial synergy between the sport and the spectacle. It seemed to be a given: "When the manufacture of ice becomes cheaper and the artificial rinks are fixtures of every college town, then we shall have a game that will rival foot ball."[38]

In the Pacific Northwest, hockey promoters gushed with optimism about a new rink's ability to insure hockey's growth. In 1915, Oregon writer W. A. Kearns insisted that despite the fact that "few Oregonians" had ever "seen a hockey stick, much less a hockey match," Portland's huge new Hippodrome, built for the Pacific Coast Hockey Association (PCHA) franchise Rosebuds, guaranteed success. Despite the reality that all the professional and amateur players were Canadian or Eastern American transplants, "a year or two will undoubtedly find some native players as good as the transplanted variety."[39]

By 1920, hockey was established in the northern tier of the United States, from coast to coast. With few exceptions, the sport depended on artificial ice rinks. But there were already dozens of them, with more to come. If Boston had its Arena (rebuilt after a 1918 fire), New York its St. Nicholas Rink, and Cleveland had its Elysium, then Portland, Oregon, had the Hippodrome, and San Diego its "Ice Rink," where locals could play through the summer, occasionally against Canadian visitors. In every town or city that had tasted the game's speed, skill, science, and violence, there was a strong belief that an indoor artificial ice rink would insure long-term growth. As one Midwest writer crowed in 1917, "with new artificial rinks being erected and interest in hockey growing universal, success is inevitable."[40]

Optimism was the watchword. And with good reason. The sport was taking off at all levels. Openly professional hockey had a brief existence in the upper Midwest and Pittsburgh with the International Hockey League from 1904 to 1907. When exorbitant salaries and economic reality sunk the IHL, Pittsburgh's franchise president A. S. McSwigen worked desperately to cobble together a replacement with teams in the big markets of Canada and the United States. He had no luck, but from that day forward US writers wrote annually of "plans" to bring the professional game back to the States. McSwigen settled for the Western Pennsylvania (amateur) League, stocked by top Canadians and local stars. In the 1909 Spalding *Guide*, Edward Thierry of the *Pittsburgh Dispatch* noted that these "premier players" were "by no means amateurs." It was a Freudian slip. Ostensibly, Thierry meant "amateur" in terms of skill. But he betrayed the reality that these stars were getting paid under the table. Other writers were more explicit. In 1914 a Pennsylvania columnist wrote: "Ice hockey stars in the east are paid $800 a season." It was the underside of senior amateur hockey. At least

Frank and Lester Patrick were above board with their openly professional Pacific Coast Hockey Association. But pro hockey was short lived in both the Midwest and Far West. Until the 1920s, American pucksters developed most solidly at three levels: schools, colleges, and senior amateur.[41]

Sports were an important part of life in American schools, especially the public schools. Private schools, such as St. Paul's, had a longer tradition, but sports like football, hockey, and basketball came along just as American cities expanded their commitment to public secondary education. Typically, students organized the first teams and leagues as a way to rally school spirit. In 1896–97, for instance, New York area schoolboys organized the Interstate Interscholastic Ice Hockey League, composed of five schools, including Montclair, New Jersey, which won the first silver cup. By 1911, the Spalding *Guide* lamented the lack of a fixed league schedule, recognizing that schoolboy hockey was the foundation where "stars were developed and made possible." This was particularly true in Minnesota and New England. The Twin City area developed early high school powerhouses at St. Paul's Mechanic Arts and Central High Schools. Central's 1911 contingent won the Twin City Interscholastic championship going away; local writer M. B. Palmer called the team a "well-nigh perfect hockey machine." In Boston the Suburban High School Ice Polo League basically just rolled over its sport, expanded its membership, and became the Greater Boston Interscholastic Hockey Association. Within a few years, powers such as Melrose and Arlington High Schools cemented their dominance in the new Boston Arena. Five of seven players on the *Boston Herald*'s first "All School" team (1912) hailed from either Melrose or Arlington. Some private schools—Andover and St. Paul's in New England, Culver Military Academy in the Midwest—were stronger than local college teams. In 1917, Chicago's Hyde Park High School seven beat Northwestern University.[42]

In most cases, however, the schoolboys emulated and chased after the college teams, typically taking pride in watching their own alums move to that next level. College programs and leagues were key tenants in the new rinks. In December 1898, Yale, Columbia, Brown, and Penn met at the St. Nicholas Rink to form the Intercollegiate Hockey Association of America, with a short list of bylaws that empowered an executive committee to set a schedule and "attend to any other business." Princeton joined in 1900. Harvard waited until 1902, when the college dropped a rule restricting all competition to campus grounds. The IHAA was essentially an eastern collegiate league, leaving western schools to make their own claims on

Hotel Westminster
Copley Square
Telephone for Tables After the Game
C. A. GLEASON

WEDNESDAY, JANUARY 22, 1913

Programme

HARVARD vs. PRINCETON

HARVARD		PRINCETON	
MORGAN	RIGHT WING	PATTERSON	LEFT WING
PHILLIPS	CENTER	KUHN	CENTER
SORTWELL	ROVER	BAKER	ROVER
HOPKINS	LEFT WING	KILNER	RIGHT WING
GOODALE	COVERPOINT	EMMONS	COVERPOINT
WILLETTS	POINT	LEE	POINT
GARDNER	GOAL	WINANTS	GOAL

PRIZE CUPS
Medals, Badges, Trophie Shields, Society Jewels Emblems, Etc.
Special Designs or Catalogue sent free on receipt of particulars, or any information in regard to price or Quantities
DORRETY
Factory and Salesrooms
387 Washington St.
Boston

PATTERSON, WYLDE & WINDELER
General Insurance Agents
72 KILBY STREET
BOSTON
Telephone, . . . Main 4343
Fire, Marine, Automobile, Burglary
Yacht, Workmen's Compensation
Plate Glass, Boiler, Bonding

Harvard-Princeton lineups in Boston Arena program, 1912–13 season (Boston Arena Program 1912–13; Collection of Richard A. Johnson)

mythical "national" championships. In the 1920s seventeen Midwestern schools, including Marquette, Michigan, Minnesota, and Eveleth Junior College formed the Northern Intercollegiate Hockey Association. In certain cities college hockey was as hot a ticket as one could find in any sport at any level. When Hobey Baker led his Princeton Tigers into the Boston Arena (1911 to 1914) there was no rival on the Hub's sports pages.[43]

Of course, stars like Baker had to move on after four years. Arena managers needed the next level. In most markets that meant senior amateur leagues, which were selective. For instance, the 1898 Spalding *Guide* listed more than a dozen clubs in the New York Metro area, but only four played in the newly created Amateur Hockey League of New York. In 1899 this same league opened its championship to challenges from teams outside the area. Thereafter, it rechristened itself the "American" Amateur Hockey League, even though it denied membership to clubs in St. Paul, Minnesota, and Philadelphia. League apologists like J. Parmly Paret, *Outing*'s hockey beat writer, justified the decision on the grounds that a fixed schedule requiring long travel would pull players from their real jobs, leading to "under the table" payments for their services. A "challenge" system minimized travel time for a national title and thereby supported the purity of amateurism and spared hockey from the "leech of professionalism" that had ruined roller polo and basketball.[44]

Boston's Arena League featured intense rivals such as the Boston Athletic Association, Boston Hockey Club, Crescents, and Intercolonials. The upper Midwest had the American Amateur Hockey Association (founded 1913) with Calumet, Portage Lake, Sault Ste. Marie, St. Paul, and Duluth. San Francisco had the California Amateur Hockey Association. It was a hard business with a relatively short season and, for the Midwest, high travel costs. By 1917, Calumet and Portage Lakes had withdrawn from the AAHA. Even the strongest franchise, the St. Paul Athletic Club, had to push its members in 1916 to buy a whole box section of six seats for the season, for $25. With eight home games, that came to 40 cents per ticket, a 20 percent discount from a single-game price. This early price promotion was no panacea. A year later, a *Pioneer Press* writer warned that "the Athletic club team is proving a costly luxury for the club. . . . There is a considerable deficit already, and unless the patronage picks up largely in the remaining games it is certain that the club will not again attempt to provide the fans of this city with a championship team." While train travel (time and cost) restricted regular season competition to a regional scope (after all, even major-league baseball went no farther west than St. Louis), promoters constantly schemed at ways to claim a "national" title.[45]

American fiction writers also embraced the Canadian game. The years from 1890 until 1920 made up the heyday of American juvenile sporting fiction. Hundreds of boys' school sports stories—including, after 1896, hockey stories—rolled off pens of prolific writers such as Ralph Henry Barbour, Harold Sherman, Edward Stratemeyer, and Gilbert Patten. These included Barbour's *The Crimson Sweater* (1905) and *Guarding His Goal* (1919); Arthur Stanwood Pier's *Boys of St. Timothy's* (1904) and *Harding of St. Timothy's* (1906, both books modeled on the real St. Paul's School and written by an SPS alum); Graham Forbes's *Boys of Columbia High on the Ice* (1911); and Stratemeyer's *Dave Porter and His Rivals* (1913). Although not the most favored sport, hockey appeared conspicuously in these American narratives. Despite the fact that the rules described by these authors derive directly from the Montreal rules of 1877, no mention of Canada's influence or origin appears in these stories. To a Canadian reader, the books by Barbour, Pier, Stratemeyer, and others before 1920 are conspicuous in their depiction of ice hockey as a home-grown, indigenous *American* product. It is only after World War I, and especially by the mid-1920s, that the Canadian connection appears in the works by these authors and others.[46]

Ironically, this nationalism meant that American hockey pundits always had one eye on Canada—the home, the touchstone, the role model. From the great tour of 1894–95 on, Americans wondered how they would fare against Canadians. In 1920 they had their chance on the world stage. The 1920 Antwerp Olympics were the first that included ice hockey, as a demonstration sport (separate Winter Olympics did not begin until 1924). The American team earned a silver medal, losing gold to Canada, 2–0. The Americans were a mix from three top teams: the Boston Athletic Association, the Pittsburgh Athletic Association (PAA), and the St. Paul Athletic Club. Roy Schooley of Pittsburgh made the final selections. As historian Roger Godin explained, "Schooley was a naturalized American from Welland, Ontario, who had come to Pittsburgh in 1901. He had begun his career as a referee and subsequently managed both Duquesne Garden and the Pittsburgh team. As manager of the Olympic squad he had full power to select the players." It took a Canadian to pick America's first Olympic team. Pittsburgh mogul William Haddock called the 1920 silver medal the "greatest accomplishment" in the "most successful" season in American hockey history. "Beaten but Not Disgraced" read the *New York Times* headline. The editorial crowed, "It wasn't so long ago, when the mere suggestion of putting an American hockey team against a Canadian championship team would have been greeted as the season's best joke."[47] Within a decade, however, American college programs consciously sealed themselves off from Canadian comparisons or Canadian influence, even as they hired Canadian coaches. After three decades of madcap convergence on the Montreal game, segments of American hockey began to diverge.

8 What Game? Forging a Distinct Product: 1890–1920

At the end of the first week of January 1914, Hobey Baker, Fred "Cyclone" Taylor, and "Bad Joe" Hall must have known how each other felt. Their teams had all lost games and, for them, losses were rare. On January 5, Baker's champion Princeton University seven were beaten 4–2 by the University of Ottawa in what the *New York Times* called "the fastest hockey that has been seen at the [St. Nicholas] rink in many a day." Baker was the "peerless hero" of the match, Toronto's *Globe* reported. But he was, if anything, *too* fast for the other Tigers. "Nearly every time he made a sally on the Canadian net he had outstripped his teammates and was alone in his efforts." Two days later, Taylor's Vancouver Millionaires suffered similar disappointment on the West Coast, losing to their island rival, the Victoria Aristocrats, 6–5 in a Pacific Coast Hockey Association game that, the *Globe* claimed, included a "desperate finish." The Aristocrats went on to win the PCHA, then lose a Stanley Cup challenge to Toronto. Still, Taylor's season was far from unsuccessful. In sixteen games, the Cyclone scored 24 goals and 15 assists, earning 18 minutes in penalties along the way. That week was not much better for Quebec's Joe Hall. In a losing effort against the Montreal Canadiens, Hall and Canadiens star Edouard "Newsy" Lalonde, the *Globe* recounted, "had a fight on the ice" that inflicted some damage. Hall, the defensive heart of the National Hockey Association (NHA) champion Bulldogs, was still smarting four days later. When his team met the Toronto Blueshirts, "'Bad Joe' Hall did not play," the *Globe* declared, "his head being swathed in bandages." Hall was not often on the losing end of such exchanges, and there were many of them over his nineteen-year career. Two days later, he was back in action, but the episode was hardly tutelary. Bad Joe finished the season with 61 minutes in penalties.[1]

Beyond wins and losses, goals and rules infractions, the actions and images of Taylor, Baker, and Hall tell us a great deal about hockey during its "big push," 1890 to 1920. They were emblematic, both in the ways they captured popular attention and notoriety, sold the game to prospective fans, and branded it on the ice. They helped usher in a grand transformation. In these decades, hockey became a tightly defined and circumscribed activity whose hallmarks were speed, science, and savagery—a *serious* sport. By 1920, the game that fans saw on the ice was considerably different from what Carnival-goers witnessed in Montreal in the cold midwinters of the 1880s. While the brilliance, power, and innovation of prominent players such as Baker, Taylor, and Hall pushed form and strategy in sometimes-unintended directions, they all acted on a stage set by others. That stage included technological change; reorganization as a modern, corporate enterprise; and representations by the press. In the thirty years after 1890, hockey's first "stars" emerged; a small handful of players whose names became part of the sport's brand.

Character First—Hobey Baker

If Hobey Baker's bad week in January 1914 affected him adversely, no one would have known. Quiet and self-effacing, Baker shied away from publicity despite magnetic attention he earned from American and Canadian sports fans and press. The younger son of an elite Philadelphia family, Baker (1892–1918) learned the game at St. Paul's School in Concord, New Hampshire, where he found worth in athletics if not academics. While only a junior at St. Paul's, he burst onto the Boston hockey scene in February 1908 with a goal against the Harvard Varsity. A year later, his team made its annual trip to New York's St. Nicholas Rink and trounced rival St. Mark's, with Baker scoring seven goals. The *Times* headlined: "Baker's Play the Feature."[2]

At Princeton, he starred on the football field, where he was a deadly drop-kicker and a fearless kick returner, despite his modest size—no fair catches, no helmet. But the ice surface was his greater canvas. After Baker's sophomore year as a Tiger, the *Boston Herald* concluded that he was "without doubt the best all-around player ever developed on this side of

Hobey Baker, at the center of the Princeton Tigers, ca. 1914 (Davies Collection, Seeley G. Mudd Manuscript Library, Princeton University)

the border." In February 1913, when Baker led his Tigers into the Boston Arena against a strong Boston Athletic Association seven, local hockey beat writer and publicist Fred Hoey marveled at his "cat-like movements" that "had the BAA men literally standing on their heads to stop him." They could not, and he bagged two goals. In 1916 old hand Tom Howard, who had played in Montreal and New York and coached at Yale, said emphatically: "I consider Baker one of the most remarkable players in the history of the game." Whether they rooted for Yale, the BAA, or Harvard, fans cheered for Baker.[3]

He was dashingly handsome, his blond hair flowing as he rushed the puck. His solo flights were typical of the era's top players when the rules prevented forward passes. Though his weaving and swerving style helped him avoid checks and bring the crowd to its feet, it often trapped his teammates offside. His biographer, John Davies, claimed that teammates were sometimes upset by his "unpredictable changes in direction" that ended in their embarrassment. Sensing this, the modest Baker once complained about the crowd's adulation: "I can't hear the other fellows calling for a pass and people will think I'm a puck-hog."[4]

In life, his blemishes were too few to tarnish his status as a real-life athletic hero. In death, they have been almost wholly forgotten, particularly because of the way Baker died: too soon, and in service to his country. When the United States entered the Great War, Baker enlisted in the army and distinguished himself as a pilot with 103d Aero Squadron (formed from remnants of the Lafayette Escadrille), winning a Croix de Guerre. When he missed a kill, he wrote an old teammate that it was "just like missing a goal when you have gotten past the defense and have only the goal keeper to stop you."[5] But war is less forgiving. Baker died on December 21, 1918, when his plane crashed mysteriously on a final flight he took after he received his orders to return home, more than a month after the war had officially ended. At least one newspaper suggested he had ditched deliberately because his fiancée had dumped him: "It was whispered around the field" that Baker had just received "her marriage announcement to some 'swivel chair' bird." The published eulogies for Baker were many and moving. "Nothing could stop his rush but a goal-tender who was born with a horseshoe in his hand," said the *New York Globe*.[6]

Of all the descriptions, however, none conveys Baker's legacy better than a 1962 reflection by George Frazier, then the doyen of Boston's literati. "Always at college hockey games," he wrote, "I am haunted by the redolent remembrance" of Hobey Baker, "as he was in the sinew and swiftness of his youth, in the nocturnes of half-a-century ago at the sanctified second when he would take the puck from behind his own net and, as the crowd rose to its feet screaming 'Here he comes!' he would start up the ice like some winged messenger out of mythology, as fleet and as godlike as any of them, his bright birthright a blazing blur, and for a lovely little while God would be in His Heaven and the puck, more than likely, in the other team's net."[7]

The Value of Speed and Skill—Fred Taylor

The fact that Baker could share a bad January 1914 week with Frederick Wellington "Cyclone" Taylor (1884–1979) demonstrates just how big and broad the hockey world had become. As a skater, stick handler, and passer, Taylor matched the American; thereafter all similarities cease. A pure amateur, Baker played hockey, his biographer wrote, "*pour le sport*." Cyclone represented a growing cohort of vagabond professional and "shamateur" hockeyists who measured their success by the money they could make. Over the course of his twenty-one-year career (1902–23), Cyclone Taylor became the sport's first professional star and cashed in on the growing commercial demand for hockey spectacle. When Canadian Governor General Earl Grey saw Taylor score four goals in one game for Ottawa in January 1908, his Excellency declared Taylor "a cyclone if I ever saw one." The *Ottawa Free Press* seconded the motion: "In Portage la Prairie they called him a tornado, in Houghton, Michigan, he was known as a whirlwind. From now on he'll be known as Cyclone Taylor."[8]

Born in 1883, Taylor began playing competitive hockey as a teenager for his hometown team, the Listowel (Ontario) Mintos, but as he admitted in an interview shortly before his death in 1979, "I didn't really come into my own until I began to play for Stratford in 1902, at the age of 19." Playing against other south-central Ontario town teams, he was noticed and recruited to play for Portage la Prairie for two years in the Manitoba Senior Amateur League. Taylor quickly made his mark as a rover in one of the most competitive leagues in the world. His speed and skill opened new possibilities, including pay for play. When the Michigan-based International Hockey League (IHL) enticed Canadian players to cross the border, Taylor was among the first recruits, signing with the Portage Lake Lakers from 1904 to 1907. When that league folded, Taylor, now an acknowledged star, signed for two years with the Ottawa Senators of the Eastern Canada Amateur Hockey Association, an organization that soon ended the ruse by excising the word amateur and rebranding as the ECHA. Taylor's presence symbolized the increasingly commercial nature of the game. Years later he told hockey writer Stan Fischler, "Depending on the player, a salary would run from $1200 to $2500." When Taylor's Ottawa Senators played a 1908 two-game series against the Stanley Cup champion Montreal Wanderers in New York's St. Nicholas Rink, the spectacle kindled a media blaze, much of which focused on Taylor. Cyclone's dominating play appealed to New Yorkers as much as his rugged looks, which resembled American heavyweight boxer Jim Jeffries, then being pressured out of retirement to be the "Great White Hope" against Jack Johnson. When Taylor returned to New York in the spring of 1909, one banner in the St. Nick's Rink read "WELCOME BACK, LITTLE JEFF."[9]

Fred "Cyclone" Taylor, ca. 1919 (City of Vancouver Archives)

A marquee attraction was worth marquee money. In 1910, now a member of the NHA's Renfrew Creamery Kings (aka "Millionaires"), Taylor negotiated an unheard-of price for his services: $5,260 to play for the 1910–11 season. "If I had been one of those good negotiators," he later recalled, "I could've gotten $10,000—a real fortune then, because they wanted me real bad." His third visit to New York came in March 1910, when the Millionaires came to play a team that mixed Montreal Wanderers and Ottawa Senators. New York's *Evening Telegram* reported that among "the Renfrew players will be . . . 'Jeffries' Taylor, the man who is paid more than $10 for every minute he is on the ice. . . . His salary shames what is paid to our star baseball players for a full 154-game season."[10]

Taylor finished his brilliant career in the West, in the Pacific Coast Hockey Association (PCHA), a league hatched by the brothers Lester and Frank Patrick that lured talent from the eastern powers, employed a "syndicate" model of interlocking ownership, and generally shook up the game. Hired by the Vancouver Millionaires for $1,200 per season, Fred Taylor became the jewel of the circuit, averaging more than a goal per game in his ten seasons there. In the Millionaires' 1915 Stanley Cup playoff series against Ottawa, Taylor scored six goals in three games. He led the PCHA in scoring five times, including 1917–18, when he scored 32 goals in eighteen games.[11]

Songs of Savagery—Joe Hall

Joe Hall's bad week in January 1914 was, relatively speaking, not all that bad. A wag might say that all of Hall's weeks in hockey involved bad behavior, and the first week in January 1914 paled by comparison to, say, the final week of January 1910, when Bad Joe (1882–1919) was a formidable defender for the Montreal Shamrocks. In an NHA game against Renfrew, Hall took exception to a referee's call. The *Renfrew Mercury* noted he "became enraged and made for the official with his fists," but before he could reach him, Hall "was promptly met and knocked to the ice," which angered him further. As he lay on the ice, he "made a kick at Kennedy, the official, with his skate and tore the referee's trousers." League officials fined Hall $100 for his antics but declared him eligible to continue playing, which he did that very night as his Shamrocks defeated their townsmen, the Canadiens, 5–2, in front of two thousand fans.[12]

Joe Hall became the sort of player that the rules and dynamics of early hockey allowed. Born in England, he moved at age two with his family to Winnipeg and, later, Brandon, where he grew up and developed his own punishing style. Initially a forward, Hall's rough play suited him better as a defenseman, which he became for Winnipeg in the Manitoba Hockey League. Though rumors of secret pay circulated in 1904 and 1905, Hall was officially an amateur with Brandon (1901–03; 1904–05) and Winnipeg (1903–04). In 1905–06 he ended the mystery and joined Taylor and others in the openly professional International Hockey League, playing for Portage Lakes that season. He played as a professional for the remainder of his career: fifteen seasons with the Quebec Bulldogs, Kenora Thistles, Montreal Shamrocks, Montreal Wanderers, Winnipeg Maple Leafs, and Montreal Canadiens, including four Stanley Cup–winning teams.

No stranger to the scorecard, Hall scored 33 goals in twenty games for Portage Lakes in 1905–06, and 13 goals in nineteen games for the NHA's Quebec Bulldogs in 1913–14. But his frequent presence in the penalty box earned him his nickname. Always among league leaders in penalty minutes, he racked up an impressive 98 PIMs in Portage Lakes in 1905–06, 95 as a Quebec Bulldog in 1916–17, and an even 100 for the Canadiens in 1917–18. His offenses were both routine and irregular. In one 1906 IHL game against Pittsburgh, Hall "laid out" Pittsburgh star Hod Stuart with a stick to the jaw and later ran the Pittsburgh goaltender Winchester. "'Bad' Joe Hall was an excitable type," Cyclone Taylor recalled. "If he heard before a

Joe Hall (back row, far right) and the Stanley Cup-winning Kenora Thistles, 1907 (Lake of the Woods Museum, Kenora, Ontario)

game that someone was out to get him on the ice, he'd get charged up and go after that person first thing."[13] Hall became, for much of his career, a hired gun; the "muscle" that teams needed to carry them deeper into the playoffs. Another modern die was cast. Sadly, like Baker, Hall met his end too soon. While with the Canadiens in Seattle preparing for their Stanley Cup series with the Metropolitans, Hall fell victim in spring 1919 to that mysterious killer of the young and vigorous—Spanish influenza.

Joe Hall, Cyclone Taylor, and Hobey Baker were heroes and archetypes of hockey in an industrial age. Electric speed. Sharp, crisp, cutting shifts in direction. Hard, black, rubber pucks rifled at goal, sometimes ricocheting into the stands. Sticks crashing on bare bone. Fists, blood, gore. Pure joy of motion. Science of teamwork. And the chance for cash. In these years, players, coaches, managers, promoters, and writers took a raw pastime and gave it a modern image. It was the difference between the Stanley Steamer and the Model T.

Innovative Strategy: Positional Alignment and Tactics

In the late nineteenth century, hockey was played, one historian put it, "at a comparatively sluggish pace" with a "rather individualistic, 'scrambly' style of play." One coach described it as "haphazard."[14] The rules prohibited all forward passing. Like rugby, it was an onside game in which the puck could only be distributed to teammates laterally or backward. The rules encouraged solo rushes over combination play and left little leeway for strategizing systematic play. At the same time, contemporary skates (as "modern" as they might be) had flat blades more like today's figure skates—useful for powerful thrusts and wide turns but not for quick stops, starts, or tight turns needed for sharp passing and puck movement. And even the most skilled puck carriers and playmakers were slowed by snowy, bumpy, or mushy ice. It was an era that valued "grit" and determination. Substitutions were rare, so players tended to cruise and save energy for short bursts. Late Victorian performances were slow, dull, low-scoring affairs of attrition punctuated by episodic bursts of brilliant individual performance. But that was about to change. By 1920, the chances of audience ennui were very slim; hockey had become a widely recognizable sport composed of three central ingredients: speed, science, and mayhem.

Speed had always been a useful attribute for anyone chasing a hard object on a slippery surface. But after 1900 it became an essential attribute that separated hockey from other sports competing for popular attention. Speed was often used to sell the game to uninitiated publics. "With all due reverence for cricket, we think hockey a trifle faster," the *Victoria Times* observed after the hometown team took on the New Westminster Royals in the first PCHA game in January 1912. Hockey "is the swiftest exhibition of skill in the sporting world."[15] This was more than a Canadian's pride for his national winter sport. American publications such as *Harper's Weekly* and *Outing* echoed the feeling with articles titled "Speeding It Up on the Ice" and "Fastest Game on Two Feet."[16] Speed was vital to individuals like Baker and Taylor; team speed was equally impressive. When the upstart Kenora Thistles challenged and defeated the heavily favored Montreal Wanderers for the 1907 Stanley Cup, newspapers declared in unison the secret of success. "Speed won," the *Montreal Star* admitted; "Kenora seemed to cover twice the distance of the local men." The crosstown *Montreal Herald* agreed: "With such speed, teamwork is almost unnecessary."[17]

Almost. Players borrowed more from rugby than just padded pants, striped sweaters, and shin guards; they borrowed its pace and tactics, too.

Restricted by rules, players advanced the puck in one of three ways: singular dashes up the ice (in the same fashion that halfbacks returned kicks in American football); "lobbing" or lifting the puck into an opponent's defensive zone (like a punt); or, increasingly, by systematically passing the puck to teammates (laterally).[18] These tactics made for a few spectacular moments but more often for long, drawn-out territorial campaigns that resulted in few scores. Particularly distressing to early promoters was the tendency to rely on unappealing and collective tactics from rugby and football: interference and "mass plays." "Among some senior teams the practice of interference is becoming prominent," Arthur Farrell argued in 1899. "[It] should be severely checked, because it is an unfailing cause of unnecessary roughness." Mass plays, he continued, are "calculated to injure"; they made hockey both ugly and dangerous.[19]

After 1900, strategy became more complex, and hockey became a prettier game to watch. This paralleled the institutional changes taking place in American football, such as the idea of hiring outside, nonplaying (and sometimes paid) coaches to oversee team selection, training, and strategy.[20] During the 1880s, Montreal Winter Carnival teams were represented at meetings by their captains alone; by 1900, coaches had risen to a place of importance, especially as tacticians. A coach could see the ice and plays develop from a perspective unavailable to a player. Moreover, most coaches in these years (and ever since) were ex-players themselves. It was no coincidence that "science," or combination play, was elevated during the same years as the rise of the coach. Figures such as the PCHA's Patrick brothers and Harvard University's Ralph Winsor left important imprints. By 1912 the National Hockey Association recognized the trend and legalized "megaphone coaching" on the "sidelines."[21]

Hockey's new strategy emerged along with its first stars. Team tactics were devised to provide a combined defense against the marauding of players like Taylor and Baker. Gradually, coaches and players began to see that combination play could have a positive effect on offensive strategy as well. Adherence to strict positional alignments, and patterned and practiced passing involving several players, could both score goals and prevent opponents from scoring.

Player positions were a subject of experimentation. Until the end of World War I, seven-man hockey (an inheritance from the Montreal Winter Carnival) held sway. In 1912–13, the National Hockey Association tried out six a side in an effort to cut down salary costs. League members agreed to play six men until February 1, when seven players would be used for the season's final weeks and playoffs. But when February 1 arrived, the governors reversed their decision, leaving in place "the more popular style." Eventually, six-man hockey became orthodoxy. The Ontario Hockey Association and the New York–based American Amateur Hockey League clung to seven a side for a while; but by 1920, each had adopted the six-man format. In 1920 the Ligue Internationale de Hockey sur Glace (LIHG, founded 1908) adopted six-man hockey for international and Olympic play. In 1922, when the Patrick brothers' PCHA finally relented, the hockey world's transition was all but complete.[22]

Modern tactical innovation began, however, well before the end of the seven-man game. Four forwards—two wings, one center, and one rover—provided a team's offensive attack. On defense were three men: a cover point, a point, and a goaltender. Positional strategy focused increasingly on a strict division of labor and athletic specialization. Forwards were expected to be the fittest and best skaters on a team, the center and rover the most agile, quick-thinking, and dexterous players. The cover point was to be a team's most physical player, and the point its best puckhandler and sturdiest defender. Then, as now, goaltending had special demands: quick, cool-headed, methodical, and well positioned to cover angles, the goaltender must be a team's most reliable player. Ex-Harvard captain Trafford Hicks reminded his readers in his 1912 booklet *How to Play Ice Hockey*: "There is no one back of the goal keeper to compensate for his blunders."[23] Put together, the different positions were parts of a complementary system. "There's a science to hockey," Boston's Ralph Winsor noted in 1918: it is much more than "a general barn-yard scramble."[24]

The following figure presents in digested form variations of positional alignment and strategy that players and coaches developed in these years. In the orthodox "Canadian" formation, three designated forwards (two wingers and a center) worked in concert to pass the puck around opponents' defenders and shoot on net. The rover was expected to closely follow the attack and pick up the "loose change" if his attacking teammates got checked or lost the puck. Defenders in this system were expected to contribute little to a team's attack, though occasionally a cover point might take advantage of a chance to collect and shoot a loose puck from mid-ice. The point would rarely leave his position in front of his goaltender, who stayed in front of his cage at all times.

This alignment was the basis from which teams began to experiment in the 1890s. Positional alterations were normally subtle in these years, though

Standard or "Canadian" Formation	The Quebec Variation, 1895	Kenora Thistles "X", 1905–06	Winsor's "American System"
F C F	F C F	F C F	F LC RC F
←R→			
CP	CP CP	R	
			CP
P	P	CP P	P
G	G	G	G

Modern positional play in seven-man hockey

their effects could be profound. The Quebec Variation provides one such example. An 1895 *Montreal Herald* article, called "The Latest Style of Play," explained the change: "Some teams, notably that of Quebec, have sought to strengthen the defense by playing two men at coverpoint at the expense of one of the forwards. The change has caused much discussion in hockey circles." The wunderkinder Kenora Thistles of 1906–07 introduced another innovation that, when combined with their team speed, helped win the Stanley Cup. One Thistles historian observed: "Kenora was able to take full advantage of their skill by forming an 'X' instead of a 'T,' which ultimately redefined the play of defencemen."[25]

One important innovator was Harvard's Winsor, a varsity captain and later coach for both the Crimson and the Boston Athletic Association Unicorns. He devised what became known in the war years as the "American System," an alignment that both he and the *Boston Herald* trumpeted as "superior" to Canadian strategy. Principal among Winsor's ideas were two: four forwards abreast, all of whom attacked and "checked back," patrolling their "lanes" in both directions; and two defensemen, a cover point and a point who played almost parallel to one another, and divided the ice vertically. "On a big rink like the Boston Arena, the hockey taught by Ralph Winsor is superior to the Canadian brand," New Brunswick native and captain of the Boston Arena Hockey Club, Frank "Red" Synnott, admitted to the *Herald* in January 1918. "When a team can spread a forward line across the ice and hold its lanes, it takes a snappy combination of players to overcome this game."[26]

Surely, there were other variations in these years. But by the early 1920s, the essential elements and orthodoxies of modern positional play were in place. Right and left wingers' zonal responsibilities clung to the boundaries and ranged the whole length of the ice. A center's role now encompassed both attacking and defending throughout the rink's central corridor. At defense, two skaters now divided their position horizontally (left, right) instead of vertically (front, back) and were expected to work in unison. Finally, there was the goaltender, whose job had not changed much, except that after flopping was legalized in 1917, he was now free to do his job more acrobatically. Thereafter, at least in North America, tactics congealed and were not challenged seriously until Lloyd Percival questioned them in the 1950s and the 1972 Summit Series debacle made them obsolete.

Yet innovations in positional alignments tell only half of the story. *Dynamic* strategy was a subtler and more powerful transformation. Unlike football, hockey coaches could not craft *fully articulated* plays; the game did not lend itself to that; but they could plan *contingencies*—tactics for common situations and predictable possibilities. All of this was limited by the offside rule. What former Winnipeg Victoria star Tom Howard stated in a 1905 article was bedrock: "The off-side rule is the foundation of hockey-playing."[27] The challenge was to create sustained attack and sound defense without making what today seems the most natural play of all, a forward pass. The response lay in three tactical innovations: the development of patterned playmaking; an emphasis on team defense and backchecking; and a new logic of defense partnership.

For Montreal Shamrock Arthur Farrell, combination play was nothing less than the scientific management of player movement. Some passages in Farrell's 1899 handbook could have been written by Frederick Winslow Taylor himself: "Combination play" was the "scientific means" to "perfection," wherein "with every man working in his position, *like so many movements in a clock*, a forward with the puck, in advance, should know without looking, where each of his partners follows." Farrell championed situational proclivity: the skill and knowledge to anticipate where one's teammates and the puck were going, and to take advantage of that circumstance. Farrell's book specifically addressed common situations that forwards faced in the game: what to do with a 4-on-2 or 4-on-3 advantage; how to use the boards to pass to a teammate; where to position oneself when the puck went behind the net. Traff Hicks's 1912 volume even began to explain the rudiments of the modern set "breakout" play. The goal here was predictability, and Farrell and Hicks set down in ink what must have been voiced in many rinks. In the thirty or so years before 1920, *combination play* became an exalted term.[28]

The second major, dynamic innovation of these years involved what might be called today team defense or, more simply, backchecking. Combination attack play demanded a response. When the lob/dump tactic predominated, backchecking was not needed; it would have been a liability because it meant taking men out of position who might otherwise pounce on lobbed pucks. In those days, the designated backchecker was the team's rover, "the busiest man on the ice." By the 1900s, a more systematic approach to backchecking became de rigueur. All forwards were to play "two ways." Though not alone in promoting this approach, it was Winsor (called by his opponents "The Wizard") and his disciples, like Hicks, who best articulated the scheme.[29] "Following back is one of the first changes of Canadian hockey I established when I began coaching," Winsor recalled in 1918. "The system of play I have mapped out . . . requires a man to check back in his lane. It is sensible hockey."[30] Not everyone agreed completely; Canadian ex-pat and Boston resident Red Synnott politely demurred. Though Winsor had, in Synott's view, "revolutionized hockey in this country . . . the game I have been brought up [on] in the provinces always will be my style. . . . I believe Winsor's style takes a lot out of a player . . . when a player loses the puck he has to stop dead in his tracks and chase back the same lane. . . . The Canadians, when they lose a puck, swing off to either side and circle around so that they can take another crack at the forward with the puck. They are maintaining the same pace with a minimum effort." In truth, they were splitting hairs. By 1920 backchecking had become a permanent element of the modern game.[31]

Besides experiments in alignment, team defense also included dynamic tactics about how to handle distinctive attack situations (1-on-1, 2-on-1, and 3-on-2) and designate "on-puck" and "off-puck" responsibilities for each. Though it is unclear who first conjured such change, Kenora's Art Ross and Boston's Winsor were among the first to *describe* it. Whatever its source, the modern defensive mindset was born out of these simple adjustments in alignment and responsibility. By 1920, the dynamics of modern defensive play were in place.

Bloodshed and Mayhem

Beyond speed and science, hockey was branded as violent. Rough play was part of the game from its inception, but in this period it took on a strange sort of cultural significance as well. Hockey's roughness established it in the minds of contemporaries as a "manly" game whose inherent danger asserted the virility of its players (and followers), assuaging some fears that a prosperous, cosmopolitan, white, urban, and industrial culture might become soft and effeminate. This mentality also legitimized violence in football, lacrosse, and boxing in the same era.[32]

There was frequent debate, prompting endless hand wringing over acceptable limits of hockey's physicality, at all levels of play. One might see it as either an endemic problem that threatened to radicalize an essentially pretty game of skill, speed, and agility; for another it was no problem at all, and required no apology. The debate echoed for more than a century. By 1920, however, a general consensus had already emerged: the "best" sort of hockey must have physical violence, though not in excessive measure. The meaning of "excessive" has been hockey's puzzle ever since.

There were two sorts of violence. The routine form was permitted by the rules and became an important tactical element.[33] In the era's many handbooks, checks with the shoulder or hip were prescribed, but only for situations that called for physical play, especially on defense. Players were never to give priority to punishment over puck play, never to "run" opponents and put themselves out of position. In contemporary game accounts, roughness often overshadowed passing, puck handling and shooting, and critics argued that it hurt the game. Overly physical hockey was ugly, even when it did not technically break the rules.[34]

But the line between legitimate violence in hockey and unacceptable roughness was never very clear. The game's speed detracted from referees' abilities to monitor all players' behavior. Moreover, the effectiveness of intimidation motivated players, such as Joe Hall, to cross the line regularly. The 1911 *Spalding Ice Hockey Guide* described the conundrum:

> Hockey is a rough game at the best. Body checking is legitimate and falls will consequently be frequent. Tripping is not allowed, but often the players are so expert that it is impossible for the referee to decide if the trip was intentional or accidental, and as a consequence players often get the benefit of the doubt. With players who are disposed to be ugly there are many tricks that are used. When in close contact with an opponent the short end of the stick is used to jab into his ribs or stomach. The short end . . . can be used so effectively that no one but the injured player will know what has happened.[35]

Butt ending was an instant violation of an emerging code.

Routine physicality led occasionally to bouts of exceptional, extreme violence—brawling, slashing, slugging, stick swinging and fighting—that simultaneously thrilled some spectators and threatened hockey's legitimacy. Newspaper game reports often featured descriptions of ugly episodes. OHA president John Ross Robertson warned his charges in 1904: "We must call a halt to slashing and slugging, and insist upon clean hockey . . . before we have to call in a coroner to visit our rinks." Robertson was more prescient than he could have known. One year later, Alexandria, Ontario's Alcide Laurin was killed by a stick swung by Maxville's Allan Loney. Two years later, Charles Masson of the Cornwall Hockey Club struck Owen "Bud" McCourt of the Ottawa Victorias in the head with his stick, killing him. Both Loney and Masson were initially charged with murder, but the charges were later reduced to manslaughter. In each case, the offending players were acquitted in the courts. In Canada, between 1905 and 1918, there were eight episodes extreme enough to result in formal charges of assault, four of them in 1907 alone. These cases were the tip of a sizeable iceberg. A newspaper account of a 1907 game between the Ottawa Silver Seven and the Montreal Wanderers described "an exhibition of butchery" that resulted not in death, merely the spilling of blood. "[Ottawa's] 'Baldy' Spittal allegedly tried to split Cecil Blachford's skull" with a two-handed chop. "Blachford was carried off with his blood pouring on the ice." This decade of carnage would be matched in a second wave during the 1970s.[36]

As the mayhem escalated, some in the press blamed the referees. "Infrequently is a game played about New York which does not disclose the foulest kind of foul play," Caspar Whitney wrote in a 1903 editorial in *Outing*, titled "Hoodlumism in Hockey." "[Y]et on the majority of occasions the offender escapes free of penalty, or the penalty is . . . absurdly inadequate. . . . Newberry, of the Hockey Club, after a long series of foul plays, eventually so seriously injured an opponent he is not likely to play again this season—yet Newberry was taken out of the game for just *two* minutes!"[37] In the aftermath of McCourt's on-ice death in 1907, the *Ottawa Journal* claimed that more alert officiating would have prevented the tragedy. "Nearly all the local players express the opinion that if the referee had been more strict regarding the rough play, the trouble would have been averted."[38]

The rules themselves were a bigger problem. At the time, referees were given wide discretion on the penalty time imposed for any foul. The American Amateur Hockey League rules said, "He shall have the power to rule off for any period of the actual playing time that he may see fit any player who violates the rules." The Ontario Hockey Association had similar language: "for such time as he may deem expedient." Consistency has long been coaches' and fans' bugaboo on officiating. In this case, the rules were a recipe for complaints. Despite the debate, violence became an accepted and useful part of the game, and central to its appeal. Together with speed and combination play, roughness was among the trinity of elements making the game that came of age between 1890 and 1920: a unique construction that fused science with savagery, art with atavism.[39]

Hockey's Material Culture

Innovation arose not just from player character or coaching genius. It also flowed from fundamental changes in basic material culture—specialized skates, protective equipment, and the stick—all of which allowed players to play more quickly and reliably in combination with one other. Ready-made ice skates were no new thing to North Americans and Europeans of the Victorian era. By the 1880s, however, it was clear that hockey demanded more than what generic models could offer. Skaters needed a blade high enough to prevent the boot's sole from touching the ice when turning or cutting corners and "long enough and sufficiently flat on the ice to admit of great speed," but not so long at the heel or toe to hinder quick turning. Hockey skates needed to be lightweight and strong, Arthur Farrell noted from experience, "because the thousand twistings and turnings of a player strain every inch of the blade, each plate and every rivet."[40]

Fortunately for players, there were plenty of firms who by the 1890s claimed all of these traits for their specialized products. Halifax's Starr Manufacturing Company had been providing Maritimers with ice skates since the 1860s, but in the late 1880s it began to offer "Starr Hockey Skates," regularly introducing new models for the sport in subsequent years, including, by 1902, the "No. 5," the Chebucto, the Regal, and the Velox. Starr's "Mic-Mac" featherweight skate was promoted as "the fastest skate in the world," one that made its wearer "The Modern Mercury."[41] Starr was a power, but it had competitors, especially beyond the Maritimes. In November 1897, the Samuel Winslow Skate Manufacturing Company of Worcester, Massachusetts, ran a quarter-page advertisement in *Harper's Monthly Magazine* with a drawing of a new "St. Nicholas Skating Club

Starr hockey skates, "The Modern Mercury" (The Collection of the Darmouth Heritage Museum)

Hockey Skate," noted as "the combined judgment of the most celebrated ice hockey players."[42]

The sales of hockey equipment followed the transition from local to national. Early players purchased equipment from local hardware and cycling retailers, a relatively modest line of goods appended to larger, year-round, and more fluid sales items: bicycles and tools. Generally, any marketing that businesses did was local, geared toward a *known* audience. One example demonstrates this: in a small foot-of-the-page advertisement in February 1895, the H. P. Davies Company branch of the Griffiths Cycle Corporation offered Toronto's *Globe* readers the whole range of gear they would need to play: "HOCKEY STICKS, SHOES, PUCKS, SKATES, SWEATERS, RULES."[43]

Equipment dealers both prodded and followed the game's growth. Manufacturers expanded vertically, intensifying competition. Starr, for example, developed means to market its skates nationally and internationally. By the early 1900s, Starr advertised its wares in both daily newspapers and specialized trade journals such as "Outer's Book" and "Sporting Goods Dealer." The company also produced its own catalog—*Starr Skate Book*—and also marketed its skates prominently in Eaton's mail order *Fall and Winter Catalogue*, which distributed products across the Dominion. Starr used sponsorships, moreover, to advance its presence in the market, donating trophies to the winners of league competition in Halifax (1897) and Winnipeg (1907). National marketing seemed to pay dividends: every member of the 1917 Vancouver city-league champions wore Starr skates.[44]

Despite this commendable record, Starr paled next to Spalding, the Chicopee, Massachusetts–based sporting-goods giant whose success came from another proven Gilded Age business tactic: the "capture" of constituted authority. Spalding produced and marketed equipment for all sports, and for many nations. In hockey, they made everything one would need to play, coach, or officiate the game. A big company with big influence, the Spalding brothers created symbiotic relationships with emerging governing bodies such as the Amateur Hockey Association of Canada. In return for printing the association rules, Spalding equipment was designated as "official." The 1904 edition of the *Ice Hockey and Ice Polo Guide*, for instance, included the "Laws of Hockey of the Canadian Amateur Hockey League." Rule 13 mandated that all games be played with a Spalding puck. This practice had started in the 1870s in American baseball with the Spaldings' cozy relationship with the National League (in which Albert Spalding was a team owner). It foreshadowed the tight relationship that continued between hockey equipment makers and the sport's clubs, leagues, and organizations.[45]

The upshot was greater expense to serious consumers. According to Spalding's 1904 *Ice Hockey Guide*, players could buy a Spalding "Championship" stick for 50 cents or a polished "Shamrock" stick for 75 cents. A puck was relatively expensive at 25 cents. Shin guards ranged from 40 cents to $2.50 a pair; the better ones covered the bone with "real rattan reed" and heavy felt. Canvas pants cost from 40 cents to $2.00, and moleskin goaltender pants were $3.00. There were skates of many kinds for all prices, from 90 cents to $5.00.[46] Through fancy, illustrated advertising, companies such as Spalding and Starr managed to create consumer need. For one to be a *real* player, homemade goods would no longer do. Brand names were now the badges of legitimacy.

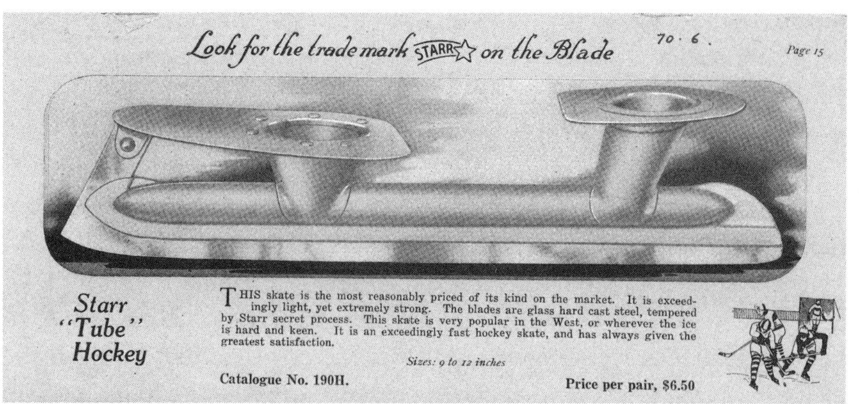

Starr "Tube" hockey skates: "Very popular in the west" (The Collection of the Darmouth Heritage Museum)

Brand names could also distribute innovation quickly. The introduction of tube skates completed the era's changes in skating technology. This was a breakthrough concept—a hollow tube of steel held the blade in place, making the skate much lighter. Starr introduced its first tubular products during World War I. The Spalding factory built and sold tubular skates as early as 1912. It took years for manufacturers to develop tubes that did not break or loosen along the blade edge. Once perfected, however, the metal tubular skate was the basic item for the next six decades.[47]

Hockey sticks, too, became the objects of improvement. In the late nineteenth century, Canada's most prolific source of sticks were Mi'kmaq natives in the Maritimes, wood carvers and craftsmen whose "Mic-Mac" brand dominated the small market. It was Mic-Mac sticks—made first of ironwood, then yellow birch, and produced in Nova Scotia—that Lord Stanley's sons and their "Rideau Hall Rebels" used in the 1880s. It is likely that Mic-Mac sticks were used by James Creighton and friends in Montreal in 1875, by Master Conover and his charges in New Hampshire, and by Tom Paton, who brought "hockeys" from Montreal to begin Toronto's experiment with the game. In the 1890s, Mic-Mac sticks were bought by the Starr Manufacturing Company and distributed in bulk, complementing their line of skates. Simple but sturdy, these sticks were made from one piece of wood, then "steam-bent" into form. Native sticks were hand cut and carved from "selected second-growth birch, grain of wood running with curve of blade." By the 1900s, Starr also advertised a new, industrial model, The Rex: factory-made and featuring a "double-groove blade." With its deeper pockets, Spalding could offer a range of models named for and endorsed by luminaries like Tom Howard, Lester Patrick, Percy LeSueur, and Didier "Cannonball" Pitre.[48]

Less critical was the rest of the sport's "kit." Handbooks in the 1890s advised players to wear a moderately heavy sweater, pants padded at the hips, thighs, and knees, and heavy stockings with a light suit of underwear. Thin gloves and shin guards completed the attire. Before the turn of the century, a hockeyist might meet these needs at home, with his own (or a family member's) skills, needles, and thread. Yet, by the 1900s, even these elements of the game were becoming standardized. In the 1890s, players might fashion their own gloves and gauntlets from spare leather and ideas borrowed from cricket batsmen; for players coming into the game by 1905, however, hockey gloves were a distinct commodity. Shin protection, once provided by rolled-up catalogues, were now "hockey shin guards," created specifically for the purpose. In this age of professional experts, specialized equipment promised performance and legitimated the sport.[49]

The Role of the Press

But legitimation came via the printed word as well. In January 1914 millions of North Americans could have learned of Baker's, Taylor's, and Hall's bad week by simply thumbing through their newspapers' sport pages. It is hard to overestimate the influence that mass-produced daily newspapers had in cultivating interest and markets for hockey. By the 1910s, from November to April, newspapers conveyed hockey stories to meet the voracious appetite of a growing audience.

Here, two important and related patterns emerged—one quantitative, one qualitative. Between 1890 and 1920 the amount of daily print dedicated to telling hockey stories increased gradually. In addition to local reportage, papers broadened their scope and began to include results of games played across the country and in other countries. Second, the reports ceased to be simple, stolid accounts of who played, when, where, and with what result. By the 1910s, hockey held a variety of narrative possibilities. Contests were portrayed thickly and with drama, canvases on which heroes and villains, favorites and underdogs, authorities, rule breakers, and subversives were cast and recast. Every game was a live stage play just waiting to be invested with meaning.[50]

By 1920, newspapers had created a sporting culture so broad, integrated, and metropolitan that one could find fans of Babe Ruth as readily on the Canadian prairies as in urban America.[51] And the same was true for Hobey Baker, Cyclone Taylor, and Joe Hall. Hockey benefited from propitious timing; it came of age just as the mass-produced newspaper went looking for copy to sell to the public. In a 1912 article in *Baseball Magazine*, titled "Ice Hockey—The Baseball of Winter," F. C. Lane wrote: "The fact that sporting sheets have of late devoted so much space to hockey is a sure indication of the popular approval of that sport. This attitude can mean only the awakening of the press to the value of this marvelous game, and the corresponding awakening of the public to its value as a genuine sport of national and international possibilities."[52]

Toronto's daily newspaper, the *Globe*, provides an interesting reflection of this phenomenon. The *Globe* could hardly be considered one of North America's "people's journals," like Hugh Graham's *Montreal Star* or William Randolph Hearst's *New York Journal*, which began to rely on sensationalist accounts and illustrated renderings of sporting (and other) events in the 1890s to broaden readership and sell more product.[53] Still, even a cursory examination of the hockey coverage in the *Globe* demonstrates the growing popularity of and demand for the game. In 1890, sporting news was still mixed in among other local news items, but in 1895 and 1900 the *Globe* dedicated a separate sports section of one or two pages. In the 1890s, hockey rarely ranked as a lead story, normally placing second to speed skating, curling, or reports from "the Turf." By 1910, however, hockey had begun its permanent ascension to top rank in the winter sporting news. In most weeks between mid-November and early April, hockey dominated, and *Globe* editors met the demand for local, national and international results by inserting a standard daily column headlined "Hockey Record: Results and Fixtures," along with occasional, chatty news segments called first "After the Puck" (1900), then "Puckerings" (1905–20). By 1915, emboldened story titles and page headlines drew readers' attention to its thickening coverage. Typical, for example, were the headlines on the *Globe*'s sports page on February 7, 1920, hawking three hockey pieces—"DENTS 5; AURA LEE 3. LEAFS SIGN DYE . . . DECISIVE O.H.A. GAMES"—and a brief report on the Dominion Football Association meeting—"SOCCER MOGULS HERE."[54]

More prominent, the stories were also more numerous in these years, tracked by a simple count (table 8.1) of *Globe* hockey reports in the first

TABLE 8.1. Hockey Stories in Toronto's *Globe* in first week of February, selected years, 1890–1920.

1890	1895	1900	1905	1910	1915	1920
2	12	21	74	80	62	75

week of February in every fifth year, 1890–1920.[55] The expanding *range* of coverage was equally impressive. Scores from professional leagues and all ranks of amateur teams—junior, intermediate, collegiate, and senior—and from all parts of Canada, the United States, and even Europe found their way onto *Globe* reports. In 1915 news from Toronto's church and industrial leagues shared space (without distinction) with those about the Quebec Bulldogs, the Pittsburgh Yellow Jackets, and the Michigan Soo. After 1910, *Globe* sports readers had the hockey world at their fingertips.

Hockey stories grew in number after 1890, then declined in 1915 and 1920. Growth until 1910 reflected not just a developing interest in the sport among readers but an increase in games to cover. There were more stories to tell. So why, then, the decline after 1910? *Globe* editors and readers hardly grew less interested in hockey news in those years; explanations lie elsewhere. In 1915, Canada's preoccupation with its efforts in World War I may have reduced available space for game reports. Moreover, in 1915 and 1920, written sports news was being squeezed by advertising (especially for train travel, male grooming products, and cigarettes) and the beginnings of photographic reportage, both of which placed a premium on space for written copy. More important, there was a qualitative change in hockey news that began to chase some game reportage to the sidelines. By 1920, *Globe* editors favored fewer, pithier, and more dramatic game accounts instead of devoting roughly equal space to dozens of contests. As the *New York Record* and *Philadelphia Inquirer* did with football coverage, so too the Toronto *Globe* in its hockey reportage. By 1920, newspapers eschewed broader "blanket" coverage in favor of spin, and even local amateur games became subjects for grand renderings by sports dramatists.

Before 1905, most game accounts in the *Globe* assumed a formulaic and predictable form. Below a leading and sometimes catchy headline appeared a brief description of the teams and the game's result, followed by team rosters and referees' names. Occasionally, reporters added footnotes about curious incidents in games, upcoming matches, or the consequences of a game's result. One such account of an OHA game from early February 1895 is typical:

> PARIS MAKES A CLEAN SCORE
>
> Hamilton. Feb. 2—(Special)—Paris and the Victorias played a Southern League game this afternoon at the Victoria rink, the Paris team winning by 6 to 0. The teams were:
>
> Paris—Gray, goal; Howell, point; Ansley, cover point; Mauer, Bridle, O'Neill, Gillard, forwards.
>
> Victoria—Sinclair, goal; Leith, point; W. Meakins, cover point; Miller, Wyndham, C. Meakins, Yorick, forwards.
>
> Referee—D.M. Cameron.
>
> In the first half the Victorias, who were overmatched, kept the visitors from scoring, but the second half Paris made six straight goals and the Victorias failed to score.[56]

This perfunctory treatment was an economical way of delivering the facts that followers sought.

By 1915, the *Globe* augmented its daily coverage with one or sometimes two lead stories that received much longer treatment. These reports were rich, thickly described, dramatic renderings that altered the function of sports coverage. Like their more skeletal neighbors, these stories also had a rough formula. They consisted (generally) of five parts: a pithy, sensational lead paragraph that drew reader interest and suggested a narrative arc; a paragraph that described the live audience; a section that depicted team play and the general flow of the game; a penultimate segment that focused on individual stars; and, finally, a summary section that listed team rosters and game officials. Sometimes ordered differently, the components were consistently present and essential. They were acts in a play—a theatrical structure that sportswriter/dramatists imposed on selected games. The recurring narratives were simple but effective themes: brain versus brawn, the favorite versus the underdog, "science" versus art, combination play versus individual effort, and order versus chaos. Occasionally, ethnic identity was played up to color the game's course and results. Though not overtly bigoted, these references leaned on accepted (though cheap) stereotypes that played on reader sympathies. The *Globe* occasionally referred to the Montreal Canadiens as the "fleet French" and the St. Michael's College OHA and Toronto St. Patricks NHA teams as "the Irishmen," as though these monikers would enlighten their largely Protestant and Anglophone readers.[57] By 1920, newspapers presented hockey to the reading public as a performance of modern life.

What's in a bad week? Much more than just rotten luck. The trials of Hobey Baker, Cyclone Taylor, and Joe Hall provide an entry into a world of sport undergoing significant change: a world going modern. Along with the rise of big stars, "scientific" strategy, and better and more uniform equipment, a new sort of storytelling sold the game's culture to the masses. Hockey became a major sport in North America in these years. A unique game, tailored by increasingly sophisticated strategy and tactics, and shaped by the market, it also developed a cultural gravitas of its own. By 1920, hockey was no longer an experiment that might fail. The only question was how well it might succeed.

9

Whose Game? Class, Language, Race, Sex, and Nation

In the years that Hobey Baker led his Princeton and St. Nick's teams into Boston, the Arena developed its own intramural rivalries among senior amateur sides. At the center of them were the Boston Athletic Association's "Unicorns," managed by George V. Brown and stocked with Harvard alums, including player-coach Ralph Winsor. The BAA's elite status was validated by Harvard's annual schedule, which featured all university teams, except the BAA. Several opponents positioned themselves (with strong press backing) to knock the Unicorns off their pedestal. One was the Intercolonials, managed by grocery magnate Charles F. Adams, led by player-coach Raymie Skilton (a local product of Rindge Tech), and laced with Canadian "ringers." When the Intercolonials dissolved, Skilton took his talents to a new challenger, the Boston Arena Hockey Club, managed by news writer and Arena publicist Fred Hoey. The press hyped these "bitter" rivalries, filled with rough, slashing play that exposed underlying social and cultural tension. Dartmouth graduate Leon Tuck was witness to it; he had played for the Arenas one season. In January 1916 he wrote to his friend, Unicorn captain (and Boston Brahmin) Frederic Huntington: "The style of hockey and some of the fellows on the Arena team are not just the sort that would make the game as enjoyable for me as it might be."[1] Social class colored early-twentieth-century hockey, even if it now included both the rough and the respectable. Teams' (and players') social origins continued to inform the way they played the game and the meaning it had for them.

For almost two decades, Montreal hockey had rested comfortably among its elite and upper-middle-class founders, all of them *male* and *white*. Social and cultural diffusion raised questions of ownership—something that all sporting (and all social) endeavors in Victorian- and Progressive-era North America and Europe faced. Tuck's letter conveys angst. Who could participate? Who *should* play the game? And, as a result, who could claim it? In the rush to secure suitable ice, equipment, teammates, and opponents, early players and promoters rarely posed the questions for open, meaningful discussion. But some of the answers are, like Tuck's letter, strewn among the primary sources of the game's "big push," 1890–1920. In those years, hockey became no longer race-, class-, language-, or gender-exclusive; but those social cleavages continued to matter. French-Canadian, female, black, First Nations, American, and European players came to constitute a cultural "other" that fortified a developing product image. The irony was this: even as hockey became more inclusive on the ice, it was becoming culturally coded in the popular mind as a rough, northern winter game played, possessed, and driven by white, male, English Canadians.[2]

Class and the Amateur Ideal

James Creighton and Arthur Farrell skated their sport in the heyday of the amateur ideal. As we note in chapter 4, amateurism's founders and governors claimed it as the purest form of sporting endeavor: sport for its own sake. These groups championed a vigorous, "manly" endeavor that could impart critical moral values to all who played it correctly. Hockey was an avenue to the strenuous life and social mobility; it built both muscle and character at a time in industrializing North America when traditional masculinity was under fire and opportunities for men to succeed in life seemed increasingly tenuous. "Speaking of . . . hockey," Farrell wrote in 1899, "a prominent banker . . . said 'that a good, clean sportsman was an acquisition to any commercial house,' and his statement is correct."[3] Farrell and many others envisioned each game, each practice, as part of a tutelary seminar where one could absorb the principles of a successful life. Like other amateur sports, hockey might teach the middle and working classes how to construct a sense of respectable public "self."[4]

Respectability and character grew from playing *amateur* sport—an avocation, free of commercialism, profit, and vice. This message echoed repeatedly throughout the era among advocates such as the OHA's President John Ross Robertson and *Outing* magazine editor Caspar Whitney. Their insistence had important social ramifications. As one historian wrote, the game belonged to a "closed circle of upper-class gentlem[en]."[5] In 1898,

Outing's J. Parmly Paret concluded that "the game has found more favor with the classes than the masses."[6]

But even as Farrell, Whitney, Paret, and others waved their flag, commercialization challenged and then obliterated exclusive amateurism. The promise of commercial gain through gate receipts, winning teams, promotable stars, advertisements, and endorsements compelled organizers to compensate players, first under the table, then openly after 1904 in the International Hockey League (IHL). By the time the professional National Hockey Association was formed in 1910, hockey in North America was a divided proposition, riven between those ostensibly committed to the purity of the old amateur ideal and "new men," for whom commerce was king.

Professionalism brought both a new ethic and new socioeconomic constituencies. In an era when both leisure time and disposable incomes increased for the middle and working classes, access to the game also broadened. Hockey was expensive, but not prohibitively so. One historian noted that among the teams of the early twentieth century were "a plumber's helpers team in Ottawa, two teams of workers from the brass department of Canadian General Electric in Peterborough, [and] the Fire Brigade in Calgary." This diffusion was fostered by a growing number of non-elite institutions and networks: the public schools, churches, and municipalities seeking to foster healthy outdoor recreation among their citizens. And the potential for making money drew players and speculators (businessmen and gamblers) from all social ranks. Moreover, as the importance of the bottom line rose, game tactics changed. Commercialization demanded winning, and, with increased frequency, winning wrought violence. With commercialization, as chapter 8 demonstrates, players and managers added *mayhem* to individual skill and combination play to complete a trinity of appeal.[7]

Commercialization introduced what (to some) was a disturbing pattern of proletarianization. After 1905, players were increasingly both rough and "rough." The rink became a place where, subtly but meaningfully, classed identities were played out and represented among skaters, spectators, and promoters. Canada's most prominent players included few scions of colonial nobility—relatively fewer McGill and MAAA men. Taking their places were newer, more plebeian and mercenary figures, new emblems such as "Cyclone" Taylor, "Newsy" Lalonde, Sprague Cleghorn, and "Bad" Joe Hall, whose style of play paralleled a harsher industrial world. The advent of openly professional leagues made disturbingly clear this change in the character of (and characters in) the game. Eastern Canadian newspapers routinely denigrated IHL play as vulgar and violent; they bemoaned, in two scholars' words, the "behaviours of professionals and the working-class patrons who frequented games in mining towns in the Upper Peninsula of Michigan." Old purists had few realistic suggestions beyond demanding that referees be of irreproachable reputation and "gentlemanly status."[8]

In the eastern United States, where gentlemanly ideals prevailed a bit longer, this contrast was made plain and sometimes construed as the difference between "Canadian" and "American" versions of the game. Turn-of-the-century "visitors from the United States accused Nova Scotians of corrupting the game," in one account, "because the version they saw was so much rougher than the version they saw at home."[9] The differences in play were brought out to American audiences most clearly in the style that Hobey Baker played. Baker was the walking, breathing model of gentlemanly conduct. He repeatedly spurned offers to turn pro. In the words of his principal biographer, when fouled, "he never retaliated, even under the most extreme provocation," though he was often provoked. One Canadian playing for the Irish-American Athletic Association seven recalled a game against Baker's St. Nick's team: "We were Canadians . . . and didn't intend to be shown up by what we thought was an overrated stuck-up society kid. He was slugged, roughed up, kneed, elbowed, and given every dirty trick in the book. Once our star, a big Indian center named Cree, banged Hobey's head against the cage and knocked him out for a few seconds." But a gentleman never retaliated.[10]

The Profession of Hockey

Wealthy, even royal, patrons like Lord Stanley and his sons were crucial promoters in the early diaspora. Still, the elite status of founders was no guarantee. After all, polo began among Newport elite, but it faded in North America. Hockey's success instead depended on the tireless efforts of people from what we would now call middle-class backgrounds. This included missionary players, arena owners and managers, journalists, sporting-goods manufacturers and dealers, association officers, and coaches, many of whom served in multiple roles at once. They loved the sport, but that was not the main attraction. Instead, they recognized that this new, special game offered opportunities for making a reputation or even a living. And so these formative years between 1877 and 1920 witnessed a first generation of "professional" experts who developed and sold

Frank Calder, NHL president, ca. 1934 (Walter P. Reuther Library, Archives of Labor and Urban Affairs, Wayne State University)

pre-formed packages of play, complete with mass-produced, specialized rules and equipment. Some, like Boston's George V. Brown, focused their work on one city. Others, such as George Meagher, traveled the world with rules and equipment.

The archetypes included journalists like Frank Calder who, like so many in this first cohort, was from immigrant stock. Calder was born in Bristol, England, in 1877, but his parents were Scots. In 1900 he came to Canada and found work as a teacher. By 1907 he was in the newspaper business, where he made a reputation as an investigative reporter and editor. He made friends and enemies in the sporting world, but he had a reputation for hard-nosed honesty. Photos of Calder almost always show a tight-lipped, dour look and small, questioning eyes. As two hockey historians describe him, "he preferred to use three words rather than three sentences if he thought he could get away with it." This was a good trait for the president of the National Hockey Association and its successor, the National Hockey League. Like the sports world of which he was so much a part, Calder was all business. He had plenty of international counterparts, like Louis Magnus in France, Emil Prochazka in Prague, and H. Newman Reid in Australia.[11]

Eddie Livingstone (1884–1945) shared several traits with Frank Calder. His father emigrated from Scotland to Canada, where he built a successful Toronto-based printing business that afforded Ed and his brother a respectable, middle-class education and lifestyle. This included playing hockey with the St. George's junior team. As his biographers have argued, "Livvy" was a plugger who overcame a small frame and myopic vision with pure grit. Injury ended his playing career, and by 1908 he was assistant sports editor of the Toronto's *Mail and Empire*, among other things writing stories about hockey games that he refereed. As was the case with Calder, Livingstone's insider interests led him to administrative positions. These included managing an amateur hockey team sponsored by the Toronto Rugby and Athletic Association. As in his playing days, rivals learned hard lessons if they equated Livingstone's physical stature with a lack of toughness. His managerial success led to his recruitment for ownership in the National Hockey Association, where he conducted business as he had played: check hard and give nothing away. He was an early archetype of the cantankerous owner always on the edge of club dissolution. He sued his league colleagues over player rights and trades. He battled over arena contracts. He feuded over schedules. Frank Calder once referred to him as a "lunatic." In 1917 the NHA owners voted to disband their old league and create another, the National Hockey League. Only the new league did not include Livingstone. Undeterred, he continued with lawsuits, rival franchises, and rival leagues for well over a decade, until the Depression cooked all expansion gooses. By all accounts, Eddie Livingstone had firmly believed in the amateur code when he began his playing career. The ensuing decades taught him that gentlemanly behavior did not work amid cutthroat competition on or off the ice.[12]

Hockey also attracted self-made or arriviste business moguls like James MacNaughton, whose Scottish shepherd father, Archibald, had immigrated to Canada, where he shifted from farming to copper mining. James was born in 1864 in Ontario but grew up in Michigan's Upper Peninsula. He quit school at age sixteen to work in the coal docks of the Calumet and Hecla Mining Company, where his father ran the company's railroad operation. James had intelligence and drive, which propelled him to the University of Michigan for a degree in civil engineering. He returned to the Calumet area where he steadily rose in the management ranks, reaching a presidency by 1926. Along the way, MacNaughton became an avid hockey booster. In 1913, he ordered the purchase of a large trophy to be awarded to the winner of the American Amateur Hockey Association—in reality an upper Midwest league. According to legend, MacNaughton insisted that "price didn't matter," and so the 40-pound, 5-gallon cup, was purchased for $2,000. Since 1914, when the Cleveland Athletic Club won it, the MacNaughton Cup has symbolized a form of "western" championship. In 1955, cup control shifted from the senior amateur to the collegiate ranks and the Western Collegiate Hockey Association. There is no evidence that MacNaughton ever played hockey with any level of competence. Instead, he is a classic example of the business mogul who sought and found wider notoriety through an affiliation with a sport.[13]

Francophones and the Birth of *les Canadiens*

Language also contoured hockey culture. Anglophones developed the sport in a city famously divided by the languages of its residents: English and French. Montreal's linguistic divide in the 1880s and 1890s was as sharp and difficult then as it is now, a division compounded by residential and occupational segregation. As Hugh MacLennan aptly wrote later in the twentieth century, language differences created in Montreal "two solitudes."[14]

French Canadians were slow to embrace the new game because they were effectively shut out of the principal venues where it first took root: the Victoria Skating Rink, the Crystal Ice Rink, and the McGill University quadrangle (though not, to be sure, the open ice of the St. Lawrence River). An even more effective barrier was cultural: in the 1870s and 1880s, as one scholar has argued, the Roman Catholic Church "condemned all cultural products of Anglo-Canadian society" and was "dubious about any leisurely activity."[15] Though a small number of French Canadians, such as the Montreal Victorias' Claude Lamothe, laced up the skates and played, it was not until the 1890s that any significant movement of this sort took place.

"The Irish taught the French to play hockey," one authority wrote, in two bilingual Catholic classical colleges in Montreal: Ste-Marie and Mont

St-Louis. By the mid-1890s, French and Irish students mingled on these college's junior-level teams. In 1894 the first all-French-speaking Canadian hockey club was formed, *Le National*, a team affiliated with the *Association Athlétique d'Amateurs le National*, a francophone multisport organization modeled after the anglophone MAAA. Made up of players nurtured at Ste-Marie and Mont-St Louis, *Le National* prospered, gaining entry to the Federal Amateur Hockey League (FAHL) in 1904 and the Canadian Amateur Hockey League (CAHL) in 1905, Canada's top tiers. In 1898 members of the francophone snowshoe club formed *Le Montagnard*, which quickly became the best French-Canadian team in senior hockey after joining the FAHL in 1905. In a few short years, these teams became the emblems of French-Canadian sport and the incubators for French-Canadian talent, having had on their rosters at one point or another the *porte-étendards* of players: Jack Laviolette, Didier Pitre, Emile Coutu, Joseph Dostaler, and Edouard "Newsy" Lalonde. When a March 1909 exhibition game was held at the Jubilee Rink in Montreal's francophone East end between the world-champion Montreal Wanderers and a francophone "all-star" team, the game's result (a narrow 9–8 win for the Wanderers) announced that French-Canadian hockey had come to stay. Moreover, the timing of this match was propitious. As part of the negotiations for the formation of a new professional hockey league in eastern Canada in 1910 (the National Hockey Association), Wanderers' owner J. Ambrose O'Brien advocated strongly for the inclusion of a French-Canadian team, to be called *Le Canadien*. His advocacy worked. The *Canadiens* became one of seven founding members of the NHA, in time an almost wholly francophone organization owned by O'Brien but managed by Montrealer Georges Kendall (a.k.a. Kennedy). French-Canadian fans did not have to wait long for success. The *Canadiens* fielded a very competitive team each year and won their first Stanley Cup in 1916. Among the *Canadiens*' first captains was Laviolette, a pioneer of French-Canadian hockey.[16]

This early success fashioned a national icon. Between 1910 and 1960, the Montreal *Canadiens* became a vessel for French-Canadian national identity in a country dominated by English culture, where French Canadians often felt like second-class citizens, "hewers of wood, and drawers of water." If not in politics, or in business, French Canadians could survive and win on the ice. It is important, a scholar argued recently, to see this phenomenon not as an example of assimilation to English-Canadian norms. "French Canadians' enthusiastic engagement with . . . hockey . . . [symbolizes] a subordinate people's appropriation of practices from the dominant culture."[17] In short, French Canadians took hockey from English Montrealers and made it their own. It has been a game divided by language ever since.

Race: White Is a Color

Like class and language, race also played an important role in early hockey's ethos and place in society. The amateur ideal assumed whiteness. In a practical sense, widespread racism confirmed that equation. Hockey found organization and structure during the same years that hosted Exclusion Acts and head taxes for Chinese immigrants; Jim Crow segregationist laws, radical racism, and an epidemic of lynching; the effective blocking of the *Komagatu Maru*, the colonization of the First Nations, and the de facto segregation (or ghettoization) of "New" Immigrants in burgeoning North American cities.[18] At the same time, amateur and professional governing bodies in baseball, lacrosse, golf, tennis, and other sports drew explicit or implicit color lines to protect the "purity" of their competition. Unlike American boxing or English cricket, hockey's whiteness in these early years was never seriously or often openly questioned. Comparatively few nonwhites played the game, and no singular nonwhite athlete challenged the racial profile of the amateur ideal. Hockey lacked a Jim Thorpe, a Jack Johnson, or a Tom Longboat—a nonwhite athlete so undeniably proficient that the sport's whiteness need be questioned or qualified.[19]

In late-nineteenth-century Canada, one author has observed, hockey's ties to aboriginal sport were played up by contemporaries; its close resemblance to lacrosse and its hyper-physicality reinforced the idealized "images of masculinity valued in First Nations culture."[20] This lent the game a certain legitimacy; to be aboriginal was to be authentically, quintessentially Canadian. Still, that Canadian-ness was an imagined and racialized construct. Another scholar saw the same thing in the rising fad of snowshoeing among the late Victorian Montreal's Anglo elite: "performing as a Native made you a native."[21] Hockey may have had aboriginal ties, but like lacrosse, the fact that it was possessed, standardized, and redefined by white men granted it the patina of respectability that it needed to thrive among the other modern sports.

Of course, many nonwhites did play hockey in Canada and the United States, even in the game's early days. In Minnesota, pioneering multisport black athlete Bobby Marshall excelled as a cover point for the semiprofessional Minneapolis Wanderers from 1907 to 1909. Known for his scoring and occasionally rough play, he was, the *Minneapolis Journal* noted in January 1907, "one of the best players in the city."[22] Similarly, Woodstock's Bill "Hippo" Galloway and Stratford's Charlie Lightfoot starred for their respective town teams in Ontario Hockey Association play in the 1890s and 1900s.[23] Even more significant, as Maritimes historians have documented, black Nova Scotians played competitive hockey on segregated teams as early as 1895. By 1900, at least seven black teams were observable on Maritime ice, notable almost as much for their colorful names as for their color: the Dartmouth Jubilees, Amherst Royals, Truro Victorias, Africville Seasides, Halifax Eurekas, and Charlottetown's West End Rangers—fifty-six men in all. These teams composed the "Colored Hockey League," a series of challenge matches that filled out winter seasons between 1900 and 1905.[24]

In the Maritime Provinces, black hockey drew the attention of white crowds and newspaper reporters, whose accounts were unflattering and sometimes racist. Their stories mentioned the usual rough checks, high sticks, slashes, and occasional fisticuffs that by this time were standard fare. Some players, like the Eurekas' Charles Tolliver, captured attention with their speed and roughness. One account emphasized his "aerial flights" over sticks, which brought "roars of laughter" (or perhaps awe), as well as his "flying body checks." But in the days of de facto Jim Crow, no newspaper was above overt racism. When the Eurekas and the Jubilees held a barnstorming exhibition in Sydney, Nova Scotia (a mining town with a strong black community), the *Sydney Post* ran a cartoon to accompany the game story, which was generally positive. The four-box cartoon strip, however, featured stereotypical "Sambo" characters with wooly hair and large white lips, including a box-seat section of "Rooters from the Coke Ovens," and a group of five monkey-like players falling over each other above the caption, "Where is the Puck?" Still, black players and fans would not allow outsiders to decide for them what the game meant. Within the African Canadian community, hockey was a "source of community solidarity and identity." Social gatherings and turkey, goose, and oyster dinners often followed games. "Camaraderie was an obvious benefit for all."[25]

In some of these years, black teams competed for the self-styled "Colored Hockey Championship of the Maritimes." As one author noted, they might as well have called it the "Colored Hockey Championship of the World."[26] While many games were on outdoor rinks, big matches occurred in white-owned indoor rinks such as the Victoria Rink and later the New Exhibition

Rink in Halifax. Without guaranteed ice time, the black teams utilized boxing's "challenge" system, which early baseball teams had also used. For example, in January 1904, the following notice appeared in the *Acadian Recorder*, a newspaper that provided regular coverage of black teams:

> The Eurekas, of Halifax, accept the challenge of the Seasides to play any colored hockey team in Nova Scotia. Games to be best two in three for championship. Dates and rink to be agreed upon later.
>
> A. F. Skinner
> Capt. Eurekas
>
> p.s. Captain Carvery can see me any evening after 7pm at 146 Creighton St. to arrange details.[27]

After some amount of wrangling—perhaps over how the rink and teams split expenses and revenues—team managers set a date or dates, then developed flyers or newspaper advertisements. When the Eurekas and Seasides finally squared off in February 1904, the game was promoted in the *Recorder* with a box advertisement that announced: "Colored Hockey Championship at the New Exhibition Rink, Set for February 26, A Great Battle for the Championship—Don't Miss It." The Crescents and the Willows played an "intermediate" game (presumably at the half), with general admission 25 cents and balcony seats 35 cents. Newspaper accounts indicated crowds ranging from 250 to more than one thousand, with typical crowds in the three hundred to five hundred range, probably just enough to meet rink and team expenses. The players were technically "amateur"; the small crowds suggest that there was little revenue to pay them under the table. After 1905, somewhat mysteriously, black teams acquired less rink time and less newspaper coverage. Their hockey rested increasingly on the unreliable ponds. The occasional "big" match might occur in a rink, especially in the early 1920s, but even before the first decade of the twentieth century was finished, the ten-year golden age of black hockey in the Maritimes was over.[28]

First Nations players left an even fainter trace. There must have been Natives who played on eastern clubs before 1920 without ever having their race identified in the public record. There are few we can identify. One rare example is Kahnewake Mohawk Paul Jacobs, one of the many famed bridge-building Mohawk "skywalkers" of the early twentieth century, who excelled as a player for the Dominion Bridge Company and Laval University teams in the Montreal City League and with New Haven and Cleve-

Dunbow (AB) Industrial School hockey team, 1899 (Provincial Archives of Alberta, B6534)

land of the US Amateur Hockey Association in the years 1912 to 1922.[29] Even fewer documents reveal hockey teams composed wholly or predominantly of Natives, from Indian Reserves or predominantly Native locations. One example is the Dunbow School Hockey Club, representing an Indian Residential School, whose teams in 1898 and 1899 impressed observers by defeating neighboring white teams. A photograph of the 1899 team reveals eight fully uniformed and equipped native hockey players (and one white), straight-faced, shorn and groomed to look like proper Canadian (read: white) gentlemen, and accompanied by their coach, Roman Catholic priest Father Albert Naessens, upon whom was bestowed the title "Father of Native Hockey in Alberta" by contemporary Albertans due to the masterful play of his charges.

The image raises many more questions than it answers. As with similar photographs from Indian industrial schools in the United States in the Progressive era (such as the famous Carlisle, Pennsylvania, Indian School), even a cursory reading of the Dunbow photograph makes it hard not to think of hockey as an arm of the school's larger "civilizing" mission.[30] But

Dunbow Indian Residential School hockey team, undated (Missionary Oblates, Grandin Collection, Provincial Archives of Alberta)

then again, perhaps like French-Canadian hockey in this era, these native players were not passive subjects but active historical agents. Perhaps they, too, appropriated the game, made it their own, and invested it with their own meanings.[31] Indeed, a second photograph of a Dunbow School team from the same era is much less racially loaded. If anything, what is most notable is how well equipped and uniformed they are for any hockey team from rural Canada in the 1890s, white or nonwhite.

When noticed at all in the popular press or by the sport's organized bodies, however, nonwhite hockey was "racialized" and marginalized as "other." On segregated or integrated teams, when blacks and Indians did play, they introduced a contrast or relief that pushed contemporary observers to confirm the game's whiteness. Black and Indian skaters were exceptions that existed dramatically to prove the rule, accepted as long as they were in the minority, subordinate, and not seriously challenging hockey's early social order. In one sense, their presence was needed by white sporting society, as rule breakers and racial role players to clarify where the cultural boundaries really lay. When New York City fans read the account of

Hobey Baker's head being "banged against the cage . . . knock[ing] him out for a few seconds," it would have made perfect sense to them that the aggressor was a "big Indian center named Cree." Could there be a better foil for Hobey Baker, the shining white knight of fair play? Race mattered in early hockey.

Women Claim Their Ice-time

As in everything, sex also mattered. In the sporting circles of colonial, late-Victorian, respectable society (circles where, at least formally, "separate spheres" doctrine still prevailed), every game was "sexed" at its founding. Some, like golf or tennis, were open to women, on their own or mixed with men. Others, like football or lacrosse, were clearly stamped as men's turf. Hockey's early champions wrote incessantly about "manhood" and "masculinity." Women would have to wend their way onto this patch of ice.

The amateur code, a gentleman's construct, had only a little room for female accomplishment. Moreover, the waning of the amateur ideal created something of a double bind. As the game became markedly more commercial and professional in the early years of the twentieth century, there was no comparable promise that women's hockey could sell tickets or foster perennial intertown rivalries the way the men's game could. As one authority noted, it was not until about 1916 that the hockey world started taking women "seriously."[32]

It was an era of first and mixed starts. For a relatively small group of women, hockey playing was consistent with a redefinition of womanhood in turn-of-the-century North America, the replacement of the True Woman with the New Woman. At the same time, women's place in the rink cast into sharp relief the fact that Canadians and Americans refused to see hockey, *real* hockey, as anything but a man's game, a vehicle for the definition of masculinity at a time of cultural crisis. And this cultural equation has cast a long shadow.[33]

One thing is clear. Women in Canada and the United States did play in this era, and they raised the possibility of playing a different *version*, a door through which their daughters would skate in the 1920s and 1930s. Ottawa was the seedbed. Women and girls skated alongside boys and men at the Governor General's rink at Rideau Hall in the 1880s, the *Ottawa Citizen* reported, and in February 1891, the first all-women's game took place in that city. Women hockeyists in Barrie, Ontario, followed suit the following year.[34] From there, women's hockey was diffused as broadly and quickly (if not as thickly) as the male game. In the 1890s, women's teams were organized throughout the Canadian provinces. Newspaper stories and photographs reveal the existence of fully uniformed and equipped women's club teams in Edmonton, Medicine Hat, and Vulcan, Alberta; Nelson, British Columbia; Montreal, Quebec City, Kingston, and Toronto; Saint John, Fredericton, and Moncton, and in many other locales. Even the tiny burgh of Millbrook, Ontario, and the borderland town Okotoks, Alberta, boasted women's teams.[35] Most games were local affairs, but intercity competition soon developed, and by 1900 the first known women's hockey league was formed in Quebec, made up of three teams, Montreal, Quebec City, and Trois-Rivières. In Ontario, women's club teams were joined in the sport by "co-eds" from Queen's University and the University of Toronto, all of whom scheduled competitions with opponents when and where they could find them. Sometimes, occupational links created rivalries. For example, the *Manitoba Free Press* of February 13, 1914, previewed the scheduled match between the ladies' sevens representing Main-Garry and St. John Fort. Both teams played in the "Telephone Ladies Hockey League."[36]

The early history of American women's hockey can be divided credibly into two general periods: the era of "first starts" before 1916 and the years between 1916 and about 1922, which began a period of more serious, structured, and perennial competition. Women began to play soon after their male counterparts. An 1896 photograph depicts female students at Mount Holyoke College in western Massachusetts skating, holding hockey sticks, and presumably playing. A newspaper report in the *Ottawa Citizen* refers to a match played between women's teams in Philadelphia in 1899. But competition took off after 1916, not coincidentally, when a three-game series between two Canadian teams, the Cornwall Victorias and the Ottawa Alerts, was held at the Cleveland Elysium. East of Cleveland, in New York and Boston, women's teams took root soon thereafter. On November 16, 1916, the *New York Times* reported that the St. Nicholas Rink had been the site of a "hockey battle" between the St. Nicholas Blues and the Manhattan Reds, "New York's first hockey game between women's teams." On March 22, 1917, the St. Nicholas Girls' Hockey Club traveled to the Boston Arena to take on the Arena Girls' Hockey team; on March 24 and 30, the Boston girls returned the favor. Despite predictions that the better-practiced New York side would sweep the series, the Boston club performed well, winning 3–2 "at home" in the Arena, and losing two close games (1–0 and 3–2) at St. Nicholas Rink.[37]

More remarkable than the scores, however, was the mixed sense of enthusiasm and curiosity in the local press reports. John Hallahan, the *Boston Herald*'s hockey beat writer, covered the game in the Arena. While play was "ragged at times," he wrote, "there were spells when some excellent work was displayed." He claimed the match was a "first time" affair in America. This is doubtful, but his overall account was positive, noting that "while hockey is altogether too strenuous a game at times for men, it did not prove too hard for women to tackle last night." In a concession to standard concerns about overexertion, the rink was shortened "to half its regular size," the three periods were reduced to ten minutes each, and free substitution was allowed "throughout the struggle." In an aside that captured the essence of old-time hockey, Hallahan noted that "of course, there were several bumps, tosses, and falls, but no serious damage was reported, only that Miss Ruth Denesha had a couple of teeth loosened."[38]

This early growth was uneven. Women's competition failed to catch on in the Maritimes and in the American Midwest, and was supported best and grew most impressively in the Canadian West and in northeastern Ontario, in rural and newly settled communities where social order was in flux and the need to fight isolation with community activity trumped matters of propriety. In these places the women's game became notably more competitive. At the Banff Winter Carnival in 1908, two women's teams battled for the Rocky Mountain Park Trophy and bragging rights for the year.[39] In 1911, women's teams from the northeastern Ontario mining towns of Cobalt and Haileybury played a four-game series characterized by "tight checking and defence" and watched by more than one thousand fans. The series reflected serious growth, as the *Cobalt Daily Nugget* noted in a double-edged statement: "The game has passed the comedy stage."[40] But everywhere it was played, women's hockey suffered during World War I. Ironically, at a time when women's suffrage was established and gender roles were expanded to support the war effort, women's inroads into the male public space of ice hockey were stemmed both in Canada and the United States. Only after 1920, with the return to "normalcy," did the women's game revive.[41]

Moreover, comments like those in the *Nugget* revealed a wider and deeper ambivalence. The rink was tilted. Women did not and could not play on the same terms as men, in part because most were still unsure of

Ladies playing hockey, Banff, Alberta, ca. 1911 (Glenbow Museum Archives, Calgary)

the game's propriety as a public endeavor. At Queen's University and at Stratford, Ontario, women's practices and games were routinely closed to the public in an effort to protect the modesty of players still trying to learn and the reputations of those who might shout, grunt, and cheer loudly as they skated, stickhandled, and scored. Women played the same rules as men, but they wore distinctive dress, including long skirts and, by 1910, bloomers. Moreover, newspaper reportage invariably supplied cultural commentary along with the description of players and scores. A February 15, 1902, *Toronto Star* report of a Belleville-Kingston women's event "turned into a bizarre commentary on players' ages and weights."[42] Male writers typically offered accents of novelty and curiosity; an inversion of sex roles was acceptable as long as seriousness was kept in check by denigrating women's talent and by humor. Accounts of the first ladies' match in Calgary in 1897 suggest "this activity was unladylike and highly injurious to a woman's sensitive constitution."[43]

As such, women's hockey posed no real challenge to those casting the sport as a masculine game.[44] One handwritten cut line accompanying a 1907 photograph of a women's team in tiny Hannah, North Dakota, described this inversion graphically. They "played against men . . . and the men had to use brooms."[45] To make this point is not to be dismissive. Female hockey before 1920 was important prologue for the game's development as serious sport in the 1920s and 1930s and a symbol for what could emerge. By 1920, rink doors had been cracked open to workers and Francophones, white men who could make the Montreal game better. But race and gender lines were harder to cross, and hockey—*real* hockey—remained, even by the end of the Great War, symbolically white and male. By 1920, though a few women played, hockey was recognized by contemporaries as a man's game. In the popular mind, it was also distinctively *Canadian*.

Nationhood

The history textbook *Sport in Canada* claims a commonly understood, almost ineluctable truth:

> While ice hockey may not presently be important to all or even the majority of Canadians, one cannot overstate its historical significance in creating a Canadian national identity. The inescapable reach of hockey into the lives of Canadians has been described as almost an organic connection, a "natural extension of seasonal rhythms." . . . [H]ockey remains central for individuals who seek to elaborate an ostensibly unified Canadian national identity. In this respect, *hockey invented Canadians as much as Canadians invented hockey*.[46]

In the popular imagination, hockey is Canada's game and always has been. And yet that equation—like all artifacts of national identity and ascription—is a historical construct. Hockey *became* "Canada's Game" from 1890 to 1920, and that "fact" has had to be proved in every generation since, against the assertions of many critics. Hockey's Canadian-ness derived from something much more than its place of origin and from the predominant nationality of its players, promoters, and audiences. It became a symbol or icon of Canada's existence, common currency that represented connectedness for many diverse people in a fragmented country. There is some irony in tracing the history of this national cultural claim: even as more and more non-Canadians embraced the game after 1895, even as it diffused broadly across international boundaries, Canada's national identification with hockey seemed to tighten. A notable gap emerged between what was athletically *real* and what was culturally *true*. Moreover, a tangential equation grew as well: not only was hockey equated with Canada, but Canadian hockey was the superior brand. By 1920, Canadian hockey became construed as the genuine article, the gold standard, and the center against which rivals in America, Britain, Europe, and other places would be measured and found wanting. In short, by 1920, Canada became the "hockey-nation" in minds of both Canadians and non-Canadians.

The timing was coincidental and crucial. A game and a nation grew together. Hockey became a natural emblem of Canadian maturation; a new sport for a new nation and, alongside lacrosse, a playful declaration of Canada's arrival in the world.[47] Moreover, unlike Britain's cricket, rugby, or soccer (or for that matter America's baseball and basketball), hockey did not follow an imperial direction from center (or mother country) to periphery (or colonies). Hockey defied the course of empire. It was, one might say, a *postcolonial* game. As Canadian historians note, Canada was in these years in a self-governing (but not sovereign) British Dominion, a country beholden to Britain for defense, trade, and cultural direction, increasingly subject to the discomfort that came with being next-door neighbor to an ostensibly friendly, wealthy, and noisy nation whose leaders did not hesitate to brandish a "big stick" (as it happens, a bat). Late Victorian and early Edwardian Canada was caught between two Anglophone empires. Internally, Canada was a nation whose populations could not clearly decide who they wanted to be. Advocates of independent nationalism (English and French) clashed with continentalists and imperialists over Canada's essence and its prospects for the twentieth century.[48]

Mired in this intractable debate, hockey seemed a benign yet common article in which many could symbolically invest.[49] Ottawa-based author J. Macdonald Oxley, a prolific Canadian writer of boys' juvenile fiction, offered this assessment in 1895:

> The part performed by Canada in making contributions to the list of the world's amusements has been by no means slight. Lacrosse and canoeing for the warm bright days of summer, snow-shoeing and tobogganing for the crisp cold nights of winter, these make up a quartette of healthy, hearty sports, the superiors of which, in their appropriate season, any other country might safely be challenged to show. But apparently this ambitious colony is not content with the laurels already won, and in the bringing of the game of rink hockey to perfection would add another to her garland; for this fine game, as played in the Canadian cities to-day, is, without question, a distinctly home product.[50]

Despite his use of the objective, third-person voice, Oxley's words reveal a sense of domestic pride in a special game—Canada's own.

Americans also acknowledged the Canadian connection. This was not only a factual observation but also a rationalization. It was hard to deny the quality of Canadian "imports," ex-patriates who had moved with their families to stock young amateur teams with their best talent: Tom Howard, Odie and Sprague Cleghorn, and Cooper Smeaton in New York, Red Synnott in Boston, Herb Drury in Pittsburgh, Ray Bonney in Minneapolis, and virtually all of the players in the short-lived IHL. They stood out because they were both more experienced and more skilled. *Outing* author J. Parmly Paret noted: "The Canadians are so old and so thoroughly tried in hockey . . . our players have yet a great deal to learn from their Canadian cousins." He added that "it is not surprising that the Canucks should be so much superior to American players, for the game is still in its infancy here."[51] There were important exceptions among American players in these years, such as Hobey Baker of Philadelphia, Gerry Geran of Holyoke, Massachusetts, Frank Goheen of White Bear Lake, Minnesota, and others. And yet they served to confirm the general rule.

There were cracks, however, in this Canadian connection, especially in the eastern and Midwestern markets that had enjoyed and nurtured similar games like polo as early as the mid-1880s. American analysts were also chauvinists. They quickly posed the challenge for the United States to catch the Canadians and match them at their own game. It was a refrain that still rings. "The quickness of American athletes to pick up new sports and excel at them has become almost proverbial and it has never been better illustrated than in hockey," Paret asserted in 1898. "The newly-imported game attracted much attention from men who had excelled at other sports, and it was only a short time before they began to improve so rapidly that even the Canadians may have to battle hard for their future laurels."[52]

To do this, American players, coaches, and commentators began to entertain the idea of developing an *American* brand, one that met their needs and sensibilities, a less violent brand than the one that Canadian expatriates brought with them. Following one especially physical 1911 game between the New York Wanderers (led by the Canadian Cleghorn brothers) and the New York Athletic Club in which 118 penalty minutes were assessed, the *New York Sun* commented: "The importation of these players seriously hurt the game here because they brought their rough style of play with them." A writer for the *Spalding Hockey Guide* in 1911 agreed:

"To keep the game a popular winter attraction something must be done to put a stop to unnecessary roughness."[53] And coaches such as Harvard's Ralph Winsor began to conceive of an "American system"—better, some claimed, than the Canadian. But most Americans who played or followed hockey in the 1890s, 1900s, and 1910s understood the Canadian claim, even if they did not wholly believe it.[54]

Between 1890 and 1920 hockey's world became broader and deeper than its inventors might ever have imagined. In most of Canada and along America's northern tier, it was on thick, expansive ice, played among amateurs on youth and school teams and in junior, intermediate, collegiate, and senior leagues. It became an overtly professional game in these years, too, offering a chance to earn an open dollar for skill and prowess. As it spread, hockey experienced important demographic changes and challenges that questioned the sport's identity and character. Though it began this era as a game for elite, Anglophone, white men, in these thirty years hockey was taken up and embraced by people beyond those narrow social and cultural confines. By 1920 it was enjoyed by peoples of several nations, all social classes, English and French speakers, whites and nonwhites, women and men. It proved a slippery item to its original owners. The genie was out of the bottle.

And yet, symbolically, hockey has never been more Canadian, white and male than it was by 1920. The sport's success celebrated its founding orders. In the popular mind, Canada was hockey-nation, and the game that skilled, fast, and "manly" white men had fashioned in central Canada was the genuine article. By 1920 an eastern establishment of writers and league administrators—many of them (like W. A. Hewitt, P. D. Ross, and Frank Calder) wearing both hats at once—had established a product that distilled current beliefs. The contrast between the image and the reality was remarkable, but image mattered, and it had long-lasting consequences. For much of the twentieth century, hockey rested in the North American public's mind as a phenomenon defined quintessentially by its Canadianness, its whiteness, and its maleness, even as its changing demography suggested a more complex reality.

10

Across the Ponds: 1895–1920

In 1899 player-author Arthur Farrell casually wrote that "even in distant Europe teams have been organized in Glasgow, London and Paris." Today's historians are still working to clarify all the details of this process. One cannot always trust the claims of Farrell's contemporaries, even famous ones who were his relatives. Take the case of George Meagher, Farrell's uncle and one of the most celebrated skaters of an early skating dynasty. Meagher's older brother Daniel played in that first, fabled 1875 game in Montreal's Victoria Rink. Perhaps young George was one of the lads who jumped on the ice, triggering a donnybrook at the game's end. In any case, he became a renowned figure skater, and by the mid-1890s he was a feature on North American and European tours, dazzling crowds with his ice skills and his stories.[1]

In December 1896 Meagher was a headliner at Brooklyn's new Clermont Rink. The local *Eagle* touted him as "the champion figure skater" and fawned over his ability to do "twenty-three different grapevines, fourteen spins, and seventy-four figure eights, and over one hundred anvils on foot without stopping." By now Meagher was also spinning hockey stories, including the notion that two winters earlier he had brought sticks on a European tour and had so whipped up enthusiasm in Paris that he left behind "a league of hockey teams, which played four times a week." From Paris, wrote the *Eagle*, the great skater moved to London, to Glasgow, to "Nuremberg, Bavaria and thence to the other European capitals, even to St. Petersburg." In each of these cities, went the tale, Meagher "and his new game found favor."[2]

Four years later, in a book titled *Lessons in Skating—With Suggestions Respecting Hockey, Its Laws, and American Hockey Rules (1900)*, Meagher reiterated part of his claim. "In Paris, London and Glasgow," he wrote, "the Canadian game of hockey was introduced in artificial ice rinks by the writer in the year 1895 . . . under the distinguished patronage of the Marquis and Marchioness of Dufferin and Ava . . . and to-day many clubs are flourishing, and 'long may they live.'" Like all good promoters, he was optimistic about the game's future, promising his readers on both sides of the ocean that when the cunning and courageous hockey player darted through the opposition, coaxed the puck with gentle skill, and finally cracked it through the goal, "a thousand, yes, five thousand throats shout and scream until the pandemonium reminds one of a dynamite factory cutting loose."[3]

The problem with Meagher's account is that modern historians have uncovered little in contemporary European primary sources to verify his claims. In fact, there is much contradictory evidence. The Canadian skater surely made headlines with his skating tours. He may well have given a few exhibitions with a stick and puck, and he may have enticed a few local skaters to join him on the ice in venues around Europe. But that is a far cry from providing a serious and lasting introduction to the sport. The facts are more complex. In the swirl of global capitalism that marked the 1890s and early 1900s, numerous teachers, engineers, journalists, and assorted bourgeoisie traveled the seas and the continents with baggage containing hockey rules and hockey equipment. Moreover, older and indigenous games like bandy were already played at various levels of organization and sophistication across Europe, especially in cities that had the indoor artificial ice rinks to support fixed schedules for leagues and tournaments—essential for a game's growth. Montreal hockey was layered on top of existing sporting cultures, including ice skating.[4]

The British Isles and Australia

England was the first stop on this transatlantic expansion. Fittingly, one of the early matches was a royal mix of the old and the new. In late 1893, Lord Stanley of Preston returned from his stint as Canada's governor general, along with his sons, who had done so much to promote the new game in Ottawa and beyond. Their skating careers back in England await more detailed research, but Lord Stanley's aide-de-camp later recalled that three of the boys played in a Buckingham Palace match within months of the family's return home. By another account, they played a more celebrated contest in early 1895. "Major" Peter Patton, the leading force in British hockey in the first half of the twentieth century, claimed (in 1936) that five Stanleys squared off against a "Buckingham Palace Team" consisting of the Prince of Wales (later Edward VII), the Duke of York (later George V), and other royalty. The story makes sense given the Prince's long relationship with ice "hockey." Recall that in January 1864, the *London Times* reported on Edward's friendly match on the lake near Frogmore Lodge.[5]

The Stanleys' skills showed, as they won easily—in Patton's words, "numerous goals" to only one for the Palace team. Patton added: "The Prince was greatly impressed by the play of the Honourable F. W. Stanley, who dribbled the puck at considerable speed while skating backward in front of the Prince." The use of a puck suggests that the teams played Montreal hockey. But Patton went on: "Strictly speaking, the game more resembled bandy, as played in those days, than hockey; bandy sticks being used with the puck instead of hockey sticks." Over the next few years, the flying Stanleys played a few other memorable matches. By 1899, however, Patton says that they "had not played for quite a long time." They yielded their missionary status to others like Major Patton himself.[6]

B. M. "Peter" Patton was born in 1876 in London, the son of a brigadier general. He was educated at Winchester and Wellington, both of them steeped in the *sports-for-all* or *games* ethos of the English public schools. He represented two important archetypes in the history of any sport: the upper-crust amateur athlete who got involved in governance; and the indigenous missionary of a "foreign" sport. Hockey historian Martin Harris wrote that Patton probably learned to skate while on holiday in Switzerland. His hockey exploits got a boost from the same bloom of indoor, artificial ice rinks that triggered American hockey in Baltimore, Washington, and New York. First came the small Niagara Hall surface in London's Westminster district (January 1895)—then, a year later, the National Skating Club's "Palace," followed by the Princes Rink in November 1896, both in affluent neighborhoods. The Princes ice surface was a reasonable size—200 by 52 feet—and here Patton helped to found the "Princes Ice-hockey Club," which was a British and European force for two decades. Harris also noted, "In 1902, through the assistance of Canadians resident in London, he helped establish a more recognizable version of the sport, using a puck instead of a ball, and long flat-bladed sticks." Patton was expanding the beachhead begun by the Stanley brothers, whom he credited (in his 1936 book) with a number of earlier matches. Even though Patton said the first 1895 match was more like bandy, he did not say that about subsequent contests. Further, the Stanleys would logically have had some real hockey sticks with them, and they could have imported others. They had both the desire and the means.[7]

There is no doubt, however, of Patton's central role in Britain and Europe. He helped organize England's first league in 1903 with five teams: London Canadians, Argyll, Cambridge, Amateur Skating Club, and Princes. In 1914, Princes and Cambridge joined with Manchester, Oxford Canadians, and Royal Engineers (Chatham) to form the British Ice Hockey Association. Patton served as BIHA president until 1934. He and his club also played at center ice in European developments. In his 1950 classic *Ice Hockey: The International Game*, Bobby Giddens described this early stage of English hockey as hockey "for the Few by the Few." The players "chased the puck for personal pleasure and physical exercise and paid much in money for subscriptions and equipment, much in travel and time for long sojourns to the open air ice of Switzerland, Germany, and France." British hockey quickly changed in the 1920s.[8]

Competition also followed rink construction in Scotland. The Glasgow Real Ice Skating Palace opened in May 1896. Local investors laid new technology inside an old theater, yielding a rich mix of sleek, modern ice surrounded by an orchestra pit, a balcony, a lush calico canopy, and finely upholstered furniture. The owners learned quickly that skating alone, especially at session rates of two to three shillings, could not keep them afloat, so by June they ran a newspaper ad requesting "applications for the use of the ice floor for curling, hockey, etc." As one historian suggested, hockey was better positioned than "etcetera" for several reasons. George Meagher had been "briefly engaged" at the rink "at considerable expense" to give lessons and performances. He probably also showed off his skills with a stick, whether hockey or bandy is not clear. In any event, a local side played the London Bandy Club in several matches, leading the local press to convey the same mixed descriptions offered in America: "ice hockey," "bandy," and "hockey on the ice," with even a "shinty" thrown in. But a June 8 reference to a "puck" suggests the Montreal game. There were other matches of bandy-hockey played at the Real Palace before it closed in May 1897 for reconversion to a new technology with a steadier and growing audience—the cinema.[9]

Surely players continued to hone their skills with various sticks, balls, and pucks, but Scotland's next chapter awaited the Scottish Ice Rink Company's 1907 opening of a pavilion at Crossmyloof, Glasgow. One contemporary recalled a bizarre design twist, which testified to the place of skating and curling as co-anchor tenants. The rink had "iron supports" running down the middle of the ice to hold up both the roof and a balcony built "to house an orchestra which provided the public skaters with the music necessary for their evolutions." For any form of hockey this was certainly an early version of the neutral zone trap! In fact, the rink sounds like it had been converted from a roller skating venue. The surface was only 140 by 49 feet. The early players had no nets and used "short sticks, after the fashion of bandy sticks." They were just as likely shinty "camans." The players generated enough interest, however, to warrant a Scottish Ice Hockey Association in late 1909 or early 1910. This group sponsored a team that battled an English side at Princes Rink in March 1910. Glasgow news reports included lineups with "rovers," a positional mark of the Montreal game. The Scots got pasted 11–1, in part because they were using the short sticks against the longer, broad-bladed Canadian models. A year later, in a rematch using real hockey sticks, the northerners tightened the score to 6–1. The Crossmyloof rink closed in early 1918. Organized Scottish hockey went under water for another decade.[10]

The British Empire's reach brought the game Down Under long before that. According to the Australian Ice Hockey Federation, the country's first ice rink opened in Adelaide at the turn of the twentieth century, under the management of H. Newman Reid. In 1904 Reid and his two sons (Andy and Hal) used field hockey rules and equipment to whip up enthusiasm for "hockey on ice," despite the presence of a large support pillar in the middle of the ice surface—Crossmyloof redux. In 1906 the Reids moved to Melbourne, where the father took over management of the new Glaciarium rink. They brought their hockey with them and it slowly attracted a following. By July 1906 there were enough confident players to support a challenge to some Americans from the *USS Baltimore*, a cruiser that had seen action with Admiral Dewey's Manila Bay fleet in 1898. Dunbar Poole, a well-known skater and recent immigrant from Britain, led the Australia side. Poole was an investor in the Adelaide rink, and he played a large role in Sydney's hockey fortunes, managing the Sydney Glaciarium, which opened later in 1907. Years on, hockey player-writer Bobby Giddens called the 1906 match an "auspicious occasion" but also added that "the hockey, in truth, was not ice hockey inasmuch as the players used stick and ball." The American players probably called the game "polo."[11] The following July, members of the touring "All-Canada" lacrosse team took on a local side in Canada's *other* national sport at the Melbourne Glaciarium and defeated them 13–1 and 13–0, diarist Frank Grace recalled, in front of a "very large crowd."[12]

When the Sydney Glaciarium opened in July 1907, the *Morning Herald* announced the rink owners' expectations: "Gentlemen to wear caps and not hats when skating and ladies to avoid using hat pins. Skaters must wear boots with skates attached, not strapped on." The last rule served to boost skate rentals, which were an important revenue stream. And it was skating, not hockey, that drove arena income. As Giddens recognized, Australia was a classic case of rink design relegating hockey to an afterthought. As in so much of the game's history around the world, he argued, "the first indoor rinks" had been "built for ice skaters." Even if the ice surface was large enough to support the end-to-end and side-to-side flow of a hockey game, there was typically "no thought in the construction . . . for seating capacity, or audience attendance," which "immediately" restricted "ice hockey promotion." Take the case of the Sydney Glaciarium, which had an ample 174-by-75-foot ice surface but other design problems. The boards in the "Glacci" were set *outside* a series of support posts, which caused many problems for players who wished to bank the puck to evade opponents. Worse yet, the early rink had a steel railing embedded in the ice at one end, something of a pamper pole for beginning skaters. This became an extra player during hockey matches.[13]

Despite these problems, within a short time Sydney had a handful of teams competing in its Glacci, enough to form a New South Wales Association, which in 1909 sent a team to Melbourne to play Australia's first interstate match. In sports-crazy Australia, the states of Victoria and New South Wales would have at it in yet another game. The small but rabid Sydney fan base got a boost in 1911 with the arrival of Jimmy Kendall, a Nova Scotian. Australian sources emphasize that his "training and ability completely revolutionized" the "Australian Ice Hockey." A 1932 game program noted: "Jim Kendal [*sic*] caused consternation and amazement with the Victorian players and selectors by his amazing speed, accuracy and powerful shooting and was virtually a match on his own for the Victorian team." More Canadians followed after World War I. Small rink sizes and the long distances between cities (600 miles), however, slowed hockey's development in Australia. Teams needed money for travel; money came from gate receipts.[14]

Continental Ice Time

In his 1950 survey, Bobby Giddens cautiously covered developments in Switzerland. First, he credited as "founder" an Englishman Tom Griffith, who helped organize Zurich's Grasshopper Club in 1886 and staged the first soccer and cricket matches in Switzerland. In 1887, Giddens claimed, Griffith "told his Zurich friends that he had the rules of a new game," which was Canadian hockey. Since the AHAC had published new rules in 1887, this account is plausible. Next, Giddens mentioned an American, Sam Pierce, who coached the Davos Hockey Club in the mid-1890s. At the same time, Giddens asked: "Was it bandy or was it hockey?" If all of these early games were bandy, then perhaps the hockey honors should go to the Princes Club of London whose members (including Peter Patton) played several friendly matches against Swiss sides in the early 1900s, leading several Swiss clubs to convert their games—and, in the case of the St. Moritz Bandy Club, their name—to Canadian hockey. By 1908 the Swiss had a national league.[15]

Switzerland became an early hotbed of international play, in part because of the spectacular alpine conditions and their attendant resorts, in part because the Swiss Hockey Union ran an "open" championship until 1913—that is, it allowed non-Swiss clubs to compete. In 1910, Montreux hosted the first official European championship. After the Great War, like other countries, the Swiss began to turn inward and closed their league championship doors. At the same time, the country continued its rich "open" tradition with Davos's Spengler Cup (1923), a European Club championship that continues today as international hockey's oldest-running club tournament, an event boosted by the 1926 construction of an indoor, artificial ice arena.[16]

Germany had some early artificial ice rinks, including a small 600-square-meter surface featured at a model exhibition in Frankfurt in 1881. Professor Carl von Linde patented this rink's refrigeration machinery. Later, Nuremburg and Cologne opened arenas using von Linde's design. In November 1910 the Berliner Sportpalast opened, giving Germany one of the world's premier indoor multipurpose facilities, complete with artificial ice for skating and hockey. The Sportpalast was soon complemented by two other facilities with large ice surfaces: the Admiralpalast and the Hohenzollern Sportpalast. Germany remained a leader in indoor-rink development.[17]

Bandy-hockey at St. Moritz, 1894 (Martin and Osa Johnson Safari Museum)

This fostered the growth of clubs, including the Berliner Schlittschuh Club (BSC), one of Europe's most dynamic vehicles for promoting skating and hockey. The club impresario was Hermann Kleeberg, himself a competitive speed skater, who moved into the management of the BSC ice hockey team after its founding in 1908. If Germany's rinks and managers were homegrown, hockey's ride to Deutschland is a good example of the cosmopolitan world of global capitalism. The most important figure in this story was Charles Hartley, an American-born, Canadian-bred, and internationally trained dentist. Born in 1883 in North Plains, Michigan, young Hartley moved with his family to Brantford, Ontario, then as now a hockey hotbed. Hartley played on two Ontario championship teams during his years at the University of Toronto's Royal Dental College. He continued his "student-athlete" ways as a member of the team at the University of Chicago's College of Dental Surgery (1904–05). His scrapbook includes newspaper stories and releases announcing that the Chicago faculty had recommended him for advanced study in Europe. He settled on Dresden, where he worked among dentists at the royal court of Saxony, learning the latest techniques in "porcelain restoration." He was not the first (or last) dentist with an eye on hockey. In his case, however, his primary interests were playing and coaching. He later recalled his initial encounter in 1906 with a German squad:

> Imagine my surprise when my first tentative investigation of the possibilities of hockey in Germany were greeted with the assurance that they already knew all about hockey there. And what hockey! They played eleven men a side and used a lacrosse ball. The ice was approximately the same size and shape as an American football field. The sticks were of about the same length as a mashie-niblick, and no one dreamed of trying to carry the ball. They just batted it down the ice to the next man.

This was certainly bandy. Hartley tried his best at stick handling, but he was quickly cautioned that he could not hold it with two hands.[18]

The next year, Hartley had a Toronto friend ship him a bundle of Canadian sticks and pucks. With this equipment, he converted local bandy players. From 1907 until the outbreak of the Great War, Hartley traveled with German club and national teams, playing, teaching, and refereeing the newer game. It was a loose, gentlemanly period for international competition, so this Canadian national was allowed to play as a German in some of Europe's first international tournaments, including one in Berlin in November 1908, where his Berliner Schlittschuh Club lost to London's Princes club. In January 1910 he played for the German national team at the European championships held in Les Avants, Switzerland. His play was "brilliant" and he was voted the tournament's best forward amid some very strong competition, including the elegant Oxford Canadians. With superior skating and stickhandling skills, he cut a striking figure on the solo "rushes" so typical in a game that allowed no passing to a teammate ahead of the puck carrier. Hartley left Germany during the Great War. His club mates honored his stature in their yearbook, which included Hartley's picture placed with the title: "Unser Meisterlehrer" (our Master Teacher).[19]

The Czech experience was a bit different. Its sportsmen (then residents of Bohemia and subjects of the Austro-Hungarian Empire) organized bandy clubs in the 1890s. These included the forerunner of the now-famous Sparta Praha Hockey Club, which was founded in 1893 as AC Královské Vinohrady. Like the Swedes, the Russians, and most Europeans, the Czechs were comfortable calling their game bandy-hockey ("bandy hokej"), even if it had little in common with its Canadian counterpart. One account holds that the Czechs entered the Montreal experience in 1905 when a Canadian visitor named Ruck Anderson gave a demonstration in Prague. Other accounts credit a connection between two journalists: Louis Magnus of France and Emil Prochazka of Prague. Impressed by Magnus's passion to spread Canadian hockey and establish an international federation, Prochazka requested that Magnus save a spot for the Czech Hockey Union, even though a union did not yet exist. As the authors of *Kings of the Ice* explained, Prochazka was "ambitious," was "an ardent fan" of Slavia (a Prague bandy club) and likely was "positioning himself to become the head of a yet to be founded hockey union to insure Slavia certain privileges in the new sporting event." Czech bandy clubs met in the ensuing months, and in December 1908 they formally established the Czech Hockey Union. One of the group's leaders was Josef Gruss, a professor at Charles University. Gruss contributed both intellectually and physically to Czech hockey fortunes. When he wasn't translating rules, he was manning the goal for the first Czech national team.[20]

Translating rules was one thing; finding equipment and learning techniques were quite another. When the Czechs arrived in France in 1909 for their first international competition, they realized they were not even playing the right game. One of the veterans Jan Palous recalled the surprise in a 1956 radio interview:

> Forty-seven years ago we left for Chamonix to take part in our first international ice hockey tournament but we had no clue about the sport at the time. It was not until we reached Chamonix that we saw, for the first time ever, a few other players—from Canada—with sticks, proper skates and a puck. We didn't even know the rules of the game. We were even extremely surprised when we saw that the goal posts were not mounted right at the edges of the rink, but with playing space behind.

Josef Gruss recalled later that he was lucky to secure a goalie stick in Chamonix. The Czechs lost all their games, but they impressed Louis Magnus, who predicted a rapid ascent as soon as they had the right equipment and techniques. They were quick learners. In 1911 they defeated the Swiss, Germans, and Belgians to win Europe's second championship tournament.[21]

Austria, which had embraced bandy in 1899, saw several clubs convert to the Canadian game only a few years later. By the time Vienna enjoyed its first artificial ice rink in 1909, hockey had reached a tipping point. Within two years, by one account, "almost all bandy players began to play hockey." In January 1912, clubs formed the Austrian Hockey Union, which three months later gained membership in the Ligue Internationale de Hockey sur Glace (LIHG), hockey's first international governing body. Hungary was a bit slower to adopt hockey, in 1925, when an Englishman introduced the game.[22]

Some early experiments went nowhere. In 1899 a Finnish professor named Leonard Borgstrom rallied enough skaters for an experiment on the frozen reaches of Helsinki's Northern Harbor. A local sporting newspaper reported "the new ice sport is called hockey." Since the account mentioned a puck and goals of "two poles over one meter high," it probably was the Montreal game. It did not catch on, however; Finnish hockey awaited a second coming in 1927. For their part, the Russians were accepted into the LIHG in February 1911, but they were dropped seven months later for inactivity. While this episode demands greater attention, one can guess that the problem was confusion over terms. The Russians thought "hockey" meant their game of khokkei, which was bandy. The Canadian version waited almost four decades before its formal adoption in the Soviet Union.[23]

Sweden joined the LIHG in 1912, a decade *before* the Montreal game took root in the country. The membership was a tactical move to garner participation of other countries in a possible hockey or bandy tournament at the Nordic Games of 1913. Clearly, the Swedes did not recognize a difference between the games. As one authority explained, "no tournament was ever staged, and the Swedish membership . . . seems to have been forgotten."[24]

Canada's game finally came to Sweden after World War I, an import nurtured by a combination of strong nationalist sentiment (seen in the Nordic Games) and shrewd promotion. One of the characters was an American film executive named Raoul Le Mat, who was opening an MGM branch in Stockholm (where MGM "discovered" Greta Garbo in 1924). Swedish historians note that Le Mat had played hockey back home, watched Swedish bandy, and soon set off to convince several prominent Swedish journalists and sports leaders to organize and send a hockey team to compete in the 1920 Antwerp Olympics, where the Montreal game was to be played as an exhibition sport. Other promoters were homegrown nationalists who saw Olympic participation as an obvious objective. One of these men was Anton Johansson, the chairman of Sweden's Football Association, which in 1907 became the governing body of Swedish bandy. Another was Torsten Tegner, "prominent Swedish sportsman, journalist, and one-time owner-editor of Sweden's largest sporting paper Idrottsbladet" who had played bandy for the Djursholm Hockey Club earlier in the century. Both men had links to the Swedish Olympic Committee.[25]

In Bill Sund's account, "the Swedish Olympic Committee was not hard to persuade, since the aim was to take home as many medals as possible and the new team, selected among bandy players and others who had tested ice hockey abroad, was considered promising." Stockholm newspapers warmed to the idea of international competition. After all, wrote one, "fairly average Swedish bandy players" had played for top-level foreign teams and emerged as stars. Le Mat agreed to coach the team, assisted by Ernest Wiberg, a Sweden-to-America émigré, now home for a visit. Le Mat held an "open" tryout at the Stockholm Stadion on January 27, 1920, which he planned to document on film. Unfortunately, the organizers had not sent out personal invitations, and no one showed up in response to the newspaper announcements. Johansson and the Football Association then got more aggressive in pursuing particular bandy players, including several who had played hockey for Berlin's Schlittschuh and Berliner Sport Clubs. Outdoor ice and equipment were lingering problems. Thaws left little time for training. LeMat ordered hockey sticks from America, but the shipment was delayed at Gothenburg Customs. Bandy sticks and a crude rubber puck would have to do. Goalkeeper Albin Jansson wore his fencing gear, including the mask, making him a forgotten pioneer in protective equipment.[26]

In April, the Swedes headed to Antwerp, where they finished fourth of seven teams. On their return to Stockholm, the Football Association honored them with a banquet and silver medals. The LIHG followed with a bigger reward: the chance to host the 1921 European championships. Soon, hockey boosters formed the Swedish Ice Hockey Association, with Anton Johansson as chairman. The Canadian game would never eliminate bandy, but it was now moving to the center of the winter sport stage.[27]

Tournaments, Olympics, and International Bureaucracy

George Meagher claimed that he introduced hockey to the French during his 1895 skating tour stop in Paris. At least one modern French account says that his visit occurred in 1894. In either case, Meagher's influence was marginal. French records indicate that Canadian hockey did not catch on until December 1902, when le Club des Patineurs of Paris embraced it and began to challenge others. The following winter, SC Lyon hosted London's Princes Club for several matches. French promoters held a "national" championship as early as 1904 and entered teams in international competitions beginning in 1905.[28]

The French genius for diplomacy manifested itself in sport a decade earlier in the guise of Pierre de Coubertin, a diminutive Anglophile who convinced delegates from a gaggle of national sports bodies to join his visionary Olympic movement. It was no easy task, and the first few Olympics were hardly the media spectacles we think of today. But Coubertin's Olympics provided a linchpin for the burgeoning world of amateur sport. Not only did each country need an "Olympic Committee" to oversee the organization of teams, each sport needed an international federation to oversee the championship competition at the Olympics. And each international sport federation needed units at the national level. This complex web of national and international amateur governing bodies opened up gargantuan opportunities for politics, tension, and intrigue. Coubertin's 1896 event kicked off a century of scramble for power at multiple levels in multiple sports. It was like America's Oklahoma Land Rush, with a rich cast of characters racing to claim turf.[29]

France had its hockey ace in Louis Magnus. Born in Jamaica (1881) to French parents, Magnus came to France in 1889 and joined le Club des Patineurs de Paris in 1897. A journalist and publisher by trade, Magnus fell headlong for skating and hockey. As the Patineurs launched their interclub competition, Magnus quickly earned a spot on the "A" team. He was also a five-time French skating champion. But he was even more adept at organizing. And he was committed to developing a governing body for hockey. Emil Prochazka, a Prague journalist, characterized Louis Magnus as "obsessed with the idea of popularizing Canadian ice hockey in Europe." In January 1905, Magnus wrote a column in the Patineurs' bulletin, musing, "It would be wise to find a solution for the unification of the rules of hockey. The question is being studied and we hope to bring a solution this year." Like W. A. Hewitt and Frank Calder in Canada, Magnus was one of a long list of journalists who looked to move from writing about hockey to running hockey. This he did by organizing a May 1908 Paris meeting at which delegates from France, Great Britain, Belgium, and Switzerland founded the Ligue Internationale de Hockey sur Glace (the English name "International Ice Hockey Federation" was not adopted until 1954). Bohemia also joined that year. For his efforts, Magnus was elected the first president, and he served in that post until 1912.[30]

Continental leaders like Louis Magnus were crucial to hockey's development. At the same time, an IIHF official history credits England's Princes Club as well as "British tourists and university people" and "Canadians studying in Europe" with driving European bandy-hockey's convergence toward the game played in North America. In October 1908, Peter Patton captained the "Princes" in a Berlin tournament. In January 1909, LIHG members met in Chamonix and established rules for competition. At the same time in Chamonix, the Princes were winning an "international city tournament." In 1910, the LIHG moved beyond club to national team levels, as sides representing Great Britain, Belgium, Germany, and Switzerland gathered in Les Avants, close by Montreux, Switzerland, for Europe's first championship tournament. The game was certainly hockey, although players lacked the specialized equipment then quite standard in North America. According to the IIHF's historians, skaters wore "gym shorts" and "football jerseys"; goalkeepers used field hockey pads; for others the padding was "cardboard sheets and old school books put inside the socks." Regardless of the uniforms and equipment, championships attracted more national teams and national organizations: Germany joined the LIHG in 1909; Russia in 1911; Austria, Sweden, and Luxembourg in 1912. In 1911, the LIHG formally adopted Canadian rules.[31]

Among the most prominent exemplars of this phase of hockey and global capitalism were the Oxford Canadians, a team of Canadians studying at Oxford University. Almost all of the players were Rhodes Scholars, the beneficiaries of the post-graduate program funded by Cecil Rhodes, an Englishman who made a fortune harvesting and exploiting the natural resources of Africa. Rhodes believed in British empire, and his engine was private enterprise. He certainly profited. His endowed Oxford scholarship program began in 1903, for students from the British colonies (present or former), the United States, and Germany—all part of Rhodes's vision for harmony among the three great powers who fit his sense of Anglo-Saxon destiny. Starting in 1906 a group of Canadian Rhodes scholars formed a team that played several games per year, traveling to London for their ice time. In 1910 the Oxford Canadians began a series of annual tours across Europe, entering various international tournaments. Their success matched their skill and flair.[32]

In January 1913 the Canadian captain of the "Oxfords" (Gustave Lanctôt) offered his assessment of European hockey. While not yet up to North American standards, the European "hockeyists"—decidedly educated and cultivated—were amateur purists who played to win but never with "second-class tricks" or "rough play." The like-minded crowd would boo "down the whole house" a player called for tripping. And according to Lanctôt, those spectators were not in the bench seats common to North American rinks. They sat along "floors laid up with tables at which you sit and drink and even dine, if you care for, while watching the matches." In the

Oxford Canadians and BSC, 1913. Dr. Charles Hartley is standing third from the left. Walter J. Pearse on far right, from Kamloops, B.C., was killed in action at Vimy Ridge, April 9, 1917. (Courtesy of Oxford University Ice Hockey Club Archives)

same month, a German sports journal volleyed the praise: "European teams playing against the Oxford Canadians have learned much. In particular the Berlin S.C. has to thank this club for their progress in Canadian ice hockey." The goodwill had limits, since such club teams often represented their nations at international tournaments. Was the Oxford team British or Canadian? The issue of national background vexed the LIHG beginning in 1910. It worsened after World War I.[33]

Antwerp 1920

Hockey's initial phase of convergence, 1877–1920, culminated in April at the Antwerp Olympics. These games reflected both the ravages of war and the efforts to revitalize. Germany and Austria were not invited to compete. Belgium still looked much like a war zone. As one Olympic historian put it, "the facilities were far from ideal . . . the track was poorly built . . . athletes complained about the inadequate accommodations and poor facilities."

Some events did not go off until September. But it was a major moment for hockey. Historians have not yet uncovered all the details, but hockey boosters successfully petitioned the Antwerp organizing committee and the International Olympic Committee to include the sport as "exhibition" competition. The decision fit within a broader discussion about including winter sports on the overall schedule. For Antwerp, this meant ice skating and ice hockey, and for good reason. Antwerp had an ice arena, the Palais de Glace. A symbol of convergence, the Palais was built in 1910 as a roller rink. As early as 1914, however, an ice skating association apparently converted the floor to ice during the winter. When the IOC announced its Antwerp pick in April 1919, the Palais offered one of the few existing facilities and management structures for hosting *any* Olympic competition. According to historian Roger Godin, the Olympic organizers only wanted figure skating on the program, but the rink's managers countered: it would be a twin bill—figure skating and hockey—or nothing. It was not the last time rink managers dictated terms to the Olympic magnates.[34]

One Belgian, Paul Loicq, burst onto the international scene at these games, as a member of the local hockey committee, as a player on the Belgian team, and as a referee. Born in Brussels in 1890, Loicq was a lawyer by training. An excellent speed skater, he adopted the Montreal game and played on Belgium's bronze-medal team at the first LIHG championships. After 1920 he gained an international presence as an LIHG executive and as a referee. For his efforts he was inducted into both the IIHF Hall of Fame and the Hockey Hall of Fame in Toronto. Since 1998 the IIHF has bestowed the Paul Loicq Award on a person honored for service to international hockey.[35]

Seven teams entered the competition: France, Belgium, Sweden, Switzerland, Czechoslovakia, the United States, and Canada (represented by the Winnipeg Falcons, winners of the Allan Cup, awarded annually to the Dominion's senior amateur champions). Tournament play (like the rest of the games) was organized under a modified "Bergvall System," named after a Swedish journalist and member of the Swedish Olympic Committee. The system was used for water polo in the 1912 Stockholm games. It seems a bit odd to our modern liking. A draw determined the opening brackets of single-elimination play, called the "A" tournament or the "gold medal" round. Teams who lost to the gold-medal winner played in the "B tournament. A third (or C) tournament pitted the remaining losers against each other for the bronze medal. While Canada and the United States were expected to finish 1-2, the other teams knew that much depended on the opening draw, held on April 22. France got a bye. The brackets and the results for the A round were as follows:

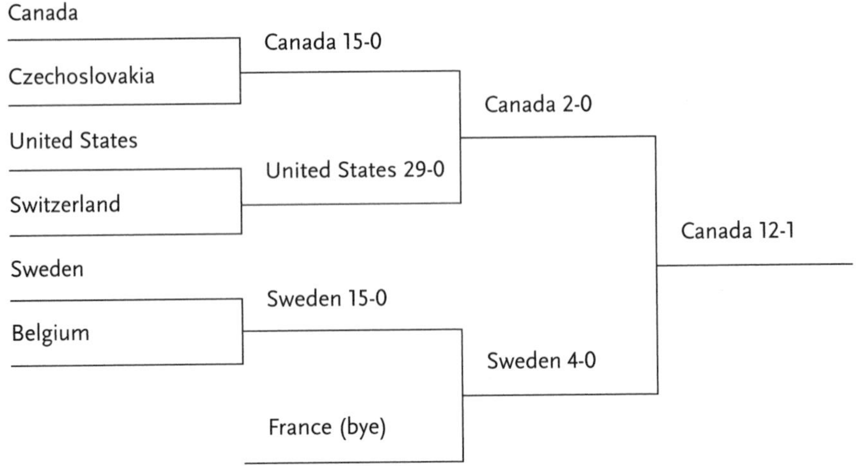

In the B, or silver-medal, round, the United States swept the Swedes and the Czechs by a combined score of 23–0. The Czechs squeaked by the Swedes 1–0 for the bronze. The rules were basic seven-man hockey, even though the ice surface was only about 60 feet wide. This squeezing of players may have contributed to some aggressive play. Canadian team manager W. A. Hewitt—long-time secretary of the Ontario Hockey Association—refereed Sweden's romp over Belgium. Play got rougher and rougher, with the home crowd booing the Swedes. Hewitt commented: "The Swedes were rough even by Canadian standards. They had a theory that the thing to do was to knock down every Belgian player and then pick up the loose puck." The Czech-Sweden game for the bronze medal on April 29 was tightly fought, but the packed house also sought blood and mayhem. A Swede caught a skate blade in the face and had to leave the ice. Although the Czech captain graciously pulled one of his own men to even the sides, tempers flared. A local reported that "the game, in fact, almost degenerated into pugilism and several players had to be excluded for brutal behaviour."[36]

The Canadians and the Americans impressed the Europeans with their skill and their equipment. Canada's Frank Frederickson and America's

"Moose" Goheen were especially awesome to the Europeans. One Swedish newswriter described the scene:

> When the boys saw the Canadians and the Americans play for the first time, they first looked silently on the play, then on one another, and then they said with one voice "I'll be darned." You see, these chaps really could play in a way that you never had known. The swiftness, the quick turns and dribbling, the recklessness and mastery with which they shot the puck with extraordinary speed into the goal, made one's head spin, it captivated and thrilled the spectators so that they could not keep quiet, but had to shout and applaud and excite themselves, as if they were a Storm and Monsen [Swedish evangelists] audience, speaking with tongues, instead of decent ordinary people with an interest in sports.

Hockey fans could speak in many tongues. A Belgian reporter added, "among the Americans, play appears second nature. . . . They are admirable and no wonder some women become slightly hysterical while watching their brilliant play."[37]

The North Americans' ready-made equipment—skates, pads, pants, gloves, and sticks—gave them added aura. As a Stockholm writer put it, comparing them to the Europeans was like comparing "fresh champagne to stale cheap lager." American Moose Goheen later recalled that, besides skates, the Czech goalie wore only "a pair of pants, a jersey, and a pair of gloves." This was in keeping with bandy rules, which by this time had taken the stick out of the goalie's hands. No wonder the Yanks scored sixteen goals against the Czechs. The North Americans were generous, however, letting the Europeans borrow equipment when they played each other. As America's Cy Weidenborner recalled on his return to Minnesota, "when the series was over they bought all the sticks, gloves and pads of the Americans and Canadians."[38]

Besides Olympic-level, face-to-face transfer of style and equipment, the Antwerp Games were a landmark in several ways. Most important, the LIHG and other hockey enthusiasts had convinced the International Olympic Committee to place their sport on the Olympic roster, even if only as an exhibition. Because rink managers continued to insist on hockey as well as figure skating, the game was secure and appeared in every subsequent Winter Olympics (separate winter games began in 1924). This gave hockey an inside position as the premier winter team sport, pushing it further ahead of bandy, which still had a strong presence in Europe. "What if" history is a hazardous game, but we can speculate about what would have happened had Europe's many national bandy associations formed an international federation (not done until 1955) and successfully lobbied the IOC before the LIHG did. What if the Antwerp games had included bandy rather than hockey? We might now watch Olympic bandy rather than Olympic hockey. Players would whack at a ball with one hand. Goalies would not have sticks. Ice-game history might have bifurcated along the lines of football, with one version dominant in North America and another version dominant in the rest of the world. Among other things, there would have been no Miracle on Ice, unless it was in bandy![39]

But hockey's promoters were successful. Equally important, the Olympic games attracted teams from the United States and Canada. Their players were celebrated both for their skills and for their national colors, which evoked memories and gratitude for the allied war effort. While neither country was a member of the LIHG before the games, they joined while in Antwerp, adding organizational status to their reputations for on-ice performance. The Canadians and the Americans became the new models for emulation, in playing styles, coaching, and equipment. While earning the second-place medal, the United States trumped Canada within the LIHG, with Cornelius Fellowes winning a vice presidency. At its post-Olympics Antwerp meetings, the LIHG also revised the international rules, shifting from seven-man to six-man hockey, at that time favored by most North Americans. The experience in the small "Palais" rink, and the mayhem of the Sweden-Czech game may also have had influence. Reduce the number of players, create more skating space, and nudge the game toward skill over brute force. The sport had converged, in rules and in governance. From this point on, hockey was truly intercontinental as well as international.[40]

At the same time, the Antwerp Games fueled the fires of national pride among continental teams. Moreover, by joining the LIHG, Canada and the United States brought credibility to what was (and would continue to be) an essentially European governing body. Neither country would ever be satisfied that its political input corresponded to its prowess on the ice. But there was no going back. International competition was too important. And so the LIHG became a separate force in rules and in competition. Hence the paradox that ends part 2 and begins part 3 of this book. At the very moment of ultimate convergence—when one version of a game on ice stood ready as the dominant version—there were already cracks and splinters in its framework. Hockey was starting to diverge.

Hockey's Positioning by 1920

James Creighton and his colleagues began a grand experiment when they codified a novel game on skates in 1870s Montreal. They borrowed here and there and kept tinkering with the rules. As we have seen, however, there was nothing unique in this process. Schoolboys were doing the same thing at St. Paul's and elsewhere. So were roller-rink owners in America and Europe, as were skaters in England's Fen district. Recent research has uncovered many other experimenters and codifiers around the world. Surely there were more. Some written rules may have been destroyed in a fire or thrown out in a move. Perhaps, instead, they are simply waiting to be discovered in some attic or library. Such is the lot of historical materials. What we do know is that a few skating games—notably hockey, bandy, and polo—emerged before 1900 as commodities to be sold and consumed in ready-made packages of rules and equipment. And by 1920, hockey was the most advanced of the three.[41]

Polo and bandy were strong alternatives. In October 1899, for instance, the *Washington Post* ran a story on plans to build a new professional roller polo league in eight prominent baseball cities, including Boston, Washington, New York, Baltimore, Chicago, St. Louis, Cincinnati, and Pittsburgh. "Boston capitalists" were fishing for investors who would bite on the following claim: "The proprietors at the various rinks and clubs in the New England Polo League reap rich harvests every winter, and their organization is established on the same systematic basis as baseball." However dubious the claim of profitability (teams continually failed in the polo leagues), these boosters recognized a real prospect on the sports calendar: winter was still an open market. In America at least, baseball filled spring and summer months; football was king of fall. Basketball had not yet developed as a spectacle. There was need, they concluded, for a "national winter sport" to be "sandwiched between" football and baseball. In their opinion, "roller polo fills the bill."[42]

The struggle for space on the calendar was particularly important during this period. The histories of bandy, polo, and hockey only begin to describe the robust sport marketplace. Between 1877 and 1920 in North America and

Europe, athletes, entrepreneurs, boosters, writers, and other assorted professional experts worked furiously to position a range of organized games, fighting over what scholars have called "sport space." As they put it, "while early arrival does not guarantee late survival, it most certainly helps." There were winners and losers. By 1920, hockey was king in Canada. Polo was still popular in many markets around the world, but in North America polo had yielded to hockey as the premier *winter stick* game. Basketball offered stiff competition at the grassroots levels, but in America's northern tier, especially in its largest cities, ice hockey had emerged as THE winter spectacle. As one promoter remarked in 1898, hockey filled the "aching void" in the calendar between football and baseball. As we have also outlined, bandy was being squeezed off to secondary status in Europe. It held its place largely in the Nordic countries and in Russia. Historical estimates of any sport's popularity—especially participation—are always problematic. But as a spectacle, as a sport that drew legions of paying onlookers and crowds of reporters, hockey was well positioned by 1920.[43]

As an earlier article in the *Philadelphia Inquirer* noted, hockey was no longer the loose "shinney" of childhood memory. It was now structured in "hard and fast rules." Like football, it had "many tricks and stratagems of attack and defense . . . plots and counterplots." Unlike football, however, there were "no slow movements . . . for the players are never still." At the same time, hockey was still a relatively simple game to follow. Fans were close to the action in almost any seat of the era's arenas. American boosters often noted that hockey's simplicity and proximity gave it an edge over football. As the Johns Hopkins University captain explained to the *Washington Post* in 1897, "every play in hockey is seen by the spectators, while many of the most brilliant points in football are overlooked by those spectators who have but a superficial idea of the game."[44]

Consumers with any level of interest or knowledge, superficial or deep, could experience hockey's central tension of science, speed, and skill against mayhem and bloodshed. But this was also a problem. The theory of branding suggests that consumers visualize and remember products in terms of single attributes. Hockey's fusion of attributes became both strength and weakness. On the one hand, there was a little something for everyone; on the other, only the most hardcore fans could rationalize the combination with any level of satisfaction.[45]

This issue played itself out in the next period, 1920–1971, as professional experts and bureaucrats in Europe and North America began to fashion separate rules. Canada continued to take center stage as the producer of the best and the most players, as the source of coaches worldwide. But governing bodies outside of Canada increasingly asserted their independence of Canadian authority. Hockey's professions of coaches, administrators, rink managers, writers, and players cleaved along both national and ideological grounds: Canadian versus Swedish versus American versus Russian; amateur versus professional versus collegiate. Some of the tensions were evident before World War I. In 1917 a Chicago enthusiast wrote that hockey's success required three lines of effort: "missionary, the teaching and organizing of the game; publicity, not of the sporadic or 'going to happen' kind; and real encouragement by the men interested in the ice game." The next five decades saw battles on all of these fronts.

PART THREE

THE DIVERGING WORLD OF CANADA'S GAME, 1920–1971

11

Hot Wars, Cold Wars, and Brand Wars

Adolf Hitler stood in Bavaria before a crowd of some fifty thousand shivering spectators and more than one thousand athletes from twenty-eight countries. The *Literary Digest* reported that "flakes of snow nestled in his close-cropped mustache" and a "driving wind whipped his brown uniform." In his distinct Austrian accent, the Third Reich's chancellor read a simple proclamation: "I declare the Fourth Winter Olympic Games of 1936 at Garmisch-Partenkirchen opened." That February afternoon, after the bands played "Deutschland über Alles," "The Badenweiler March" (the Nazi Party anthem), and the Olympic Hymn, after the church bells and cannon fire, and after the procession of nations, the American ice hockey team opened that sport's competition with a 1–0 win over Germany in a sparkling new outdoor, artificial-ice arena that packed in ten thousand fans.[1]

The twin alpine villages of Garmisch and Partenkirchen lie near the Austrian border on an ancient trade route spiked by several of Germany's highest mountains. Their natural assets for a Winter Olympics were compelling. As historian David Clay Large noted in his *Nazi Games*, however, building an infrastructure was no simple task. When the International Olympic Committee awarded the winter games to Germany in June 1933, "GaPa" (the local nickname) required significant investment in modern facilities for skating, ski jumping, and bobsledding. The German Olympic Committee, the Reich, the state of Bavaria, and the local organizing committee all jockeyed to avoid assuming the estimated cost of 800,000 to 900,000 Reichmarks, a hefty sum made more problematic by Hitler's clear commitment to build and showcase new facilities for the 1936 summer games in Berlin. But the job got done. In addition to state subsidies and ticket sales, the organizers cultivated and garnered revenue from corporate sponsors, including Coca-Cola (an "official" sponsor of the games) and Ovomaltine (the "official" drink of the German athletes, which Large claims was "so vile that none of them would drink it").[2]

Overall attendance totaled near 650,000, although most were Germans and many were trucked in for show. Only forty-four hundred foreigners made the trip as spectators. Still, this was all a great improvement over 1932's Lake Placid Winter Olympics, which drew only fourteen thousand attendees. Equally important for the GaPa events, about five hundred print and broadcast journalists showed up, including some of the era's most celebrated writers, such as America's Westbrook Pegler and Paul Gallico. The Alpine vistas and venues blended the latest in technology with the quaintest of traditions—excellent story material. *News-Week* wrote that "at every turn, foreign visitors see evidences of Teutonic thoroughness and efficiency." Public officials and shopkeepers were bilingual. Bands used weatherproof sheet music. A three-hundred-seat press box included forty-four new telephone lines that could handle two thousand long-distance calls per day. Gallico wrote a feature for *Vanity Fair* describing the warm and cozy atmosphere of the local cafés, filled with the sounds of accordions, zithers, and yodeling, the smells of beer and tobacco, and the sight of old men in lederhosen. "You doubt," he concluded, "whether you will ever be in a better place." The *New York Times*'s Berlin bureau chief Frederick T. Birchall was also covering the games. Birchall had won a Pulitzer for his reporting, much of which cast the Nazis in a respectful, even positive light. In this vein he predicted that most tourists would return home "averring that Germany is the most peace-loving, unmilitaristic, hospitable and tolerant country in Europe and that all the foreign correspondents stationed here are liars."[3]

It was not so tranquil beneath the surface. The height of the region's beauty was matched by the virulent anti-Semitism of its inhabitants. Even Nazi officials had difficulty getting the locals to remove signs and serials (like the *Stürmer*) that promised to rid the Reich of all Jews. As *Time* magazine reminded its readers, the United States had come close to boycotting the German games because of Hitler's racial policies. The Olympic world was tense. The 1918 Armistice ending the Great War did not end conflict. Europe and the Mediterranean limped through the 1920s only to be pummeled by the Great Depression. Many countries turned toward authoritarianism. Dictators ruled in Germany, the Soviet Union, Italy, Greece, Portugal, Cuba, Argentina, Brazil, and other countries. Demagogues rallied mass support in the United States and Great Britain.[4]

Collisions On and Off the Ice

The GaPa Games were not immune to tension. Winning was too important. Italians raged when the IOC ruled their bobsledders ineligible because they were professionals (in auto racing). Austria's Karl Schafer, world champion in figure skating, was investigated for taking endorsement money. But out on the gleaming new ice rink—with its 12 miles of deeply chilled, carbonic-acid-filled piping (capable of keeping a hard surface at 50 degrees F) and its gargantuan electric clocks—hockey was a special magnet for strife. *News-Week* noted that hockey "spiced the Olympics with a sour flavor."[5]

Europeans, who fawned in 1920 over the brilliant play of Canada and the United States, were no longer so deferential. In the first round, Italy upset the Americans in overtime, 2–1, before a record afternoon crowd. Associated Press reports focused on the "dogfights in front of the nets" and the Americans' "vicious body-checking defense." The Italian bench "repeatedly booed the bespectacled but pugnacious Gordon Smith" who "accused an opponent of deliberately knocking off his glasses in a scramble." The *New York Times*'s Albion Ross admitted that the "United States team does not appear to be the crowd's idol. It is a rough team, because North American hockey is a rough game." Not to be outdone, a Frenchman bit a Hungarian's arm. Frederick Birchall wondered "whether hockey is a game really suited to the Latin temperament." He described the scene when American referee Walter Brown disallowed an Italian goal against Switzerland. Amid the "howls of dismay from the Italian section of the stand . . . there was a small scuffle in the press seats." An Italian writer was taking "careful aim with his typewriter at the referee" until he was "disarmed by his colleagues."[6]

The greatest battle was over eligibility and bureaucratic control. Canada protested Great Britain's lineup, which was stacked with British-born-but-Canadian-raised stars, including Alex "Sandy" Archer and Jimmy Foster, who had been lured back "home" to play in the English National League. In late 1935, Canada's amateur governing body, the CAHA, woke up to the fact that the British team might be a threat. Using their franchise power, the CAHA suspended Archer, Foster, and a number of other players, claiming they and the ENL never obtained releases for the players to play outside

CAHA jurisdiction. This notion of franchise rights and sanctioning power over players lay at the heart of international amateur sport. Leagues in one country were expected to respect the rights of another country. Poaching without permission was ungentlemanly.[7]

Journalists smelled a good story. Albion Ross wrote that the American team arrived in Garmisch after an exhibition tour "playing against Canadians under all manner of disguises." Great Britain's entry was "an all-star combination made up of ten Canadians and two Englishmen." But the case had complications. The vagabond players were technically eligible for two reasons: they were born in England and the LIHG rules only prohibited jumping clubs without permission *during* the season. The decision between home rule and international federation rule finally rested with a meeting of all delegates held on the tournament's eve. Technicalities aside, USA's Avery Brundage candidly conveyed the general sentiment: "The Americans will have enough on their hands meeting one Canadian team. They don't want to face two." LIHG delegates sided with Canada. Britain threatened to boycott, but backed off when Canada agreed to waive the suspensions during the Olympics.[8]

Canada had won on principle, but its magnanimity had limits, especially after Britain got through the qualifying round. In a public appeal for "sportsmanship" (in other words, for Britain to relent), CAHA president E. A. Gilroy focused on "two players," whom the press recognized as Archer and Foster. Gilroy particularly objected that the British Ice Hockey Association had "sent an agent to Canada, sometimes taking two to four players from one particular team." That agent was a wily Irishman named John "Bunny" Ahearne, who soon became the kingpin of international hockey and a constant spear in Canada's ribs. If Gilroy hoped Great Britain would withhold its stars from further play, he was wrong. They did not budge; Britain had Canada's waiver in hand. The LIHG decided that in the future no transplanted player could return and play for his native country until he had done at least five years' residency. This was too late for Canada in 1936. Foster's brilliant net play led Britain to a 2–1 upset in the second round. Canada still went through to the final round, along with Britain, the United States, and Czechoslovakia. But there would be no revenge match. An obscure playoff system held that teams in the medal round would not replay teams they had already beaten. Stranger still, the second-round victory also counted for points in the medal round. If Britain could defeat the United States and the Czechs, Canada could only watch from the sidelines while the gold medal slipped from its grasp. This is exactly what happened, as Canada lost its Olympic supremacy for the first time. The *Manchester Guardian* summarized the outcome as well as anyone: "Canada lost the title under its own name but won it under Britain's."[9]

The hockey world had changed dramatically since the Antwerp Olympics, expanding across Europe and beyond, symbolized by Japan's admission to the LIHG in 1930. Nippon sent representatives to Lake Placid in 1932, part of its careful planning for an Olympic entry. American goaltender Franklin Farrell III later recalled, "They were very thorough . . . they came in and measured every bit of equipment that I had from tip to toe." Leaving nothing to chance, "they felt the muscle of my calf and thought it was padding and wanted to know what I had there." The emerging empire's pucksters were embraced in Garmisch. If he questioned the notion of "Latin" hockey, Frederick Birchall gushed over the Japanese players, who were proving themselves to be "fine all-around Winter sportsmen."[10]

As the eligibility squabble showed, however, sportsmanship was finite. When medals were on the line, techniques and tactics shifted from the rink to the boardroom. Canadians "of all disguises" still dominated the ice, but they could not control the international sports bureaucracy. In historian John Wong's words, Canada had "paid little attention to matters outside the nation's borders." The 1936 Games were a wake-up call from Europe. It would not be the last in the decades between 1920 and 1972. But North Americans generally paid little attention to Europe outside of Olympic years—at least until 1972 and the Summit Series. Forty years after the GaPa debacle, Ken Dryden wrote his classic treatise on hockey, filled with theory and whimsy about the game's history. His most telling line was a lament that "a game we treat as ours isn't ours. It is part of our national heritage, and pride, part of us; but we can't control it." One suspects that CAHA president E. A. Gilroy felt that same way in February 1936.[11]

In 1920 at Antwerp, Europeans applauded the speed, skill, and generosity of the North Americans, even as they criticized the Swedes and Czechs for their brawling. Four decades later, the images were drastically different, especially those of Canadian hockey. According to one Finnish scholar, his countrymen pelted the Belleville McFarlands with snowballs when they appeared during a 1959 tour, and "local newspapers branded them as 'a hooligan gang' who played 'like a bunch of hoodlums, ramming down everything that came in their way.'" A few years later a Swedish Hockey Federation official vented that "Canadians aren't hockey players—Canadians are murderers." What drove such striking shifts in image over the five decades after the Antwerp Olympics? That is a fundamental question for part 3 of this book.[12]

Home Rules and Global Sport

In her analysis of "globalizing sport" in the 1930s, Barbara Keys clearly outlined the tensions between international or "universalist" frameworks like the Olympics, the LIHG, or FIFA (world football's international governing body) and the many "countervailing pressures to assert national, local, and particularist identities" that played themselves out in the cultural and sport marketplace. The GaPa Olympics were a case in point. Canada and Great Britain had their national identities at stake in the appeals they made over player eligibility to the LIHG, the rising international governing body that had the final say.[13]

Keys's book emphasized a convergence of structure and interest in the worlds of the Olympics and top-level football (FIFA). As she put it, "The onset of a world-wide Depression and the turn toward isolationism and autarky in many countries might suggest that modern sport's internationalizing momentum would have been halted in the 1930s. Instead it accelerated." In May 1936 the *New York Times*'s Arthur Daley said the same thing as he wrote about the expansion of international sports tours and tournaments. "In recent years there has been a trend toward internationalism," he noted, "and there has been hardly an athletic activity that had not been affected by it." In many ways, this was true well beyond sports. Recent historical research has outlined the steady growth, during world tensions and wars, of intergovernmental organizations like the League of Nations and the UN, as well as international nongovernmental organizations like the Red Cross.[14]

Maintaining the framework was never an easy exercise. Moreover, in some sports the diverging local and particularist elements prevailed over the universalist. Ice hockey was one such sport. If convergence toward one form (the Montreal game) marked the years from 1877 to 1920, *divergence* colored the five decades after Antwerp. To borrow a phrase from a scholar of the American Revolution, the process involved two issues: "Home Rule" and "Who Should Rule at Home." In the case of hockey (and other sports between 1920 and 1972), these may be translated into two questions: How would any nation frame a sport to represent *its own* interests vis-à-vis those of other nations? And who would control development of a sport *within* each particular country? Garmisch-Partenkirchen offered examples of both issues, which were not new, but which had greater emphasis after 1920.[15]

The broad context for answers lay in the economic, military, social, cultural, and political turmoil that so clearly marked this period. Postwar trauma was followed by a depression, another hot war, and a cold war. There was little relief. While the 1920s were "roaring" in parts of the world, they were not universally positive. As historian Tony Judt put it, "Europe in the Twenties and especially the Thirties entered a twilight zone between the afterlife of one war and the looming anticipation of another. The internal conflicts and inter-state antagonisms of the years between the world wars were exacerbated—and in some measure provoked—by the accompanying collapse of the European economy." The 1920s reopened some elements of global trade, but the framework was shifting. Russia closed its borders with its revolution in 1917. Several empires (notably, the Austro-Hungarian and Ottoman) disintegrated. New nations emerged, such as Turkey, Finland, and Czechoslovakia. And as one historian put it, "After the war, ethnic hatreds had found fresh outlets, and the newly independent nations appeared to take perverse pleasure in thwarting one another's ambitions. They seemed bent on establishing distinct identities regardless of the costs to themselves." Czechoslovakia, Yugoslavia, Romania, and especially Hungary looked to high tariffs and self-reliance as the routes to economic salvation.[16]

By the 1930s, the stakes for home rule grew higher. When the Great Depression swept over the world's economy, it both spawned and reinforced regimes that declared their independence from Western capitalism. Fascists, socialists, communists, and nationalists on all continents promised to go it alone and build their economies independently. Scholars label this "autarky"—what Jeffry Frieden called "forcible separation from the rest of the world." In the face of the Great Depression, even John Maynard Keynes reduced his long commitment to free trade. "Ideas, knowledge, art, hospitality, travel—these are the things which should of their nature be international," he argued. "But let goods be homespun whenever it is reasonably and conveniently possible; and, above all, let finance be primarily national." As Barbara Keys suggested, sport was both an international art show and a national treasure to be protected. The Depression did not hinder the expansion of international sporting competition, but the era's geopolitics heightened awareness of a new tool for national identity. It is no surprise that the long disconnect of the Depression, World War II, and finally the Cold War also encouraged sporting autarky. National identity mattered. Flags that flapped with blood could also furl with medals.[17]

New Technologies and Visual Turns

The GaPa games showed that mass media were central to these developments, as every major political figure of the time understood. Breakthroughs in communication technology had been linked to sports for some time. As we have noted, hockey's first two periods (to 1920) ran in broad confluence with a heyday of both global capitalism and what Benedict Anderson called a "lexographic revolution" of literature, music, and education in "national" languages. This supported the national-international tension that Keys so carefully outlined. The modern Olympics (starting in 1896) provided the template for other world championships at which rivals could display their worthiness. As Keys put it, once in the system, "each nation could claim that its participation in any international contest, though outwardly conforming to the same rules and conditions as every other nation's, was nevertheless fundamentally an expression of intrinsically national characteristics." Mass media drove much of this dynamic.[18]

If global capitalism collapsed in general after 1914, international media expanded to cover the story. New technologies of production and distribution enhanced the importance of various print forms, which would be supplemented by radio and television. The 1920s and 1930s especially saw staggering advances in the use of visual technology. The rise of the motion-picture industry was just one example. Equally important was the merger of photography and journalism, made instantaneous and widespread in newspapers and magazines that utilized innovative electronic equipment to send photo images via telegraph and telephone lines. Wire services such as the Associated Press, Hearst International, and the New York Times Wide World hired electrical engineers to keep pace with the competition for speed, clarity, and economy of picture transmission across continents. This meant that daily newspapers could now run something closer to actual photos rather than line drawings of the day's events. A single picture could command up to $10,000. In our age of cable, satellite, LCD, HD, 3-D, and 4K, we still respond to sharper, clearer images that help to tell a story. Our ancestors were no different.[19]

In February 1936, for instance, as the Winter Olympics began in Bavaria, *News-Week* magazine included a two-page self-promotion of its three-year run. With a growing circulation already at 160,000, there was reason to gloat. While not mentioning the competition from *Time*, *Life*, *Look*, or their foreign counterparts, *News-Week* outlined the formula. It was a fusion of "the Articulate and the Visual, redeeming cold type with the communicable conviction of photographic fact"—the result of a weekly gathering, selecting, and blending of the pictures and stories from thousands of photographers and correspondents around the world. It was a new kind of storytelling where "no words are wasted that can be given to pictures . . . neither are pictures allowed to interfere with necessary facts." Predicting the attacks against "mindless" entertainment masquerading as news, the magazine also applauded its own readers as the type that "do their own thinking and refuse to submit to the anesthesia of regimented opinion." In the end, of course, there was another benefit. *News-Week* would not exhaust the reader: "They stay for the Ads."[20]

Language and image, flashing instantaneously across and between continents, became weapons of battle between warring regimes in geopolitics, as *Fascism* or *Communism* faced off against *Democracy*, consciously or carelessly enabling consumers to recognize clearly *us* against *them*. Sport was a vessel of this process, in the battles over home rule and rule at home, as accounts of the GaPa games displayed. It was no surprise that boxing, baseball, horseracing, and football (in all codes) became staples of motion-picture newsreels. *News-Week* understood this clearly. Of the seven photographs surrounding its self-promotion, two were from sports. One was of Joe Louis. The other was taken at a New York Rangers practice.[21]

Brand Wars

Hockey's wars were brand wars. If part 2 of this book outlined the development of the Montreal game as a distinct sport, the five decades following the 1920 Antwerp games centered on building brands *within* hockey. As today's marketing experts suggest, brands are built on slogans and symbols intended to trigger emotions in the consumer's mind, emotions that lead to awareness and loyalty. Branding links with positioning, the effort to create distinctions in consumer minds about one product vis-à-vis another. Language and image are the tools of the trade. From 1920 to 1972, journalists, coaches, and administrators employed language and image as they wrote books, articles, rules, and committee minutes that distanced their game or their players or their governing body from some other entity. There had been earlier such occasions: the rise of the Pacific Coast Hockey Association as a bandit league, the portraits of Eddie Livingstone as a malcontent, Ralph Winsor's American system. The five decades after Antwerp, however, heightened the rhetoric and the boundaries between hockeys: collegiate versus senior amateur versus outright professional versus Olympic and international; Swedish, Soviet, or Czech versus North American; men's versus women's.[22]

World football was the great exemplar. Language and image mattered almost as soon as the game circulated in the flows of global capitalism. Nationhood demanded translations into the vernacular. As one football historian found, people who adopted Britain's gift moved quickly to revise key terms into their own language. For instance, when the Deutscher Fussball-Bund was founded in 1900, it faced strong national antagonism to most things British, including sports. And so began the "Germanization of football language." In this way, "captain became *Führer*, free-kick became *Frei-Tritt*, and goal turned to *Tor*." Something similar happened in Turkey. When a reform-minded Committee for Union and Progress assumed power after the death of Sultan Abdullhamid II in 1908, there was a football boom in Istanbul. But the country's new sports periodical *Futbol* (1910) was careful "to ingratiate itself with the hyper-nationalism of the new government by searching for Turkish alternatives to the standard English vocabularies."[23]

The age of autarky raised the stakes for this process. In 1922, Mussolini's Fascists took power in Italy. Their strategy for regenerating a great empire included cultural as well as economic and military tools. Among other things, cinema newsreels were to be distinctly Italian and fascist. So would football. Clubs with English names came under fire—and went Italian. Genoa became Genova; Milan, Milano. Fascists were not alone in their title tweaking. In Czechoslovakia the communists who took power in 1948 forced the longstanding Slava Prague football club to change its name to Sokol Slavia Praha VII, a slap at the club's links to the city's liberal political and professional classes. On the other hand, Sparta Prague was spared a name change because of its association with workers. Likewise, in East Germany and Poland, old bourgeois sports clubs lost both their names and their support after World War II. Legia Warsaw became CWKS.

Security forces, the army, and industry became the sponsors of once-proud private clubs whose names were now Chemie Leipzig, Lokomotive Stendal, or Turbine Erfurt.[24]

These years also spawned the notions of national styles in football—Italian versus Dutch versus Brazilian versus English. In Argentina, David Goldblatt found, writers for a new weekly sports magazine *El Gráfico* (1919) "transformed the raw material of *porteño* football into an entire national mythology." Players from the past and present were "characterized and evaluated, lineages and golden ages were constantly being constructed and reconstructed." And most important, the characteristics of *criollo* football were carefully distinguished from their British counterparts. By the time Argentina created a national professional league, "in the hands of the new popular press, like *El Gráfico* magazine and the newspaper *Clarín*, a working mythology of a unique national playing style had been articulated."[25]

A similar process unfolded in hockey. What's more, commentators and broadcasters in the decades after Antwerp seemed to *look for* and accentuate the differences. Somehow, the ways that Italians played football or Canadians played hockey *had to be* different from the ways in which others played the game. Sport was seen to reflect political economy. Politics demanded it. This would be especially true during the Cold War after 1945. As one Finnish scholar put it: "From a Cold War viewpoint, the roster of participants in international hockey was perfect: the Soviet Union and its satellites Czechoslovakia and the German Democratic Republic (GDR, East Germany); capitalist superpower USA with two of its central NATO allies, Canada and the Federal Republic of Germany (FRG, West Germany), the most important European bulwark against communism, and finally, several hard-pressed neutrals like Sweden, Finland, and Switzerland." As he further noted, championship venues were often central to Cold War stories: Prague, Moscow, Geneva, Helsinki, Stockholm, and Vienna. It was all an elegant script for national branding.[26]

Within and across continents and nations there were other battles over control and identity, as the CAHA-LIHG standoff in Garmish suggested. Who exactly would rule at home? In a forty-year period, a form of ice hockey had spread from Montreal to America, Europe, and even Australasia, under one basic set of rules—those of the Amateur Hockey Association of Canada, the game's first (1886) real governing body. When American magazines and newspapers began writing about hockey in the early 1890s, they specifically referenced the AHAC rules. When Americans in Baltimore and

Washington, DC, first played the Montreal game in 1895–96, they played under the rules of the AHAC. Hockey's first guidebook, published by the Spalding empire in 1897, included rules of the new Amateur Hockey League of New York. They were almost a verbatim copy of the AHAC rules. By 1920, when players, writers, and fans in London, Zurich, Prague, Boston, St. Paul, or Seattle used the term "ice hockey," they typically meant the Montreal game, as developed by the AHAC.[27]

This uniform vision changed first in Canada, with the development of commercially oriented senior clubs (of questionable amateur status) and avowedly professional leagues, which prompted a splintering and reconfiguration of governing bodies over the first two decades of the twentieth century into a veritable alphabet soup of organizations: CAHL, IHL, FAHL, ECAHA, ECHA, CAHA, NHA, OPHL, MPHL, and PCHA. Within the amateur ranks themselves, there was frequent bickering among regional associations and the CAHA. The selection of the 1936 Olympic team was a complex case in point. Starting at Antwerp in 1920, Canada's Olympic representation had gone to the club in possession of the Allan Cup, awarded since 1908 to the nation's senior amateur champion. In 1936, that should have been the Halifax Wolverines, who swept Port Arthur's Bearcats in the 1935 Cup finals. But Haligonians had no Wolverines in 1936. The team had dissolved, in their view because of draconian CAHA eligibility rules enacted by western and central Canadians jealous or ignorant of realities in Maritimes hockey. So Port Arthur went to Garmisch instead, to its bitter defeat (albeit bitter*sweet* in Halifax). As we shall see, by 1936 Canada's whole amateur establishment was teetering.[28]

Europeans and Americans had their own ideas about who should rule the game, as the following chapters show. For instance, the LIHG (known after 1954 as the IIHF) fashioned separate authority over international competition. Anyone interested in World Championship or Olympic glory needed to defer to and negotiate with its executives and delegates, who themselves were evolving in backgrounds and approaches. Take the British, for example. The patrons and moguls of Montreal hockey were initially royals and Oxbridge types—the Stanley boys, the Prince of Wales, "Major" Peter Patton, Canadian students at Oxford. By 1936, however, British skaters (even those raised in Canada) represented a very commercialized, semi-professional industry controlled by rink owners and promoters like the Irish-born travel agent John "Bunny" Ahearne. In many ways, ice hockey was replicating, at a faster pace, the history of football.

In the United States, the NCAA slowly wrested control of school and college competition from any rivals. This began in 1926, when the association organized an ice hockey rules committee. Rufus Trimble, a faculty member at Columbia University, served in the powerful role as secretary-editor. Two years later, the *Official Ice Hockey Guide* (a Spalding publication since 1897) moved under the aegis of the NCAA, becoming part of the association's "plan to issue rules on all sports participated in by college teams." The Committee claimed that in their short existence, the NCAA ice hockey rules were already "in general use by the amateurs throughout the United States, including school, college, club, and industrial teams." For the next four decades, the NCAA committee consciously worked to distinguish its game from other forms of hockey, especially the professional forms. Among its central goals, it wanted to promote "greater appreciation" of skill in contrast to the "approval, and even encouragement, of reprehensible rough play now sometimes unfortunately manifested by spectators." In a clear jab at the NHL, the committee concluded: "The extension of professional hockey in the United States should not interfere with the improvement of intercollegiate play in this respect." To be sure, every governing body kept a close watch on its rivals, adopting or refuting rules changes as they saw fit. On balance, however, the years from 1920 to 1972 saw a divergence of brands.[29]

Women sought their own space. Language and image were vital to their efforts. Women's hockey often expanded out from under the control of men's organizations. For instance, the Preston Rivulettes, the most successful hockey machine in the interwar years, competed under the banner of the Dominion Women's Amateur Hockey Association and the Ladies Ontario Hockey Association. There is much to parse in these names. One is hard pressed to find any governing body in any sport, anywhere, which includes the term "Men's." But most attempts by women to develop their own sports included some inclination to attach a gender descriptor. Even if the leadership of the DWAHA or LOHA was female, with laudable goals of "girls' sport run by girls," such names inevitably prompted comparisons to the *real* governing body and the *real* game. For instance, the DWAHA tried to force teams hosting a championship to provide a money guarantee to their traveling opponent. In 1934 the Rivulettes could not scrape up the required $1,500 to host the Edmonton Rustlers for the Dominion championship. Edmonton therefore won by default. Such problems in governance led Alexandrine Gibb, a sympathetic sportswriter for the *Toronto*

Daily Star, to pan the DWAHA for a policy "put in when they apparently imagined they were as powerful and financially as strong as the C.A.H.A.," a body that needed no gender descriptor.[30]

Industry Infrastructure

As part 3 outlines, the NHL, the IIHF, the NCAA, the DWAHA, and others continued a process begun by predecessors traced in part 2. Each of them fashioned industry models with particular approaches to three elements: developing, organizing, and disciplining labor, including players, coaches, officials, and administrators; generating revenue, capital, or state subsidy; governing and regulating member organizations and events, with rules and standards of conduct. One critical analysis proposed a dichotomy of alternative models within Canadian hockey between *community* and *commercial/capitalist* (in other words, NHL) traditions. In the authors' words, "a community team, amateur or professional, existed to provide hockey for the enjoyment of the community. A commercial team existed to make money." As late as the 1930s, they claimed, local amateur, collegiate, regimental, worker, or business teams of *community* ethos outnumbered professional (*capitalist*) teams by ratios of 10:1 or even 15:1. The relative numbers, popularity, and autonomy of those clubs eroded drastically by the late 1940s, all in lockstep with the NHL's rise.[31]

From a global perspective, however, it would be a mistake to overestimate the NHL's dominance—at least until after 1972. The most significant alternative in the Cold War period was the state-socialist model, which was entirely separate in its logic. Were the Soviet or Czech players "amateur" or "professional?" The International Olympic Committee and the IIHF repeatedly dodged the vexing question. Models help us to make sense of the past. But they can also confound it. As Richard Gruneau and David Whitson argued, "Hockey has always had a range of different meanings and intended uses for various groups. . . . The game has variously been a form of backyard play, a type of 'civilizing' amateur sport, an opportunity to drink and gamble, a source of profit, and a community symbol. Moreover, these different uses of hockey have often blended together in complex ways." Our challenge is to recover those alternatives. In other words, we must return to a more fundamental question, well parsed in an elegant history of the NHL's first fifty years: How did the hockey business grow, and why did it take the particular form it did?[32]

This game of exquisite skill, speed, science, and brutal violence took on particular meanings in places like Eveleth, Minnesota; Örnsköldsvik, Sweden; and Sherbrooke, Quebec, which were among a number of places that took to thinking of themselves as "hockeytowns." Sport geographers have argued that places are ensembles of landscapes, artifacts, memories, ideologies, rituals, and other elements. They all have historical roots. In the same way, places became "hockeytowns" when their economies, demographics, and institutions conspired to create an environment where hockey had a central place in a town's sporting infrastructure, where characters cemented it into civic culture, and where a shared meaning of the game developed.[33]

Towns, cities, and arenas of all shapes and sizes were incubators for identities based on social class, neighborhood, region, nation, gender, ethnicity, and race. They also included a growing assortment of entrepreneurs, promoters, coaches, and journalists who believed in the game, in the power of rink technology, and in their ability to prosper as hockey professionals. Their ideas about the game matured in the practical life of rinks, dressing rooms, and committee meetings and were made manifest in daily newspaper stories, in feature magazine articles, in public relations campaigns for arenas and teams, and in the precise wording of rules and regulations.

It is no surprise that this generation of hockey professionals included a number who had either worked in journalism or education. They were trained to the power of language and image. This included the NHL's Frank Calder, who had been a newspaper editor; Canada's W. A. Hewitt, who doubled as journalist and bulldog of the Ontario Hockey Association; Alexandrine Gibb, sportswriter for the *Toronto Daily Star*, who claimed to have a direct hand in founding the Preston Rivulettes; and Rufus Trimble, Columbia professor and long-time editor of the NCAA Hockey Rules Committee. It also included coaches like Dick Vaughn of Princeton, Eddie Jeremiah of Dartmouth, and broadcaster-entrepreneur Lloyd Percival, all of whose instructional manuals became bibles for generations of players. These people were among hockey's organic intellectuals who knew how to write and to fight for their particular hockey nation. They understood that the pen and the picture were mightier than the stick. Their stories are central to hockey's era of divergence, 1920–72.

12

North American Core Brands: 1920–1945

On January 1, 1922, the mining community of Eveleth, Minnesota, opened a new $50,000, three-thousand-seat, indoor artificial ice arena called the Hippodrome. For the next forty years, the small city was one of the world's most productive hockey towns. Lying some one hundred miles south of the Canadian border, on the edge of the Mesabi Iron Range, Eveleth's ore began feeding America's industrial growth in the late 1890s. While raw material flowed out on the Duluth, Missabe and Northern Railroad, laborers flowed in, mostly from Croatia, Slovenia, Serbia, Italy, and Finland. Montreal's game swept over this cauldron of global capitalism early in the twentieth century. Open and covered natural ice rinks spawned talent for competition against rival mining towns like Virginia and Hibbing. By 1919, Mayor Victor Esseling and businessmen formed the Eveleth Hockey Association to organize teams at all levels for play in a new Recreation Building.[1]

Within two years, however, that venue was inadequate for the EHA's plan to enter its senior team, the "Reds," in the newborn United States Amateur Hockey Association (1920). The USAHA was a product of entrepreneurial energy and necessity, hatched largely by rink managers in the Northeast and Midwest. America's recent Olympic team (filled with Minnesotans) was organized and sanctioned by the International Skating and Hockey Union, an affiliate of the Amateur Athletic Union, which controlled American Olympic efforts. Despite the team's silver medal, USAHA founders wanted their own governing body. In their opinion hockey was "entirely foreign to those in either speed or figure skating." The USAHA sought sanction from the AAU, the American Olympic Association, and the LIHG so that it could control America's international ventures and negotiate agreements with its Canadian counterpart to prevent senior-level players from jumping the border in search of a better deal. Once formed, the USAHA quickly made alliance agreements with the AAU and with the Canadian Amateur Hockey Association.[2]

Like other national governing bodies, the USAHA established a championship and trophy to cultivate dependence from its affiliated teams. Absent professional rivals (the National Hockey League was still all-Canadian), the USAHA showcased the most skilled American talent along with some recruited Canadians. Teams played in one of three "sections," whose regular-season champions played off for the national title. Group One included the Boston Hockey Club, Boston Athletic Association, New York, and Philadelphia. Group Two was all upper Midwest: Calumet, Sault Ste. Marie (Michigan), Eveleth, and Portage Lakes. Group Three included Cleveland, Duluth, St. Paul, and Pittsburgh. The USAHA was top draw in these American markets and the pinnacle for most U.S. players. Annual dues were $10 per team; players registered for 50 cents per year. To encourage stability, one league rule spelled out penalties ($25 fine plus the visitors' expenses) for forfeiting a scheduled match without at least three days' notice. In a nod to revenue sharing, the home team had to guarantee the visitors a payment of 15 cents per mile, one way, for ten players. Members were also required to keep cash books and ledgers available for inspection.[3]

Eveleth's Reds played to packed houses in the new Hippodrome, and they attracted top Canadian players like Ivan "Ching" Johnson and Percy Galbraith. How could a little mining town recruit such talent? Simple. They paid them. Surviving records show that the overall 1924–25 budget of almost $42,000 included $17,511.23 for "salaries and labor." The 1925–26 budget of $42,302.98 included $11,963.65 for "salaries—players." The 1923–24 report listed specific player disbursements, including $200 to Johnson in 1923 and $2,146.55 to Galbraith over two seasons. Galbraith's 1923–24 "amateur" salary of $1,511 was less than the $2,500 the NHL's Boston Bruins offered him in November 1924. But it was more than the $1,350 Kansas City's minor-league Americans offered Norbert Steele for the 1941–42 season. The Eveleth Reds were not the rare senior amateur franchise secretly paying players. The rarity is that their financial statements have survived.[4]

Given the higher living costs in Boston, Galbraith would have been economically better off staying with the Reds. The lure of the big-time, however, was too much to pass up. Percy Galbraith's choice told a larger tale. When the NHL finally opened American franchises, 1924–26 (in Boston, New York, Pittsburgh, Detroit, and Chicago), professional hockey became a hot commodity, attracting new audiences and new investors. From 1920 to 1945, boom times and hard times led to growth and instability across North America hockey. Individual teams (like the Reds) and leagues sprouted and died with regularity, artifacts of free-market capitalism both embraced and challenged during these years. In business terms, hockey experienced an era of brand warfare.

Yet, the same era has come to represent a "golden age." Expanded sports sections, news bureaus, motion pictures, and radio produced and distributed heroes to wide swaths of consumers. The effect was integrative and pervasive. Western Canadians in Edmonton or Regina could easily follow Babe Ruth's antics in Gotham. Americans in many major northern cities could track the multisport achievements of Toronto's Lionel "Big Train" Conacher.[5] Those images have stuck: "old-time hockey"—an era when the game was first played *right*. To conjure that sentiment, today's fans need only list their litanies of heroes: Eddie Shore, Howie Morenz, Georges Vézina, Busher Jackson, King Clancy, Aurèle Joliat, Dit Clapper, and others. But, as symbols, their images are also misleading and facile. The era's game was not simple, or ageless, or even "golden." In truth, the central tensions are illustrated best not in the character and color of icons such as Shore and Clancy and Morenz, but in the circumstances of myriad lesser-known players, nonheroes like Percy Galbraith, George Owen, and Dave Trottier.

Two Paths to the Pros

Born in Hamilton, Ontario, George Owen Jr. (1901–86) moved at age ten with his family to Newton, Massachusetts, when his father, an accomplished engineer, accepted a position at MIT. Owen was an "all-rounder." At Newton High School he gained a local reputation as a sportsman. At Harvard he exemplified the scholar athlete, earning a record nine varsity letters, never losing to Yale in football, and captaining both baseball and hockey. A smooth-skating defenseman, he was Harvard's best in the Crimson's first half-century on the ice.

The Toronto St. Patricks reserved his NHL rights, but Owen refused to sign, playing senior amateur for the Boston Hockey Club (1923–24),

George Owen flanked by Eddie Shore and Lionel Hitchman
(Courtesy of the Boston Public Library, Leslie Jones Collection.)

Boston Athletic Association Unicorns (1925–26), and the University Club (1926–29) while he worked full-time with a local investment firm. In January 1929, however, he relented, signing a contract with his hometown Bruins (who had traded for his rights) and beginning a five-season career in the big league. Early on, Owen dressed as a sub, supporting Bruins stalwarts Eddie Shore and Lionel Hitchman, but when his opportunity arose, he seized it. Owen had speed, tenacity, a passing and scoring touch, and he was clever enough with the stick around his own net to make up for a want of physicality. Among the first college-bred players in the United States to make the NHL, he was also the first big-league player to regularly don a helmet, his old Harvard football "leatherhead." Owen was a favorite with the press, for whom he always had time and a few bon mots, a rare gift among his peers. He retired at the end of the 1932–33 season, when new blood augured his demotion to the minors. Mostly a second-stringer in the days when a starting defense pair logged the lion's share of ice, Owen nevertheless posted respectable big-league numbers: 46 goals and 38 assists in 204 NHL games.[6]

David Trottier (1906–56) was born in Pembroke, Ontario, a lumber town in the Ottawa Valley, an early incubator of hockey talent and home to early star Frank Nighbor, the "Pembroke Peach."[7] Trottier was a left-winger with a deft scoring touch who did not shy away from rough stuff. He first rose to prominence as a junior playing for Toronto's St. Michael's Majors (1923–25) in the Ontario Hockey Association. From 1925 to 1928 he became a dominating presence with the Toronto Varsity Grads.[8] In 1926–27 he tallied 33 goals and 10 assists in just twelve games, leading the Grads to the Allan Cup, Canada's senior championship. Moreover, as was custom then, Allan Cup winners in the season preceding an Olympic year won the right to represent the Dominion in the Games. The Grads did not disappoint. Playing just three games (the Canadians were granted a pass through the qualifying round), the Grads won them by a combined score of 38–0 en route to a gold medal. Trottier himself tallied 12 goals and 3 assists.

Trottier's performance abroad sparked a bidding war among NHL teams. In November 1928 he signed with the Montreal Maroons for $10,000, embarking on an eleven-year NHL career in which he recorded 125 goals and 116 assists in 476 games, and 556 penalty minutes. When the Maroons folded in 1938, Trottier's rights were taken by Detroit, where he toiled for part of a season (1938–39) before ending his time as a big leaguer.[9]

Not heroes, Owen and Trottier were effective players whom contemporaries regularly praised. For us, the context of their careers is instructive. They reflect the unstable relationship between the professional and amateur ranks in North America, as well as widespread concern about the creep of professional control. Even in the late 1920s, the decision to "go pro" was saddled with baggage, especially for elite amateurs. Owen repeatedly rebuffed offers of professional contracts; in 1927, the *New York Times* reported that he had "turned down an offer of $5,000 to play . . . for a few months."[10] Trottier was one of only two Varsity Grads to go pro.[11] One chatty piece of speculation in Toronto's *Globe* in late February 1928

Toronto Varsity Grads 1928 with Dave Trottier (University of Toronto Archives)

related that players on "the ex-Blue combination stated emphatically that they would not become pros, while one of them . . . roundly denounced the impudence of the 'reserve rule,' which . . . made him the property of a club which he would not join under any circumstances."[12]

Elite hockey players could reject the notion that professionalism was the natural outcome of a distinguished amateur career. What's more, players who made the jump in these years were not without bargaining power. When he finally signed with the Bruins in 1929, Owen insisted that he keep his in-season day job. Trottier had even more leverage. Both the Ottawa Senators and Montreal Maroons claimed him, a competition that was settled officially by an NHL president-brokered "gentleman's agreement." Actually, as the press showed, it was Trottier's own decision.[13] Beside a photograph of Trottier with the cutline "Business Man," the *Globe* reported that "Trottier said he would play with Montreal or not at all in the N.H.L. or other pro circuit." To him, the gentleman's agreement was an "affront." "Young Mr. Trottier . . . carried his point."[14] His example was not missed by other pros, including Pittsburgh's Roy Worters, who used Trottier's case as leverage in his own contract negotiations.[15] In 1941, when a thirty-five-year-old Trottier decided that he had exhausted his pro career but not his love for the game, he was successfully reinstated by the CAHA as an amateur.[16] The NHL did not own him.

The 1920s opened North American hockey's fifty-year era of brand expansion, divergence, and warfare, when powerful organizations—local, provincial, national, and international; amateur and professional—came to order and effectively control the game. Gradually, the NHL gained supremacy, but its rise was neither assured nor easy. Governing bodies like the USAHA, the NCAA, and others built their own gravitational force to attract players, coaches, and fans.

The Amateurs

By 1920, Canadian amateur hockey was a pyramid of associations that spread across the breadth of the country. It was the original brand. Power resided in perennial governing bodies built on formal constitutions and annual meetings, staffed with executive councils producing standard rules, certifying and assigning referees, and policing players' amateur status with tools that included a blacklist for those caught breaking the code. The first of these organizations, the Ontario Hockey Association (formed in Toronto in 1890), was until the onset of World War II the world's most powerful hockey body and the model for other amateur associations in Canada. Led by the iron-fisted John Ross Robertson (d. 1918), the OHA enforced a "scarlet letter" rule: once a professional, always a professional. Any player who had ever received pay for play (in any sport) could never again compete with or against OHA teams. The OHA was the first to sort amateur hockey by caliber (senior and intermediate) and by age (junior and minor), giving administrative order to a potentially chaotic situation on the ground.[17]

Other regional and provincial associations adopted the same bureaucracy. Alberta formed its amateur hockey association in 1907 (only two years after becoming a province), and others followed: Saskatchewan (1912); Manitoba (1913); British Columbia, Quebec, and Northern Ontario (1919). The Ottawa and District AHA followed in 1920, the product of a jurisdictional scrap with the OHA.[18] In Atlantic Canada, organization came in 1928, when leaders in Nova Scotia, New Brunswick, and Prince Edward Island formed the Maritime Amateur Hockey Association, an arrangement that functioned for forty years until the provinces each created their own governing bodies.[19]

Crowning these provincial organizations was the Canadian Amateur Hockey Association, a national body formed in 1914. Born months after the onset of war, the CAHA became the nation's nerve center of amateur hockey, its semi-annual deliberations the focus of kudos and scorn alike from managers, players, parents, and sportswriters. In the interwar years this national bureaucracy had force, though it always claimed more control than it could possibly exercise, and its public face reflected more harmony among its affiliates than really existed.[20]

Organized, officially sanctioned competition grew everywhere in Canada. Evidence is scattered and partial, but still, enough of it remains to demonstrate the pattern. The Alberta AHA registered forty-one clubs and 387 players in 1923–24; by 1931 their numbers had grown to 785 players.[21] In the Ottawa District alone, there were, by 1935–36, 115 registered teams and 1,650 "carded" players.[22] Quebec's AHA grew meteorically in the 1930s: in 1930–31, it recognized 207 clubs with 2,573 players registered, and by 1938–39 it had almost doubled its player registrants, to 4,735.[23] The OHA had similar growth.[24]

Still, organization was limited. AHAs only began to register youth players by the mid-1930s: juveniles and midgets first, the younger divisions to follow.[25] At the senior and intermediate levels, there was as much competition outside of the AHAs' jurisdictions as within. When OHA secretary-treasurer Bill Hewitt reported in 1931 that registration had never been better (199 teams and 4,230 players), he did not include players from northern Ontario, the Toronto Amateur Hockey Association, the St. Catharines district, and the Toronto and District Secondary Schools. Unregistered players made up "probably 6,000 more players."[26] Teams and leagues departed the OHA even as others joined it. This was the case with the Ontario Rural Hockey League, which first affiliated with the OHA in 1932, then departed in 1936 when affiliation no longer suited its needs.[27]

The AHAs' reach was always bigger than their grasp; but their grasp was considerable. They required all registered teams to abide by their definitions of amateurism and playing rules or face being blackballed. Outlaw teams were denied access to postseason tournaments and trophies. AHAs policed their terrain with a complex of tools, including a "carding system" that compiled and kept track of eligible players and allowed associations to control player transfers from team to team. Residency rules insisted that players must live in the towns for which they played, and reinstatement rules governed the return of players who had played pro. The OHA was first and strictest in its use of these tools. It had a comprehensive carding system in place by 1923 and was the most unforgiving in its treatment of teams and players who had gone astray.[28]

Throughout the 1920s, AHAs were the sentries for the amateur ideal, and the press rarely hesitated to take their side. "Tourist" players were roundly decried in the press as threats to the idea that local hockey should be made up of locals, as were professional teams who filched the best amateur players. When the Boston Westminsters, an American senior amateur team, was smeared in the Canadian press in 1921 for being a "tourist mecca" for Canadian players, its manager was outraged and demanded that Canadian authorities undertake a probe to clear the team's name.[29]

In Ontario, until the end of the 1920s, getting reinstated as an amateur was an almost impossible task. But few other AHAs were so exacting. Outside of Ontario the amateur ideal was less rooted, and the game was regulated less severely. In Alberta, where disdain for centralized power was part of the political culture, OHA-like control was only an aspiration. The guarded tone in the Alberta AHA's mission statement, expressed at its annual meeting in 1920, was revealing: "It is the aim of the officials to promote the game extensively in the country towns and they hope to have all amateur clubs and leagues affiliate."[30]

All AHAs could agree, however, that openly professional teams were too aggressive in cherry-picking players and repeatedly called for fairness and a retreat from tampering. The OHA passed a motion at its 1928 annual meeting proposing that the NHL be prevented "from placing the names of O.H.A. players on the lists of its clubs, unknown to and without the consent of these said players."[31] Gradually, by the end of the 1920s, the CAHA took the lead in governing hockey across the nation. Its control of the national championships persuaded regional AHAs to adopt CAHA playing rules to ensure their teams' eligibility for Dominion honors.[32] Moreover, a national registration protocol was worked out: regional AHAs would collect player registrations and fees every fall and transfer those documents to the national organization by February 1. By the early 1930s, the CAHA operated a national clearinghouse of eligible players.

In the United States, amateur play also expanded, but with less sweeping consolidation of power. At its lowest levels—high school and college—the game involved comparatively few players and short (if vigorous) seasons. As a result, most competition resided in isolated markets, each with its own rules and culture. Elite seniors, however, followed the Canadian pattern of regional and national organization, in this case under the watch of old hands in the management of sports and their facilities, men like Boston's George V. Brown, Pittsburgh's William Haddock and Roy Schooley, St. Paul's Frank Weidenborner, and Philadelphia's George F. Pawling. In 1920 these were the men who formed the USAHA, the nation's marquee senior amateur loop. Hockey was typically just one of many sports in their agendas as managers. George V. Brown, for instance, may be more famous for his stewardship of the Boston Marathon; Schooley for his work in Pittsburgh baseball.[33]

While the USAHA recruited players from Canada—like Eveleth's Johnson and Galbraith—it was largely a showcase for American talent and a site where local heroes like Boston's Owen or St. Paul's Francis Xavier "Moose" Goheen could flourish. At 5'9" and 170 pounds, Goheen impressed writers in all USAHA markets with his speed, skill, and physical play, just as he had done at the 1920 Antwerp Olympics. He "played big." Covering the 1922 national finals between St. Paul and Boston's Westminsters, John Hallahan, the doyen of Boston hockey writers, praised Goheen for hooking "the puck away from an opponent about as often and as cleverly as any player who has appeared in the Arena, who 'jumped' with astonishing speed for so large a man." He also had a "wicked" shot—a threat both for speed and misdirection. This was high praise from a hardened analyst who had watched Hobey Baker in that same arena.[34]

From 1920 to 1925, the USAHA brought big-time play and a national playoff to a circuit that ran from the Northeast to the mid-Atlantic, to the Midwest and the old Northwest, that great hockey basin that swooped around the banks of Lake Superior down to the Twin Cities. The USAHA was no small achievement in a time when the World Series of professional baseball had only sixteen teams and a smaller geographic footprint. But questions about its claim to amateur status lingered. The league defined "amateur" in terms of what a player could *not* do: play in open competition against players or teams not sanctioned by the USAHA or CAHA; play for a share of admission money, or a "stake"; teach or pursue sport as a livelihood; be remunerated for play with a non-hockey job or sinecure; or receive any kind of payment, even for the loss of work time, except for actual travel expenses. Like most amateur groups, the USAHA employed negative due process. Accusations of professionalism rendered a player guilty: "the onus of proving his innocence shall rest with the accused."[35]

There was tough talk, but not much enforcement. After all, the association's leaders were rink managers who counted on star power to draw crowds. In February 1924, Boston's gossipy "Bob Dunbar" column quoted one prominent amateur: "I simply cannot afford to play professional hockey." That December, in a montage of images about "scenes we'd like to see," one Boston cartoon featured a uniformed player holding his glove out toward a cigar-chomping, fedora-capped boss. The scowling player says: "$100 increase or no game." The cartoonist's suggestion: "Salary limit for all amateur hockey players." In 1925 one Boston amateur sued his club for nonpayment of salary. Columnist W. O. McGeehan noted that the Hub defined an amateur as "an athlete who does not sue when he is not paid off." "Bob Dunbar" concluded: "This mercenary side of 'amateur' hockey . . . is one of the many reasons why some of our leading sportsmen and clear thinkers want to hurry the arrival here of pro hockey of the honest and above-board stamp."[36]

The debate about what constituted an amateur (and whether that ideal was worth saving) haunted the USAHA's Canadian cousins as well and led to a monumental shakeup. In 1935–36, in a shocking triune movement, amateur authorities abandoned their attachment to strict definitions, withdrew from their two-decade affiliation with the umbrella Amateur Athletic Union of Canada, and aligned themselves formally with the NHL and its professional affiliates—a 180-degree turn. The changes produced deep rifts among amateur sportsmen and restructured governance for the remainder of the twentieth century.

The change happened swiftly, but its causes were longer term. First, openly professional hockey (the NHL and other leagues) had gradually become legitimate in the public eye. In the 1920s, Bruce Kidd wrote, "A whole new galaxy of stars, lionized by the commercial media, descended on the hearts and minds of Canadians."[37] Next came the Great Depression. By the early 1930s, joblessness, material want, and declining purchasing power affected everyone. Fewer players and teams could pay their carding fees, and fewer fans could afford to pay to watch tournament and playoffs games on which the associations had built their coffers. The AHAs suffered. In British Columbia no annual meeting took place in 1933 because "the Association was broke."[38] Even the OHA felt the pain. Despite experiencing growth in membership in 1935–36, the organization finished the year $5,862 in debt.[39] The CAHA saw its own funds dwindle from a robust surplus of $50,000 in 1930 to $5,000 in 1936. Financial trouble weakened the AHAs' ability to police their ranks and depleted their willingness to impose simon-pure rules on needy players. Players inclined to amateurism in principle could no longer afford it; pay for play became logical.

In response, the AHAs liberalized their codes. The OHA opened the door to reinstating a small number of professionals in 1929; by 1933 the CAHA moved toward allowing reinstatement for any former pro and allowed for pros and amateurs to mingle in charity games.[40] But monumental change came in 1935. At the annual parliament of the AAU of Canada, hockey officials pressed for a formal relaxation of the code, so that all amateur sportsmen could play with and against professionals, without penalty. Their case was defeated, but CAHA men were determined. At their annual meeting in Toronto in spring 1936 the CAHA passed four proposals that legitimized a form of professionalism within the amateur ranks. These included allowing players to "capitalize on their ability as hockey players for the purpose of obtaining legitimate employment"; to "accept from their clubs or employers payment for time lost from work while competing for amateur clubs" (in other words, "broken-time" payments); and to "play exhibition games against professional teams under such conditions as may be laid down by the individual branches of the CAHA." When the AAU of Canada vetoed the proposals, the CAHA disaffiliated, becoming an independent body.[41]

Freed from the bonds of strict amateurism, the CAHA then signed a formal agreement with the National Hockey League in May 1936. There was something for both parties. For the NHL, the CAHA agreed to adopt the playing rules of the NHL in their entirety and to observe suspensions that the NHL (or its minor-league affiliates) had meted out to individual players. For the CAHA, the NHL agreed to curtail tampering with amateur players and regularize its selection and use of CAHA-affiliated players. No player registered with a CAHA junior club could now be hired away from that team unless it had the consent of the club's management. Moreover, NHL teams would now provide notice of intention to sign senior amateurs to tryout contracts by August 15 preceding a season, and all such players not signed to a regular-season contract by November 15 had to be returned to their clubs. The deal, by one account, "gave the NHL the decision-making power to mold the product, and implicitly acknowledge the superiority of the NHL brand as well as its authority in the production of commercialized hockey games."[42]

Life at the Top

For the NHL, this was "monopoly's moment," when characters and circumstance conspired to shift control into the hands of businessmen and their media promoters. The NHL *captured* hockey and reordered it, placing a crown of professional control atop the pyramid of once-thriving amateur organizations. As Bruce Kidd wrote, "[In] just two decades, the NHL became the best-known sports organization in Canada, with its players household names and the term 'professional' synonymous with 'excellence'."[43] Hockey became big business in the 1920s and 1930s, and with it came rationalization: mergers, combinations, market competition, and product undercutting. Specifically, the NHL ascended via two critical events: the collapse of its only rival professional leagues by 1926, and the NHL-CAHA agreement of 1936. Still, there was nothing ineluctable about this process. The NHL's success was slow, uncertain, and hotly contested.

Professional hockey expanded in a variety of major and minor leagues that produced an array of acronyms matching FDR's New Deal. The effect must have been as confusing for readers of the sports pages then as it is for historians today. Three major-league circuits operated in the early 1920s, the oldest of them being the Pacific Coast Hockey Association, the Patrick brothers' syndicate. Since 1911, PCHA teams in Victoria (Cougars), Vancouver (Millionaires), Seattle (Metropolitans), Spokane (Canaries) and Portland (Rosebuds) had thrived and provided rivals to eastern powers, largely by raiding their franchises for top talent. Between 1914 and 1922, the PCHA winners played annually against the NHL champions for the Stanley Cup. Seattle actually won it in 1917.[44]

The newest was the Western Canada Hockey League, created when four nominally amateur teams in Calgary, Edmonton, Regina, and Saskatoon declared themselves pro in 1921. From 1922 to 1926, WCHL winners were invited to play PCHA and NHL victors for the Stanley Cup. But having two western major leagues was not sustainable. When the PCHA's Seattle franchise folded in 1924, the Patricks dissolved their association and merged their Victoria and Vancouver teams into the WCHL. The Victoria Cougars won the Stanley Cup in 1925, but the hybrid experiment was short lived. In May 1926 the WCHL folded as a big-league pro circuit. Two teams were liquidated, their players sold to NHL franchises (Frank Patrick, for example, sold his Cougars roster to the new Detroit NHL franchise owner for $100,000) and the prairie-based league reverted to minor-pro status.

The most prominent professional organization throughout the era was, of course, the NHL. Formed in Montreal in 1917 from the ashes of the embattled National Hockey Association, the league soldiered through the Great War, wracked by instability and infighting but steered masterfully by its president, Frank Calder. A small but profitable business, by 1919 it had four franchises, all in central Canada: Ottawa Senators, Toronto Arenas (sold in 1919 and renamed the St. Patricks), Montreal Canadiens, and Quebec Bulldogs, who moved to Hamilton (and became the Tigers) in 1920. Compared to the PCHA and the WCHL, the NHL was in decent financial shape and poised to become bigger by expanding to eastern US cities.

The most stable franchise was the Canadiens, whose appeal as an *équipe nationale* provided a steady French-Canadian following. In Toronto the St. Patricks (renamed the Maple Leafs in 1927), operated on a bedrock of local support. Ottawa's Senators thrived in the Roaring Twenties but fell victim to the Depression and suspended operations in 1931–32, later moving to St. Louis (as the short-lived Eagles, 1934–36). Another team, the Montreal Maroons, catering to Anglophones in that city, took to the ice in 1924 and lasted fourteen years, until 1938, when financial straits caused its owners to suspend operations. Until 1924, NHL hockey was central Canadian hockey, a business supported by the strength of the nation's commercial and industrial heartland.

New Venues and New Markets

The NHL's most significant change came when it expanded to the United States. By 1923 the league's magnates—Canadians all—set their sights on big American markets with promising fan bases. This meant particularly Boston, New York, Pittsburgh, Chicago, Detroit, and Philadelphia. The 1920s were boom years for these cities, which enjoyed staggering economic and population growth. Prosperity was uneven, but many workers, especially white-collar professionals, enjoyed more leisure time and income. American spending on recreation increased 300 percent during the 1920s. Speculation in sport spectacle spurred a new wave of facilities, including a new Madison Square Garden (New York, 1925), Detroit's Olympia (1927), the Boston Garden (1928), and the Chicago Stadium (1929).[45] In these new venues, hockey shared time and synergy with prize fighting, newly legitimated by its wartime use in training soldiers and legalized by 1917 in twenty-three states.[46] New arenas were the vessels for a first age of grand spectacle; built of steel, concrete, and brick, they were monuments to their host cities.[47]

Expansion to America put pressure on Canadian franchises. Older venues gave way to newer, larger, and more luxurious rinks. Toronto's Arena Gardens had been a showcase when it opened in 1912 as the city's first artificial ice facility. But its capacity and bench seating could not match popular demand in the 1920s as Toronto's swelling population (376,471 in 1911 but 631,207 in 1931) enjoyed more prosperity. When Conn Smythe became managing partner of Toronto's NHL club in 1927, he gave them a new name: Maple Leafs. A new arena was next, but Smythe needed public support and investors. In 1929 he circulated ninety-one thousand promotional booklets playing on Torontonians' civic pride. New York and Boston had each built new arenas and then went on to win the Stanley Cup. "Toronto dare not lag behind." In one cartoon, a woman welcomed the promised improvements, such as better heating: "I used to go to all the games but I don't like the cold rink."[48]

Selling options for U.S. franchise rights involved intricate machinations among NHL president Frank Calder, owners, and interested local parties. A central figure was Tom Duggan, a Montreal boxing and racing promoter who had orchestrated the building of the Mount Royal Arena in 1920. Often on the edge of insolvency, Duggan played at the margin of the NHL operation, and he wanted in. With no Canadian franchises available or in his price range, he looked south and enlisted American-born Canadiens owner Léo Dandurand to present a US expansion plan at the league meeting in January 1923. A month later, Duggan had an agreement with NHL president Frank Calder: $2,000 for options on two franchises to be placed among Boston, New York, and Brooklyn. Duggan then traveled extensively over the next eighteen months, haggling for deals and holding press conferences—always saying he was on the cusp of something big. The top Boston investor prospect was Charles F. Adams, a grocery-store magnate who had managed a team in the Boston Arena's early days and was on the board of the New Arena Corporation. With one eye on owning the franchise himself, Adams brokered a contract for Arena ice time, despite the concerns of Arena manager George V. Brown that pro hockey would diminish the value of USAHA operations. For this help, Duggan promised Adams the Boston franchise at cost, provided he could land something in New York or Brooklyn. With little hope for an arena large enough in Brooklyn, Duggan needed the Madison Square Garden and its manager, Tex Rickard.[49]

George Lewis "Tex" Rickard (b. 1870) had risen to prominence in the early twentieth century by promoting big boxing bouts, including the 1910 "match of the century" between Jack Johnson, the first black heavyweight champ, and Jim Jeffries, the retired champ returning as a Great White Hope. Rickard was an old cowboy, but he dressed in fine suits, shiny shoes, and stylish hats and always carried a fine Malacca cane. He smoked cigars, talked with a western twang, and played the press like P. T. Barnum. After his sudden death in 1929 the *North American Review* declared him "The Master of Ballyhoo."[50]

In September 1924 the NHL governors approved new franchises in Boston (bought by Adams) and Montreal, to begin that very season. A month later they refused Duggan an extension on his original New York option. He had three weeks to make a $6,000 down payment. Duggan had one franchise option—Tex Rickard, who had both the Garden and time on his side. Duggan soon worked out a contract with Rickard and his assistant John Hammond, and it dripped leverage. Duggan got ice time for games and practices at the brand-new (1925) Madison Square Garden. In return, he agreed to pay $500 per game night toward operating expenses, *plus* 50 percent of the gross admissions gate, *plus* 50 percent of net revenue from away games or playoff games, *plus* half the cost of a refrigeration system (estimated at $80,000). Beyond this, Duggan promised to help Rickard grab an additional New York franchise, thus cannibalizing his exclusive market rights. As in Boston, Duggan did not have the money to actually buy the franchise, and so he brought in a partner, a notorious bootlegger named Bill Dwyer. Duggan's hunger to get into the NHL business trumped his better judgment. He never recovered the full value of his New York or Boston interests, despite a series of lawsuits.[51]

For his part, Rickard was all in for Canada's game. The New York Americans helped open the new Madison Square Garden in December 1925. The following year, the MSG's own franchise was ready to go. The press (likely with Rickard's coaxing) took to calling the team Tex's "Rangers." The name stuck. That same year, he bid unsuccessfully for an NHL franchise in Chicago while trumpeting his plans for "Madison Square Gardens" in Chicago and Philadelphia. None of that panned out, but he *was* behind the building of another "Madison Square" Garden, this one in Boston (1928). In all cases, hockey and boxing were central to his public vision. In Chicago he pushed the ice game, claiming that "in New York, society comes to the games in evening wear . . . the sport takes hold of the women as well as the men." In 1926 he boldly predicted: "Within five years it will be drawing more money than boxing."[52]

Between 1924 and 1926 NHL hockey came to Boston, New York, Pittsburgh, Chicago, and Detroit. All cities save Pittsburgh were home to new indoor arenas seating eleven thousand and more. There was money to be made, and it attracted hardened and savvy entrepreneurs Adams, Rickard, and "Big Jim" Norris, baron of a lucrative shipping and grain enterprise in the Great Lakes region. Norris's Chicago franchise bid clashed with that of Frederic McLaughlin, whose family had made a bundle in coffee. But Norris's commodities gave him deeper pockets. He lost the Chicago franchise bid to McLaughlin, but when the economy crashed and burned, he ended up owning the Chicago Stadium, Detroit's NHL franchise and arena, as well as equity interests in New York and Boston.[53]

The Minor Pros

Minor-professional teams spread across North America, especially after 1926, when the consolidation of big-league franchises opened old markets for lower-level teams. In these places, hockey knowledge mattered less than the willingness to pay for the spectacle. In medium and small cities, they aimed to capture civic pride and transmute it as a local symbol. But smaller venues always meant modest returns and transiency—the unpacked suitcase and the omnipresent moving truck.

In 1926 four minor leagues emerged in North America's hockey heartland. One of them was the Canadian Professional Hockey League (1926–29), established in Hamilton in June 1926, partially as a response to the OHA, which had declared more than twenty senior players ineligible for violating the residency rule. The league brought open pros to its five charter Ontario cities: Hamilton, London, Stratford, Niagara Falls, and Windsor. However, the CanPro was short lived. Only two of the original franchises (Niagara Falls Cataracts and London Panthers) survived the league's three seasons. At its annual meeting in 1929 the governors voted themselves out of existence but then reformed as the International Hockey League.

Two other circuits opened in the prairie West. In 1925 the USAHA could no longer keep up the ruse that it was anything but professional, and it folded. Some teams reconstituted as the Central Hockey League (CHL) in 1925–26, rechristened as the American Hockey Association (AHA) in

1926–27. The AHA lasted until 1942, when it collapsed under the weight of the war. Its longevity masked internal volatility. Six franchises inaugurated AHA play in 1926 (Chicago, Detroit, Minneapolis, Duluth, St. Paul, and Winnipeg). From 1927 to 1933 the league flirted with the NHL, seeking a formal affiliation, only to be denied that status because it refused to vacate cities—Buffalo and Chicago—where NHL teams or affiliates already resided. In 1933, AHA leaders knuckled under and became an NHL-recognized minor league for the remainder of the decade. Beyond its founding cities, AHA teams performed across the American Midwest, from Buffalo in the northeast to Omaha, Kansas City, Oklahoma City, St. Louis, Dallas, Wichita, and Fort Worth.

The other western minor pro league, the Prairie Hockey League (PHL), was shorter lived—just two seasons. It was western Canada's answer to the demise of the Western Hockey League. In its first season the PHL iced five entries: Calgary Tigers, Edmonton Eskimos, Moose Jaw Warriors, Regina Capitals, and Saskatoon Sheiks. When the two largest cities (Calgary and Edmonton) declined the invitation to return for the 1927–28 season, the loop folded, many of its players returning to the senior amateur ranks.

The Canadian-American Hockey League (1926–36) was more successful. It opened in 1926 with five teams: Boston Tigers (later Tiger Cubs, then Cubs), New Haven Eagles, Quebec Castors, Providence Reds, and Springfield (Massachusetts) Indians. The five originals lasted through the era (with brief one- or two-season Depression-related respites) and were joined by shorter-lived teams in Philadelphia, Newark, and the Bronx. The league's footprint in the medium and large cities of the American northeast may have been the key to its relative stability. Short bus or train rides kept costs low, and comparative longevity built rivalries among the league's fans. In 1936 the Can-Am merged with the five-year-old International Hockey League, itself an amalgam with the Can-Pro League. This loop had totaled thirteen franchises in eleven cities across southern Ontario, western New York, Pennsylvania, and northern Ohio—all supposed to act as feeders for the NHL, a plan that worked better in theory than in practice. Following the 1935–36 season, three Depression-wracked IHL teams folded and two others merged, leaving only four entries. These teams combined with (or more accurately rejoined) their former mates in the Can-Am to form a new group: the International American Hockey League (IAHL), which operated under that name for four seasons, 1936–40, with almost all of its entries in the American northeast: Providence, New Haven, Philadelphia, Hershey, Springfield, Syracuse, Pittsburgh, Cleveland, Buffalo, and Indianapolis. In 1940 its moguls rebranded as the American Hockey League.[54]

It is tempting to see minor-professional hockey in this era as already and naturally part of the NHL's orbit, an integrally connected network wired to train up its best players for the game's highest tier. But that didn't happen systemically until the 1940s. Most minor pros never made it to the NHL; for many, that was never the ultimate goal. Clearly, Frank Calder and some NHL managers, such as Lester Patrick and Conn Smythe, regarded the minors as proving grounds, but that opinion was hardly universal. Minor-professional team owners, coaches, and fans could see their teams as creditable enterprises, affiliated with but apart from big-league hockey.[55]

Beginning in 1926, however, the NHL began to lay the groundwork for a minor-league system. *Sport Story* magazine editor Handley Cross explained it as vertical integration, "in much the same manner as the minor leagues are affiliated with the major leagues in professional baseball."[56] That wasn't *quite* right. Between 1926 and 1936, Calder negotiated affiliation agreements with each of the developing leagues to secure labor supply to the NHL and to prevent minor leagues from locating in NHL cities. While owners and managers in the Can-Am League were largely compliant with NHL wishes, a rockier relationship existed with the solons of the AHA and Can-Pro. The agreement that Can-Am executives signed adopted the NHL constitution and playing rules, a standard player contract similar to the NHL's, a provision whereby NHL teams could loan players to Can-Am clubs and a clause that allowed an NHL team to draft minor-league players for $5,000. For Can-Pro's president, Charles King, these last two details rankled. On-loan players in the Can-Pro who were summarily recalled to the NHL without notice created instability in King's league's product. When Can-Pro renewed its NHL affiliation agreement in 1927, it included a no-recall clause.

Territorial rights were another bone of contention. Eddie Livingstone, ousted when the NHA dissolved and reformed as the NHL in 1917, led a charge in the AHA to establish a franchise in Chicago (the Cardinals) and started a war with the NHL Black Hawks, both clubs signing "claimed" players and cutting ticket prices. It was a battle he could not win, since he lacked both the deep pockets of McLaughlin and the support of other AHA owners. He was forced to sell in 1933 before the NHL would agree to sign another affiliation agreement with the AHA.[57] Thus, minor-profes-

"The Little Ranger Schoolhouse," cartoon (Walt Ball/*Toronto Star*, used with permission)

sional leagues developed an ambiguous relationship with the NHL in the 1920s and 1930s. Their affiliation agreements indicate a willingness—like all functional trusts—to cooperate rather than compete, but not on just *any* terms. "The relationship between the major and minor leagues," John Wong wrote, "was often dialectic rather than dictatorial."[58]

Although the NHL began to allow its clubs to own and run minor-league teams in the mid-1930s, few were ready to take advantage of Calder's affiliation agreements. "Only two clubs, the Leafs and the Rangers operate farm teams," the *Montreal Gazette* observed in December 1936, but "the chain store system has proven its worth in baseball. . . . [I]t will eventually be shown to be a necessity in major league hockey.[59] The system soon took shape. By 1939, Lester Patrick oversaw what sportswriters called his "4 Rs"—Gotham's (NHL) Rangers, the (C-AHL) Philadelphia Ramblers, the Eastern Hockey League New York Rovers, and the (CAHA Junior) Edmonton Roamers—a string of networked teams that kept his NHL squad stocked with top talent.

By the onset of World War II, North American hockey had a core system, with the CAHA as its base and the NHL its crown. But there was much to be worked out. NHL moguls had only begun to dabble with sponsoring CAHA junior teams, and some, like the impatient Patrick, complained that too many wouldn't release players for big-league tryouts. "If they aren't more equitable in the future," he warned, "they are likely to wake up some morning and find that organized professional hockey has scrapped the whole treaty."[60] Ironically, war-era player shortages served to expand and deepen NHL farm systems. By 1943 the *Ottawa Citizen*'s Charles Edwards predicted that a "Gigantic Farm System" would "Make NHL Boss of Amateur Hockey."[61] It did. The 1936 CAHA-NHL deal centralized power and opened amateur hockey to a long train of abuses of youngsters and their families. CAHA Secretary Gordon Juckes later lamented his predecessors' decision to go to bed with the NHL, calling the system a "gigantic slave farm."[62]

The Pro Brand

In a February 1936 *Literary Digest* article, Lester Patrick captured the NHL's essence after two decades of expansion. "We're professional showmen . . . interested in J.Q. Public and, when J.Q.P. fills all the seats, we know we're right."[63] Patrick had started selling hockey in 1911 in the Pacific Northwest. New technologies helped him and many others move the pro game from local to mass culture. Newspaper stories could attempt to articulate the game, but a picture was worth a thousand words. The advent of the 35mm Leica camera in 1925 and the development of flashbulbs and wire photos produced compelling, if pixelated, images that educated readers about this new brand of spectacle.[64]

Radio also assisted market expansion, especially in Canada, where radio set ownership exploded from some ten thousand in 1923 to one million in 1934. An impressive 348,507 sets were sold in 1939 alone. The NHL brand expanded along a network of radios, beginning with the broadcast of a Canadiens–Ottawa Senators Stanley Cup match in 1924. Conn Smythe was an early convert: "I knew we should broadcast," he told Scott Young. "People who were interested enough to listen to our games on the radio were going to buy tickets sometime." His savvy was repaid. While other hockey franchises in Canada and America slowly embraced local broadcasts, Smythe moved aggressively. By 1933, Leafs broadcasts traveled through a twenty-station network that reached across Canada. For Anglophones, the Leafs became Canada's team. Bruins owner Charles Adams also experimented with radio and target marketing. Bruins games appeared on Boston's WBZA and Springfield's WBZ in 1926, with hockey writer Frank Ryan doing the play by play. Adams himself joined the campaign with pitches to female fans in his press interviews. Demand rose so high that the team began a season-ticket program.[65]

Patrick, Smythe, and Adams understood sport as spectacle. They developed and sold their game as a brand that combined several elements—speed, science, violence. NHL teams and their media allies pushed speed foremost. When the Montreal Canadiens made their first stop in Boston in 1924, the focus was on Howie Morenz and Aurèle Joliat, in Boston manager Art Ross's view "the two fastest men in hockey skates in the world." After Joliat's two unassisted goals sunk the Bruins, 4–3, writer Stanley Woodward concluded, "never before has a Boston hockey crowd seen such amazing speed."[66]

In 1929 the NHL began to allow forward passing within, but not between, each of three zones. Players and coaches responded, but perhaps not as intended. Enterprising forwards like Boston's Cooney Weiland simply hung near the opponent's net waiting for a teammate to bring the puck across the blue line and make a 50-foot pass to an all-alone sniper. By December, goal production was double its norm. So the NHL changed the rule mid-season, prohibiting players from crossing the offensive blue line before the puck: modern "offside" was born. Still, the pro game moved at dizzying speed. During the Detroit Cougars' first season, a Chamber of Commerce newsletter championed hockey over football: "In football, the ball is actually in motion only about 11 minutes out of the 60 . . . but in hockey there must be a full 60 minutes of actual play."[67] For Lester Patrick, hockey was *still* too slow. In 1939, he pushed for a delayed or tag-up offside rule.[68]

Pro hockey's promoters also emphasized a higher level of "science," or combination play. While Art Ross prepared his Bruins for their inaugural season, one *Boston Herald* story emphasized how the "old fox" had installed a level of regimen little seen among the amateurs: "scoring plays, defensive tricks, and all that goes with an effective and well-balanced professional team." The pros also oozed higher levels of skill and courage. After the Black Hawks home opener in November 1926, the *Chicago Defender*—a nationally distributed African American paper—described hockey as a "game of skill, brains, judgment, and speed." Three weeks later it added "courage," "danger of collision," and "numerous scars of battle."[69]

For *New York World*'s Gertrude Lynahan, violence was the paramount feature. "Hockey offers more chance for men to lame, maim, bruise, batter, smash and slash each other than any other game." The popular physical culture magazine *The Arena and Strength* featured a stern-looking player on its January 1934 cover and three-page narrative. "The players usually put on a double feature," writer Morry Stiles declared, "a game and a fist fight." A February 1927 issue of *The Sportsman* asked in one title, "Ice Hockey—A Game, or Assault and Battery?"[70] Writing in 1929, one Philadelphia writer held that the hockey fan "sees for his money many fights and near-riots . . . fought . . . with the same vigor that Tunney fought Dempsey." In these years, NHL games etched fighting into the script of expected action.[71]

The pro brand captured local but loyal pools of rabid fans in America. Canada was an ocean of devotion that crossed the continent. By 1939, professional and senior amateur hockey cut a wide swath across North American sports markets. Most players and fans, however, recognized a hierarchy of power and prestige. By World War II, the NHL enjoyed a position of dominance in the broad hockey market. But as political, economic, and cultural theorists have long articulated, power is seldom total. It is constantly contested.

13

Diverging North American Brands: 1920–1945

On January 19, 1919, hockey solons met in Montreal Amateur Athletic Association rooms on Peel Street near Sherbrooke, steps from McGill University campus and blocks from the site of the old Victoria Skating Rink and the elite Anglophone neighborhood of Westmount. Their purpose: to launch the Quebec Amateur Hockey Association (QAHA). "Among those present," the *Montreal Gazette* recalled, "were major Hartland B. MacDougall, outstanding Montreal athlete, James A. Taylor, president of the Amateur Skating Association of Canada, T. Yates Foster; W.R. Granger, president of the M.A.A.A.; T. Slattery of the Shamrocks club; C.S. Fosbery, principal of Lower Canada College; and William J. Morrison, sports editor of the *Gazette* and representing the M.A.A.A."[1] Over the next two decades the QAHA's constituency broadened beyond this base; so, too, did its leadership, shared roughly equally between Anglophones and Francophones. Historians have largely ignored the QAHA and what we know has come from occasional inferences and a tendency to link the QAHA's difficult past to the turbulent era of post-1960s language politics. The association was, according to one modern study, "an anglophone agency within which francophones had no power."[2] That belief motivated Quebecers after 1960 to reorganize amateur hockey in the province and led, by the mid-1980s, to the transformation of the QAHA to a wholly francophone organization, *Hockey Québec*. Still, linguistic tensions in the era of Quebec's Quiet Revolution should not be read backward. In the 1920s and 1930s, the QAHA was a functionally bilingual organization that had numerous colorful beefs with the CAHA, but language was not the cause. Not yet.

In the interwar years NHL power grew over a range of leagues and associations in North America, but there were limits to this control. As one expert wrote, while the "NHL brand came to dominate . . . it was not the only brand."[3] There were important sites in North America where the NHL could not reach and where the game grew in *divergent* directions. In both the United States and Canada, teams, towns, leagues, and associations vied for space and control. These included the QAHA, the Canadian Intercollegiate Hockey Union (CIHU), and National Collegiate Athletic Association (NCAA), whose organizers, coaches, and players skated against the cold breeze of consolidation.

Perennial Rogue: The Quebec Amateur Hockey Association

The organization governing in hockey's "birthplace" was also, ironically, its worst tenant. The relations between the CAHA and its regional affiliates were never completely steady, and the blanket semi-annual meeting reports that they were "all in it for the good of the game" masked a more persistent antagonism. For the regional organizations, the CAHA was never doing enough (about "tourist" players or amateur reinstatements), always doing too much (making accusations of professionalism), or, as Maritimers claimed in 1936, biased in favor of central Canada. For most affiliates, these were routine complaints that were adequately handled (if not resolved) behind closed doors and only occasionally laundered in the press. But some complaints grew louder and developed a perennial axis of tension. Every family has a black sheep; for the CAHA, it was Quebec.

The QAHA was regionally unbalanced in these decades: Montreal players, teams, leagues, and administrators dominated. In 1938–39 the association's registrants numbered 4,735; fully 68 percent of them (3,221) belonged to the Montreal District, with only 14 percent (647) from Sherbrooke and 18 percent (867) from Quebec.[4] Like other regional AHAs, the QAHA governed the game in its region, annually tweaking its laws to suit local circumstances, such as the availability of ice and officials.[5] It was no less dogged than Hewitt's OHA in identifying and stamping out violations such as residency rule infractions and professionalism. When Raymond Hawkins, a player in Montreal's Railway Telephone Hockey League, violated the residency rule in February 1928 by playing for the Canadian Pacific Railway team in the league championship tournament without having been resident for the requisite time, the QAHA threatened to suspend all players participating in games in which he had played. In its own domain, the QAHA was king of the castle. Twenty-two players in Montreal found that out in January 1934, when President Alcide Gagnon suspended them for playing "outlaw" hockey in unsanctioned *Ligue de L'Est* games.[6]

The QAHA quarreled regularly with its neighbors, the Ottawa and District Hockey Association, over the affiliation of teams, occasionally accusing each other of poaching across the Ottawa River, their shared boundary. Its sovereignty stretched to other matters, too. When, in 1933, the CAHA banned all of its teams from playing games against the Eastern Hockey League's Atlantic City Seagulls (US amateur champions), the QAHA objected loudly. The Sea Gulls, a notorious club composed of Canadian "tourist" players, had played several games against teams in Quebec; the QAHA looked upon the CAHA ruling as arbitrary and discriminatingly punitive.[7]

The main cause of the rocky QAHA-CAHA relationship was simple mistrust. The dynamic paralleled a larger antagonism in Canadian political culture between Canada's two largest metropoles—stolid and proper "Toronto the Good" versus gritty and cosmopolitan Montreal. The QAHA never missed a chance to accuse the parent group of favoritism toward the OHA (its biggest constituent) and all things Toronto. When the QAHA invited teams from Ontario to play in its senior series in 1925–26, Toronto's *Globe* was outraged over this attempt at poaching and supported the OHA's efforts to protect its turf. The QAHA declared that it would not be dictated to by the OHA and threatened to break away from organized hockey in Canada.[8] Though that measure was averted, raw feelings remained and the incident deepened suspicion. When the QAHA's Montreal junior team lost to the curiously mature-looking Copper Cliff (Ontario) Redmen in the 1937 Memorial Cup playdowns, QAHA president Alphonse Therrien demanded that the CAHA check the Redmen's birthdates.[9]

The QAHA clashed with the CAHA in other episodes regarding jurisdictional authority. In autumn 1937 the CAHA questioned the eligibility of two Quebec senior league players from Ontario who hadn't received proper transfer credentials. Don Willson played in Canada for the Kirkland Lake, Ontario, seniors in 1933–34 but then played two seasons in Europe. When he signed with the Verdun Maple Leafs, he assumed his European sojourn eliminated the need for a transfer of his card from the OHA to the QAHA. At the same time, Cy Allen, a center who played with the OHA Toronto Goodyears in 1935–36, refused to return to that club and signed with the Montreal Royals. Both Willson and Allen met the CAHA's residency rule to play in Montreal, but the question of protocol remained and the QAHA chose a unilateral course. On December 8, 1937, QAHA president Art Lapierre declared: "Willson and Allen are hereby allowed to participate in any future games, regardless of any decision by the Canadian Amateur Hockey Association."[10] In doing so, both Lapierre and Quebec Senior Hockey League president George Slater knew what they were courting. "The CAHA has no alternative than to throw us out at their next executive meeting," Lapierre stated. Slater added: "We're tired of being dictated to by the C.A.H.A. for the past 15 or 20 years. . . . We're not going to leave our necks under the C.A.H.A. heel any longer."[11] Their prediction came true. On December 9, 1937, CAHA president Cecil Duncan formally suspended the QAHA and declared all of its affiliate teams ineligible for Allan Cup and Memorial Cup playdowns. Meantime, he set up an alternative "commission" of amateur hockey in Quebec and invited all teams in that province interested in competing for national titles to join it. When asked if he held out hope for the return of the QAHA, Duncan was openly irritated: "I don't care."[12]

Happily, Lapierre reconsidered his original ruling. And the CAHA responded in kind, reinstating the QAHA in January 1938.[13] Even after losing the battle, however, Lapierre earned kudos in Quebec, and he was elected for two more terms as QAHA president. The biggest casualty in the affair was CAHA president Duncan, who resigned in April 1938, his term marred, the *Globe and Mail* assessed, by his "battle with the Quebec Amateur Hockey Association."[14] In the interwar years, the QAHA had a peculiar posture. Recognizing the argument over the need for nationwide administration, it accepted affiliation with the CAHA. But more than any other regional AHA, the Quebec branch was sensitively jealous of its jurisdiction and leapt at any issue that smacked of intrusion, especially if it involved "Toronto."

Whither Amateurism? A New Collegiate Space

For intercollegiate hockey in Canada, it was an era of paradox. At first, the university game grew steadily, and its top teams played at the highest rung in the elite amateur ranks. The Depression era, however, brought hardship. As professionalism spread, universities were held out as the one place where simon-pure amateurism might remain. The Depression and its effects pushed universities to think hard about their place in the hockey *market*, and their programs developed an ambivalence with respect to the CAHA: how to uphold the image of amateurism even as "amateur" hockey was drawn into a commercial orbit?

By the end of the 1920s, more schools than ever sponsored teams. Intraschool play flourished among faculties and professional schools. Some squads, such as the University of Toronto's School of Dentistry—the Dentals—did so well that they competed in the senior ranks of the OHA. The Maritime Intercollegiate Athletic Association (MIAA), founded in 1910, grew to ten member schools. St. Francis Xavier University, in Antigonish, Nova Scotia, was one early MIAA powerhouse, winning in 1928–29 its first in a string of thirty-two regional titles. Mount Allison University dominated in the Depression decade, winners of six MIAA hockey championships between 1930 and 1939. The game flourished among western Canadian universities who in 1919 formed the Western Canada Intercollegiate Athletic Union, which organized a formal schedule of league games and a championship title among its four schools (the Universities of Alberta, British Columbia, Manitoba, and Saskatchewan). In 1922, University of Saskatchewan's Dr. J. Halpenny donated a prize—the Halpenny Trophy—for the winner of the WCIAU series.[15]

But the most widely celebrated university hockey was played in central Canada, in the Canadian Intercollegiate Hockey Union (CIHU), formed in 1903 and re-established after the Great War. Small but vigorous, it included six university teams from Ontario and Quebec (McGill, Montreal, Laval, Queen's, Toronto, and Western Ontario) who competed for the Queen's Cup. Here, the storyline was simple. University of Toronto dominated the senior intercollegiate play throughout the 1920s, the sole holders of the Queen's Cup; McGill University was tops throughout the Depression decade, winning the Cup in every year except one.

Across the Dominion, the *quality* of university hockey was impressively high. School teams were among the country's best senior amateurs. Toronto's Varsity Blues won the Allan Cup in 1920–21; University of Manitoba did so in 1927–28. The University of British Columbia reached the Allan Cup playdowns in 1921 after winning the provincial Senior A crown, as did the University of Saskatchewan varsity in 1923 after winning the Western Canada senior title. Moreover, universities often sponsored junior amateur teams that went deep into the Memorial Cup tournament. The Manitoba squad won the Memorial Cup in 1923, and in 1926 Queen's was runner-up. Most celebrated were the former University of Toronto students (with a few fictive alums added in) who played as the Varsity Grads, winning the Allan Cup in 1926–27 before going on to dominate the 1928 Olympic tournament in St. Moritz as Team Canada. University hockey had a conspicuous place in the press. In Toronto's *Globe* and *Star*, games of the U of T, McGill, Queen's, and other teams received top billing alongside the latest events in the NHL.

Despite their popularity, university teams had an uncertain place in governance. Some embraced CAHA affiliation, because the winner of the intercollegiate (CIHU) crown was offered an automatic berth in the Allan Cup tournament, bypassing the regional playdowns that other elite amateur teams went through. Brash university coaches registered their teams in both the CAHA and their regional AHAs, but doing so created a sort of jeopardy. The CAHA might rescind its invitation to a team whose record was marred by a loss in the regionals. In 1925, Toronto Varsity rejected membership in the OHA—its regional AHA—because, as its coach Conn Smythe explained to bewildered OHA executives, "Varsity might win the Intercollegiate but lose to the OHA senior champions and not make it to Allan Cup."[16] By the 1930s (after Smythe's departure to the pros) that sort of pride had abated, and Varsity joined the OHA. Other teams weren't so strategic. Saskatchewan saw no trouble in 1923 in playing in (and winning) both the provincial amateur championship and the Allan Cup.[17]

But the affiliation question had other consequences. By 1930, CAHA senior hockey was becoming more transparently commercial and professional. With the Depression, the amateur ideal sagged and the once-negative connotation that marked "pay for play" disintegrated. University teams in OHA series, for example, frequently matched up against teams that were anything but amateur, resembling little the fresh-faced gentlemen scholars who laced up the skates for the honor of their schools. In places such as Trail, British Columbia (where the "Smoke Eaters" represented resource industry communities and their employers), in Sudbury, Kirkland Lake, and Hamilton, Ontario (where the Wolves, Miners, and Tigers, respectively, plied their trades), hockey was a working-class obsession, and the players reflected the character of those communities. The relaxation of the standards and policing of amateurism (through a more generous reinstatement policy and, eventually in 1936, the approval of broken-time payments) exacerbated the class and cultural differences within the sport and isolated the *real* amateurs even further.

The dark clouds that presaged the CAHA-NHL Agreement in 1936 cast a broad shadow. School officials must have developed some suspicions about the direction of "amateur" hockey. Among them was Dr. W. G. Hardy, professor of classics at the University of Alberta, coach of the university's "Golden Bears" (1924–28), president of the Alberta AHA from 1931 to 1933 and first-vice-president of the CAHA during the NHL negotiations.[18] Hardy was the principal author of the CAHA's Four Points in spring 1936 and, as an educator, had to have felt the tug of conflict. His day job was to prepare gentlemen; at night and on weekends he helped govern professionals. Perhaps it was remorse that pushed him to try to get the CAHA to re-affiliate with the Amateur Athletic Union of Canada (AAUC) late in 1937. It was too late; his colleagues on the CAHA Executive Committee outvoted him.[19]

Though listing badly, the amateur ideal still resonated in the country's largest universities, whose leaders were unwilling to compromise on the old equation of sport and gentlemanly character. Out of step, they were, at least, sincere. Even by the mid-1930s, the press understood that these schools had a mission greater than wins and gate receipts. No one complained when the University of British Columbia Thunderbirds, champions of the provincial Senior A series and winners of the Savage Cup in 1921, had to forego the Allan Cup tournament because it conflicted with final exams. When the QAHA president "ordered" McGill to play a 1934 senior-league match in Quebec City against the wishes of university officials, one *Globe and Mail* editor scoffed: "Alcide Gagnon Has Sense of Humour."[20] Even so, it was a posture that couldn't last. When the CAHA disaffiliated from the AAUC, university teams were forced to choose. Staying with the CAHA meant continuing to play competitive championships, but it also meant, de facto, that its players would be skating against outright pros, in violation of the AAUC rules. For McGill coach R. B. Bell, the obvious choice was to stay with the AAUC to avoid risking his players being "barred from other sports through the playing of 'outlaw' hockey."[21] These sorts of considerations motivated university officials to step outside of Canadian hockey's core marketplace.

But where? For some, the answer was south, where the amateur ideal remained firmly in place—in the old, elite schools with long traditions of gentlemanly sport. In February 1936 four Canadian university teams (McGill, Queen's, Toronto, and Montreal) reached agreement with Dartmouth, Harvard, Princeton, and Yale to form the International Intercollegiate Ice

Hockey League. Each team played a ten-game schedule, which, in the case of the Canadian squads, was supplemented by CIHU play.[22] For four years, from 1937 to 1940, the IIIHL operated with good success, but the war brought its promising start to an end. McGill carried its CIHU dominance to the IIIHL, winning the league's Thompson Trophy in the first three years with a record of 28 wins and only 2 losses; Toronto captured the hardware in the final season.[23]

The IIIHL was a small but significant ideological success. For a short time, it succeeded in preserving a vision about the purpose of hockey that stretched back to Arthur Farrell's soaring 1899 declarations about the connections between "Canada's Royal Game" and preparing gentlemen for the trials of life. Even as that noble dream wavered, Canadian universities could look for support to their American counterparts where amateurism was, rhetorically at least, safeguarded and secure.[24] If shining, that moment was brief. When, after World War II, Canadians returned to play college hockey in the United States, they did so most often as recruited players for American teams, a practice that was accompanied by rancor from both sides of the border.

America: The AAU and the NCAA

Amateur hockey also diverged from the NHL in many American markets. In 1930, for instance, despite the Depression's rising hardships, Texas boosters were optimistic, announcing the creation of the Texas Inter-City Hockey League as a "step nearer the eventual formation of a professional circuit." In truth, it was no league at all, but a tournament that pitted regional champs from San Antonio, Houston, Dallas, and Tulsa. These operations lacked the luster of the NHL, yet they earned the support of local businesses and fraternal associations. That same year, the Atwater Kent team of Dubuque, Iowa, reported a twenty-one-game schedule against the likes of the Clutes of Waterloo, Silver Radio, Boy-rites, and Links Studio. And the Bank Italy Club of San Francisco reported games against the Athens AC and the Italia Vertus Club.[25]

Such activity caught the attention of a major sport organization, and it wasn't the NHL or its affiliates. In 1930 the Amateur Athletic Union (AAU) moved into a void left by the USAHA's collapse. The AAU had firm control of American Olympic efforts in some two dozen sports, but this did not yet include hockey. Sixteen of the AAU's regional districts were already sponsoring hockey championships, and the next step was to assert control over the Olympic team and (re)establish an amateur model for governance. It promised—in a slap at the likes of the Eveleth Reds—"any overenthusiasm of locally patriotic citizens or others with commercial motives will not be permitted to result in a team with any players of doubtful amateur standing."[26]

But someone was going to make money. In 1935, Frederick Rubien, the AAU's ice hockey committee chair, sounded like Tex Rickard when he declared that "under AAU supervision" ice hockey had "firmly established itself as America's national winter sport." His supporting numbers dripped with dollar signs: "More than 2,000,000 spectators witnessed sanctioned contests during the 1934–35 season," with regular crowds packing large venues such as Madison Square Garden. The AAU, whose offices depended on a percentage of the gate receipts from senior competition, staged and hyped playoffs at big arenas. That year the Chicago Baby Ruths edged Walter Brown's Boston Olympics in a two-game, most-goals showdown. Rubien's one lament was that the big rinks shut down their ice before the AAU could negotiate a North American championship with Canada's Allan Cup winner. Such a match would have "become one of the major sport attractions of the North American continent." The AAU intended to grow its own game, independent of the NHL.[27]

AAU senior leagues, however, had a festering flaw. Upon his return from the 1936 GaPa games and the governance brouhaha, American Olympic Association treasurer Gustavus Kirby announced with disgust that amateur hockey was "becoming a stench in the nostrils of honest sportsmen." American sportswriters sneezed their own disdain—at Kirby's hypocrisy—but they also hacked at the AAU. The *New York Daily Mirror*'s Dan Parker blasted the "phony purity" of the Eastern Amateur Hockey League. Players were getting paid. Eveleth's Connie Pleban recalled his mid-1930s experience with the Chicago Baby Ruths, a team sponsored by the Curtiss Candy Company, whose eye was on winning a national championship. This meant getting the best talent. "I was paid $25 a week," Pleban recalled, "to do some fictitious job like cutting out paper dolls."[28]

AAU hypocrisy was a hot topic. And it brought challengers. Today, the NCAA is the favorite piñata for journalists to brickbat on issues of exploitation, commercialism, and duplicity. But in the 1920s the NCAA was the underdog, the new face on the block, only a decade old, and it was determined to control its sports. If the NCAA wanted to win a war of governance, it needed traction as a superior brand. This led the association to begin developing rules for sports beyond football, its initial focus. Collegiate hockey programs had used the rules of other governing bodies. In November 1920, for instance, representatives from Penn, Princeton, Yale, Cornell, and Dartmouth met with an eye on creating a "national association" to serve as a "governing body for all intercollegiate hockey" and to "increase the general play of the game in the west." At that point the group simply adopted the rules of Canadian universities "with minor changes."[29]

The NCAA started its own hockey rules committee in 1926. It was chaired by Albert Prettyman, coach and athletic director at Hamilton College. Rufus Trimble, a faculty member at Columbia University, served as secretary-editor. For any governing body, rules were crucial in developing "brand identity." The NCAA launched a brand war, and language was a crucial tool in this struggle. But language needs a medium, and so in 1928, the association took control of the three-decades-old Spalding *Ice Hockey Guide*, thus assuring a national circulation of its rules and its philosophy. From the beginning, Rufus Trimble maintained that his committee and its brand would nurture skill over "rough play" and thereby distance "intercollegiate" from "professional" hockey.[30]

At times, there were missteps, such as with the offside rule. The Montreal Game had swept away its early competitors—ice polo and bandy—in part because its *restrictions* on forward passing made it seem more "scientific." By the 1920s, however, professional leagues (led by the PCHA) were liberalizing their rules to allow forward passing within (but not across) defensive, center, and offensive zones. In the meantime, American collegians stuck stubbornly to their purist sense of a scientific game. This required clarifying multiple situations of "onside" and "offside" play. For instance, the 1928 NCAA rulebook contained eight pages of detailed diagrams that explained the numerous offside situations, including such esoteric moments as "offside or onside following a rebound against the end boards," a shot, or an intercepted pass.[31]

The branding battle demanded close attention to language. In 1929, Trimble bristled at the NHL's use of the term "forward pass." He was quick to remind his readers:

> The new [NHL] rules retain the ambiguity of the term "forward pass." A "forward pass" would naturally be taken to mean the passing of the puck forward. This has always been permitted under all rules. It is off-side

play that has been prohibited; that is, the passing of the puck forward *to a player ahead of the player who made the pass.* While it may not be of great importance, it is regrettable that the draftsman has not used greater phraseiology [*sic*] in this regard.

For the NCAA Ice Hockey Committee, every word was a face off.[32]

In 1930, Trimble and his colleagues adopted NHL rules on offside. At the same time, however, they erected two fundamental distinctions in their brand. The first involved limits on body checking. NHL rules had no limits on *where* bodychecking was allowed, and earlier collegiate rules had a similar approach. In 1928 the NCAA committee changed this, adopting a two-minute penalty for body checking *outside* the defensive zone. This meant that both defensemen and forwards could pass or rush the puck up two-thirds of the ice surface without fear of being (legally) crushed by a hard shoulder or hip. Collegiate supporters suggested that this brought more skill to the game. NHL supporters suggested that it hampered the development of two key skills: delivering and avoiding checks.[33]

Fighting was the subject of even greater divergence. The original rules of Montreal hockey (1877) did not include fighting among its catalog of egregious fouls: "charging from behind, tripping, collaring, kicking, or shinning." In the decades that followed, the list grew longer, but a referee had full range to penalize objectionable behavior "for any time in his discretion." By the early 1920s most governing bodies were spelling out penalty types and times with more detail, and "fighting" or "slugging" were now among them. In 1921, for instance, the NHL rules listed fighting as a "match" foul that merited a punishment ranging from a ten-minute penalty to a game disqualification—"such length of time as in the opinion of the referee shall constitute an adequate penalty."[34]

The very first set of NCAA rules (1926) was unequivocal: "Slugging incurs a five-minute penalty and disqualification of the offending player for the remainder of the game." Two years later, the phrase was expanded to include "slugging, fighting, fisticuffs, or attempting to hit or slug." Meanwhile, in 1930, the NHL reassessed fighting from a discretionary match penalty to a "major" penalty of five minutes' duration with no disqualification. The NCAA Hockey Committee was clearly aware of this divergence. New editor Louis Keller wrote in 1933 that "in some cases fighting and 'dirty' play may add interest and increase attendance, nevertheless the type of rough play that develops into slugging, kicking, and near riots on the ice is not in harmony with the principles of sportsmanship which are advocated by schools and colleges and hence should be strictly ruled out of the game." This "firewall" has been in place ever since.[35]

In these ways, the NCAA Committee created clear lines between American collegiate and professional hockey. Yale's coach Larry Noble recognized this divergence in a 1929 interview published in the *Boston Globe*. He was not afraid that the NHL would "smother" the collegiate game. The pro hockey fan, he said, "looks for and tries to stimulate the 'fighting instinct' of the players" so that an initial duel of sticks and fists expand to a team "fracas" followed by a "glorious riot," which would leave the fan "particularly gorged with delight." College hockey was quite different. The core interest, he claimed, "is centered around the team and the college, not around the spectacle or the gate receipts." Noble's naivety notwithstanding, for the next forty years NCAA rules increasingly defined hockey for the vast majority of American players and many fans, who came to appreciate a style that had far less hitting and fighting than the Canadian-dominated NHL and its minor leagues. The divergence seriously reduced the chances that Americans would get the chance play in the NHL. By the 1950s, almost none did.[36]

The NCAA did not sponsor a national championship until 1948, so colleges competed in regional associations and leagues as they had done since the 1890s. But programs mushroomed in the 1920s. Eastern hockey sprouted in New York and New England. Midwest hockey grew steadily, with a band of small colleges like St. Olaf and large universities, including Michigan, Minnesota, and Wisconsin, composing the Western Collegiate Conference.[37] The Far West was a hotbed of growth for two decades. Cal, USC, and UCLA had teams by 1929, along with Saint Mary's and Occidental. UCLA's correspondent to the *NCAA Guide* was optimistic: "Due to added interest shown by the public and student body, ice hockey, a winter sport, has come to hold a place in intercollegiate athletics of sunny Southern California." Coached by hockey pioneer Dr. Charles Hartley, who had brought the Montreal game to Germany in the years before World War I, USC's Trojans put up a thirty-five-game win streak from 1930 through 1933, produced by players imported from places such as Brandon, Manitoba; Ely, Michigan; St Paul, Minnesota; and Boston. Not a single Californian was on the squad. With a limited number of indoor rinks, however, West Coast hockey was difficult to sustain. Cal briefly dropped the sport in 1936–37. A correspondent wrote in the *NCAA Guide* the following year that attempts to resurrect the program enjoyed "only slight progress" largely "due to the presence of a professional team in San Francisco and inadequate rink facilities." A decade later, there was only Cal, which in 1949 had to play all its games on the road. By 1951, even it had disappeared.[38]

Most high schools adopted NCAA rules. Their programs grew in the old hotbeds of Michigan, Minnesota, Chicago, New York, and New England. For instance, the Bay State Interscholastic Ice Hockey League, which formed in 1932, contained schools that once belonged to other leagues in Greater Boston, some even back to the days of ice polo: Needham, Waltham, Walpole, Boston College High School, and others. The eight-team league held a round-robin schedule and a playoff. In all, more than thirty thousand fans attended league games in 1937. A year later, the total attendance for league play had doubled. The desire for titles drove hockeytown schools like Melrose High School, long a Greater Boston power. In 1923 the *Spalding Guide* reported that Melrose claimed the "national interscholastic championship," then hunted for greater glory by taking on the Earl Grey club of Quebec for the international crown. After losing, Melrose claimed that Earl Grey had "ineligible players and thus they should forfeit the title." All of this parroted the collegians and senior amateurs.[39]

Grassroots growth was limited by the lack of indoor, artificial ice arenas. Not everyone could practice or play in the Boston Arena, Boston Garden, Madison Square Garden, or St. Paul Hippodrome. But rink building, both outdoor and indoor, still advanced. It is fair to say that schoolboy hockey grew in the 1920s, staggered during the Depression, but survived with a solid base. Although not a true census of American hockey, the *NCAA Guide* of 1938–39 included a list of teams hosted by schools, colleges, and amateur clubs; 387 of them, representing twenty-three states, with the bulk from Massachusetts (87), Minnesota (53), and New York (59). Teams from high schools totaled 201, amateur clubs 110, and colleges 76. It was a strong foundation for a postwar surge.[40]

Founding the Amateur Hockey Association of the United States (AHAUS)

The AAU and NCAA each offered their constituents order and organization for a growing *American* sport outside the NHL and Canadian orbit. They succeeded, generally, in staying out of each other's way. But the interwar years spawned one last American battle over who would rule outside of collegiate and school hockey—the AAU or an upstart competitor, the Amateur Hockey Association of the United States (AHAUS), a commercially oriented operation that developed close ties to the CAHA.

The AAU's problems were largely self-inflicted. Take the case of AAU senior hockey at Madison Square Garden (MSG), under the watch of Thomas F. Lockhart, described as "an Irishman of great energy and humor." In 1971 Lockhart recalled his early days at the Garden working for Tex Rickard's protégé John Reed Kilpatrick: "My experience had only been running boxing shows at the Garden," he emphasized, when Kilpatrick tapped him to strengthen the amateur hockey card, which was not "paying off." "My idea to promote hockey was the same I had used for boxing promotions," he said: "cut rate tickets and contacts." It was a formula for success. In 1933 Lockhart helped create the Eastern Amateur Hockey League, which included the Atlantic City Sea Gulls, the Baltimore Orioles, the Hershey Bears, the Bronx Tigers, the NYAC, St. Nicks, and Crescent Hamilton AC. In 1935 the Crescents moved from Brooklyn to MSG and became the New York Rovers. They were successful on the ice and phenomenal at the gate, often packing MSG with ten thousand to twelve thousand fans.[41]

Packing the Garden meant putting top talent on the ice, and that meant Canadian players. This triggered troubles with the AAU. In 1937 hockey writer Thomas Deegan noted that the Rovers had only one American-born player; "The others are from Alberta, Ontario, Saskatoon and Vancouver." It did not take a muckraker to wonder why "amateur" hockey attracted such a group. The AAU should have launched a wholesale investigation of the league, but it did not, and the reason was economic. The EAHL paid a percentage of gate receipts to the AAU, whose approach to control was typically to pounce on a single or small case to make a point for public consumption. In March 1937 it picked the Baltimore Orioles of the EAHL. It was a mistake.[42]

As the season was reaching its conclusion, the AAU's regional office ruled the Orioles "ineligible" for further play because it "was not satisfied with the amateur status of the players and questioned their means of livelihood." Loss of the AAU "sanction" meant that any club playing against the Orioles would also become ineligible. Lockhart responded that his league would "continue to function whether the AAU sanctions it or not" and would "refuse to pay to the AAU office the percentage of the gate receipts it has been collecting." He then announced a meeting with representatives of the Quebec [Amateur] Hockey Association to form an independent international league for two seasons. The gloves were dropped. AAU hockey chairman Frederick Rubien was in a tight spot. He kept quiet as the 1936–37 season wound down, but in December 1937 he bellowed the AAU position in an open threat to all senior teams and players: compete against the EAHL or a new renegade group in Michigan, and you will lose all eligibility for national or international competition. This power, he claimed, was "recognized by the Ligue Internationale de Hockey sur Glace."[43]

Lockhart was not alone in his battle with the AAU. In Boston, thirty-two-year-old Walter A. Brown ascended to become general manager of the Boston Garden and Arena after the sudden death of his father, George V. Brown, in October 1937. Walter had led American contingents, under the AAU umbrella, in World and Olympic tournaments since 1931, but he now switched his allegiance.[44] In March 1940 the Boston Arena hosted the "first annual national championship of the United States Amateur Hockey Association," which fielded eight teams from New England, New York, and New Jersey, including the all-Francophone St. Dom's from Lewiston, Maine. A *Boston Globe* story—likely written by an Arena publicist—predicted that the tournament "shapes up as the finest 'pure' tournament to be staged here in years." The word "pure" was code for players who were real amateurs, a level down from the Rovers or the Olympics. More interesting was the USAHA brand name. That association was long defunct. The writer intended to say the Amateur Hockey Association of the United States (AHAUS), a title conjured in defiance of AAU authority.[45]

Walter Brown's Boston Olympics soon joined the Rovers in the EAHL, and news accounts suggest that winning the EAHL also meant winning the AHAUS crown. Meanwhile, the annual AAU championships attracted teams from across the nation. AHAUS was at first a weak brand, with limited recognition and no real power. Later "official" accounts carefully articulated the AHAUS founding on October 29, 1937, in New York City. But the attendees were almost all from the EAHL and the Metro area. Official histories say little about the next decade of AHAUS—because there was little activity. An AAU-AHAUS war did not break out because there was soon a real war going on. With no Olympics or World Championships, there was no national team to fight over. Squabbling about sports governance receded to the margins of popular interest. That changed soon after the American troops returned in a postwar mass that included army staff officer Lt. Col. Walter A. Brown.[46] There would be Olympics in 1948 and a battle over who would name and sanction the American team.

How to Play: Diverging Hockey Styles

Central to the story of NHL ascendancy was a harmonizing of rules. The movement to standardize began in earnest in the late 1920s, and the CAHA-NHL agreement of 1936 insisted on it. NCAA limits on checking and fighting were important exceptions, but after 1936, NHL rules governed the widest swath of players. However, it would be a mistake to conclude that because one set of regulations increasingly governed the sport, the *playing* of hockey was everywhere the same. In fact, as rules changes opened up the ice for forward passing and as the sheer numbers of players, coaches, and hockey thinkers expanded, the ice pad became a place of remarkable innovation.

By 1945, hockey was a faster and more tactically rich game than it had been in 1920. It may have been one of those eras when the game naturally *evolved*. More likely, changes were attributable to other, more measurable causes: material factors and new values. These included more indoor, artificial, and reliable ice, providing more practices and games; greater demand for "science" among consumers; and bigger and fitter players.[47]

Lamentably, much of the discourse of innovation is irretrievably gone. Canada's great "hockey men" from this era were frustratingly mum on what made their teams successful, unlike the modern day, where youth hockey schools, coaches clinics, radio and television commentators, the daily press, and online chat lists hash out strategy and tactics in minute detail. "All during my younger days as a hockey player and later as a coach and referee," post–World War II Canadian hockey guru Lloyd Percival recalled in 1951, "in practically any other major sport many and varied books were available, but in [Canada, in] hockey there was none."[48] Perhaps most Canadians felt as New York Ranger boss Lester Patrick did. Canadians didn't need such things; to them, "hockey is inherent."[49]

If Canadians didn't need instruction, many Americans *did*, and so numerous experts published an expanding series of popular articles and textbooks explaining the game to interested neophytes and inviting them to take it up.[50] Two volumes stood above the rest in popularity and in authority: *Hockey: The Fastest Game on Earth* (1938), written by Manitoba-born Mervyn "Red" Dutton, who played for the Montreal Maroons and the New York Americans before becoming the latter team's coach and general manager in 1936; and, *Hockey, for Spectator, Coach and Player* (1939), the largest compendium of all of them at 367 pages, a surgically precise breakdown of every aspect of the game, authored by Princeton head coach Richard F. Vaughan and former Yale coach Holcomb York.[51]

Overly technical and laden with diagrams, these manuals parsed hockey into minute segments and robbed its real attraction: flow, intuition, and anticipation, the skills that couldn't be taught. Vaughan and York's 1939 tome was encyclopedic. Scattered among chapters on "individual elements," "defensive elements," "offensive elements," and "fundamentals of goaltending" (among others), were sixty-two figures and 157 diagrams. It must have sucked the life out of the game for its readers. Still, these volumes are important historical documents. They show us how contemporaries thought. Between vapid instructions on "how to hold the stick" and perform a "give and go," we can see something of the philosophy of the day, an attempt to apply "system" to chaos. "Dick Vaughan is not a Canadian," Lester Patrick quipped in the perfunctory foreword to Vaughan and York's *Hockey*, "but an American and one boasting no experience or background in the sport other than that of an intercollegiate player or coach. Dick Vaughan never played professionally. . . . But . . . [e]ndowed with a keen analytical mind, Mr. Vaughan has made an intensive study of hockey in all its phases . . . and even after thirty-five years . . . as player, coach, and manager, I have learned a lot of things from . . . this book."[52] Talk about feinting him with damn praise. Had he looked closely, Patrick would have seen that Vaughan was, indeed, an astute student of the game and its changes. *Hockey* was the product of four years of focused study—in person, in documents, and in film—of all levels of play. It provides a snapshot of how far the game had come by 1939, especially as to systemic planning.

By the 1930s the days of old-style, free-for-all, unplanned action had long passed. Now, for Vaughan, all teams played (with variations) one of three *systems*: "defensive, offensive, and wide-open hockey." The defensive system was heir to the old, prewar onside game, in which teams did little forechecking and waited for individual chances to counterattack. The offensive system focused wholly on devil-may-care attacking, dumping the puck, and using all five skaters to pursue and pin opponents in their own zone and maximize scoring chances. The most novel system, and in Vaughan's estimation the most creditable one, was the wide-open system, which involved "pressure, checking back against counterpressure . . . skating fast and hard . . . in all three zones."[53] Wide-open hockey was, for him, the "true" game, a symbol of all that was modern, strategic and attractive about the sport.

Vaughan's depiction was necessarily overdrawn and neat, but there is evidence that *real* hockey was planned and played in each of these three ways. The old, defensive system was always purportedly on its way out, but in truth it survived the era. US-born Frank "Shag" Shaughnessy, legendary coach at McGill (1919–27), described what he called "five-man defense" in a rare interview in *Sport Story Magazine*, a juvenile fiction serial. A style of play invented by the 1915 NHA Ottawa Senators, the five-man defense, had a simple, defend-first–counterattack-second premise. "The moment one of your forwards misses a shot for goal," Shaughnessy explained,

> your forwards dash back to their own half of the ice, form a defensive line, and wait for their opponents to bring the attack to them. Your center blocks off the opposing wings out toward the side boards. If an opponent gets through your first line, the defense men are waiting for him. If you are able to intercept a pass, or get the puck by a poke check, you are all set to start another offensive. Your opponents seldom are able to get well started. You keep the puck in their territory, or in center ice, and they haven't had a chance to score.[54]

This is akin to what today's coaches call a "1–4 forecheck" or "trap," perhaps the most conservative system a team can play. McGill shifted tactics after 1924, but other teams persisted, with variations on the theme.[55] The Senators continued the scheme with success well into the 1930s, much to the chagrin of opponents' fans and journalists alike. After one Senators-Leafs tilt that the home team lost, the *Toronto Star*'s Charlie Querrie chirped: "We have often remarked that the best defensive is the offensive and we still believe it even if Ottawa won on Saturday."[56]

The general trajectory in strategy favored Shaughnessy's transition (and Querrie's sentiment). "Offense-first" was swept in by a new generation of players. "When I came into professional hockey," WHL (1923–26) and NHL (1926–37) pro Bill Cook remembered, "the old rough-and-tough boys were . . . on their way out. Younger players, coming into the game with new ideas, had begun to change things."[57] "Play as much of the game as you can on your opponents' half of the ice," Springfield College coach (and former University of Manitoba player) George B. Affleck admonished young readers in *Sport Story Magazine* in 1926. "The team that can keep the puck in its opponents' territory, and that keeps the enemy goalie busy, is the team that wins hockey games."[58]

Offense-first was simple in principle and a product of the new rules that allowed forward passing in all three zones. There was a tightening of penalty calls for interference and a softening of physical play. All of this opened up the game for offense. "The first major change," wrote Vaughan, "took the form of fore checking as an offensive measure."[59] Forwards were now encouraged to harry opponents in their defensive zone. As they did that, their defensemen followed up the play and joined the forecheck—all five players within the attacking zone. "When I first played hockey the defenseman was solely a player used for body checking and blocking," Red Dutton recalled in 1938. "Today . . . defense positions are further up the ice and there are no . . . traditions riveting the defensemen back in the positions they held near the goal when they were known as point and cover point. The winning hockey team now is one with five forwards." The best example of a player using this new style, in Dutton's view, was Eddie Shore, "who carries a big load of the Boston Bruins attack."[60]

The newest scheme was more radical. "Wide-open" hockey envisioned the game in the same ways that West Point–educated Civil War generals conceptualized strategy. For them, winning battles was about geometry and pace.[61] Articulators of this style saw the ice as a series of three vertically divided geometric zones, the defending, neutral, and attacking zones in which each player had different responsibilities. Most novel, however, was that wide-open advocates also divided the whole ice horizontally, into three "lanes" to be patrolled by each of the three forwards. Forwards were admonished to "skate your lane." "In pro hockey," Dutton observed, "it is generally accepted that wings never cross the ice, but protect their own areas—which puts the burden of protecting center ice on the all important center man. . . . The wings should never unnecessarily roam from the alleys that run the length of the rink from one corner to the other."[62] From their respective lanes, forwards could fashion breakout plays from their own zone, passing plays to methodically move the puck up the ice and toward their opponent's net. Forwards' zone play was designed to confront defenders who had the challenge of covering the whole breadth of the ice and carving out space for an uncontested shot on net.

Pace was equally important. In the wide-open system, when the puck changed hands, forwards were expected to back check along their lanes with vigor and determination. Speed was critical. No opponent was to be allowed the luxury of uncontested possession of the puck in any area on the ice. Equally, speed was critical to this system's concept of attack. Lane play—spreading out forwards horizontally—was designed to find attacking forwards space to move, but they had to move quickly. The wide-open system called explicitly for defensemen to jump into the rush and outnumber their opponents in an attack, to switch quickly, once their team gained possession of the puck, from defender to attacker. That idea was new in the interwar years, and it redefined the sort of work expected of defensemen. The *Toronto Star*'s Andy Lytle noted this in his account of a convincing Leafs' victory over the St. Louis Eagles in 1935. "Toronto's defence four occasionally complain because they are under orders to protect [goalie George] Hainsworth at all times and yet must rush whenever such an opening confronts them. . . . [But t]he sound nature of this school of hockey thought was beautifully illustrated Saturday night . . . the Leaf defenders swept down the ice and made the odd man, as used to be done in lacrosse."[63] The Leafs were a sound model for "wide-open hockey" in the 1930s, but it was Lester Patrick's Rangers who perfected the system. It was a style well suited to the city in which they played. After one game in which the Rangers trimmed the defense-oriented Senators, the *Globe*'s Bert Perry gushed: "The Rangers are playing hockey as it should be played, and the way the fans want to see it played. . . . The death knell of defensive hockey is being sounded in the N.H.L."[64]

Wide-open hockey privileged the game's gifted scorers and, for the first time, *whole lines of forwards* whose combination play resulted in goals. The wide-open system of hockey helped make heroes of the Leafs' Kid Line (Charlie Conacher, Busher Jackson, and Joe Primeau, 1929–36), the Rangers' Bread Line (Bill Cook, Bun Cook, Frank Boucher), the Montreal Maroons' "S" Line (Babe Siebert, Nels Stewart, Hooley Smith), the Bruins' Dynamite Line (Cooney Weiland, Dutch Gainor, Dit Clapper) and Kraut Line (Milt Schmidt, Woody Dumart, Bobby Bauer), and the Montreal Canadiens' Speedball Line (Howie Morenz, Aurèle Joliat, Johnny Gagnon). Collective glory took its place alongside individual celebrity.

And yet, opening up the game by no means meant the "death knell of defensive hockey." The offensive, five-man system and "wide-open hockey" were simply too risky for some teams, especially those with a deficit of talent. Then, as now, why not just hunker down, keep it close, and see if the puck bounces your way on a counterattack? Old-school defensive hockey remained too useful to discard completely. Coaches never forgot that if half of the challenge was scoring, the other half was keeping the puck out

249

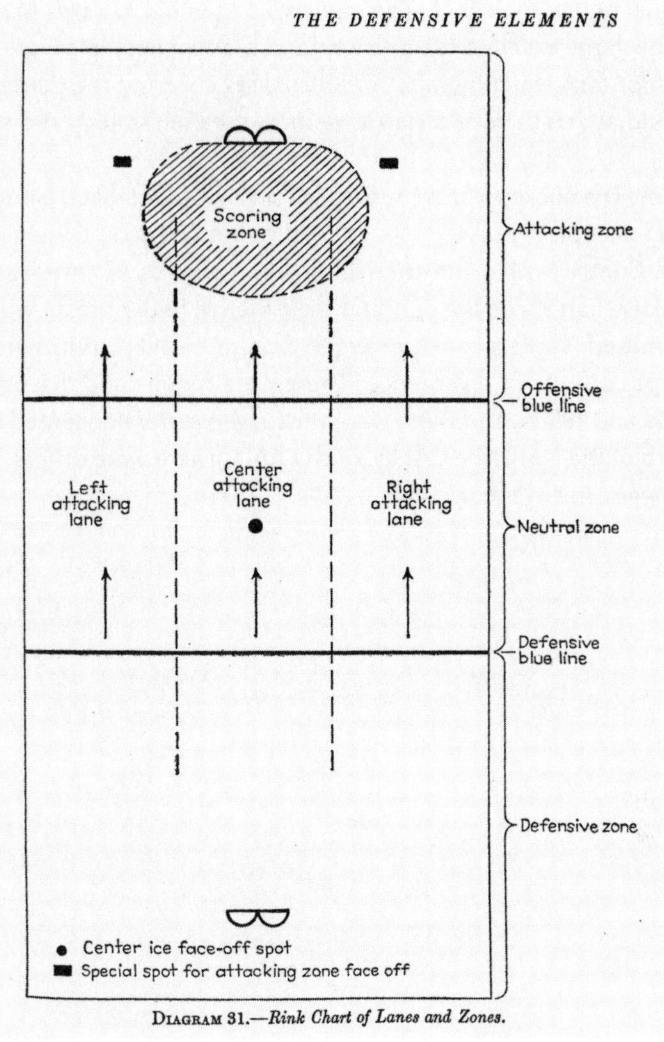

"Rink Chart of Lanes and Zones" in Richard F. Vaughan and Holcomb York, *Hockey for Spectator, Coach and Player* (New York: McGraw-Hill, 1939), 123.

of your own net. Depending on the time of the season, injuries, and varying opponents' strengths, a team normally committed to a "wide-open" system might adopt a defensive posture; or, an old-fashioned "five-man defense" might throw caution to the wind and play a five-man attack. To stick slavishly to one system would be foolish; good teams needed more conceptual agility than that. The effect was exciting. No two teams ever played the game exactly the same way, and that opened up a world of possibilities for fans watching and for journalists covering the games, those who would attach their own narrative meanings to strategy and style.

By the time the hockey world churned within a global conflict, a broad market stood occupied, bureaucratized, and rationalized: a new regime for a new era. Control in North America, however, was at all times uncertain and shakier than some bosses (and their friends in the press) would ever have admitted. While a core converged around the NHL, one can also see important currents of divergence. There were rogues and discontents in the 1920s and 1930s, and there were those who never consented to living in the orb of the NHL, the CAHA, or the AAU. There were others still who weren't welcome in those places.

14

Teams and Leagues of Their Own: 1920–1945

In March 1928 the *Brantford (Ontario) Expositor* was impressed with the hockey skills of "foreign-born . . . boys, who seem to have a little more punch than some of our own lads." The names of Italian-origin players on the Northern Ontario Junior Hockey League winners from Sault Ste. Marie included Delabbio, Adamo, and Dorazzio. "Many good boys are being produced by the parents who came here from farther east in Europe than the British Isles. . . . Color or creed does not matter if you have something above the ordinary in you." It was overstated, but the writer's sentiments represented something bigger about belonging and the ownership of the game. Many children of 1880s- and 1890s-era "new" immigrants from central, eastern, and southern Europe *became* North American by playing North American sport.[1]

In the interwar years, hockey writers often acknowledged diversity among players, though they rarely elaborated on their comments. To be Icelandic Canadian (like Frank Frederickson and the 1920 Canadian Olympics entry), or Italian Canadian (like the Canadiens' Silvio Mantha)—white ethnics—meant nothing pertaining to performance on the ice or *style* in performance. Their sort of diversity was nothing more than an intriguing trait used by sportswriters to spice their game narratives. In one 1928 *New Haven Journal-Courier* piece, the New York Americans' "Jewish Hockey Star" Sammy Rothschild was championed as an exemplar of his race, "certain to become one of the most popular players in Manhattan, where a Hebrew athlete never fails to draw crowds to the gate." But there was no claim that his Jewishness influenced the way he approached or played the game.[2]

The same sort of discourse shaded the old central-Canadian shibboleth matching the Dominion's two founding peoples in a simulated ethnic war on the ice: *les Canadiens* versus either the Anglo-Montreal Maroons or the Maple Leafs from of white, British "Toronto the Good." These mashups were mythical, commercial bunkum. Toronto's *Globe* promoted one March 1933 game between the Canadiens and Leafs, asking, "Can the Experience and Speed of the Latin-French Habitants Withstand the Determined Assault of the Anglo-Saxon Leafs? Tonight's Battle Will Tell the Tale." Readers would have understood that language as only imagined symbolism. The reality was different. "The Canadiens, called the 'Habitants,' are the heroes of the French-Canadian residents. The Maroons are the red-hot favorites of the citizens of English, Irish, and Caledonian extraction," sports columnist John Kieran noted in the *New York Times* in December 1933. "However, the managers and owners will go only just so far in . . . applying the language test to a hockey player who may help them. Thus the Maroons enlisted the services of M'sieu Dave Trottier and the Flying Frenchmen have a Riley and a Burke on their side. . . . Howie Morenz, of course, is a lineal descendant of the Swiss family Morenz." For Anglophones, Francophones, and other white ethnics, this discourse was playful but empty.[3] Hockey's embrace of diversity, however, did not extend very far; the game was still essentially white and male. Black, Native, and women skaters were marginalized on the ice and off, exceptions that existed dramatically to prove the rule, acceptable as long as they were few in number, subordinate, and not a serious challenge to the sport's social order.

Maracle on Ice

Race hovered over North American hockey in the 1920s and 1930s. Even as the sport's whiteness widened to embrace new immigrants, its boundaries also thickened. Those who remained outside its color lines—blacks and Natives—became even more "other." Color was made to matter and racial difference was equated with how they played the game. Even Baltimore's "All-Negro Weekly," the *Afro-American*, adopted this qualifying language in 1931, in its ambivalent "praise" of one schoolboy (probably Dickie Johnson), a standout hockey player at Rindge Tech in Cambridge, Massachusetts. "Brother, that's going some, if you ask me. I'm not exactly a 'suth'n gentleman' but I'm surprised. Our people do not take to winter sports, and when one of our boys deliberately steps into this field almost unknown to us as a group and makes good, he deserves three long cheers."[4] No doubt Johnson and others would have preferred to be recognized for their skills as hockey players, full stop. Surely, the same was true for Bud Maracle.[5]

Elmer Henry "Bud" Maracle's career sheds light on this process. He was born in 1904 in little Ayr in south-central Ontario. His family was of Haudenosaunee (Mohawk) descent and moved when Bud was a boy, first to Midland and later Haileybury, a hockey hotbed in the northeastern part of the province. There, Bud Maracle began a career almost a quarter-century long, in which he played and excelled at every position but goaltender. In 1921–22 he led Haileybury High School to the Northern Ontario Hockey Association (NOHA) junior series title, once scoring 6 goals in a game against neighboring rival New Liskeard.[6] Maracle's performances landed him a spot at left defense with the regional NOHA junior powerhouse North Bay Trappers, where he toiled for three years, leading them in 1923–24 to the Copeland Cup.[7] In 1925–26, he returned to southern Ontario to play for the Goodyears in the Toronto Industrial League, one of the many loops that had not yet become affiliated with the Ontario Hockey Association and, therefore, operated outside of its strict policy of amateurism. It must have been in Toronto where Maracle was noticed by big-league scouts. In August 1926 he signed a tryout contract with the NHL's New York Rangers.[8] When he failed to make the big club at the Rangers' October training camp,[9] he was assigned to the their Canadian-American Hockey League affiliate, the Springfield Indians, where he excelled for six seasons (1926–32) and helped the team to consecutive Can-Am League championships in 1927 and 1928. In February 1931, Maracle's NHL moment arrived. Called up from the Indians to buttress the Rangers in their playoff run, he played creditably in fifteen games and contributed 4 points, as the Rangers lost to Chicago in the Stanley Cup semifinals.[10] But he didn't stick. In fall 1931 he returned to the Can-Am for three more seasons before he migrated westward, playing out his career for minor-pro teams in Tulsa, Detroit, Toledo, and, finally, San Diego.[11]

If Toronto was where Maracle got his big break, it was also there—in big-city, white, prosperous and Protestant Toronto—where his race became a matter of public interest and a perennial descriptor that followed him everywhere. After 1926 the press routinely identified him as "Maracle, the Indian,"[12] "the full-blooded redskin,"[13] "Chief Maracle,"[14] and other variations. Thrice he was featured in Associated Press wire blurbs that declared him the professional game's first and only Native player; his ascension to

Bud Maracle and the Springfield Indians, ca. 1927–28 (Courtesy of Angus Carroll)

the NHL in March 1931 occasioned an AP news blast titled "Redskin Icer" run by dozens of American newspapers.[15] Though these brief blurbs championed his talents as a skater and checker, his race made him newsworthy.[16] There was an expectation that being Indian made his game different. "Buddy Maracle . . . is a full-blooded Indian," the *New Haven Journal-Courier* noted in February 1928, "and his racial characteristics—hard to hurt and untiring—make him one of the most colorful players."[17]

In Springfield and New Haven he was a clutch goal scorer, sure-handed in tight situations in front of the net.[18] In the Indians' 1928 Can-Am Fontaine Cup final series against Quebec, Maracle "played . . . brilliantly," according to the *New York Times*, and scored the winning goal.[19] In the 203 games he played over six seasons in pro hockey's best minor league, Bud Maracle scored 42 goals and 33 assists and earned 240 minutes in penalties.[20] Why he didn't stay in the NHL is not wholly clear, but there are clues. At 5'11" and 195 pounds, he was bigger than the average player. But at least one rumor circulated that he wouldn't willingly play a hard game and, in Springfield, had to be threatened in order to get the desired result.[21] Taciturn, insular, hard to coach: the contemporary stereotype of Native American athlete would have been hard for Maracle to escape—just as it was for Tom Longboat, Fred Simpson, and Louis Sockalexis.[22] The rumor is belied by the facts. The newspaper record of his games reveals him as a physical player and, more than occasionally, a willing combatant when the gloves were dropped. In one Springfield-Boston game in February 1927, Maracle and the Tigers' George Redding were given matching minors for roughing in the game's overtime period. In the box "for only a few seconds," the *Boston Globe* reported, they began to fight. It took fifteen minutes and three policemen to stop them.[23] "Soft" is hardly a fitting descriptor. In truth, injuries plagued Maracle and came at the worst possible times. He was apparently dropped from the Bronx Tigers in December 1931 because "mishaps had kept him from the line-up." Springfield was willing to give him a chance that year, but as coach Frank Carroll stipulated, "he must show that he is right in practice before the club will offer him a contract."[24] Healthy? Compliant? "Right" was a loaded word.

Color and Control: The St. Catharines Orioles

Maracle's example is instructive because of his prominence and the willingness of the press to imply that his race had something to do with how he played. But the branding of nonwhite hockey was even more conspicuous when whole teams of nonwhites played and captured the attention of the press. In the 1920s and 1930s, a handful of black and First Nations teams assembled in North America, most often as commercial novelty. Their promoters banked on the idea that contests between "Colored" and white teams would sell tickets. White spectators and the press puzzled at the racial incongruity (how do *they* play hockey?). But they already had a preferred answer. A nonwhite *style* had to be different, and less, than the establishment game.

The expectation of aesthetic difference was attached to any all-black team. It motivated Northern League minor-baseball owner and Minneapolis resident R. L.Voelz's proposal to organize an "all-Race" squad to tour the States in 1934–35.[25] The same curiosity attended the games of the Niagara Falls (Ontario) Swallows, later called the "Coloured Ambassadors," who played a series of nonleague matches against commercial teams in 1937 and 1938, and an all-Chinese hockey team that played in Montreal in the 1930s and 1940s.[26]

Black style was at the center of another hockey story, one that resurfaced decades later in newspapers, popular sports history books, and a 2000 *Maclean's* magazine issue that used it as an example of black progress in Canada's white national game.[27] The St. Catharines Orioles were an all-black squad that played two seasons in the Ontario Hockey Association's Niagara District Hockey League, in 1937 and 1938. "The first non-white hockey team on record was recently formed . . . and is creating a sensation in ice rink circles," the *Baltimore Afro-American*'s Niagara Falls correspondent reported in March 1937. "There have been players on white teams before, but this entire group is drawing crowds at every appearance."[28] The writer was wrong on both fronts. Though not numerous, black teams had indeed existed before 1937, most notably in the Colored Hockey League that thrived in the Maritimes, 1895–1930.[29] Moreover, the Orioles' biggest problem was that, after an initial surge of interest, they could not maintain fan interest. Their story shows that hockey as racial novelty could only go so far, and winning games trumped all.

The St. Catharines Orioles were a group of fifteen young men, members of the local British Methodist Episcopal Church, an institution central to the identity of the city's small African Canadian community of two hundred. Among them were some able players, including Amos and Laverne Dorsey, and the three Nicholson brothers (Hope, Doug, and Dick). In the mid-1930s these men played on an outdoor rink, on an abandoned lot near the Grout Silk Mills in downtown St. Catharines. It must have been there where, in 1936, they were "discovered" by local white sportsmen and transformed into the Orioles.

On February 19, 1937, the *St. Catharines Standard* announced that a new aggregation was formed: "Canada's Only All-Colored Hockey Team."[30] Clad in new orange-and-black sweaters and stockings, the team was a late entry into the intermediate division of Niagara District Hockey League, a collection of six local outdoor teams. The NDHL was venerable—the oldest continuously operating league in the province whose victor advanced to OHA playdowns.[31] The Orioles played their home games in the City Box Bowl (now Haig Bowl), an outdoor rink open to Niagara's winter weather.

Re-fashioning a group of black friends and co-parishioners as the Orioles was the brainchild of local white men, including Harold "Touch" Woods (1893–1941), the owner of a successful trucking company and a prominent figure in amateur sport in southern Ontario. Known for his organizational skills, he was manager in the late 1920s and early 1930s of the St. Catha-

St. Catharines (Ontario) Orioles, February 1937 (St. Catharines Museum, St. Catharines Standard Collection S1937.37.3.2)

rines Grads intermediate basketball team, seven-time provincial titleholders and Dominion champions in 1929. He founded the Niagara District Baseball League, a semiprofessional circuit, and operated the Transport Athletic Club, a local boxing fixture where some of the Orioles members trained.[32] In the mid-1930s he served as a district boxing commissioner for the Amateur Athletic Union of Canada. He was appointed a member of the Canadian Olympic Committee in 1939[33] and to the Ontario Athletic Commission[34] in 1940, just months before his widely mourned death at age forty-eight.[35]

Woods was also known for his beneficence and community spirit. One example of his philanthropy stands out. When George Bird, an unranked local boxer, qualified to represent Canada in the 1936 Summer Olympics by upsetting heavyweight favorite Tommy Osborne, he did not have the funds to get to Berlin. Woods found the money for Bird to go.[36] Woods was also one of a small handful of St. Catharines sportsmen who raised money for the construction of the city's first indoor rink with artificial ice,

Garden City Arena (1938); Woods himself loaned the funds needed for the rink's seating.[37] Woods then convinced Conn Smythe to move the Toronto Maple Leafs training camp to St. Catharines in 1939 and 1940, bringing big-league exhibition games to local fans.[38] And according to Hope Nicholson, Woods was among those who appeared one morning at the BME Church and convinced its members to form a hockey team.

The press plugged the Orioles as a curiosity; news of their existence spread quickly and widely.[39] Only one day after the *Standard*'s unveiling, the *Toronto Globe and Mail*'s Tommy Munns ran a column trumpeting the "Orioles . . . the only all-colored puck brigade cavorting in the Province." The *Toronto Star* ran a lengthy feature titled "Negro Puck Club" that included four photographs and a full-length column of text.[40] By late March word had reached Baltimore's *Afro-American* and the *Chicago Defender* (another prominent national black newspaper), who declared the Orioles beacons of racial progress.

Conversely, the white press's announcements and the few game reports that survive were tainted by overt racism. The *Niagara Falls (N.Y.) Gazette* referred to them as the "Duskies,"[41] and the *Standard* repeatedly called them "boys," worrying at one time that the team's biggest challenge would be to keep its star player, Amos Dorsey, from halting hockey game play to do a tap dance. Even as he lauded them, the *Star*'s feature writer noted that no one on the team was gainfully employed and that their talent was doubtful. "They may not get anywhere as pucksters, *but the club suah has colah . . . yeah mam*!" The *Globe and Mail* suggested that rather than Orioles, they should have been dubbed the "Black Birds" and said that they presented a "picture which would delight the eye of Octavus Ray Cohen," a 1920s writer from the American South whose novels played with the Sambo stereotype.[42] The use of grotesque, caricatured dialect was not uncommon in the pre–civil-rights-era press and was likely fueled in Canada by the exoticism of black subjects in a lily-white country. Still, the language betrays an unwillingness to consider the Orioles as serious athletes.

The Orioles were hardly a commitment to racial progress. They were created and then effectively abandoned because of money. They failed as a commercial commodity in an era when so much relied on revenues. First, they were not very good. In their inaugural "season" (shortened because of their late formation and then warm weather that melted outdoor ice), the Orioles played five games, losing four and tying one. In 1938 they played eight games and lost every one of them, going 0-6 in NDHL play.

Their final game involved a much-hyped trek to Guelph, Ontario, to play against a team of intermediate all-stars.[43] The result was grim. The Orioles were down 6–0 at the end of the first period and ultimately lost 17–7, even after they had agreed to take on two Guelph players for the last half of the game. Fans, disgruntled by the mismatch, "went after their money [they had] paid to see the game." One Guelph sportswriter who had hyped the game to boost ticket sales was embarrassed and claimed that he had been hoodwinked by mischievous advance press.[44]

The all-black Orioles, dressed up, registered in a proper league, and taken on the road, failed on the scoreboard. But aside from a few game promoters, most white fans would not have expected the Orioles to succeed and would have been surprised if they did. The newspapers described the Orioles as exhibiting a "lack of coaching and of condition"[45] and "loose play"; of playing the game with "careless abandon."[46] In their debut, a 10–6 loss to the Weston Bread team of the local commercial league, "several of the Orioles displayed a lack of acquaintance with the sticks they were carrying."[47] Occasional individual plays earned praise, such as Hope Nicholson's blistering shots or the frenetic skating of George "Ninny" West, "a whole show in himself."[48] But nothing would have convinced reporters that the Orioles were the real deal. Modern hockey—*white* hockey—involved speed, system, and science, the attributes the Orioles sorely lacked. Their white opponents, such as the Thorold Arena team that defeated them 9–2 in March 1937, all seemed to have "too much finish."[49] That the Orioles could not win against all-white teams must have been interpreted by readers as a convenient confirmation of the popular "truth": *real* hockey was the brand of hockey fashioned by the all-white NHL.

The Orioles experiment failed also because of bad timing. What was good news to most of the hockey community in St. Catharines, the coming of indoor ice, was bad news for the Orioles and probably their coup de grâce. The outdoor City Box Bowl was no place to stage a commercial venture, which required reliable ice, where admission could be charged. In 1938, St. Catharines built Garden City Arena, a state-of-the-art indoor facility with artificial ice and three thousand seats, making the city a viable platform for competitive commercial hockey.

Garden City Arena changed the meaning of hockey locally. Not all teams gained access (there was only one pad and too many teams). Those who played indoors were legitimized; those who did not were devalued. The local newspaper was remarkable in the early 1930s for the range of reporting on Niagara district hockey schedules and scores, but after the arena opened in 1938, if hockey did not happen there, in effect, it could not have been important. The Orioles never got to play in the arena, and reports of their games disappeared from the *Standard* completely after 1938. The mercurial rise and fall of the Orioles played out in just two seasons; there is no evidence that they took the ice in 1939. In the end, the Orioles made an important cultural statement about the color of "real" hockey in 1930s Canada, and they brought out among white sportswriters the general feeling that there was only a marginal place for nonwhites in Canada's national winter game. And it was in the margins where another interesting episode illuminating hockey's race played out.

The Cree and Ojibway Indian Hockey Tour

Between December 1927 and February 1928, sixteen hockey-playing members of the Cree and Ojibway First Nations in northeastern Ontario undertook a barnstorming tour of twenty-two cities and towns in Canada and the United States. Traveling by charter bus, the "Cree and Ojibway Indian Hockey Tour" was a well-promoted and cleverly planned road trip that began in Timmins and swung through southern Ontario before it crossed the US border and performed in Michigan, Ohio, Pennsylvania, New York, Connecticut, Rhode Island, and Massachusetts. In some cities, the players divided themselves into two "tribes," the Crees versus the Ojibways, and billed their games as the "Indian Hockey Championship of Canada." In other locations, only one team went on the ice to face a local side. In every place, the Natives wore buckskin jerseys with fringe and (in pregame warmup) ceremonial headdresses made of feathers. Invariably, the hype oversold the actual product, but the spectacle was more important than the quality of play, for this tour was unique. While barnstorming was a frequent feature of American baseball and football, it was rarely done in hockey. And though individual First Nations players, like Bud Maracle, were sprinkled through amateur and minor-pro hockey, all-Natives teams were virtually unknown.

The tour is fascinating for the relief in which it cast the subject of hockey's color. Certainly, it demonstrated Natives' agency, particularly the business acumen of tour organizers Joe and Willie Friday, two Ojibway hunting and fishing camp operators who organized the road show around two decades' worth of contacts among wealthy white sportsmen from southern Ontario and the northeastern United States (men whom they had guided

Cree and Ojibway hockey tour, 1928 (City of Toronto Archives/TTC Fonds, series 71, item 5619)

in Temagami's wilderness in seasons past). For them, the tour was a cleverly orchestrated enterprise designed to cement clients, drum up new contacts, and build their tourism business in northeastern Ontario.[50] For full effect, the Fridays and their hockey tourists "played Indian,"[51] dressing up in garb that white audiences expected of real Native guides and *performing* their "authentic" culture, part of which was hockey.

The Cree and Ojibway tour was grueling. On the road for a little more than two months, these young men played eighteen games and traversed more than 1,700 miles on winter roads. The itinerary included huge American metropolises—Philadelphia and Boston—as well as tiny Ontario towns—such as Longford Mills and Blenheim, and several medium-sized cities in between. If press reports can be believed, the teams skated in front of a capacity crowd of five thousand at Cleveland's Elysium and two thousand at the New Haven Arena; twelve hundred at Springfield's West Side Arena and three thousand at Philadelphia's Arena.[52] When they were not on the ice (and when local YMCAs and service clubs afforded them time and space), these Natives performed specially orchestrated "Pow-Wows"—demonstrations of canoe paddling, bow-and-arrow whittling and shooting, birch-bark canoe construction, moose calling, snowshoe making, and other skills, a spectacle for which they charged a small admission fee.[53]

But hockey was their centerpiece. Their playing talents are hard to gauge. Some, such as the Anderson brothers—Roy and Harry—were experienced players who, as Toronto's *Globe* noted, "played for Stock Yards in the Mercantile League at the beginning of the [1927–28] season until the lure of the wide open spaces proved too strong and they went back North." As a whole, they were judged in London, Ontario, to be "as good as many intermediate O.H.A. sextets."[54] The overall tour record shows that the Crees bested the Ojibways (4 wins, 2 losses, 1 tie), and against local opponents, the Indians (appearing alternately as "Crees" and "Ojibways") posted a losing record (4 wins, 5 losses, 2 ties). In some games, the Crees or Ojibways played against younger junior teams (ages sixteen to nineteen) and lost (Timmins); in other games they fared well against competitive intermediate OHA teams (Ingersoll). In Boston they suffered their most embarrassing defeat to a collection of former American collegiate stars, including Harvard's George Owen.

In the end, scores mattered less than spectacle. To sportswriters, the Cree and Ojibway teams screamed "Wild West" or a contact tale in the style of James Fenimore Cooper. "From the pine-clad . . . shores of old lake Temagami, a feather-crested tribe of Cree redskins will sweep into the Border Cities Monday night to do battle with the Windsor Chicks hockey brigade," the *Star* announced. In Pittsburgh, one editor forecast bad blood in the coming Cree-Ojibway game: "Their enmity on the ice is reminiscent of the days when the tribes battled with tomahawks and arrows."[55] And in Philadelphia, each "brave battl[ed] with the stoic pertinacity of his race for victory. The ice was dotted with Redskins as the Indians wielding their sticks in tomahawk fashion sliced each other to the ice. . . . [T]he battle had the color of a primitive combat staged upon a natural river rink in Northern Canada."[56]

Amid this commentary was an assertion that Indian hockey was *authentic* hockey, that these teams offered a glimpse of the modern sport's ancient forebears. White sportsmen, reporters, and promoters wanted to believe that when they played it, Natives played the *original* game. The *Cleveland News* waxed nostalgic about this fiction in its pre-game announcement:

> Canada is the home of hockey and the Indians of that country were the first to play it. . . . It was taken up by the French and English settlers of the Dominion and gradually developed into the king of winter sports. The Canadian Indians never lost their love for the sport and many of them are

> skil[l]ful players, although the number engaged in professional hockey is very small. But far up in the North woods, they play in their villages, on the ice of lakes and streams.[57]

In taking this line, newspapermen promoted a chance to see real Native culture unveiled. Moreover, the presence of renowned First Nations athletes at some of these games helped to prove their authenticity. In Toronto the Cree-Ojibway contest was made legitimate by the presence of Tom Longboat, an "interested spectator [who] lent much vocal encouragement to the battle." In Springfield, the game was refereed by Bud Maracle, the "real Redskin of the champion Springfield Indians of the Canadian-American League."[58]

Convinced of authenticity, reporters looked for a distinctive *Indian style* of hockey; an *ancient* style. Many reporters described their game as lacking one or more of the essential elements of modern hockey: speed, "science," and mayhem. Indian hockey was fast at times and skillful at others, but it represented an archaic version of the game long ago eclipsed by white sportsmen. Cree and Ojibway players were congratulated for their persistence and determination. "Hardy" and "tireless skaters," they were "hard to hurt." Excellent skaters, the *Cleveland Plain Dealer* asserted, the Indians were also "adept at stick handling and masters of the poke check." The most impressive parts of Indian hockey were the separate talents—speed, aggressiveness, tirelessness, stickhandling, and stick checking—that individual players brought to the rink.[59]

Where Indian hockey was judged more harshly was in the traits that made the game *modern* according to contemporaries: strategy or combination, and violence. Too individual and not very physical, Indian hockey had not progressed much past shinny. A full-column write-up on the Cree–Woodstock Intermediates game spelled out this contrast. "The game was interesting all the way through," the *Sentinel Review* reporter noted, "because it was a demonstration of the old and new styles of hockey." The Crees surprised the Woodstonians by playing three forwards in the Woodstock defensive zone, attacking at all times. "They showed . . . all kinds of speed and an uncanny method of holding the puck and getting their shots away fast from almost any angle." In the end, Woodstock won 3–1, the reporter concluded, by virtue of its combination play.[60] A reporter for the *Cleveland Plain Dealer* drew a similar conclusion when the Ojibways trimmed the Crees 6–5 in the Elysium, and in Windsor, the headline writer for the *Border*

Cities Star stated bluntly: "Crees Lack System."[61] Finally, despite impressive size, these Indians played the game in a remarkably placid style, a trait that belied the overblown Wild West discourse. A writer for the *Providence Journal* told audience members to expect "little or no body checking."[62]

These white reporters imagined an Indian style of hockey and projected it onto the Crees and Ojibways. This was hardly new; the same sort of musing had gone on in other sports. American football writers developed their own implicit racial taxonomy. The tactical style of the 1920s Haskell (Kansas) Indian Institute teams carried out was routinely described as "colorful," "wily," "crafty," and "tricky."[63] Hockey reporters' observations reveal a search for racial order in the hockey world, an order that celebrated the white game as modern and progressive and the Indian game as archaic and quaint, a "vanishing" style played by a "vanishing" people.

These stories about race are few, but they are telling. Hockey had a race, and it was white. White hockey meant modern hockey, a distinctive brand that packaged speed, science, and physical play. The Crees and Ojibway tour was designed as a deliberate burlesque, but the white press would not leave it at that. They assessed the Natives' game seriously and determined that, as hockeyists, they were yesterday's men. Pitched as good-natured fun, the tour stirred deeper feelings about the color of real hockey. What is more, real hockey had a sex, too.

. . . and Sex Is Everything

The cover of the American humor magazine *Judge* for the week of February 18, 1922, presented a very intriguing image: three young "flappers"—thin, athletic women clad in stylish hats, sweaters, and bloomers—playing competitive, fully uniformed and equipped, team ice hockey.[64] Drawn by prolific French artist René Vincent in the Art Deco style, the image presents a telling contrast: two opponents in the background doggedly pursue the puck toward an empty goal, while the would-be goaltender, in the foreground, takes a time out to apply lipstick. Vincent's complex images of the New Woman in America capture an important conundrum of the era. In the Jazz Age, competitive women's hockey made great strides even as it carried the burden of traditional male doubts about the propriety of its presence.[65]

In 1920s North America, women's ice hockey emerged as a legitimate, promising expression of athletic prowess. In the United States, that promise went unfulfilled. But in Canada, the game spread like wildfire, spawning

"Making Up the Team," *Judge* magazine, February 18, 1922
(Chronicle / Alamy Stock Photo)

both local and national rivalries, and a women's hockey *culture*. In both countries, however, the women's goal was challenged by economic pressure and by a gender bias that had them, their games and leagues, subordinated to those of men and boys.

The interwar period followed an era of "first starts" for women's hockey (1890–World War I), when women first formed teams and formally reported game results in the press. A new period of more serious, structured, and perennial competition began to take shape about halfway through the conflict.[66] The Great War shook the ground in which prevailing gender roles were rooted. Women took on unconventional, "manly" positions as munitions workers, medics, and ambulance drivers to help "make the world safe for democracy."[67] Some advocates of women's athletics saw entry into the war as a test of strenuous womanhood and an opportunity to cement the doctrine nationally. If the postwar popularity of women's sport and physical education (alongside the new physicality of the flapper) is any indication, it was a test that North American women passed with flying colors. Athletes such as Bobbie Rosenfeld, Babe Didrikson, Hazel Wightman, and Glenna Collett became "respectable heroines" of the age.[68]

Women's ice hockey was fueled by this transition. By the early 1920s, it became something more than a series of sporadic contests and a makeshift pastime. There were two potential places for growth. The first was in universities, where the gathering of young women opened new doors for the pursuit of sport. Here, two different perspectives developed. In the United States many universities placed restrictions on vigorous sport for women, which, some held, overtaxed their delicate mental and physical constitutions and morally endangered them by exposure to the brutish, unseemly excesses of manly sport.[69] Women's physical education faculty in these colleges developed a guarded approach. Their concerns were central to the American Physical Education Association's Committee on Winter Activities in Snow and Ice, whose members hailed from Skidmore, Mount Holyoke, Minnesota, Michigan, and Wisconsin in the United States, and from McGill and Margaret Eaton School in Canada. As Helen Driver of Wisconsin put it, health, happiness, and enthusiasm for the outdoors were the goals of winter activities. Winning and publicity were not part of the equation. Hockey's role in this was "only as a device to improve skating ability and satisfy the group-game urge."[70] Such philosophy limited the women's game to intramural affairs in places such as Smith College and the Universities of Minnesota and Alaska. But even intramural or "exhibition" hockey could gather a crowd. Zerada Slack of McGill described the tight control at her school: no gate receipts, no trophies, chaperones on away trips. Still, the matches on the rink bordering a busy Montreal thoroughfare were "always watched with interest—sometimes more than is welcome!"[71] The APEA rules allowed body checking in the defensive zone, but the general understanding was that women would not "play rough" and that the game needed to be slowed down.

Canadian educators had fewer concerns in this vein, or maybe Canadian women students simply disregarded them. In 1920 the Western Canadian Intervarsity Athletic Union (WCIAU) sponsored a formal women's league involving the Universities of Alberta, Saskatchewan, and Manitoba. A team from the University of British Columbia joined in 1923. Among the earliest women's university stars was Saskatchewan's Genevra "Ginger" Catherwood.[72] In central Canada, teams from the University of Toronto and McGill and Queen's Universities formed the Women's Collegiate Ice Hockey League, whose victor was awarded the Beattie Ramsay trophy. Ramsay, a Torontonian, OHA star for the U of T (1919–23) and one-time Maple Leaf (1927–28), would generally have been pleased with the outcome. The University of Toronto women dominated the league, winning all but one championship over fourteen years.[73]

Organized competition also spread outside the academy to urban clubs and industrial leagues. Here, without the financial support and facilities that higher education institutions could offer, and squeezed against men's teams for ice time, women's hockey entered uncertain territory. In the United States, rinks were commercial creatures where women's teams were organized and sold as spectacle—first and foremost. By December 1920 they were a regular fixture in New York and Boston. Moreover, with the construction of the Ice Palace in 1919, groups of Philadelphia women were interested in challenging the teams from Boston and New York. So optimistic were members of Boston's Back Bay Hockey Club that they initiated plans for the development of a formal intercity league and had notices published in the *New York Times* and the *Philadelphia Inquirer*.[74] But by 1922, the American experiment was over, largely because it failed to deliver a product similar to the one that audiences had come to expect from men's games. "Women may be good skaters," one *Boston Globe* sportswriter wrote in late January 1921, "but their inability to shine as hockey players was demonstrated when the Back Bay Hockey Club defeated the Girls' A.A., 2 to 1, last night at the Arena. There was a small attendance."[75] In this environment, where gate receipts were a measure of worth, no statement could be more damning.

Canadian women's clubs were much more successful. Prewar clubs such as the Ottawa Alerts and Cornwall Victorias were rejuvenated in the postwar years and joined by several new entities. In the West, the annual Banff (Alberta) Winter Carnival hosted a women's tournament from 1917 until

1939. Prewar teams from places such as Fernie, British Columbia (Swastikas), and Calgary (Regents) and Edmonton (Monarchs) carried over their enthusiasm and were joined by teams such as the Vancouver Amazons, who played for the Alpine Cup, the carnival's women's championship, in 1923.[76] News of the women's tournament at Banff traveled far: one *Boston Globe* weekend pictorial spread in January 1921 featured ladies' play at Banff and a photograph depicting fully uniformed teams in bloomers, striped stockings, shin guards, and gloves, entertaining a sizeable crowd that ringed the outdoor rink.[77] In big-city Toronto and Montreal, participation grew steadily among teams such as the Aura Lee club, Toronto Patterson Pats and Northern Electric Verdun.

As with the men's game, tournaments and challenge series were soon outgrown, and women's teams desired more permanent fixtures run by formal associations, with playing rules, constitutions, executive boards, and annual meetings—the sorts of structures that men had built in the previous decades. In 1921, Calgary's Regents Ladies Hockey Club petitioned the Canadian Amateur Hockey Association for permission to enter a tournament sponsored by a commercial firm, the P. Burns Company. The Ladies assumed that the CAHA was their natural parent body—an assumption the men did not share. President H. J. Sterling was puzzled, and he promised to consult with ladies' clubs in Ottawa and Winnipeg before deciding on a course of action. Tired of waiting, perhaps, the Regents went ahead and played, and then proceeded to spearhead their own regional association, rounding up other women's teams (such as the Calgary Hollies, Edmonton Monarchs, and the Patricia Ladies Hockey Club) and sponsoring a provincial crown.[78]

In Ontario a more ambitious operation took root. In 1922, twenty women's clubs from across the province met to form the Ladies Ontario Hockey Association. For nineteen years, the LOHA administered and controlled their sport in the province. Its constitution followed the OHA's model, and it affiliated with the Amateur Athletic Union of Canada in 1922. But in 1923, when LOHA executives sought affiliation with the CAHA, they were denied, President W. H. Fry arguing that full-contact hockey was an inappropriate sport for women. Still, throughout the 1920s the LOHA was the strongest women's sport organization in Ontario (if not the whole Dominion). Its membership grew throughout the 1920s and declined only when the Depression wrought its worst effects in 1934, when the league could claim only seven teams. The organization soldiered on, however, largely on the strength of its leadership, including presidents Fanny "Bobbie" Rosenfeld (1934–39) and Roxy Atkins (1939–40). One of the greatest appeals of the LOHA was its year-end championship tournament—at first for senior teams only, later adding an intermediate series. Though an unofficial (yet widely publicized) national series for the Canadian title began as a challenge match,[79] in 1933 elite women's teams created a formal organization, the Dominion Women's Amateur Hockey Association, to oversee a national championship game and its hardware, the Lady Bessborough Trophy.

As with men's, women's hockey spawned some impressively dominant teams. Toronto's Pats was one, sponsored by the Patterson Chocolate factory, and led by Rosenfeld, a multisport star. At the Montreal Winter Carnival in 1929, the Pats took on Quebec's women's powerhouse Northern Electric Verdun, defeating them in front of a reported twenty-nine thousand spectators. Edmonton's Monarchs were another such collection, winners of the Alberta provincial title in 1928, as were Ottawa's Solloway Mills, Ottawa and District champions in 1929. A rare but impressive Maritime team was the Charlottetown (PEI) Islanders, who challenged for the Lady Bessborough Trophy in 1939.[80] Noteworthy, too, were the Toronto Ladies Hockey Club and the Montreal Royals, who played—to critical acclaim—a six-game series against one another in American cities in December 1939.[81] Far and away the most dominant team in the era, however, were the Preston Rivulettes, who joined the LOHA in 1931 and immediately took control, winning ten provincial championships and four Canadian titles. In the Depression decade, they won 350 games, tied three and lost two. "Other teams," one authority wrote, "had little hope of defeating the 'queens of the ice lanes.'"[82]

Many of these women were remarkably able athletes who had made names for themselves in multiple sports. America's Agnes Seamans, of Somerville, Massachusetts, and the Boston Girls' Hockey Club in 1920, was the New England speed-skating champion, 1913–16, and a challenger for the US speed-skating championship in 1917.[83] Among the Philadelphia women players was Phyllis Walsh, listed in "Big Bill" Tilden's 1921 book *The Art of Lawn Tennis* among the "Famous Women Players in the U.S."[84] And New York's Elsie Muller was a champion speed skater who won titles as North American Outdoor Champion (1928) and International Outdoor Champion (1931). In 1932 she represented the United States in the Winter Olympic Games at Lake Placid. In hockey, according to game reports, Muller scored goals in virtually every game she played.[85]

In Canada, women's hockey was a platform for athletic heroism. Marion Hilliard starred on the 1924–25 University of Toronto team that first won the Toronto Ladies Hockey League and followed that up by winning the LOHA title. She played for seven seasons at U of T, four as she completed a baccalaureate degree in arts and science, and three more as she pursued her doctorate in medicine.[86] Calgary's Margaret "Prudie" Pruden played for the Patricia LHC, helping them earn an Alberta title in 1925 before moving to Edmonton in 1928 and leading the Monarchs to provincial honors. However, three women stars stood out above the rest. Toronto's Rosenfeld was an acclaimed softball player and track runner who, as a member of Canada's Olympic team in 1928, won a gold medal in the 400-meter relay. As a hockey player, she starred for the North Toronto AAA in the early 1920s but by the middle of the decade was captain of the Patterson Pats, leading them to perennial success in LOHA competitions. Two women stars of the era knew each other well because they played on the same team, the Rivulettes. Hilda Ranscombe was a fast skater with a dangerous shot; "Marm" Schmuck was a tough, speedy forward who once dropped the gloves with a Winnipeg player in a title game. Captain of the Rivulettes, Schmuck was a poster girl for the women's game. When the Rivulettes visited St. Catharines' Garden City Arena in February 1940 for an exhibition game against the Toronto Ladies HC, her picture was featured in the local press underneath the headline "Best in Canada."[87] These players and others were regularly championed by female sports columnists, such as the *Toronto Star*'s Alexandrine Gibb, who wrote on women's sports for a dozen years, 1928–40, and Myrtle Cook, who, beginning in 1929, wrote "In the Women's Sportlight" for the *Montreal Herald* for forty years.

For all of this growth, the male press and promoters treated women's hockey with ambivalence. A mixed sense of enthusiasm, curiosity, and uncertainty attended their matches, leagues, and championships. Women's hockey was, like all ice hockey, a physical sport, and men (and some women) were unsure how to deal with that spectacle. Play often got rough. LOHA officials often advised team reps to tone down the physical play, lest women's hockey be shunned by the sports establishment.[88] It had a "reputation," one scholar wrote, lacked respectability, and was looked upon by some as a "crowd of roughnecks."[89] The game's physicality appealed to many women, however, particularly working women, who, another scholar noted, "flocked to the cities in search of employment, sought recreational opportunities in their spare time, and . . . turned to sport."[90]

Clearly, the quality of play in women's hockey improved over time, with the growth of its organizational structure. It all mimicked men's hockey, which stands to reason: men managed and coached most of the teams.[91] This was true of fledgling teams in the United States as much as it was of Canadian squads.[92] As managers and coaches, men pushed women to the play the game the only way they knew how: with speed, science, and physicality. However, though a few female star players could skate fast, shoot accurately, pass the puck in quick and timely ways, and, when necessary, mix it up, not many could match popular expectations of what "real" hockey should look and feel like.

North American sportswriters portrayed women's hockey as "other"—a different game. Male writers could not see it as a part of the modern brand. Reportage was brief, cursory, unserious, and often condescending. Even game reports that contained some element of serious narration fell into an easy, critical style that diminished the women's athletic accomplishments. "The time worn and venerable old saying, much favored by sport generations that 'Woman's place is in the home,' is quite passé these modern days," began the *Montreal Herald*'s March 1928 story about the Metropolitan League Championship game between the Verdun "500" and Northern Electric (two of the best women's hockey teams in Canada in the 1920s). It was "no pink tea affair," as Northern won by 3–0, and the referees "had the rare experience of keeping eighteen girls quiet for an hour." An accompanying cartoon depicted one player holding a powder puff.[93]

In Canada, the demise of women's hockey in the late 1930s was complicated. Without doubt, the Depression hurt many teams, who found scratching together funds for travel, practice ice, and league fees increasingly difficult. In Ontario, the lack of parity was a dissuading factor. Fewer and fewer teams registered with the LOHA because doing so was merely signing up to get creamed by the Preston Rivulettes. The onset of World War II reset priorities for the whole hockey world, male and female; for women, the war delivered a near-knockout blow. By 1941 not a single women's league remained in operation in Toronto, and in Winnipeg there were no teams at all.[94] Most profoundly, after twenty years of growth, women's hockey failed to achieve legitimacy in the eyes of the men who controlled the sport. Perhaps because of this, it ran out of momentum. The way the game was viewed, understood, and constructed in these years, to borrow Carly Adams's words, "sustained the gender polarities in hockey." No number of individual stars or dominant teams could alter the mythologies built around the men's game, that hockey was "the rightful place of boys and men."[95] And only them. "It is the dominant view," a sport sociologist wrote some years later, "that men's hockey is the 'real' game."[96] She might also have said *white* men's hockey. As all of the stories above tell us, the strength of a core brand overshadowed the promise of nonwhite and female players and kept them on the margins. But it didn't obliterate their experiences. Rather, significant reform to the supremacy of whiteness and maleness was merely postponed.

15

Europe, the LIHG, and Olympic Hockey: 1920–1945

In April 1919 the International Olympic Committee tapped Antwerp to host the 1920 Games. Peace, hope—and retribution—filled the air of postwar Europe. The games began with a mass release of doves and the first-ever competitors' oath, taken for all by Belgian fencer Victor Boin: *"We swear that we will take part in the Olympic Games in a spirit of chivalry, for the honor of our country and for the glory of sport."* Chivalry had limits. The IOC allowed the Belgian organizers to decide whether to invite Germany, whose 1914 invasion of their homeland triggered the vast slaughter. Germany was not invited.[1] Belgian revenge was a tiny window on the larger postwar panorama of ethnic struggle launched in the dissolution of old empires and economic volatility. As one historian put it, submarine warfare literally sank the global economy—with thirteen million tons of shipping. "International trade, investment and emigration all collapsed" and were forcibly opposed by "revolutionary regimes" that favored plans and protection over the free market.[2]

This did not stop the sheer growth and flow of international sports systems; hockey kept expanding. Leagues and championships multiplied across Europe and beyond. Canadian coaches and players swirled in greater numbers within their prewar networks. In 1923 the LIHG admitted Romania, Spain, and Italy to membership. Poland, Hungary, and Finland soon joined. By 1930, membership included Japan. But postwar antagonisms did intrude. While LIHG members found the spirit to readmit Austria in 1924, they held out two years longer against Germany, a position that led Sweden to quit in protest. Twelve years later, the Garmisch-Partenkirchen

(GaPa) Olympics showed that the wages of world war included heightened nationalism. And this clearly played itself out on the ice.[3]

Antwerp was also filled with battles over organization and management. The games were officially pitched to the Belgian and International Olympic Committees by a "Provisional" group of established sportsmen. At the same time, a local cohort of bankers, merchants, and shipbuilders organized their own "Festivities Committee" to supplement the sporting events with an air show, exhibitions, and a trade fair. It was an early, massive, and (to the Provisional Committee) outrageous effort in what is now called "ambush marketing"—making money by posturing as an official Olympic affiliate. This caught the attention of Olympic "founder," Baron Pierre de Coubertin, who warned in an August 1920 report to his Olympic brethren about the dangers of opportunists who "come forward to manage [sporting events] and whose only dream is to use someone else's muscles either to build upon his own political fortune or to make his own business prosper." Of course, such motives thrived as far back as the ancient Greek tyrants who promoted great athletic festivals in order to boost their own popularity. And Coubertin's fear of crass commercialism might have seemed odd to many North Americans who believed that hockey's expansion rested on indoor rinks, which required revenue streams, which in turn required investors and tactics that often clashed with the tenets of pure amateurism. Europeans clung longer both to outdoor venues and to notions that sport should be pursued for its own sake.[4]

European Clubs

The European "sport-for-gentlemen-amateurs" model was, however, slowly challenged. Sports clubs multiplied after 1900 with variation and complexity. It was not a uniform system of old fuddy-duddies. Take workers' sports. The decades after World War I saw greater organization and hardening of lines against "bourgeois" (read: amateur) models that both neglected and exploited the proletariat. Worker-based club membership exploded. One estimate counted more than one million members in German clubs by 1929; Austrian almost one-quarter million, and Czechoslovakian two hundred thousand in 1931; French one hundred thousand in 1934. International festivals, meets, and tournaments looked to rival their bourgeois counterparts. These included Workers' Olympiads in 1921, 1925, and 1931. By most measures, they were highly successful. The 1931 festivals enjoyed levels of participation and spectators that "compared favourably or better with the 1932 Olympics in Lake Placid and Los Angeles." But workers' sports did not unite all workers. Organizations split along the hardening lines of ideology—social democracy, socialism, and communism—and name calling took place even among associations like the Lucerne Sport International and the Red Sport International.[5]

European sports clubs were culled over, refashioned, and militarized by fascist and communist regimes in ways that would have been incomprehensible to the Montreal Victorias. In Göttingen, for instance, football clubs that had affiliated with worker associations were dissolved by the Nazis in favor of clubs that had aligned with established bourgeois groups under the aegis of FIFA. But even survivors had to adopt Nazi protocol. Club officers were addressed as "Führer"; club meets closed with "Sieg Heil." Old Russian clubs experienced different ideology but similar morphology. Hockey clubs experienced parallel pressures and changes.[6]

What European sports, including hockey, did not experience, however, was the cartel found in America's major leagues of professional baseball. This was the model adopted by Canada's National Hockey League—where a group of owners staked out exclusive territories, where an owner's market and an owner's profits were largely an owner's business, where the "big league" dominated the "minor" leagues, and where players had no rights to move once they were "owned." European football certainly had professional sides and leagues, sanctioned by established governing bodies, starting in England in 1885. Still, it was a limited form of professionalism, often embedded in a larger, multisport club and governed by a board of directors. In England the Football League even set limits on the amount of revenue that could be siphoned off to dividends, and it prohibited payment of directors. This would have seemed absurd to MLB or NHL owners, but it made sense in the club system, where a strict profit motive seemed too crass a denial of the dominant sporting creed. European intellectuals were at once aghast and supercilious at the sliminess of America's commercialized college football, with its routine exposés of academic fraud, slush funds, and payoffs. European hockey played in this ideological environment. For half a century, only England experimented with the North American model.

Europeans of all stripes devised strategies for negotiating North American products and North American culture. Jazz, motion pictures, Mickey Mouse, Coca-Cola: all of them were part of a much larger dialog. What to reject? What and how to adapt, revise, and embrace as their own? These were age-old questions in the history of cultural diffusion. Mass media made the discussion very public and very powerful. Canadian ice hockey became part of this mix. In the decades between the wars, the game still appeared as a novel and foreign product. Players and coaches from Kenora or Halifax or Toronto were recognized and coveted as experts. But that did not mean complete deference. Hockey was not a patented or even trademarked good, and European governing bodies put their own stamp on the sport.[7]

The English League and Bunny Ahearne

The bridge—or halfway house—between North America and continental Europe was England and the English National League, a quasi-professional operation filled with imported Canadians, some of whom, as we have seen, were able to suit up in a British uniform and beat their homeland in the 1936 Olympics. The English League was entrepreneurial in nature because it depended on artificial ice and imported players, both of which required significant revenue. One of the imported Canadians was Rene F. G. "Bobby" Giddens, whose hockey career crossed many of the boundaries that grew more rigid by the 1950s. An Ottawa native, he learned the American college game at Harvard, where he graduated class of 1930. Three seasons later he sailed east to play for the Stade François club in Paris, then to England as player-coach of Streatham. For the next two decades he was a fixture in British and international circles, largely on the basis of the weekly newspaper, *Ice Hockey World*, which he founded in 1935, and which reached a peak circulation of thirty-five thousand two decades later. He also published and edited an eponymous annual from 1947 to 1955. His book-length history and reflection, *Ice Hockey: The International Game* (authored as "Robert Giddens"), appeared in 1950 as a number in the Foyles Handbook series.[8]

It often takes an "insider-outsider" to fully appreciate the dimensions of a culture, a nation, or a national sport like hockey. Bobby Giddens was one such character. He understood the key ingredients for what is now called "growing the game." The first was rink building. Giddens attended Harvard at a time when hockey was the top spectacle of Greater Boston's winters—solely because of the Boston Arena. During his junior year, he might have watched the mammoth construction project at North Station, which included both a new railroad depot and Tex Rickard's fourteen-thousand-seat Boston Madison Square Garden. Odds are he attended the Garden's first hockey game in November 1928. The Athens of America was now a two-rink Hub of Hockey.[9]

England needed the same infrastructure. Like many promoters, Giddens argued that his audience, the people, had all the right stuff of champions. If only Great Britain had colder winters, their native sons "would now be some of the finest ice hockey players in the world, Canadians and Canada notwithstanding." Absent another ice age, the future rested on artificial ice. But even the early rinks, he lamented, "were few, small and exclusive. The Niagara, the Princes and the Brighton rinks were built by ice skating interests for ice skating enthusiasts—not for ice hockey." For the most part, he claimed, the managers "discouraged hockey" because they thought it was "too rough and too tough." This changed in the 1920s and 1930s, a period of high hopes for building hockey as a commercial success. Westminster's Ice Club (1926) triggered a rash of new rinks. Park Lane Ice Club, Golders Green, Hove, Richmond, and Hammersmith opened in 1928–29 alone. Ice sizes varied, and seating was an afterthought. Then the Depression dumped a harsh reality on any plans. Golders Green became a cinema, Park Lane a ballroom. The Hammersmith ice rink was converted to the Palais de Danse (later made punkishly famous by The Clash).[10]

In 1934, however, confident Wembley promoters built the Empire Pool and Sports Arena, which held ten thousand seats and a full-sized sheet of ice—quite attractive for hosting international championships. It was a marvel of structural concrete, with the roof counterbalanced by huge concrete fins that were modernism's answer to flying buttresses. The design provided unobstructed sightlines for spectators.[11] New rinks followed Wembley. Empress Hall, Brighton, and Harringay were the most notable. Teams of this era had livelier brand names: Hammersmith Lions, Wembley Lions, Earls Court Rangers, Kensington Corinthians, Richmond Hawks, Brighton Tigers, Grosvenor House Canadians. It would, however, take skill to sell the show. And how to get it? As Giddens knew, the answer was the same in Britain as it had been in New York in 1896: "In order to give the public the best in thrills, rink executives have gone to Canada for their manpower."[12]

Grosvenor House won the 1933 league crown with an all-Canadian team. With such talent in short supply and hot demand, rink and team promoters used every means to lure and retain it. Gerry Heffernan, who played in 1937–38 for the Harringay Greyhounds, told hockey writer (and longtime Giddens assistant) Phil Drackett: "English clubs were paying more than double that being paid in amateur circles in Canada and the United States. . . . For my previous season with Montreal Royal Seniors (1936–37), I received $300 (65 pounds). Harringay paid me 10 pounds weekly, a total of almost $1,000 for the season 1937–38." Wembley Lions player Jo Jo Grabowski agreed: "Most Wembley players received 10 pounds weekly, plus two pounds for a win, one pound for a tie." The better the player, the higher the pay.[13]

The British Ice Hockey Association (BIHA) had a rocky adjustment to the new reality. Successful administration required someone with guile and gusto, with ambition and energy, with a sense of the business chance in a quasi-regulated environment. It took someone like John Francis "Bunny" Ahearne, who, like many kingpins of the amateur establishment, had never played the sport he helped to build and exploit. Ahearne was born in Ireland in 1900 and moved to London in 1927 to work in the travel business. According to one biography, Ahearne "never wore skates himself," but after watching a game in 1931 at the Golders Green rink, "he immediately recognised the sport's great possibilities and began handling the transport requirements and arrangements for visiting teams from North America."[14]

For more than forty years, Ahearne was a central character in the drama of international hockey. His broad dome and receding hairline were matched with long black arcs of eyebrows that mirrored his take-your-chances smile. He was less the leading man than the cabaret master. His crucial move was an association with the American Walter Brown, whose father, George V. Brown, was managing both the Boston Arena and Boston Garden and was at the center of Boston's amateur sports establishment. Ahearne shared more than Irish heritage with the Brown family. Together, they represented the adolescent profession of sport managers, entrepreneurs who had to match wits (if not fortunes) against the entrenched, often aristocratic, sometimes royalist interests of "sport for the sake of sport." The Brown-Ahearne partnership pricked the establishment on numerous occasions. It apparently began in 1931, when Walter Brown organized and managed the Boston Hockey Club on a European tour en route to the World Championships in Poland, where the Yanks finished with only one defeat, to Canada. Two years later, his Massachusetts Rangers represented the United States in Prague, going undefeated to win the LIHG's gold medal. The warm-up for that performance was, by one account, "an ambitious four-month, 50-game tour of eight European countries covering 26,000 miles." Ahearne arranged both the 1931 and 1933 trips.[15]

The alliance strengthened in 1934 when Ahearne traveled to North America to stock both the English National League and the British National Team. The key was to find amateurs who had been born in the United Kingdom, giving them a path to international eligibility. The Brown family farm in Hopkinton, Massachusetts, became Ahearne's base and Walter his personal driver as he traveled into Quebec and the Maritimes. Tom Brown later said that his brother Walter had "crossed into Canada so often that the border guards called him by his first name." In one year of trawling from Brown's launch, Ahearne landed fourteen Canadians for the English League, including Moncton goaltender Jimmy Foster, a native of Glasgow, Scotland, who featured prominently in the 1936 Olympics eligibility squabble.[16]

Ahearne became assistant secretary of the BIHA before the 1933–34 season, a move that made great sense for someone looking to build a sports travel business. The international amateur network required national governing bodies to register players and certify the purity of any traveling team. Far smarter for an entrepreneur like Bunny Ahearne to monitor that process from the inside. His timing was perfect. In the early thirties, Phil Drackett later recalled, the BIHA "was a somewhat shaky edifice run on very amateur lines, the leading officials being mainly university men or army officers." This changed when Ahearne's firm agreed to provide the organization with "free office space and secretarial assistance for two years." The paperwork included floats of money. According to Drackett, "Since the BIHA had cash flow problems, the tour agency would finance bringing over Canadian and American teams and wait for payment." By 1935 Ahearne was the BIHA's general secretary, which drew him into the orbit of the LIHG, whose council he joined in 1947. From 1951 to 1977 he served a series of top posts in the LIHG (renamed IIHF in 1954).[17]

Once inside the IIHF, Ahearne became more aggressive in blending his private business with that of the IIHF. As was the case in most of the amateur sports world, national teams were pawns in the action. American hockey mogul Walter Bush later explained the 1950s math: "Bunny would call Walter [Brown] and arrange these tours, but Walter never got that involved. Bunny set up a schedule of 30 games and we drew over 300,000 people. If they paid one dollar apiece, that's 300,000 bucks and we got $30,000. Bunny made a bunch of money off hockey." Bush, however, was a quick learner and soon demanded an appearance-fee increase from Ahearne, from $1,000 to $3,000 per game. "Of course," he recalled, "Bunny was very, very angry with me because it was cutting into his business."[18]

Most Canadians first learned of Ahearne during the 1936 Olympic battles, both off and on the ice. From that point on, he was something of a lightning rod and villain. In 1992 two Canadian hockey writers captured their nation's collective anger, fifteen years after Ahearne's retirement from hockey:

> Ahearne may have been capricious and unpredictable, but two things were certain as long as he ran international hockey: he knew exactly where every dollar came from, and if you didn't book through his travel agency, you didn't play international hockey. Teams who didn't use his agency found their permissions . . . revoked at the last minute. When a protest was made, no record of any request for a permit could ever be found at IIHF headquarters. Teams that booked through Ahearne's travel agency had no problems.

They were not alone in this assessment. American national team coach Murray Williamson took this one step further in his memoir, claiming that Ahearne inflated his take by adding extra and unnecessary legs on team itineraries.[19]

Ahearne was controversial on all hockey continents. Fritz Kraatz played on the 1928 Swiss Olympic team. He later served two terms as IIHF president. His description of Bunny was interestingly balanced: "an Irishman, fiery-haired, arrogant, quick on the uptake, a fine businessman, obstinate, capable of warm feelings and then acting unscrupulously in pursuit of his own advantage." Hockey writer Scott Young later concluded that "Bunny Ahearne, as interpreted through sports pages and sports broadcasts, is a pompous Englishman who wears vests and is always taking sides against Canadians. A more accurate image would be of a man who can be pompous, wears vests, is English, and is not intimidated by anybody, especially Canadian sports columnists."[20]

On the whole, Europeans had fewer issues with Bunny Ahearne. They were not so dependent on his travel agency. More important, he was a master negotiator who seemed quite capable of beating the North Americans at their own game. That was good for European hockey. And it was precious for Britain. Ahearne's management of the 1936 Olympic team—coupled with rink building—spawned something of a golden age for British hockey. The crowds and the atmosphere for some events were seared into memory. Phil Drackett recalled "queues at Harringay for the World Championships winding twice around the giant building, and an enterprising salesman chanting 'Telfer's hot pies' as people shivered and stamped their feet in the cold night air." In Britain between the wars, hockey was a hot pie indeed.[21]

Continental Nationalism

For at least three decades after Antwerp, and well beyond Britain, the favored currency in hockey's growing network remained Canadian: people like Tommy Darling, who coached in Switzerland in the 1930s before playing in England (Streatham), Scotland (Fife and Dunfermline), then England again (Brighton), between which he sandwiched war service in the Canadian Army. By 1953 the *Ice Hockey World Annual* reported that he was off to Johannesburg with an appointment as coach to the South African Ice Hockey Association. Canadian coaches on the Continent during this time included John Dewar (Hungary), Howie Grant (Czechoslovakia), Bobby Bell (Germany), Frank Trottier (Sweden), Bud McEachern (Norway), and Mike Buckna (Czechoslovakia). This was not surprising, given Canada's dominance at the 1920 and 1924 Olympics. The Winnipeg Falcons scored 15–0 and 12–0 wins over the Czechs and the Swedes in Antwerp. Four years later in Chamonix the Toronto Granites pounded their way to an aggregate 104–2 smashing of Sweden, Czechoslovakia, Switzerland, and Great Britain. In both cases Canada's only competition was the United States. For the near term anyway, European clubs and national teams looked to emulate the Canadian game, employ Canadian coaches, and (like England, Italy, France, and Poland) recruit Canadian players of European birth (or some credible bloodline) to gain eligibility to represent the "home" country.[22]

In these ways, Canadian imports were used for European nationalist projects. Czechoslovakia was a case in point. In fact, it was a new country, a postwar amalgamation of Bohemia, Upper Hungary (Slovakia), Moravia, Austrian Silesia, and Carpathian Ruthenia. Following its readmission to the LIHG in 1920, the Czech national team won European championships in 1922, 1925, 1929, and 1933. The country's first artificial ice arena, in Prague, opened in 1931 with LTC Praha hosting a University of Manitoba team headed to Poland for the World Championships. That same year, the Slovakian Hockey Union merged with the Czech Hockey Union to form an even greater Czechoslovakian entity. In 1935 Mike Buckna left Trail, British Columbia, to take a job as player-coach with LTC Praha. Over the next decade, his presence cleaved by war, he led that club and the national team. Such a connection lent gravitas in the eyes of a well-traveled North American promoter like Walter Brown. "Take Czecho-Slovakia for example," Brown reported in the 1936 *NCAA Guide*, "Ten years ago the only team in the country was that of the Lawn Tennis Club in Prague. The Prague team practically was the entire Czech hockey federation. Now, however, this Prague team is but one member of a federation which boasts of eighty teams."[23]

Brown had especially high praise for Josef Maleček, a Prague native born two years before Brown, in 1903. One biographical sketch says that Maleček "grew up on the vast Letenska plain in the Moldau region, near a point where it overlooks the river. He got his first skates even before he went to school. In the winters, it was possible to skate on the river." His father and uncle were among the founders of AC Sparta Praha. Sports were in his blood: all sports. And he competed at elite levels, at a young age. He set a Czech hurdling record at age sixteen. As a twelve-year-old, he suited up for Sparta's junior ice hockey team. Five years later he was on the senior side, and soon the Czech national team, where he was a fixture for the next seventeen years. One researcher calculated that over the 107 games Maleček played for the Czech team, he scored 114 goals, a production pace that he matched in grace and skill with the solo "rushes" that defined a game of limited forward passing. Canadians praised him. In 1939 Dick Kowcinak was a member of Canada's World Championship entry, the Trail Smoke Eaters. His team played a total of fifty-six games on their tour of Europe (perhaps arranged by Bunny Ahearne). Along the way Kowcinak was asked by the Polish newspaper *Warszawsky Przeglad Sportowy* his opinion of Europe's best player. "The best player so far," said Kowcinak, "has been Josef Maleček, the Czech forward. He is what we back home call a 'hockey brain'."[24]

In 1927 Maleček and others left Sparta Praha amid an intramural squabble and helped launch a new hockey side for LTC Praha. Such player defections were impossible in the North American cartel system (short of a rival league), but it worked for Maleček and LTC Praha. The contingent, mentioned by Walter Brown in his 1935 report, soon became one of Europe's most famous teams. Both LTC Praha and Maleček gained popularity by the team's willingness to barnstorm the country with exhibition games and by the start of hockey radio broadcasts, which coincided in 1931 with the opening of artificial ice at the new Štvanice stadium. As a later Czech Radio reflection put it, "for the first time, Czech hockey was freed from the shackles of changing weather." The sentiment was doubtless inflated by memories of the 1925 European Championship, when a January thaw forced a venue change from Prague to a frozen lake in the Vysoke Tatry Mountains. Few spectators made the trek. But Josef Maleček and reporter-announcer Josef Laufer enjoyed rink and radio technologies that pushed the game and its personalities across Europe and North America. One biography noted that "Maleček became the first hockey player who was used in various commercials, be it tires or building material." This was of course a violation of the strictest amateur rules. But who was watching? By 1933 the great No. 5 was crowned by a major daily newspaper as the country's most popular athlete. Mike Buckna must have been pleased with the skill he found on Prague's teams in 1935. Surely Europe was not dependent on Canada for top talent. They could and would grow their own.[25]

Switzerland, with its beautiful, frozen vistas and its established resorts, was a natural for hosting tournaments, beginning with the first European Championship in Montreux in 1910. That same year the Akademischer Sports Club of Zurich joined the Swiss Hockey Union, opening a pipeline into the German cantons. Warm weather, however, could still muddle progress. For instance, the 1928 Olympic tournament at St. Moritz saw close matches, less because of talent equity than slushy ice conditions. Still, the Swiss League grew from twenty-three clubs in 1919 to forty-three in 1939. The Swiss national team slowly developed strength and by 1926 gained the European crown. While the Swiss embraced Canadians like Tommy Carling, they were (like the Czechs) concerned to produce and proud to acclaim homegrown talent. Davos, which enjoyed the country's first indoor artificial ice rink in 1926, was especially fertile. In 1935 Walter Brown called Davos natives Ferd Cattini, Bibi Torriani, and Hans Cattini the "finest forward line on the continent, and one of the best the writer has ever seen." Walter Brown had seen every NHL team come to play in Boston, so that was saying something. Bobby Giddens, another expert analyst, described the three as "immortals" whose "hockey was beautiful to watch and their lateral passing was the result of much practice, patience and determination."[26]

Another immortal Davos product was the annual Spengler Cup tournament, prompted in 1923 by a trophy donation from Dr. Carl Spengler, a Davos native who gained world renown for innovation in tuberculosis treatments. Spengler hoped that the Cup competition would boost the prospects for German-speaking teams who had been ostracized after the war. In his own way, Spengler was pushing the official creed of Olymp-

Russell Hopkins, Oxford Canadians, makes a kick save at Spengler Cup in Davos, ca. 1934 (Courtesy of Oxford University Ice Hockey Club Archives)

ism, which the Olympic magnates had abandoned in their desire to punish Germany. Without question, the Berliner Schlittshuh Club (BSC) was the main beneficiary, finishing first or second six times between 1923 and 1931. Oxford, Cambridge, HC Davos, LTC Praha, and Diavoli Rossoneri Milano were other top teams in the first two decades of the Spengler Cup competition. Carl Spengler fashioned a template for European club competition. Four years later, Austria's Hugo Meisel took this to another level with football's Mitropa Cup.[27]

Germany's expulsion by the LIHG hardly dampened hockey's popularity, especially in Berlin, home of the Sportpalast and the BSC. Once reinstated in 1926, the national team (stocked with players from BSC) competed hard in international competition, earning silver at the 1930 Worlds, bronze at the 1932 Olympics, and bronze at the 1934 Worlds. Their European ranking was quite strong in the 1930s, with a No. 1 finish in 1930 and 1934 and third-place finishes in 1933, 1937, 1938, and 1939.[28]

Germany's best-known players of the era were Gustav Jaenecke and Rudi Ball. Jaenecke's was a classic sporting tale. Born in 1908 in the household of a Berlin cobbler, Jaenecke's athletic skill got him on the BSC team and on the national team, where he earned widespread acclaim. He also won the German tennis title in 1932 and played on five Davis Cup teams. By one calculation, Jaenecke scored one-fourth of all German national team goals between 1928 and 1939. A contemporary wrote that "he could shoot from any direction, and it was as if his skates were grown on his feet like the pedestal on Bismarck's statue." Rudi Ball was two years Jaenecke's junior. As a youth, he watched Canadian Blake Watson play for Wiener EV against the BSC. He was smitten by Watson's grace and skill. A speedy right wing, Ball worked his way up to the BSC first team in 1928, where he joined his older brothers Gerhard and Heinz. Rudi Ball was good enough to play beyond the local or national levels, as he also joined Josef Maleček, Bibi Torriani, and Jaenecke on several all-star teams that faced off against touring Canadians. As a twenty-two-year-old at the 1931 LIHG championships in Chamonix, Ball tallied five points in five games as Germany earned a silver medal. The following season he led his national team to Olympic bronze in Lake Placid. A French newspaper story in December 1931 listed Ball as the best player in Europe.[29]

But January 1933 brought Hitler to power, and the Ball brothers were half-Jewish. Following a suspicious February torching of the Reichstag, the Nazis began to squeeze a wide array of enemies, most especially Jews. By April, new anti-Semitic laws were in full force. Jews were expelled from universities, the civil service, hospitals, and sports clubs. *Der Stürmer*, the Nazi newspaper, made things quite clear: "We need waste no words here. Jews are Jews and there is no place for them in German sports." Rudi, Heinz, and Gerhard Ball moved to St. Moritz and then Milan, where Rudi led Diavoli Rossoneri to the Spengler Cup title in December 1935. In the meantime, Germany faced growing criticism for its anti-Semitic policies. On the sport side, this included boycott threats against the 1936 Olympics. In a scenario that deserves more research, the German national ice hockey team that had neglected Rudi Ball for several years suddenly invited him back, just in time for the games at Garmisch. At one level, this was an obvious public-relations maneuver to reduce the protest. At the same time, according to hockey historians Birger Nordmark and Patrick Houda, the most crucial pressure was internal: "Gustav Jaenecke wouldn't play without Rudi," and even the highest-ranking goose-stepping Nazi hockey mogul knew that without Jaenecke and Ball, "the team would be virtually useless." More interesting than his Olympic participation, however, is the fact that Rudi Ball returned to Berlin and played for BSC and Germany until 1944. Hockey skill had somehow trumped the Aryan Laws.[30]

Sweden maintained its policy of neutrality up to and through the coming war. As with its politics and diplomacy, Sweden found a middle (or "third") way in sports, in this case between the two winter sports of hockey and bandy. Swedish representatives to Antwerp joined the LIHG, along with Canada and the United States. The bandy-based team (only three members had played any hockey before the Olympics) finished fourth and, along with its fans, had a conversion experience after watching the North Americans' skill with the puck. The LIHG tapped Stockholm to host the 1921 European Championship, which was played under the lights on an outdoor rink. Some six thousand fans cheered the home team to victory over Czechoslovakia—the only opponent to show up. This did not mean that Swedes were ready to dump bandy, which itself expanded both in geography and demographics. In the 1920s and 1930s, teams from outside the Stockholm-Uppsala area began to challenge for the bandy championships, Västerås, Karsland, Skutskär, and Nässjö among them. The working class soon embraced bandy. As one historian put it, "the sport that . . . was first played by the nobility and military officers of land and sea had finally become, up and down the length of Sweden, the sport of industrial workers in communities far from the capital." This process benefited from a 1919 labor law that reduced the workday to eight hours, from the development of workers sports clubs among mining, steel, forestry, railway, and other industrial enterprises, from bandy's promotion in newspapers, and from increased availability of cheaper, ready-made equipment.[31]

Hockey made quick advances along the same lines, but it essentially skipped bandy's early, tight alliance with noble, wealthy, and highly educated players. By one account, Canada's game was quickly dominated by "teams from Stockholm's inner city and from working class districts" like Södermalm and Södertälje. Hockey's physicality matched the worker's world—the checking, the roughness, the clash of stick on stick, all of which were restricted in bandy. And so "aristocratic bandy soon gave way to dashing ice hockey, with its special aura of being associated with American culture." By 1922 seven Stockholm-area clubs founded the Swedish Ice Hockey Federation, which immediately began to sponsor a national championship. Raoul LeMat donated the trophy, which still bears his name. *Total Hockey* indicates that Sweden's first artificial ice rink "was built into an airplane hangar in 1931 and it remained the country's only indoor arena until 1938 [when it closed]." The rink hosted more than one thousand games in its short life. It would be two decades before Sweden enjoyed another indoor artificial ice arena, Rosenlundshallen in Jönköping. Only slowly did hockey move to outlying areas such as Leksand, Örnsköldsvik, and Gälve. It took until 1957 for a non-Stockholm team to win the Swedish Championship. Bandy continued as a popular sport; hockey grew as a commercial product.[32]

Hockey in any form wasn't played in Finland until 1927. One expert claimed that speed skaters were "unhappy with bandy because the huge surface" of ice required for play always crowded off other activities, even on massive outdoor rinks. Once again Antwerp's Olympics turned the tide, as the Finnish skating contingent saw that hockey's smaller ice surface might allow skaters to share space back home. Still, it was seven years before the first club game was played in Tampere. A year later, in 1928, Finnish hockey (under the banner of the Finnish Skating Union) joined the LIHG. This triggered a control grab by the nation's football union, which published a set of rules, began sponsoring its own tournaments, and invited Stockholm's IK Gota (the Swedish national champions) to play in Helsinki. The skating and football unions negotiated a rapprochement in 1929 that created the Finnish Ice Hockey Association. Swedish coaches nurtured the game's advance, but as in Sweden, ice hockey was slow to expand beyond an urban base in Helsinki-Tampere-Turku. The game did not really boom until after World War II, aided by the opening of Tampere's artificial ice rink and by the rise of a robust equipment industry. Replicating the American experience, Finland's market was technology based, and it was manufacturers who could bind the aspirations of grassroots youth and club teams to the big-time success of the national team.[33]

Soviet *Khokkei*

While the Finns and Swedes returned from Antwerp marveling over Canadian skill, across the Gulf of Finland, Russia was embattled in civil war (1918–1921). As numerous historians have emphasized, that experience had great and long-term effects on sport in the Soviet Union. Military preparedness and state security were formally and deeply engraved in the objectives for physical culture of all varieties, including the two most popular sports—football and hockey. Old, prerevolutionary clubs gave way to the emerging forces, especially the Red Army (TsDKA) and the state police (Dinamo). In the early 1920s there was also an ideological struggle over what was called "a properly post-revolutionary culture for the masses" in areas such as film, literature, and exercise. The Proletarian Culture Movement attacked all "bourgeois elements" and looked to start anew with socialist projects. For their part, "Hygienists" wanted to emphasize mass participation over mass watching. In 1925 the Central Committee of the Communist Party settled the issue, at least for sports. As one authority put it, "Rejecting the utopian and experimental tendencies, the leadership decided in favor of a high-performance, competitive approach that could inspire proper values and instill respect for authority." Thus, by fiat, bourgeois spectator sports were re-anointed as healthy and socialistic so long as they were properly organized. This decision spawned an "amateur" club system sure to befuddle governing bodies like the IOC and the IIHF.[34]

The cruel hardships of central economic planning left little time for leisure or sport, but by late 1935 Stalin proclaimed that "life has become better; life has become more joyous." Free time was to be filled with appropriate activities, including watching loosely assembled national leagues in football and bandy. The top performers in both sports were Dinamo and Central Army, as well as industry-based clubs like Spartak, Metallurg, Krylia Sovetov, and Lokomotiv. Historian Robert Edelman found that all of the clubs "supported women's teams as well." Russian *khokkei* (bandy) was not as well organized as football, but in both cases club play was largely local, with all-star teams and occasional tournaments set for battles over regional or national titles. This replicated the early development of sport in the West. There were other parallels. Khokkei was rough, with stick work that would have suited even Bad Joe Hall. Spectators were loud and aggressive in their verbal assaults on officials. Finally, the ostensibly amateur clubs (especially in football) secured top talent by every possible means, including secret salaries and sinecure jobs, just as in the United States and Canada. A popular Moscow sports newspaper, *Krasny Sport*, complained in January 1939 that "half-trained sportsmen should not receive extra money for fictional 'work'; they should not receive subsidies and all manner of gifts for success in competition. That is a bourgeois practice that has crept into Soviet sport." As in the West, this "shamateurism" wilted under public scrutiny, but it never disappeared. Unlike the West, the Soviets transformed the practice into something called "state amateurism." That waited, however, until the late 1940s, when the USSR formally entered international sports networks.[35]

In the meantime, Soviet authorities were closely watching the West. As early as 1934, one historian found, the state Physical Culture Council established a Foreign Department that "carefully monitored western sport, acquiring and translating training manuals, rule books, physical education journals, films and newspapers." It also hired foreign trainers and coaches. It was a new campaign to beat the bourgeoisie at their own games. Part of the new openness involved travel and tours, both out of and into the country, for individuals and teams in an array of sports, including swimming, wrestling, skating, football, boxing, track, and cycling. Canadian ice hockey was among the imports. Soviets recognized its popularity, in part because of Canada's success at the 1928 St. Moritz Olympics.[36]

By most accounts, the first USSR exhibition of the Montreal game occurred in March 1932, when workers from the German trade union *Ficheti* squared off against bandy sides of the Moscow Selects and the Central Red Army Sports Club. This prompted an immediate debate on hockey's merits. The *Soviet Fizkultura i Sport* magazine offered an unflattering analysis comparing hockey to bandy. "With the rules such as they are," wrote the author (referring to the restrictions on forward passing), "hockey appears to be purely individualistic and primitive." After watching the solo rushes so common at the time, it seemed obvious that "the game is very poor in combinations and in this regard cannot be favorably compared to bandy." In a collectivist society, there seemed to be little "need to cultivate Canadian hockey." The themes of the individual versus the collective echoed at higher decibels after World War II.[37]

But the new game did have supporters. While some rules seemed to favor bourgeois ideals, hockey's smaller rink dimensions had the same appeal as they did in Sweden and Finland. A November 1931 article in Leningrad's *Spartak* magazine recognized that with "the size of the ice fields . . . it would be possible to set up a hockey ground on any skating rink." This might work to collective advantage. Research has identified several attempts to jumpstart Canadian hockey before the war. One followed a letter in *Krasnyi Sport* from the captain of the Moscow Bandy Selects calling for organized play "as soon as possible." In 1939, members of Moscow's Physical Culture Institute planned to introduce the game into their curriculum: "Arrangements were made to stage demonstrations of games, seminars were planned for players to share their experiences and experts in the manufacturing of hockey equipment were invited to Moscow from the Soviet Baltic republics of Latvia, Estonia and Lithuania." But there was no eruption of the Canadian game.[38]

There were scattered visions and aspirations. For instance, in December 1936, Mikhail Iakushin traveled to Paris with the Dinamo football team for a match against Racing. During the visit he and his teammates attended a hockey game. Iakushin also played on Dinamo's hokkhei team, so he must have had a keen eye on the action. Impressed with the Montreal game, he wrote in his diary: "The game was very interesting. How would we do against these teams? Surely we would lose. But if we were to cultivate Canadian hockey, we would soon reach the level of the European teams." One expert concluded that "had not the war intervened, there probably would have been a Canadian hockey season in the winter of 1941–42." That winter, however, saw a different and deadly set of battles on ice.[39]

The LIHG-IIHF and European Nationalism

Europe supported an expanding network of players, coaches, and competition in the 1920s and 1930s, with continued interest in (and deference to) Canadian expertise. With the exception of the USSR, there was free flow of sports across borders. But there were also elements that accentuated nationalist and trans-European sentiment, laying the foundation for a proto-Eurozone mentality vis-à-vis North America. Some of this was seen in the desire to develop and promote "home-grown" talent that could proudly hold the flag in medal ceremonies at Olympic or World Championships. Hockey, like most sports of the age, was a simple tool for national pride and nation building, especially on a continent where "nations" were sometimes little more than newly carved, postwar boundaries. Mass media were crucial to this process.[40]

The Italian press, for instance, covered the GaPa games closely, rejoicing or whimpering with every victory, every defeat, every questionable decision by an official. As one scholar wrote, Italy came to the games eager to build on the success of "Mussolini's Boys" at the Los Angeles summer games in 1932 and of the 1934 Azzurri's World Cup victory over Czechoslovakia, held in the Holy City itself. Italy's presence at Garmisch included political considerations—for example, "an act of friendship toward its new political ally" and the need to "build up its image at home" after the invasion of Ethiopia and the resultant international backlash. A 2–1 hockey victory over America was a statement of national pride and resourcefulness in the face of economic sanctions. Headlines back home morphed sporting victories into military success: "The Glorious Alpine Soldiers Come Out at Garmisch as Being the Best Soldiers in the World, Proving the Efficiency of the Army in Every Field." One can find similar (if slightly deflated) headlines in the home papers of other victorious teams.[41]

International championships provided regular opportunities for national revanche in icy wars without deadly weapons. Take the 1937 World Championships, when the Kimberley Dynamiters represented Canada, eager to avenge the Olympic loss to Great Britain the year before. The long-awaited rematch was played before a crowd of ten thousand at Harringay in London. The tension exploded when Britain's winger Chirp Brenchley was downed by a Canadian stick. Bobby Giddens later recalled that "when Brenchley crumpled, the roaring crowd went berserk" in a booing, feet-stamping, and fist-shaking frenzy. Some fans littered the ice with "oranges, paper and coins." A game official rushed to the microphone to plead for "any British sportsmen in the House" to step up—to no avail. The arena bandleader finally pulled order out of chaos by playing "God Save the King."[42]

Hosting a tournament was an opportunity for building notions of nationhood, especially for a young and tenuous amalgamation like Czechoslovakia. The 1938 World Championships in Prague occurred under the growing cloud of German claims on the Sudetenland territory. By one account, the Czechs fashioned "a festive occasion unequaled to that point in hockey history." President Edvard Beneš, who had been for decades the voice and face of Czech nationalism, served as honorary chairman of the competition. His government sponsored a lottery, selling some two hundred thousand tickets to cover the expenses, which Bobby Giddens estimated to be eight hundred thousand Czech Kroners. Among the costs were improvements to Štvanice stadium, including new radio and telephone facilities. The Czech postal service opened a stadium office just for the event and also issued hockey stamps. Not to be outdone, a tobacconist created a hockey-brand cigarette. The national railroad did its part by offering steep discounts to hockey tourists. The event promotions included the widespread distribution of a special poster, chosen from a strong competition of artists. According to Giddens, the poster "was sent to tourist agencies, railways, clubs and associations throughout the country and Europe." Event organizers prepared an elegant publication for LIHG members attending the federation's 25th Congress. Among other bits of data, readers could find the claim that Czechoslovakia had more hockey clubs (361) than any other country in Europe.[43]

Europeanism concentrated in the labyrinth of governance—the LIHG. The federation proved an excellent steward for growing the game in Europe, which was its logical focus. The North American markets had their own internal battles over governance. The LIHG was wise to stay out of them. From 1910 until 1930, then, the term "international" really meant European, since World Championships only occurred in conjunction with the Olympics, in 1920, 1924, and 1928. This changed at the 1929 Congress in Budapest (held during the European Championships), where the LIHG decided to hold an annual World Championship, with two provisos: there must be at least one non-European team to invoke "world" titles, and the highest-placing European team would win the European title. Twelve countries participated in the 1930 affair, including Japan. It was a long haul for all teams, though, as Chamonix's outdoor natural ice suffered a slow melt that forced a move to Berlin and Vienna. In 1932 the LIHG held its championship outside of Europe for the first time when it was contested in conjunction with the Winter Olympics at Lake Placid. There were predictions of a record level of participation, but the fast-growing Depression dashed such hopes. Only four teams competed for ice hockey medals: the United States, Canada, Poland, and Germany. Canada went undefeated, with its only blemish a tie in the medal match against United States, which took the silver, Germany the bronze. North America did not host another LIHG event for three decades.[44]

The LIHG's Eurocentrism also showed in the roster of its executive council. America and Canada had joined with great fanfare in 1920. Canadian coaches and players were in hot demand all across Europe. But that did not translate into influence in governance. North Americans never held more than one of two VP slots until the 1948 election to the presidency of Canada's George Hardy. Given the body's membership, this was logical. Logic, however, did not always resonate during disputes. After one eligibility spat at the 1932 Olympics, American Rufus Trimble, editor of the NCAA rules committee and guidebook, complained about the LIHG and its "archaic and unsound ideas of amateurism . . . preserved in well-nigh inflexible rules and precedents." The CAHA ratcheted up the language after its loss at the 1936 Olympics. The LIHG, then, was basically a European organization. To North Americans, it could be counted on to support Europe in any spats with Canada or the United States.[45]

Like the NCAA, the LIHG understood the importance of rules in carving out a distinct game brand that reflected the membership's philosophy. There was, to be sure, some deference to history. An introductory note to the 1931 rules began with concise authority: "Ice hockey originated in Canada." This much everyone agreed upon. But the LIHG was in its own way more conservative than even the NCAA. Take the offside rule. By 1931 the

NCAA (like the NHL) allowed a player to "play or receive" the puck from anywhere within one of the three zones (although there was still no legal pass across the blue lines). The LIHG rules were a throwback to the old view of "scientific" play. Players, Rule V-b noted, "must always do everything possible to remain between the puck and their own goal (on-side). A player in front of the puck is off-side" and " . . . cannot, without committing an infringement, take part in the play in any manner." Offside players had to try to get onside or risk a penalty for loafing. The only concession to thirty years of innovation was that a player could not be offside in his own end zone. The LIHG rule represented a belief that the game of lateral and drop passing was more challenging.[46]

If forward passing was a debatable component of science, body checking was something to be minimized. On this plane, the LIHG moved in tandem with the NCAA, carefully proscribing contact. Like its North American predecessors, European hockey developed amid an amateurist ethos on violence that favored limited rules but wide referee discretion. Some things were simply ungentlemanly. "Charging, tripping, collaring, kicking, cross-checking, or pushing shall not be allowed"; these terms went as far back as the 1873 field hockey rules. "Unfair" or "rough" play was punishable to varying degrees, including expulsion, whatever the referee decided. But such haziness (and resultant inconsistency in the eyes of players, coaches, and managers) could not last when national or international championships were on the line. Hockey was by its nature a game of contact. What was an illegal charge or push? Like the NCAA (and unlike North America's professional or senior amateur leagues), the LIHG made things easier for referees by restricting *any* body checking beyond the defensive zone. *Total Hockey* claims that "body checking was introduced in the defensive zone" as a rule change for the 1926 European championships. The more appropriate words might be "restricted to the defensive zone." A game with such limits on checking was a fundamentally different game. While the LIHG had not yet seen the need (like the NCAA) for a firewall on fighting, this divergence in checking rules slowly but forcefully created a cultural boundary between continents. European players, managers, and officials such as Belgium's Paul Loicq, Czechoslovakia's Josef Maleček, Switzerland's Bibi Torriani, and Britain's Bunny Ahearne played a part in crafting a hockey brand that began to diverge from the one played at elite levels in Canada and America. This triggered enormous frustration and passion in the international events after World War II.[47]

In his 1950 survey, Bobby Giddens hinted at a trend that was beginning to rend historic bonds between Europe and hockey's mother country. The Swiss initially adopted Canadian rules for their league, he noted, because President Raymond Gafner was "impressed and influenced by the Canadian touring teams." By 1948, however, Gafner cautioned his charges that "care must be taken to fight at all costs and with all the means in our power, against the rough and sometimes almost brutal character which has signaled out certain ice hockey matches in Switzerland." One English league (Streatham) manager recalled to Giddens the problems in Zurich with a local team that "tried to play the Canadian way." "They held us, skated interference, bodychecked everyone but the puck carrier," he complained. When the English (with their heavy Canadian influence) started to hit back, "the Swiss were chagrined." Afterward, the *Neue Zuecher Zeitung* complained about Streatham skating too many "Canadian woodcutters" who "unfortunately attempt to make use of their strength in a way which does not meet with the taste of the public." To Giddens's eye, it was more a case of getting what you asked for. The Cold War prompted a more fervent discourse on national styles of play and their links to national character.[48]

16

Strength Down Center—North American Brands: 1945–1971

There is no better distillation of hockey's postwar meaning to Canadians than a ten-minute, forty-second, 1953 film called *Here's Hockey!* Directed by Leslie McFarlane, author of several of the famous Hardy Boys novels and dozens of hockey yarns in pulps like Street and Smith's *Sport Story* magazine, the film portrays hockey's Canadian anatomy from the bottom up: "the 65,000 players registered with the Canadian Amateur Hockey Association."[1] At each level we see more sophistication: from kids at local outdoor rinks to juvenile and junior players who play an expensive, equipment-heavy, and strategic game dependent on indoor arenas and ice-making technology. Here, players are picked and groomed for stardom, first to minor-league teams such as Jean Béliveau's Quebec Aces, then to the bright lights and big business of National Hockey League teams like "Gordon" Howe's Detroit Red Wings. McFarlane illustrates a tightly integrated national pyramid of pyramids, each part dependent upon the others. "In the games back home, you watch your cousin or your brother or the grocery boy; here [in the big leagues] the bond between the crowd and the players is forged by the stars of the game." Made the year after *Hockey Night in Canada* was first broadcast on television and the year before the East York Lyndhursts stumbled badly against the Soviets in the World Championships, *Here's Hockey!* has an unmistakably triumphal tone. "Our goal, our team, our town, our game," the narrator chants, "for Canadians, the greatest game in the world: hockey!" Few Canadians doubted the superiority of their brand even as international results began to suggest otherwise. For them, hockey's strength was at its center.

Galaxy NHL

Driving this culture was the NHL, the sport's pole star. The New York Americans' demise during World War II ushered in an era of relative stasis: 1942–1967, the age of the mythic "Original Six," the survivors of depression and war.[2] In 1967 the NHL began a series of expansions, adding six new franchises in that year, two more in 1970, and two more still in 1972, totaling sixteen teams by 1972.[3] Despite its progressive image, the move was essentially defensive, adopted to head off any rival major league. It was aimed, too, at securing a national television contract, which by the mid-1960s was a necessity for survival in the North American entertainment business. Expansion changed the way that NHL teams recruited and maintained their rosters, but not much changed in how the game itself was played. Expansion added colorful new names and uniforms, but it wasn't until after 1972 that much new happened on the ice. A more central change was administrative consolidation, an imperative that shaped NHL dealings throughout the 1940s, '50s, and '60s, when the league entrenched its control over North America's core brand.

NHL power resided in three places: the personality of its president, its commercial success and brand recognition, and its chokehold on labor supply and working conditions. When NHL chief Frank Calder died suddenly in 1943, league owners convinced the affable Mervyn "Red" Dutton, one-time WCHL and NHL defenseman and coach-manager of the New York Americans (1935–42) to serve as acting president, which he did reluctantly until 1946. Before he left office, Dutton convinced the governors that his assistant, Clarence Campbell, should succeed him as president. A Rhodes scholar who had played for the Oxford Canadians in the 1920s, Campbell was an accomplished lawyer and an NHL referee in the 1930s. During World War II he rose to the rank of lieutenant colonel in the Canadian Army. His war work was so highly esteemed that, in 1945, he was appointed prosecutor for the Canadian War Crimes Commission.[4]

Still, Campbell did not inherit the gravitas that the NHL presidency later held. In his first decade in office, he was little more than a spokesman. One event, however, elevated him to the status of league boss. On March 13, 1955, Montreal's Maurice "Rocket" Richard was cut by a high stick from the Bruins' Hal Laycoe in a game played in the Boston Garden. Richard had long been the target of abuse from opponents, but with Laycoe's offense, Richard snapped. Attempting to get at Laycoe, the Rocket swung his stick, breaking it across a Bruin's back. When linesman Cliff Thompson tried to restrain him, Richard punched Thompson, committing one of hockey's few cardinal offenses. Referee Frank Udvari ejected Richard from the game, but the real drama came days later. After interviewing the principals involved in the melee, Campbell wielded the might of his office, banning Richard for the remainder of the 1954–55 NHL season as well as the playoffs. The decision set off a welter of protest, particularly among French-speaking Quebecers, who interpreted the decision from the Anglo-elite Campbell as yet another racist insult to the French-Canadian underclass and their hero. For Campbell, the decision was just, and he was determined not to shrink from unrest and personal threats. On March 17, accompanied by three NHL secretaries, he proceeded to his regular seat in the Montreal Forum midway through the first period of the Canadiens game against the Red Wings. Identified by the partisan crowd, Campbell was booed, pelted with eggs and tomatoes, and punched by a fan. Shortly thereafter, an irate partisan set off a tear-gas bomb, causing the Montreal fire chief to evacuate the building and end the game. From the safety of the Forum's medical clinic, Campbell added insult to injury by declaring the Red Wings the game's winner. But the mob was not finished. Demonstrators took to the streets for hours outside the Forum, smashing store windows, looting, overturning cars, and chanting "À bas Campbell." The Richard Riot resulted in $100,000 in damage and dozens of the Rocket's supporters arrested.[5] "Campbell should not have been at the game," referee Red Storey recalled years later, "and if he'd not been at the game, we would have had no riot."[6] When the dust settled, when Richard's public plea for a return to order was heard, Campbell was quietly triumphant. In a way, the Richard Riot made Campbell's presidency. English-language media in Canada and the United States swung in favor of law and order and afforded the NHL president new respect. So did his bosses. "It's funny," Campbell told one hockey writer long after his punishment of the Rocket, "but until I made that decision, I was never really acknowledged as the head of the NHL."[7]

For the remainder of his career (until 1977), Campbell *was* the NHL. To old-time hockey men, he was a maddeningly erudite figure who spoke with over-polished diction. He seemed inaccessible, "austere," "dictatorial."[8] He was a "traditionalist,"[9] an upholder of the ancien régime put into place by the 1936 NHL-CAHA agreement and cemented by wartime attrition. Campbell effectively defended professional hockey in his testimony to U.S. congressional antitrust inquiries in 1957, 1958, 1961, and 1964, and against the claims made by the Canadian government in 1969 that the NHL's Reserve Clause was draconian and exploitative. He negotiated professional-amateur agreements with the CAHA in 1958 and 1967. He steered the NHL through expansion in 1967 and meted out punishment to players for on- and off-ice transgressions. Campbell's image and the orange-and-black shield were interchangeable NHL icons.

But the NHL also drew strength from its prosperity. Despite rocky years in the early 1950s for its American clubs, the league flourished. Gate receipts increased. NHL fans paid $3,681,020 in ticket purchases in 1946–47, a figure that experienced a slight swoon in the early 1950s, falling to $3,425,028 in 1951–52 before it rose again, to $4,282,541 in 1956–57. Thereafter, steady growth was the pattern: $5,244,874 in 1958–59; $6,356,346 in 1961–62; and $9,568,427 in 1965–66, the year before expansion. And expansion upped the flow. In 1967–68 the league netted an increase of more than $1 million in gate receipts; after that, it boomed—$23,784,900 in 1968–69 and $26,805,605 in 1969–70. One historian claimed: "The arenas were bursting."[10]

To those figures, the NHL added income from radio and television. Its clubs pulled in a total $187,429 in media revenues in 1951–52, a number that grew to $308,575 in 1954–55 and $1,442,810 in 1965–66.[11] The CBC's *Hockey Night in Canada* (in English Canada) and *Soirée du Hockey* (in Quebec) brought in sponsorship revenue. By 1948 every U.S.-based team had home-game broadcast arrangements, but they experienced uneven results. Television pulled customers away from the rink and hurt the gate. It was a poor trade off. For example, Chicago's annual $5,000 broadcast franchise fee in the early 1950s came nowhere near the amount of its estimated loss at the gate. The NHL finally struck national deals with CBS (1956–60) for a limited number of weekend games, with NBC (1966) for playoff games on Sunday afternoons, and with CBS (1967–68) for twenty in-season games. The immediate gains were modest; their real importance rested in their capacities to grow future markets.[12]

This bigger picture papered over marked differences among NHL clubs. Throughout the Original Six era, there were haves and have-nots. Business boomed for the Montreal Canadiens, Toronto Maple Leafs, and Detroit Red Wings, and their successes on the ice were matched at the box office.[13] Less impressive were the Bruins, Rangers, and Black Hawks. In the early 1950s, Chicago's finances were so alarming that the team pleaded for revenue sharing from other franchises. Its principal owner, James Norris, estimated that he had lost millions trying to keep the franchise afloat. But the structure of the league—a multi-owner cartel directed by a board of governors made up of principal owners and a president—fostered a feeling of fraternity and common purpose. Occasionally some of them, like Toronto's Conn Smythe and Montreal's Hartland Molson were overprotective of their interests, but generally the group recognized that they were all in it together. In 1971, a year after the second expansion admitted franchises in Buffalo and Vancouver, Detroit owner Bruce Norris lamented that league meetings had "lost all the feeling for the partnership and fellowship that existed when there were only six teams."[14] The NHL brass was tight, and at least some of their success stemmed from that fact.

Finally, NHL strength was measurable in the control it asserted over labor supply and the conditions of work. After 1945 the league tightened its grip on the North American pyramid, building its minor-league farm system and using the provisions of the 1936 CAHL-NHL agreement to influence root-and-branch how hockey was organized and played, from novice boys to Senior A men. The NHL's sponsorship system was designed to feed the big league. But it also became a lightning rod for discontent among Canadians who saw a public good stained by profit motive and continental influence.

Minor Pros

In the generation following the war, the NHL reestablished the entente with the three best minor-professional circuits. The steadiest among them was the American Hockey League (AHL), whose leaders had been uncomfortable as junior partners to the NHL before the war. New among the minor circuits was the Western Hockey League, heir to two earlier conglomerations: a second iteration of the Pacific Coast Hockey League, which jump-started back to life in 1944, and the Western Canada Senior Hockey League, which merged with the PCHL to become the WHL in 1952. In the east, in 1953, the Quebec Senior Hockey League ended its pretense of being amateur, disaffiliated from the QAHA, and became the openly pro Quebec Hockey League (QHL). When it stumbled financially in the late 1950s, its best teams became the core of the Eastern Professional Hockey League (EPHL), a small-city circuit subsidized and directed by the NHL. But it, too, struggled at the gate, and in 1963 four of its five franchises relocated to the US Midwest, where they formed a new NHL farm league, the Central Professional Hockey League (CPHL).

Initially, NHL relationships with minor-pro leagues were piecemeal and disjointed, but in 1954 the big league consolidated arrangements in a uniform Joint Affiliation Agreement signed by the three main minor-pro groups (AHL, WHL, and QHL). The JAA bound minor-pro teams to participate in an interleague draft and protected all pro teams' "territorial rights." The first JAA lapsed when its five-year term expired in 1958, but the impetus remained through bilateral agreements that the NHL penned separately with the WHL (1959–65), QHL (later EPHL, 1959, and CHL, 1963), and AHL (1960). In 1967 the NHL orchestrated a second JAA that formally integrated the minor-pro leagues into the NHL's player-development system and prevented leagues from raiding each other's players. The 1967 JAA completed a process that Lester Patrick's "farm system" had been constructing for some time.

The NHL also established order by establishing a Central Registry, a master list of all players signed and claimed by pro and minor-pro teams. First proposed by Campbell in 1946, it was only agreed to by minor-pro leagues in 1948. For NHL teams, a master list was essential for forecasting talent supply, avoiding tampering charges, and maintaining interleague peace. When a professional sought to be reinstated as an amateur to play internationally (as one-time Maple Leaf Sid Smith did in 1958), he was "released" from his pro status by being stricken from the registry.[15] Located in the NHL office and updated by its staff, the registry symbolized the growing dependence of minor leagues on big-league leadership.

Sponsorship System

More controversial was how the NHL handled *new* talent. In the postwar years, the league carefully constructed its sponsorship system, articulated in agreements it signed with the North American amateur hockey authorities—the CAHA and AHAUS (but most significantly the CAHA). The principles of the arrangement were simple, the details complex. It traded money for control. In the first Pro-Am Agreement of June 1947, the NHL (speaking for all the professional leagues) promised $30,000 annually ($2,000 from each NHL club, $1,000 from each minor-pro team) to amateur hockey authorities as a payment for "player development."[16] In return, the amateurs agreed to allow each NHL club to sponsor (fully or partially bankroll) two amateur teams, where they could locate and train their prospects. The amateurs agreed not to impede the pros' movement of players across leagues and jurisdictions and to play according to NHL rules. In turn, the NHL forbade its clubs from signing prospects younger than sixteen years old. The first Pro-Am deal expired in 1955, and it took until 1958 for the NHL, the CAHA, and AHAUS to pen a successor pact. The 1958 agreement replicated the terms of the 1947 deal with some fine-tuning, including an increase in NHL payments to the amateurs for player development. Thereafter, the CAHA's annual transfer steadily grew; between 1946 and 1966, it amounted to $708,000.[17] The sponsorship system expired in 1967. With expansion on the horizon (and the need to evenly populate new big-league teams with talent), and with complaints about the cost of operating farm systems,[18] NHL brass adopted instead a universal draft of amateur players.

Still, for twenty years after 1947, the sponsorship system held sway. Though an NHL team could sponsor only two amateur clubs, its sponsored teams could sponsor their *own* clubs. Junior A teams could sponsor Junior B teams, which, in turn, could sponsor midget teams, all of them using money that originated from an NHL parent. This chain allowed the NHL to reach deep into the amateur system.

It was nearly impossible for talented teenagers to go unnoticed and unclaimed, to elude the dragnet. After 1946, all pro teams had a reserve list of players whom they had signed to contracts—forty players and four goaltenders per NHL team, thirty and three for minor-pro teams. In addition, each NHL club had a negotiation list, the names of four players (twenty per team by 1958) with whom they had the exclusive right to negotiate contracts (or, simply, to protect them from other teams accessing their rights). Once a player signed, he was moved to his team's reserve list. If he was unsigned by the end of the year, he was fair game for other teams. When one added to these lists the thirty-six amateur players on sponsored teams, NHL teams each had direct control over about eighty players, and many more indirectly.[19]

But the teeth of the NHL's grasp were located in its exploitative contract system. The 1947 agreement described three types of recruitment contracts—A, B, and C forms. The first two were comparatively innocuous. A player who signed to an "A" form committed himself to an exclusive tryout with a professional team, nothing more. "B" forms replicated "A" forms but gave pro teams the option to sign a player who had performed well in a tryout to a playing contract in return for a signing bonus. Most invasive was pro hockey's "C" form, a contract that committed a player's professional rights exclusively to an NHL (or minor-pro) organization. The C form was the most widely employed, and the most controversial. Players had to be sixteen years old (raised to eighteen in 1950) to sign on their own; otherwise, a player's parent or guardian could sign on his behalf. A C contract was renewable each year at the club's option, making it, in theory, an indefinite commitment.

The system was archaic, unjust, and oppressive. NHL scouts sought to tie up talented youngsters, even before they reached junior age (sixteen to twenty). Reggie Fleming became the property of the Montreal Canadiens at age thirteen; Bobby Hull, a Black Hawk at fourteen; Mickey Redmond, a Leaf at thirteen. Players who did not like it had little recourse if they wanted to play the professional game. And it played havoc on junior rosters. Signing a C form with the Toronto Maple Leafs in 1949 meant that sixteen-year-old Danny Lewicki could no longer suit up with his Stratford, Ontario, Junior A team. When Stratford president Harold Wyall protested, a blusterous Conn Smythe told the *Winnipeg Free Press* that Lewicki "would line up with one of the Leafs' pro or amateur clubs 'or he won't play at all.'"[20] Gary Butler, a Regina boy signed to a C form by the Montreal Canadiens and assigned to the Habs' junior-affiliate Regina Pats, changed his mind about a pro hockey career in 1960, wanting to forego his final junior season and take a scholarship at the University of Michigan instead. When the Pats refused to release him, Butler's father appealed directly to Canadiens' vice president Kenny Reardon: "Gary has certain fundamental rights," C. N. Butler pleaded, taking the high ground, "and one of these is to pursue his life as he sees fit."[21] There was no way through the situation, only around it. Some junior managers and coaches, such as the Edmonton Oil Kings' Leo Leclerc and St. Michael's College Majors' Father David Bauer, told their players to delay signing with pro teams until they had all their cards (including U.S. college scholarship offers) on the table.[22] To sign or not to sign was a question with very high stakes for talented athletes who were not yet old enough to appreciate the consequences.

Popular esteem for the NHL blinded Canadians to what common sense should have told them. But many saw the NHL contract system for what it really was. In 1949, Dr. G. E. Hall, president of the University of Western Ontario, declared: "Schoolboy hockey players are being exploited 'with the viciousness of the mill-owners of the early 1800's.'"[23] Newspaper columnists such as Louis J. Fusk of the *Quebec Chronicle Telegraph*, Charles Mayer of *Le Petit Journal*, and Maurice Smith of the *Winnipeg Free Press* joined the chorus.[24] And the cause was taken up by prominent voices in civil life, including Rev. Canon R. L. Seaborn, Anglican Dean of Quebec, and Quebec Premier Maurice Duplessis.[25]

But NHL leaders fought back with equal vigor. Exploitative? Clarence Campbell countered: "ridiculous and absurd"; "utter falsehoods."[26] The C form is "our protection against bootleg amateur clubs and operators . . . [who try] to chisel in," Smythe argued in 1949. The newspapermen who complained about the system were mere publicity hounds "trying to sell their columns."[27] Ultimately, the thrust and parry didn't change anything, and pro hockey's contract system stood firm.

Players talented and lucky enough to make it in the pros signed another contract, called the Standard Player Contract, a feature introduced by Campbell in 1947 and later adopted by other pro leagues. Outwardly innocuous, again, the details mattered. The standard contract was a bureaucratic rationalization that treated players as interchangeable units of labor. It presumed no special cases and offered little leeway for players' circumstances or demands. Like the Central Registry, the NHL head office warehoused all of its player contracts. Players were not routinely issued copies of their own contracts. Why would they need them? As Campbell claimed to a 1957 U.S. Congressional committee, "a very large number of them would be happy not to have the contract. . . . Players don't have any troubles . . . their wives . . . have the troubles."[28]

Even more repressive was the reserve clause, a feature common in professional sports contracts in North America since baseball's National League instituted it in 1879. The reserve clause held that when any contract between a franchise and a player expired, the team retained the exclusive right to re-sign him, trade him, or sell his rights. A player who didn't wish to re-sign had no real choice short of holding out until his team's owner traded him, sold his rights, or agreed to renegotiate on more favorable terms. Between 1945 and 1972, with so few big-league teams and an abundance of players seeking roster spots, those who held out were either extraordinarily confident or reckless. For the NHL, the reserve clause was "essential," Campbell told the congressional committee in 1957. When a 1969 Canadian government task force proposed to study its legality, Campbell defended it hammer and tongs,[29] with the help of sympathetic friends in the media and some NHLers. In 1968, after seventeen years with the New York Rangers, NHL veteran Harry Howell offered only mild complaint when he was traded without consultation to the Oakland Seals. "In my opinion, a reserve clause of some kind is necessary. After 10 years, though, I don't think a club should have the right to trade a man without offering him his freedom."[30] The reserve clause took advantage of a player culture that was reluctant to challenge the league.

Remarkable, then, that some of them did. It was central among the issues raised by the first National Hockey League Players' Association (NHLPA) formed in 1957 at the instigation of Detroit's Ted Lindsay and Montreal's Doug Harvey. Led by players on all six teams, the body initially pushed the NHL for higher contributions to players' pensions. But soon it added another demand: a no-trade clause after six years of service, plus no compulsion to sign a contract after it had run out and arbitration had been sought. The reaction from NHL owners was vitriolic. Lindsay's boss, Detroit GM Jack Adams, denounced him as a "cancer" and traded him to lowly Chicago. Campbell refused to acknowledge the existence of the NHLPA. Intimidated, the players backed down and, team by team, voted themselves out of the union. When the NHL revised the terms of the standard contract in 1958, the reserve clause remained intact. The NHLPA failed in 1957, but its treatment shook players' and fans' faith in the league's benevolence.[31] When a second NHLPA emerged in 1966 under the leadership of owner-friendly Alan Eagleson, the reserve clause was not on the table.[32]

The Long Shadow of 1936

Below the tip of the pyramid, the CAHA and its affiliates governed the core brand. More than the NHL, the CAHA was closer to the people and it received a good deal of sports-page ink. The organization remained federated: a national executive that managed, negotiated with, and sometimes bullied the leaders of nine regional associations. Most conspicuous in the press in these years were the CAHA presidents, but real power was concentrated in three men who were appointed secretary-manager and registrar-treasurer (later executive director): William Hewitt (1922–60), George S. Dudley (1945–60), and Gordon Juckes (1960–77). They kept the CAHA's books and registration cards, penned its voluminous correspondence, brokered peace among its members, threatened sanctions against outlaw organizations, managers, coaches and players, and helped select and sanction teams to represent Canada internationally.

Of all the routine business conducted by the CAHA, most taxing was its job of keeping track of player carding and transfers among regional organizations and international amateur bodies—for example, AHAUS and the British Ice Hockey Association. Mundane, it was nevertheless essential to controlling the sport. In an age when junior and senior clubs abounded, young men convinced themselves that they could slip across jurisdictions undetected. They rarely could. Hewitt, Dudley, and Juckes applied carding rules strictly and didn't hesitate to suspend outlaw players.[33] Only occasionally did carding matters rise to a crisis level, such as in 1961, when the CAHA temporarily dissolved its agreement with AHAUS in protest against its inability to crack down on unsanctioned Canadian players playing with US teams.[34]

More challenging was CAHA control over international play. Until 1968, when the government of Canada created Hockey Canada, the CAHA recruited, financed, and selected national teams to play in tours and tournaments. It was a tough job. Few elite amateur teams wished to play abroad—it cut into their schedules and gate receipts, and by the late 1950s, winning in Europe was no longer a sure thing. Between 1962 and 1970, CAHA executives agreed to try something new, a vision of former Toronto St. Michael's College star turned Basilian priest and educator, Father David Bauer. Instead of sending under-motivated Allan Cup champions, Bauer developed a Canadian National Team of young, elite, amateur players who trained and studied together at the University of British Columbia. But problems abounded. Elite amateurs were like hens' teeth, and it was nigh impossible to pry players away from sponsored teams. As a result, Father Bauer's noble experiment returned lukewarm results: champion of the Centennial Tournament in Canada (1967), a bronze medal in the Grenoble Olympics (1968), and a fourth-place finish at Innsbruck (1964).[35]

The real success of the CAHA after World War II was in how steadily it grew the game. Amateur hockey registrations were 67,541 in 1948–49, but after a temporary decline in the early 1950s, registration began a steep increase: 85,840 in 1956–57, 143,000 in 1961–62, 245,348 in 1966–67, and 540,837 in 1971–72.[36] After 1945, hockey became the country's pride—its best players stars, their images conveyed in newspapers, on radio and in specialized pulp magazines—*Hockey Pictorial*, *Inside the Blueline*, *Hockey Illustrated*, and *Hockey News*—and delivered in the saccharine biographies of Howe, Béliveau, Richard, Hull, Orr, and other stars, and in the juvenile fiction of Scott Young.[37] It came in the flotsam and jetsam of material culture: sweaters ordered through Eaton's catalog, table-hockey games featuring NHL teams, Beehive Corn Syrup player picture-posters, Esso Power Player sticker books, and the ubiquitous hockey cards printed by chewing-gum companies Parkhurst, Topps, and O-Pee-Chee. And it came in the radio and television broadcast voices of *Hockey Night in Canada*'s Foster Hewitt and *Soirée du Hockey*'s René Lecavalier and, for those close enough, a visit to the Hockey Hall of Fame, a brick-and-mortar pantheon of "greats" conceived early in this era (1943) and finally constructed on Toronto's Canadian National Exhibition grounds in 1961.[38]

The NHL might have sold the game too well. By the 1960s, continentalization was an ominous concern for Canadians, whose manufacturing base and unions, foreign policy, and cultural industries were under siege by "Americanization."[39] Hockey too: by 1964, only four out of twenty-six professional teams played in front of Canadian audiences. Canada was training players for export to the United States, with very little in return. When Vancouver's 1967 application for an expansion NHL franchise lost out to six American cities, Canadians were angry: "How spineless can we get?" one *Toronto Star* epistle read.[40] "What this country needs," *Maclean's* journalist Bob Bossin wrote in 1970, "is a sport it can call its own. We used to have one: Hockey."[41]

On the ice, hockey's "strength down center" produced a coaching myopia. NHL capital's ability to integrate, organize, and rationalize labor, its top-down control, and its invasive sponsorship system stifled tactical creativity and reinforced old doctrine. NHL and CAHA teams all seemed to play the same style, one conceived at the game's highest levels and trickled down through minor-pro and amateur coaches, players, and parents. Integration worked against innovation.

Lloyd Percival's Alternative Vision

Few dared challenge the orthodoxy of NHL training and coaching techniques. One of them was Lloyd Percival. Over three decades, his "Sports College" broadcasts on CBC radio and television, alongside his pamphlets, books, and newspaper articles, made him a prominent voice on health, fitness, and hockey. His round, high forehead, small chin, slightly beaked nose, and horn-rimmed glasses projected owlish wisdom, which was offered on air in nasally but confident and casual conversation. He was trustworthy, especially when bolstered by mounds of statistics and research.

Percival was born in 1913 and grew up in Toronto's leafy Rosedale neighborhood. Despite an aptitude for tennis and cricket, he pursued hockey and boxing with passion. In 1929 he got an itch to coach, so he began a long international apprenticeship that included coursework at America's

Springfield College and England's Loughborough College. He learned the rudiments of survey research and analysis, attended coaching camps (including one of Knute Rockne's last) and major sports events (Berlin Olympics), and conducted interviews with popular media personalities like the American Ted Husing. He began a newspaper column for the *Toronto Star* and created Toronto-area radio shows, including quiz-based features "Sports Club," "Mental Athletics," and, in 1941, the thirty-minute "Sports College," which begat a weekly newspaper cartoon "featuring 'Ace Percival, the world's most versatile athlete."[42] By July 1944, "Ace" could be heard on the CBC across English-speaking Canada and parts of the United States. Meantime, the YMCA National Council helped him produce and mail study bulletins and sport instruction pamphlets, called "Playbetters," for any youth who requested them.[43]

Percival covered all sports, but his audience responded most enthusiastically to hockey, especially when he featured guests such as Gordie Howe, Terry Sawchuk, Syl Apps, and Bobby Bauer (who had played for Coach Percival on a youth team). In 1950, Percival's printed hockey advice crossed the border in the annual American *Ice Hockey Guide*: sixteen "Hints for Goalkeepers," including one to "play plenty of fast table tennis, handball, or badminton" to keep the eyes and muscles "right on the beam." In 1951 he compiled his thinking in a compendium, *The Hockey Handbook*, covering well-worn subjects like skating, puck carrying, shooting, and goaltending. But his presentation was different from that of other hockey gurus. He peppered his arguments with statistics from his Sports College research. And he coupled the science with a strong message: educated hard work could turn a young dreamer into an NHL success.[44]

In 1950–51, Percival was invited by the NHL's Red Wings and the OHA's St. Michael's Majors to provide special training sessions. He and his research team conducted tests and offered prescriptions for players, coaches, and trainers on exercise, nutrition, motivation, skill development, and strategy. According to Percival's biographer, his Red Wings report was one hundred pages long. In his work for St. Michael's, he gathered game statistics on body checks, shooting, passing, and positional play, as well as puck possession—common fodder for today's "analytics" but unheard of in 1951. Many on those teams, including Jack Adams, Red Kelly, Gordie Howe, and Bill Dineen, praised his work.[45]

But Percival earned the scorn of others at the top of the hockey pyramid. Journalist Douglas Fisher zeroed in on the main problem: "Percival's personality. He is . . . without much patience for unscientific coaches or for the pundits who have kept sports writing in the shallows of anecdote and community rivalry." Percival attacked shibboleths such as the steak-and-eggs pregame meal, restrictions on water during training and games, and disdain for off-ice training. In 1951 his "scientific tests" showed that Gordie Howe was the "best right wing in hockey" and Maurice Richard a "poor second." In response, Canadiens coach Dick Irvin called Percival's work the product of a "three year old child."[46] Despite this, Percival's voice resonated. Eventually, most elite programs heeded his call for more scientific coaching, better nutrition, and year-round conditioning—ideas the Russians used effectively by the end of the 1950s. As different as they were in tone and perspective, Leslie McFarlane's *Here's Hockey!* and Percival's *Hockey Handbook* inhabited the same space in postwar Canada. If McFarlane celebrated the strength and glamour of hockey's Canadian empire, Percival pinpointed its flaws, predicted its decline, and pointed a way forward.

The American Orbit, 1945–1971

American hockey had its own disruptions in the postwar decades. Here, strength down center was visible in two important developments. The first was the rise to dominance of AHAUS, the national body that mimicked the Canadian system in the way it governed senior hockey and negotiated creeping professionalism. The second was the entrenchment of hockey's unique American signature, the "college" model—with its emphasis on pure amateurism and an imperative to develop a distinctly *American* version of the game.

AHAUS's rise came about from one critical event: the knockout blow it dealt to the AAU at the 1948 Winter Olympics. Two US teams arrived in St. Moritz, each carrying the flag: one, an AAU team sanctioned by the International Olympic Committee; the other, an AHAUS team, sanctioned by the local Swiss Organizing Committee and the LIHG. The American feud started in 1937 when a group of rink managers, including Boston's Walter Brown and New York's John Reed Kilpatrick, organized AHAUS to challenge the AAU's control of senior hockey and its status as a governing body with the right to select national teams. AHAUS favored a liberal approach to amateurism (permitting swift reinstatement of ex-pros and the mixing of amateurs and pros in game play) to encourage a freer flow of top talent and top teams.[47] In 1947 the LIHG formally recognized AHAUS as national governing body for hockey in the United States.[48]

But the LIHG didn't have the only say. Avery Brundage, chairman of the US Olympic Committee, vice president of the IOC, and amateur purist, smelled a rat. His USOC had sanctioned the AAU team, and though the LIHG controlled most international hockey tournaments, the IOC controlled the Olympics. It would be the AAU team, spewed Brundage, or no US team at all. For him, St. Moritz was a showdown between amateur and commercial interests: "The future of . . . the Olympic Games are at stake." Worried, IOC president Sigfrid Edström wrote to Brundage: "If there is no Ice Hockey, there can be no Olympic Games." Brundage recalled that he was "practically public enemy No. 1—there was little or no understanding" of his position especially among the "Press and Radio." In the end, Brundage and the IOC reached a strange compromise with the LIHG: Olympic hockey would go on and the AHAUS team would represent the United States in the record book, but only if it did not win a medal. As it happened, the US team finished fourth.[49]

The 1948 imbroglio began the death spiral of AAU hockey and the ascendance of AHAUS, whose future looked bright. The association's 1948 guidebook listed sixteen affiliated elite amateur leagues, including five from greater Boston; five from Minnesota (with clubs in Wisconsin and North Dakota); one on the Pacific coast that ranged from Vancouver to San Diego; an international league that comprised teams from Detroit, Toledo, and Windsor, Ontario; one all-Wisconsin; one Metro New York; and an Eastern league with franchises in Boston, New York, Atlantic City, and Baltimore.[50]

Senior amateur teams shared two principal attributes, the same as their Canadian cousins. Local attractions, they were also *commercial* enterprises. For instance, the Maroons of Berlin, New Hampshire, were heirs to a hockey tradition dating back to the early twentieth century, populated by French-Canadian immigrants who came to work in the town's paper mills. Known for great speed and skill, they were led by Father A. Lauziere, who managed and financed the operation, sometimes from his own pocketbook. His 1947 replacement was another priest, Father Omer Bousquet, who spearheaded a campaign for a new arena, built in time to host the 1948 New England Senior tournament, which the Maroons won in front of thousands of fans.[51] Likewise, a vibrant enthusiasm motored senior hockey in Warroad, Minnesota, a hamlet of fourteen hundred people that produced some of the America's top postwar talent, including Olympians Gordon, Roger, and Bill Christian. While Warroad had long enjoyed amateur hockey success, in the postwar years the senior Lakers benefited from the work of the Warroad Recreation Association, boosters who in 1959 raised $15,000 in cash (and much more in labor, equipment, and materials) to renovate the town rink, adding six hundred new seats, four locker rooms, and a concession stand. Lakers games were a weekly expression of community strength. As one article explained, "The entire population—1400 strong—made it for the 1958 game with the US Nationals."[52]

Not far behind *community* was *commerce*, and attention to expenses and revenue. Among the most pressing costs were player payments. Take, for instance, the Northern Amateur Hockey League, an industrial loop that foundry and shipyard employees and Coast Guard personnel in Duluth, Minnesota, had formed during the war. It was reorganized in 1945 to include the Williams Coolerators, Eveleth Rangers, Virginia Amerks, Hibbing Barons, and Fort Frances (Ontario) Maple Leafs. According to historian Jim Coughlin, "NAHL players . . . received expense checks based on reputation and fan appeal. Sam LoPresti, the Chicago Black Hawks goaltender when war broke out, drew the largest—$100–125 per game. In Eveleth, the hometown players divided up the gate receipts after expenses."[53]

The constitution of the International Hockey League, an AHAUS-governed senior "amateur" league that included the Minneapolis Millers and the St. Paul Saints, betrayed the confusion about paying players. Article 2 claimed it would follow the rules of AHAUS, though on-ice rules were those of the NHL. More confusing, article 16 put a limit on weekly player "salaries"—$1,800 per team or $128 per man. A 1960 official league "salary" list showed that most players earned more than $128, but almost all of them less than $200. To collect *any* "salary," of course, violated every existing amateur code.[54]

But AHAUS was willing to look the other way because senior amateur hockey supplied needed revenue. In one account, NAHL teams "were asked (not required) to contribute 10% of their gate receipts to AHAUS. Teams that 'passed the hat' instead of charging admission were asked to kick in $10 a game."[55] In 1961 the IHL Minneapolis Millers were to pay 2 percent of their gate receipts to AHAUS. Seemingly small change, the aggregate effect was enormous for AHAUS. An August 1960 bulletin celebrated an increase from the previous year of 243 registered teams, to a total of 732. Of that total, only forty-one teams (less than 7 percent) played to a "paid gate," but their 2 percent fees "really support the other 93%." The AHAUS financial report for 1963 conveyed the importance of the paid gate: of its $99,531.35 in revenues, 43 percent came from "percentages received."[56]

A decade earlier, IIHF president Fritz Kraatz recognized the monetary value of senior amateur leagues in a roundup he wrote for the *Ice Hockey World Annual*: "In the U.S.A. only 38 teams play to a paid gate, while 266 do not. One eighth of the members support the other seven eighths"—a real Robin-Hood operation. "The AHA of US is really contributing toward the advancement of ice hockey by helping out the youngster who is coming up." And growing participation numbers suggest that AHAUS was an effective steward.[57] In Minnesota, for example, media scion Bob Ridder and Twin Cities youth league convener Don Clark founded the Minnesota Amateur Hockey Association in 1947 and soon gained AHAUS sanction. By 1951 the MAAA had 560 teams registered and became a seedbed for America's biggest crops of talent over the ensuing two decades.[58]

An American System

Throughout the 1950s and 1960s, AHAUS shaped a distinctive brand, remarkable for its steady growth and its ambivalent relationship with its partners in the NHL and CAHA. From 150 registered players in 1937 it grew to twenty-four thousand in 1963, who played coast to coast on more than sixteen hundred teams. AHAUS was a bargain for youth teams, which into the 1960s paid only $2 for registration in return for access to regional and national tournaments and, after 1959, *United States Amateur Hockey*, a national service magazine filled with tactics, tips, and news.[59] More practically, AHAUS offered its members a hospital-plus-dental insurance plan that covered hockey injuries at rates ranging by age from $1 to $17 per player.[60] AHAUS built the base of an American pyramid, where thousands of boys (and some girls) learned to skate, shoot, and stickhandle. This base fed talent to high schools and they, in turn, to college programs, senior leagues, and the national team—the pinnacle of success.

It was an American hockey *system*. In 1961 a *United States Amateur Hockey* editorial declared: "The height of hockey desires in the United States is to play in college, on a good high school team, or get a shot at the National team."[61] Unlike Canada's system that connected minor hockey to NHL "farms," or Europe's "siloed" club system, America was driven by a *college* vision, heirs to the amateur ideal rooted in turn-of-the-twentieth-

Cover of *US Amateur Hockey Magazine*, 1959 (Courtesy of USA Hockey)

century Ivy League schools and mythical figures like Hobey Baker and Frank Merriwell.[62] In the mid-twentieth century there emerged new versions, like Pete Dawkins, the all-star, sixty-minute defenseman on Jack Riley's U.S. Military Academy teams (1957–59). In 1959 Dawkins racked up 25 goals and 38 points, the same year he earned honors in the classroom, served as president of his class, captained the football team, won the Heisman Trophy, and received a Rhodes Scholarship at Oxford.[63]

Despite its common vision, the American system was not neatly governed. AHAUS supported the base of the pyramid but shared power with other important stakeholders including the NCAA Hockey Rules Committee and the American Hockey Coaches Association (AHCA). The AHCA was formed in May 1947, when fifteen college representatives met in New York City to create a permanent body dedicated to giving order to the amateur game by organizing college hockey officials, encouraging adoption of NCAA rules, promoting rink construction, and establishing a code of ethics. Its first president was former NHLer (then Yale coach) Murray Murdoch. In 1960, AHCA president Harry Cleverly (Boston University) reported a membership of "700 coaches from colleges, private schools and high schools, officials, [and] ex-coaches."[64]

The AHCA also focused on establishing a national tournament sanctioned by the NCAA, whose executive committee needed persuading. The challenge, AHCA secretary-treasurer (and Michigan coach) Vic Heyliger later recalled, was to "find a location that would be suitable to hold a large crowd . . . easily accessible, and . . . let us get some expense money to cover our costs." The challenge was met in 1948 when Thayer Tutt, owner of the Broadmoor Hotel and the Broadmoor World Ice Arena (both in Colorado Springs), agreed to host and to pick up all expenses (including travel, meals, and housing) for the tournament's first ten years. The event's Broadmoor years were luxurious. Michigan player (and later coach) Al Renfrew recalled: "The Broadmoor was a first-class facility . . . a beautiful sight—like dreamland." His team responded on the ice: five championships in ten years.[65]

Beyond governance, the American system's integrity resided in rule-making and officiating an American *code*. Among the first to articulate this was 1951 NCAA committee chairman Louis Keller, who noted that his rules were both distinctive and exemplary. "[H]igh schools and other amateur organizations accept and use our recommended rules. . . . Our . . . game . . . conforms to educational ideals and promotes . . . sportsmanship, co-operation, respect for authority. . . . When we allow . . . fighting, brawls, etc., we are certainly not living up to our assumed obligations."[66] Defending the American brand required dedicated referees' associations. Formed in 1928, the first regional group, the Eastern Hockey Officials Association, took its work seriously. It screened applicants via a written exam, recommendation letters, and sometimes-direct observation. They were vigilant amateurists. "Certainly," one section president wrote in 1950, "no official should be accepted as a member who works games in which professional rules are used." In 1955, regional officials' associations formed the National Ice Hockey Officials Association, which worked closely with NCAA colleges and high schools. The circle of American hockey tightened.[67]

In the 1950s and 1960s, traditions took root in record and ritual: perennial team dynasties and signature tournaments gave distinction to the American game. Among the symbols were the Bowdoin College Polar Bears, coached by the inimitable Sid Watson, 1959–83, who demonstrated how small college teams could compete against teams from large state universities that sometimes had ten times their student enrollment.[68] A former NFL football player, Watson was among a wave of coaches who took the high school and college reins from an earlier generation. They included Jack Kelley (Colby College and Boston University), Bob Johnson (Colorado College and Wisconsin), Ed Burns (Arlington, Massachusetts, High School), Jim Fullerton (Brown), Herb Brooks (Minnesota), and Charlie Holt (Colby and New Hampshire). Many had played and coached football. They wanted more science in the game; all of them were interested in "systems": forechecking, power play, break out, and defense.[69]

Their teams were organized in loosely structured leagues that competed for mythical "championships." In the East, these included the Pentagonal or Ivy League, the New England League, and the Tri-State League, all of which were consolidated in the early 1960s in the Eastern College Athletic Conference. Elsewhere, schools such as Macalester, St. John's, Hamline, Bemidji State Teachers College, and others formed the "Minnesota College Conference," with schedules of about fifteen games each.[70] Out west, college action focused after 1951 on the Western Intercollegiate Hockey League that pitted Michigan, Michigan Tech, Denver, Michigan State, Minnesota, Colorado College, and North Dakota against one another. Reconstituted as WCHA after 1958, its members dominated the NCAA championships for years.[71]

Beyond regional rivalries, media and fan spotlights focused, too, on a growing list of brand-name tournaments. Beginning in 1952, Greater Boston had its Beanpot, limited to Harvard, BC, BU, and Northeastern, which soon developed a unique local intensity. Long-time Boston College coach "Snooks" Kelley put it simply: "You have to know the Pope to get a ticket."[72] But the ultimate American tournament was the NCAA championship that pitted the best NCAA teams from east and west. Selecting the teams was controversial. In the West, beginning in 1959, WCHA teams participated in a tournament that produced national bids. Tournament slots were allotted to eastern teams by NCAA committee selection until 1962, when the ECAC held its first playoff event.[73] The league tournaments became big regional spectacles that triggered the development of new programs.

Secondary school programs fed the dream. Independents (or preps) continued to lead, in part because they invested in on-campus rinks. One exemplar was Lawrenceville (N.J.) School, which held its first "Invitation Tournament" in 1948, a showcase for college recruiting. Its 1958 tournament program lists entries from New England, New York, New Jersey, and Canada, with competition established "on the firmest possible basis of friendly invitation." Alongside the preps, the greatest surge of interest was among public and parochial high schools. The three decades that followed World War II were golden years for American high-school boy's hockey. The explosion of postwar suburban and ex-urban housing triggered a school-building boom, and hockey was a beneficiary.[74]

One measure of this growth could be found in state and regional tournaments. The New England Interscholastic Tournament, for instance, dated to 1941. It had struggled and lost money, but by 1958, its sixteenth annual affair, held at the Rhode Island Auditorium, enjoyed standing-room-only crowds. That year, tiny Burrillville (Rhode Island) High School defeated powerhouses Melrose (Massachusetts), St. Dominic's (Lewiston, Maine), and Arlington (Massachusetts) en route to the title. First iced in 1940, Tom Eccleston's Burrillville Broncos practiced on frozen ponds or on a crude rink frozen over an asphalt surface and surrounded by a tight mesh fence designed to combat the sun's glare.[75] In Minnesota, high-school hockey was boosted in 1945 when St. Paul Schools' athletic director Gene Aldrich hosted the first statewide tournament. It was an immediate success. More than eighty-four hundred fans watched three days of games, including those involving Granite Falls, who, one historian wrote, arrived "without regular uniforms" since they "were accustomed to playing in long pants and sweatshirts . . . [and] stuffed newspapers into their pants for shinguards." A local program loaned them uniforms, but they were no match for mighty Eveleth, who romped 16–0.[76] By the late 1960s the tournament had reached capacity in the old Auditorium, so the boys moved in 1969 into Bloomington's Met Center. Attendance jumped to 79,868.[77]

Boom times had arrived. Fenton Kelsey Jr. captured the feeling in a 1962 *Hockey* editorial. In the coming year, he predicted, "600,000 youths and adults will play some kind of hockey . . . from casual pick-up games to those attended by the thousands." Hockey was already a $25 million business in America. By 1971, he said, "there will be over a million and a half U.S. men and boys playing ice hockey." Kelsey's optimism papered over rising tensions concerning Canadians in the U.S. college ranks. And the focus on males reflected hockey's long gender bias and its preoccupation with money.[78] Still, his self-congratulatory tone was warranted. In three decades, American organizers, players, and coaches carved out space within hockey's North American core.

17

Cold Wars and International Ice: 1945–1971

The 1948 Winter Olympic Games opened on January 30 in St. Moritz, Switzerland, a country that stayed neutral during the war. The participating nations were more or less the same as those at GaPa in 1936. But Europe was not the same. Cities, towns, and villages across the Continent were reduced to rubble. Factories, railways, roads, bridges, and lines for telegraph and telephone blown up. Farms and vineyards destroyed. More than thirty-six million Europeans were dead. Humanity had succumbed to mass extermination, mass rape, and mass looting at levels beyond imagination. War's end only extended the suffering for millions of the displaced, the homeless, and the diseased. The year 1947 was particularly difficult in Europe. Food shortages were exacerbated by a bitterly cold, icy, snowy winter, followed by a summer of record drought that dropped the harvest's yield by a third. Currency crises across the Continent conjured the bleak years after the Great War. The Marshall Plan, announced in 1947, offered some hope for a sustained recovery, at least among those states that accepted American aid. Stalin refused to play along, thus steeling the curtain that slowly dropped around Czechoslovakia, Poland, Hungary, Rumania, East Germany, and others.[1]

Amid this atmosphere, the Olympics were a small measure of normalcy. Swiss hockey legend Bibi Torriani stood on a platform before the assembled athletes and spectators, touched the Swiss flag, and read the oath of fealty to the IOC, an oath that brimmed with notions of gentlemanly sportsmanship and amateurism. A Canadian hockey player, Hubert Brooks, wrote in his diary about those opening ceremonies, which included Swiss President Enrico Celio's declaration that the games were "a symbol of a new world peace and good-will." The notion must have been irritating, and much worse, to those still in misery. Ironically, the oaths of Olympic peace resounded just as news circulated of Mahatma Gandhi's assassination in India, which triggered riots, civil war, and an eventual partition between a Hindu India and a Muslim Pakistan. As Brooks noted in his diary, goodwill did not pervade these Olympics, at least when it came to hockey. St. Moritz returned to the spotlight two "control" issues that had simmered before the war: commercial interests off the ice and North American brutality on it.[2]

The first controversy was the bizarre American civil war between the teams from the AAU and AHAUS. Beyond the bluster of Avery Brundage and the apparent initial victory for IOC control of Olympic eligibility and competition, the fact remained that the AHAUS team was the team of record: a team representing a new governing body more aligned with rink managers and "commercial" interests; a team officially recognized by the LIHG, if not the IOC. In this respect, the St. Moritz games may be seen as an early moment in a movement among the various sports federations for more control of Olympic events. We see its fruits today, where eligibility rules vary widely between Olympic sports because the IOC has formally ceded its control. To some degree, hockey was an early agitator.

Once underway, the 1948 tournament showcased the divergence of playing styles beginning to differentiate European from North American hockey. Hubert Brooks mused in his diary about his team, other teams, refereeing, as well as fan and media responses to the competition. His entry about Canada's game versus Sweden contained comments that resonated more loudly in the next few decades. The Swedes, he noted, had a "scrappy club with two 60-minute defencemen, big and rugged but not so tough." While Tre Kronor might "lack the fitness of our Canadian squad," he added, they compensated with "aggressiveness—minus the body check." The Swedes were not alone in this. To North Americans, slashing and hooking, not rugged checking, marked the European game. "By Canadian standards," Brooks wrote, "we never thought we participated in a rough game." European referees and media had other views. Canadian Wally Halder, Brooks claimed, "played throughout his entire University of Toronto career without a single penalty." In St. Moritz, however, he was "nicknamed 'The Brute' and described as 'vicious' by some segments of the European press." Brooks's diary is peppered with comments on brawls in games involving America or Canada. As he noted following Canada's victory over Great

Britain: "The fans got into the action hooting and yodeling with each new penalty call. The refs and the European teams were not ready for the North American 'body checking' style of hockey which they considered 'dirty.' We, on the other hand, were not used to players getting away with holding, hooking and spearing." Thus, St. Moritz sparked tensions over "systems" in international hockey. In the quarter century that followed, amid the ebbs and flows of the Cold War, multiple disputes—over eligibility, club and national team support, playing, coaching, and training styles—slowly coalesced around broader imperatives of political economy and culture.[3]

The Short New Life of the English League

English hockey skated through the war in relatively good shape, thanks in large part to the presence of so many high-quality Canadian players stationed with the burgeoning Allied Expeditionary Force. By the early 1950s, the English senior circuit was re-established with franchises at Earls Court (Rangers), Empress Hall, Streatham, Wembley (each of them Lions), Harringay (Racers), Brighton (Tigers), and Nottingham (Panthers). Harringay, Wembley, and Empress Hall rinks each seated some eight thousand fans. *Ice Hockey World* reported that most rinks were smaller, but all were "accustomed to capacity or near-capacity crowds." League play was initially minimal; it entailed "two major tournaments annually [that] consisted of three home and three away games between each team." The holiday recess between tournaments allowed the rinks to book lucrative ice shows and the teams to tour the Continent.[4]

The United Kingdom had additional rinks in Ayr, Perth, Dundee, Dunfermline, Durham, Falkirk, Grimsby, Belfast, Kirkaldy, Manchester, Edinburgh, Paisley, Glasgow, Southampton, Blackpool, and East Twickenham. Almost all had full-sized ice surfaces, and seating ranged from two thousand to three thousand. But would this be enough to build a grassroots foundation of young players who brought families to watch the game at various levels? Could hockey lure football fans indoors? Could elite-level spectacle thrive without a grassroots base? Would strong grassroots play insure attendance at the top? That was the ongoing conundrum. For the English Senior League, a showcase of talent meant Canadian imports. In 1952, for instance, *Ice Hockey World*'s "Big Six" English Senior League all-stars were all Canadian: goalie Earl Becker (Yorkton, Saskatchewan), defensemen Jack Leckie (Powassan, Ontario) and Tommy Jamieson (Toronto), and forwards Les Anning (Rimouski, Quebec), Chick Zamick (Winnipeg), and Les Strongman (Winnipeg).[5] As it had before the war, the English Senior League operated on a North American–style commercial model. While technically amateur, players received wages both above and below the table. Rink and team owners expected their investments to fetch a profit.

Indoor, artificial ice rinks required high levels of revenue to pay both capital and operating costs. Senior amateur leagues and public skating could not keep the lights on every night. Rink managers and owners like Sir Arthur Elvin of Wembley, Frank Gentle of Harringay's, and Claude Langdon of Empress Hall looked to any and all ways to attract consumers. One sure bet was ice shows that featured top figure skaters sprinkling their skill among acts of chorus lines and clowns. A pure hockey promoter like Bobby Giddens could only grit his teeth when the ice shows grabbed most of a rink's advertising budget for Day-Glo posters in transit terminals and advertising copy in programs. He challenged the rink bosses to have their admen and press secretaries "probe the ice show market for ice hockey fans." No one was listening.[6]

Demand for hockey did not keep up with cost. In 1954 *Ice Hockey World* estimated that the average gate at the average rink was £770 per game. Of this, an "entertainment tax" took £160. The team roster in the British League was twelve, of which ten (on average) were Canadians. One of them was Ken Johannson, an Edmonton native who, like Bobby Giddens, chose the American college route (North Dakota) before crossing the Atlantic. Johannson recalled that his 1953–54 compatriots included "some very, very good players and guys who could have played in the AHL in those days and maybe the Western Hockey League and would have been potentially called up to the NHL." He also recalled their pay at about £22–23 per week—that, on top of room and board with a family. This matches *Ice Hockey World*'s estimate of top salaries at £20 per week, with British players making more like £12 per week. The total average travel cost, including transporting the Canadians before and after the season, was £100 per player. Sticks, uniforms, skates, tape, medical supplies and other necessities ran some £100 per player. On top of these were the arena's fixed and operating costs, as well as administrative and staff salaries. The magazine concluded glumly, "Is there money in ice hockey? What do you think?" Slashing labor costs was not an option. Phil Drackett, Giddens's right-hand man, recalled decades later that "it was no good getting less expensive players because a public reared on good-class hockey would not accept the lowering of standards."[7]

By the mid-1950s the league was down to five teams: Harringay, Wembley, Brighton, Nottingham, and Paisley. By 1960 the league was dead. Years later, Drackett remembered a sad irony: in 1959 the New York Rangers and the Boston Bruins played two exhibitions in England at the start of a European Tour, just "as British big-time hockey was about to breathe its last." It was also the end for *Ice Hockey World*, which Drackett claimed reached a weekly circulation of fifty thousand, stocked with national advertising. As he poignantly recalled, "with deep regret" he "slid the case on my trusty typewriter," shook Giddens's hand, and settled in as a sportswriter on Fleet Street. Giddens died only a few years later, his dream of homegrown English hockey unfulfilled.[8]

Continental Nationalism Redux

Fifty years later, we can say that the English League employed the wrong model, in the wrong place, at the wrong time. A strictly commercial operation, stocked with Canadians, had little financial or cultural leeway. Amid an economy that was being nationalized, investors slashed and burned assets that drained their portfolios. And consumers, like the broader world they lived in, were awash in national pride and interest. If the negotiations of 1919 marked out new borders and new nations while leaving people intact, 1945 brought something different and more sinister: what we now call ethnic cleansing. Across the continent, millions were removed and displaced in the name of nationalism. Such a storm also blew across Europe's hockey rinks.[9]

An early signal came from the British Ice Hockey Association, which changed course in 1950 on the composition of its national team—in this case, on its use of Canadian transplants. "This year," wrote Bunny Ahearne, the BIHA's powerful secretary, "the Great Britain team for the first time on record is composed entirely of home-bred players who have learned and played all their hockey here in Great Britain." This included eleven Scots, whose development Ahearne attributed to a policy requiring each senior team to roster at least three native players. Unfortunately, local development was too slow to save the English Senior League.[10]

In 1953, LIHG President Fritz Kraatz offered his own simple blueprint for building European hockey. Nations had to invest in artificial ice rinks. Then they could develop native talent. He was quite sanguine about the first step. France planned new rinks in Lyons and in Paris; Italy was finishing twin rinks in Cortina d'Ampezzo, site of the 1956 Winter Olympics, as well as one in Balzano. There were high hopes for another in Trento. Yugoslavia was finishing rinks in Belgrade and Zagreb; Vienna promised a mammoth facility that could seat twenty-five thousand—part of its bid to host the 1957 World and European Championships. Sweden's federation was "fighting hard to get a rink of its own in Stockholm." Denmark and Netherlands were in similar modes. Oslo's new arena was "doing very well." Both West and East Berlin enjoyed covered rinks, and West Germany planned for two more. Switzerland looked to build in Lugano, La Chaux-de-Fonds, and Geneva. But new rinks could not build "European" hockey if they were filled with Canadian players. "Ice hockey on the European continent," he warned, could "only exist if the different nations concerned breed their own native players." While everyone knew that Canada was the "greatest ice hockey nation," and its players might be "very welcome as instructors," it was equally clear that "the import of complete teams would ruin Continental ice hockey in a very short time." Kraatz was a shrewd observer. Canadian players were still valued on club teams, but there had to be limits.[11]

Canadian *coaches* were still especially attractive assets, even for national teams. Within a decade, however, the most powerful national teams wanted "national" coaches. Sweden was a good example. In November 1948 the Swedish IHA invited Bunny Ahearne to visit as a consultant: in part to discuss plans for Stockholm's hosting of the 1949 IIHF championships, in part (wrote Bobby Giddens) to tap Ahearne's "wide international experience on how best to establish and popularize ice hockey throughout the country." While Giddens did not spell out a strategy, it seems the Swedes and Finns (and others) had picked up a central notion to recruit Canadian coaches who had dual nationality. Of course, Ahearne was well versed on issues of passports and visas. He had smoothed out, among others, the immigration problems of Canadian-Finn Gunnar Telkinnen who played for Harringay in the ENL. The Swedes had already used Canadian Vic Lindquist as a coach in the 1930s. In 1950 they tapped Ahearne's pipeline and hired as their national team coach Frank Trottier, an Ottawa native who had played in the ENL since 1936. According to Giddens, Trottier took Swedish-language lessons in London before his move, ordered top-level Canadian equipment and uniforms, and "arranged with the Canadian government's Department of External Affairs to have films and still pictures of ice hockey action to supplement his practice lectures" to the national team. He also brought his own hockey primer, translated into Swedish, which was widely distributed to supplement the lectures he gave around the country as he preached the game and scouted for talent.[12]

Trottier may have helped Swedish hockey in general, but his Tre Kronor national team played to close losses against Canada, Great Britain, Switzerland, and the United States at the next World Championships. Fifth place was not enough to save his job. It was a matter of control, said Rudolph Eklow, vice president of the SIHA, who told *Ice Hockey World*, "Mr. Trottier will not permit managers and officials in the player's box. We appreciate that he has great English, Canadian and International experience, but he does not yet know the Swedish play and players." Bobby Giddens recognized the real issue was "more than a deadlock between coach and officials." It was "a clash between two points of view; the Canadian one and that of the European or Scandinavian outlook." The Swedes wanted their own national stamp on hockey. While Canadians Ed Reigle (late 1950s) and Billy Harris (early 1970s) had the Tre Kronor helm briefly, Swedish glory came under the watch of natives Folke Jansson (World Championship gold medal in 1957) and the inimitable Arne Stromberg, (one gold, six silvers, and two bronze medals at World and Olympic events between 1961 and 1971).[13]

Sweden had three divisions of organized amateur play in 1950, with the first division centered in the Stockholm area, including A.I.K., Gota, Deisel, and Atla. Each Division I team was allotted 2½ hours of ice time per week on Stockholm's sole artificial surface. All other play was on natural ice. D-I teams carried twelve players. Giddens claimed that the average ticket cost 2.50 kroners, with matches averaging three thousand fans. As in most national-league operations, the Swedish Association took a percentage of gate receipts for its operating expenses.[14] Bunny Ahearne felt strongly that postwar Sweden would become a power. As *Ice Hockey World* reported in 1952, "He sees the day not too distant, and despite Bandy, the national pastime, when ice hockey will loom big, popular and first-class in Sweden." To push that process, Ahearne commissioned a cup in his own name, played for annually in a Swedish tournament. Canada and the United States sent clubs to the first affair, which Canada won.[15]

To become a consistent international power, Sweden needed artificial ice rinks. An unnamed correspondent submitted a telling anecdote to the *Ice Hockey World Annual* for 1954–55. Sweden's King Gustaf had attended the Sweden-Canada match at the 1954 World Championships in Stockholm. A good sport, the seventy-year-old monarch stayed through the match despite the heavy snow that cascaded onto the outdoor facility. At one point, sixteen thousand fans started to chant, "We want a covered ice rink," to which the king turned and "showed that he was of the same opinion." In the next two decades, Swedish communities and clubs responded, especially beyond the original hockey bulwark of Greater Stockholm.[16]

Simple numbers tell the story of Swedish investment and its payoff. A 1969 article spoke of a "10-years explosion" in rinks and participation: from six rinks in 1955 to one hundred in 1965, and to 140 by 1969, including twenty-five large indoor stadiums. In 1955 there were some nine hundred clubs and fifty thousand players. By 1969 there were sixteen hundred clubs and 110,000 players in five thousand different leagues affiliated with the SIHA. This did not count the one hundred thousand youth playing in local community events. By the late 1960s, Tre Kronor ranked with the USSR and Czechoslovakia among the Big Three in world competition. The Swedish national league produced a train of talent, starting with forward Sven "Tumba" Johansson. When the Soviets first appeared on world championship ice at Stockholm in 1954, their first big match was against the home team. It was back and forth in the first period until Tre Kronor scored first. One Russian account described the ensuing scene, doubtless replicated many times over the years: "The spectators, led by an employee of the stadium, who wielded a rod for want of a baton, cheered wildly as the figure 1 appeared on the score tower. 'Tumba, Tumba, Tumba,' they shouted." The Swedes had other stars, including forward Ulf Sterner and defensemen Lars Lasse Bjorn and Roland Stolz. All were more than six-feet tall, all combined speed, skill, and toughness. Their physical play has been characterized as "Viking" hockey. Johansson and Sterner caught the eye of NHL scouts and were invited to try out for the New York Rangers. Although neither lasted long on the roster, they were a harbinger of future migration.[17]

As Swedish historian Tobias Stark has argued, during the 1960s hockey became a metaphor for the "Swedish model" of life under the Social Democratic Party that brokered compromises between industry, agriculture, and organized labor and thereby transformed the country "from a poor and traditional agrarian society, on the social and political periphery of Western-Europe, to a hyper-modern industrial nation, widely considered as one of the world's leading welfare states." And "sossehockey" became a middle way between North American individualism and Soviet collectivism.[18]

Finland rose more slowly than Sweden, in large part because it lacked indoor artificial ice rinks. All of the country's venues had natural ice until 1956, when compressors and chillers arrived in Tampere. But there was no roof. True indoor arenas did not arrive for another decade. By one account, as late as 1970 "Finland had two ice stadiums and a few artificial skating rinks." By that time the Swedes had "32 arenas and 124 artificial rinks." The Finnish economy was slower to rebound from the war. While the socialist state supported health and fitness, hockey was one of many sports vying for public dollars, and rinks were a daunting expenditure that faced "strong resistance amongst the distributors of public funds." A rink-building boom waited until the 1980s.[19]

The Finns won a silver medal in the 1962 European Championships, but it took another decade, and more rinks, for their arrival as a consistent threat. As they struggled to catch up with their neighbors, the Finns looked to Canada for coaching. In 1968, for instance, the Helsinki Ice Hockey Club team recruited NHL stalwart Carl Brewer to run things. Brewer only lasted one season, but, as several Finnish scholars put it, "he was in many ways unmatched as a pioneer of professional ice hockey in Finland." His encouragement of NHL-style physicality even influenced the Finnish national team whose "style of play changed" and "became tougher" during Brewer's tenure.[20]

While the Swedes and the Finns were ascending the ranks, the Swiss were in a slow decline. Like Sweden, the Swiss remained neutral during the war. Unlike Sweden, they did not use that economic advantage to boost their hockey infrastructure. During one postwar season, a hockey insider told Bobby Giddens that the Swiss "will have to do an overhaul job." Among other things, he said, their equipment was outdated. "The pants don't even have 'charley-horse' pads. The skates the boys use are two and three sizes too big for them." He also noted the biggest problem: "They'll have to put roofs over their rinks. The players will have to practice more. To-day they have two workouts a week, which isn't enough for a high school kid." As late as 1961, however, the Swiss hosted international competition in a converted Lausanne outdoor swimming pool. In March 1971 coauthor Steve Hardy coached a visiting American team that played outdoors in both Davos and St. Moritz. Beautiful vistas, but dicey odds for good ice.[21]

Despite such limitations, Switzerland drew Canadian talent, especially at the coaching level. In 1953, for example, the following clubs had Canadians at the helm: the National Team, Zurich Grasshoppers and Schlittschuh Club Berne, Neuchâtel, Basel, Davos, and Arosa. As Stan Obodiac (who coached SC Berne) wrote in the *Ice Hockey World Annual*, he and

American Sports Ambassadors in Switzerland, 1971 (author's personal photo)

his countrymen loved the setting. "There are wonderful rinks," he noted. "There is snow grandeur. The fine sun allows you to play outdoors and never be cold. The country is small and you can be anywhere for games in five hours. The kids are crazy about puck chasing." The Swiss themselves wanted better results. By 1954, Dr. M. Thoma, president of the Swiss Ice Hockey Federation, saw his nation's program in the second tier of European play with Germany, Norway, Finland, and Italy—clearly below Russia, the Czechs, and the Swedes. Despite the growth of teams (from 198 in 1949–50 to 262 in 1953–54) the Swiss were having trouble adjusting to what he called the newer "rushing" style of play. In his opinion, overuse of Canadian coaches was no help. "Many clubs engage them purely because they are good players and not because they are good coaches." He expected that a motion to bar them, narrowly voted down the year before, might soon "be carried." Switzerland remained a magnet for North American players and coaches, but after winning three consecutive bronze medals in World Championship play, the national team slumped to second-tier status until winning silver in 2013, beating Canada along the way, with Canadian Sean Simpson behind the bench.[22]

Germany, a prewar power, faced the longest odds for continued success. Torn asunder in postwar politics, the two Germanys were still a single entity to the LIHG, which expelled them in 1946. West Germany slowly rebuilt its club programs and by 1947 had a new Oberliga—the top division (replaced by the Bundesliga in 1958). In 1951, the LIHG reinstated West Germany (FRG). By 1963, 323 teams reorganized into the German Hockey Union. The rebuilding process opened doors to Canadians. The national teams (A and B level) that entered the 1955 European and World Championships (held in their own country) were selected and coached by five Canadians who worked in the German League: Frank Trottier of Füssen, Lorne Trottier of Garmisch-Partenkirchen, Andre Girard of Krefeld, and Joe Aitken of Bad Toelz, and Clare Drake of Düsseldorf. Canadian coaches, however, could not play for the German national team, which spent the next decades out of the medal running.[23]

East Germany (GDR) entered the IIHF as a separate nation in 1956. In subsequent years, its national team, like the FRG, played on the margins of the medals, competitive but not quite there. As one German historian wrote, the GDR faced a tougher road to sports success: "The GDR had started with worse conditions than had the FRG. While the FRG received Marshall Plan Aid, the Soviet occupation forces dismantled many useful things, like train lines and factories and transported them to the Soviet Union as reparations. . . . While the FRG continued to use the expertise of Nazi sport leaders, teachers and coaches, the GDR tried to replace all Nazis." When the communist regime decided to build its international sports presence in the 1950s and 1960s it was along the Soviet model, with centrally controlled clubs, coaches, and scientists running a nationwide "dragnet for talent selection." But hockey took a backseat to gymnastics, track and field, and swimming. The system goal was "medal intensity." Hockey required investing in eighteen players for a single medal. Why not give the ice time to speed skaters who "could win twelve times as many medals."[24]

Soviet *Khokkei* Reinvention

The Soviets enjoyed a different calculus. For one thing, they won the war. In the words of historian Tony Judt: "After two decades of effective exclusion from the affairs of Europe, Russia had resurfaced." The Red Army and Mother Russia repulsed the world's most powerful war machine. Victory "brought Stalin credibility and influence, in the counsels of governments and on the streets." The USSR was gearing up for confrontation with the West. And in a new twist, this included sports, where central planning proved both nimble and effective (unlike agricultural policy). And so, in December 1948, the Central Committee of the Party issued this resolution: "Soviet sportsmen, in upcoming years will surpass world records in all major sports." In 1949 a party serial turned prediction into fact: "The increasing number of successes achieved by Soviet athletes . . . is a victory for the Soviet form of society and the socialist sports system; it provides irrefutable proof of the superiority of socialist culture over the moribund culture of capitalist states." The stakes were high.[25]

The Soviet sport authorities were aware of Canadian hockey as early as 1928. For a variety of reasons, however, they had supported their own "khokkei," or bandy. A new policy to pursue international medals required a conversion, since there was no Olympic bandy. But it was conversion and not invention. The first generation of Soviet hockey players emerged from a combination background of bandy-khokkei and football. This included Vsevolod Bobrov, who could score in bursts both on the pitch and on the ice. He switched hands with the hockey stick as he executed wide dribbles left or right, a common bandy move, but much harder to execute with the longer hockey stick. Other converted stars included Yevgeny Babich, Alexander Uvarov, Valentin Kuzin, and Yuri Pantyukhov. All had great speed, maneuverability, and vision, which are crucial in bandy.[26]

Bobrov was a good example of the crossover. According to a Russian biography, he grew up in the town of Sestroretsk, near Leningrad. His father, Mikhail, played on the bandy-khokkei team of a local factory "built in the days of Peter the Great," and he "passed his love of Russian hockey on to his sons." The sports genes deferred temporarily to football prowess, however, when Bobrov debuted with Central Red Army in 1944 and was quickly a phenom. His football experience "helped him develop his tactical skill—the marvelous ability to keep the rink in his field of vision while skating at whirlwind speed." In a passage that would have been first written for a Soviet audience, Bobrov's biographer captured key differences in the games: "Imagine that instead of a spacious ice-field with plenty of room for twenty players, if need be, and where a wicker ball rolls lightly and softly, you are taken to a small rink, which, besides everything else, is completely enclosed by tall boards. Here, there is hardly any elbow room for as few as ten players and instead of a ball a solid rubber disc is passed around with lightning speed. And if such a puck hits you, it will seem to be made not from rubber but from lead." It was a game for a man like Bobrov.[27]

By most accounts, the Soviet conversion began in February 1946 at the Moscow Institute of Physical Culture, where a small rink opened for experimental play. A symposium for players, coaches, and officials occurred that autumn in Leningrad, which was deemed enough training to launch a "sixty-day season" in December. After the premier game, *Sovetskii sport* was ebullient: "This first game showed that Canadian hockey can swiftly gain the sympathy of fans and players, with its tempo, quickly changing momentum, and intensity of play." But then, who had a choice?[28]

Among the pioneers were player-coaches Anatoli Tarasov of Air Force (briefly) and Central Army and Arkadi Chernyshev of Dinamo. These two men guided Soviet national hockey fortunes for more than two decades, alternating as head coaches and ultimately serving as co-coaches (although Chernyshev was technically the head coach). In the words of well-known hockey writer Igor Kuperman, "It was almost impossible to imagine how two such different personalities would work side-by-side. Chernyshev, the 'hockey professor,' always retained composure and elegance. He loved his stars and knew how to deal with the most talented players." By contrast, "Tarasov was the volcano of passion, sometimes angry, sometimes sarcastic, but always trying to bring out the best from his players." Under their leadership, the Soviets made quick strides. In February 1948 the great Czech club LTC Prague traveled to the USSR for some "friendly" matches. The team was stocked with a dozen players who had just won a silver medal at the winter Olympics. When they saw their first opponents, the Moscow Selects, they were underwhelmed. As Gustav Bubnik later recalled, "When we first saw their equipment, we would not stop laughing. They had soccer uniforms, leather bicycle helmets, and very long sticks." The laughing stopped on the ice, where the Soviets split a three-game series, 1-1-1, but outscored Prague 11–10. The Czechs were among the first to recognize that a shift in international power was at hand.[29]

Lack of quality equipment and ice time continued to be major problems. The Soviets lacked an indoor arena until 1956, so the coaches employed exotic but effective dry-land training to build the muscle and motor skills required on the ice. American coach Murray Williamson recalled visits with Tarasov at the height of his successful tenure. At the Central Army training center, he saw small groups working at high pace through a series of drills "on a crude wooden basketball court." The players were

> jogging, rolling, jumping, and hopping while tossing five-pound weights to each other . . . doing a series of hops across the basketball floor using medicine balls to pass under legs . . . hopping and skipping exercises while playing catch with heavy discs from the end of barbells . . . stickhandling with weighted hockey sticks with an elastic-type rope tied around their waist and attached to a fixed pole just off the edge of the basketball court.

Williamson was even more startled to witness high-paced calisthenics in the Soviet locker room just prior to their 1968 gold-medal game against Canada. Anatoly Firsov—one of the world's greatest forwards in the late 1960s—recalled that Tarasov once interrupted a team field trip that was intended as a break. Everyone was hunting for mushrooms when Tarasov boomed advice to Firsov (and everyone else). Mushroom hunting was not to be a leisurely jaunt. "You must pick up mushroom!" Tarasov insisted. That meant "to sit down on one leg, on another leg, land on one buttock, and then tear off the mushroom, not only with one hand, but with another as well, and keep an eye to make sure, that nobody else could pick the mushroom up!" Training opportunities were everywhere. Tarasov insisted that the key to his coaching system was to be "a very good musician," conducting his players in staccato. Over time, the Red Machine enjoyed better facilities and equipment. It is doubtful the team ever had better coaches than Tarasov and Chernyshev.[30]

To most sports fans and media, the Soviets came out of nowhere. LIHG president Fritz Kraatz knew better. In 1953 he wrote a European roundup for the *Ice Hockey World Annual*. The Soviets, he noted, are "our youngest member." Although they had not yet entered the IIHF championships, he went on, they "may very well be a great surprise one day." Swedish fans at the 1954 World Championships in Stockholm, however, were not expecting much, and they might have laughed at a cartoon depicting an outsized Canadian player seating a pint-sized Soviet (who looked much like captain Vsevolod Bobrov) at a desk. The cartoon caption read: "Today the Canadians will give the Russians their first lesson in hockey." This image was soon shattered. Wearing their odd, leather helmets and their unstylish uniforms, the Soviets blew through the opposition and then trounced Canada's entry 7–2 before more than seventeen thousand fans. The *Ottawa Journal*'s headline lamented ominously, "Russians Teach Canadians Lesson in Stickhandling." The student was now the teacher.[31]

Canadians tended to blame the CAHA for sending an inferior club when their rivals were preparing true national all-star teams. Former NHL player Joe Cooper griped, "Let's face it: Russia didn't send a team until she thought she had a chance to win. The United States didn't send a team at all because they knew they couldn't win with the caliber of players they had. Yet we send a second-rate team as though it was some insignificant exhibition jaunt." It was a mistake of hubris that Canada made repeatedly. Joe Mathewson, an old-timer from Winnipeg, admitted the obvious: "You know, there's no reason why Russia shouldn't have a good team. Their climate is similar to ours." Future Hall of Famer Lionel Conacher captured a common sentiment: "This is a catastrophe. We can send to Europe exactly what we've got, and that's the best hockey players in the world, or we can stay right out of these championships." It took almost twenty years before Canada's top professional players faced the Soviets.[32]

Many sensed that the balance of power was shifting. As a German correspondent wrote in a preview of the 1955 World Championships, "The Russian victory in last year's World Championship has stimulated interest and the quantity and quality of entries for the 1955 Championships is greater than ever before." The events were at four German locations: Krefeld, with its newly covered Rhineland Halle that seated 10,500; Dusseldorf's newly enlarged, sixteen-thousand-seat arena; Cologne's outdoor facility (seven thousand seats); and Dortmund's fifteen-thousand-seat Westfalenhalle. "For the first time since the war" he went on, "radio announcers of Eastern Germany and Czechoslovakia will broadcast direct to their respective countries, the Network of Northern Germany having made available to them one of its most modern radio cars." Would there be another upset?[33]

Ice Hockey World Annual reported that "all of Europe" seemed to converge on the four German host cities. Canada's team—the Allan Cup–winner Penticton (British Columbia) "Vees"—were bolstered by some all-stars. Feeling intense pressure from journalists, political pundits, assorted "back-slappers and hangers-on," they turned surly and "unsociable, short on humour, suspicious of all." The Canadians whipped the Soviets 5–0, but their popularity suffered when Clem Bird, Penticton's president, was quoted, "We made [the Russians] look like a bunch of ham and eggers. Those guys quit cold. This was a good one for democracy." Bobrov, Russia's captain, was more diplomatic, conceding, "They are different from us, too hard and, let's admit it, awfully good." Georgi Ragulsky, vice chairman of the Soviet Sports Committee, was more analytical, in search of lessons for the future: "I think we are still superior in teamwork and at least equal in technique and stickhandling but the Canadians are faster and shoot harder. We'll be back next year to show what we have learned in the meantime." The next year was an Olympic year, with the winter games at Cortina d'Ampezzo, Italy—a test to see who had learned more lessons. The Soviets took Olympic gold, with the United States close behind. Canada won gold medals in 1958, 1959, and 1961, but the Maple Leaf was in decline on the world ice. In contrast, the Soviets were setting the foundation for almost three decades of domination.[34]

Czech *Agonistes*

Perhaps the most complicated postwar story—both tragic and triumphant—was that of Czechoslovakia. Hockey was on the rise in the late 1930s, and the national team continued to provide inspiring victories during times of duress. One history reported that in 1940 the Germans, who now controlled the country, promoted two matches between their team and the Protectorate of Bohemia and Moravia, to be held at Prague's winter stadium. The intent was for the Reich "to give the Czechs a lesson in the superiority of the Aryan spirit." The confident Germans allowed live radio broadcasts since they had "absolutely no doubts" about the outcomes. The Czech team won by scores of 5 to 1 and 3 to 0.[35]

From 1945 to 1948 Czechoslovakia endured a complex metamorphosis, from Nazi protectorate to ostensibly free democracy (albeit with a strong communist party) to communist satellite of the USSR. In hindsight, the final shift seems to have been inevitable, but as one prominent historian wrote, "At least until the autumn of 1947 Stalin left Czechoslovakia alone." And so, as an independent nation, Prague hosted the 1947 IIHF World Championships. The Canadians stayed home, making the Czechs and the Swedes the favorites. The Czechs won gold on aggregate goal differential, even though they lost to the Swedes, 2–1. Over the next year, however, their fortunes quickly froze amid the rapidly changing landscape of the Cold War.[36]

American player John Garrison captured the last months of the old regime in a poignant account of his experience on the controversial AHAUS group that Avery Brundage so opposed at St. Moritz. In late 1947 the team played a series of exhibition games as an Olympic tune-up, the handiwork of old friends Walter Brown and Bunny Ahearne. The tour started in Czechoslovakia, with games in Prague, Bratislava, and Brno, where Foreign Minister Jan Masaryk "delivered a most heart-warming greeting to the American team over the public address system." Masaryk was well known from his diplomatic posting in America, his marriage to an American, and his London-based opposition to the Nazis. The Americans even traveled on Masaryk's "private train" back to Prague, where they played the Prague Lawn Tennis Club (LTC Praha), the "strongest of all Czech teams." This trip came at the end of an era for Eastern Europe and its sports. Democratic structures like "Parliament" and bourgeois clubs with names like "Lawn Tennis" quickly dissolved behind the Iron Curtain, which descended around Czechoslovakia via a communist coup shortly after the Olympics. Masaryk was found dead—dressed in his pajamas—below the window of his bathroom in the Foreign Ministry. He had been murdered.[37]

The postwar atmosphere was hot with retribution against anyone accused of collaborating with the Nazis. Even a national star like Josef Maleček was not immune from attack. In one account, Maleček was "charged with collaboration." Perhaps his accusers were affiliated with Sparta Praha and were still bitter about his 1927 jump to LTC Praha. Perhaps they were socialists, bitter at his successful sporting goods store located "in the heart" of Prague, where he sold CCM Canadian equipment—the top of the line. In any event "although his enemies were unable to prove their allegations, he went into exile," coaching HC Davos in the Swiss League. In another story, he attempted to cross the border using a fake Peruvian passport. The border guard recognized the famous athlete but let him go with only a wisecrack: "Mr. Maleček, you're certainly the last Peruvian ever crossing this border!" He played and coached hockey and tennis in Switzerland and Germany until he moved to the United States, where he worked as editor and sports commentator for Radio Free Europe and Voice of America. The power of radio, despite communist efforts to jam the signal, rekindled his fame back home. Maleček died in America in 1982. He was inducted into the IIHF Hall of Fame in 2003.[38]

The Czech hockey team earned a silver medal at St. Moritz, and their scoreless tie with Canada's entry was a real victory given the 7–0 pasting they took from the Maple Leaf at the 1936 Garmisch games. The 1948 Czech team was coached by Canadian Mike Buckna, who had coached LTC Praha before the war and returned in 1946. He recalled the postwar state of hockey in a 1958 interview: "We had 20,000 kids in Czechoslovakia [playing hockey] between 1946–47 and 1947–48." In fall 1948, however, he returned to his home in British Columbia. "I wasn't too hot about coaching a 'satellite' team," he noted. "I could have stayed. But I'd been getting used to being the head man in hockey over there, and I got the feeling that I wouldn't have the same freedom to operate." Frank Trottier felt the same rejection in Sweden two years later.[39]

New types of nationalism were swirling in Eastern Europe. As Anne Applebaum has argued in her history of how the "iron curtain" descended, communist leaders were totalitarian in their outlook. Like the founder of totalitarianism, Mussolini, "they wanted very much to create societies where everything was within the state, nothing was outside the state, and nothing was against the state—and they wanted to do it quickly." This meant grabbing control of police, radio, church, schools, and independent groups such as sports clubs. And this also meant changing the names of football and hockey clubs. Slava Praha football was forced to change its name to Sokol Slavia Praha VII, a slap at the club's old links to the city's liberal political and professional classes. HC Sparta Praha endured a series of rebrandings—Sokol Sparta, Sokol Bratrství Sparta, Sokol Sparta Sokolovo, Spartak Praha Sokolovo, Sparta ČKD Praha—until returning to its original name in 1990 amid the Velvet Revolution.[40]

LTC Praha, long the centerpiece of Czech hockey, suffered a worse fate. Several team stars beyond Josef Malaček defected at the 1948 Spengler Cup tournament in Davos. Defections were a serious issue for Stalin and his communist allies, especially in the wake of his troubles with Tito and Yugoslavia. Consequently, the years 1948 through 1954 saw a number of celebrated show trials as the Soviets increased pressure for regime loyalty. In Bulgaria the "traitors" were the leaders of the Protestant church. In Czechoslovakia it was Catholic priests. In Albania, Hungary, and Bulgaria it was communist apparatchiks who had become too independent. The trials, the prison sentences, and the executions accentuated the dangers of patriotic limelight for anyone but Stalin.[41]

The national team was under a close watch. Despite losing six players in a plane crash, the team won gold in Stockholm in 1949, beating the Canadian entry for the first time, 3–2. A year later, however, there was no Czech entry at the LIHG's tournament in London. One player, Vaclav Rozinak, recalled the details:

> In London, we wanted to prove that the team was good, that the world title we won in 1949 had not been a coincidence. But, then some people appeared and said that we would not be going because visas for the reporters had not been obtained. Two days later it was clear we would have to stay. Of course, we were annoyed. The whole thing peaked at a pub when undercover secret police showed up. Somehow a fight broke out and we ended up at the police station. We thought it was all a joke and thought we'd only stay there over night. Even in court, when we were suddenly found guilty of treason and espionage, we laughed and didn't take the charade seriously. But the fun was over when we ended up in prison with our hair shaved off. We realized then they truly were not going to let us go.

Rozinak and his teammates were sentenced for treasonous "attempt to defect," with prison terms ranging from one to ten years. Czech Radio noted later: "In 1955 the players were released under amnesty, and were officially rehabilitated in 1968. But seven players died later from forced labor suffered in uranium mines." A number of those players had played for LTC Praha. This episode brought a tragic end to a famous hockey club.[42]

The Czechs seemed to vanish from the scene. In 1953, Fritz Kraatz wrote ominously: "From Czechoslovakia, which used to be one of the strongest European ice hockey nations, no news about the progress of the sport has been received." But hockey was alive and rebuilding under the new regime. The Czechs came to the 1954 IIHF Championships and finished in fourth place. They stayed in the running or on the medal stand from that point forward. Some existing players made the transition from democracy to socialism, including Vlastimil Bubnik, who emerged as a twenty-year-old star on a team decimated at the recent show trials. "The continuity was broken," he recalled. "We were starting from zero." Bubnik, like a number of the Soviets, was a football-hockey player who could score in either sport. He ended his career in 1971 with a total of 300 goals on Czech club teams and 57 goals on the national team (in IIHF championship play)—just under a goal-a-game pace. Karel Gut was a converted defenseman with offensive flair. Gut came up in 1949 in time to be around the old guard. He became a fixture on the national team and was voted best defenseman at the 1955 IIHF Championships. When his club career on Spartak ended in 1964, he moved behind the bench. In 1973 he began a ten-year stint as head coach of the Czech national team and followed that as top man in the Czech Hockey Union.[43]

A new generation of stars also emerged in the late 1950s and early 1960s. These included Jaroslav Jirik, who first appeared in the late 1950s, scored 300 goals for club teams and 37 in world championship play. Known for parking himself solidly near the opponent's net, his nickname was "Brambor," or Potato, and he was difficult for any defenseman to dig out. Jirik was tough enough to draw attention from the St. Louis Blues, who brought him over in the summer of 1969. That season, he played three games in the NHL and fifty-three for their AHL affiliate, the Kansas City Blues. From 1963 to 1979, Jan Suchy scored 162 goals in Czech club play, remarkably as a defenseman. That offensive flair was matched on the national team, where he scored 21 goals in sixty-five championship tournament games. He was one reason his club, Dukla Jihlava, dominated the Czech national league. One of Suchy's club teammates was Jiri Holik, who played a record 319 games on the Czech national team—141 in World Championship play, where he scored 55 goals. He attracted attention from the Detroit Red Wings, but like many of his generation behind the Iron Curtain, he was reluctant to defect. "At the time," he recalled, "I thought communism would never come to an end." He admitted that he "didn't have the courage to emigrate."[44]

The Iron Curtain separated Czechoslovakia from Western Europe. The country was formally a member of the Warsaw Pact, a Moscow-led alliance that had little room for nationalism, especially after Marshal Tito moved Yugoslavia on its own path. But there was irony in Stalin's assault on bourgeois nationalism just as he decided to enter the world stage of international sports and compete with capitalists in bourgeois sports like hockey. What would happen when a satellite such as Czechoslovakia played against the Soviet Union? How would nationalism play out in those moments?[45]

One such event occurred in March 1969 at the IIHF World Championships in Stockholm. Less than a year earlier, Soviet tanks had rolled in to crush a democratic movement, the Prague Spring of Alexander Dubček. The Czechs were scheduled to host the hockey event, but they declined to do so in the aftermath of invasion. In a new double-round-robin format, the Czechs and Soviets faced off twice, and bitter nationalism was on display. The Czech players altered their official jerseys, covering the Soviet star that had been added, post-1948, above the traditional lion image. At one point the crowd, full of Czech sympathizers and ex-patriots, began to chant: "Dubček, Dubček, Dubček." Most chafing of all, amid the two glorious victories over the Red Machine (2–0 and 4–3), was the raucous taunt of "Your tanks, our goals." The Soviets had never lost two matches to the same opponent in this way. The victories were not enough, however, to steal the crown, as the emotionally spent Czechs lost twice to Sweden and ended with a bronze medal. Czechoslovakia might have been a political satellite, but on the ice it was a sovereign nation.[46]

The years between 1945 and 1971 saw a rearrangement in European hockey. For a variety of reasons, Great Britain, Germany, Switzerland, and a few other prewar hockey powers fell to secondary status. Sweden, Czechoslovakia, and Finland strengthened their positions, each under different circumstances. And the Soviet Union emerged as the most dominant force of all. In each of the latter cases, hockey structures supporting the national team also supported nationalist sentiments. This tended to reduce an earlier dependence on Canadian expertise. Within the IIHF, the ethos of old-school "sportsmen" like Paul Loicq or Fritz Kraatz gave way to the entrepreneurial spirit of Bunny Ahearne and Walter Brown. International hockey became a successful business that required juggling the interests of multiple product brands, especially those of "Canadian" and "European" teams. It also required compromise between the ideals and realities of old models like amateurism. The Cold War entry of the Soviet Union in 1954 heated up hockey's brand wars.

18

Postwar Brand Wars: 1945–1971

In February 1952, Olympic hockey skated into Oslo's new, indoor, twelve-thousand-seat, artificial-ice rink—the Jordal Amfi. The competition also served to determine the LIHG (soon to be IIHF) World and European crowns. So there was much on the line. Nine teams competed. Canada's undefeated Edmonton Mercurys won World and Olympic gold. The Americans took silver, and Sweden beat the Czechs in a controversial, sudden-death playoff for Olympic and World bronze as well as the European title. Tensions on and off the ice pitted Europe against North America. A Russian commentator wrote in *Ice Hockey World Annual*: "The Americans beat up their opponents, tripped them up and made fun of them whenever they scored a goal." Spectators were "so enraged, that some members of the American team had to arrange to leave the Stadium secretly. Orange skins, apple cores and snowballs were thrown by the crowd." American team manager Bob Ridder, a Midwest amateur hockey leader from an influential publishing family, was moved to question the wisdom of future international play. CAHA president Doug Grimston clashed with LIHG and BIHA magnate Bunny Ahearne, long a blade in Canada's ribs. Ahearne in turn resigned his position as a CAHA liaison to Europe. *Ice Hockey World Annual* speculated: "European criticism of Canadian style of play may also lead to a CAHA decision to withdraw Canada from international competition." Grimston concluded, "There is no use in carrying on any longer" since the divide over legitimate body checking was too vast.[1]

The period from 1945 to 1972 saw both an escalation and a shift in the rhetoric of divergence, from hockey as a game to hockey as political or national or cultural metaphor. Russians altered the description of North

American hockey from simply "brutal" to "capitalistic." Western democrats in turn cast Soviet players as communist "robots." Amateur governing bodies battled over the meaning of their core principles. Who was "pure" and who was a "cheat"? American university coaches endured bitter debates over the dangers of recruiting Canadian players who would bring "Canadian" hockey into the "American" game. And pundits around the world questioned whether women could or should ever play such a "manly" sport. Amid the fray, however, certain corporate names like CCM, Jofa, and CBS operated with limited interest in these squabbles. Their focus lay in sales to any and all consumers. They slowly emerged as a force of convergence.[2]

Soviets vs. North America

A biography of Vsevolod Bobrov characterized American play at the 1955 World Championships as "rough and frankly dangerous." The 1956 American team earned higher praise for intelligent counterattacks, but its hallmark was still hard hitting: "The boards groaned under the impact of human bodies. The moment a Soviet player gained the puck, he was tackled by the Americans, who did all they could to wrest it from him."[3]

North American Olympians—groomed in senior amateur leagues—were used to body checking all over the ice. The IIHF and its European leagues, on the other hand, restricted checking initially to the defensive third and later to the defensive half of the ice. It was a recipe for resentment. Take, for example, the East York Lyndhursts, the senior amateur side that represented Canada in the 1954 World Championships. As one player recalled, "Because of the European rules our guys couldn't hit them in the centre zone. . . . Knowing they couldn't be hit legally until they crossed the blueline they'd skate with their heads down." This was apparently too appetizing for defenseman Ben Chapman, who positioned himself cleverly enough so that a Swiss attacker "skated right into" him. Chapman probably did a tad more than stand still; he ended the game with a half-dozen penalties. Incidents like this contributed to what Swedish papers called "rough-house tactics" and Radio Moscow labeled "shocking behaviour."[4]

By 1954 both sides of the Iron Curtain had reconfigured and expanded their propaganda apparatus to fight what some called the "Culture Wars." Academic and popular writers, both East and West, who had once together pitched their stories against Fascism, now turned their intellectual fire against one another—Communism against Capitalism. The main antagonists, the USSR and the USA, cranked it up. Their arsenal included radio networks, movies, newspapers, serials, and books. The Soviets had TASS (the state information agency) and *Pravda* (the party newspaper); America had its US Information Agency. Together, they had thousands of employees. In these culture wars, the Soviets and their communist allies fought a rear-guard campaign against American and Western jazz, rock and roll, and motion pictures. Commissars kept Mickey Mouse off the screen and jammed the airways to block the music of Elvis Presley. But there was a problem with competing for victory in sports. You could not simultaneously engage and exclude. It was one or the other. So both sides moved down a path used for decades by boxing, racing, baseball, and football promoters: they turned teams, individuals, and events into symbols of something bigger.[5]

At the 1954 World Championships in Stockholm, Soviet coach Vladimir Igorov told the media that his team's "collective playing" would counter the rough play of Canada's Lyndhursts. He was correct. But just what was "collective playing" and just who would refine and articulate the specific components of a "Soviet style"? The man most associated with this effort was Anatoli Tarasov, now commonly known as the "Father of Russian Hockey." A first-generation soccer-bandy-hockey player, Tarasov found his niche as coach of Central Red Army and then as co-coach of the national team. With his bushy eyebrows, prominent nose, broad frame, and ebullient personality, Tarasov was the perfect Russian bear in the era's hockey dramas. He emerged from a Soviet educational system that included several famous Institutes of Physical Culture, whose mission was to train instructors for grassroots exercise programs, coaches for specific sports, and athletes for international competition. The oldest was the Lesgaft Institute in Leningrad. But Moscow's Institute was better funded and closer to the center of power and population. As a Moscow graduate and as coach of Moscow's top team, Tarasov enjoyed a home base with links to the best research facilities. He wrote regular commentaries in Soviet journals. He published his first book in 1950. For the next three decades he was the most visible and vocal representative of a *Soviet* game.[6]

As part of his research, Tarasov closely studied the Canadians, taking notes on what to emulate, what to revise, and what to reject. There were already books available: memoirs, histories, and instructional guides among them. But in 1951 Lloyd Percival published a different kind of tome, *The Hockey Handbook*, based not on just his own experience but on interviews, detailed game observations, and experiments. Percival's research was a six-year international effort, and it was exactly the template that any Soviet sport "scientist" would find attractive. Tarasov later called Percival "the outstanding world hockey theoretician." He inscribed his own book-gift to Percival: "Respectively to Lloyd: Your wonderful book which introduced us to the mysteries of Canadian Hockey, I have read like a schoolboy." The schoolboy soon became the teacher.[7]

The 1950s were an era of relatively good feelings between Soviet and North American hockey, despite complaints about violence and Cold War tensions. Canada, the United States, Switzerland, and others boycotted the 1957 World Championships in Moscow to protest the USSR's invasion of Hungary, but this did not cause a serious backlash. Further, while no Canadian or American wanted to lose to the Soviets, the characterizations of *play* between east and west were not so highly politicized as they would later become. Tarasov himself criticized early Soviet play for its lack of aggressive shooting. Some of the stylistic differences, he wrote, were vestiges of bandy. Some were based on rules differences. American Olympic star Bill Cleary insisted that differences in play derived from factors in sports, not politics. This included the Soviets' tendency to regroup with backward and lateral passes rather than play straight ahead (in other words, dumping the puck or shooting it). For Cleary, it was a product of European football heritage as well as a bigger rink size. The differences in style were therefore not yet painted in bright tones of capitalism versus communism.[8]

The 1960 Squaw Valley Olympics marked a transition. The games themselves were a success. The sunny California weather neatly paralleled a thaw in Cold War relations. Most pundits expected the Canadians and the Soviets to battle for gold. But the USA team performed a "Forgotten Miracle," upsetting both Canada and the USSR along the way. One of the most widely circulated and remembered stories, however, accentuated East-West friendship. After the second period of the gold-medal game, with the United States down by a goal against the Czechs, Soviet captain Nikolai Sologubov came into the US locker room and pantomimed putting on a mask. Several players recognized the gesture as a suggestion to use oxygen, which some Soviets had tried in the high altitude. A few American players did so. Initial reports questioned both the power of the oxygen and the purity of "Solly's" altruism (a Czech victory would knock the Russians out of a medal). But the United States scored six unanswered goals to win gold. And the *New York Times* headline ran: "Russian Tip Helps U.S. Win Olympic Hockey." Tarasov himself praised the Americans for their "simplicity and restraint . . . their honesty, their great heart for sport, and their excellent behavior both on and off the ice." He hoped for continued exchanges, for joint practices, and for "an intensified exchange of literature between our hockey federations."[9]

The good feelings soon ended. The Cold War went red hot in May when the Soviets shot down an American U-2 spy plane. Summit talks were cancelled. Cuba's Fidel Castro announced trade agreements with the Soviet Union, which prompted a US embargo. In turn, Castro nationalized $850 million in American-owned property and business. The year 1961 was even more inflamed, with a failed invasion of Cuba, a failed Kennedy-Khrushchev summit in Vienna, construction of the Berlin Wall, and Soviet resumption of nuclear weapons testing in the atmosphere. Hockey slid into the tension. In 1962 the Soviets and the Czechs boycotted the IIHF World Championships in Colorado after the East German team was denied visas, a snafu triggered by the Berlin Wall.[10]

The Soviets, now four years without a gold medal, shook up their program. As Bill Cleary recalled, "After '60 . . . the Russians went back and really started to analyze the style of hockey that they played." And change it, too. Tarasov was sacked as the top coach, replaced by his rival Arkadi Chernyshev, who had no better luck at the 1961 Worlds, where Canada regained the crown. According to one later account, this slump prompted Leonid Khomenkov, the administrative head of Soviet hockey, to suggest importing Canadian coaches. Tarasov, who returned to co-coach with Chernyshev, reacted aggressively. He wrote: "A person from another country would find it more than difficult to teach us if he did not know our people, their character, their tendencies, the peculiarities of their national behaviour." And in the early 1960s Tarasov became more strident in his characterizations of difference between Soviet and Canadian styles.[11]

His triumphant *Road to Olympus* (1969) opened with the 1963 IIHF Championships in Stockholm, where the Soviets finally recaptured the gold medal after a seven-year famine. He told two stories to set up his rhetoric on collectivist hockey. Channeling Percival, he noted that "in the game against the Canadian team, the players of the USSR squad made 110 passes, while the Canadians made 60 passes." The bottom line was this: "Our players did not go in for individualism." This was reinforced when the IIHF failed to select a single Soviet for the all-tournament team. According to Tarasov, "the President of the Hockey Federation, Mr. Ahearne, explained this decision by the fact that on [the Soviet] team there were no stars, and therefore, no one could merit such an award." Puzzling to a westerner, but a key point for Tarasov.[12]

He then explained the political roots of pass-happy Soviet hockey. When a Canadian or a Swede attacked open ice, "he will sooner plunge through himself with the puck" than pass to an open teammate. That meant that four other players were dependent on one. By contrast, he argued, in looking to pass first, the Soviet puck-carrier was dependent on his four skating teammates. Tarasov claimed that this "collective" approach emanated from Socialist culture: "Real teamwork, comradeship and readiness to help a teammate is cultivated, first of all, by the very atmosphere of our life." His players learned the lessons well. Goaltender Vladislav Tretiak recalled Tarasov grilling Valery Kharlamov (by some accounts, the most dangerous forward of the 1970s) about the dynamics of passing. "Tell me, please, when you have the puck, who is in charge?" Kharlamov mistakenly answered, "I am in charge." Tarasov angrily responded, "Wrong! You are a servant of your teammates. You play on the Soviet team to benefit your comrades. . . . Don't put yourself first."[13]

In this era of divergence, there were clearly differences in styles of play between European amateurs and North Americans who played under NHL rules. European restrictions on checking and a bigger ice surface encouraged a game with more flow, passing, and puck possession. But some of the notions of "national" difference seem inflated. For instance, Tarasov's insistence that Canadians were puck hogs is belied by the fundamental credo of Toe Blake's great Montreal teams: always look to "headman" the puck. Likewise, America's hockey "bible," *Ice Hockey*, written in 1942 by Dartmouth's Eddie Jeremiah, included the cardinal offensive principle to "Pass the Puck Up Ahead to Any Uncovered Teammate." Jeremiah also championed the "weaving" patterns of offensive play so often associated with Tarasov's teams. While the Soviets passed and swirled and regrouped far more than North Americans, so did other European teams.[14]

The "Soviet" system succeeded not from any decidedly *unique* approach to team tactics. The Soviets' novel divergence lay in an authoritarian and regimented system of training, possible in a socialist state that made its athletes full-time professionals. Their devotion to rigorous and innovative land drills stemmed more from a lack of artificial ice rinks than from scientific ingenuity. In this system, the head coach of a national team had extraordinary control over his players. One Russian television director recalled in 1977, "Tarasov's tight rein as a coach reflected Soviet life in microcosm: submission, flattery, and smiles to his face; envy, hatred, and denunciations behind his back." But whatever the realities of their "system," Tarasov and Chernyshev produced rosters of highly skilled players who competed at a high pace. Their string of international victories that began in 1963 at Stockholm is a testament to its effectiveness. It was Tarasov's job to develop and articulate the brand. It was the players' job to win in the only team sport that pitted serious contenders from North America against those of the Soviet bloc. In the Cold War, the coolest game was hot.[15]

The Canadian Problem in American Hockey

Within North America, another brand war erupted over the increasing presence of Canadians on the rosters of American college and university teams. Contemporaries in the United States and Canada called it the "Canadian Hockey Player Problem." College hockey had long connected Canadians and Americans, from the days when Hobey Baker's Princeton seven challenged Canadian teams. But Americans played by rules distinct from the core NHL/CAHA brand. And while some Canadians played on American varsity teams, they were rarities.[16]

This changed dramatically in the quarter century after World War II, triggered by the 1947–48 events establishing the American Hockey Coaches Association and the NCAA Championship. The number of participating schools increased steadily from there. Having dipped to twenty-one in 1945–46, it rose to forty-two in 1954–55, 56 in 1964–65, and ninety in 1974–75. More and more spectators cheered in new, modern arenas built on college campuses. Team fortunes appeared regularly in the national print media, on radio, and, by the end of this period, on television. The pressure on athletic directors, coaches, and players to produce winners grew in tandem.[17]

In the 1950s and 1960s, many, like Michigan's Vic Heyliger, looked to Canada's amateur ranks as a bottomless talent reservoir. Murray Armstrong (Denver University, 1956–77), Amo Bessone (Michigan State, 1951–79), Ned Harkness (Rensselaer Polytechnic Institute, 1953–61, and Cornell University, 1961–70), Jack Kelley (Boston University, 1962–72), and many others tapped their Canadian connections to recruit young talent. The most active was undoubtedly Armstrong, whose Denver Pioneers were quite successful, earning national championships in 1958, 1960, 1961, 1968, and 1969.[18] The effect was hard to miss. In February 1955, *Sports Illustrated* attributed the growth of college hockey's respectability to the "annual invasion by hundreds of Canadian students . . . who swap their talent for a scholarship." In 1950, Michigan State's team roster listed only one Canadian; by 1958 it had nineteen. North Dakota's first varsity squad (1948) had no Canadian players; by 1966, twelve "Fighting Sioux" hailed from north of the border. At Cornell, three Canadians played varsity in 1957; there were seventeen by 1967, when the Big Red won their first NCAA championship. That same year, a headline from Toronto's *Globe and Mail* reported "400 Canadians Playing in U.S. College Hockey."[19]

Canadian recruits produced better hockey, but they also prompted tremendous rancor among American athletes and administrators who complained about their game, their rinks, and their scholarships being captured by foreigners. Their loud objections were matched by Canadian officials who loathed the idea of Canadian-trained boys being lured away from their homes and commitments to Canadian amateur teams to delight audiences in American arenas. "The team that most experts rate the best in the U.S. has yet to use a single American," *Time* magazine reported in January 1961. "The supremacy of Denver's Canadians . . . is hard enough on U.S. pride," let alone the "other top U.S. teams manned almost entirely by Canadians. The Canadian hockey invasion has set off one of the bitterest fights in U.S. college athletics."[20]

At issue was more than just turf or who should have the privilege of playing in American collegiate rinks. The Canadian Hockey Player Problem also implicated the *way* the game should be played, and it called into question the NCAA brand. Canadian recruits were more experienced and better trained. Their game was faster, more competitive (though more violent), and more exciting to watch. *New York Times* writer Dean McGowen's 1971–72 season forecast made an awkward admission: "In most cases, by the time the Canadian boy is ready for college he has left his American competitor far behind in skills and stamina."[21] Some Americans emphasized the benefits of imports. St. Lawrence University coach Ole Kollevoll stated in 1955: "Our players are improving all the time, and much of the credit should go to the Canadians for setting such good examples of how hockey should be played."[22]

But Kollevoll's views were hardly typical. Long-serving Dartmouth coach Eddie Jeremiah (1930–67) noted in 1955: "The wholesale importation of

Canadian stars to some colleges are making a farce out of the NCAA championships." Harvard coach Ralph "Cooney" Weiland (a Canadian himself) was more blunt: "Canadian athletes are ruining U.S. College hockey." The feeling was even more deeply felt among American collegians who played alongside Canadian "hired guns." The talented, well-trained Canadians brought a game that was not just faster but also more violent. An increase in on-ice fracas and in routine violence was not just coincidental with the rise in Canadian recruits. It seemed they superimposed *their* game on the American root. "I viewed that RPI game on Saturday," former Harvard player and US Olympian John B. Garrison complained to Harvard coach Bill Cleary (1971–90). "The very worst elements of the Canadian game were on display. . . . Board checking and charging were rampant all evening and how those officials figured they earned their fees I can't understand." The villains here—the officials and *Canadian* hockey—shared equal blame.[23]

Just as troublesome for Canadian observers was what happened to the carefully developed skills of their players once they accepted scholarships across the border. The American game threatened to "spoil" Canadian talent. First and foremost, players could not body check beyond their own defensive zone (changed in the 1960s to their defensive half). Moreover, they could ice the puck legally after they cleared their own blue line, in contrast to the Canadian amateur and NHL game that required clearing the center red line. The perceived effect was profound. "U.S. college hockey deteriorates the skills of the best Canadian players," long-time scout and Minnesota North Star general manager Wren Blair declared in 1969. The game "makes players 'soft' and unsuitable as recruits for the National Hockey League." More convincing was the testimony of the players who had actually experienced the difference. A rookie with the Toronto Maple Leafs in 1963, Denver University product Johnny MacMillan agreed. "I think my advancement to the NHL was set back to some extent by the fact I played college hockey. . . . You'll find college players to be very good skaters, but they aren't aggressive enough for the pros. Our rules . . . de-emphasize roughness, close checking, and aggressiveness. You can skate hard all winter and never really get hit hard."[24] To Canadian minds, American collegiate hockey was too offense minded and dainty—hardly the sort of hothouse environment where talented players could perform at their peak level or prepare to play professionally. In his 1973, US-published autobiography, one-time Denver University star and Chicago Black Hawks standout Keith Magnuson called the NCAA brand "your rinky-dink version of our game

. . . 'foreigners' like me are regarded as traitors in my own country for taking the soft way out."[25]

Beneath all of this nationalist hubris and hyperbole was a reality of change. The NCAA Rules Committee had worked aggressively for decades to accentuate distinctions in rules, always proclaiming the superiority of their brand. They maintained this position in private and against strong pressure, in one case against Clarence Campbell, who launched a campaign at the NCAA, as part of his expansion strategy. He clearly described his goals in a 1966 report to the NHL's board of governors. The league, he argued, needed to "exercise its maximum influence" to align NCAA rules on checking and passing with those of the NHL, in order to groom high school players—a key segment for American player development. The high schools were aligned with the NCAA, and even Campbell recognized that any NHL effort to create its own rival programs "would probably be black-balled by the high schools." Thus in 1966–67, Campbell and Boston Bruins owner Weston Adams sent letters to the NCAA ice hockey committee recommending that the college game make two radical rules changes: permit body checking all over the ice and adopt a restriction on "two-line" passes. The NCAA committee rebuffed the proposal. Its minutes reflect a belief that requests from the NHL should have "no influence" on the college game: "Our game under the present rules is so much better than the professional game." But belief in the value of difference soon diminished.[26]

Brand difference depended on the NCAA's willingness to defend its culture from external influence—*Canadianization*, perhaps—a task that it was committed to do. Before 1972 the Canadian Hockey Player Problem was addressed only incrementally, and clumsily at that. In the 1950s and 1960s, representatives from the CAHA, the AHCA, and the Western Collegiate Hockey Association established gentlemen's agreements to avoid tampering with Canadian recruits committed to Junior A or professional hockey in Canada. By the late 1960s, however, these were insufficient and gave way to more formal NCAA legislation, including an age-limit restriction on foreign athletes (1965) and by 1971 an outright ban on athletes who, as junior players in Canada, had received room-and-board stipends that effectively made them professionals. Only by the mid-1970s did the Canadian Hockey Player Problem subside—solved, as it was, by a demographic boom in talented American-born collegians, by the effects of the NCAA's restrictive legislation and, ironically, by AHCA and NCAA committee votes to harmonize playing rules on checking. Despite the NCAA's triumphant protectionism, convergence in the "way" of North American hockey began to creep back in, and the American collegiate brand, so carefully crafted in the 1940s, '50s, and '60s, was again in jeopardy.[27]

The Vagaries of Amateurism

If some Americans doubted the amateur status of Canadian imports, skepticism was tenfold about the Soviets. How could they get so good so fast? The question was hardly limited to hockey. In the postwar years, the International Olympic Committee and its associated sports federations grappled with the question of permitting the Soviets to compete. While there was rising pressure to do so, there was equal awareness that the Soviets awarded cash prizes to athletes who broke records. This was a frontal assault on the IOC's amateur code, which in 1947 prohibited "material gain of any kind, direct or indirect." Few put much stock in an official Soviet resolution in 1947 that banned financial rewards. But Olympic politics followed a crooked path. The USSR's new national Olympic committee (NOC) was admitted to the IOC upon its first application in 1951. Its head, Konstantin Andrianov, was elected an IOC member. The Soviets then entered the 1952 Helsinki Summer Games and garnered enough medals to make a plausible claim to "winning" the overall competition. Soviet supremacy at the 1956 Winter Games in Cortina (a runaway triumph with seven gold, three silver, and six bronze medals) set off greater alarms. Their continued success opened a larger debate about the legitimacy and practicality of amateurism itself.[28]

Popular writers, politicians, and Olympic officials suggested that such staggering success *must* reflect a distortion of Olympic values. In 1960, *Sports Illustrated* published a major story on the "soul" of the games—basically an examination of state amateurism. A lieutenant in the Red Army explained that his military obligations during hockey season were only a few hours per week. The rest of the time "he is completely free to train and practice with his team." He was also provided a small apartment in Moscow for himself, his wife, and his young daughter, an annual "vacation at a fashionable Black Sea resort," and "a medium-priced car." Clearly, he was no amateur.[29]

The problem for international hockey was that the CAHA, AHAUS, the English League, and the Swedes all played loose with rules and oversight on amateurism in their elite leagues. In 1953, one year before the Soviets' entry, IIHF president Fritz Kraatz recognized that the "conception of amateurism in the various countries" was "quite a problem" the IOC was "making a great effort to solve." He was not sanguine about a solution, however, because of the "mathematical aspect." That meant money.[30]

The code of pure amateurism had been under assault for some time, even within the Olympic movement. The cracks came early. Under pressure from soccer's FIFA, the IOC allowed broken-time payments (compensation for loss of wages from players' "real" jobs) in soccer at the 1928 Olympics. Avery Brundage and others, however, counterattacked at the next Congress. No soccer in 1932. The issue did not abate in the postwar sports world, especially when so many suspected the Soviets of paying their athletes. Under more pressure, in 1962 the IOC Congress allowed NOCs to provide up to thirty days' pay to dependents "suffering hardship" because of an athlete's salary loss.[31]

The IIHF was a leader in this battle to loosen the impossibly pure (and naïve) amateur code. For decades, the federation had given its national affiliates great leeway in determining who was an amateur. It was one reason Brundage viewed hockey as an outlaw. By the early 1960s, the IIHF bylaws, while prohibiting "prizes of money," allowed the "refund of living expenses when traveling for ice hockey purposes," as well as the "refund of loss of salary," provided "the refund be paid only through or controlled by the National Association to which the player is affiliated," and "all receipts and vouchers [be] delivered to that body for examination." Giving autonomy to each national association was a gentlemanly concession that blistered under Cold War allegations. Oversight was limited and sporadic. For instance, one writer discovered that most of the 1961 Canadian national representatives, the Trail (British Columbia) Smoke Eaters, were employed by a local mining company that paid them for their hockey sacrifice: $90 per week for family expenses and mortgages.[32]

The amateur Finnish League had similar problems, as one historian found. An increase in commercial approaches during the 1960s and 1970s (such as putting sponsors' names on jerseys) eroded the old morality. Player payments came under the table, away from the eyes of sports and tax authorities alike. There were no written contracts. Rather, "payment arrangements were negotiated orally during confidential conversations. Stories of payments made in 'brown envelopes' were widespread. In reality, the growing player salaries were a public secret."[33]

Americans were no better. In February 1966 a recently graduated Harvard goaltender named Godfrey Wood wrote a manifesto in the *Boston*

Globe calling for more uniformity in the amateur rules. "Some players on 'amateur' teams in the Eastern Hockey League," he argued, "can make up to $250 per week in 'expense money.' They may, however, be making more than a lot of rookies and second year men in the professional leagues." In Wood's opinion, Americans had adopted "the Canadian idea" that "no matter how much expense money is given, a man is not a professional until he has signed a pro contract." Despite well-parsed distinctions in the amateur code, national and Olympic teams began to eliminate the practical differences between "expenses," "broken-time payments," and "salaries."[34]

By the late 1960s, disputes about ideal and real amateurism spurred pressure to make hockey an "open" sport, which would allow professionals to play in championship events. Wimbledon—hallowed ground for amateur tennis—had gone "open" in 1968. The United States Tennis Association followed suit a few months later. The philosophy behind open play was to see the best athletes compete for the prize, regardless of their amateur or professional status. It was also a solution to rampant hypocrisy. Canadians had pressed for more openness in hockey since 1954. Let Canada's best play against the Soviets' best. By 1969 even Tarasov agreed. "To this day," he wrote, "I do not understand why the best Canadians cannot meet the leading European selected teams from time to time at some interesting type of tournament. Both sides would win from such a meeting." Such a summit series came soon enough.[35]

Divergence and Disappearance: Women's Hockey

Collective/individual, Canadian/American, amateur/pro—these were prominent binaries. To this list, we add male/female. Women's hockey in postwar North America and Europe was first denigrated by contemporaries and later, to add insult to injury, forgotten. In North America, many daughters of the Preston Rivulettes, Vancouver Amazons, Montreal Northern Electric, Boston Back Bay, and other clubs chose not to skate in their mothers' lanes. Even in much of hockey-mad Quebec, World War II led to a two-decade *disparition*. What's more, a rhetoric of difference marked the description of girls and women as they were compared to men and boys, who played the *real* game. And yet, despite all this, fragments of experience remained—important artifacts for historians, since they act as a tattered link between the "golden" years in the 1920s and 1930s and a modern renaissance after 1972.[36]

Fragments included the wartime three-team Montreal Women's Hockey League, a four-town Prince Edward Island women's league, and the Moose Jaw (Saskatchewan) Wildcats, whose search for opponents pushed them to play men's town teams.[37] By 1951 the Canadian women's senior national championship—once virtually owned by the Preston Rivulettes—was revived and featured the Wildcats along with the Port Arthur (Ontario) Bearcats and the Winnipeg Canadianettes. Colleges and universities hosted sporadic competition, such as the February 1950 game that featured the University of Toronto varsity "girls" and a Queen's University team. At youth levels, this pattern was replicated: occasional challenge games, one-off tournaments, and charity nights that treated girls' games as novelties.[38]

Perhaps the most telling story of the decade involved Abby "Ab" Hoffman, who in 1955 disguised her sex so that she could play in the boys' Toronto Hockey League. When, at season's end, her secret was revealed, she was banned from playing with the boys the following season and forced onto a prospective girls' team, which ultimately collapsed for want of opponents. Ab's story grabbed headlines across Canada, but it was exceptional in many ways, not least because of its notoriety. There was a paucity of press interest in women and girls on the ice; as Brian McFarlane noted, "newspapers all but abandoned women's hockey."[39]

In the 1960s, something of a slow return took place, on the shoulders of a society then undergoing a demographic boom, a new age of prosperity and consumerism, and the contemplation of new spaces for female agency. In colleges and universities, women's teams returned to the ice: by mid-decade, they could be found at Queen's, Western, and Toronto universities and Guelph's Ontario Agricultural College, forming, at its height, an eight-team league. Quebec experienced a renaissance that found expression in the reformation of organizations such as the *Ligue Féminine de Hockey Les Canadiennes* (Canadian Women's Hockey League), a four-team, French-speaking circuit in East Montreal.[40] Across the border, in Brown University's Pembroke College, the first American collegiate varsity team was iced in 1964, joined later by its Ivy-League sister Cornell. By 1972, Brown and Cornell stood alone as schools that offered women's intercollegiate hockey, playing against each other and a variety of local men's and, occasionally, Canadian teams. The revival was slow and uncertain, largely because of cost. Cornell's women footed their own bills for the four road trips they took in 1972. Significantly, the 1960s (re)emergence was motivated wholly by grassroots interest among women. At Queen's, it was a student—Kay

"Cookie" Cartwright—who convinced the school's athletic director, Marion Ross, that a team was warranted and sustainable. Likewise at Brown and Cornell, where students Nancy Shieffelin ('67) and Linda Fox Phillips ('68) successfully lobbied the administration. The trend accelerated after 1972.

Opportunities grew slowly in youth hockey. League play among all-girl teams remained restricted in the 1960s principally to those urban areas (such as suburban Toronto) with a critical mass of potential. One example was Brampton Ontario's Canadettes Girls Hockey Association, which consisted of a four-team league formed in 1964 by Roy Morris. More striking was the growing number of invitational hockey tournaments for girls' teams, hosted by a variety of southern Ontario communities. The 1960s saw the Picton Provincial Women's Hockey Tournament, the Kingston Invitational, the Wallaceburg Jaycees Tournament and the massive Wallaceburg "Lipstick" Tournament (1967), which featured three days of play and about four hundred players. In the same year, Morris's Canadettes hosted the ambitiously named Dominion Ladies Hockey Tournament in Brampton Ontario, with twenty-two teams in three divisions. To historians Joanna Avery and Julie Stevens, these sorts of youth tournaments were critical building blocks: "Aside from promoting and developing the players' skills, the first hockey tournaments provided supporters of women's hockey a breeding ground for sharing stories and stimulating ideas."[41] Their weakness, however, was their ephemeral nature; without many formal league structures and affiliations with perennial governing bodies, girls' hockey in the '60s was still on shaky ice.

Beyond the numbers lay issues of attitude, strewn throughout the reportage on women's play. Commentators assumed inferiority even before they had seen a game. This was apparent at one University of Toronto–Queen's University tilt in February 1950, at which Toronto prevailed 7–2. "The large number of male onlookers who came to scoff," read one newspaper account, "remained to cheer on to victory the feminine counterpart of the Blues."[42] "These ladies," one Montreal newspaper announced in the headline of its October 1966 feature on the *Ligue Féminine Les Canadiennes*, "quit the kitchen for the rink."[43] Perhaps nowhere was this rhetoric of difference expressed more bluntly than in an editorial written by Scott Young in a January 1962 edition of Toronto's *Globe and Mail*. "If anyone would care to see me in a wide variety of attitudes of sheer horror," the noted columnist and author of popular boys' hockey fiction wrote, "the one sure way would be to trick me into attending a girls' ice hockey game."

The prospect of an eighteen-team tourney in nearby Alliston took Young back to his early days as a cub reporter in Winnipeg where, when asked to cover a University of Manitoba women's game for the *Free Press*, he was appalled to watch as forward Grace Harling, "one of the prettiest girls I ever saw," was body checked and upended.

> Some big beast on defense would belt her one and . . . she'd fall flat on her back, and they'd have to hold me down in the press box or I would have blown up the rink . . . It is in this light that I appeal to the citizens of Alliston to strike a blow for femininity and plan to be out of town on March 2–3 when the 1962 all girls tournament will be held. Further, I appeal to everyone who enjoys watching a pretty girl trip daintily down the street—how would she look, with [a] black eye and a charley horse?[44]

Young's editorial—a clumsy attempt at humor—was cloaked in a traditional chauvinism that seems more in tune with 1926 than 1962 (written just one year, after all, before North Americans greeted Betty Friedan's now canonical argument, *The Feminine Mystique*). Tellingly, he drew many irate responses. Female hockey players were neither "beasts" nor brutal, responded readers from Ajax and Alliston; "All girl hockey players have been slapped in the face," wrote one.[45] On the surface the exchange seemed a minor flap, but in truth it merely exposed the larger challenge for recognition and rights that female athletes had been seeking since the turn of the twentieth century.

Finally, women's and girls' hockey was challenged by more than want of perennial leagues and governing bodies, by more than a lingering chauvinism. It was compromised from within, by the emergence of ringette, a game designed expressly for girls. Invented in 1963 by Sam Jacks, director of parks and recreation in North Bay, Ontario, ringette spread slowly through the network of municipal recreation directors in Ontario and Quebec, who soon formalized a set of common rules. Ringette looked like hockey in important ways; it was played with five skaters against five (plus goaltenders) in full hockey gear in a standard hockey rink. But it differed in other key elements: players used a straight stick shaft (with no blade) and a rubber ring instead of a puck; no body checking was permitted; the ring had to be passed at each blueline and teams had to shoot on goal before thirty seconds of possession expired. Finally, zone restrictions limited contact: from the top of the faceoff circles to the end boards only three-on-three play was allowed. The earliest promoters emphasized participation but struggled to explain it to Canadians who had memories of competitive women's hockey. The *Toronto Star* described it as "basketball on ice" and "similar to floor hockey but played on skates": "It's not very popular yet." But girls and women rapidly threw themselves into the game. In 1971, Toronto schoolgirls had a citywide championship, and Oshawa, Ontario, hosted an invitational tournament for club teams. By 1973 ringette had a large-enough following to spawn provincial governing bodies in Ontario, Quebec, and Manitoba. The game's growth enthused Canadians who believed that girls could excel in and control a segregated version of the game, *their* game. But the rise of ringette almost certainly slowed the revival of women's hockey by siphoning away a good many of its most able prospects.[46]

In Britain and France the 1920s saw the rise of vigorous enthusiasm for female challenge series, leagues, and annual tournaments. In both countries, women's clubs scheduled friendly challenge matches against their countrywomen and club teams from abroad. The heyday stretched from 1926 to 1938, when a cross-Channel hockey culture took root. Women skated in Manchester, Brighton, Southampton, and London, where a team called the Lambs played in Wembley Stadium and drew fans and press coverage.[47] Across the water, competitive teams such as the Chamonix (France) Sporting Club Edelweiss and the CSHB in Brussels, Belgium, took to the ice, but Paris was the core of continental women's hockey in the 1920s and 1930s, where the Flêches Noires, Droit au But, Club de Sport d'Hiver, and Gros Caillou Sportif clubs played challenge matches in the Vélodrome d'Hiver and the Palais de Glace that were routinely covered in *Le Figaro* and *Le Dimanche Illustré*. Finally, from 1931 to1936, England and France put up national teams to play against each other for a purported European championship that was closely covered in the press.[48]

As in North America, hockey playing represented a new, liberal outlet for women. In France, in particular, the game became a platform for the expression of a new modern womanhood. Hockey was both an activity and an aesthetic—an arena for new ideas about female movement, grace, style, verve. French female hockeyists were among the first athletes to travel to their events in England by airplane, the technological symbol of modernity in the 1930s. Reports of the on-ice successes of the Paris Droit au But ("On Target") were featured in a fashion magazine (*L'Officiel de la Mode*) alongside posed team photos of what were easily the most stylish hockey uniforms of any era. One surviving photo of the French national team de-

Paris-soir

LE HOCKEY INTERNATIONAL FEMININ

Hier soir, à Londres, un match passionnant de hockey féminin sur glace opposait l'équipe britannique à l'équipe française. Voici un instantané de cette rencontre qui nous a été transmis par avion.

English and French women's teams face off for International Honors, 1932 (*Paris-Soir*, March 4, 1932)

planing at South London's Croydon Airport on Valentine Day 1931 shows eight smiling women in cloche hats and fur-trimmed coats over skirts walking arm in arm, carrying fashionable handbags, flowers, and bundles of ice hockey sticks. One British aviator who was on hand at Croyden described it: "On Saturday, we witnessed the arrival of a French *ladies 'Ice Hockey* team.' They do not look so athletic as our own countrywomen, who take up sports, but, perhaps, one had better leave it at that." In contrast, the English team was stolid and sturdy, led by its robust captain and goaltender, Miss "Bubbles" Umney, whom London's *Daily Mirror* headlined as "6-ft WOMAN ICE Player," and by Mona Friedlander (later a Word War II aviatrix), whose imposing physicality on defense was noted in the *Daily Mail*. "When Miss Friedlander charged, somebody knew all about it. Once it was M[ademoise]lle Tollin . . . the referee blew his whistle and the casualty was removed from the rink."[49] Vive la différence.

In both Britain and France, war decimated the women's game. It was disrupted in England by the need to reallocate labor power, resources, and space. In postwar Britain it was shouldered aside by a new cultural definition of the game as even more strenuously masculine, aggressive, and violent, personified by the rough-hewn Canadian troops who dominated wartime competition. English audiences must have concluded that women could not conceivably return to *that* game. In France, the end of women's hockey was even more blunt: it was simply outlawed. One historian noted, "Women's ice hockey in the Hexagon disappeared brutally due to the Second World War, though men's ice hockey somehow continued. . . . The Federation of Ice Sports added an article in its rules expressly forbidding the practice of female ice hockey."[50] Organized competition also disappeared in Belgium and Australia.[51] Only after 1972 did winning conditions revive the culture of female ice time.

Harbingers of Corporate Hockey

Brand notions of hockey—Canadian or American or Soviet, manly or feminine, amateur or professional—were divergent in their effects on the game. There was one set of brands, however, that looked to transcend the squabbles among hockey's national governing bodies and their representatives. These were corporate entities with visions of global markets. Their game plan was one of convergence. They were harbingers and triggers for what followed after 1972.

Skate and stick manufacturers, for example, had one central, abiding interest: growing their markets. They aligned with any and all who might help their cause. By the 1950s, Spalding and Starr had faded, and a handful of firms controlled North America's hockey equipment market. Top-line skates included the CCM Prolite "Tackaberry" that graced the feet of so many NHL stars, and the Bauer Style 92 "Probilt" that was a rival among elite players. The top American skate was the HYDE-Style 795-Pro made of kangaroo leather, tempered steel shanks, and an "indestructible waterproof solid leather box toe." By the mid-1960s a Swiss ski boot company named Fesl introduced a product promising both the protection and feel of the finest leather ski boots. North Americans skaters, however, were not ready to channel Jean-Claude Killy. Fesls fizzled. Within a few years, however, the Lange company succeeded with a similar, plastic design.[52]

The best-selling sticks were Canada's CCM and Hespeler, and America's Northland Pro. Regional and local sporting goods dealers and even hardware stores sold sticks with their own or other nondescript name brands. It was a sleepy market primed for a shake-up. Two examples demonstrate this well. In Sherbrooke, Quebec, Léopold Drolet, a clerk in a local auto parts store that sold sports equipment (including hockey sticks) alongside tie-rods and carburetors, observed one of World War II's peculiar consequences in the Eastern Townships region: "Une certain pénurie de bâtons de hockey"—a particular shortage of hockey sticks. It was his main chance. Opening up his own stick factory in 1949, Drolet created Sherbrooke Woodcraft, a quality brand that enjoyed a sharp rise in sales and became Sher-Wood in 1961. The greatest challenge in the company's first half-decade was establishing brand legitimacy: local skaters had always preferred Hespelers, made in Anglophone south-central Ontario, and had even shunned the CCMs produced in St-Jean-sur-Richelieu, southeast of Montreal. "They didn't want to lose their money," Drolet recalled, and were convinced that only "in Ontario, where there was plenty of money, could they produce the best quality." But quality spoke, and with it, the local chauvinism was reversed. From $46,900 in 1950, the company's sales rose to $154,000 in 1955, $708,100 in 1960, and $1,739,400 by 1969, when a fire ravaged the stick factory and forced Drolet to sell part ownership to an American company. By the 1990s Drolet had sold everything, and the shift toward composite sticks pulled much of the company's production from Sherbrooke to overseas.[53] Still, the brand survived, even if its local raison d'être had passed.

South of the border, Olympians Bill and Roger Christian turned their hockey celebrity, their name, and their woodworking skills into a successful stick-making company in their hometown, Warroad, Minnesota. By 1969 stock floats and stick sales supported the construction of a dedicated manufacturing facility that housed an engine of innovation. One result was the laminated shaft, which the Christian brothers had first seen while playing in Finland. This was followed by an aluminum design in partnership with the Easton Company. In 1972, Christian Brothers unveiled a synthetic stick. By the early 1990s they employed sixty-five full-time workers who turned out sticks for players in North America, Europe, and even Japan, with total annual sales of more than $7 million.[54]

Equipment manufacturers looked to sell to any player, at any age, in any league, in any country they could. Like Volvo, IBM, and British Petroleum, their abiding sense of capitalism transcended loyalties to any "national" interests. For example, the Swedish Jofa firm was founded in 1926 to make leather products. In 1963 they began producing plastic hockey helmets that soon were part of the Tre Kronor brand image. Jofa did not rest with a Swedish identity. Its eyes were on North America, where within two decades its helmet was most associated with Wayne Gretzky. Jofa was a force of convergence. But such tides could become an uncontrollable vortex. Jofa was soon swallowed up by larger, Swedish and North American companies in the merger manias of the 1970s, '80s, and '90s.[55]

In the 1950s the CBC in Canada, CBS in the United States, and national networks in Europe all televised top-level hockey. *Ice Hockey World* reported that television rights to the March 1955 World Championships in Germany had "already been sold at a figure rumored to be in the region of 50,000 Swiss francs, roughly £3000 sterling." At the same time, any member country of the IIHF maintained "the right to veto or 'blackout' telecasts in their own country." It seemed like a failsafe system. TV could boost any national brand. But broadcasts, especially after 1972, beamed across lines of nations, governing bodies, or genders, thereby supporting convergence.[56]

In North America, NHL and Olympic broadcasts spiked interest, which supported rink-building and youth participation. This opened a market for experts to sell their knowledge at summer camps. West Point and Olympic coach Jack Riley ran a very successful program in Worcester, Massachusetts. Called the Eastern Hockey Clinic, Riley's camp mixed American boys with Canadian NHL pros. The coaching roster included Ralph Backstrom, Jacques Lemaire, and Charlie Hodge. Drake McFeely (who starred at Amherst College in the mid-1970s) recalled his awe of the flashy Lemaire, who drove a "very impressive car (Corvette?) . . . always had a pack of Marlboros in his back pocket," and dazzled the campers at evening "lectures" well-salted with the word "shit."[57]

What's more, myriad summer hockey camps staged in Canada catered heavily to an American clientele. In summer 1966, Roger Crozier's Muskoka Hockey School, the *Toronto Star* reported, offered a six-week course for three hundred boys, "almost entirely . . . U.S. youngsters, most of them from the Baltimore and Washington areas." In 1969 the hockey-oriented Bobby Orr–Mike Walton Sports Camp on central Ontario's Lake Couchiching projected enrollment of 750 campers, "75 per cent American"—including 40 percent from greater Boston—and only 15 percent total from Toronto.[58] It was a convergent and profitable experience all around. Promising, too. In 1966 the *Boston Globe* reported that the Eastern Hockey Clinic "has already had one of its students," a Lynn native named Larry Pleau, "grabbed by the Stanley Cup Champions, Montreal Canadiens." With NHL expansion coming the following year, Harvard coach Cooney Weiland recognized that camps like his own could fuel dreams "of a professional career."[59]

In 1959, *US Amateur Hockey* magazine proclaimed its mission to develop an American market. Much of its line ink over the next few years pushed an American brand, and it published "official" columns for AHAUS and the AHCA. But it also had to sell copy to all consumers. It had to grow the game overall. One way was to use NHL stars to write instructional columns. Thus, in the very issue wherein Princeton's coach Dick Vaughan challenged his colleagues to reduce their Canadian imports, *USAH* featured a column by Detroit Red Wing Marcel Pronovost on "effective Defensive Play." Teammates Gordie Howe, Alex Delvecchio, and Terry Sawchuk soon appeared. Hockey knowledge was a commodity that crossed brand lines. It was a force of convergence.[60] Even as the sport seemed terribly frayed—by disagreements over violence, playing styles, gender, and amateurism—commerce promised to mend the tears in hockey's fabric. It was a one-world vision whose time was near.

PART FOUR

THE RISE OF CORPORATE HOCKEY, 1972–2010

19

The Old Order Disrupted: 1972

In 1971, *Atlantic Monthly* published a long profile of Bobby Orr, the outstanding Boston Bruins defenseman who the magazine claimed had revolutionized his sport. The article captured the state of the NHL as it was just beginning a transformation of expansion, continental television exposure, increased salaries, and a new wave of owners, sponsors, and fans. In 1971, however, much of the old NHL culture still dominated. Orr's flamboyant teammate Derek Sanderson spoke of the Boston Garden's "lunch-bucket crowd, guys who slug their guts out all week long and whose only enjoyment is a few beers and a hockey game." Author Tom Dowling noted "there is no reference for managerial leadership here, no mirroring of middle-class aspiration, no hungering for upward mobility." Pregame introductions did "not trumpet the hockey players' college pedigrees, since, as it turns out, many of them have no more than a ninth-grade education." In some ways, the 1971 NHL had not changed since World War II. The players were almost all like Orr in one respect: Canadian born and bred, they were products of a development system controlled by NHL franchises.[1]

In other ways, however, the old regime had started to change a half-decade earlier. In 1966 the NHL's governors approved a doubling of teams, with franchises in Pittsburgh, Philadelphia, St. Louis, Bloomington (Minnesota), Oakland, and Los Angeles. That same year, the docile NHL labor market was shaken when Orr and his lawyer-agent Alan Eagleson negotiated a whopping two-year rookie contract allegedly worth between $50,000 and $100,000, with a $25,000 signing bonus. Two years later, Orr's new three-year deal was worth some $200,000, a figure that forced owners to open their pocketbooks (at least a little) for other players. Parsimonious owners like Boston's Weston Adams planned to pay for this with revenues from expansion fees and television. The results were mixed. Overall Nielsen ratings for CBS's NHL game of the week increased from 4.1 in the first season of expansion to 5.6 for the 1969–70 season. The problem, however, was the uneven distribution of fan interest. Localized demand translated into uneven local media deals and associated revenues. For instance, in 1971 the Boston market registered a 16.1 rating, while the Los Angeles market was 2 and Atlanta was 3.8. While the Bruins got "around" $75,000 for their share of the CBS deal, they pocketed $375,000 from their local TV partner, Channel 38. The rich were getting richer.[2]

The *Atlantic* also described a division over how to market the game. Derek Sanderson was "interested in bringing hockey into the mainstream of American life, with all the wealth, celebrity, and crass vulgarity that the phrase implies." On the West Coast, the expansion franchise in Oakland had struggled and been sold in 1970 to the eccentric baseball owner Charlie Finley, who changed uniform colors to match those of his Athletics, including flashy skates (first green and gold, then white). On the other hand, old owners, like the Bruins' Adams and his counterparts in Montreal, Detroit, Chicago, New York, and Toronto, cherished "the game's traditional values, the independence from corporate life and TV domination, even the savagery of the game, which, unless diluted, is too raw to gain even middle class respectability." Of course, it was easy to embrace tradition where demand was higher than supply.[3]

Bobby Orr's arrival pushed boundaries both on and off the ice. Change was in the wind, like the wet chill before a nor'easter. No one, however, was prepared for the changes triggered in 1972. Divergence among hockey's various governing bodies had marked the era from 1920 to 1971. Some of this stemmed from national and continental politics; some from differences in rules and philosophies of play. Some were based on gender biases. Some differences were clear on the ice. Some were figments of rhetoric. But they all mattered. More important, however, was their solubility. Differences are not all permanent, and this was very true in hockey. Just when Anatoli Tarasov was hammering away at North American individualism and just when American college coaches were raising cautions about Canadian imports and just when males were lampooning female abilities, events began to turn the flow of hockey culture from divergent to convergent. After 1972, both on and off the ice, North Americans and

Europeans slowly began to embrace similar structures, similar rules, and similar styles of coaching and playing.[4]

Convergence in Rules

The first swing point was playing rules. Recall the fundamental difference between NHL-rules hockey (which meant virtually all of Canada and US senior amateur) and those of Europe or the American colleges and high schools: NHL rules allowed checking all over the ice; the others limited checking, first to the defensive zone and then to the defensive half of the ice. While the Canadians complained about this distinction, they were not alone. In 1949, American Olympian John B. Garrison argued that North American and European versions "could benefit by incorporating some of the proven features of the other," leading to a game with a more robust combination of physical contact, speed, and "clever stick-work." By the 1960s, the Swedes began to lobby for checking all over the ice. Tarasov, among others, stood firm against this change, arguing that offensive-zone checking could reduce the role of skill. It took stronger and more concerted lobbying to change the rules. That came through the person of NHL president Clarence Campbell.[5]

Rules convergence was a key piece of the league's expansion strategy, part of a vision for greater influence on the IIHF and the NCAA, two reservoirs of potential talent. At the same time, the NHL engaged in more heated debate within Canada about the nation's participation in international hockey. The CAHA seemed too weak to return the Maple Leaf to glory. In 1969 it was replaced by a new entity, Hockey Canada, which took control of national teams, and which included representatives from both the NHL and the NHL Players' Association. Clarence Campbell reported to his Governors that it was "highly desirable" that Hockey Canada succeed, since "it will be the natural forerunner of trans-Atlantic competition in which the NHL is certain to have a prominent place." In July 1969 Campbell led a delegation to the IIHF Summer Congress in Switzerland, where they showed a film on NHL hockey and successfully lobbied for checking all over the ice.[6]

It was a transformative moment. In his final memoir (1997), Tarasov claimed that the Canadians used "powerful pressure" that was "mainly directed against us." In his view, "the Canadian coaches wanted to deprive us of an easy performance, speed maneuver[s], well organized forechecking and that habitual freedom that enabled our players to play collective, creative, winged hockey." There may have been truth to that, but clearly many European members projected their own benefits from liberalized checking. The IIHF itself concluded that "aligning the game with the NHL" was one of "the most substantial and dramatic rule changes in the history of international hockey." Among other things, "without this rule in place" it was doubtful "that Swedes Borje Salming and Inge Hammarström could have even attempted to play in the NHL, when they became European pioneers in 1973." Equally important, the change "paved the way for the historic interaction between the IIHF world and the NHL; the 1972 Summit Series between the Soviet Union and Team Canada."[7]

The Summit Series

Campbell and the NHL needed more than rules changes to facilitate a showdown between the NHL and the Soviets. They needed IIHF approval to allow the Soviet "amateurs" to play against salaried professionals. Campbell pushed for this at the 1969 IIHF Congress. As one expert wrote, the IIHF did not approve "open" hockey—the vote was 20 for and 30 against—but it did "allow nine professionals on national teams as an experiment for one year, provided that the players were not from the NHL but from minor-league clubs." By several accounts, the deciding vote for this experiment was cast by none other than Bunny Ahearne. A Canadian team that included pros went to the Moscow Izvestia Cup tournament in December 1969, taking home silver on the strength of a 5–2 win over Sweden, a 10–1 thrashing of Finland, and a 2–2 tie with the hosts. Even though the Canadian pros were considered "mediocre," their performance was "bad news for the 'amateur' establishment."[8]

What followed, however, was bad news for Canada, which had earlier been tapped to host the 1970 IIHF Championships. Behind the scenes, Avery Brundage and the IOC were making their last stand in letters and phone calls with Bunny Ahearne. If outright professionals were allowed to play in IIHF championships, Brundage threatened, none of the competitors would be eligible for Olympic competition. At their January 1970 meetings, the IIHF leadership reversed course and resurrected the ban on outright professionals. Hockey Canada's representatives directed their venom at Ahearne, the Soviets, the Swedes, and the entire establishment of "phony" amateurs. Then they announced they would not host the IIHF championships and would not send a national team to any international championship until the playing surface was leveled.[9]

What no one said out loud was that Brundage had *not* prohibited "friendly competition" or exhibitions between amateur and pro teams from Europe and North America. A year before, Tarasov had written that "both sides would win in such a meeting." Tarasov was not alone in these beliefs. It took three more years of negotiations before all the rhetoric about styles finally moved onto the ice in September 1972, in an epic Summit Series between the Soviet National Team and a set of NHL All-Stars doing business as "Team Canada." Four games across Canada; four games in Moscow. All the pieces were in place, except one. Anatoli Tarasov was no longer national team coach. That role was taken by Vsevolod Bobrov. Some said that Tarasov had become too outspoken in his columns and media appearances, that he had demanded a better deal for himself. Ironically, he was becoming too "individualistic."[10]

There was much on the line, even if few pundits gave the Soviets a chance. There was a potential television audience of some twenty-five million people in North America and one hundred million in the USSR. Corporate sponsors paid $25,000 per minute to advertise on the North American telecasts. There was no shortage of takers, either for TV time or for arena signage. The Gillette Razor Company explained its purchase of Moscow signage: "Every time the players swoop down the ice, line up before the game, or face off in the centre of the rink, the company's advertising is plainly visible to the millions of television viewers."[11]

The Soviets drew first blood with a surprising and dramatic 7–3 victory at the Montreal Forum. The Canadian people and their media were expectedly distraught, spewing lots of David and Goliath metaphors. But perhaps the most telling comment was uttered by Johnny Peirson, a Canadian and Bruins alum who was now color commentator for Boston's Channel 38 telecasts. The station was anchor to an ad hoc American network set up for the series. Peirson and his colleague Fred Cusick were the personalities that American viewers saw and heard. During the wrap-up of game 1, Cusick asked Peirson, a World War II veteran, for his final thoughts: "Well Fred, I always hoped I would someday see history unfold, but I never thought it would be Dunkirk."[12]

Canadian coach Harry Sinden planned to beat the Soviets with an aggressive NHL-style game: high pressure, hard hitting, and hard shooting

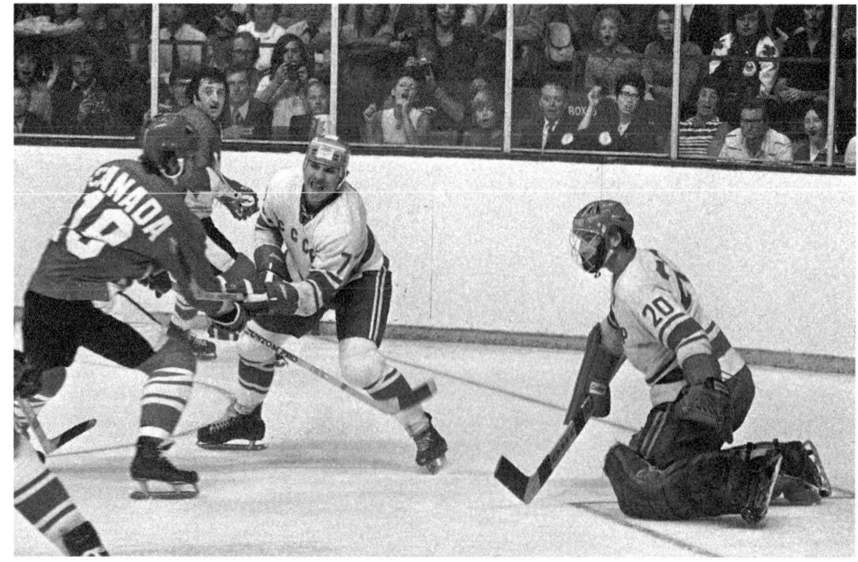

Henderson Shoots on Tretiak, 1972 Summit Series (THE CANADIAN PRESS/Peter Bregg)

from any angle, because his scouts had marked Soviet goalie Tretiak as "questionable." Big mistake. After four games, the Soviets led 2-1-1. When the Soviets won game 5 in Moscow, things looked bleak. The Canadians, however, doubled down in aggressiveness—forechecking, shooting, and hacking their way back to tie the series after seven games. In his memoirs, Tretiak offered the Soviet appraisal of games 5 and 6: "Those games gave the Moscow spectators the opportunity to see first-hand the inside of professional hockey. The dirty tricks, punches, threats to the referees, and after-the-whistle hits were all tactics that the Canadians demonstrated without any trace of shame. Our fans, who were used to a different kind of competition, were literally shocked." The finale, game 8, went down to the wire before Toronto's Paul Henderson scored the winning goal—on a rebound.[13]

North American hockey fans rejoiced. But something had changed. In the preface to his series memoir, published later that fall, Harry Sinden recognized the need for concession and change—for convergence:

> Hockey has been the Canadian game. We fostered it, loved it, nurtured it, thought it would be ours forever. This series showed that there are

> many nations now who want to share this great game with us at its top level of excellence. We should feel proud of this, not threatened by it. We should feel we have groomed a beautiful child whom the rest of the world wants to love with us. For years, the Russians, Czechs, Swedes and others studied our game and the way we developed it. They have learned their lessons well. Now it's time for us to learn a few from them—especially from the Soviets, who I feel have invented new methods which transcend some of those that are still an integral part of the Canadian style . . . I salute the Soviet players, and their coaches, for their dedication to the game. In many ways, they are, right now, the best players in the world.

The next decade reinforced Sinden's analysis.[14]

The issue was how much and how fast to change. Ken Dryden tended goal for Canada in that series. In 1971, as an NHL rookie, he stoned Bobby Orr and the Big Bad Bruins in the Stanley Cup playoffs. Yet he developed into one of the world's best goaltenders while playing at Cornell in the late 1960s under Ned Harkness. He understood the challenge the Soviets posed to North American hockey. In his 1983 reflection, *The Game*, he outlined the clash of styles:

> We dominated those parts of the game to which our style had moved—the corners, the boards, the fronts of both nets, body play, stick play, faceoffs, intimidation, distance shooting, emotion. In the end it was enough. But disturbingly, the Soviets had been better in the traditional skills—passing, open-ice play, team play, quickness, finishing around the net—skills *we* developed, that seemed to us the essence of hockey, but that we had abandoned as incompatible with the modern game.

When he wrote his book, Dryden did not believe that Canada had shifted tactics much since 1972. But he recognized that the numerous encounters between Soviet and NHL teams in the mid-1970s had done something else: "The Soviets fundamentally changed their approach to the game," shifting from a predictable (if still hard to defend) possession game to the transition game favored in North America. And the Soviets had learned to shoot, to play more aggressively, to counterattack more quickly. "It was," said Dryden, "our game played their way. . . . It was the final irony. In countering our game, they discovered they could play theirs more effectively." The Summit Series marks the beginning of a half-century convergence in coaching and playing, both across the Atlantic and within North America.[15]

The World Hockey Association

Team Canada escaped humiliation by a few minutes and sheer willpower. Both the Canadian media and populace quickly shifted from sighs of relief to second-guessing. The generous analysis emphasized that, yet again, Canada lacked its best players. Bobby Orr was hurt. And Bobby Hull was ineligible. Along with Derek Sanderson, Gerry Cheevers, and J. C. Tremblay, Hull had been on Harry Sinden's original roster. But there was a hitch. All were leaving the NHL for more money in the new rival World Hockey Association. Campbell gave them until August 13 to sign NHL contracts if they wanted to join Team Canada. It did not look promising, and Hull's case looked the bleakest. A month earlier, he had signed a ten-year contract with the WHA's Winnipeg Jets. Canadian fans flooded newspapers and radio stations with protests over Hull's exclusion. Even Prime Minister Pierre Trudeau made an appeal, but to no avail. The NHL held firm. While Campbell admitted to the *New York Times* that "public opinion is against us," he emphasized that the NHL owners were "making nothing from the series. Further, the only way the players themselves had agreed to the series was if their liability for injury was covered by the NHL." That meant that only players under NHL contracts would play. Hull had defected to the enemy. "He has openly suborned the players of the NHL," said Campbell, "and urged them to leave and join the WHA. He abused the NHL. We're certainly not going to provide him with the sounding board platform from which to extol the virtues of the WHA for six or seven weeks around the world."[16]

The World Hockey Association was the second major event of 1972. The league's name reflected the bold and brash hucksterism of its founders, Dennis Murphy and Gary Davidson, who had also concocted the American Basketball Association in 1966 as a rival to the established National Basketball Association. Both the ABA and the WHA were modeled after the American Football League, which in 1966 was winning a six-year war against the established National Football League, a war that ended in a merger, earning early AFL investors a windfall expansion of asset value. It was all about national footprints and national television deals, requiring expansion into new markets. Pro sport franchises seemed to be a solid (if not a sure) bet for hustling investors.

The WHA was filled with hustlers, from the top down. The sporting brain was Murphy, a serial start-up guy who did not stop with the ABA and WHA. He also founded World Team Tennis, Roller Hockey International, and the International Basketball Association. He groomed his showmanship as mayor of Buena Park, California, and as a fundraiser for Governor Pat Brown. His sporting ambitions stemmed from a friendship with Al Davis, long-time coach and owner of the Oakland Raiders and founding member of the American Football League. Murphy's burly frame, strong nose, wavy black hair, frumpy dress, and ebullient personality made him something of a doppelgänger to Anatoli Tarasov. Davidson was a different sort, a young Orange County lawyer who was the front man for the ABA and WHA and later the World Football League.[17]

One scholar summarized the Murphy-Davidson modus operandi as a series of six steps. First, "incorporate the league." Second, "line up investors and sell them franchises while reserving franchises for themselves." Third, "call press conferences and act like the league was a going concern." Fourth, "sign some star players to make the league appear viable." Fifth, "announce rule changes or gimmicks or anything that would make the new league distinctive from the competition." Finally, "sell off their franchises (which was how they made money on these projects), let the league run on its own and then go on to the next enterprise." Getting investors was the perfect job for Murphy. As he recalled, "It was easy for me, because I'd done it before with the ABA. Every town has a high roller, a guy with money who was involved in sports. I'd go into a town and find out who those guys were. Then we need to make our pitch." By November 1971 the WHA announced high rollers and franchises in Calgary, Chicago, Dayton, Edmonton, Los Angeles, Miami, New York, St. Paul, San Francisco, and Winnipeg. Some of them didn't last a year, but such vagaries were part of the Murphy-Davidson model.[18]

The WHA needed a star, and its focus quickly moved to Bobby Hull, who in 1969 had waged a rancorous contract battle with Chicago's Black Hawks that included a one-month holdout of his services. Like Joe DiMaggio three decades earlier, Hull learned the hard way that players had no leverage against teams and leagues that lacked competitors. Major-league sports operated a monopsony, employing a "reserve system" that essentially bonded players to their owners in perpetuity. Teams in the same league system could not bid openly for players, whose contracts could be unilaterally extended forever by owners exercising what was called an "option" clause. In 1969, after getting nowhere with his holdout, Hull came to his senses, apologized to the Black Hawks, and accepted a $17,000 loss of salary. His 1969 contract, however, formally ended in the spring of

1972, just as the WHA was looking for players. That prior season, Hull had scored 50 goals and made his tenth appearance as an NHL All-Star. He was everything the WHA hoped for. As Dennis Murphy recalled, "Bobby was perfect for us. I've never seen a guy who was better at PR. He'd sign autographs for hours. He was always smiling. He had this charisma. He just looked like a star."[19]

In June 1972, Hull signed a ten-year, $2.75 million contract with the Winnipeg Jets and the WHA, which included a $1 million up-front bonus for personal services to the league. The *New York Times* reported NHL president Clarence Campbell's earlier warning that if the WHA enticed NHL players to jump leagues, "we will fight them from the ramparts." In fact, Hull's whole signing process was cat and mouse, since the Black Hawks were chasing him with an injunction. The next day, Campbell told the *Times*: "As far as the N.H.L. is concerned, Hull has broken his contract with the Hawks."[20]

NHL clubs pursued their case in various courts, seeking restraints against jumpers like Hull on the grounds that an NHL contract included an additional option year that could be exercised unilaterally by the club. Some courts agreed with this. Others did not, particularly if players countersued with claims that such a system violated American antitrust laws. Professional sports contracts and reserve systems were very much in the public imagination during the summer of 1972. In June, the US Supreme Court upheld baseball's reserve system, which the Court had exempted from antitrust law in 1922. The decision was a slippery one, made on the basis of *stare decisis*, or standing by earlier decisions. In essence, the Supreme Court dodged a decision on the merits of baseball's reserve system and instead urged Congress to act. At the same time, the Court noted that other sports had no such exemption.[21]

In the fall of 1972, a number of *NHL v. WHA* player cases were aggregated into a single hearing at the federal district court in Philadelphia. There, on November 8, Judge A. Leon Higginbotham granted a preliminary injunction preventing the NHL from using its reserve system and its option clause as a basis for legal challenges against players who had jumped to the WHA. In short, Bobby Hull and the others were now legally free to play in any American market. The NHL might have taken its case back to Judge Higginbotham for a permanent ruling. It did not do so. The WHA and Judge Higginbotham forced the NHL to begin serious negotiations with the NHL Players' Association that ultimately led to forms of free agency undreamed of a decade before. Because of the WHA, professional hockey was now a freer players' market than baseball. This fact was not lost on Marvin Miller, the head of the Major League Baseball Players Association, who told *Jet* magazine: "If the language of the decision is to be interpreted to mean that a team can no longer control a player for the rest of his life, but just until his contract expires, then it has a great deal of significance." Within a year, Miller used this logic to begin dismantling baseball's reserve system.[22]

Some were not happy with the WHA's progress. *New York Times* columnist Dave Anderson expressed disdain shortly after Hull's signing. His immediate issue was a conflict of interest created by the collective funding of Hull's $1 million bonus. While no one had the exact details—whether each team paid $90,000, or the amounts were uneven—the point was that "no matter what the amount, each W.H.A. club owns a piece of Bobby Hull's magnificent muscles and curved stick." If Hull was the marquee player because of his scoring prowess, Anderson pondered, how could other teams feel free to assign a "shadow" to prevent his freewheeling play or otherwise hinder his scoring? That would be against their financial interests. Anderson's other beef could have been written by NHL publicists. Professional hockey, he claimed, was about to become "the most diluted major league sport," expanding from the "compact strength of six major league teams to the expanded weakness of 28 alleged major league teams—16 in the NHL, 12 in the WHA." Anderson seemed to pine for a return to the so-called Original Six of one hundred players. By his count, the NHL and WHA were "advertising 500 players of major league caliber. It's false advertising." Canada, he went on, could not be expected to produce five hundred quality hockey players. With a population of twenty million, that meant producing twenty-five major leaguers per million. America, he noted, with its population of two hundred million, needed only a ratio of ten per million to stock the two thousand slots needed for the NFL, NBA, and MLB. He concluded that hockey was engaged in "reckless expansion," which "produced parody before parity." Anderson was onto something. At the same time, he revealed himself to be ignorant of hockey's wider world. He made no mention of international sources such as Sweden or Finland, and he completely ignored the American collegiate leagues, which had managed to produce a star like Ken Dryden. Both the WHA and the NHL soon began to siphon talent from both the international and the collegiate pools.[23]

Checking All Over the NCAA Ice

Grooming new talent pools, however, required some convergence in rules. Recall that Clarence Campbell and the NHL had in the late 1960s urged both the IIHF and the NCAA to change the checking rule to align with the NHL. The IIHF had complied in 1969, and Europeans had since then been checking all over the ice. In theory at least, this provided players like Börje Salming better preparation for a professional career. The NCAA rules committee, on the other hand, had rejected the notion in 1967, saying, "Our game under the present rules is so much better than the professional game."[24]

Pressure continued. The following year (1968), the NCAA committee allowed body checking up to the offensive blue line. And at its 1972 meeting, the members finally allowed body checking all over the ice, despite a "long, detailed, thorough discussion" about the potential for "more fights, more injuries, jamming, interference, retaliation." In the end, the committee appeared to accept the position of member Al Renfrew, then coach at the University of Michigan: "Let's be honest; let's legalize what already is going on." Ironically, the year before, the same committee had ordered its secretary-editor to warn the ECAC and the WCHA (the college leagues that produced representatives to the national tournament) that "the continuance of high sticks endangers the whole future of American hockey." In fact, the greatest threat to a distinct "American" game was body checking all over the ice. There was no going back.[25]

One Boston writer reported that AHCA members endorsed the change by only a 21–20 vote. Local coaches echoed the split opinions. Boston University's Jack Kelley, just off consecutive NCAA championships, was positive because it would provide uniformity "from the Pee Wees right up to the pros." On the other hand, Harvard's Bill Cleary saw "no way" the change would help. It would bring, he predicted, "more cross-checking, charging, and high sticking." His job was "coaching American college hockey . . . not trying to get kids ready for the pros." Six local college players (including two of Cleary's) were all "in favor." They doubtless agreed with Boston State coach Eddie Barry, who stated flatly, "We'll be giving our kids a better chance to make pro hockey. With all the new pro teams being formed there has to be plenty of openings and the college kid will be sought after even more now."[26]

In the same year, the ECAC (which controlled eastern college hockey) moved to allow freshmen to play on varsity teams. The NCAA had liberalized its freshmen eligibility rules in 1968, with the exceptions of football and basketball. Most hockey programs kept their freshmen off the ice, but by 1972 there were proposals to allow freshmen in NCAA football (which happened). Hockey programs jumped on the bandwagon. The arguments were largely about cost savings and greater opportunities for "ready" players. Threats of litigation were also in the air. In some cases, attorneys were claiming that the chance to showcase talent and land a pro contract was a property right, perhaps even guaranteed in the Constitution. In any event, for college hockey, it all meant that an incoming freshman could now play immediately on varsity, under open-checking rules, where he could develop and display skills to pro scouts from the now-expanded landscape that so pleased Eddie Barry and so worried Dave Anderson. *Boston Globe* writer Joe Concannon sensed that it all might bring "the end of an era." As he accurately put it, "the college campus, once virtually un-trod upon by the pro scouts, has now become a very happy hunting ground." It would be difficult, he added, to gauge the "earthquake effect" until the 1972–73 season ran its course, but it was "safe to say . . . because of the signing and pending signing of so many undergraduates, the balance of power in college hockey could shift almost overnight." The bottom-line question, which became so much a part of college basketball, was: Who could keep their players long enough to find a core group of championship leaders? A half-decade before, few college players or coaches even thought of, let alone hoped for, a pro career. The earthquakes of 1972 changed that.[27]

Title IX

In the early 1970s, ice hockey was rocking with major events—at least for men. In Canada and Europe, one cannot easily find an epochal event or new league that altered the landscape for women. As we shall see, it was more a matter of players, coaches, and promoters at the grassroots steadily working for more space on rinks and in the media.[28] In America, however, 1972 saw President Richard Nixon sign a bill of education amendments to the Civil Rights Acts of the 1960s. Title IX of those amendments banned, in simple terms, gender discrimination at any American educational program that received federal money. Most of the people who promoted Title IX expected its focus to lie in more equitable hiring, promotion, and salaries for faculty and graduate students at colleges and universities. But historical contingency altered the evolution of federal regulations articulating what the simple law would mean in practice. In 1971 a group of highly competitive and highly committed female coaches and administrators created the Association of Intercollegiate Athletics for Women. At the time, the NCAA was a male-only operation. Competitive teams for college women typically existed within departments of physical education, where the notion of national championships—with pressures and scandals tied to the "male model"—was still suspect in the minds of many female administrators. Female leaders were also aware, however, of the NCAA's growing (and threatening) interests in women's sports. So the AIAW emerged as something of a compromise: a national enterprise with national championships, but with clear limitations on the recruiting and scholarship awards that were so controversial in NCAA play.[29]

Female collegiate athletes now had a broad range of national championships. But there was one big hitch. The men's programs controlled all the money. In the spring of 1973, *Sports Illustrated* ran a three-part series on "Women in Sport." Part 1 laid out details on existing discrimination. For instance, at the University of Washington, 41.4 percent of the students were women, yet less than 1 percent of overall athletics expenditures went to women's sport. Part 2 conveyed examples of old attitudes that held women back: for example, the notion that sports would permanently injure a girl's reproductive system and render her less "feminine." Part 3 looked more at the prospects for greater equality of opportunity. Some girls had already won court cases under the aegis of equal opportunity law. Male administrators worried that a rise in female participation would create "catastrophic" problems with facility usage. "But an even worse storm is brewing," wrote the authors. That storm was Title IX.[30]

And so, in 1974–75, as the US Congress held hearings on Title IX regulations, female athletics administrators began appearing and laying out just how impoverished their programs were. The numbers were staggering. At Ohio State, the men's budget was $6 million; the women's was $43,000. At Texas, reported Women's Athletics Director Donna Lopiano, the men spent $2.4 million, while the women had all of $128,000. According to Lopiano, that amount equaled the men's phone budget. Boosters of men's programs quickly turned up the heat in an effort to protect football and other men's "revenue" sports. This only clarified the stakes and focused Title IX attention on athletics. By 1979 the Office for Civil Rights hammered out policy interpretations that became the most important lever of opportunity that American female athletes ever enjoyed. As we will see, they used Title IX with courage and tenacity in a host of sports, including ice hockey. By 1998 four American universities, well-stocked with Canadian players, competed for a national championship in Boston's Fleet Center. That same winter, an American team took the very first women's Olympic hockey gold medal, at Nagano.[31]

Corporate Hockey

The year 1972 held one more landmark. Bruce Kidd and John Macfarlane published *The Death of Hockey*, a book that warned Canadians they were losing "their" game. For Kidd and Macfarlane, hockey enjoyed its best days under a "community" model, where local, grassroots initiatives built rinks and players and teams, where identity was local. Kidd and Macfarlane predicted that a rising "commercial" model would siphon money and loyalty to the big leagues (in other words, NHL and WHA), to the detriment of the grassroots. Would Edmonton, Quebec, or Winnipeg (all in the WHA) be able to compete, they asked, with bigger American markets thirsting for major-league sports? Fans in Quebec and Winnipeg found the answer soon enough.[32]

Kidd and Macfarlane were onto something important. Their book deserves re-publication because it signaled a swing in hockey's history, toward a convergence of forms and approaches around the world, creeping in alignment with something closer to the National Hockey League's version. After a half-century of diversification, with nodes of power growing across Canada, America, and Europe, with a balance of interests among the professional, amateur, Olympic, and collegiate ranks, distinctions on and off the ice began to collapse toward a central model. While we share Kidd and Macfarlane's sense of change and their embrace of an ideal type, we choose not to use the term "commercial" or "capitalistic" (the term Kidd used later).[33] After all, hockey first developed and spread within vast flows of global capitalism between 1880 and 1920. In that sense it had always been a commercial and capitalist game. Anatoli Tarasov repeatedly insisted that he was building a model *in opposition* to some dominant, capitalistic form.

Between 1972 and 2010 there were three flows of convergence toward what we call "corporate" hockey. The first was part of a broader movement of grassroots and youth sports away from unorganized play toward highly structured, adult-dominated, privately operated programs and leagues. To be sure, adults had been coopting children's games and sports for more than a century, on public playgrounds, in school gyms, and on club fields. Pop Warner football, Little League baseball, OHA hockey—all made claims to offer better experiences and training than kids could enjoy on their own. In light of the Summit Series, the West looked to the East for ideas. In mid-September 1972, the *New York Times* published a short story by John Nelson Washburn, "a student of Soviet affairs in general and Soviet sports in particular." It was one of many attempts to parse the secrets of the Russians' early Series victories. Washburn focused on Moscow's Children and Youth Sport School for Hockey, run by the TsSKA, or Red Army team, and directed by no less a figure than Tarasov. The school's most prominent alumnus was Vladislav Tretiak. According to Washburn, the school was the base of national team development, beginning with Tarasov's "scientific search" for talent—a necessity "because the discovery of an excellent player cannot be trusted to luck." Players as young as age six could be admitted to the school, provided they passed an "entrance examination" administered by Tarasov and some associates, who included Vladimir Brezhnev, brother of the Communist Party chief. Washburn provided no details on the examination or the training in the school. It was enough for him to know that Tretiak had other school alumni as teammates on the Soviet national team, including the estimable defenseman Alexander Ragulin. "The end result," Washburn warned, "bodes ill for Soviet hockey opponents." Tarasov and the TsSKA's youth hockey school "may already have succeeded in laying the foundation for making Moscow the future hockey capital of the world."[34]

But most pundits missed the underlying irony of Washburn's story. Tarasov and the Soviets were channeling old North American concepts: the NHL's scouting and signing system; the hockey school operated by big-name coaches and players. In the following decades, youth skill development worldwide would be increasingly measured and influenced by distant experts and organizations. As we shall see, this often triggered conflict between local, regional, and national governing bodies. And in some cases, it was the national offices pushing the locals to bring more fun and more pure play—rather than more matches—onto the season schedule of precious ice time.

The second aspect of "corporate" hockey was an increased willingness to embrace business partners to underwrite costs in return for the opportunity to market their products through an affiliation with a team, a player, an arena, or an event. Today's marketers call this "sponsorship." It is an expected and necessary practice at almost all levels. In 1972, however, coaches and administrators of many teams or leagues (especially school and college) considered the practice to be "commercialization" that contaminated the game on the ice. These concerns, of course, did not prevent governing bodies from securing lucrative deals with corporate partners. In many ways, the Europeans led the North Americans down this path. Even the Soviets had their hands out, as Ken Dryden discovered when he arrived in Moscow in September 1972. In the heart of Soviet socialism, the fourteen-thousand-seat Lenin Sports Complex's "Palace of Sport" hockey rink was resplendent with the logos and marks of North American corporations. "Most Russians," he wrote, "probably have never seen a commercial or an advertisement of any sort. Yet there are 16 messages on the boards now, selling everything from Jockey shorts to Turtle Wax to Heineken beer." He understood the deal to be sixteen signs at $12,000 each, a pittance today but a tidy sum then, especially in Western currency. There would have been seventeen had the hosts been able to keep the Molson image at center ice. But Labatt was sponsoring the Canadian telecasts to the tune of $800,000. Labatt would not underwrite telecasts that featured constant images of a rival brewery. Alan Eagleson explained to the Soviets the fine points of "exclusivity," and the Soviets, who were adept at removing images, said goodbye to Molson.[35]

These commercial intrusions were anathema to the NCAA hockey committee in 1960. By 1990, however, it was difficult to reject corporate dollars and their related logos. In 1960 it was unthinkable for the Soviet players to compete in anything but socialist-made uniforms. But such notions began to crumble like the Berlin Wall. By 1996, the IIHF gave Reebok the rights to supply *all* of its championship competitors with Reebok-brand uniforms.

The third aspect of "corporate" hockey involved the decisions of players, coaches, and promoters at all levels to admit and even encourage tighter and tighter linkage, formal or informal, to a small system of governing bodies, leagues, teams, and associations run by a burgeoning cast of managers and marketers who embraced and adopted what Julie Stevens called "professional and corporate management practices." Over time, this system swirled more clearly around the NHL. Byproducts included the development of university-based training programs, professional associations, academic and trade journals, and metrics or "analytics" by which to measure individual and organizational performance. Another aspect was the growth, especially in the 1990s, of giant, international and multinational firms like Nike, IMG, AEG, and Disney that expanded both horizontally and vertically to control bigger markets and longer chains of supply, manufacture, and distribution. Nike thus bought Bauer to get into the hockey market; Disney bought a new NHL franchise and called it the "Ducks." The phenomenon crossed many sports, and by the millennium's end, one could find numerous examples of CEOs, COOs, CFOs, and CMOs who bounced around the sport industry from media company to professional team to equipment manufacturer to collegiate conference. In the case of hockey, the path for player development increasingly led to the NHL, and the most important decisions rested directly or indirectly, but always consciously, on the interests of the NHL. This would have been inconceivable to American Olympic star Bill Cleary in 1960 or to Soviet Valery Kharlamov in 1970. Playing for their country was the ultimate goal.[36]

In all three of these areas, the era of corporate hockey was one of convergence in the way the game was organized, marketed, and played. Corporate hockey was not any worse or any better than other or earlier versions of the game, whatever they were called: community, recreational, socialist, collegiate, or amateur. Nor did a convergence toward one form eliminate all the diversity that had blossomed in the five decades after the 1920 Antwerp Olympics. But, in any measure, 1972 clearly marked a swing away from difference and toward sameness.

The Revolutions Would Be Televised

If the obvious triggers of change were within sport (the Summit Series, the WHA, and Title IX), other factors were geopolitical and economic. The Cold War softened, the Iron Curtain fell, the Soviet Union crumbled, and the European Union grew. The old verities of nationalism became less compelling—at least until the new millennium. After the early 1970s the world opened up. Some of these changes were linked to new technologies in transportation and communication. Computers, satellites, and cable networks could move data and money at speeds undreamed of only decades earlier. Products, including sports equipment and teams, moved more efficiently and cheaply in jumbo jets and seaborne containers. In the 1980s, as Jeffry Frieden wrote, "a new ideological wave swept the world. Politicians, analysts, and interest groups attacked government involvement in the economy after generations of general acceptance." Investors both pushed and profited from these developments. In the last three decades of the twentieth century, foreign investment by multinational corporations went from $10 billion to $1 trillion per year. Money flowed to more productive regions and industries, and to cheaper labor. Product components now came from many areas. In Frieden's words, "goods previously made in one country could now be divided into a dozen parts, with each part manufactured in a different nation." An "American" Barbie doll sold in Topeka, Chelmsford, or Johnstown might contain Taiwanese plastic, Chinese cloth, and Japanese hair—all assembled in Malaysia. Capitalism, as another scholar wrote, is a "system constantly reinventing itself, a set of prescriptions peculiarly open to disruption, a work in progress." Hockey, like capitalism, reinvented itself in the decades after the Summit Series.[37]

At the same time, the increasingly wider net of global communications, beginning with satellite television transmissions in the 1960s, allowed for the instant circulation of cultural performances and products. Soviet goalie Tretiak wrote of the Summit Series: "The Soviets made an unforgettable impression on millions of television viewers around the world." Europe's hockey-playing countries televised the games, which eased angst for some Canadian fans who had traveled to Moscow on package deals only to find that their tickets had been given to Soviet officials. One told a reporter that sixty-eight of them would "fly to Copenhagen where they understand they can watch the games on television." Their friends and compatriots back home also watched the live action. In fact, watching Team Canada play in Moscow on TV became a moment of national bonding for Canadians.[38]

Their experience rested on satellite technology, which had orbited since the 1960s. Some events at the 1964 Tokyo Olympics, for instance, enjoyed live international transmission. Improved launch vehicles, signal transponders, and antenna receivers, coupled with international agreements, spawned new corporations like the International Telecommunications Satellite Organization (INTELSAT), which facilitated a live audience of one-half billion for the July 1969 Apollo 11 moon landing.[39] More consumers everywhere were watching the tube. By 1970 the Western Europe ratio of televisions to people stood at 1:4. The Soviet bloc was no different. In historian Tony Judt's words: "Two East German households in three possessed a television (whereas less than half owned a fridge); Czechs, Hungarians and Estonians (who could watch Finnish television broadcasting from as early as 1954) were close behind." By 1980 television penetrated most of

Europe. While football was the leading sport production, hockey was a close second in many countries.[40]

North America was further ahead. By the late 1960s the cable industry was emerging as something more than a means of carrying a few local broadcast stations to homes in valleys blocked from line-of-sight image transmission. Microwave towers and signal boosters enabled the distribution of some broadcast stations to locations far beyond their normal market. For instance, in 1971 author Hardy was able to watch Boston Bruins games in a small hotel in Claremont, New Hampshire. But microwave technology was too expensive to be the backbone of truly regional or national cable networks. The answer would lie in more satellites. In late 1970 the Hughes Corporation filed a proposal with the FCC for the development of two satellites, each of which could transpond ten video channels, including sports events from the "Hughes Sports Network." In a formula that became tiresome to most consumers, the business model anticipated extra monthly fees passed on directly from the cable company to its subscribers. In 1972, TELESAT CANADA launched the first domestic communications satellite. A year later, on June 18, 1973, the first coast-to-coast transmission from satellite to cable included a championship boxing match, live from Madison Square Garden, produced by a new company called Home Box Office, which had run its first transmission nine months earlier to 365 cable subscribers in Wilkes-Barre, Pennsylvania. Those first shows included a hockey game. A decade later, four domestic satellites carried forty such programming services, including ESPN. By 1995, 65.8 million of America's 95.4 million television households that dwelled along cable lines purchased monthly services. Canadians grabbed cable even faster, with 80 percent of them connecting in the 1980s. Europeans were uneven, with some countries (Netherlands, Belgium, Switzerland) above two-thirds penetration and others (Great Britain and France) under 2 percent.[41]

For sports fans, cable was an acceptably expensive way to get more diverse and more reliably transmitted content, especially for championship events and tournaments like the Summit Series. For sports moguls, better television technology promised a broader fan base. The decades-old model of percolating influence returned in new guise. Televised professional games would develop young fans who would yearn to learn to skate and play, which meant more business opportunities for rink building, equipment sales, instructional camps, teams and leagues, and new professional opportunities in the development and showcasing of player talent. In many ways, television was the central engine of corporate hockey.

The 1970s and 1980s saw a swell of media packages at local, regional, national, and international levels. A good local example was something called Hockey Night in Boston. In 1972 two enterprising entrepreneurs—Darby Yeager and Lance Lofaro—began a television show called *The Face-Off Circle*, which aired on cable television in a few Boston suburbs. The following season, they moved to WCRB-AM radio as *Hockey Night in Boston*, which ran delayed broadcasts of high-school games, and quickly expanded to include live coverage of games three nights per week, as well as the annual state tournament. With a growth in broadcast rights, *HNIB* jumped to the more powerful station WBOS-FM, whose signal reached fans as far as Cape Cod. Not content to cover someone else's property, Yaeger and Lofaro developed a summer all-star tournament and a March banquet tied to all-scholastic team announcements. In 1978–79 they were back in the television business, with a Saturday late-night slot on Channel 25. *HNIB Magazine* soon followed: a thrice-yearly roundup promoting high-school hockey. In some ways they were way ahead of the sport industry with their integrated control of both an event and its distribution. The 1982 summer tournament ran for three weeks at the Stoneham Arena, attracting more than twenty-five thousand fans, scouts from all twenty-one NHL teams, and coaches from more than one hundred colleges, all to watch top schoolboys from Massachusetts, southern New Hampshire, and Rhode Island. College coaches vied for the chance to lead one of the four teams filled with talent that included goaltender Tom Barrasso (soon to be the No. 5 pick in the NHL draft) and future Cy Young winner Tom Glavine (who was also a top NHL prospect). HNIB enterprises attracted top corporate sponsors like Brigham's Ice Cream, Control Data Corporation, the Massachusetts National Guard, and Christian Brothers Hockey. *Hockey Night in Boston* is alive and well in 2018, an exemplar of convergence toward corporate hockey and the NHL.[42]

Scholars of nonsports television content have questioned notions of simple media domination by "imperial" powers from America and Europe. The worldwide distribution and popularity of *Dallas* in the 1980s, for instance, did not signal or trigger the dissolution of national, regional, or local culture in Italy or Iraq, on or off television. But what of sports championships and sports stars? As we shall see, some media impressions triggered convergence, as North American coaches sought to unravel Tarasov's formulas of success. At the same time, in an age of instant global images, how long could a teenaged European player rebuff the allure and the examples of Bobby Orr, Wayne Gretzky, and the NHL?[43]

In the four decades after the Summit Series, hockey's laborers and capitalists created a world much more fluid and connected than ever before. Even if players and fans did not renounce their local identities and loyalties, they appeared more willing to try out others. If coaches and administrators clung to beliefs that *their* systems were the best, they also made changes here and there to be more like the NHL, changes that were more fundamental than may have first appeared.

20 Restructuring North America: 1972–1988

Amid the raucous aftermath of a 4–3 semifinal victory over the Soviets' Big Red Machine, USA Olympic team coach Herb Brooks strained to hear President Jimmy Carter offer telephone congratulations. Afterward, Brooks explained: "He said we had made the American people very proud, and reflected the ideals of the country." Carter called again the next day after a win over Finland sealed the gold medal. Brooks answered, "It's a great win for the American people, Sir. . . . Just shows that our way of life is the way to carry on." Their fellow Americans celebrated everywhere with chants of "USA, USA!!" It was, the *New York Times* explained, "a kind of national vindication after years of tensions with the Soviet Union and adversity in Afghanistan, Iran, the Middle East and other world arenas."[1]

The 1980 Miracle on Ice was a central hockey moment of this era, lying half way between the iconic 1972 Canada-Russia "Summit Series" and the 1988 Calgary Olympics, when, for the first time, the IIHF and IOC allowed professionals to play. In 2000, ESPN ranked it as the "greatest game of the century." The IIHF listed it as number one in importance. Most North Americans remember it as a vindication for Western capitalism against Soviet socialism. To that extent, one could say that little had changed in the world of hockey. Systems on the ice represented broader cultural and ideological differences, just as Anatoli Tarasov had been preaching for two decades. But if we peel away the veneer layered only *after* the game (for no one had given the United States much chance of a medal, let alone gold), we can see that American hockey had changed dramatically in the two decades following the 1960 Squaw Valley miracle. Brooks, his players, their technical and tactical preparation, and their administrative support structure had all moved closer to a professional and even a Soviet approach. They were a bundled example of wider flows of convergence.[2]

Brooks grew up on the east side of St. Paul, Minnesota, and played among a cohort at Johnson High School whose state titles in 1953 and 1955 were rare exceptions to North Country domination. At the University of Minnesota, he was a smooth skater and a decent playmaker but, like most American college forwards of the day, not very physical, in part because the rules prevented forwards from checking beyond the defensive zone. One teammate noted: "Hitting was not Herbie's game." Brooks was famously cut late from the 1960 Olympic team but went on to play for the national team in the next two Olympics and six of the next eleven World Championships.[3]

The international exposure influenced his philosophy when he began coaching at his alma mater—as an assistant in 1968 and after 1972 as head coach. He developed a "hybrid" system of discipline and creativity, in many ways similar to that of Anatoli Tarasov, whom he studied closely. Like Tarasov, Brooks believed that success rested on attention to detail, tough conditioning, and tight control of player psyches. He pushed his teams to the limit. Amid all the postmedal euphoria of 1980, *Newsweek* noted with understatement: "Brooks is not well liked by his players." As his biographer wrote, Brooks believed in disciplined defense, but his offense was built around "creative" players. Steve Christoff, 1980 Olympian (and ex-Gopher), noted that, offensively, "We were pretty much free to do whatever we wanted."[4]

Hollywood movies and popular amnesia suggest that Brooks's miracle innovation lay in his mastering the Russians' system and using it against them. Brooks was a brilliant coach, but he was not the first to bring Russian methods to the US national team. He followed his old Gopher teammate Murray Williamson, who had coached Brooks on the St. Paul Steers and the 1968 Olympic team. Part of Williamson's blueprint was to use conditioning drills he had learned from Tarasov on a visit to the Central Red Army training center in July 1971. Tarasov showed Williamson that the "real key to the Russian training system" was pace: "Every drill the Russians did, either on or off the ice, was at a brisk tempo that required each player to push himself to the limit and do it quickly."[5]

Williamson's 1972 Olympic team's 5–1 upset win over the Czechs led to a silver medal, which has been forgotten in large part because the game time in Japan was 2:00 A.M. EST, and NBC provided minimal highlights.

But it was a big deal in Sapporo. One writer even claimed that the phrase "Do you believe in miracles?" was first uttered there by announcer Curt Gowdy (whose young assistant was Al Michaels). In another account, Tarasov was so moved that he gave Williamson "a big bear hug and a kiss on the lips in recognition of America's defeat of the Russians' hated Eastern Bloc rivals." Hugging Russians was not so preposterous in 1972. Three months after Sapporo, Richard Nixon became the first American president to visit Moscow. Hockey was ripe for détente, especially after the strong Soviet showing in the Summit Series revealed that North Americans had much to learn from the Russians.[6]

Lou Vairo was another influence on Brooks. A congenial, outspoken New Yorker, Vairo blew onto national AHAUS circles in the mid-1970s when he moved to Austin, Minnesota, to coach the local Mavericks, one of a growing number of Junior A teams, a novel tier of corporate hockey in America, competing with high schools for players, ice time, money, and loyalty. Vairo's background was mostly in roller hockey on the streets of Brooklyn, but he knew he could coach. In 1974 he had "emptied his savings, borrowed money," flown to a Soviet clinic that included Tarasov, and there began a two-decade friendship. In 1976 his Mavericks won the national championship and caught wide attention because of their European style. By 1979 he was working for AHAUS. Brooks grew to trust him, so Vairo served as an observer and an advance scout for the 1980 team.[7]

Some NHL coaches studied Tarasov just as closely. On the eve of the epic 1975–76 series between two Soviet clubs and eight NHL teams, New York Islanders coach Al Arbour observed: "The Russians play a very controlled, disciplined style brought about through their intensive practice and drills." Philadelphia Flyers coach Fred Shero felt the Soviets' greatest advantage was in coaching education. "To be a coach in Russia, you have to be a top player, then go to the University and learn to be a coach. . . . Over here, you see a lot of people coaching who don't know anything . . . [and] are afraid to learn."[8]

Other attitudes and approaches had changed since 1972. By 1980, America's hockey moguls no longer drew their national teams from senior amateur leagues. America's best now came from Division I college programs that were funneling talent directly to the NHL. Brooks's lineups were full of players already being groomed for careers in the rigorous and commercial world of pro hockey. Prior to Lake Placid, 1980's "young college kids" played a schedule of sixty-plus games against a range of college, amateur, minor-league, NHL, and national teams. In addition, AHAUS paid each of them "a salary of at least $7200 for six-months, plus expenses . . . better than, or on par with, minor league clubs."[9]

Moreover, most of the team already had agents, the most prominent of whom was Arthur Kaminsky. Even Brooks was a client. In the Olympic run-up, Kaminsky (and his associate Bob Murray) counseled the players to remain amateurs and keep their eyes on a bigger payday. After the gold medal, however, he played hardball on endorsement deals. His strategy backfired when he could not reach agreement with AHAUS for sharing rights and revenues. Hence no Wheaties box cover for the greatest team of champions in 1980 (that had to wait for a Wheaties "Legends" series in 1997). The young college kids—armed with a seasoned agent—were now playing corporate hockey.[10] For Brooks, Kaminsky shopped around after the Olympics, triggering rumors about interest from the Rangers and the Colorado Rockies. In the end, Brooks landed in Davos, Switzerland, for a year and then returned to coach the Rangers for four more. The rest of his career was a model of convergence, where the old dividing lines eroded: St. Cloud University, Minnesota North Stars, New Jersey Devils (and their Utica affiliate), Pittsburgh Penguins (as scout and coach), French and US Olympic teams.[11]

Herb Brooks and his Miracle team represented many things: Cold War tensions, economic frustrations, and pent-up desire for some kind of victory, this one accentuated by a classic David-and-Goliath narrative arc. At its center, however, was a broader process: the softening of the divergent hockey systems and attitudes that had evolved over five decades in North America and Europe. Openly paying monthly salaries to American Olympians was unthinkable in 1960. So were agents, even for the top-level players in the NHL. Watching so many Olympians jump to professional careers would have been a far-fetched fantasy. The structures of the hockey industry—styles and strategies, amateur and professional—were converging.

The Professional Ecosystem Unsettled

At first blush, professional hockey in the decade after 1972 appeared to be anything but a model of corporate convergence. It was more like chaos. For fans, the 1970s were a decade of zany franchise openings and relocations. The NHL added new teams in 1970–71 (Vancouver and Buffalo), then countered the WHA by opening additional franchises in Atlanta and Long Island (1972) and in Kansas City and Washington, DC (1974). The WHA itself expanded to fourteen teams in 1974 but started a downward spiral after that. As one scholar argued, the WHA simply lost the larger markets to its established rival:

> The NHL had teams in 15 of the top 20 US markets, and in the three largest Canadian ones. In contrast, the WHA failed in most of these areas. Only Houston (#13), Minneapolis (#16), and Cleveland (#17) offered any kind of lengthy WHA presence, and all of those teams collapsed over time. . . . Overall, the WHA drew about two-thirds of the attendance of the NHL, averaging 5,300 per game in its first year, and reaching 8,100 in its last season [1979].

During the same period, the NHL's average attendance dwindled from 13,700 to 11,400.[12]

League and team budgets strained under the competition for talent. Free agents enjoyed both freedom and wage escalation, long restrained by the NHL's tight control of playing opportunities and, more recently, by a weak union. For instance, Pat Stapleton had played in the Summit Series, yet (according to WHA president Gary Davidson), his Black Hawks salary was only $55,000. The WHA offered him $270,000 over three years. Davidson claimed that in year 1, the WHA signed seventy-eight NHL players who made up 23 percent of all WHA rosters. The media naturally focused attention on the huge deals for a Bobby Hull or a Derek Sanderson, but the greater impact was at the level of the journeyman. Houston Aeros coach/GM Bill Dineen explained the situation: "Most of those guys were making about $12,000 in the minors. We offered guys $30,000. I didn't have to make a big sales pitch." The hemorrhage of talent forced the NHL to raise its own pay scales. The average NHL player salary jumped from $28,000 to $44,000 in 1972–73 and to $96,000 by 1978.[13]

The financial bleeding was heavy. Davidson estimated that the WHA "as a whole lost $15 million its first season" and "most teams probably lost $500,000 to $750,000." NHL owners were also distressed. In April 1973 a group led by Rangers president William Jennings met with Davidson to negotiate an agreement, but there was still too much anger among other NHL governors. Eventually, the economics of competition forced even the old guard to accept a solution, a merger hammered out between

Howard Baldwin (WHA president and Whalers owner), Ed Snider (Flyers owner), and John Ziegler, the new president of the NHL. Edmonton, Quebec City, Winnipeg, and New England would enter the NHL in 1979, but at a high cost, each paying an expansion fee of $6 million plus reparations of $750,000 to Birmingham and Cincinnati. Each could protect two goalies and two skaters, then hope for the best in an expansion draft.[14]

This market mania triggered new rink construction, which included the Hartford Civic Center, Edmonton's Northlands Coliseum, the Richfield (Ohio) Coliseum, and Cincinnati's Riverfront Arena, part of a broader wave of "civic" multisport investment. Most WHA franchises played in less desirable rinks: from tiny, recreational facilities in Cherry Hill, New Jersey, to ratty, old dens like the Cleveland Arena and the Chicago Amphitheater. At the same time, five of the NHL's own Original Six teams played in worn-down relics from the 1920s. By spring 1988, major-league hockey had settled down, with twenty-one NHL franchises parceled into four regional divisions branded with founders' names: Adams, Patrick, Norris, Smythe. Thirteen teams now played in arenas either new or renovated since 1966.[15]

Big-league expansion battles shook the ecosystem of the minor leagues as teams came and left. Long-established markets like Vancouver, Pittsburgh, Minneapolis, Indianapolis, Buffalo, Cleveland, and Kansas City faced long odds to support both NHL/WHA franchises and minor-league teams. Providence, Springfield, and Cincinnati lost and regained minor-league teams, even as they built new arenas in search of franchise stability. Hope sprang eternal in old, smaller markets such as Binghamton, Erie, Johnstown, and Utica, which played in the North American Hockey League (1973–77) and served as the real-life backdrop for the movie *Slap Shot*. Southern cities like Greensboro, Charlotte, Richmond, and Winston-Salem welcomed the Southern Hockey League (1973–1977). The system shuffles continued in the 1980s with new circuits like the Atlantic Coast Hockey League, formed in 1981 from the remnants of the Eastern Hockey League, with locations ranging from Winston-Salem to Baltimore to Cape Cod. In 1984 the ACHL revamped itself into a "rookie" league to reduce costs and level roster strengths. It experimented with shootouts, substance-abuse programs, and tougher penalties for fight instigators. It attracted some talented young coaches with names that resonated for years: Rick Ley, John Tortorella, Dave Hanson, and Rick Dudley. But by spring 1987, it was dead. In the era of corporate hockey, minor-league teams continued to churn.[16]

Television Power Plays

While other leagues floundered and faded, the NHL's grinding success was well told on network television. In Canada, the national franchise had been *Hockey Night in Canada* (*HNIC*) since the Saturday night show's 1931 inception on radio as *General Motors Hockey Broadcast* (later *Imperial Esso Hockey Broadcast*). Well before its CBC television debut in 1952, the show was simply *Hockey Night in Canada*. In 1965, Canada's first commercial network (CTV) bought rights to a Wednesday-night game of the week. With NHL expansions and the WHA merger, *HNIC* enjoyed a bloom of broadcast venues beyond Montreal and Toronto. The realities of corporate hockey, however, intruded on the desires of some fans. Molson Brewing owned the Montreal Forum, the Canadiens, and a piece of *HNIC*'s production company, the Canadian Sports Network (CSN). It was not good business for them to televise from Quebec City, whose Nordiques were owned by rival brewer Carling-O'Keefe. By 1986, Molson went on a bigger power play and took full control of CSN, soon morphing the firm and name into something more fitting to its corporate interests: Molstar Productions Ltd. This company soon began a very public and very controversial dance with CTV over the rights to *HNIC*.

Would the nation's most sacred marriage of winter evenings and winter sport leave the hallowed carriage of the CBC and move to CTV? It was big news in Canada in the spring of 1988. As explained by hockey writer Scott Young, in the final six-year deal with CBC, "Molson got the commercial concessions it wanted," including corporate signage "on or near the ice-surface boards and arena entrances within easy camera range, the Molson logo as part of the televised scoreboard," and the biggest coup: "calling the show *Molson Hockey Night in Canada*." Foster Hewitt had always plugged his sponsors. Now the whole game was pitched outright as a corporate property.[17]

In mid-1970s America, *Monday Night Football* was the focus of national sports passion. Some local markets, like Boston, had extensive media coverage and strong ratings for their NHL franchises, but the league as a whole lacked a presence. In the 1960s, NBC had carried some Stanley Cup playoff games across a national platform, and CBS carried from 1968 to 1972 a weekend game as well as some Stanley Cup tilts. In the 1970s and 1980s, the league bounced between NBC, ESPN, and USA networks, never quite finding solid ice. When it could not land an established network, the NHL patched together its own syndicate for special events like the Super Series over the New Year of 1975–76 and the Challenge Cup of 1979. Executives had the nagging worry that Americans simply did not understand the game. In 1973, NBC had introduced a between-periods cartoon character, Peter Puck, "here to lay some facts on you about hockey—the world's fastest team sport." This "poke-check professor" was the brainchild of NBC executive Donald Carswell. Animated by the famous Hanna-Barbera studio, he appeared in nine three-minute clips to introduce viewers to a cartoon world of players, penalties, tactics, and techniques, all the while trying to avoid a hard check. It was yet another chapter in efforts to sell hockey in America.[18]

Labor Market Turbulence

After 1972, rules changes, international play, professional expansions, and increased media presence widened expectations about who could play professional hockey. Scouts, coaches, executives, and especially young players began to believe that the reservoir of talent was no longer restricted to the Canadian junior leagues. Table 20.1 displays some simple statistics that convey these changes. US collegians and Europeans had practically no place on NHL rosters until this expansion in league size and mentality. By the mid-1970s, however, both leagues were drafting dozens of collegians and a handful of Europeans each year. As with any draft, only a minority actually made it to the big leagues. But it was the dream that mattered. And the lure of the salaries.

While the system of talent recruitment became more tightly integrated, there was a growing sense in the 1970s that professional players (and prospective ones) were emerging from their long-held status as the exclusive "property" of team owners. The WHA had cemented players' right to jump leagues if they were free agents. Even within leagues, the tide was turning, largely because of collective bargaining. Baseball led the way, despite a June 6, 1972, US Supreme Court decision (*Flood v. Kuhn*) that upheld Major League Baseball's reserve clause. The MLB Players' Association, directed since 1966 by Marvin Miller, was undeterred. As Miller wrote in his memoir, the publicity and pressure surrounding the Curt Flood case led the owners to make a gargantuan blunder in the 1970 agreement: "In order to maintain in court the fiction that baseball was governed impar-

TABLE 20.1. WHA and NHL Drafting of NCAA Collegians and Europeans in Amateur Drafts over First Ten Rounds

Year	NHL Collegians	WHA Collegians	NHL Europeans	WHA Europeans
1968	3		0	
1969	7		1	
1970	14		0	
1971	20		0	
1972	21		0	
1973	21	16	0	0
1974	27	32	0	0
1975	36	24	4	5
1976	24	15	5	9
1977	37	27	4	3
1978	44		3	
1979	15*		6	

* Only 6 rounds
Source: "NHL and WHA Draft History," HockeyDB.com, http://www.hockeydb.com/ihdb/draft.

tially and not by the commissioner, a paid employee of the owners, the owners had to concede that any disagreement about the . . . provisions of the collective bargaining agreement would be resolved by impartial, binding arbitration." By 1975 several arbitration decisions provided what the courts would not: free agency. The owners were now forced to negotiate a whole new system. Player salaries skyrocketed as they reflected a free marketplace for talent. Players in other professional leagues, including the NHL, took notice.[19]

Alas, there was no Marvin Miller in the world of hockey. Instead, the players got Alan Eagleson. By one account, he grew up in the 1930s and 1940s a scrawny, scrappy kid, better in class than on the field or ice. When he bloomed physically, he became a brawler, ready to duke it out with anyone who crossed him. By one account, "Eagleson did everything in extremes. He talked louder and swore louder and more frequently than anyone his friends had ever met." But his cockiness, his combativeness, and his guile were the perfect ingredients for a players' savior who might free them from the shackles of the owners. As Bobby Orr wrote in his memoir, Eagleson came into his life in 1964 at a spring hockey awards banquet. There were no flocks of agents in those days, so when he approached the family, Orr's mother asked him what he would charge for services. As Orr remembered, "he responded with a look of great sincerity and answered, 'Mrs. Orr, I'll make money only if your son makes money.'" Eagleson was soon agent, adviser and *consigliore*. He controlled all of the finances for Orr and others in a growing stable of players.[20]

When the NHL players unionized permanently in 1967, "the Eagle" was the logical choice for executive director. Several of his law-firm partners had quietly done most of the organizing. He leveraged his position as executive director of the NHLPA for a place at the table with Team Canada and other international hockey ventures, including the Summit Series and the Canada Cup. As he negotiated ever-rising contracts in the 1970s, he seemed a dream come true. But the players might have paid closer attention when the Maple Leafs owner Conn Smythe said, "I don't like unions, but I'm glad it's Eagleson at the head of the Players Association rather than somebody else." Soon Eagleson set up a series of interlocking companies—Sports Management Ltd., Nanjill Investments, Rae-Con Consultants—which recycled players' money into greater assets for Eagleson, who parleyed his sports fame into political equity as president of the Ontario Progressive Conservative Association. Some viewed Eagleson as hockey's king. But even a casual economist could sense that rising salaries stemmed more from WHA competition than from Eagleson's negotiating.[21]

The open market attracted dozens of new agents like Art Kaminsky, who gave players more choice and Eagleson's firm a big headache. Some wondered how Eagleson could simultaneously and fairly represent *all* players (as boss of the NHLPA) and *his* players (as head of his law firm). Some of his own clients wondered why he charged a 10 percent commission when competitors charged only 3 percent. And others questioned the size of his entourage, whose lavish travel was always paid out of the gross revenues from international events like the Canada Cup, leaving less to go into the players' pension fund. In 1976 he led his top client Bobby Orr to leave Boston for Chicago. There was grumbling in Beantown that Eagleson himself was getting a better deal from his old friend, Black Hawks owner Bill Wirtz. A year later, Orr's knees forced him to retire. He soon realized that he was hardly the millionaire Eagleson had promised. Players who left Eagleson's agency found little support from the NHLPA. More important, while Marvin Miller was steering his players through a series of work stoppages and victories in free agency, NHL players (and their agents) got little in free agency and groused that Eagleson provided no financial reports on NHLPA expenses or retirement funds. By 1989 the players were in open revolt against their own association. They commissioned a special report by rival agents, which claimed Eagleson had been misusing pension funds.

Eagleson was still elected to one more term as executive director and, as if to spite the players, the Hockey Hall of Fame inducted him the same year, as a "builder." The Order of Canada named him an officer.[22]

Both American and Canadian journalists dug into the story and published shocking accounts, most notably Russell Conway's series in the *Lawrence (Mass.) Eagle Tribune* called "Cracking the Ice," a 1992 Pulitzer Prize finalist. It became clear that Eagleson had been double-talking players while cashing in with the owners. Among other things, it emerged that he had refused (without consulting his client) a 1976 Bruins offer to give Bobby Orr 18 percent of the franchise's equity! Conway charged fraud and embezzlement. Canadian journalists added to the claims. The FBI and RCMP jumped in. After a decade of legal maneuvering, Eagleson pleaded guilty to a series of charges in America and Canada. Among other penalties, he served six months in a Toronto correctional facility. The Order of Canada expunged him and, after players like Brad Park applied pressure, Eagleson resigned from the Hall of Fame. A year later, Russell Conway was awarded the Hall's highest honor for journalism. It was a moral victory, but it did little to reimburse the players whom Eagleson had swindled—especially Orr, who lamented: "I am . . . angered by what he did to so many people, and embarrassed that I was one of them."[23]

Eagleson's example is important for more than what it says about his appalling exploitation of the athletes whom the NHL had relied on as compliant laborers for so long. Eagleson was as much a creature of the players' own push toward control as he was its creator. By the end of this period, the pendulum of power had swung a great distance, so great that budding Canadian superstar center Eric Lindros could refuse in 1992 to report to the NHL team that had drafted him (the small-market Quebec Nordiques), forcing a trade to the big-market Philadelphia Flyers. Four decades earlier, that sort of audacity from any professional athlete would have been wholly inconceivable.

American Colleges Go Corporate

In American colleges, the old east-west power structure came under stress. It had been dominated in the 1960s by the Eastern College Athletic Conference and the Western Collegiate Hockey Association, whose champions automatically went to the NCAA championship—a single event of four teams representing schools that ranged from small liberal-arts colleges of one thousand students to state research universities of thirty thousand. Growth was steady both in numbers and in geographical footprint: the forty-three schools who competed in 1956 grew to 102 by 1982, and their traditional Midwest and northeast locations expanded to Ohio and Alaska in the mid-1960s, Illinois, Missouri, and Pennsylvania by 1976.[24] In 1978 the NCAA added a Division II national championship. That same year, for the first time, a new conference (the Central Collegiate Hockey Association) sent a representative to the Division I tourney. In 1984 the east split at the top when seven programs left the ECAC to form Hockey East, with a separate league tournament and a separate schedule, including a novel experiment of regular-season interleague play with the WCHA. Founding commissioner Lou Lamoriello had played and coached at Providence College before serving as athletic director. He promised a simple vision of better hockey. He added that he would "be awfully surprised" if the league did not have a television package. That soon came, in a deal with the New England Sports Network when that new regional entity was launched in March 1984 under the joint ownership of the Boston Red Sox and Delaware North (which owned the Boston Garden and the Boston Bruins). Professional sports and college sports were aligning.[25] Occasionally, it destroyed old rivalries. Between 1967 and 1971, for instance, Sid Watson's Bowdoin Polar Bears regularly played and occasionally beat the likes of Providence, Northeastern, Vermont, and New Hampshire. By the mid-1980s the Division I programs could not afford to schedule any but their own.

NCAA hockey moved in other ways to reduce the barriers once separating the American college game from the pros. In 1971, for the first time, the NCAA Championship moved to a major NHL arena, the Boston Garden. From its inception in 1948, the event was held at either the quaint Broadmoor World Arena in Colorado Springs, at campus sites like Minnesota's Williams Arena, or at small historic venues like the 1932 Lake Placid Olympic rink. The effect of moving to the Boston Garden in 1971 was impressive. The *Boston Globe*'s Joe Concannon described the scene before the championship: "The lobby . . . was jammed and the large mass of people slowly edged its way up the ramps into the arena . . . a very special night in college hockey." The crowd was tallied at 14,995. The transition from campus rinks to an NHL venue reflected both larger monetary goals and a more professional brand. A few coaches complained about the loss of intimacy, but their voices were soon silent. In the decade ahead, only two campus facilities hosted the event.[26]

Local television stations carried a smattering of college games in the 1960s. By the mid-1970s, there were regional packages. For instance, in 1976, the ECAC announced its first-ever regular-season television game of the week. It was an all–Division I affair, produced by Boston's CBS affiliate, Channel 7, with live Saturday action beamed from college rinks in Boston, Providence, New Haven, and Durham, New Hampshire, featuring top teams from all around the east. New York State Public Broadcasting's station WNET also carried the games, which grabbed between 12 percent and 17 percent of the TV market share. In March 1979 the series culminated with a live telecast of the league championship at a packed Boston Garden, hyped by month-long publicity. In the 1980s new cable channels and networks jumped in to produce college games, like Boston's Now Preview and StarCase channels, and a young ESPN that covered the NCAA championship as early as 1982.[27]

Another episode reopened the long dispute over Canadian imports and emphasized the limits of corporate convergence in US college hockey. Bill Buckton and Peter Marzo came to Boston University in 1972, two top Canadian recruits in a long train that started in the mid-1960s under Jack Kelley. Buckton and Marzo had played briefly on Junior A teams, long characterized by American administrators as professional operations. A 1973 late-summer eligibility screening—prompted by accusations from a rival school—disclosed that Buckton and Marzo had received not only payments for room and board and books, but also small weekly allowances. Cash transactions made them professionals under NCAA rules, and BU ruled them ineligible. The players sued in federal court, winning a preliminary injunction and then a consent decree with the ECAC, as the presiding judge doubted there were any real differences between expenses paid by ECAC-NCAA member schools and those paid by Canadian junior-hockey programs.[28]

The case begged for clarity in NCAA rules. When Eastern schools circulated results from an NCAA questionnaire, it appeared that anywhere from twenty-four to fifty players might be deemed ineligible, some for accepting tryout expense money. Western schools initially said their players were pure, prompting Brown's athletic director to quip, "I can't believe [it]. . . . There aren't two Canadas." Estimates of potentially ineligible players spiked upward to two hundred, including six from Harvard. The ECAC petitioned the NCAA for relief, perhaps hoping to avoid another court battle. The NCAA seemed fixed in its hard-line position about amateurism. Later that fall, however, it modified the rules to allow Junior A players to play, so long as they received no more than "actual and necessary expenses."[29]

The NCAA eventually drew the line at Tier I Junior A (later Major Junior). Sign there, and you are ineligible. With that firmed up, the Canadian controversy faded away. Meantime, Herb Brooks's Minnesota Gophers, with an all-Minnesota lineup, won national titles in 1974 and 1976 (sandwiching a second-place finish in 1975). A story by Art Kaminsky in the *1977 Official Ice Hockey Guide* crowed: "Over 75% of the participants in the 1976 NCAA tournament were American-born players." In the next four decades, as more young Americans set their sights on professional careers, as more chose Canadian Major Junior over NCAA, the problem for American college hockey would be less about keeping Canadians out than keeping Americans home.[30]

Canada's Amateurs Regroup

There was agitation north of the border, too. By the late 1960s, elite Junior A leagues began to chafe at the structure imposed by the CAHA. Foremost among them were western teams who played in small, provincial leagues and were often handled by teams from Ontario and Quebec in national playoffs. For Bill Hunter, owner of the Junior A Edmonton Oil Kings (and later the WHA's Oilers), a bigger league would pool western resources and bolster the region's chances for the Memorial Cup. In 1966, Hunter convinced the Junior A Calgary Buffaloes and six junior teams from Saskatchewan to bolt and, with his Oil Kings, form a new circuit, the ambitiously named "Canadian Major Junior Hockey League" (renamed the Western Canada Hockey League in 1967). Hunter's circuit raised its age limit to twenty-one, which openly defied the NHL-CAHA agreement. The CAHA declared it "outlaw" and banned its teams from national playoffs.[31] But the league persevered and, eventually, rapprochement came about. The CAHA was either inspired by the WCHL's concept of a Canadian Junior A super league or scrambling to head off a total jailbreak. In 1970 the CAHA announced the creation of a new tier of junior hockey, "Major Junior A," a three-league partnership that included Ontario Hockey Association Tier I junior teams (reorganized as the Ontario Hockey League in 1974) and those from the Quebec Major Junior Hockey League, itself a new league cobbled in 1969 out of two junior circuits in that province. The leagues formalized their affiliation in 1974, becoming a national organization, loosely under CAHA control.[32] Major Junior grew steadily from thirty-one teams in 1972–73, to thirty-four in 1978–79, and to forty in 1983–84, where it remained into the 1988–89 season.[33] The majors left their regional CAHA branches in 1980 and formed a self-controlled enterprise, the Canadian Hockey League, to which the CAHA entrusted the Memorial Cup in 1985.

This new model for elite junior hockey in Canada was plainly commercial. The franchises were almost all privately owned enterprises run, as sportswriter Scott Young wrote in his history of the OHA, by "businessmen accustomed to regular business practices."[34] Each league appointed its own new commissioner to look out for its members' financial interests. Quickly, the leagues acted to ensure control of their most valuable resource: players. A draft of midget-age players was put in place in Ontario in 1969, and (until 1975) each team was allowed a "protected list" of midget-age prospects. In all leagues, teams made arrangements with area Tier II Junior A and B clubs to develop their prospects, just as big-league teams had done before expansion. Rostered players signed standard player agreements with their junior clubs, and each team developed scouting systems and protective eyes to ward off tampering. And the majors played long, pro-like schedules: seventy games for OHL teams in 1983–84; and seventy for teams in the "Q" and the "Dub" in 1987–88 (NHL teams played eighty). That busy schedule maximized ticket sales and generated advertising revenue in game programs and local promotions. The OHL inked a "game-of-the-week" TV deal with Global Television Network in 1982, which ran throughout that decade.[35] And though its commissioners persisted in calling their players amateurs, they made no bones about remuneration: players received modest monthly stipends, money they couldn't otherwise earn in part-time jobs. In a short span, the major juniors became the world's best incubator for NHL players, organized like an NHL writ small.[36]

Here, something was gained, but something was lost. Major-junior teams became commercial implants, their rosters filled largely with seventeen-to-twenty-year-old imports, guests who billeted with local families and enrolled for a short time in area schools and colleges. The junior, juvenile, and midget teams below them were filled with local kids who had played together through the ranks of local minor hockey in front of local followers. Major junior added spectacle to local hockey scenes, but its players never stayed long enough to become *our boys*; and *our boys*, the cream of the local hockey system, were scattered among major-junior teams in *other* cities.

Beyond the reorganization of junior hockey, the 1970s and 1980s witnessed a corporate readjustment of amateur hockey in Canada. The creation of an elite super league rationalized and compressed junior hockey. A self-sorting began to divide players: pro-driven ones pursued major junior; those who sought US scholarships were steered toward Tier II Junior A, where stipends weren't paid. Also, the withdrawal of major-junior teams from their provinces' amateur hockey associations had a noticeable financial effect, reducing both membership dues and playoff revenues. When the OHL left, the OHA had to reduce its operating budget by fully one quarter.[37] While Junior C ranks survived the pinch, Junior D teams and leagues collapsed across the country. As a result, less-competitive juvenile hockey ranks grew, and the CAHA responded by providing a national championship.[38]

Minor hockey in Canada in the 1970s and 1980s experienced a paradox. While growing in funding and following at the highest ranks, its grassroots began to wither. On one hand, the period hosted remarkable growth in infrastructure. Communities across Canada invested unprecedented sums in new, well-lit, and clean facilities; players had more ice available to them than ever before. One rink census reported "756 arenas built in the early 1970s."[39] But the building boom overestimated long-term public demand. In the 1970s, CAHA player registrations grew slowly but steadily (from 540,837 registrants in 1971–72[40] to 599,480 players in 1979–80[41]). And then they stopped: 1980 constituted a high-water mark, and registrations fluctuated annually between five hundred thousand and six hundred thousand for the remainder of the decade. There were more rinks but fewer players and, worryingly, a declining desire to play the national game.

What caused the loss of popular faith in this national symbol? Canadians held their own views, but four of them were common: unjustifiable violence, increasing costs (equipment, ice time, and registration fees), hypercompetitiveness, and overlong schedules. A 1979 government-backed report called "Canadian Hockey Review" stated that the sport was "in deep trouble."[42] To these causes, contemporaries might have added another factor: demography. In the two decades after Prime Minister Pierre Trudeau's *Multiculturalism Act* (1971), Canada welcomed an influx of "New Canadians" whose cultural backgrounds knew little of hockey and for whom a self-professed "tolerant" society encouraged them to celebrate their own, transplanted sporting traditions. Hockey's image as a *white* and *establishment* sport appealed little to newcomers.[43]

Francophone Revolutions

In Quebec a corporate rebranding of amateur hockey tapped into an explosive nationalist agenda. The Quiet Revolution had, since the era of the Richard Riot, plowed a way toward modernization and liberation for francophone Quebecers. This involved a new *statism*. Starting with the Jean Lesage government (1960–64), politicians began to replace Catholic Church–run social welfare and education institutions with secular, province-operated replacements, promote francophone entrepreneurship and state-directed (Crown) corporations, and encourage a collective desire to be *maîtres chez nous* (masters in our own house), a self-aware, French-speaking society intent on calling its own shots.[44]

Francophone hockey in Quebec had always been political, but the Quiet Revolution stimulated changes to the operation of amateur hockey in Quebec. In 1968, business and lay interests formed the Association de Hockey Mineur du Québec (AHMQ), which snatched control of grassroots programs from local parishes and called into question the authority of the Quebec Amateur Hockey Association, which AHMQ directors felt it had outgrown. Born in 1919 in the leafy Montreal neighborhood of Westmount, the QAHA had long been seen as a tool of Anglophone power, and so the AHMQ's emergence had nationalist resonance. In 1969, popular pressure forced the QAHA to make a name change to Association du Hockey Amateur du Québec (AHAQ). But French names did not dissolve bureaucratic tensions over turf. In 1976, in the same year that René Lévesque's separatist Parti Québécois came into office, the AHAQ and the AHMQ merged, becoming the Fédération québécoise de hockey sur glace (FQHG). In the early 1980s it changed its name to Hockey Québec, a unilingual francophone organization with the province's sanction and sizeable public funding. Hockey Québec was more than a functional bureaucracy, it was a national sports symbol of the new Quebec. If Québécois hockey talent once relied on the happenstance of eager youth, volunteer coaching by priests or parents, and whatever skate-able ice was available, new generations could now be developed rationally and systematically with province-wide standards, educated coaches, and funding.[45]

The aura of the Quiet Revolution gave Quebec hockey a push to test its mettle against other Canadian regions and teams from around the world. The best examples of this are the *Tournoi Internationale de Hockey Pee-Wee de Québec*, which since 1960 has invited eleven- and twelve-year-old players to the Old Capital during its winter *Carnaval*. By the early 1970s, teams from across Canada as well as the United States and Europe competed in several divisions, including, after 1976, an "International Cup."[46] In 1965 a similar annual tournament for fifteen- and sixteen-year-olds was started in Drummondville, which by the late 1970s featured teams from across Canada as well as from Michigan, Sweden, Czechoslovakia, and, in 1991, Russia.[47] For some, Quebec international hockey ambitions were even greater. In June 1976, Quebec City lawyer and founding member of the Parti Québécois, Guy Bertrand, pitched the idea of a Quebec national team for IIHF annual championship. To advocate for it, he created the *Comité Équipe-Québec*. No stranger to the sport (he was agent for several Québécois players in the 1970s), Bertrand was connected politically. In 1977 he presented a memorandum to Canada's Parliamentary Committee on International Hockey proposing the creation of a Team Quebec for elite international tournaments. Alas, the idea stumbled. Parliament demurred, influenced perhaps by the intransigence of CAHA (now called Hockey Canada), raw feelings in English Canada, and the daunting task of seeking IIHF approval. Few outside of Quebec could separate the hockey proposal from the goal of political independence in Quebec.[48] In 1981, Bertrand resurrected the *Comité*, recruited sports celebrities (including Canadiens star Guy Lafleur) to the cause, secured the support of the FQHG and the provincial government, and published a manifesto in *La Presse*, a popular Montreal daily. This second iteration also fizzled, but the idea hasn't died.[49] Whether or not it ever comes to fruition, the idea reflects how in Quebec corporate hockey leaned heavily on the state and on prevailing nationalist winds.

CIAU: A Refreshing Contrast

Cast in relief against all of this stood Canadian university hockey, a neglected gem since its pre–World War II heyday. When York University's Yeomen defeated Western Ontario to win the 1988 University Cup in front of only thirty-four hundred spectators in Toronto's Varsity Arena, local journalist Kellie Hudson wondered: "Where were all the hockey fans?" The problem rested with universities' unwillingness to promote their sports. What we need, Canadian Interuniversity Athletic Union president Gib Chapman noted, is a "professional approach" to college sports. "Let's look at how it's done south of the border."[50] But the article missed an important point. In an age when the culture of Canadian hockey was moved increasingly by corporate governance and money and was marked by the specter of stagnation among youth, university hockey remained a refreshing contrast. Canada's university teams drew little press attention and paltry attendance, but still they had a solid presence and a respectable pedigree. The game held its own on Canadian campuses (thirty-four teams in four conferences vied for the nation's University Cup in 1986–87, for example), and it hosted regional rivalries. It was good hockey, played largely by early-twenty-something ex-junior players who had been overlooked or rejected by the pros.

For a few, it was a stepping-stone to the big league. Perennial powerhouses Alberta and Toronto each sent nine graduates to the NHL, including the Golden Bears' Randy Gregg and the Varsity Blues' Dave Reid. Other NHLers who honed their skills there included Manitoba's Mike Ridley and Stu Grimson, Dalhousie's Paul MacLean, and Queen's University's Morris Mott. What's more, Canadian universities were sometimes cradles for professional coaches, some of whom reached the highest levels of achievement in the sport: Tom Watt and Mike Keenan started their careers at Toronto, Clare Drake at Alberta, Dave King at Saskatchewan, Jean Perron at Moncton, and George Kingston at Calgary. "The talent and skills are there and we play an exciting brand of hockey," UBC athletic director Rick Noonan told the Canadian Press in 1985. "Three years ago we beat Denver twice at home and the year before that we went into North Dakota and won twice at their homecoming weekend."[51] But in funding, financial aid, and public notice, Canadian universities were no comparison for their American counterparts; they were the Rodney Dangerfields of the hockey scene.

American Amateur Change-Ups

North American professional leagues had opened their minds on the talent feeder system; they were now beckoning more Americans straight from high schools and colleges, as well as through Canadian junior leagues. This encouraged a boom at the American grassroots levels—more rinks and players. Greater Boston was a case in point. The area had a dozen or so indoor, artificial ice rinks before the Bobby Orr era. But No. 4's Messiah-like arrival in 1966, his exquisite skill showcased on Channel 38 Bruins telecasts, and his nationally broadcast, Stanley Cup–winning goal on Mother's Day 1970 spurred a generation of kids who wanted to be him.

Investors rushed to join local and state agencies to build new ice surfaces. As a 1979 *Boston Globe* story put it, "From 1968 to 1975, amateur hockey never had it so good . . . 52 privately owned rinks and 44 state-operated rinks." High schools added programs to parallel growth in youth hockey. AHAUS youth registrations in Massachusetts jumped to 54,480 in 1970.[52] A bigger boom happened in Minnesota. New-rink construction, especially in the Twin Cities area, shifted the state's player production southward, but the game was booming everywhere. By 1976 there were one hundred indoor artificial-ice rinks supporting eighty thousand registered players. By 1982, 154 schools supported boy's hockey teams; state tournament attendance hit a peak in 1985 at 103,096.[53]

More rinks, with more hockey, for more players. It was an old song of promise. But some were worried. John Mariucci, Eveleth native and legendary Minnesota coach, complained in 1976 of too many players "waiting for one hour of indoor ice when they could use the natural ice God has given them for five or six. . . . The result is that they can't skate." Top-level coaches like Amo Bessone agreed: let them have more fun and more ice. Avoid too much organization—avoid corporate hockey. Mariucci believed in a system that channeled players through high school and college. At least then they had access to an education. "When I talk to groups in other states . . . I warn them . . . 'don't start up a junior program.'"[54]

But junior hockey was on the rise in America, and Herb Brooks was among the pioneers. In 1971–72 he coached the Minnesota Junior Stars, one of the many corporate alternatives to high-school hockey. Brooks's Stars were, his biographer wrote, "first sponsored by the Win Stephens Buick dealership and then later owned and operated by KSTP radio and television owner Stanley Hubbard." Junior teams sprouted in Rochester and Austin, Minnesota, and then into Nebraska, Iowa, and Wisconsin, the core of what became the United States Hockey League. It was a very Canadian model, but in America the financial challenge was greater, since high school programs were so entrenched. American juniors' fan base was very small—some teams played before crowds of fewer than fifty. Gradually, advocates like Brooks and Vairo gained a foothold, promoting junior hockey via testimonials from alums like Joe Mullen, who emerged from the New York–based Metropolitan league to become an All-American at Boston College before starring in the NHL. By the late 1980s the USHL was already becoming a grooming salon for NCAA Division I recruits, and its franchises were vibrant businesses with highly paid coaches and administrators.[55]

Corporate influence affected American hockey well beyond its juniors. In the 1970s and 1980s the national governing body—the Amateur Hockey Association of the United States—moved to a more corporate approach. In 1972, Thayer Tutt became AHAUS president, replacing longtime boss Tom Lockhart, who had run the organization "out of a shoe box" from its inception in 1937. The AHAUS office soon moved from New York City to Colorado Springs, close to Tutt's Broadmoor and the US Olympic Committee. One official history noted: "The organization needed to be operated more like a business." As president, Tutt expanded the organization and hired an executive director, first filled by an old hockey hand and well-known referee named Hal Trumble (1972–86). Trumble needed only himself and a secretary in 1972. By the end of his tenure, however, the staff had increased to fifteen full-timers; so had team registrations, from 7,015 in 1972 to 11,543 in 1985. In 1986, AHAUS changed its name to the more regal USA Hockey. When David Ogrean became executive director in 1993, USA Hockey had about two hundred thousand members. By 2010 that number had grown to 474,592, with 70,000 of them female. By 2011 the national offices held ninety employees.[56]

Throughout the 1970s, AHAUS's revenues came largely from team registrations and NHL subsidies calculated from the number of Americans drafted. To support a national framework, AHAUS refined its financial strategy. In 1979, Trumble checked off a list of revenue sources: "We get grants from the NHL. We sell merchandise. We have an insurance program. We earn interest on money we have in the bank. We get some help from the US Olympic Committee. We sell our mailing list. We sell advertising in our brochures, our guides and rulebooks, just about anything we can to raise money." That same year, AHAUS moved to control its brand by purchasing Fenton Kelsey's magazine *United States Hockey and Arena Biz*, which had a circulation of thirty-two thousand. The magazine's name followed the organization's name changes: first to *American Hockey Magazine*; then to *USA Hockey Magazine*. In 2012 it was mailed to more than 425,000 players, coaches, and officials in the United States.[57]

Herb Brooks and his 1980 miracle cohort of "college kids" represented an American system that was just starting to converge nationally across the old divides of youth, high school, college, amateur, and pro. Their Canadian counterparts had slightly different components, but they were on the same general path. The process was uneven and often contentious, and it spawned a paradox that grew in the decades ahead. In Canada and America, both the CAHA / Hockey Canada and AHAUS / USA Hockey increased messaging and programming that emphasized fun and fundamentals at the youngest level, only to be largely rejected by local parents and coaches who insisted on more games and more travel as the best path for their children's expected climb to the NHL. No one recognized this inversion of values more clearly than Bobby Orr. As he pulled himself back from the Eagleson fiasco, he committed time to become chief ambassador for the "First Goal" campaign, a fifteen-minute movie as well as clinics across North America, sponsored by Nabisco Brands, sanctioned by AHAUS and CAHA, with Orr preaching a simple gospel: "My parents bought my equipment, drove me to the rink and rubbed my feet when they were cold. I can't ever remember them saying that I was going to be a professional hockey player." Ever since, Orr has been committed to "de-professionalizing" youth hockey, even as he built a very successful agency for top-level talent. It was a tight arc. Few could skate it as cleanly as Bobby Orr.[58]

21 Global Visions of Open Ice: 1972–1988

Swedish blueliner Thommie Bergman excelled at the Sapporo Olympics in February 1972. The next month he signed with the Red Wings as a free agent. The NHL became even more real to Swedes in September when Team Canada, on its way to Moscow, played two "friendly" exhibitions in Stockholm. The buildup was immense, especially given the Soviets' dominating performances in Canada. Top tickets sold for eight times their face value, despite live television. The matches were gruesome. Canada won the opener 4–1 by playing their aggressive, hard-checking style. The Swedish media called them "Team Ugly." Game 2 ended in a draw—both on scoreboard and in blood. Sweden's Ulf Sterner slashed Canada's Wayne Cashman in the mouth. Vic Hadfield retaliated and broke Lars-Erik Sjöberg's nose. Canadian ambassador Margaret Meagher publicly lamented the violence. Canadians, including Harry Sinden and Ken Dryden, complained that the Swedes were "sneaky" dirty, playing to the referees' incompetence. But Canadian coaches and scouts, despite their public declarations, watched carefully the skill of Swedish players like Börje Salming, who recalled: "It was during these months that I started to wonder—or perhaps dream is the word—about the NHL." A year later, he signed with the Toronto Maple Leafs. For his part, Sterner (who had had a brief NHL tryout in 1965) announced that he hoped to get noticed by the WHA. And a younger generation of Swedish hockey executives like Ove Rainer moved the Swedish Ice Hockey Association toward a friendlier posture vis-à-vis the NHL.[1]

If American and Canadian hockey began to converge in the 1970s and 1980s, it is also fair to say that Europe turned more North American in its embrace of corporate models. Some of this was defensive strategy, to dissuade players from signing with the NHL or the WHA. There was even the specter of new European leagues run by North American owners. In 1971, for instance, Red Wings owner Bruce Norris and his team counsel John Ziegler announced plans for the European International Hockey League, which would feature top clubs that affiliated with NHL counterparts. The plan went nowhere, so Norris hatched the London Lions, who played seventy-two matches from October 1973 into March 1974, at Wembley and around the Continent. Norris got support from Bunny Ahearne, who registered the club as amateurs. A London meeting in July 1974 promised something more, when host Ahearne corralled representatives from Finland, Holland, Belgium, and Sweden to meet and discuss the league. The EIHL died aborning, but its publicity splash had ripples.[2]

European Regime Change

Bunny Ahearne's dalliance with Bruce Norris came at the end of the Irishman's influence. He had arrived on the international scene in 1936 as representative for the British Ice Hockey Association. After 1951 he was almost continually either the IIHF president or vice president. By 1975 his reign was over. A 1998 IIHF history says that members were increasingly agitated that Ahearne ran the federation "just like his travel office as the 'boss.'" When he pushed for a Dutch ally to succeed him, "the delegates elected his opponent Dr. [Gunther] Sabetzki," a German. Long a burr on Canada's blades, Ahearne was nonetheless inducted into the Hockey Hall of Fame in 1977—as Martin Harris wryly noted, "perhaps because he had finally retired." He was described as a "professional sports manager," part of a new breed like his friend Walter Brown. "Ahearne was very skilled in combining his official function with his business. He used his own travel agency, he had a share in the 'Association of Eastern Ice Arenas' and took an active role in the board advertising and TV rights." This was code for saying that Bunny openly pushed the boundaries of "gentlemanly" behavior, especially against the Olympic establishment, itself inherently corrupt and hypocritical. He saw and exploited revenue streams before others did. As one authoritative Olympic history found, in 1955 he pressed the IOC to adopt a television policy that "allocated equal shares of television revenue" to the IOC, the international sports federations (for example, IIHF), and the local organizing committees (such as Squaw Valley). This was well ahead of the rights fees explosion in the 1970s and 1980s. Avery Brundage and the IOC were slow to move. By 1963, Ahearne threatened the organizers of the 1964 Innsbruck games with a hockey boycott unless the IIHF got at least one-third of all television revenues. Brundage called the demand "blackmail." No wonder Brundage hated ice hockey. In many ways, Ahearne was at the vanguard of open recognition that amateur hockey, and amateur sport, was a business. He died on April 11, 1985.[3]

Ahearne's successor, Sabetzki, served as IIHF president from 1975 to 1994. He came into hockey via journalism—a throwback to the early days of journalist-administrators like Louis Magnus, Frank Calder, and Bill Hewitt. But Sabetzki was progressive in his negotiations with the IOC, the NHL, and Canada about the use of professionals. He was in position at the right time. The 1970s were years of rapprochement between the International Olympic Committee and many of the international sports federations, including the IIHF. For one thing, sour and dour Avery Brundage retired in 1972, giving way to a genial and more malleable Lord Killanin, a.k.a. Michael Morris, a man of privilege who came of age in 1930s journalism, writing on gossip and politics for London's *Daily Mail*. He was no bulldog for amateurism, and as one Olympic historian put it, "one of the new president's ambitions was to adjust the amateur rule to the realities of sports in the late 20th century." And so, while the IOC Charter of 1978 technically still outlawed professionalism, by the decade's end it also allowed athletes to garner endorsement money so long as it was kept in trust by their national Olympic committees, which could then pay their living expenses. The IOC also finally authorized "broken-time" payments for loss of "regular" wages while training or competing. The IIHF and other federations had been moving further for some time. England's Football Association deleted the word "amateur" from its rules in 1975. Ahearne's IIHF allowed professionals to play in the Summit Series. Sabetzki allowed them at the 1977 World Championships. It was all in the fine print about "exhibitions" versus "championships" and "reinstatements" of amateur status. It was all done with a wink and a nod. In 1980, Killanin was followed by Juan Antonio Samaranch, who intended to maximize IOC revenues, which meant totally opening the Games to the world's best professional athletes. The IOC soon allowed each international federation to determine how far to open its doors.[4]

Sabetzki was at home in this environment. And so he pushed, by one account leading the agreements to allow professionals at IIHF World Championships, which occurred later in the calendar year to allow "suitable player selection from among the NHL teams eliminated from the Stanley Cup." America and Canada also "relinquished their application to host any world championship tournaments" in return for which the IIHF sanctioned the Canada Cup, a tournament played five times in North America between 1976 and 1991 featuring teams from Canada, the United States, and the top four European national teams from the preceding World Championships. Every entry could use professionals. Beyond this, the officiating system was NHL-style, with one referee and two linesmen, as opposed to two referees. The Canada Cup was the Summit Series on steroids, especially for Canadian fans whose team won four out of five, thereby in their minds returning the hockey world to its natural order. The tournaments also required ongoing cooperation between the IIHF, the NHL, and the NHL Players' Association. By 1988 the Calgary Olympic hockey games were completely open to professionals. The problem was how to synch the NHL schedule with the Olympics. The orbit was swirling more tightly.[5]

Swedes and Finns Go Pro

Börje Salming's career represents the shifts in Swedish and European hockey as global flows moved them closer to North American models. He grew up in the northern mining town of Kiruna. Börje and his brother Stig played for Kiruna AIK, the workers' club, whose rival was IFK, the club for engineers and civil servants. A prodigy, Börje often practiced with the "A" team, even while on the junior roster. Much as in Sudbury, Ontario, and Eveleth, Minnesota, hockey seemed a ticket out of the mines. Salming's ticket arrived in 1970, when he was purchased for 25,000 kronor (about $3,500) by Brynäs, a top-level club in Gävle. His personal deal was for about $145 per month, at least formally. He later admitted that "players received money under the table, free cars, and other secret benefits." By 1973, to counter NHL and WHA offers, the Swedish federation announced an increased tournament allowance for national team players, from "5,000 to 11,000 crowns." At that year's World Championship, Maple Leafs representatives approached Salming about a two-year deal, with annual salaries of $50,000 and $60,000—"staggering sums" for a young Swede. When he asked national team coach Kjell Svensson for advice, Svensson said: "You should go if you get the chance. It might not come again."[6]

As one Swedish authority argued, Salming was attractive to Toronto because he played a style that was more than the stereotyped Swedish "sossehockey" (an abbreviation for "social democratic ice hockey"), which was typified by "a disciplined and adaptable two-way-player, with great skating and puck-handling skills, who preferred to blend into the group, rather than 'flying solo' and/or being in the center of attention." He played rougher and tougher than the normal Swede. The assistant coach of Tre Kronor, a Canadian, said, "Salming is more Canadian than the Canadians themselves." Early on in Canada, however, as he played for the Leafs, Börje often heard taunts of "Chicken Swede." He quickly proved them wrong and was soon embraced in Toronto and elsewhere for his total, almost reckless commitment to shot blocking as well as his passing, shooting, and willingness to drop his gloves. Salming played for Sweden in the Canada Cup of September 1976, and Swedes watching back home took notice when he earned standing ovations during introductions at Maple Leaf Gardens. As a Swedish journalist later put it, Salming may have been embarrassed at the applause, but Sweden "got a confirmation of what we had long known: [Börje] was the king of Toronto!"[7]

The growing success of Swedes like Salming, Thommie Bergman, Anders Hedberg, and others led the California Golden Seals to pick Björn Johansson fifth overall in the 1976 draft. He did not pan out, but others did, including Anders Kallur and Stefan Persson, who had their names Stanley-Cupped with the 1980 New York Islanders. Some Swedes were elated at this success. Others were troubled. The NHL and WHA success stories had mixed play back home, as the Tre Kronor national teams kept losing talent to professional contracts, leading to a term "proffsflykt" ("escape to professionalism") and a push by the SIHA to upgrade support via "landslagspengar" ("National Team-money") grants to elite clubs to pay their best players. In October 1975 they opened a new "Eliteserien" or elite league for these top clubs and players. Loosely called the Swedish Hockey League (SHL), the official, very corporate name was "Eliteserien om Volvo Cup." Two Swedish scholars emphasized that "this was, and still is, an aberrant step in the history of Swedish sport. Up to then, no sports league had sold or even been interested in selling its name or 'brand' to any commercial business interests." Brynas IF won the first three league titles. "In Sweden," wrote Tobias Stark, "the infected professionalization debate came to a first close in 1976" when the SIHA withheld Tre Kronor from the Innsbruck Olympics "on the grounds that the players in the Swedish Eliteserien were not true amateurs." Most people, however, felt "the real reason" was a cold calculation by the SIHA and its clubs: "It was too costly to have two international tournaments (the Olympic Games and the World Championships) impinging the domestic schedule the same season, as that might hurt their gate receipts." A decade later, the NHL began facing the same decision. In 1990, Börje Salming returned to Sweden and stepped on the ice for AIK. The Swedish Elite League welcomed him home.[8]

In 1975, Finnish hockey moguls opened a new Elite League, called SM-liiga (or "Finnish Championship League"). It was a logical move, like that of the Swedes, to keep the country's best players away from the NHL and WHA by paying them openly. The top clubs essentially stepped away from the Finnish Ice Hockey Association, the vast majority of whose members adhered to the principles (if not the practices) of amateurism. They faced new problems, however, when the WHA started signing Finns in the mid-1970s. This included established stars like Veli-Pekka Ketola and young phenoms like Matti Hagman. It forced the sport and tax authorities to accept and regulate professional hockey. The Elite League, with open professionalism, was the answer. The league also differed in its acceptance of in-season player trades, a longer season, and playoffs. In short, the Elite League moved toward the North American model.[9]

Finland still lacked an adequate supply of indoor, artificial-ice arenas necessary both to develop talent and to attract paying spectators and sponsors. The central planners of this Nordic welfare state saw limited return on such massive capital investments. In 1981 the FIHA finally launched its own push to build one hundred new indoor arenas; the country had about two hundred by 2000. Along the way, by one expert account, resident hockey clubs continued a commercial development that began in the 1960s when corporate sponsors' names were "sewn into club jerseys," a practice begun on the football pitch. The next stage involved banner ads on the boards. Into the 1970s, corporate sponsors began to demand more "concrete value" for their support—what today's marketers would call return on investments (ROI). This included "the use of star players in advertisement" and in public appearances. It also included the production and distribution of collectible player cards, which naturally included corporate logo images. Despite old-school critics who "denounced marketing" in its use of sponsor images on jerseys and boards, Finland (like much of Europe) went corporate before North America did.[10]

USSR—Hockey Bread and Circus

In the 1970s and 1980s, the Soviet Union had no place for Western-style corporations or marketing—at least not officially. All players in the Major League of the USSR Hockey Championship were amateur—at least officially. At the time, the Major League housed the ten top teams, most of which were fixtures, like Moscow's Central Army (TsSKA), Spartak, Wings, and Dinamo. There were two tiers below the top, and after each year's thirty-six-game schedule, the bottom and top teams of each tier switched places—a process called relegation/elevation, used widely in Europe, especially in football. Moscow's big teams played home games in the fourteen-thousand-seat Palace of Sports arena, which *Sports Illustrated*'s Mark Mulvoy described in 1976 as "a cold, drab building with sight lines little better than Madison Square Garden's." Unlike the Garden's $12 reserved bench seats, however, a Soviet fan paid only about $1.50, with end-zone seats considerably less. Unlike North American rinks, there were "no air horns, organ grinders, banners and, best of all, no vendors bawling and blocking the aisles." And much like football stadiums and hockey arenas across Europe, fans entertained themselves with their own songs and chants: "Mol-od-tsy, mol-od-tsy, mol-od-tsy—Good boys, good boys, good boys" or "Sudya Na Mylo"—"Referee to the Soap Factory," or the universal prod to players "Shaibu, Shaibu—puck, puck." Those willing to wait in line could buy a 75-cent meal that included "a sosisky (a kind of hot dog) or a sausage sandwich, an ice-cream bar about twice the size of an Eskimo Pie and either tea or coffee."[11]

If fans sang and chanted their way through a distinctly European game experience, the players were beginning to go Western. "Except for the goaltenders," Mulvoy noted, "Soviet players generally use only one piece of Russian-made equipment: their dentures." Goaltenders wore "bulky Russian-made chest protectors," but all else was imported. Skaters wore Jofa helmets "because the hockey federation recently worked out a 'good deal' with the Swedish manufacturer." The favorite skates were Super Tacks. A Central Army player insisted that "one of the best things" about playing in North America "is that we'll all come back with a couple of pairs of new skates, dozens of new hockey sticks, new sweat suits, new shoes and a lot of other equipment—all compliments of the manufacturers." These were the entitlements of a real pro, despite the party line about state amateurism. Spartak player Alexander "Sasha" Yakushev acknowledged a monthly salary of roughly $400 per month (300 rubles), "about twice the salary of the average Soviet worker," with extra benefits like a discount on new Volga autos and free family vacations on the Black Sea. But when told he could earn the equivalent of 200,000 rubles in the WHA, Yakushev answered like a good socialist: "I've thought about it. The money, I mean, not leaving my country. I read about all those salaries, but I don't understand them. Why does someone need all that much money, anyway?" Attitudes changed dramatically in the next decade.[12]

The Soviets dominated international competition throughout the 1970s and 1980s. Despite losing some championships like the 1980 Olympics or exhibitions like the 1972 Summit or the Canada Cup in 1976, 1984, and 1987, the Soviets, not the Canadians, were still the team to beat. And by the mid-1980s, comrades across all eleven time zones watched state television, including fifty to sixty hockey games per year. Of course, there were some limits to what they saw. For instance, as one authority explained, during the 1984 Canada Cup, Peter Stastny (a Czech defector) played for his new country, Canada. Soviet viewers never heard his name mentioned: "Although the international feed showed Stastny several times during the game against the Soviet team and although his name was spelled out on the back of his jersey, Soviet announcers were forbidden to mention his name, even when he scored or assisted."[13]

There were well-documented troubles in the Soviet league, a consequence of authoritarian approaches to the national team. Across a nation with long winters, hockey talent was funneled to the four Moscow-based clubs and especially to TsSKA. In the Tarasov years, 1948–60 and 1962–75, Central Army won eighteen USSR championships. The Soviet Ice Hockey Federation accepted this imbalance because it facilitated national team training and travel at short notice.[14] By 1977 a new boss named Victor Tikhonov held the reins of both the Central Army and national teams. Tikhonov (b. 1930) grew up during the war playing soccer and bandy, like many Soviet boys. He first played the Canadian game with the VVS team. He was as successful, and as demanding, as Tarasov. But if Tarasov was full, fat, feisty, and funny, Tikhonov was cold, flinty, and stiff. He did not care about popularity. Years later, when asked on a Swedish documentary about battles with his players, he responded: "If you get results, then you're right. If not, it doesn't matter if you are generous, beautiful or kind—or how many people like you." Despite the loss in 1980, the Soviet national team still got impressive results in the 1980s. But it all imploded in 1989.[15]

Soviet sports media grumbled about the league's imbalance. In 1982–83, TsSKA won its seventh-straight crown, sweeping forty of forty-four games. The club controlled twelve of twenty-two players on the 1984 Olympic team and fourteen of twenty-three on the 1988 team. The result was a noticeable reduction in fan interest. In one account, the Central Army team had "rinkside support of only a few strategically seated battalions, who utter not a sound unless authorized by their commanding officer." The focus on the national team had another bad result: a neglect of grassroots development. By 1988 one report claimed that Canada had ten thousand indoor skating rinks, in contrast to the Soviet Union's 102.[16]

Glasnost and Perestroika

A published report on Soviet inferiority would have been unthinkable in 1978. But things changed—perhaps too quickly—with the 1985 rise of fifty-four-year-old Mikhail Gorbachev. He inherited a mess: Afghanistan, falling oil prices, steadily rising foreign debt, a shrinking domestic economy; in short, a fundamentally failing system. His general approach to reform included the difficult-to-translate notions of *glasnost* (openness) and *perestroika* (restructuring). They were complementary since, as one historian wrote, "in order to break the stranglehold of the Party *apparat* and drive forward his plans for economic restructuring," Gorbachev needed "official encouragement for public discussion of a carefully restricted range of topics." Among his moves were orders for the police to "cease jamming foreign radio broadcasts" and a general relaxation of censorship. Gorbachev was appealing to the public and pushing the party at a time when 90 percent of Soviet households had television. Dissidents like Andrei Sakharov, freed from house arrest in December 1986, now appeared on national broadcasts demanding more freedom and change. It was a heady time, now almost forgotten in the West. Soon it affected many areas of Soviet life, hurling the people into unknown territory. And this included hockey.[17]

A noted Western analyst wrote in 1990 that critics were harping about "the dark side" of elite sports, including "match fixing . . . bribery of referees, drug taking and other nefarious activities hitherto only mentioned in the context of capitalist sport." Top athletes began to agitate for honesty about professionalism so that "athletes no longer have to compromise themselves." Openness was easier than restructuring a society and economy where a central party controlled almost everything: production, consumption, incomes, expenditures. But there *was* innovation. Plans were announced for a Formula One track and a golf course—both long prohibited as decadent bourgeois practices. The NFL and the central sports committee cut a deal for a September 1989 Redskins-Cowboys game, for the "Glasnost Cup." Funding was the biggest issue for Russian sport managers. Where the old state system provided significant support to established clubs, the new age meant self-sufficiency. Hockey clubs had always counted on gate receipts, but they were dwindling, especially with TsSKA breezing to championship after championship. Before the decade's end, Spartak and Dinamo were wearing corporate logos on their uniforms.[18]

The players, especially those on the national team, found their own forms of openness and restructuring. The NHL and the WHA coveted Soviet talent after 1972 and began drafting Soviet players with the hope that some might defect or be allowed to leave. Ken Dryden had been a close observer of Soviet hockey for two decades. In 1989 he published a book that updated his musings on all things hockey. He recognized that openness was appearing in the Western lifestyle of the Soviet's best players: "Fetisov drives around Moscow in his blue Mercedes wearing an ABC-TV Calgary Olympics ski jacket. At Archangelskoye, Krutov and Larionov lounge around reading newspapers, Krutov in a sweatshirt that reads 'The 40th NHL All-Star Game Edmonton, Alberta,' Larionov in one from the Quebec City's Rendez-vous '87. . . . Five years ago their look would have seemed disloyal, but no more. They are contemporary Soviets. They see no boundaries on their horizons. They look outside, not in." Soon all three were living and playing outside.[19]

Czechs Unchecked

By 1988, Czechoslovakia was further along the road to openness in hockey. It had been a rough journey. After 1968's Prague Spring and August's Soviet invasion, the Communist Party doubled down on its control of speech and behavior, especially in response to protests at home and nearby (Poland) about free speech and civil society. Intellectuals, academics, and playwrights all felt the sting of purges. Central planning spawned overproduction of steel and heavy industrial products. But it also built some extraordinary hockey players on national teams that, beginning in 1969 and continuing through the 1970s and 1980s, moved into a consistent place among the world's top three. This run included gold medals at the IIHF championships in 1972, 1976, 1977, and 1985, with upset victories over the Soviets in 1969, 1972, 1977, and 1985. Two such wins in 1969 prompted a crowd to swarm Prague's Wenceslas Square with chants and songs and one banner that read BREZHNEV 3, DUBČEK 4. In Bratislava, mobs surrounded and taunted Soviet troops in their barracks. One television announcer drank a special toast, saying, "This is not only a victory in sports but also a moral one." For this, she lost her job.[20]

As in numerous European countries, hockey was Czechoslovakia's number-two sport, following football. The early 1970s saw a slump in attendance, which one report attributed in part to "a qualitative shift in spectator expectations" and linked to the "screening on television of the best ice hockey matches from the Soviet Union and Canada." Still, by late 1980s there were 891 clubs with more than fifty-five thousand active players. The club teams played in one of three tiers: a top "national division" of twelve teams, and two lower divisions in separate Czech and Slovak leagues, with additional subdivisions in each region. The top hockey teams were facets of old-school multisport clubs. Sparta Praha, for instance, had ten thousand members across a range of sports, including soccer, hockey, rugby, basketball, and softball. Slovakia's Slovan Bratislava had more than six thousand members across fifteen sports. Playing or rooting offered some measure of relief from the regime's repression. With increased media images of life in the West, however, there were also increased yearnings for freedom. The Czech government had allowed Jaroslav Jirik, at career's end, to sign with the St. Louis Blues in 1969. After one year he returned home. In 1974 star player Vaclav Nedomansky did something different. He defected, following the script from 1948 with Josef Malaček and others that led to the hockey purge of 1950.[21]

"Big Ned" Nedomansky was thirty years old. At 6'2" and 205 pounds, he *was* a big man for that era. A strong skater and shooter, he starred for a decade on both Slovan Bratislava and the Czech national team. He scored 78 goals and added 32 assists in ninety-three Olympic-World-European Championship appearances—an amateur career capped by his "best forward" performance at the 1974 World Championships, leaving Western scouts thirsting for his offensive skills. The WHA's Toronto Toros and the NHL's Atlanta Flames had negotiating rights, but the Czech authorities were not in a negotiating mood. Nedomansky then secured a travel visa, ostensibly to visit Switzerland with his wife and son. Once there, he contacted the Flames and Toros, who each sent negotiators. The Toros prevailed to the tune of a five-year, $750,000 deal. *Sports Illustrated*'s Mark Mulvoy called Nedomansky "the most famous Communist-bloc athlete to defect to the West since 1956." Nedomansky later insisted that his defection was not political. He simply wanted, he said, to "continue my career on the highest possible level and lead life according to my ideas." The Czechs and the IIHF were not happy with these ideas, which did not include compensation for transfer. Bunny Ahearne threatened to withhold approval of the scheduled summit between the Soviet national team and the WHA's All-Stars. The bluster did not stop the series. And Big Ned had an excellent nine-year run (for a player in his thirties) with the Toros, Birmingham Bulls, Red Wings, Blues, and Rangers. Off the ice, however, he suffered the same fate as Bobby Orr, signing on with Alan Eagleson, whom he later sued.[22]

A year after Nedomansky defected, Peter Stastny played his first games for Slovan Bratislava along with his older brother Marian. They were soon joined by their younger brother, Anton. Nedomansky was their inspiration in many ways. By 1980 Peter and Anton were fed up with their Bratislava team and were looking west. The Quebec Nordiques, newly merged into the NHL, were looking east for talent. President Marcel Aubut hired Gilles Leger as director of personnel development and charged him with securing the Stastnys. *Sports Illustrated*'s E. M. Swift described Leger as a "suspicious looking character" whose "thick lips" always held a cigar, and who wore tinted glasses and a trench coat. In August 1980 the brothers were in Austria with the Czech national team. They called Aubut, who flew immediately with Leger and enlisted the help of someone called only "007." Soon came clandestine meetings, high-speed driving, James Bond–like encounters with Czech intelligence, and expedited Canadian Embassy work. The atmosphere was frantic, but by August 25, Peter, his wife, Darina, and Anton were in Canada. Brother Marian went home and was banned from his club and national teams, punished when he refused to denounce his brothers. The Stastny parents also suffered. Peter and Anton were castigated as "sell outs" and became nonpersons in the Czech hockey annals. A year later Marian defected with his family. Others followed.[23]

While the Stastnys and Nedomansky claimed their defections were not politically driven, their exploits were well covered by Western political interests. As a chronicler of Czech hockey defections wrote: "It was important that Nedomansky set a strong precedent for the countless countrymen secretly following his exploits back home on Radio Free Europe." And "thanks mostly to secret rallies around the radio to listen to Radio Free

Europe, tales of the Stastnys' NHL exploits began coming into Czechoslovakia. Before long, their countless accomplishments in Quebec motivated other Czechoslovakian players."[24]

Through the 1980s the Czech communist regime was slow to restructure most of the economy. Perhaps because of defections, they made hockey an exception. Attendance at "national league" games steadily rose from an average of 4,875 in the late 1970s to 5,490 during the 1987–88 season. One study attributed the attendance rebound to a new league playoff system "copied explicitly from the successful Canadian format." In 1988–89, Czech authorities formally recognized the national division as openly professional. Teams were finally allowed to *sell* their players to Western owners, but not before the players had turned twenty-eight years old. League teams shed their old communist sponsors (factories, government ministries, or trade unions) and cut deals with Western firms. As in Sweden and Finland, it was cash in return for "advertising both on the club shirts and on the boards around the ice rink." Slovan Bratislava embraced Metal Frankfurt and had a side equipment deal with adidas. Zetor Brno joined with Fiat. And, most notably, Sparta Praha—whose worker-related club name was spared trauma under Communism—now skated in stride with that most decadent symbol of capitalism: Levi Strauss. The collapse of state subsidies required new economics.[25]

Flows of Convergence

Amid the contentious Thatcher era, Britain's economic rebound in the late 1980s contained a hockey boom, with dozens of new rinks and an expansion of organized leagues, from youth levels through the senior Premier division. In the era of corporate hockey, this top tier was aptly called the Heineken League, launched in 1982 with the announcement of a television deal between the BIHA, Thames TV, and ITV. As late as 1988, the league restricted each team to only three foreign "imports." The home-grown strategy was rewarded with Edmonton's 1986 drafting of Tony Hand, whom Phil Drackett toasted as "the first British Heineken League player to be drafted by an NHL professional club." Hand represented the central dream in a hockey world of converging interests.[26]

Over the years, of course, many have been drafted but few have played. Still, it is always the tales and statistics of success that feed the dreams. Newspapers, magazines, television, and radio filled the air with stories about Hand, Salming, Nedomansky, the Stastnys, and others. Simple numbers were also alluring. By the 1986–87 season, NHL rosters included forty-five Europeans: twenty-five Swedes, eleven Finns, eight Czechs, and one West German. Others skated in the minor leagues. And North Americans crossed the Atlantic in the other direction, as Canadians had been doing for decades. In 1976, for instance, Joe Bertagna was at the start of a long, successful career as a "hockey guy." A stellar goaltender at Arlington High School ('69) and Harvard ('73), he was earning a master's degree in journalism when he wrote a lively piece for *Hockey* magazine about the "many former collegians" who were "packing their skates, gloves, and Berlitz dictionaries and heading for Europe." Bertagna left a teaching job to play for SG Cortina in the Italian League. Austria, Germany, and Spain were favorite places for others. The money wasn't great, although the "expense" policies on some clubs "put a strain on the word 'amateur.'" An additional word of advice: those who sought a continental hockey tour needed to "establish the appropriate contacts" and mine their network of coaches and players with international experience.[27]

Joe Bertagna leveraged a personal network. By 1980 there were corporate entities offering these services. That year's *International Ice Hockey Guide* included an ad for the CAN/AM Hockey Group of Guelph, Ontario, which represented "a select number of professional North American players who are interested in a European hockey career starting in the 1981–82 season." CAN/AM boasted a stable that was "carefully screened from 100s of talented players," all with "high technical skills to fit the European style of play" plus "strong leadership characteristics both on and off the ice." CAN/AM would find the right players, conduct negotiations, write the contract, and "arrange all releases and travel." It emphasized to the European teams: "You do not have to spend a fortune for a top pro player."[28]

By the 1980s, players and products flowed in all directions. The 1987–88 *IIHF Yearbook* reported a federation membership of thirty-seven but a global reach of "fifty nations" stretching across all continents—a perimeter circling from Alaska to Argentina to Australia up through Japan and China to Russia through Scandinavia and the Baltics and back across the Atlantic. Within that circle were leagues of all sizes and types. And fan groups: West Germany alone listed fifty-four fan clubs. In a new market like Israel, the attraction might simply be shinny. That country's first rink opened in January 1986 in a suburb of Haifa. Soon a Canadian national was giving hockey skills instruction. Transplants from the Soviet Union, Canada, the

United States, "and other traditional hockey countries" began their own shinny sessions. In May 1988 a "new and larger" rink opened near Tel Aviv. That same year saw the birth of the Israel Ice Hockey and Figure Skating Association.[29]

Ads and stories in European yearbooks and North American magazines pushed a vision that de-emphasized national systems of play and highlighted something more vertical and universal: a ladder of development that rested on expertise dispensed by international corporations and individuals who hoped to build their own corporations. At the top of the ladder was the NHL. A good example of this vision was the *International Hockey Guide*, which began shortly after Gunther Sabetzki took the IIHF reins from Bunny Ahearne. In 1979, Sabetzki wrote inside the cover that it was "the official yearbook of the International Ice Hockey Federation." The guide clearly represented a notion of global, corporate hockey. In fact, within a year the guide became a joint venture between the Finnish Ice Hockey League, *The Hockey News* (long an NHL mouthpiece), and Sports Representatives Ltd., a marketing, licensing, and publishing firm headed by Bob Haggert, an old Maple Leaf trainer and staffer. The NHL's CEO John Ziegler wrote a "Message from the President." It was short and glib. He congratulated the publishers and editors for their pleasing job of making comprehensible for fans like him the "varieties of League systems, languages and statistic compilations" in a time when "interest in international hockey" was "ever increasing." But while the guide included twenty-five pages on the Olympics and World Championship All-Star teams, there were more than forty pages of NHL stories and statistics. Ads for the new Louisville stick, used "12 hours a day for 2 full months" at the CAN/AM Hockey School in Guelph, Ontario, were matched with ads for the plastic, ski-boot-like Daoust "Futura" skates promising that the "horse and buggy days are over." Together, a coterie of manufacturers, agencies, rink construction firms, and publishers made the guide an arcade of international products and services that continued through the 1980s.[30]

Female Pressure and Male Pragmatism

The story of girls' and women's hockey after 1972 emphasizes two themes: pressure from the grassroots (especially from players and their parents) and pragmatism from established governing bodies. Female players and their allies in Canada, America, and Europe pressed for more opportunities under differing national circumstances. Within two decades, however, they converged on a global vision of IIHF World and Olympic championships.

Canada continued its late 1960s growth pattern, mercurial and patchy, here and there. The West was a good example. "Every small town had a team of girls in the 1970s," recalled Lila Quinton of the Saskatchewan AHA. Senior competition was the engine of credibility. University hockey returned, in some places, after almost thirty years of dormancy. Teams were iced in Alberta, Manitoba, British Columbia, and Saskatchewan, where a tournament called the Labatt Cup began in 1979 and three years later became the Western Canada Cup, the regional women's championship. Outside of universities, women established senior hockey clubs, such as those in the five-team, thirty-game Winnipeg Women's Hockey League. The Melfort (Saskatchewan) Missilettes, the Alberta Wild Roses, and the Edmonton Chimos also traveled around rural Alberta, playing men's teams.[31]

Female players in Quebec, "perhaps inspired by the new Nordiques club," were particularly active. By 1974, Quebec City clubs played others near Ottawa, Montreal, and Rimouski. At Lévis, a tournament began in 1978. College hockey reemerged in Quebec among the newly created CEGEPs (akin to America's junior colleges) and at the province's established universities, such as Montreal's Concordia, which hosted an annual tournament starting in 1968. In Quebec, elite senior hockey included sponsored teams such as Montreal's Le Titan (backed by the stick maker) and Quebec City's Belvédère (supported by the cigarette maker Rothman's) and an annual Festival de hockey Molson—a "world's championship" pitting those intraprovincial rivals against teams from Ontario and Massachusetts.[32]

But it was in Ontario where the women's game made its greatest grassroots gains. It was rooted in local teams (the province boasted some three hundred girls' teams by 1983), regional leagues (like eastern Ontario's competitive Picton League), and occasional tournaments, like the annual affairs in Brampton, Picton, Kingston, Oshawa, Downsview, London, and Brantford. The most prestigious was the Dominion Ladies' Hockey invitational tournament, which started in 1968 and featured two hundred teams by 1996. A formal Canadian National Championship began in 1982, complete with a sponsor (Shopper's Drug Mart) and a trophy: the Abby Hoffman Cup.[33]

In most CAHA jurisdictions, female hockey operated under the existing structure for boys and men—considered yet another constituent, a single voice among many. This seemed acceptable in regions with low numbers of registered female players and teams. Not so in Ontario, which had both the greatest numbers and the legacy of the interwar Ladies' Ontario Hockey Association, led *by* women *for* women. Prompted by an inquiry from a provincial government consultant and the prospect of government funding, the Ontario Women's Hockey Association was founded in 1975 at that year's Dominion Ladies' Tournament, held in Brampton. Its founders believed that female players had fundamentally different interests. They needed to publicize the virtues of their game and push for better ice times, sometimes in opposition to boys' hockey and girls' ringette. From 1975 until 1980 the OWHA established its own governance structure, recruiting mechanism, finances, and public relations campaigns. Only in 1980, after establishing its base, its personality, and protections for its constituents, did it affiliate with the OHA. Questions about representation and "voice" continued. Even though the CAHA had formed a "women's council" by 1981, it refused for years to consider allocating a national board position for female hockey. CAHA chairman Clair Sudsbury stated: "Female hockey doesn't have the numbers. . . . The women must learn to walk before they run."[34]

The feminist movement raised critical questions that even a conservative sport like hockey could not escape. Did gender equality mean separate but equal opportunities for girls and boys? Did true equality mean integration—boys and girls playing together? These questions were handled unevenly and clumsily, in ad hoc ways across the country. In Manitoba, MAHA president Don Mackenzie called it a "problem" that four eleven-to-fifteen-year-old girls had registered to play on Winnipeg boys' teams: "I am still hung up on integrated hockey," he said in 1981. But it was in Quebec and Ontario, where a good many more women and girls played the game, that the question became especially acute.[35]

In 1976 thirteen-year-old goaltender Françoise Turbide played for an almost all-male team in Notre-Dame-de-Grâce, a Montreal neighborhood. Her presence and play became an issue several months later when the Fédération québécoise de hockey sur glace (FQHG) expelled her from playing with boys, concerned that her health and safety were at risk. When Françoise's father raised the case in front of Quebec's Human Rights Commission, that body declared the FQHG's decision discriminatory. In 1978, Quebec's Superior Court ratified the commission's judgment and ordered that girls be allowed to play on boys' teams if separate and equal facilities for girls didn't exist. Françoise didn't return to the ice, but the precedent was critical.[36]

Similar issues bubbled up in Ontario and reached a boil in 1981. Twelve-year-old Justine Blainey earned a spot on a boys' team in the competitive

Metro Toronto Hockey League, but the Ontario Hockey Association blocked her skating lane. Blainey's case was more than a matter of merely wanting to play somewhere; she aimed to play *boys'* hockey specifically, which featured slapshots and bodychecking, both of which were outlawed by the OWHA. Blainey took the MTHL and the OHA to court—first in a complaint to the Ontario Human Rights Commission, which was rejected, prompting her to appeal the law (the Ontario Human Rights Code) in the Ontario Supreme Court, where her case also was unsuccessful. She persevered and took the case to the Ontario Court of Appeal, where she won in 1986. That court ruled that the OHA's "no girls on boys' teams" rules contravened the Canadian Charter of Rights and Freedoms. In the time elapsed during these proceedings, she went ahead and played in the MTHL, sometimes registered as "Justin" Blainey. The press covered every stage closely.[37]

Blainey v. Ontario Hockey Association (1986) split the hockey community, especially feminists. Arguing in favor of Blainey was the newly founded (1981) Canadian Association for the Advancement of Women in Sports, which looked upon the case purely as a Human Rights matter.[38] Arguing *against* Blainey was a motley collection of vocal traditionalists,[39] old-time hockey stalwarts, *and* the clear-eyed OWHA, which saw potential damage to the female hockey brand should Blainey win. What would prevent the very best female players from jumping ship to join up with competitive boys' teams, which would beggar many fledgling girls' teams who needed their best players to compete and serve as role models? Which road to equality? That question did not disappear. Still, on balance, the 1970s and 1980s gave women a new confidence in, ownership of, and aspiration for *their* game. In 1987 the OWHA successfully staged a first-ever, seven-team "world" tournament in North York. For established hockey authorities, for the press, and for girls and women who played and watched, the tournament was an inspiration, a benchmark, and a catalyst.

In America, collegiate women led the pressure for more athletic opportunities, which were becoming a touchstone for gauging the progress of promises embedded in Title IX. It was a long, hard campaign. A March 1974 *Time* magazine story offered examples of both progress and problems. For instance, Laurel Brassey at San Diego State had earned a spot on the men's volleyball team. On the other hand, the two-year-old women's ice hockey team at Colby College was "allotted two practice periods per day—at 6:15am and 11:30pm" and "unlike the men, women pay for their own uniforms, hockey sticks and gloves." The struggle was similar at other pioneer programs, often located at established men's powers like Brown, Cornell, Harvard, Providence, and Dartmouth, some of which had only recently gone co-ed.[40]

The University of New Hampshire offers a case study in the themes of pressure and pragmatism. In October 1974 a small group of students requested help from the campus recreation office in their goal of forming a women's ice hockey team, either intramural or club (that is, nonvarsity but playing against other university teams). At the time, UNH was only starting to build a formal intercollegiate varsity platform for women. Initially rebuffed, the students appealed to the vice provost for student affairs, who asked campus recreation officials to review their initial decision, in part because of "the questions we have raised about this with regard to TITLE IX." After two weeks of meetings, the women gained status as the "Women's Ice Hockey Club," with a modest allotment of ice time and access to some intramural equipment. They also secured a coach. Within two years the Wildcats had a varsity team, with a fifteen-game schedule, regular ice time, new uniforms, and a new head coach named Russ McCurdy, a BU grad and veteran of the 1962–63 US National team. The Wildcats finished the season 15-0, outscoring the opposition 120–32. Lesley Visser was a rising-star journalist, and her *Boston Globe* story captured both the joy and frustration of these early days. Talent, ice time, coaching, and equipment produced a team that McCurdy felt came along only "every ten years or so," with a "chemistry I will probably never see again." For all their success, however, UNH would not play in Cornell's big March tournament despite receiving an invitation. The annual team budget covered everything but postseason play. As McCurdy admitted, "No one had any idea we'd be this good."[41]

Two years later, McCurdy's Wildcats participated in the nation's first women's intercollegiate championship, sponsored by the Eastern Association of Intercollegiate Athletics for Women. Eleven schools had varsity programs—Boston College, Brown, Colby, Cornell, Dartmouth, Harvard, New Hampshire, Northeastern, Princeton, Providence College, and St. Lawrence University—and four made the tournament. In 1984 the ECAC took over the championship. From 1980 to 1988, UNH won six titles, its success a result of great players, strong coaching, and institutional support, including athletic grants in aid (a clear advantage over Ivy League opponents). Through the 1980s the "national" championship was an all-eastern affair. Women at Minnesota and Wisconsin could not break through institutional barriers. That changed in the next decade.[42]

The grassroots were also growing. Visser's December 1977 article in *Hockey* reported that AHAUS-registered girl's teams in the previous five years had surged from thirty-five to 164. National championships began in 1975. Two years later, two dozen teams competed for titles across three divisions. Growth was coast to coast. In the mid-1970s, Hollywood even had a girls' league for players ranging in age from eight to eighteen. A women's league there was short lived, but *Hockey* reported that "two teams still hold practice sessions with players that included a lawyer, an actress, a dancer, a teacher and a grandmother." Warner Brothers studios sponsored one team.[43]

Europe lagged behind North America. A 1989 IIHF yearbook reported that while "women's ice hockey has already become well-known sport with thousands of players in the USA and Canada, the sport just manages to keep alive, if at all, in Europe and other parts of the ice hockey world. Not because there is no interest in women's ice hockey, but because there are no fixed practice times yet, and neither the associations nor the clubs are particularly interested." The reasons matched North America's: protect ice time for boys and men. Thus, women received the odd, available times, especially early morning, which in cold winters was "certainly not amusing." In order to provide access, some federations allowed girls to play on boys' teams and let mixed teams compete in championships. In Germany, some managers protested and "demanded to annul the results of those teams and to prohibit such 'mixed teams.'" In a compromise, mixing was allowed until age twelve.[44]

The German Ice Hockey Federation reported thirty-five teams registered in 1988. The Netherlands reported six official teams as well as a national team. Sweden saw thirty-two teams compete in a national-championship league, won by Nacka HK. Denmark reported twelve women's teams, with a total of 230 registered players. For the first time, in 1987–88 Denmark established an official national team, which played matches at the Ochsner Cup in Switzerland against sides from Great Britain, Switzerland, Guelph (Ontario), and Nacka (Sweden). France reported 492 women playing across eighteen official teams, which competed for a national championship won by Grenoble. Great Britain reported twenty teams, who had founded their own division of the British Ice Hockey Association, the Women's Ice Hockey Association. Czechoslovakia was the only Eastern Bloc country reporting women's teams (twenty); unofficial standings showed the top team to be Beroun, followed by Pilsen, Sparta Prague, Slavia Prague, and Kladno.[45]

One problem was the lack of uniform rules: "Some teams play with body check and slapshot while this is not allowed to others. Some let women play with their long hair showing from under the helmet, while others have to hide their hair under the helmet in order to prevent an opponent from tearing the hair of others in a turmoil or the height of a battle." Feminists noted that the Swedish men's national team was stocked with players "wearing sometimes shoulder-long hair." Some leagues required breast protectors, believing the players would thus "avoid cancer through hits and blows against the breast." One referee allegedly "refused to find out by touching whether the ice hockey players wore a breast-protection and rather did not start the game." As the women's market grew, manufacturers produced better-fitting equipment. The questions about body checking, safety, and "femininity," however, proved more difficult to resolve.[46]

By 1988 female hockey players earned a significant expansion of opportunities for practice and competition. Most of that progress resulted from agitation at the grassroots. There were still huge and obvious goals to reach, the most glaring of which were championships. In 1988 the world's best players (and their fans) could not look forward to titles sponsored by either the IOC or the IIHF. That was soon to change, a product of pressure from below and pragmatism from above.

The hockey world started to converge in the years between the Summit Series and the Calgary Games. European players and leagues adopted attitudes, aspirations, and policies that drew them closer to North America and the NHL. The world also opened up, with more opportunities to play at just about every level. European players broke old bonds in order to follow their NHL dreams. North Americans moved in greater flows eastward to grab spots in Europe. And women on both continents began to push in greater numbers for more ice time and more support. At the time, many representatives of the old order—national federation executives, collegiate athletic directors, professional league owners, club administrators—felt adrift upon the sea of change. In hindsight, it was only the beginning of the voyage.

22

The Game on the Ice: 1972–1988

There is a hilarious scene (one among many) in 1977's frighteningly popular film *Slap Shot*. Like so many successful comedic spoofs, it contains a telling grain of truth—this one about the state of hockey tactics in the 1970s and how far out of balance the game's central components of speed, science, and mayhem had drifted. In a playoff race, with a lack of skating and scoring talent, and facing the prospect of his Federal League team being folded, Charlestown Chiefs player-coach Reg Dunlop (Paul Newman) decides that the only chance for success (on the ice and at the box office) is to goon it up. Leading a rag-tag collection of Canadian minor-league lifers, three bespectacled simpleton brothers (the Hansons), and an ex-college star, Dunlop has his work cut out for him. But his cynical tactics begin to bring wins. Toward the end of the film, the Chiefs visit the Hyannisport Presidents, and the gong show reaches new heights. Ahead 7–1, a Hanson brother's goal celebration is interrupted when a foreign object thrown from the stands hits him in the head, knocking off his glasses. In response, he does the only logical thing. He climbs over the glass and goes into the stands after the fan. Several teammates follow, starting a huge melee that leaves the Presidents bemused and leads the Hansons to jail. Sensing an opportunity for splashy press, Dunlop happily gives them over to the local police who show up at the dressing-room door. "I throw up my hands. I can't control 'em any more. They gotta be punished. Will you do me a favor and put 'em behind bars?" In the next breath, he tells Chiefs general manager Joe McGrath (Strother Martin) on the phone: "They're puttin' the Hansons away on a trumped-up charge. Someone threw a monkey wrench. Yeah, it hit Jeff right in the face. No, they were defending the honor of Charlestown at the time. The boosters are behind us 100 per cent." When McGrath shows up in Hyannisport to arrange the Hansons' bail price, Dunlop objects to the GM's dickering:

DUNLOP: "You can't leave those guys in there. They're folk heroes."
DESK SERGEANT: "They're criminals."
DUNLOP: "Most folk heroes started out as criminals."

Overblown caricature, to be sure. But to unpack the scene is to parse something central to North American hockey's public image in the 1970s. The game had become a running joke, a modern Roman Forum, a safety valve for the stress of modern life. A surrogate for *real* violence outside the glass. The "new" brutality delighted many and drew deep concern from others. And *Slap Shot*, the film, had an odd career. The film's intended mockery of gratuitous mayhem faded. The dark humor, tribalism, and hypermasculinity grew magnetic among many players and fans. It all became a weird source of identity, a positive assertion of toughness and rule flouting. It was a celebration of hockey gangsterism, for which real examples were all too easy to locate. These included Philadelphia's Broad Street Bullies; designated "hitmen" on professional and major junior teams; and, in one life-imitating-art moment, Boston Bruins player Terry O'Reilly and others *really* jumping the glass in a December 1979 game at Madison Square Garden to get at a fan who had sucker-punched teammate Stan Jonathan. "O'Reilly's after somebody in the crowd. And they have sticks. There go the Bruins," one MSG television commentator said. "You hate to see this."[1] But of course, many didn't hate it at all.

The Big, Bad Years

Violence took center ice for two decades. "Right after Paul Henderson scored his famous goal in Moscow," went one frenetic account, "hockey caught a bad cold that just kept getting worse."[2] It was most visible among the pros. There was more violence generally, and especially in the form of fighting (no longer referred to in the NHL rules by the gentlemanly term fisticuffs)—always illegal, but punished so lightly in the NHL, WHA, and Canadian juniors that its strategic intimidation value outweighed the immediate deterrent of a major penalty. During the 1980s, one journalist claimed, NHL fans were virtually guaranteed at least one "bout" in every tilt.[3] But fighting was even more prominent a feature of the game in the

WHA, a league made up of a handful of ex-NHL stars such as Bobby Hull, Gordie Howe, and Derek Sanderson, but also a great many less-talented players for whom the "rough stuff" helped compensate for a want of skill. "In the WHA . . . fighters brought in the casual fans," one league history noted, "and many teams hyped the confrontations to sell tickets."[4] Hull, Winnipeg's (and the WHA's) marquee player, staged a one-man, one-day strike in October 1975 to protest "goonery," but he earned a good deal of derision from his contemporaries and fans, and resolved nothing. "I think Bobby Hull should have kept his mouth shut," rugged entertainer Eddie Shack responded, "because now guys will be aiming for him."[5]

Fighting became so intrinsic that it spawned a new specialization, the enforcer, or goon, whose role it was not to skate, pass, or score well, but to protect a team's vulnerable stars from becoming strategic targets of assault (a pattern that has only recently begun to decline). Moreover, media commentators clung to a handful of exceptional on-ice incidents as proof of serious compromise in the game's values. So egregious were some big-league altercations and vicious assaults—such as the butt-end delivered by the Bruins' Dave Forbes to the head of North Star Henry Boucha (1975), the drubbing taken by Maple Leaf Brian Glennie at the hands of Red Wing Dan Maloney (1975), the WHA Calgary Cowboys' Rick Jodzio's beating of Nordiques star Marc Tardif (1976), Colorado Rockies Wilf Paiement's devastating two-handed slash to the face of Red Wing Dennis Polonich (1978), and the stick attack by North Stars' bad boy Dino Ciccarelli on Toronto's Luke Richardson (1988)—that they merited formal legal charges, occasioned court cases, and made public spectacles of a game gone over the edge.[6]

Moreover, routine violence—in-game hooking, slashing, and elbowing—remained everyday occurrences, despite an old argument that the threat of fighting worked to reduce stickwork and cheap tactics of the sort that Canadian and American players encountered when they played against European teams in international competition, where fighting merited a game suspension.[7] It all ran to both the extraordinary *and* the mundane, a fact reflected in the statistics for penalty minutes per NHL team per game. In 1972–73 the NHL's sixteen teams amassed 15,610 minutes in penalties in seventy-eight games, or 12.15 penalty minutes per team per game. Thereafter, that latter figure rose: 14.62 in 1975–76; 14.49 in 1978–79; 19.91 in 1981–82; 18.61 in 1984–85; and an amazing 26.42 in 1987–88, before beginning a gradual decline.[8] And, for at least some teams, the tactics delivered results. From

1972 to 1982, the Flyers were the NHL's most penalized team, and one of its most successful, earning ten playoff appearances and two Stanley Cups.[9] "They say that everything is fair in love and war," four-time Stanley Cup–winning Toronto Maple Leafs coach Punch Imlach quipped in 1973, "and as far as I'm concerned this is war. If I know you've got a bad arm, I'm going to take a stick to it. If I know you've got a bad ankle, I'm going to try to get at it. . . . If you can't play because you're hurt, that's tough."[10]

The pros were the most egregious, but the trend invaded amateur ranks as well. In an October 1976 Alberta Junior Hockey League game in which forty-three penalties were called, a Spruce Grove player, who was returning to action after sitting out a five-game suspension for spearing, was ejected (again) for spearing a Pincher Creek player and cutting his face for twenty stitches. And yet the league president refused to see it as anything more than a one-off incident. "It's unfortunate that . . . junior hockey in Alberta is being branded violent," Jim Scoular said in response to concerns expressed by MPPs in the Alberta provincial legislature. "The AJHL is not a violent league."[11] The Alberta government disagreed and asked crown attorneys across the province to observe junior games and lay charges where necessary. In Massachusetts, high-school hockey came under the influence of Channel 38 and its coverage of the "Big Bad Bruins." "Some of the things that happen in hockey defy belief," Silvio Cella, Revere High School athletic director, was quoted in one 1977 *Boston Globe* exposé. "Put a stick in the hands of some of these kids, and they go crazy." Eastern Massachusetts Schoolboy Hockey convener Mickey McGuire concurred: "It has become our biggest problem. These kids are just becoming more aggressive all the time."[12]

The Response: Smoothing the Game

The response to this epidemic came in a variety of forms: searching and saccharine lament for what had become of a once-beautiful game and widespread alarm about its polluting effect on North American children;[13] scholarly study of the relationship of on-ice violence to real-world crime and social anomie;[14] intense debate over whether on-ice assault should be prosecuted in the courts; and, notably, a scattershot of accusations from journalists and public intellectuals about the root causes. In the last area, most commentators pointed the finger at a sinister combination of interests among mass media moguls (whose sales benefited from sensational stories) and hockey entrepreneurs, foremost among them NHL and WHA owners, for whom brawling sold tickets and expanded TV viewership and in some cases seemed the only way to compete in a talent-thin environment. "We've got to mold a lineup that can take on a bunch of goons," Maple Leafs owner Harold Ballard told *Sports Illustrated* in November 1975, six months after the Flyers' Stanley Cup victory. "I'm looking for guys you toss raw meat to and they will go wild."[15]

The situation drew the attention of legislators in several jurisdictions. In Quebec, a 1977 study commissioned by the provincial ministry of Youth, Leisure and Sport reported that alarming rates of brutality were the result of (among other things) misguided coaching at the junior levels.[16] In Washington, DC, sports moguls appeared in fall 1980 at multiple hearings before the Congressional Committee on the Judiciary's Subcommittee on Crime that focused on "Excessive Violence in Professional Sports." Hockey was a prime offender.[17] But it was in Ontario where the state tried to enter the fray most substantially. Triggered by a particularly egregious brawl-filled game between minor teams from Hamilton and Bramalea in April 1974, the Ministry of Community and Social Services commissioned respected jurist William R. McMurtry to undertake a comprehensive "Investigation and Inquiry into Violence in Amateur Hockey." Published later that year, the thirty-eight-page McMurtry Report surveyed recent studies and drew upon interviews of leading academics as well as coaches, players, and officials. "Hockey need not be a symptom of a sick society," it concluded. To ensure that it didn't, McMurtry recommended a clearer articulation of the sport's aims, more research into why and how social tensions were being manifested on the ice, more and better training for coaches and referees, embedding programs in public schools where they could be monitored more closely by the province, and finally the establishment of an Ontario Hockey Council, a supervisory body made up of representatives from the game's various constituencies, including government.[18]

Public alarm and the specter of government intervention motivated hockey authorities to alter their regulations on violence, if not their attitudes. For example, the NHL introduced a "third-man in" rule in 1977 that steepened penalties for players who dangerously intervened in ongoing brawls. OHA brass responded to the McMurtry Report by recommending one-game misconducts (in other words, ejection) for combatants, though notably, its membership voted that down decisively. Fighting would remain, but other antiviolence rules were introduced: a ten-minute aggressor penalty for fight starters, stiffer rules on high sticking and checking from behind, and a new verbal-abuse penalty to protect referees.[19] Other bodies across the country followed suit with similar crackdowns.[20] In the end, however, the prospect of government intervention alarmed hockey organizations so much that it served to blunt significant reform. Once funding was secured, it seemed, the state was to have no place in the ice rinks of the nation. If more policing was to be done, only hockey men would do it. "If you guys want to run hockey," OHA executive Cliffe Phillips remarked mischievously to an Ontario government official promoting the Ontario Hockey Council, "appoint the referees!" In Manitoba the unwillingness of the Attorney General's office to assert a clear policy on prosecuting on-ice violence "hamstrung" Winnipeg police and kept them from intervening, even in the most serious cases. "Let's face it," Superintendent Herb Stephen admitted in 1982, "it's a grey area."[21]

But in the larger historical picture, it is important to see the game's two decades of hyperviolence as something more than a phenomenon brought about solely by cheap commercial pandering or cynical on-ice tactics. Something bigger, something culturally significant was going on here, too. For Canadians (and many Americans), hockey fighting in the 1970s became a symbolic act of masculine Western chauvinism, a knee-jerk rejection against the fear that, despite the scoreboard outcome in the Summit Series, North Americans were being eclipsed. Canadians could no longer lean on the old standby that their disappointing performances in the IIHF World Championships occurred because their best players were ineligible. The Summit Series was way too close a shave for anyone to really believe that anymore. The real talent gap between Canadians and their European foes was closed; the Soviets, Swedes, Czechs, and Finns were already at the door. Then, what to do? The reaction of many in the game (and some in the press), was conservative retrenchment. Team Canada won, after all, and there were lessons to be learned from what Harry Sinden's Canadians had done effectively.

As post-series memories congealed, Team Canada's ability to intimidate the Soviets was seen by one faction as the main reason the Canadians ultimately prevailed. Violence had long been a central characteristic of Canada's game, and now it was also a cultural rampart, an article of faith. Fighting, in these years, became rich with meaning. In every brawl, Canadians claimed the game as their own and labeled other versions—ones that outlawed fighting and favored a different combination of speed, science, and mayhem—inauthentic. In this way, the hyperviolent 1970s and 1980s constituted a circling of the wagons. But it was an autarkic, backward-looking, defensive impulse that could not last.

By 1987 the tide had turned noticeably. Fighting lacked its once-strong purchase on consumers and organizers, its base. In that year, the Canadian Amateur Hockey Association petitioned the Canadian Radio-Television Commission, the federal government's broadcasting regulator, to ban National Hockey League telecasts if the league refused to clean up its act.[22] Even more telling was an episode involving amateurs. In that year's World Junior Championships in Czechoslovakia, Team Canada's gold medal bid against the Soviet Union was cut short when a bench-clearing brawl ended the game. By one account, after an on-ice fight broke out, a Soviet player left his bench to join in, so Canadian players responded in kind, following hockey's "code." The result was ugly. Dumbfounded by the bedlam, game officials responded by turning off the arena lights. Both teams were disqualified from the tournament, players and coaches suspended from international competition for months. The 1987 team was excoriated in the press, by Hockey Canada, and by the IIHF, its tournament record expunged and forgotten. This event reflected a new mentality. Although CBC hockey analyst Don Cherry loudly defended their actions and one hockey writer mused two decades later that the boys "were punished for something you've been taught you have to do," a quieter majority of others believed that the brawlers got what they deserved. Times had changed.[23]

The Course of Convergence

Despite its colorful and magnetic qualities, violence masked what was, in the long run, an even more significant trend: tactical convergence. To understand this, we must return again to the Summit Series. The discourse that aired in North America during and after that iconic affair involved a central Canadian *apologia*, the need for Canadians to make comprehensible their near-death experience. The shocking success of the poorly equipped, "amateur" Soviets in the opening games, journalists reported, had little to do with Soviet superiority. It had everything to do with their conditioning, which badly eclipsed that of the portly Canadian professionals who had shown up for their brief pre-series training camp looking "prosperous." When one added a decidedly un-Canadian measure of high self-worth, Canadians told themselves, the result was understandable. It should have been expected. Too fat and too confident. But slowly some commentators, including Harry Sinden and Ken Dryden, recognized the fault in how Canadians had come to play the game over the previous three decades, and that the Russian approach to hockey might have made the difference.[24] Just as a sadly declining fin-de-siècle Britain had become anchored with the hybristic and material legacy of being the "First Industrial Nation," Canadian hockey, too, had become a victim of its glorious past.[25]

In the fifteen years after the Summit Series, the game converged on the ice. The North American "helter-skelter," dump-and-chase, intimidation tactics began to merge with the European game—the one characterized, as the 1972 Russians represented so well, by its flow, meter, pace, and geometry. There are several aspects that are essential to note about this change. First, though unmistakable, the on-ice convergence was uneven, halting, and messy. In truth, it predated September 1972 and came not in a comprehensive wave but in fits and starts, here and there. Only gradually did innovators and strategic borrowers make headway in North America. Second, the convergence (like the effects of "contact" during the Age of European Exploration) went both ways. The influences of European hockey were felt increasingly in North American rinks; and vice versa. By the end of the 1980s, the styles that Europeans and North Americans played were increasingly similar. Just as the sparkling tactical innovations that Napoleon's generals demonstrated on early nineteenth-century European battlefields became de rigueur in military academies by the time of the American Civil War, hockey's late-twentieth-century global tactical convergence produced a strategic orthodoxy that has since become evident—in the game's coaching manuals and clinics, in dressing-room discussions, in sports columns and call-in sport-radio talk shows.[26] The years between 1972 and 1988 were critical hosts to this fundamental transition.

Hockey Style

But what, exactly, was converging? The question is important. Like "middle class" or "globalization," the notion of hockey style is abstract. Much of the game's attraction has always been its chaotic nature and its speed. As we described in chapter 18, the "Soviet system" or the "Canadian style" were omnibus terms that columnists and coaches employed expecting their audiences to know what they meant, without defining them exactly, and at the height of the Cold War they lent themselves very easily to caricature and metaphor. Canadian style symbolized Western tastes for individuality, flair, and passion; the Russian emphasis on system revealed their game as socialistic and their players as interchangeable robots.

The North American style under the spotlight in 1972 was the product of almost a century of incremental growth and change. "We learned to play hockey by accident," former NHL player and then Toronto Toros coach Billy Harris wrote in 1974. "It evolved on lakes and rivers. The Russians learned scientifically. . . . The whole European approach is that way."[27] Though an oversimplification, the Summit Series pitted individual one-on-one skills against a collective system that constantly emphasized regrouping to gain numerical advantage; spontaneous creativity against extensive planning; and reliance on emotion, violence, and aggression against patience, poise, possession, and precision. "Canadian hockey prefers to use a hard hitting style of play involving much body contact which tends to limit the tempo of play both in individual and team play," Czech expert Vladimír Kostka wrote in 1978. "European hockey is based upon an attempt to combine a high tempo of play with a tougher style of play."[28]

Beyond these sweeping generalities, the contrast between the European and North American games was a multitude of small differences—to borrow that hackneyed expression from postgame interviews—the "little things" on which a grand strategy was built. Three aspects stand out most: geometry, possession, and the use of personnel. In North America before the 1970s, coaches conjured a game of imagined zones, each forward exhorted to "skate his lane," each defenseman instructed to tend to his corner when the puck went there, or to cover the front of the net when it didn't. "Stay on [your] wings on offense," three-time-Cup-winning coach Punch Imlach told his NHL charges in Toronto and Buffalo in the late 1960s and early 1970s, "because then everybody has an idea of where everybody else is."[29] In Europe the chains were off. Positional play was looser and less restricted. Forwards and defenders were taught to move to open space, much as football players did on the pitch. "Europeans taught . . . our forwards to not be so structured staying on their side of the ice," longtime NHL coach and commentator Harry Neale recalled. "Their wingers crisscrossed, skated to open ice, and hopefully, they'd get a pass. . . . [T]hat was a difficult tactic to defend against."[30]

Some of the European style rang a bell for older Canadian hockey experts, like Foster Hewitt, who told *Montreal Gazette* columnist Dink Carroll in 1986 that the 1972 Soviets reminded him of the style played by the New York

Rangers line of Frank Boucher and the Cook brothers, Bill and Bun, in the 1920s and 1930s. "They crisscrossed, used drop passes, and handled the puck so well. . . . 'The Russians . . . play this game the way the old Rangers used to play it.'" But few were still around to share this memory.[31]

Connected to the varied ways that North Americans and Europeans mentally mapped space on the rink were their differing attitudes toward possessing the puck. North Americans were willing to strategically give it up in order to win it again in a better scoring position—to dump and chase. "Most clubs today . . . like to shoot it into the corner and chase it," Imlach wrote in 1973. "One wingman takes the defenseman out of the play, and the centerman comes in and takes the puck. The third man moves into the slot."[32] "Throw it in deep and go in and forecheck," Don Cherry allegedly told his Boston Bruins players in the late 1970s. "Just rap it around the fucking boards. And you better be there."[33]

European players were schooled to avoid ever giving up the puck, to always maintain possession. When a puck carrier encountered odds that were not in his favor (a 3-on-3, or 2-on-3, for example), his impulse must always be to retreat, regroup, and recommence an attack with a better numerical advantage. If they "didn't like a play," coaching guru Roger Neilson commented, "they turned back. . . . The Europeans were so good at it."[34] The result was more continuous flow with a premium on creative passing and finding open space. Finally, the European game utilized players in a fundamentally different way. For North American coaches, the central challenge was to get the team's best five on the ice as often as possible, and in situations—on power plays and against opponents' weaker lines—that maximized their chances to score. "Everything depends on the individual skills and personalities of my players," Imlach asserted. "Great players will usually carry a team regardless of what a coach does." In Europe the approach couldn't have been more opposite. Impressive to Shero were the Russians' "five-man units constantly working together on offense and defense." "European teams never engaged in matchups," Neale recalled of that era. "They put their three five-man units out . . . and they stuck with them."[35] System trumped stars.

A New Look: North Americans Incorporate European Styles

Writing in 1974, *Vancouver Sun* sports scribe Jim Kearney argued: "Nothing changed. The basic fire-and-fall-back, show-biz NHL style remained the same. If anything new was learned from the eight-game series with the Russians it was never made evident in the NHL."[36] But the next decade and a half proved Kearney wrong. By 1988, North American hockey gradually adopted and embraced many features of the European game.

Influences came in several ways. The most colorful were the international series that featured North American pros against European nationals. In 1974 the WHA (whose players were excluded from the 1972 games) staged their own eight-game series against the Russians, one largely passed over in Canadian hockey lore because of its unflattering outcome: four Soviet wins, one Canadian win, and three ties.[37] In December 1975 and January 1976 two Russian club teams, the Red Army and Soviet Wings, visited North America, each playing four games against NHL teams, including the lauded "greatest game" in which the Red Army and the Montreal Canadiens battled to a 3–3 tie.[38] This format—the "Super Series"—proved so popular that it was replicated the following year featuring WHA opponents, and for several years thereafter. Russian clubs returned to play NHL teams in 1978, 1979, 1980, 1983, 1986, and 1989. In 1979, the Soviet national team played NHL All-Stars in a one-off "Challenge Cup" as they did eight years later in what was called Rendez-Vous 1987. For its part, the WHA hosted touring teams from Russia, Czechoslovakia, Finland, and Sweden in the late 1970s, and even included games with them in their standings in 1977–79.[39] Most intriguing, perhaps, were the international games that featured national teams. In summer 1976, Hockey Canada and Alan Eagleson organized the "Canada Cup," an occasional six-team tournament that pitted teams from the world's best hockey-playing nations. The Canadians won four of the five tournaments in the competition's fifteen-year span (1976–91), including a dramatic 6–5 final against the Soviets in Hamilton, Ontario, in 1987, the memorable winning goal scored by Mario Lemieux on a pass from Wayne Gretzky.

In all of this, elite players and coaches from both sides of the Atlantic became increasingly familiar with one another. Their engagement not only encouraged imitation and experimentation, but demanded it. Billy Harris, the coach of the ill-fated WHA All-Stars, tinkered with strategy to combat the Soviet style as early as 1974. Russian goaltender Vladislav Tretiak recalled: "Even the Canadians quickly learn[ed] the lessons we gave them. The majority of the Team WHA players were trying to play the combination style. This team's tactics were much more diverse [than] those of the team we played two years [before]. Harris taught players quick, sneaky moves, and team play."[40] And the Philadelphia Flyers, the most violent NHL team and standard bearer for the Canadian style in the 1970s, changed their play against the Soviets. According to most contemporary accounts, they defeated Central Red Army 4–1 on January 11, 1976, largely because they physically pummeled the Soviets (prompting the visitors to leave the ice temporarily and threaten to quit). But in reflecting on their win (the only NHL team to defeat the Red Army in the series), Flyers coach Fred Shero attributed their success to Xs-and-Os, not trench tactics. "The Russians passed the puck beautifully, but they do a lot of retreating and unnecessary skating, hoping to lure you out of position." As Shero put it, "There is only one puck and we just waited. Eventually, they had to try to beat us. That's when we bumped them off the puck." *Bumped*, to be sure. But they also adapted to the Europeans, using a defensive, counterattack posture that the Czechs had refined and that the Swedes later adopted in their "left-wing lock"—all of them versions of today's "trap." Against the Soviets in 1976, other NHL teams followed Imlach's dictum to "not worry about your opponent's system"—and lost.[41]

European influence also came through Europeans themselves, recruited in increasing numbers in the 1970s and 1980s to play in North American rinks. Oddly, if it was the Soviets who principally confronted North Americans with a new way to play, it was Swedes who demonstrated the European approach. Though individual European players had skated with North American teammates in earlier decades, the wedge of Swedish, Czech and Finnish imports that arrived in the mid-1970s had profound effects. In 1973 the NHL's Toronto Maple Leafs signed Swedes Börje Salming and Inge Hammarström, Minnesota signed their countryman Roland Eriksson in 1976, and the New York Islanders inked Göran Hogösta and Stefan Persson in 1977. Perhaps not surprisingly, it was the WHA that was most open to the novelty of Europeans in their midst. In 1974–75 its Winnipeg Jets signed Swedish stars Ulf Nilsson, Anders Hedberg, and Lars-Erik Sjöberg, and Finn Veli-Pekka Ketola; its Hartford Whalers signed twin brothers Christer and Thommie Abrahamsson. In the same year, Vaclav Nedomansky and Richard Farda defected from Czechoslovakia to join the Toronto Toros. Seeking more recruits, the Jets held a training camp in Finland in 1975; the Toros did the same in Sweden. Coach Glen Sather took his Edmonton Oilers to both countries.[42]

A second wave of Europeans came to the North American pro ranks just after the WHA-NHL merger in 1979. This spurt saw an even larger and deeper contingent cross the pond, including Czechs (Peter, Anton, and Marian Stastny signed in Quebec, 1980; Miroslav Frycer in Quebec and Toronto, 1981), Swedes (Thomas Steen was recruited to Winnipeg, 1981; Anders Eldebrink to Vancouver, 1981; Mats Näslund to Montreal, 1982; Tomas Jonsson to the New York Islanders, 1981; Pelle Lindbergh to Philadephia, 1981; Håkan Loob to Calgary, 1983); and Finns (Reijo Ruotsaleinen with New York Rangers, 1981; and Jari Kurri [1980] and Esa Tikkanen [1984] with Edmonton).[43] Nilsson and Hedberg, who skated with Canadian superstar Bobby Hull on the Jets' "Hot Line" in the mid-1970s, make the point best. "They revolutionized the game," recalled Canadian André Lacroix, who played on five different WHA teams and became the league's all-time leading scorer. "They said, Just because you play left wing doesn't mean you have to go up and down your wing like a robot. You can use the whole ice. It was exciting."[44]

Even more important for convergence at lower levels were the myriad clinics, coaching exchanges, and academic studies that North Americans undertook in Europe and, especially, Russia, in a decade-long wave following 1972. The Summit Series spawned an almost fanatical curiosity about how the Europeans did it. North Americans both traveled to Europe and recruited European coaches to come west to explain their game. American amateur coaches Vairo and Brooks each spent time in Russia; so did WHA coaches like Glen Sather and NHL coaches like Shero. New York Islanders coach Al Arbour admitted in 1975 that he had "spent considerable time" in Russia studying hockey philosophy. "I would like to think that the Islanders combine the best of both the North American and European styles."[45] In Canada, though coaching clinics had been around since at least 1965, a surge followed the launch of the government-sponsored (and CAHA-partnered) National Coaches Certification Program, which coincided with the European hockey infatuation. At NCCP seminars in the 1970s, European coach-instructors, such as Swedes Per-Olof Åstrand and Hans Lindberg, and Czech Luděk Bučak, became a regular feature.[46]

A flowering of spring and summer hockey schools featuring European techniques enchanted young players and their parents, who were looking to find an edge for their kids' chances at the Big Show. One of them, sponsored by the OHA and held at Maple Leaf Gardens in September 1980, promised a "Swedish-style clinic" for coaches, focusing on the "five-man attack" for youth teams ages sixteen and under, and led by Swedish coaches Curt Lindstrom and Peter Johansson: "Only 60 places available;

cost: $10 each."[47] Other, similar offerings focused on Eastern secrets to better skating. Dr. Yacov Smushkin, a former Soviet national skating coach and a refugee from the Soviet Union is one example. After landing in Massachusetts in 1973, he moved to Toronto to practice his trade. For almost a decade beginning in 1974, he promised Toronto-area youth noticeable results through innovative balance drills and "edgework"—ideas drawn from his work with figure skaters.[48] Smushkin, like other European hockey coaches, was outspoken—loud and flamboyant to mild-mannered Canadians—and his secrets became highly sought at a time when NHL All-Stars suffered defeat after defeat to the Russians. In December 1976 he even worked one-on-one with several Toronto Maple Leafs players, including Jack Valiquette and Dave "Tiger" Williams. Alas, some mountains are too high to scale. The Leafs finished 33-32-15 that season and lost in the second round of the playoffs.[49]

George Kingston and New-Style Coaching

Some of this infatuation was fleeting and faddish and played on ordinary Canadians' curiosity with exotic hockey "others" and their collective anxiety about the status of "Canada's game." But a good deal of this cultural transfer had staying power. These programs gradually opened the minds of North American coaches to doing things differently. Much of what Smushkin preached, for example, resonates still in the myriad power-skating programs that pervade North American rinks today. The fascination with Eastern European methods also traveled much further up the North American hockey pyramid, where it inspired some to study and absorb European ideas and put them on the ice. Brooks, Vairo, and Murray Williamson were among these pivotal conduits; but George Kingston's journey went even deeper.

Born in Biggar, Saskatchewan in 1939, Kingston was a decent minor player who was signed to a "C" form by the Detroit Red Wings in 1953 but chose to play university hockey at Alberta instead. Shoulder injuries shortened his playing days, but when he accepted an assistant coaching job at University of Calgary in 1967, he found a second career in hockey. Kingston paced the pine boards on both sides of the Atlantic: from 1968 to 1986 as head coach of the Calgary Dinosaurs; 1988–89 as an assistant with the Minnesota North Stars; 1989–91 as head coach of the Norwegian national team; 1991–93 as the first head coach of the San Jose Sharks;

1999–2007 as an assistant coach with the Atlanta Thrashers and Florida Panthers. He also guided Canada's national team as an assistant at the 1984 Olympics and head coach of Canada's gold-medal-winning teams at the 1987 Spengler Cup and the 1994 World Championships. He was CIAU Coach of the Year in 1974 and 1981.

Known by his players and others as a teaching coach (a rarity in the late 1960s and 1970s), Kingston characterized himself more a *student* of the game, inspired by the Soviet challenge. "As a player and physical educator, I appreciated that there was an awful lot going on in Soviet hockey that we didn't know about," he recalled in 2004. His curiosity prompted him to fly with his family to Europe in 1971. Packed into a rented Volkswagen van, the Kingstons spent five months there, including three-and-a-half weeks inside the Soviet Union, where George watched the national team play. He "bribed" his way into the closed practices with Canada lapel pins. Based on his observations, he later predicted that Team Canada would lose the Summit Series by one game, for which he was "regarded as somewhat of a traitor in Canada."[50]

The experience whetted his appetite for more study. While piling up wins at Calgary, he completed a master's degree. In 1974–75 he took a sabbatical from his work as a coach and assistant professor to tour the Soviet Union, Czechoslovakia, and Sweden "to find out what is really happening in their hockey programs."[51] In 1976 he was one of six coaches assigned by the IIHF to study a team in the Canada Cup tournament, to assess them, and to write a comparative report.[52] The result was his 1977 doctoral dissertation: "The Organization and Development of Ice Hockey during Childhood in the Soviet Union, Czechoslovakia, Sweden and Canada."

Regularly sought as a clinic instructor and event speaker, Kingston became a recognized expert on European hockey.[53] His absorption of European influences was not faddish but focused. He admired European skills training, especially skating technique, and sought to introduce his own version for Canadian youth.[54] He didn't buy everything about the ways the Russians, Swedes, and Czechs approached the game. In important ways, he felt, North Americans had gotten things right, especially regarding the adoption of "system." Reflecting on forty years of strategic convergence in 2004, his comments expressed a view that the pendulum had perhaps swung too far. The European "focus on system and system play misses the target in the game of hockey . . . the game is too fast, too dynamic, too changing, too fleeting, and momentary. . . . Players can use some structure as a start point to initiate offensive or defensive play, and also as a foundation to rebound from when tough times occur in a game. Beyond these start points, the speed and dynamism of hockey takes over."[55] As with Herb Brooks, Kingston's coaching was a critical site for the post–Summit Series convergence of hockey strategy.

North American Influences in Europe

Though the convergence of style involved two-way exchange, the ways in which Europeans influenced North Americans and vice versa were hardly identical. There was a notable asymmetry marked largely by the fact that, like all younger siblings regarding an older brother, European hockey authorities knew much more about the North American scene than the sometimes myopic North American "big brothers" knew about their European relations. As such, the Summit Series of 1972 didn't (and couldn't) ignite a *new* curiosity among Europeans about North American hockey. Still, in Europe as in North America, one could measure a similar set of reactions—conservative and reactionary on one hand, liberal and open to change on the other. In some quarters of the Continent, the results of 1972 confirmed what many had claimed for some time: their version had improved the Canadian root and needed no revision. For others, the lesson of the series was plain: Europeans needed to get tougher.

Aside from Canadian successes in Moscow in 1972 and in the 1987 Izvestia Tournament, North American national teams showed little in Europe to recommend change. Absent from IIHF World Championships from 1970 until 1977, Canada meagerly scratched out bronze medals in 1978, 1982, 1983, and 1986, and a silver medal in 1985. The United States won none. The performances of North American professionals were marginally better. Team Canada (a collection of European-based, Canadian-born pros) won the Spengler Cup in 1984, 1986, and 1987 (claiming second-place in 1985 and 1988). In 1988 the USA Selects won gold.[56] In Europe's other prominent midwinter club tournament, the Soviet Union's Izvestia (1967–96), Canadian teams earned three medals: bronze in 1978, silver in 1986, and gold in 1987. Still, Europeans watching these pros were justified in being "underwhelmed." And the fourth-place finish of Bobby Hull's lauded Winnipeg Jets at the 1976 Izvestia tournament was a disappointment to both European and North American followers. While the Jets' mere appearance provided evidence of the sport's globalization, contemporaries might have viewed it differently: that even a European-injected roster couldn't propel a star-studded North American pro outfit to victory.[57] Clearly, at its elite level, European hockey had gotten better.

Ironically, at least some of this European flourish stemmed from a continued presence of North Americans in Western European hockey circles—as coaches, advisors, and players, and with the increase in North American touring teams. No longer "evangels" bringing a new game to a new audience, these travelers were nonetheless carriers of the North American style and flesh-and-blood symbols of it as well. Fifteen-year NHLer and OHA coach Billy Harris had credentials impressive enough to recommend him to the Swedish Hockey Federation, which hired him as national team coach in 1971–72; Finland followed suit the next year and hired the Canadian-born perennial minor-pro Len Lunde to coach its national team in 1972–73.[58] Below the national-team level, North American coaches directed European club teams in a variety of countries, Switzerland perhaps most of all, and with varying results. Canadian and journeyman NHLer Kent Ruhnke performed as player-coach for Zurich's Swiss B division team. Thunder Bay, Ontario, native Cliff Stewart coached in Europe for ten years (including the EVZ club in Zug, Switzerland) before returning to Canada to take the helm of the OHA's Ottawa 67s in 1984.[59] Montreal Canadiens star center Jacques Lemaire famously quit the NHL in 1979 to coach for two years at HC Sierre in Switzerland. Ottawa native Paul-André Cadieux completed an impressive nineteen-season career as player-coach in Bern, Davos, Geneva, and Fribourg (1970–89) before hanging up the skates and coaching in Switzerland for another seventeen years. In 2014 the Lausanne daily *Le Matin* declared that the sixty-six-year-old Canadian ex-patriate had "made" Swiss hockey for forty-four years.[60] Herb Brooks, architect of the 1980 Miracle on Ice, had tougher sledding. Hired in 1980 to coach Davos in the Swiss elite, he resigned in January 1981, only six months into his contract, with a .396 winning percentage and amid public criticism for conducting "rough practices."[61]

"Some of our best hockey players are European," read a special feature in a May 1980 issue of the *Lethbridge Herald* detailing the lives of six Canadian ex-pros (including Lemaire and one-time Maple Leaf Jim McKenny) playing across the Atlantic. "Now some of theirs are Canadian."[62] Scores of other North Americans played on European club teams, exemplary by their presence and their play. European sports beat writer Bob Koep's piece in a February 1979 *Toronto Star* claimed: "Canadian Hockey Players in Europe Spearhead Teams to National Titles."[63] In that year, former Quebec junior star Serge Martel, in the midst of a six-year Swiss pro career, led SC Berne to the Swiss national championship while former Toronto Marlie and Boston University Terrier Dick DeCloe, in the middle of a nine-year run as a perennial scoring leader in the German Bundesliga, helped Cologne capture the league title. In these years, most European pro leagues limited their teams to one or two non-nationals each, and North Americans most often filled those spots. But because those slots were coveted and preserved for the most talented, the North Americans who filled them drew inordinate attention from opposing teams, and carried added expectations for performance from their teams' owners, teammates, and fans.[64] In this spotlight, a good many achieved conspicuous success. Among them were Gary Prior, who, born and raised in Montreal, played collegiately at Penn and Vermont before competing professionally in Germany and Finland, 1980–86, and then commenced a coaching career in Europe;[65] Pembroke, Ontario-born George Galbraith, whose play in goal for Vojen IK earned him Danish League Player of the Year honors in 1979–80;[66] and Arlington, Massachusetts, native and Harvard University standout goaltender Joe Bertagna, whose play helped SG Cortina win the Italian national club championship in 1975. And there were many, many others.

Canadian and American minor, junior, and university teams were also drawn to tour Europe in these years and to compete in European tournaments, unmistakable standard bearers of the North American style of play. These tours included the excursions organized by Varsity Blues coach Tom Watt and an all-star selection of Canadian university players in 1983, and the one involving the whole University of Toronto team that traveled to Switzerland, Germany, Czechoslovakia, and the Soviet Union over the Christmas holiday in 1988. A new enthusiasm grew for this sort of experience. Even IIHF red tape couldn't stem the convergence. When Toronto's Upper Canada College team was refused timely CAHA sanction to play in Sweden in January 1975, UCC and their Swedish hosts in Gothenburg pulled an end run and registered the team formally with the Swedish Ice Hockey Federation for the duration of their six-game tour.[67] The episode must have embarrassed the authorities, because no such hurdles were reported when the St. Andrew's College (Aurora, Ontario) private-school team toured Finland, Russia, and Sweden in 1982.[68]

It is difficult to measure the depth of cultural transfer that came from watching North Americans play in Europe or playing alongside them. They were expected to be proficient, to be exemplary, but even in their difference, they lacked the sort of novelty and exoticism that Europeans possessed when they came to play or coach in North America. Europeans already knew the other style (and many resented it). Sometimes, North Americans earned notoriety for the sort of bad behavior (especially abuse of officials and violence) that their national teams had exhibited at international tournaments. Undoubtedly, when SC Riesserssee coach and Winnipeg native Mike Daski "blew his stack" at game officials at the end of a German second-division game against VL Bad Nauheim in January 1975, fans were treated to what must have seemed a familiar spectacle: a "rambunctious Canadian" calling out the referees. "This sort of refereeing is going to kill the game here," Daski declared. "I'll keep on beefing until they throw me out or do something about this idiotic situation."[69] North Americans in Europe had a hard time biting their tongues. Though otherwise positive, UCC prep-school coach Brian Proctor couldn't contain his evaluation: "The referees were abominable, but that's nothing new."

Clearly, the most notable transfer from North America to Europe was physical play. Though the European press decried loudly the over-the-top intimidation tactics of the Canadian "assassins" and "thugs" in 1972, European strategists began to quietly consider the merits of a more robust style of play. Gradually, almost imperceptibly, it made its way into European hockey at all levels. One reason was because Europeans began to believe that continued success at the highest levels required more toughness. On the eve of the 1975–76 exhibition series between the Soviet Red Army and Wings clubs and eight different NHL teams, *Toronto Sun* writer George Gross recalled watching Tarasov run a practice at Maple Leaf Gardens years before. Periodically, Tarasov whacked or slashed a player with his ever-present stick. "We do these things," he explained, "so our players get used to the tactics of the Canadians."[70] But physical play was not reserved only for North American teams. Soviet players expressed it domestically, too. "In one of the tightest races in years," the *Toronto Star* reported in February 1977, "Spartak Moscow is in grave danger of losing its crown, and its players are resorting to good, old-fashioned Canadian style hitting to keep the opposition at bay. . . . In one game, [Summit Series veteran Alexander] Yakushev drew two roughing penalties and a misconduct."[71] Lars-Erik Sjöberg pinpointed the 1972 series as a turning point for European hockey: "Ever since the Canada-Russia series Europeans have become rougher. . . . [For one, t]he Russians are playing more of a Canadian style now."[72] Bill Flynn, a former Boston University Terrier recruited to play for the Bremerhaven Owls of the German Second Division told an American reporter in May 1978: "Even in Europe, violence on the ice is part of the sport. There are some dirty German players. But that is part of the game."[73]

Violence and virulence continued to brand hockey in the popular imagination long after the 1970s and 1980s passed. The sport's "bad cold" hopped the Atlantic. "Just as Swedish and Soviet-Russian ice hockey have taken up elements of the Canadian and American style of hockey," one Swedish scholar wrote of the 1980s, "the North American game has incorporated what it recognizes as the most valuable elements of European hockey."[74] In this era of convergence, hockey became at once more global and smaller.

23 From Calgary to the KHL: 1989–2010

Vyacheslav "Slava" Fetisov stood in Red Square near St. Basil's Cathedral, holding a trophy alongside his longtime Central Army and Soviet national team comrade, Igor Larionov. It was August, but a cold, blustery wind buffeted that stage of so much Russian history. Together, they had won many trophies since 1980, when they watched the young Americans celebrate in Lake Placid. Six World Championships, two Olympic golds, and nine Soviet League crowns. This, however, was different. In 1997 they were hoisting the Stanley Cup they won two months earlier with the Detroit Red Wings. Fetisov and Larionov were joined that day by Vyacheslav Kozlov, the third of Detroit's "Russian Five" unit, who, along with Sergei Fedorov and Vladimir Konstantinov, had dazzled crowds with their precision passing and close collective play—the kind that Anatoli Tarasov claimed was so representative of socialist society.[1]

The Stanley Cup was still engraved with its original purpose: to celebrate the amateur championship of the Dominion of Canada. It had long since been appropriated by the NHL. It had journeyed across North America, and to Sweden, and had even been dumped in swimming pools. But Moscow? The time had come. Fetisov's wife Lada felt the strangeness of the occasion as her husband walked through the Square amid a curious crowd: "Even a couple of years ago no one could have imagined the Stanley Cup here, as part of this scene. What's next?" There was still a line waiting to shuffle past the showcase mummy of V. I. Lenin, the USSR's founder. But the queue no longer snaked way back beyond the Square. And by one account, the "hundred or so pilgrims . . . waved and smiled when they recognized the three Russian hockey superstars." A decade earlier, the Soviet honor guard would have quickly snuffed out such disrespect to Lenin. On this day, however, even a guard could not resist the temptation to take a picture of the Cup as it sat on the mausoleum's steps. "It's a real thrill to have our guys come here and bring the greatest hockey trophy with them," said Sergeant Andrei Chursakov. "Since all the stars left, there isn't as much interest in hockey as there used to be. But I watch the NHL games with interest, just to see our guys play." The stars had been leaving since 1989. Fetisov was one of the first. He remembered the earlier days of standing with his Olympic mates and saluting Lenin. But no longer: "No way. I want people to see the system has changed. There is more freedom. You can feel it."[2]

Slava's Journey

In a 2014 ESPN documentary, Fetisov relived the journey since Lake Placid, where he watched Mike Eruzione score his famous goal. Yes, the Americans had enjoyed a miracle. But he became agitated after three decades of prodding for his reflections on the American victory. It was nothing like his experience in August 1997: "To stand in Red Square, Moscow, with the Stanley Cup in your hands, and the Russian names engraved on this great trophy; you want to talk about miracle, that's a Miracle."[3]

Fetisov's path began at the Central Army club hockey school for youth. He pursued a playing style that led many to compare him with Bobby Orr. At 6'1", 220 pounds he had the thick thighs and butt often linked to a powerful skating engine. As a twenty-year-old at the 1978 World Championships he was voted best defenseman. His coach, Tikhonov, included Fetisov among his top unit, called the "Green Five" for the color of their practice sweaters. With Alexei Kasatonov on the other point and a forward line of Sergei Makarov, Igor Larionov, and Vladimir Krutov, they seemed unstoppable.[4]

They were also aware of the westward flow of European players. Fetisov wanted his chance; so did Larionov. By several accounts, they were promised their freedom if the USSR won gold at Calgary. After the victory, however, Tikhonov reneged; the Motherland needed them. That October, Larionov published a scathing article in the popular magazine *Ogonyok*, calling Tikhonov a tyrant who kept the team prisoners in the Archangelskoye "baza" (training camp) three hundred days a year between club and national-team schedules. "It's a wonder our wives manage to give birth," he complained. Tikhonov rebutted in *Sovetsky Sport*. There would be another Super Series in North America later that year. According to Fetisov, he was promised freedom after that: "You're going to finish the season in the NHL." As it happened, Central Army was hosted by the New Jersey Devils, who had drafted Fetisov. Why not defect? Impossible, said Fetisov. "I cannot run away from my country." Instead, he sat out the Soviet Championship League season in protest.[5]

State television carried pictures of Fetisov sitting in the stands while Central Army competed. Fittingly, in that year NHL games began to appear on Soviet television, financed, one authority explained, "by the sale of commercial time to foreign firms interested in the Soviet market. Six minutes of commercials were shown during a one-hour program of taped highlights." Fetisov and Tikhonov patched things up enough to allow his participation on the national team at the 1989 World Championships. And then the logjam broke. Young Soviet star Alexander Mogilny defected from Stockholm and surfaced with the Buffalo Sabres, where he lashed out: "Here people enjoy life. Everyone has their own home, their own cars. . . . Here people live for themselves. And there, I lived like a homeless dog." Finally, the economics of perestroika and the reduction of state subsidies forced the hand of Soviet hockey. *Krylia sovetov*, a trade-union club, sold Calgary its rights to Sergei Priakhin. And Fetisov finally got his freedom. Soccer and hockey players also won the right to transfer between teams in the domestic leagues. Was there a more appropriate symbol of communism's collapse than the rise of free agency?[6]

Fetisov was traded in April 1995 from New Jersey to Detroit, where his career took its swing toward the Stanley Cup. Legendary coach Scotty Bowman had moved from Pittsburgh to Detroit in 1993, where he took over a team on the rise, in part because of young Russians, including Fedorov, Konstantinov, and Kozlov. By October 1995, Bowman had added Larionov (from San Jose) and Fetisov. Taking a page from Tarasov's books, he made them a unit, dubbed variously the "Russian Five" or "Red Army," which played with the offensive creativity familiar to fans of international hockey. Bowman recalled two decades later: "I just let them do what they wanted to do." In that first season, the Red Wings set a new record for team wins (62). The next season brought the Cup, Detroit's first since 1955. They won again in 1998, after which Fetisov left the ice for the bench, as an assistant coach with New Jersey.[7]

The NHL's Network Shakeup

August 1997 was not Slava's first trip home. Fetisov, Larionov, and others played briefly in the Russian League during a labor lockout that shortened the 1994–95 NHL season, as new NHL Commissioner Gary Bettman dueled over the league's economics with new NHL Players' Association executive director, Bob Goodenow. Both men were young lawyers (born in 1952) who reflected the mentality and calculus of corporate sports. Bettman was no "hockey guy." He was plucked from his position as senior vice president and general counsel for the National Basketball Association, where he learned his trade in the orbit of David Stern, professional sport's strongest commissioner at the time. NHL owners were tired of John Ziegler and his short-lived successor, Gil Stein. Salaries more than doubled after 1990 to an average of $572,000. Owners wanted to stem that tide, and Bettman had experience with salary caps. Goodenow was a Michigan native with a distinguished playing career at Harvard. He moved into the agency business in the 1980s and in 1991 negotiated a contract for Brett Hull that blew open salary doors across the league. Goodenow replaced the disgraced Alan Eagleson in January 1992, promising to get tough in ongoing collective bargaining. There was no breakthrough, and on April 1 the players voted to strike. It was no fool's joke, especially for the owners who had already paid most of the players' salaries for the year and who depended on playoff money for their own profits. The league settled with a one-year deal, but it only moved the showdown to September 1994, when a lockout resulted in no NHL hockey until January 1995. There was nothing new about labor strife in North American professional sports. But here were two Americans—one of them a basketball guy—squaring off in a war of words over Canada's game.[8]

After the Calgary Olympics, as the NHL became the center of a global hockey system, all of its once-internal eruptions had ripple effects. By the early 1990s, more than 10 percent of players on NHL rosters were European. An NHL lockout prompted some of them, like Fetisov, to play in their home leagues. Fedorov and Jari Kurri joined Wayne Gretzky and his barnstorming team, the "Ninety Nine All-Stars," which in December 1994 played seven games across Finland, Sweden, Norway, and Germany. European fans anticipated watching more NHL hockey that season after the NHL signed a distribution deal with ESPN International to show two or three games per week, either live or tape-delayed, in seventy-seven countries. Wayne Gretzky was a live appetizer.[9]

Player-owner sparring continued for another decade, until a bigger showdown and a full-season lockout in 2004–05. This one exposed rifts and weaknesses within the union, which settled for a salary cap that most pundits declared a clear victory for Bettman and the owners. Goodenow (who had always opposed a cap) was the fall guy, later squeezed to an abrupt resignation because he could not hold player factions together. On February 17, 2005, the day after Bettman announced the season's cancellation, the *Boston Globe* included rueful stories with headlines like "Stalemate Turns Off Fans" and "Greats Could Be Goners." Writer Kevin Paul Dupont suggested that only stupidity or greed could explain the union's refusal to accept a "reasonable" cap of $42.5 million in aggregate compensation per team (the final cap was $39 million per team and $7.8 million per player). "At last count about 60 percent of the rank and file were playing in Europe." A sidebar listed the whereabouts of fifteen Bruins. Ten were in Europe, scattered to England (two), Russia (two), Finland (two), Czech Republic (two), Sweden, and Switzerland. Worse yet were the slugs who had grabbed jobs "on this side of the Atlantic, muscling minor leaguers and even minor minor leaguers out of jobs." Solidarity had its limits.[10]

Pessimists worried. But those who felt the 2004–05 lockout would kill the league were in for a surprise. The 2005–06 season saw an aggregate attendance increase of 2.4 percent, to an average of 16,955 per game. Thirteen teams enjoyed near-full capacity in their arenas, and the league averaged over 90 percent capacity. Attendance levels held up the following season. Improved revenues meant a salary-cap increase. Corporate hockey was thriving. Bettman grew his staff from fifty to several hundred, with the main office in New York and a satellite in Toronto. By 2013 his employees topped 450. They all kept their focus on solidifying a wide North American "footprint" anchored by NHL teams in major markets, promoted by eager broadcast partners and a robust presence on internet and digital platforms, and with strong synergies with corporate sponsors and governing bodies like USA Hockey and Hockey Canada.[11]

To be sure, there were franchise struggles at every professional level, most notably in Phoenix, where the NHL Coyotes were in bankruptcy by 2009. A top trade magazine concluded: "Just how bright hockey's future will be in the Sun Belt remains unknown. To date, it has been successful in some markets but unsuccessful in others." On balance, however, statistics suggest that there were robust returns for the NHL's American strategy. A Harris Interactive Poll, begun in 1985, tracked sports popularity among American adults. In the inaugural year, 2 percent of respondents said hockey was their "favorite" sport. By 2005 that number jumped to 5 percent and held between 4 percent and 5 percent through 2010. By this measure, hockey was as popular as basketball. And the NHL was a key driver from both the top and the bottom. According to one USA Hockey account, NHL expansion "helped spawn youth programs" in associated areas. After five southern franchise launches, regional district player registrations rose from 6,718 in 1991–92 to 39,807 in 2009–10—a 492.5 percent spike. The Rocky Mountain District went up 276 percent after new teams arrived in Dallas, Phoenix, and Colorado.[12]

The Global Force Field

The NHL's international force field steadily expanded. By 2002 the league was televising five to seven games per week, plus the All-Star Game and the playoffs, to some 260 million households across 180 countries. The following year, distribution grew to 217 countries. The golden road for more and more players led to the NHL. A 2004 *Sports Illustrated* article offered statistics: "Twenty years ago, 8.7% of NHL players were born outside North America. Today that figure is 32.4%. Of the league's top 15 goal scorers in 2003–04, seven were European." Aspirations had changed. A national team or an elite league was no longer enough. As eighteen-year-old Czech goalie Marek Schwarz put it, "You want to play against the best in the world. Everyone knows that is [the] NHL." And North American money talked. In 1990 top Soviet players Andrei Khomutov and Vyacheslav Bykov had rejected the NHL to play in Switzerland. By 2007, one expert explained, the higher NHL salaries meant that "general managers of teams in Sweden, Germany, Finland, and Switzerland are happy if they are able to attract interest from the top scorer of the American Hockey League's Calder Cup playoffs."[13]

In the years after Calgary, more players were moving in *all* directions—and not just during NHL lockouts. European governing bodies had concerns. In 2006 the IIHF complained that the NHL was drafting too many marginal players simply to stock their reservoir in the minor leagues or in major junior, to the disadvantage of the European clubs. Data collected since 1995 showed that of 621 Europeans drafted, 62.5 percent (388 players) were non-impact, marginal, or below average; 133 did not play one NHL game; and 286 (46.1 percent) had (as of September 25, 2006) returned to Europe without reaching four hundred NHL games.[14] Canadian "dual nationals" were hot commodities in Europe. They helped Great Britain make the IIHF A-level pool for the 1994 World Championships. They were more problematic to Germans who worried about the effects of "duals" on homegrown talent, especially in the face of declining results at world tournaments.[15]

In 1995 the European Court of Justice weighed in on a case brought by a Belgian football player Jean-Marc Bosman, who sought the freedom to switch leagues. The ruling in his favor blew up key components in the old system of national restrictions—in particular, quotas on foreigners from other EU countries. Switzerland, for instance, had banned all foreigners from its national leagues between 1959 and 1970.[16] The ruling contributed to a broader convergence. Leagues like the Deutsche Eishockey Liga and the British Superleague were becoming, as Finnish scholars noted, hotbeds of "North American" hockey, "not only the style of play but also the business and organizational models, rules and other influences." The key move was establishing an avowedly professional top tier. But there were other NHL-like facets to the change. By the early 1990s, several of Sweden's top teams in the Elite Series had agreements with clubs in lower divisions to create "farm" systems. And while most European leagues maintained the elevation/relegation system so familiar to football fans, the Finnish SM-liiga abandoned that automatic process in 2000, bringing the premier clubs more stability and control, just like the NHL.[17]

In the Soviet Union, restructuring came with a vengeance. Vast state assets in gas, minerals, oil, heavy industry, and more were transferred at "fire sale" prices into the hands of a few dozen cronies and apparatchiks who by 2004 controlled some 25 percent of Russia's domestic economy, about $110 billion worth. These "oligarchs" soon moved from controlling factories, refineries, and pipelines into hockey and other sports.[18] The old Soviet League imploded in 1992, becoming the International Hockey League, then the Russian Professional Hockey League (RHL), whose top tier was called the Superliga. Names mattered in a global market of players. Among other things, in the New Russia one could find NHL-like mogul owners, including Roman Abramovich, the oil oligarch whose Avangard Omsk team was among the long list of "industrial" hockey franchises that pried Moscow's Red Army, Dinamo, and Spartak clubs from their stranglehold on league titles.[19] Vladimir Putin rose to power in 2000, aided by a steady, global rise in the price of oil and gas. He promised a return to Russian greatness in all sectors of economy and culture, including hockey, a game he publicly supported as both player and überfan. In the next few years, the Superliga battled the NHL more publicly for players and recognition. Lokomotiv president Yuri Yakovlev told the *New York Times*, "Sooner or later, the National Hockey League is going to have to reckon with our league, because, despite everything, we are getting stronger, not only in terms of players but in terms of our legal and financial protections."[20]

In 2008 the Superliga was reconfigured and rebranded as the Kontinental Hockey League (KHL), directed by Gazprom oligarch Alexander Medvedev, whose club entry was SKA St. Petersburg. One story claimed that Putin, serving then as prime minister, "stated frankly that the league should be used as an instrument of foreign policy." The twenty-four-member clubs were almost all in the Russian Republic, but league officials projected an expansion "west into the European Union and east to China." By early in the 2011–12 season, when there were "only 18 Russians . . . listed on NHL rosters," the KHL claimed thirty-one North Americans, twenty-seven Finns, thirty-four Czechs, and twenty-six Slovaks. In a global marketplace, the tide of player migrations swung dramatically.[21]

The IIHF adapted to the times. In 1994, newly elected President René Fasel wrote in the federation yearbook: "For the future, a co-operation with the National Hockey League seems unavoidable because only this co-operation will ensure a quality improvement of the ice hockey world championship." He cautioned that "only joint efforts can make ice hockey even more attractive," which would require "strict adherence to the rules" to control "physical violence and aggression" and protect "players with high technical skills." Like Bettman and Goodenow, Fasel represented a new generation: born after World War II, ready to embrace new global realities and challenges. Over two decades, Fasel moved from Swiss league club player to international referee, Swiss federation president, and IIHF leader.[22]

Fasel and the IIHF were fluid and effectual in their strategies. In 1970 the total IIHF membership was twenty-one. By 2007 forty-six men's national teams vied for medals. There was more parity at the top. Between 1993 and 2003 six different countries won gold. And this built a bigger audience. In 2010 the IIHF announced that its championship in Germany reached 735 million viewers through "almost 190 broadcast partners in more than 100 territories."[23] In 1996 the federation launched the European Hockey League, a continental affair channeling football's "Champions League," in which

American Mark Mowers with HC Fribourg-Gottéron (Mowers Family Collection, photo by Cristophe Colliard)

twenty clubs from twelve countries were grouped into five divisions with double-round-robins yielding eight teams for playoffs, the inaugural one won by TPS Turku. Three years later, Fasel announced a new corporate partner and a new name: the Skoda Auto European Hockey League. Action shots in the league guidebook showed players wearing uniforms pasted with sponsor logos and marks—a babel of boodle.

A companion internet league promised "a new millennium of exciting hockey games," where fans could predict outcomes and win prizes (such as luggage) in return for giving up personal information. The EHL fizzled after four seasons, but this was high-tech, progressive strategy for "growing the game." So was growing the administrative structure, which Fasel moved from Vienna to Zurich. In 1986 the IIHF had only two full-time workers. By the new millennium there were sixteen, organized in six "departments": general secretariat, in-line, finance, sport, PR and marketing, and EHL. Along the way, the IIHF also signed with a European marketing giant, CWL Holding AG, to push its various sponsor concessions. This was the new world of corporate hockey.[24]

Corporate Games

Nagano in 1998 saw the first completely "open" (professional) Olympic hockey competition. Many fans in Canada and the United States felt the Olympics would at last provide a fair test for *their* teams, now stocked with NHL talent. They were surprised and chagrined when the medalists were the Czech Republic, Russia, and Finland. Salt Lake City in 2002 pleased them, with Canada and USA finishing first and second. But this made Torino (2006) a greater disappointment. Both of them went home without medals. The Americans in particular played without the spark that a world arena should inspire. Veteran writer Kevin Paul Dupont vented a common frustration: "They're no longer young men on a mission, playing for country, desperate to find a career path to the pros. Instead, they're two-week NHL loaners, most of them made-in-the-NHL millionaires." And there was no talk at all of national systems. Except for the Latvians and the Swiss, it was all NHL-style play, minus the hardest checks and the fights.[25]

On another level, it was not even NHL hockey. It was Nike Bauer hockey. The global giant now owned the rights to supply *all* the uniforms to *all* the men's and women's teams. Players may have had real passion for wearing their nations' distinctive colors, but they all wore the same swoosh. In late 1994, Nike had purchased Canadian equipment manufacturer Canstar (which owned the Bauer and CCM brands) for $535 million, providing a quick wedge into the American ice and roller hockey markets, at the time growing at rates of 29 percent and 43 percent, respectively. Nike then invested millions into a deal called "Nike/NHL Street," an effort to propel a half-million street hockey players onto roller blades and then onto ice skates. Nike brand skates came next, launched via player deals with the likes of Sergei Fedorov, Brian Leetch, Jeremy Roenick, and Cam Neely. There were figurative cracks in the strategy and literal cracks in the skate blades, but Nike kept on with an aggressive marketing forecheck. A deal with the IIHF was a no-brainer. Not to be outdone, Reebok in 2004 bought the already giant Hockey Company, which owned the CCM, Jofa, and Koho brands, and also had deals to supply apparel and equipment to the NHL, ECHL, AHL, and CHL. By 2008, Nike exhausted its hockey interests and sold its Bauer operation, fittingly, to a private Canadian investor.[26]

In the decades after Calgary, multinational corporations like Nike and CWL Holding AG were joined by a host of rivals—from the media, from marketing, from events—all looking to grow either horizontally (from one industry segment into another, as Nike did with hockey) or vertically (buying up or down the chain of supply-manufacture-distribution). Disney, not content with acquiring ABC and ESPN, next bought an NHL franchise and named it the Ducks, which resonated with a popular Disney movie about hockey. Media/marketing firms and corporate sponsors had always been strong partners with sports leagues, associations, and federations. But now they wanted their names out front. And sometimes that meant outright ownership.[27]

Nowhere was this clearer than in the new wave of rink building. Names like Montreal Forum, Boston Garden, and Chicago Stadium gave way to Molson Center, Fleet Center, and United Center. Why not? The corporate partners were footing much of the construction bill. Northern Ireland offers a case study. The Belfast Giants Ltd. were born in 1997 as a partnership between a Canadian named Bob Zeller and a London banker named Albert Maasland. Their first home game was in December 2000 in their new Odyssey Arena, a ten-thousand-seat facility built for sports, concerts, and other entertainment, and nestled amid a cinema, restaurants, shops, and technology buildings. The arena cost £92 million of both public and private money. Its name, however, linked it to a corporate parent, the Odyssey Trust, a charitable entity developed "to hold, manage, safeguard and develop the investment in the Odyssey Project for the benefit of all of the people of Northern Ireland." The arena was managed by SMG, an American firm hatched in 1996 by Philadelphia Flyers owner Ed Snider and cable giant Comcast. The Belfast Giants played in the Sekonda Superleague, which included teams from Sheffield, Nottingham, Cardiff, and London. Heavily stocked with Canadian players, the team over the years has included more homegrown talent. It is a prime representative of corporate hockey in the twenty-first century.[28]

In another symbol of the new calculus, Anschutz Entertainment Group (AEG) bought the Eisbären, an East Berlin team that had its roots in the Stasi, the ruthless secret police of the GDR. AEG was the same firm that owned the Los Angeles Lakers, LA's Staples Center, and other sports properties. Little could better dramatize changes in economic and sport systems over a few decades—from the socialist-worker model of sport governance to the new realities of international capital. The Eisbären purchase was part of a global strategy that included building new arenas. The old Stasi affiliate had fittingly played in the Wellblechpalast (the "Palace of Corrugated Iron") located in the same East Berlin neighborhood that housed the Stasi prison. It was quite a spot for AEG's new fourteen-thousand-seat palace, O_2 World.[29]

College Conversions

North American college hockey evolved and prospered amid the changing, more competitive, and global landscape. The American Hockey Coaches Association (AHCA) reported that forty-seven Europeans played on NCAA rosters in 2004–05.[30] Shifting to bigger (NHL and AHL) venues moved the men's D-I tournament to a place as second-highest revenue-producer for *all* NCAA championships (behind men's basketball). The *NCAA News* reported that the 1997 tournament netted $749,517, "not including television rights or other sponsorship fees." The following year it earned $824,776. Better yet, everything was televised on either regional cable or ESPN. The NCAA even branded its finals as the "Frozen Four." Tickets got so hot that in 2004 the association shifted to online purchasing modeled after the men's basketball "Final Four." Individual programs followed a similar strategy of bigger, more lavish arenas, promoted with bigger media and marketing budgets.[31]

The objective was not simply to attract and please spectators. More fundamentally, it was to attract the best players. NCAA hockey was now part of a system that pointed clearly to the NHL, whose gravitational pull grew stronger by the year. More players left school early for pro contracts. The NHL was getting more aggressive in drafting young American players. Fifty were taken in the 1999 Entry Draft, second only to the 107 Canadians drafted.[32] Canadian Hockey League (Major Junior) teams were increasingly recruiting top American talent at ages as young as fourteen. In 1997 the AHCA developed a marketing brochure—*Check It Out*—filled with action photos and inserts of ex-collegians Brett Hull, Adam Oates, and Brian Leetch (wearing NHL All-Star jerseys) and strong pitches about NCAA hockey representing the "Best of Both Worlds." College recruiters had for years used this kind of language to persuade Canadian players to come south, but such an overt marketing brochure would have been unthinkable forty years before, especially to keep Americans home.[33]

In November 2009 the commissioners of the Division I conferences took things one step further. They hired Paul Kelly as executive director of a new entity, College Hockey Inc., whose objectives were to "raise the profile" of American college hockey, to "manage" relationships with "other hockey organizations," and to "aggressively identify and inform" young, elite players about the value of a college-first career. Kelly, whose two-year tenure as executive director of the NHLPA had just ended quickly and unhappily, noted an alarming statistic: "111 elite U.S. players [were] playing in the CHL," representing a greater than 25 percent increase over three years. Some of those players had been signed to junior (and by NCAA standards, professional) contracts at age fifteen. All were them were ineligible for NCAA hockey, some of whose players received free education on campuses that were also producing an average of six or seven players per NHL active roster, and also such prominent NHL coaches and executives as Lou Lamoriello, Brian Burke, George McPhee, and Dave Poile. College Hockey Inc. took up the cause for all the college coaches. Corporate hockey required new corporations.[34]

Canadian Interuniversity Sport (the CIAU's new name after 2001; now "U Sports") also became increasingly connected to the NHL system. But unlike the NCAA, Canadian universities provided a landing strip to players on the *downside* of their careers, *after* their junior careers and professional experiences had expired. The phenomenon was facilitated by CIS hockey's lack of age-limit restrictions. More important, the Major Junior Leagues began to offer their former players scholarship funds. In theory, a player who had begun his junior career at age sixteen and played out his eligibility could earn four-year funding to enroll at any Canadian (more recently, North American) school he chose.[35] The system was a counterweight to the claims of NCAA recruiters that playing Major Junior meant sacrificing a boy's education. Signing a pro contract nullified the commitment, and players were required to commence their studies no later than eighteen months after their junior careers had finished. In the 2009–10 season, one CHL press release reported that 1,040 players were awarded academic scholarships, with its teams contributing $4.5 million in funds.[36] CHL scholarships also populated CIS hockey with elite athletes (estimated to be 65 percent of rostered players in 2005; 90 percent in 2015) who had played seventy-game schedules under professional coaches. At the same time, the program *aged* university hockey: "It's not unusual to have 25- or 26-year-olds," CIS CEO Marg McGregor noted in 2010. University hockey, Allan Maki, a columnist for Toronto's *Globe and Mail* wrote in 2010, had become a "major-junior alumni league."[37]

Canadian university hockey was also for players whose big-league careers had concluded. It was possible for full-blown professionals to play in the university ranks, but only under certain conditions. For every pro season played after age twenty-one, a player sacrificed one year (out of a possible five years) of eligibility. For example, an NHLer who played two seasons in the bigs could return to CIS play at age twenty-three with three seasons of eligibility still ahead of him. One condition remained: reinstated players had to sit out one full season after their last pro game. Examples were rare. It was an exceptional player who could swallow his pride and exchange life in the big-league arenas for that in modest CIS venues. The university option appealed more to ex-*minor* leaguers; a great many others resorted to university hockey after a season or two in the AHL or somewhere else below that level. Hockey's Canadian branches were not at all far removed from one another, and it was no great feat to jump from one to another. "Going pro" (to Major Junior or the big leagues) was not a one-way street in Canada. The amateur-pro divide had been paper thin since 1936. By the late 1980s it began to vanish entirely.[38]

New Models of Grassroots Development

As College Hockey Inc. warned, parents and young players were making decisions with significant financial consequences about whether and where to sign up for a junior-level team. The most talented might opt for Major Juniors in Canada. But there were other junior tiers and leagues in Canada and America that promised more competition without sacrificing a possible NCAA scholarship. They seemed like the best of both worlds. In 2006 the *Portland Press Herald* ran a long story about the situation in Maine. In 1991 the NCAA powerhouse University of Maine Black Bears roster had thirteen players "who were products of prep school and high school programs, and only one from the U.S. junior." By 2006 that ratio had shifted to 3:7. Some top players were leaving their local Maine high-school program to train and play with the Portland Junior Pirates, live with an area family, and attend (but not play for) a nearby high school. The lure was more games, more practice, higher competition, and, ultimately, an NCAA scholarship. By 2006 the USA had seventeen junior leagues with teams ranging from the old New England and Midwest recruiting haunts to Fairbanks (Alaska), Odessa (Texas), Lincoln (Nebraska), and Affton (Missouri). All were private, for-profit operations. In 2006 the Portland Junior Pirates charged each player $5,500 for hockey expenses. The average cost for the Eastern Junior Hockey League was $3,500. High-school and college coaches appreciated the value of junior teams as a postgraduate experience, but they denounced aggressive marketing that prompted some players to abandon their high-school programs.[39]

In Canada, the issues went beyond money. In the late 1990s and the early 2000s, Canadians reeled with stories about the sexual exploitation of junior players by their coaches. Many in the media felt the whole system was exploiting boys, some of whom were drafted at age fourteen, "removed from their families . . . lavished with attention by local, and sometimes, national media, fawned over by adoring fans, and immersed in a male-dominated culture where older men control their lives." Well-known hockey writer Roy MacGregor called it "child labour." The full-season NHL lockout in 2004–05 boosted attendance, profits, and franchise values for Canada's junior teams. From the standpoint of supply and demand, Ottawa 67s owner Jeff Hunt hit the mark when he noted: "Junior hockey is everything, to a certain extent, that the NHL aspires to be." That same year, however, Hockey Canada announced the Canadian Development Model (CDM), which placed tighter age restrictions on junior hockey, largely with an eye on protecting the local midget-age programs. Under the CDM, only a few "exceptional" fifteen-year olds would be allowed on junior rosters, and the numbers of sixteen-year olds, Americans, and non–North Americans would be cut back.[40]

Whose Game?

By the 2000s, top-level leagues in North America and Europe were attracting and enlisting players and coaches from a wide international network.

But there were limits to achievements in diversity, especially for players of color. The NHL and other groups made efforts to provide ice time, equipment, coaching, and star-power support. In 1996 the NHL tracked down Willie O'Ree, who broke a color barrier when the Bruins called him up in 1958. Now, the league signed him to become a director of youth development for the NHL/USA Hockey Diversity Task Force. *Sports Illustrated* offered cause for optimism. In fall 1999 there were twenty black players among the NHL's 650 rostered positions. Across its first seven decades of its existence, the NHL had iced a cumulative total of eighteen. By 2007, O'Ree was promoting more than forty inner-city programs across the continent, including Ice Hockey in Harlem and the million-dollar Disney "GOALS" in Southern California. A *Boston Globe* story lauded O'Ree's passion but also quoted local directors who claimed the NHL was not fulfilling many promises and commitments. There was much work to be done. At a time when athletes of color were dominating football, baseball, and basketball—as competitors and fan idols—it was still unusual to see black or First Nations players on the ice.[41]

Challenges were just as difficult for disabled athletes. By most accounts, the game of sled (or sledge) hockey emerged in the 1960s from a Stockholm, Sweden, rehabilitation center, where enterprising athletes modified sleds and short poles to allow skilled movement and competition on a local lake. It is a game that requires not just arm strength to propel the sled by varied drives of the metal picks on the "butt end" of the short pole, but also the same levels of "soft" hands, strong wrists, balance, and "heads up" play of a Gretzky or Orr to gain speed, navigate, swirl, stickhandle, pass, and shoot with the "blade" end of the pole, all while avoiding hard checks—which are legal. By 1994, Great Britain, Canada, the United States, Estonia, and Japan joined Sweden and Norway with national teams at the Lillehammer Paralympic Winter Games.[42]

The speed, skill, and collisions drew larger, more rabid audiences in European, World, and Paralympic competitions. More than five thousand watched Norway edge Canada 2–0 in Nagano. In 2005, Hockey Canada stepped in with official recognition and support. Veteran player Todd Nicholson later recalled the immediate change from the days when players each paid $10,000 to $20,000 per season for ice time, equipment, and travel: "Until Hockey Canada took over, I could never figure out why I was never able to afford a house or buy things new." The payoff came quickly at Torino, where Canada won its first Paralympic Gold.[43]

It was still a struggle, however, at the grassroots level. Less than a year before the Vancouver 2010 Olympics, the president of the Colorado Sled Hockey Association lamented that facilities and retail outlets were not keeping up with the robust growth of participation and interest. "There's only one rink in the entire country" that offered sleds in its retail shop, he told a prominent sport industry magazine. "A lot of people don't want to deal with it." There were no companies making kits to quickly and effectively adapt player benches for the access and movement of sleds. "There's nothing published anywhere," he added, "no guidelines for rinks to follow."[44]

In the decades after Calgary, the most explosive hockey story belonged to girls and women. Players at all levels fought courageous battles, for ice, recognition, and support. Among American college women, that sometimes meant wielding a Title IX–brand stick. In 1979 Colgate University's women's club team began petitioning for varsity status. In 1988 they finally sued, arguing that Title IX policy interpretations compelled Colgate to give them the same hockey opportunities as the well-supported men's team. The case dragged through several appeals until Colgate finally settled in 1997.[45] The very next season saw the first truly US national championship, sponsored by the American Women's College Hockey Alliance, a partnership between USA Hockey, the ECAC, and Hockey East. New Hampshire skated away with the crown. A month earlier in Nagano, Japan, five Wildcat alums helped the USA to win the first Women's Olympic gold medal.[46]

It was also the first time that the United States beat Canada at the World Championship level. Olympic competition represented a decade of pressure from below and pragmatism from above. The swirl of action was personified by ten-year-old Samantha Holmes of Mississauga, Ontario, who attended the 1988 Winter Olympics in Calgary, where Canada failed to win a gold medal in any sport. Upon her return home, Holmes was moved to write a set of handwritten letters to government and sports officials, including Brian Mulroney (Canada's Prime Minister), Murray Costello (president of the Canadian Amateur Hockey Association), and Juan Antonio Samaranch (IOC president). In each letter, she pushed: "While I was at the Olympics, I saw six hockey games. I did not see any womans hockey teams. When I get older I want to be able to compete in hockey with other countries from all over the world. . . . Will I have that chance? . . . I don't want to give up my dreams." Samaranch promised only to pass her letter on "to our Sports Department." But the *Toronto Star* kept the story alive.[47]

Young activist Samantha Holmes (Samm Holmes Family Collection)

Girls and women at the grassroots were applying pressure. But powerful people were also advocating in high places, including three men who supported Samantha's goal. The first two were friends and counterpart presidents of amateur hockey in the United States and Canada: Walter Bush and Murray Costello. As Bush recalled in 2014, women deserved world-level competition, not only for equity's sake but also, given the slim hopes for U.S. men, because it "would be a great way for the U.S. to win a medal." Together, Bush and Costello pressed the issue. The IIHF had already sanctioned a European championship for 1989. Bush and Costello lobbied hard for a World Championship. After they showed their IIHF colleagues some videotape of women's games, one official accused them of running the tape on "fast forward." Undaunted, they convinced the federation to approve an official IIHF Championship for 1990 in Ottawa, a first step toward Olympic inclusion.[48]

Samantha Holmes was among those who attended the Ottawa tournament and celebrated Canada's gold medal. She sent her observations to her new pen pal, Brian McFarlane, a veteran *Hockey Night in Canada* broadcaster and author of dozens of hockey books. He spread the word about the young crusader who had written that "the games went down in history and women's hockey is here to stay." She was more than right. After continued lobbying from Bush, Costello, and others yielded another IIHF championship in 1992—in Finland, won again by Canada—the IOC voted to include women's hockey at the 1998 Nagano games. Pressure and pragmatism had paid off.[49]

In three years after Calgary, CAHA female memberships rose from roughly seven thousand to fourteen thousand. Those numbers certainly paled compared to the male CAHA membership of 424,785. But the key point lay in *trending*. The CAHA had actually lost nearly sixty thousand male members in the previous two years. One reason may be that Canada loved winners. If the men were falling short, women were grabbing gold. As one Toronto recreation director put it, "the success of our international teams has sent out a message that playing hockey is an acceptable thing for girls to do."[50] By the new millennium, CAHA's female registrations topped fifty-one thousand, and USA Hockey's reached 39,693. A semi-professional league, the National Women's Hockey League (NWHL) had four franchises around Toronto, two in Montreal, and one in Ottawa.[51]

For Samantha Holmes, there were always new hockey barriers to break. After starring at and graduating from New Hampshire, she moved home and played for the Brampton Thunder in the NWHL, then moved to Calgary, where she worked for the Flames, trained and played with the Canadian national team and the Calgary Oval X-Treme. She later owned, operated, and played for a team in the Western Women's Hockey League. When the WWHL folded, she added a Calgary team to the Canadian Women's Hockey League, serving as team general manager and later director of hockey operations for the league. Her career was both a catalyst for and a signal of the new corporatism that embraced the women's game and propelled it forward.

Speed Kills

In the thirty years following Calgary, hockey's principal attributes—speed, mayhem and science—were rebalanced, a correction to the brutal decades of the 1970s and 1980s. In this new equilibrium, speed was ascendant, violence repositioned; science, now *system*, reacted to the new order. The reasons for this transition included rules changes, the continued trans-atlantic convergence of elite players and coaches who elevated skill, and technology—innovations in equipment that transformed a sometimes-halting affair into a frenetic phenomenon.

Violence didn't go away in the 1990s and 2000s; it morphed. Debates over fighting continued, but they were eclipsed by concern over routine brutality. Unsavory episodes on the NHL stage echoed hockey's past: a pregame donnybrook in May 1987 between Philadelphia and Montreal; Red Wing Darren McCarty's March 1997 drubbing of Colorado's Claude Lemieux; Bruin Marty McSorley's vicious February 2000 slash to Canuck Donald Brashear's head; and Todd Bertuzzi's March 2004 mugging of Colorado forward Steve Moore from behind.[52] Though an "instigator rule" (1992) rolled out extra punishment for fight starters, fisticuffs remained a useful tool to police and market professional hockey.[53]

This culture spread beyond North American big leagues. Fighting and rough play stained the men's Olympic hockey tournament in Albertville.[54] In Europe, one brawl-filled January 2010 Czech Extraliga game between Sparta Prague and PSG Zlin resulted in 439 minutes in penalties and fourteen player ejections. In a bench-clearing fight in one 2011 exhibition game between Ukraine's Donbass Donetsk and Slovakia's HK Nitra, Donetsk goaltender Evgeny Tsaregorodtsev beat an opponent from behind with his stick.[55] And the culture held fast among North American amateurs. In a March 2008 brawl between the QMJHL Quebec Remparts and the Chicoutimi Saguenéens, Remparts goaltender Jonathan Roy skated 200 feet and attacked the opposing goalie.[56] Even more evocative was the case of Don Sanderson, a Whitby Dunlops player in Ontario's senior league who, having lost his helmet in a December 12, 2008, fight with a Brantford Blast player, tripped, hit his head on the ice and fell into a coma from which he never recovered.[57] In the aftermath, a *Maclean's* article wondered: "Can We Please Now Ban Fighting in Hockey?"[58]

More urgent, however, was a need to eliminate routine, clutch-and-grab tactics that slowed the game, stymied talented players, and made it hard to watch. It was time to let the skaters skate. Molson brewery-sponsored "Open Ice Hockey" summits gathered the world's hockey leaders to consider this challenge in 1999 and again in 2010. A volcano of ideas erupted: adopting Olympic-sized rinks; banning icing the puck during short-handed situations; enlarging space behind the net; shrinking the neutral zone; reintroducing "tag-up" offside; restricting goaltenders' ability to play the puck behind the net. A call to reduce the size of NHL goaltenders' equipment bore fruit in 2003, as did an appeal two years later to "remove" the red line (in place in the NHL since 1943) to open up the neutral zone to faster transitions. But by far the biggest change made was the crackdown, first attempted by the NHL in 1995, then reintroduced in 2002, on "obstruction interference"—the restraint of opponents who don't have the puck. NHL vice president Colin Campbell argued, "[We need to] give the gifted players more room."[59] Virtually all of these rule proposals privileged speed.

The greatest consequence of this push to unfetter the game involved strategy: how to combat speed. Everyone favored stamping out obstruction, but no one wanted a *total* free-for-all. In response, coaches followed two paths: first, slow down the fastest players with zone defenses; second, because more obstruction penalties were expected, bolster special-teams play. The first of these was epitomized in the abominable "Neutral-Zone Trap"—a defense-first counterattack strategy employing a single forechecker to channel an opponent's breakout pass along the sideboard, where defenders could outnumber the puckcarrier and create a turnover. Akin to the trap was the Left-Wing Lock, which used one hard-charging forward to flush the puck out from behind the net toward the forechecking team's left wing, stationed on the half-boards and ready to cause a turnover. In the defensive zone, rather than chase puckcarriers below the red line or at the blue line, big-league teams settled into "box-plus-one" coverage to keep the puck outside the slot and occupy shooting lanes with bodies and passing lanes with sticks. These tactics were hardly new; they were first devised by Czechoslovakian and Swedish national teams to combat the Red Army in the 1960s and 1970s.[60]

In smaller, North American rinks, the strategies were effective but stultifying. *Hockey Digest* summed up the New Jersey Devils Cup victories in 1995, 2000, and 2003: "Boring is Beautiful."[61] Equally successful were Scotty Bowman's Red Wings, who rode the Left-Wing Lock to Stanley Cup victories in 1997, 1998, and 2002.[62] Defense ruled. Low-scoring games predominated in the NHL's "Dead Puck" era, 1993–2005.

Pace quickened regardless. Technological innovation and new materials helped increase on-ice speed. One skate company, Bauer, helped fund research at McGill University's Ice Hockey Research Group to test mechanics and improve performance.[63] Tuuk skate bladeholders and boots made of molded plastic, synthetic leather, and ballistic nylon all buoyed skaters' feet.[64] Wooden sticks were replaced with lighter synthetic models—first aluminum, then graphite, carbon fiber, and wood-laminate composites. Players were convinced that the sticks allowed them to shoot harder and that made some of them trigger-happy. Devils goalie Martin Brodeur observed: "Look at Mats Sundin," who had adopted a Louisville composite. "He used to never take a shot beyond the circles . . . [Now] he's shooting from everywhere."[65]

Lightning pace increased the risk of injury. In 2002 one journalist called hockey "the most dangerous team sport in the world": thirty-seven thousand injuries per one million participants (compared to football's eighteen thousand or skiing/snowboarding's eleven thousand).[66] A 2002 study authored by Swiss orthopedic surgeon Nicola Biasca counted seventeen major spinal cord injuries in every year between 1982 and 1996.[67] Boston University's Travis Roy suffered paralysis when he slammed into the end boards head first during his very first shift as a Terrier.[68] As a result, the spotlight on danger intensified and made every attempt to tinker with hockey prone to second-guessing by safety advocates. When Hockey Canada followed the NHL in 2006 by moving the goal lines from 13 feet to 11 feet from the end boards, Dr. Charles Tator, renowned Canadian spinal-cord injury expert, predicted disaster: "If there is no turning room back there . . . we will see more broken necks."[69]

More and better equipment seemed a solution. Helmets, used for decades in Europe and youth hockey, became mandatory for incoming NHL players in 1979, but it took time; Craig MacTavish went bareheaded until he retired in 1997. Face protection had a more checkered history: AHAUS youth players wore full-face cages after 1976; NCAA players after 1980, as did all youth players on CAHA teams.[70] In 1981 the Canadian Hockey League's teams followed suit, but in the early 1990s they allowed players to wear visors instead, a response to the argument that cages encouraged players to carry their sticks high.[71] Mandatory in European hockey since the 1980s, visors came to the ECHL in 2003 and the AHL in 2006. By 2013 more than 70 percent of NHLers were wearing them. But face masks, hardened plastic shin pads, shoulder pads, and elbow pads all emboldened players to block more shots and to race for loose pucks against ever-faster skaters in close quarters.[72]

Hockey's directors responded by thickening the rulebook and promoting risk-reduction behaviors. The NHL introduced major penalties in 1991–92 for checking from behind, and other leagues followed suit. Equally effective was a broad public education campaign started in 1995 by a longtime Windsor (Ontario) Minor Hockey Association referee and coach Kevin Stubbington. His idea was simple: sew octagonal red STOP ("Safety Toward Other Players") patches on the backs of his players' team sweaters just below the neck. The idea caught on quickly and was adopted first by all youth teams in Ontario and, later, all of Hockey Canada, as well as by individual teams in the United States and Europe.[73] New rules and a new consciousness about player safety were important counters to the dangers of speed. This is hockey's new normal.

Vancouver 2010: The Natural Order Returns

Sunday, February 28. The Vancouver Olympic men's hockey final was set for 12:15 P.M. Pacific Time. Canada versus USA at the home of the NHL Canucks: General Motors Place, temporarily rechristened Canada Hockey Place. A victory would give the host country fourteen gold medals, a Winter Olympics record. National emotions were high. Undaunted, Father Glenn Dion told the *New York Times* he would *not* cancel the 12:30 P.M. Mass at Vancouver's Holy Rosary Cathedral. On the other hand, he *did* promise to shorten the 11:00 A.M. Mass, telling a packed sanctuary: "I'll try to get you out of here so you can get yourself in front of a TV." Sidney Crosby answered Rev. Dion's prayers "for the good fellows." His overtime goal gave Canada its second leg of a hockey trifecta. A few nights earlier the women had dispatched America, 2–0, for their gold. Two weeks later, the nation's sled hockey team would defend its Paralympic crown. All was well in Vancouver—in the stands that swayed with flags and on the streets that filled with "the painted, tear-streaked faces of fans" who seemed "desperate to share the experience."[74]

The gold- and silver-medal winners reflected the statistics in a 2010 IIHF survey. Sixty-two national federations reported an aggregate of some 1.5 million registered players. Canada and the United States each accounted for about a third of that total. Only twenty-eight countries reported more than one thousand registered players. Only eleven could boast a high (1:<1000)

TABLE 23.1. Hockey Hotbeds (by nation) in 2010.

Nation	Population	Total registered	Population per registrant	Total female	% registered female	Indoor rinks	Players per indoor rink
Austria	8,214,160	10,465	**784.92**	644	6	45	232.56
Canada	33,759,742	577,077	**58.50**	85,624	**15**	**2,475**	233.16
Czech Republic	10,201,707	99,462	**102.57**	2,089	2	**157**	633.52
Estonia	1,291,170	1,510	**855.08**	92	6	6	251.67
Finland	5,255,068	67,336	**78.04**	4,694	7	**240**	280.57
Latvia	2,789,132	4,691	**594.57**	79	2	17	275.94
Norway	4,676,305	6,256	**747.49**	482	8	40	156.40
Russia	139,390,205	53,280	2,616.18	308	1	**316**	168.61
Slovakia	5,470,306	8,671	**630.87**	288	3	45	192.69
Sweden	9,074,055	59,504	**152.49**	3,425	6	**327**	181.97
Switzerland	7,623,438	25,000	**304.94**	1,043	4	**156**	160.26
United States	310,232,863	474,592	**653.68**	61,612	**13**	**1,800**	263.66

Bolded emphasis added. Adapted from IIHF Survey of Players (2010); http://www.iihf.com/iihf-home/the-iihf/survey-of-players.html.

ratio of registered players to total population: Austria, Canada, Czech Republic, Estonia, Finland, Latvia, Norway, Slovakia, Sweden, Switzerland, and the United States (table 23.1). Canada was the hottest hockey hotbed with one registered player for every 58.5 people. Finland was next with a ratio of 1:78, followed by the Czech Republic (1:102.6) and Sweden (1:152.5). Russia—with a ratio of 1:2,616—continued to wring out its top talent from a relatively small slice of the population. Only two of the top eleven countries reported a female player population that was at least 10 percent of the national total: Canada and the United States. And only two countries reported more than one thousand indoor rinks: Canada and the United States. They seemed to be proving a notion made famous in an American baseball novel written by a Canadian, W. P. Kinsella: "Build it and they will come."

The Vancouver games had problems, to be sure, including warm weather that threw off outdoor schedules and raised safety concerns, especially after the death of a Georgian luger. Protesters took to Vancouver streets against "the Olympic industry," but they got little traction: the *Vancouver Sun* scoffed at the "black-clad anarchists." Pride swelled in most Canadians. One Toronto-based institute reported that a "majority of respondents" to a "mid-Games poll" felt the 2010 Olympics were a "more defining national moment" than even the 1972 Summit Series. Those feelings were not diminished when the sled team lost to Japan in the medal round, opening the way for American gold. Hockey Canada's director of national teams explained paradoxical feelings: "It's odd, but the fact that people are upset, maybe that's a good thing. It means people care. At the end of the day, that's what you want. For any sport." There was solace and pride in the widespread support for Paralympic athletes.[75]

A few shadows lingered over Olympic hockey's future. IOC president Jacques Rogge complained about two-nation dominance in the women's competition. Canada and the United States had blown out all other rivals by aggregate goal differentials of 46–2 and 40–2. "There is a discrepancy there," said Rogge. The IIHF pointed out similar scores for men's hockey at Antwerp in 1920, but Rogge's problem was in the trend. North American victories in 2010 were double the margins at Nagano in 1998. "I would personally give them more time to grow, but there must be a period of improvement. We cannot continue without improvement." The IOC had just dropped softball (and baseball) from its roster. Would women's hockey be next?[76]

The NHL was not sanguine about its partnership. More than half of the 276 men were league property. Closing down for two and a half weeks in midseason was no small sacrifice, especially when the NHL gave up all control for no monetary return. At a joint pretournament media event with the IIHF's René Fasel, Commissioner Gary Bettman dryly noted that it was "all good" if "you look at these Games from 30,000 feet." On the other hand, "you do have to take a step back at ground level and look at the impact on our season." Brian Burke was general manager of the American team. He had a long résumé as a player, coach, and executive in the NHL. He was aggressive in siding with Bettman, who was criticized widely as a scold, looking only to leverage the next set-to with the NHLPA. "From a business perspective," Burke warned, "it does not make sense."[77]

Plenty of businesses held another view. In the age of corporate hockey, it was fitting that companies like the Royal Bank of Canada, Rona Inc., Hudson's Bay Co., Samsung Electronics Canada, General Mills Canada, and Bell Canada were prominent "partners" at Vancouver—linked via ads, promotions, and events with the games, the teams, and individual athletes like Jen Botterill, Hayley Wickenheiser, and Jarome Iginla. Global giants Coca-Cola and McDonald's Corp. had their usual big Olympic footprint. As one ad executive explained to Toronto's *Globe and Mail*, it was crucial to "weave yourself into the fabric of sport."[78]

The fabric of Slava Fetisov's Big Red machine was frayed. Russia finished fifth, a performance that included a 7–3 drubbing from Canada. It was the worst-ever performance for Russia's winter teams in general. An American foreign correspondent sent remarks from Moscow. One mother said her son's hockey teammate was "so disappointed" that he "was surgically removing a tattoo of the Russian flag." There was nostalgia for the old Soviet machine. President Dmitry Medvedev (by all accounts a proxy for Vladimir Putin, who was constitutionally forced to step aside for a term) insisted that national investment in sports was "unprecedentedly high." The problem was structural. Russia had "lost the old Soviet school . . . and we haven't created our own." Top sports ministers were held responsible and forced to resign. Three-time gold-medal champion figure skater Irina Rodnina had moved to the United States in 1990 to pursue a coaching career. She blasted the laziness and corruption back home. "They have no more fear," she stressed. Openness and freedom were not working so well for Russian sports.[79]

For North American hockey, 2010 signaled a return to the natural order of things. Much had happened in the ninety years since Antwerp, where the Montreal game secured Europe's embrace, where Canadians and Americans wowed the crowds with their sparkling play and fancy equipment. Montreal hockey was no longer Canada's game. Canadians had shared their creation with a host of other countries and had lost their once-monopolistic control of rules to a handful of other governing bodies located elsewhere. Canada had, in the course of those decades, mixed dominating wins with humiliating defeats on international ice. The center of its "national" professional league had moved to New York. And, for a time, the game's most innovative coaching seemed to move from Europe west. Yet for all this, Vancouver proved a showcase for Canada and America. Russian legend Slava Fetisov had the final, ironic word. The Russians "weren't ready," he said in one television interview. In the last, thrilling game, Canada and the United States "showed the hockey of the future: fast, dynamic, and extremely skillful." And ultimately, Canada had the "speed, skills, and fury" necessary to win. Modest and gracious, Fetisov was channeling his best Tarasov. It was no longer an old form of collective hockey that earned his respect. He had seen the game change over four decades. He was excited about the future.[80]

EPILOGUE

Back to the Future?

In fall 2012, a funny thing happened to the start of the National Hockey League's ninety-sixth season of operation. It didn't. Negotiations to renew the collective-bargaining agreement with the players union stalled, so the twenty-nine franchise owners imposed a lockout. It was the third since 1993 for Commissioner Gary Bettman. The league wanted a reduction in players' share of hockey-related revenues, a ten-year minimum of service before unrestricted free agency, a five-year limit on players' contracts, elimination of salary arbitration, and other measures. The NHLPA balked, taking the NHL to Canadian provincial courts in Quebec and Alberta to contest (unsuccessfully) the lockout's legality. After three months of harsh words and schedule cancellations, the groups reached a tentative agreement on January 6, 2013, for a ten-year deal. Scores of top players scrambled back from Europe, where they had transformed—however briefly—rosters in Russia's KHL, the Swiss National League A, the Czech and Slovak Extraligas, and the Finnish SM-liiga, among other elite leagues. The NHL worked to salvage something, cobbling together an abridged schedule of forty-eight games. The playoffs for the vaunted Stanley Cup, the league's signature spring showcase and cash cow, were *not* abridged.

Both the league and the players' association promised a new partnership. There was optimism. And yet, for three months the lockout shook a global sport, exposing its structure and meaning. Historians who study the effects of earthquakes, famines, hurricanes, and other "dreadful visitations" know this well: a social organism's parts are never laid bare more clearly than when catastrophe strikes. The lockout highlighted a series of themes and questions that continue to characterize the sport since the

Vancouver Games of 2010. When NHL games stopped in October 2012, players, coaches, entrepreneurs, media commentators, fans, and historians asked together: So, now what? The variety of answers to that question was telling.[1]

We have argued that hockey's global history can best be understood as having unfolded in four great periods, and that those periods were held together by a pendular swing. From a diffuse variety of stick-and-ball games played on ice before the 1870s came successive eras of *convergence* (1875–1920), *divergence* (1920–72), and *convergence* (1972–2010)—in styles of play, purpose, and organization. So, now what? Does our model provide any guidance for the new era we now inhabit? Historians, like economists, are notoriously bad at predictions, but that fact won't stop us.

From our view, "high atop the gondola," as Foster Hewitt said from Maple Leaf Gardens on countless Saturday nights, the 2012 lockout illuminated five important areas of change and continuity, areas that both echo and challenge earlier trends. These five are corporatism, diversity, Canada's hockey identity, play on the ice, and globalism versus nationalism. In the future, will these themes and practices experience convergence or divergence? Will they have a centrifugal or centripetal inclination? Or both?

First, we see no change in the global swell of corporate hockey: the movement of grassroots and youth sports toward highly structured, adult-dominated programs and leagues; the willingness to embrace business partners who underwrite costs in return for the chance to market their own products through affiliations with teams, players, arenas, or events; and the decisions of players, coaches, and promoters at all levels that encourage tighter and tighter linkage, formal or informal, to a small system of governing bodies, leagues, teams, and associations run by a burgeoning cast of managers and marketers, and swirling more clearly around the NHL.

This integration is the sum total of countless human decisions, some of which stem from the expansion of new technologies—in equipment, in digital connectedness, in instruction—which generate new dependencies. Indoor rink building, for instance, is still essential to player development. Bigger and better rinks require deeper commitments to corporate organization and support. But factors like technology are never ends in themselves. Humans make decisions for complex reasons. In the case of sport, we can never forget that the objective is to win: for personal satisfaction or glory, for financial gain, for national pride. A corporate model may well appear to be a more efficient and nimbler apparatus in the pursuit of victory. In

North America and Europe, this means drifting further away from older models of player development, especially for teenagers. Long-established community, school, and club programs are increasingly challenged by junior and academy teams, run as businesses with associated costs and a focus on revenue streams, but always with a powerful siren song: you too can be a star (or a proud hockey parent).

Corporate hockey has certainly elevated the quality of play and will continue to do so. Players and parents are opting for the new model, but not without regrets. A 2016 TD Ameritrade survey of one thousand parents with children in elite sports clubs and programs found most families paying between $100 and $499 per month. Twenty percent paid more than $1,000 per month. One Phoenix father said he was "spending about $5,000 a season" to support his fifteen-year-old son's hockey dreams—by suspending his contributions to a retirement account and building up his credit-card debt. He admitted to relief when his son was cut from an elite travel team: "I was kind of dreading the upcoming season, knowing I'd go deeper in the hole."[2]

And there is evidence of local resistance to the global, corporatizing trend. Boston's Beanpot Tournament, for example, grows even stronger without corporate branding. To be sure, the tournament's venue changed from the Boston Garden to the Fleet Center to the TD Bank Garden. The players are now older, products of junior or national development programs (rather than just high school or prep school). And many fans (as one coach said) "just want to say they went to the Beanpot." But the event holds one firm line, articulated by Bill Cleary, a Beanpot fixture over many years as a player, referee, coach, athletic director, and fan. Cleary and his colleagues have never sold the event's name. "We don't have to be called the 'Tostitos Beanpot,'" no matter how much money they leave on the table.[3]

Recognition of high costs and high risks—in time, money, and emotion—along with frustrations about the "corporate suits" who seem to run (and ruin) everything, spawns widespread nostalgia for some purer, more authentic hockey experience. Don Cherry's popularity, "retro" sweaters, memorabilia auctions, and eBay frenzies over the "oldest" stick are all supported by nostalgia that we expect will continue. Of course, the contradiction is that many experiences of hockey "as it was meant to be" are products of corporate structure. This includes "Winter Classic" or "Centennial Classic" matches at huge outdoor venues like Ann Arbor's Michigan Stadium or Toronto's BMO Field. There is nothing new about playing in a famous venue not designed for hockey. Harvard did it in 1910. The Detroit Red Wings did it against the Marquette (Michigan) Prison "Pirates" in 1954. European clubs played in football stadiums before and after World War II, including the IIHF's 1957 title match in Lenin Stadium. Recent efforts, however, escalate a paradox. Thousands of shivering fans attend games where they can barely see the puck, played on NHL-quality surfaces requiring what a league ice-crew chief called "hundreds of workers and thousands of man-hours."[4]

Pond hockey tournaments are another example of this yearning for some notion of a purer past, pursued in paradox through modern corporate and commercial means: sponsorships, social media, entry fees, official host hotels, and spectator accommodations. But none of that seems to matter in places like Plaster Rock, New Brunswick, home of the World Pond Hockey Championship, or Minneapolis, home of the Labatt Blue U.S. Pond Hockey Championships, as long as the players paying the entry fees fulfill their quest for a piece of freedom or authenticity. For the players, it is (as the U.S. website calls it, with no apparent sense of irony) "Hockey. The Way Nature Intended."[5]

Hockey rinks and hockey culture—on ponds, in mammoth stadiums, in small-town arenas—can build community, something that scholars like Harvard sociologist Robert Putnam call social capital: "connections among individuals . . . social networks and the norms of reciprocity and trustworthiness that arise from them." Such networks and norms can *bond* people of similar backgrounds or *bridge* differences between groups, or sometimes both. In either case, dominant, national cultures will influence whether and to what extent the ice will be offered to minority groups. Entrepreneurs will continue to cultivate and promote hockey in nontraditional places and among nontraditional (to hockey) people, continuing a longstanding mantra about "can't-miss" success as soon as the Zamboni finishes its first coat of shiny, artificial ice in a new, indoor arena. Internationally, the sport continues to set down new roots. Between 2010 and 2015, China tripled its indoor rinks and doubled its registered players. Hong Kong's registered rosters expanded tenfold. India grew rinks at that same pace and tripled registrations. Turkey, Mexico, and South Korea increased indoor ice and participation.[6]

Opportunities for females, for people of color, for LGBTQ people, and for the disabled will continue to expand through player pressure and administrative pragmatism. Progress will require a mix of optimism and tenacity. In March 2017, for instance, the American women's national team went toe to toe with USA Hockey, announcing a boycott of the impending IIHF World Championship unless they received higher stipends and prize money, better insurance and travel arrangements, and greater commitments to grassroots training for girls, among other things. It was a hard shift. By some accounts the IIHF "was pushing U.S.A. Hockey to find replacement players to field a new team in case the boycott continued." Over a two-week period, however, the players stood their ground, won widespread public support, and a better deal. There is much still to be done. The number of registered female players in IIHF affiliates increased more than 10 percent between 2010 and 2015. Alas, that number is just about half the overall growth rate of registered players. So females by one measure are actually losing ground. But aggregate numbers never tell the whole story.[7]

Kelley Steadman's journey since 2010 reveals the qualitative differences unfolding for women who want to follow their hockey dreams. A Plattsburgh, New York, native, Steadman played on youth teams near home, then in September 2005 enrolled at Lake Placid's Northwood School, a hockey incubator since the 1932 Olympics. Her hard work earned her a scholarship at Mercyhurst University. After graduating in 2012 she played for the Boston Blades in the Canadian Women's Hockey League and also played (and won two IIHF gold medals) with the US national team. She was a controversial, late cut in the lead-up to Sochi. But in fall 2013 she had an option—the Russian league—where in fact she earned more money than she would have made as an Olympian. Internet-savvy, she published a blog, which documented her impressions as an athlete *errant*: "Sometimes I have to pinch myself because I can't believe I'm so far from home, seeing a completely different part of the world and being able to play hockey." In fall 2014 she joined the Robert Morris University women's program as a graduate assistant and director of hockey operations. She also landed a spot on the Buffalo Beauts of the new National Women's Hockey League, a rival to the CWHL. In January 2016 she was voted MVP of the first NWHL All-Star game. The boundaries will keep opening for players like Kelley Steadman, but it won't be easy. The very top players earn between $25,000 and $50,000 in compensation. Even as they plan expansion—the CWHL announced the addition of China's Kunlun Red Star for 2017–18—the leagues struggle financially, leading one North American writer to quip over "the alphabet soup of defunct women's pro leagues: the WBL, ABL, WBA, WUSA, WPS,

COWHL." But we remember a similar acronymic jumble in men's hockey about a century ago.[8]

Diversity will expand in other ways. Sledge hockey will continue its slow but steady growth. As USA Hockey's executive director Dave Ogrean noted in December 2015, the crucial lever will be "the force of will of a person or group of people" to get things "off the ground." For its part, USA Hockey found a corporate partner in Labatt USA, which will help new programs with the costs of ice time, uniforms, and equipment. Overall interest rose during the Sochi Olympics and the US team's run to gold, which NBC broadcast live. Media exposure will also continue to boost connectivity among Canada's Sikh community, who, in the "tens of thousands," watch *Hockey Night in Canada*'s broadcasts in Punjabi on Saturday nights, begun "as an experiment during the 2008 playoffs." Hockey knowledge has not only bound Sikh families together, it has made them feel more Canadian, more "a part" of workplace "water-cooler conversations—and even hockey betting pools."[9]

Already, gay hockey leagues in Toronto, Ottawa, Montreal, Vancouver, Chicago, New York, Boston, Los Angeles, and other places draw players to new sites, in new organizations, for games with new, inclusive meanings that help to combat the sport's lamentable image among some as bigoted and hypermasculine. Team GForce speaks to a broad audience: "The GForce team is comprised of gay male ice hockey players from across North America, many of whom have played in the junior or college ranks and a couple who have semi-professional experience. We all share a common goal: to play the game competitively as gay athletes with all the courage, strength, commitment, passion and heart of our straight opponents." While almost all affiliates in the Gay Hockey Alliance are North American, the Stockholm Snipers signal the emergence of a global movement.[10] In this way, LGBTQ teams and players are reflecting what First Nations teams and tournaments have meant to Indigenous Canadians for a long time: that hockey can be a place where minority communities collect and unite in struggle and in fun; that playing is a way of "re-purposing" mainstream culture and the national symbolism of Canada to meet their own needs.[11]

Will the sport retain its imprimatur as *Canadian* phenomenon? There is an old joke that Canada has, in fact, three national sports: lacrosse in summer, hockey in winter, and worrying about hockey year-round.[12] Since 2010, that assertion continues to resonate, despite national team successes at Vancouver and Sochi, and the junior men's team's World Championship gold-medal wins in 2015 and 2018. In one particular vein of newspaper and talk radio discussion, Canada's grip is perennially slipping. But the worry is not wholly irrational; some hard evidence exists to support the claim. Hockey Canada's male registrations have continued their pre-2010 decline, and one 2010 survey revealed that golf ranks highest among sports "most practised" by Canadians (hockey was second).[13] Speculation over the current dip repeats earlier generations' complaints: the game remains too dangerous and too expensive, it fails to adapt to a changing demography, and its hypercompetitiveness contributes to the pandemic overstructuring of children's play. As a result, questions remain about hockey's ability to be a symbolic national unifier in the country, a vehicle for the expression of national strength. In spring 2016 an inordinate amount of Canadian ink was spilled decrying the fact that none of Canada's seven NHL franchises made the playoffs and that fans in the sport's home country would have to endure eight weeks of watching *their* game on television broadcasts from rinks in Tampa, San Jose, Dallas, and Los Angeles. Toronto's *Globe and Mail* released a torrent of angst in a staccato string of articles that mixed elemental homerism with criticism of Canadian teams' coaching and organization, sympathy for the plight of players toiling in the country's nightly white-hot spotlights, and a familiar reprise of a national lament that Americanization continues to expropriate Canada's game.[14]

But for all of the handwringing, it is clear that Canada's special place in the social construction of hockey remains uncontested—at least in the short term. Today, in no other country does this sport continue to mean so much to so many—as a pastime, a rite of passage, a patriotic symbol, or as a metaphor for national life (as hackneyed as that sounds). It is no small statement that the Canadian Museum of History, the national repository of the country's heritage and identity, staged an eight-month exhibit in 2017 called "Hockey in Canada—More than Just a Game." The exhibit's description read: "For millions of Canadians, winter means hockey, and hockey means everything."[15] Outside of the country, Canadian hockey remains the "gold standard" to the rest of the world, and in many places Canada is the sport's "bête noire." In those places, Canadians' penchant for self-flagellation passes strange, and whatever cracks there are in the edifice seem comparatively minor. Will hockey continue to be as important to Canada as Canada is to hockey? That will depend on what future generations of Canadians need to extract from *their* game as touchstone of identity, or whether, in journalist and hockey writer Lawrence Martin's words, the country's emerging twenty-first-century "zeitgeist" will be "with other sports."[16]

Whatever its status as symbol, as national proxy, as national id,[17] it is on the ice where hockey is stripped of its baggage and takes a common form. What is happening now to the game on the ice, to the pattern of convergence that gripped tactics at elite levels, from 1988 to 2010? In those years, the three central elements were reshuffled and reordered, with speed given the dominant place, violence experiencing a decline in relative strategic importance, and the rise of tactical schemes implemented to neutralize speed. Since then, not much has changed. In the NHL, Los Angeles Kings' move toward a heavy, more physical lineup (echoing the style of the early 1980s) explained some of their playoff success in 2013 and 2014, but it is more likely that the recipe that propelled the Pittsburgh Penguins to the Stanley Cup in 2016 and 2017 will be the more lasting trend. "If there was one factor that overrode all others in the playoffs and the Stanley Cup final," *The Hockey News*' Ken Campbell wrote in mid-June 2016, "it was speed. Speed kills." More intimidating than physical size and force, one *Toronto Sun* writer noted, "is having players, like [Penguins Phil] Kessel and Carl Hagelin, fly down the wing at unhittable speeds who are scoring threats each and every time they step on the ice." In the words of Penguin general manager Jim Rutherford, "It's a better brand of hockey."[18] This is not news to Europeans, for whom speed has long been paramount and, on its larger rinks, will remain so. In response, the tacticians' challenge remains the same: how to slow down an always-accelerating game.

Beyond tactics, and below the elite levels, *form* is less and less rigidly defended. The arbiters of the game are more compromising about what exactly constitutes "hockey"; that it needn't be everywhere and always one game with one set of rules. This is a positive trend. The sport demands that variations be encouraged as permanently healthy alternatives to the version that has body checking, slapshots, and full-sized ice. Regarding the first two of these "essential" elements, youth administrators are discovering what female players and many "old-timer" recreational players have known for some time: one size doesn't fit all. In 2009, USA Hockey introduced its ambitious "American Development Model" for educating young players, which among other things, banned body checking until bantam age (thirteen years old). The move made sense north of the border too: Hockey Alberta and Hockey Nova Scotia followed by banning body checking in Peewee hockey (ages eleven and twelve), and in 2012, Hockey Canada spread that ban across the country. But that age-specific ban (targeting age groups at which growth rates among boys are so uneven) did not go far enough. In 2015–16, minor hockey organizations in hotbeds such as Winnipeg, Edmonton, and Toronto outlawed body checking for all players at the recreational level. In the Greater Toronto Hockey League, the largest minor hockey league in the world, the ban covers all players younger than eighteen, preserving hitting only for elite players on travel teams. "We think it's a good move," Hockey Manitoba director Peter Woods asserted. "It'll keep kids in hockey . . . we need to tailor our programs to fit the needs of our membership."[19] (Not all agree. The GTHL's ban vote passed 326–195, with a little less than 60 percent in favor.)

The same sort of definitional loosening concerns slapshots and rink size. A ban on the boomer has been in place in many adult rec tournaments for years on both sides of the border. But at youth levels there is no consensus: USA Hockey prohibits windups higher than the waist for all youth and girls age ten and younger (but allows it for Peewees, Bantams and Midgets).[20] In Canada, no blanket ban exists for any age group—the CAHA tried that in 1977 but soon reversed its course when the rule proved too hard to police consistently.[21] Today, a few individual local associations and coaches in Canada have instituted their own prohibitions because they feel slapshots stanch creativity.[22] And for the sport's youngest players, more and more associations now shrink the rink. A central staple of the USA Hockey's ADM (and in Hockey Canada's coach training) is four-on-four cross-ice competition: reconfiguring the playing surface to allow youth players to contest, pass, and shoot the puck more frequently.[23] With all of these changes, playing "hockey" today has assumed a degree of structural diversity that it hasn't had since its earliest years.

Finally, we expect to see continued, dynamic tension between global, national, and local elements of hockey culture. The 2015 IIHF Census of 2015 shows that since 2010 there has been solid growth in national membership (11 percent), total registered players (19.7 percent), registered females (10.5 percent), and indoor rinks (39.5 percent). The rates are particularly impressive when compared to the general world economy, which the World Trade Organization reported to have grown between 2010 and 2014 at an average rate of around 3 percent.[24] The expansion of infrastructure opened new, global opportunities for players like Kelley Steadman and for Auston Matthews, the NHL's No. 1 draft pick in 2016. Cast as the "next one," a long-awaited savior for the Toronto Maple Leafs, he first skated in his hometown of Phoenix, Arizona, on a tiny sheet of ice, playing small-sided games, European style, learning puck control and puck protection in crowded spaces. His most influential coach was a Ukrainian immigrant. Discovered at age fifteen, Matthews moved to the U.S. National Team Development program in Ann Arbor. But rather than play Canadian Major Junior or American NCAA, he opted for a big paycheck with the Swiss league, his last stop before the 2016 draft. Almost as nomadic was the path of Misha Song—from small rinks in a Beijing mall and an old war bunker, to youth hockey in Toronto, to schoolboy hockey at Lawrenceville (New Jersey) Academy and Philips Andover (Massachusetts) Academy, to a sixth-round 2016 draft selection by the New York Islanders. He is but one of a cohort of young Chinese players with a dream, and the parental wealth to support that dream, to hurdle national borders. Song and his friends have endured racial taunts and nagging suspicions that their American coaches gave fewer shifts than warranted to Asian players. One of them remarked: "At end of the day, we reached a consensus that we have to bear down, pay the price, because we're working our butts off for Chinese hockey, for our country. A little adversity is nothing." The NHL is their ultimate goal, but so, too, is representing China when Beijing hosts the 2022 Winter Olympics. A global network of corporate hockey will not diminish national pride and competition.[25]

In history, patterns and trends can change quickly. More than two decades ago, when the Berlin Wall and the Iron Curtain collapsed, scholars and pundits began to write—positively and negatively—about the apparent victory of global capitalism, the "end of history," a "flat" world, and the expansion of sameness. The disgruntled claimed that agencies like the World Bank, the World Trade Organization, and multinational corporations were squeezing cultural diversity. In the words of one (now defunct) protest organization: "Diversity is an enemy because it requires differentiated sales appeal. . . . Mass marketers prefer homogenized consumers." Sport sociologists and journalists debated this. Was global capitalism homogenizing sports? Would it lead to the death of the *local* ways that people played and organized their games? Would British snooker and trap ball die the death of the Maltese salamander and give way to NBA Europe? Despite abounding pessimism, many writers rejected simple dichotomies and suggested instead that sports are much more complex cultural products. One scholar offered a cogent range of possibilities for sports types:

local, national, global, international, glocal, and cosmopolitan.[26] The years since Vancouver have reduced the certainty and the worry about sameness. And we must consider that sports like hockey will again be instruments of divergence, as it was so clearly in the years from 1920 to 1972.[27]

We have argued that the NHL moved to a central, gravitational spot in the years between the Summit Series and Vancouver. This will continue. Confident that its "southern" strategy pays off, the league expanded with a hugely successful franchise in Las Vegas in 2017–18, much to the chagrin of boosters in Quebec City. And the league now sets its sights on Europe. Step 1 was the return of the World Cup of Hockey, a joint NHL-NHLPA venture that accompanied talk of training camps and regular-season games across the Pond. As league COO John Collins put it in March 2015: "There's . . . a real opportunity for the NHL to be a global brand and a global business. . . . I think the World Cup is the first big indicator of that new vision."[28] This vision did not include the Winter Olympics. In April 2017 the NHL ended negotiations with the IIHF over costs and media rights and announced its own boycott. No current NHL players skated at the 2018 games in Pyeongchang, South Korea. The NHL Players Association joined the line of outraged constituents: "N.H.L. players are patriotic and they do not take this lightly." Alex Ovechkin declared that he would represent Russia no matter what.[29] He didn't.

One way or another, the NHL will expand as a global brand, although not without serious challenge, especially from the KHL. While the KHL has dueled with the NHL over players since its 2008 birth, 2013 changed the storyline when the Helsinki-based Finnish league franchise Jokerit announced a deal to enter the KHL the following season. Until then, the KHL's footprint was restricted to Russia and the old Soviet bloc. It was now in the Eurozone. In 2016 the league expanded to China with Beijing's HC Kunlun Red Star, and it continues to explore the prospects of expansion into London.[30] Even as the KHL expanded its reach, it struggled with keeping its best players. In May 2015, Russian Federation Council senator Slava Fetisov reacted aggressively to a story that "40 players are leaving Russia to join North American leagues." He believed that his homeland still had the "most talented" players, "the ones who the people come to see." Like Columbus Blue Jackets phenom Artemi Panarin, however, they were "going to the NHL because we haven't spelled out the rules!" Slava had a rule in mind: no Russian could leave the KHL until he was twenty-eight years old. American writers noted the irony of Fetisov's stance on free agency given his own history of struggle in escaping Soviet shackles to reach the NHL.[31]

As the NHL and the KHL battle for global space, the IIHF and its national federations will counter maneuver, both in their actions and their language. In 2010 IIHF president René Fasel responded aggressively to the notion of NHL expansion into Europe: "I will fight like hell and not let anybody come from abroad." Such insularity may erode in the face of power and pragmatism. For instance, when faced with the prospect of losing a top franchise (Jokerit), Kalervo Kummola, former chairman of the Finnish Ice Hockey Federation, remarked that the result would be improvement in the Finnish national team. And Fasel himself was quoted with a similar response to HC Kunlun's deal with the KHL.[32] Divergence can coexist with convergence. For instance, the IIHF and the NCAA still maintain a firewall on fighting—the penalty still calls for automatic expulsion. We hope that doesn't change. But we also hope to see continued collaboration, such as the officiating seminars run jointly by the IIHF and NHL.[33]

Convergence and divergence, in tandem. That is what we see ahead. As one world historian wrote, "It is the complex interaction of these forces that needs to be considered if we are to make sense of the past and present." Both off and on the ice, the game and the structure become more corporate and more influenced by the NHL. But there is greater diversity in *who* plays hockey and *where* it is played. And it is also clear that convergence does not mean uniformity or loss of autonomy for the many local, national, and international organizations thriving in Dave Bidini's vast Tropic of Hockey. Roller hockey and bandy are alive and well. Every winter there is still black ice on frozen ponds that conjures visions of shinny as compelling as Arthur Farrell's in 1899: "What laughing, calling, cheering and chasing there was to be sure! With their bright eyes and rosy cheeks they dart now in one direction, now in another, till finally the vast struggling crowd surges toward the goals, surrounds them, and a fierce, lucky swipe knocks it through, while a hundred lusty voices cry their loudest: 'Game! Game!'" Happily, hockey is no longer restricted to "boys" and "men." The ice is more open, even if it is often surrounded by corporate signage.[34]

NOTES

Chapter 1. Searching for Hockey's History

1. David Bidini, *Tropic of Hockey: My Search for the Game in Unlikely Places* (Guilford, Conn.: Lyons, 2002), xviii.

2. Don Bell, "Hockey Night in Métabetchouan," in *Ice: New Writing on Hockey*, ed. Dale Jacobs (Edmonton: Spotted Crow, 1999), 33, 37.

3. Michael Farber, "Wild Times," *Sports Illustrated*, May 19, 2003, 42, 45.

4. Richard Gruneau and David Whitson, *Hockey Night in Canada: Sport, Identities and Cultural Politics* (Toronto: Garamond, 1993), 26.

5. Stephen Hardy, "Two-Way Hockey: Selling Canada's Game in North America, 1875–1935," in *Playing for Change: The Continuing Struggle for Sport and Recreation*, ed. Russell Field (Toronto: University of Toronto Press, 2015), 199–228.

6. Ken Dryden, *The Game: A Thoughtful and Provocative Look at a Life in Hockey* (Toronto: Macmillan of Canada, 1983), 231.

7. Jeff Klein, email communication to listserv of Society for International Hockey Research, August 16, 2005.

8. Morris Mott, "Flawed Games, Splendid Ceremonies: The Hockey Matches of the Winnipeg Vics, 1890–1903," *Prairie Forum* 10, no. 1 (1985): 178.

9. http://www.ballgame.org/main.asp; William Baker, *Sports in the Western World* (Urbana: University of Illinois Press, 1988); Robert W. Malcolmson, *Popular Recreations in English Society, 1700–1850* (Cambridge: Cambridge University Press, 1973).

10. Melvin Adelman, *A Sporting Time: New York City and the Rise of Modern Athletics, 1820–1870* (Urbana: University of Illinois Press, 1986); Richard Holt, *Sport and the British: A Modern History* (New York: Oxford University Press, 1989).

11. J. A. Mangan, ed., *The Games Ethic and Imperialism* (London: Cass, 1998); William J. Murray, *The World's Game: A History of Soccer* (Urbana: University of Illinois Press, 1996); Walter LaFeber, *Michael Jordan and the New Global Capitalism* (New York: Norton, 1999).

12. Benedict Anderson, *Imagined Communities*, rev. ed. (London: Verso, 1983, 1991), 84.

13. Joseph Strutt, *The Sports and Pastimes of the People of England* (London: Bensley, 1801); William Clarke, *Boy's Own Book: A Complete Encyclopedia of All Athletic, Scientific, Recreative, Outdoor, and Indoor Exercises and Diversions* (London: Vizetelly, Branston, 1828; Boston: Munroe and Francis, 1830); Jean Jules Jusserand, *Les Sports et jeux d'exercises dans l'ancienne France* (Paris: Plon-Nourrit, 1901).

14. Grant Jarvie, *Sport, Culture, and Society: An Introduction* (New York: Routledge, 2006), 91–129; C. A. Bayly, *The Birth of the Modern World, 1780–1914: Global Connection and Comparisons* (Oxford: Blackwell, 2004), 12–19.

15. Allen Guttmann, *Games and Empires: Modern Sports and Cultural Imperialism* (New York: Columbia University Press, 1994), 179; Dryden, *The Game*, 231.

16. Julie Stevens, "The Development of the Canadian Hockey System: A Process of Institutional Divergence and Convergence," in *Putting It on Ice: Vol. 2, Internationalizing "Canada's Game,"* ed. Colin D. Howell (Halifax: Gorsebrook, 2001), 53.

17. Allen Barra, "Canada Hits a Cold Spell," *Wall Street Journal*, May 17, 2002; Nancy Marrapese-Burrell, "Bruins Believe They Scored," *Boston Globe*, June 27, 2004; Rob Gloster, "Many NHL Players Head for Europe," *Boston Globe*, September 17, 2004; Michael Farber, "Tampa Bay to Tatarstan," *Sports Illustrated*, January 10, 2005, 58–64.

18. Samantha Holmes, letter to Stephen Hardy, August 12, 2003.

Chapter 2. Folk and Field Games

1. Foster Hewitt, *Down the Ice: Hockey Contacts and Reflections* (Toronto: Saunders, 1934), 1; Harold McNamara, "First Hockey Game in History, in 1837, Described by Local Man," *Montreal Gazette*, February 5, 1941; Harold McNamara, "Montreal Octogenarian Tells How Canadians Won 1837 Title," *Montreal Gazette*, February 6, 1941. Thanks to Michel Vigneault for providing copies of the original story.

2. Nancy Howell and Max Howell, *Sports and Games in Canadian Life: 1700 to the Present* (Toronto: Macmillan, 1969), 33–34.

3. J. W. "Bill" Fitsell, *Hockey's Captains, Colonels, and Kings* (Erin, Ontario: Boston Mills, 1987); Garth Vaughan, *The Puck Starts Here: The Origins of Canada's Great Winter Game Ice Hockey* (Fredericton, N.B.: Goose Lane, 1996).

4. *Ottawa Citizen*, August 17, 2006; *Backcheck: A Hockey Retrospective*, Library and Archives Canada, https://www.bac-lac.gc.ca.

5. "The Birthplace or Origin of Hockey," http://www.sihrhockey.org.

6. See Carl Giden, Patrick Houda, and Jean-Patrice Martel, *On the Origin of Hockey* (Stockholm: Hockey Origin, 2014); "Stick and Ball Game Timeline," http://www.sihrhockey.org/new/p_timeline.cfm.

7. Hewitt, *Down the Ice*, 1.

8. Giden, Houda, and Martel, *On the Origin of Hockey*; George Fosty and Darril

Fosty, *Splendid Is the Sun: The 5000 Year History of Hockey* (New York: Stryker-Indigo, 2003).

9. http://www.fih.ch/hockey-basics/history; and http://www.touregypt.net/historicalessays/ancsportsa1.htm.

10. http://ancientolympics.arts.kuleuven.be/eng/TC009EN.html; H. Gillmeister, "The Origin of European Ball Games: A Re-evaluation and Linguistic Analysis," *Stadion* 7 (1981): 19–51.

11. Allen Guttmann and L. Thompson, *Japanese Sports: A History* (Honolulu: University of Hawaii Press, 2001), 36–39.

12. Leah Niederstadt, "Of Kings and Cohorts: The Game of Genna in Ethiopian Popular Painting," *International Journal of the History of Sport* 19 (March 2002): 57–71; Robert W. Henderson, *Ball, Bat, and Bishop: The Origin of Ball Games* (New York: Rockport, 1947), 23, 32.

13. Nancy Struna, *People of Prowess: Sport, Leisure, and Labor in Early Anglo-America* (Urbana: University of Illinois Press, 1996), 40; John Arlott, *Oxford Companion to World Sports and Games* (London: Oxford University Press, 1975), 482; Morris Mott, "Games and Contests of the First Manitobans," in *Sports in Canada: Historical Readings*, ed. Morris Mott (Toronto: Copp, Clark, Pitman, 1989), 21; Ralph L. Beals and Pedro Carrasco, "Games of the Mountain Tarascans," *American Anthropologist*, new series, 46 (October–December 1944): 516–22.

14. Henderson, *Ball, Bat, and Bishop*; Heiner Gillmeister, "Golf on the Rhine: On the Origins of Golf, with Sidelights on Polo," *International Journal of the History of Sport* 19, no. 1 (2002): 1–30.

15. Art O'Maolfabhail, "Hurling: An Old Game in a New World," in *Sport in the Making of Celtic Cultures*, ed. Grant Jarvie (London: Leicester University Press, 1999), 148–65 and introduction ("Sport in the Making"), 1–11; Hugh Dan MacLennan, *Shinty* (Nairn: Balnain, 1993). Thanks to Grant Jarvie for sending these sources.

16. Gerald Redmond, *The Sporting Scots of Canada* (Rutherford, N.J.: Fairleigh Dickinson University Press, 1982), 266.

17. Alice Bertha Gomme, *The Traditional Games of England, Scotland, and Ireland, in 2 Volumes, [1894, 1898]* (repr., New York: Dover, 1964), 1:16.

18. *The Compact Edition of the Oxford English Dictionary* (New York: Oxford University Press, 1971), 1314.

19. *The Book of Games; or, A History of the Juvenile Sports Practiced at the Kingston Academy* (Philadelphia: Johnson and Warner, 1811), 13.

20. Nancy Struna, *People of Prowess*; Ronald A. Smith, *Sports and Freedom: The Rise of Big-Time College Athletics* (New York: Oxford University Press, 1988), 10; Henry Barnard, *Practical Illustrations of the Principles of School Architecture* (Hartford: Case, Tiffany, 1851), 165.

21. Jacob Abbot, *Caleb in Town: A Story for Children* (Boston: Crocker and Brewster, 1839), 37–38, 115, 122.

22. Nathaniel Beverley Tucker, *The Partisan Leader* (New York, 1836), qtd. in Michael Oriard, *Sporting with the Gods: The Rhetoric of Play and Game in American Culture* (New York: Cambridge University Press, 1991), 92.

23. "Winter Sports," *Journal of Health* 2, no. 9 (January 12, 1831): 131.

24. Brian Fagan, *The Little Ice Age: How Climate Made History, 1300–1850* (New York: Perseus, 2000).

25. William FitzStephen, *A Description of London*, transcription in Henry Thomas Riley, ed. *Liber Custumarum*, Rolls Series 2, no.12 (1860): 2–15, http://www.trytel.com/~tristan/towns/florilegium/introduction/intro01.html.

26. Breughel paintings in Kunsthistorisches Museum, Vienna; Musée des Beaux-Arts (Museum van Schone Kunsten), Brussels, Belgium. For Avercamp, van de Velde, and van der Neer, see WebMuseum, Paris: www.ibiblio.org/wm/paint/auth/avercamp; and Art Encyclopedia: www.artcyclopedia.com/artists. Toole, National Gallery of Art, https://www.nga.gov/Collection.

27. Horace M. Lippincott, *Early Philadelphia: Its People, Life, and Progress* (Philadelphia: Lippincott, 1917); Jennie Holliman, *American Sports, 1785–1835* (Durham, N.C.: Seeman, 1931), 95; John Adams qtd. in Struna, *People of Prowess*, 76.

28. Olaus Magnus, *Historia de gentibus septentrionalibus* (*Description of the northern peoples*) 1:25 Romæ 1555; 3 vols., trans. Peter Fisher and Humphrey Higgens, ed. Peter Foote, with annotation derived from the commentary by John Granlund (London: Hakluyt Society, 1996), 3:58.

29. Mike Speak, "The Emergence of Modern Sport, 960–1840," in *Sport and Physical Education in China*, ed. James Riordan and Robin Jones (New York: ISCPES, 1999), 61.

30. Luna Lambert, "The American Skating Mania," *Journal of American Culture* 1, no. 4 (1978): 691–92.

31. Freeling Diary, January 1843, Library and Archives Canada, http://www.bac-lac.gc.ca; Peter Lindsay, "A History of Sport in Canada, 1807–1867," PhD diss., University of Alberta, 1969, 44.

32. Tim Fashion, "Winter," *The Acadian / Literary Mirror* (January 1827); *Backcheck*; Society for International Hockey Research, "Report of the Sub-Committee Looking into Claim that Windsor, Nova Scotia Is the Birthplace of Hockey," *Hockey Research Journal* 6, no. 1 (Fall 2002): 1–14.

33. Vaughan, *Puck Starts Here*; "Cradle of Hockey," www.gameofhockey.com.

34. "Cradle of Hockey."

35. Fitsell, *Hockey's Captains, Colonels, and Kings*, 26–29.

36. Qtd. in *Brooklyn Eagle*, January 28, 1864.

37. For the St. Paul's story, see ch. 7 in this volume.

Chapter 3. The Montreal Birthing: 1875–77

1. *Gazette*, March 3 and 4, 1875. Our thanks to Michel Vigneault for these sources.

2. J. W. Fitsell, *Hockey's Captains, Colonels, and Kings* (Erin, Ontario: Boston Mills, 1987), 36.

3. Luna Lambert, "The American Skating Mania," *Journal of American Culture* 1, no. 4 (1978): 692; "Starr Mfg. Co.—Oldest Makers of Fine Skates," *Financial Post*, November 28, 1929; Melvin Adelman, *A Sporting Time: New York City and the Rise of Modern Athletics, 1820–70* (Urbana: University of Illinois Press, 1986), 257; Peter Lindsay, *A History of Sport in Canada, 1807–1867*, PhD diss., University of Alberta, 1969, 52.

4. George Beers, "Canada in Winter," *British American Magazine* 2 (1864): 176, qtd. in Lindsay, *A History of Sport in Canada, 7*, 50; Adelman, *Sporting Time*, 257.

5. http://en.wikipedia.org/wiki/Edinburgh_Skating_Club; Patrick Houda and Dr. Carl Giden, "Stick and Ball Game Timeline," pt. 7, "Stick and Ball Games on Ice—1861 to 1875," pp. 6, 23, Society for International Hockey Research (SIHR), http://www.sihrhockey.org; Alan Metcalfe, *Canada Learns to Play: The Emergence of Organized Sport, 1807–1914* (Toronto: McClelland and Stewart, 1987), 145; Lambert, "American Skating Mania," 684.

6. *Detroit Free Press*, September 29, 1860, January 27, 1861, and January 22, 1861; *Detroit Post*, December 11, 1867.

7. Alan Metcalfe, *Canada Learns to Play*, 145.

8. James Bird, *The Diagram: Containing Plans of Theatres and Other Places of Amusement in Boston* (Boston: Harper, 1869), 37; Lambert, "American Skating Mania," 685–86. Thanks to Paul DeLoca for sharing the Bird source from his manuscript on skating, "The Ice and the Eagle: Skating's Shift from Saint to Show and from Chaos to Science, 1380–1915."

9. C. A. Bayly, *The Birth of the Modern World, 1780–1914: Global Connection and Comparisons* (Oxford: Blackwell, 2004), 19; Don Morrow et al., *The Concise History of Sport in Canada* (Toronto: Oxford University Press, 1989), 1–5; Robert Lewis, *Manufacturing Montreal: The Making of an Industrial Landscape, 1850 to 1930* (Baltimore, Md.: Johns Hopkins University Press, 2000).

10. Morrow, et al., *Concise History of Sport in Canada*, 1–22.

11. "George Alfred Meagher," http://web.comhem.se/~u87152366/GeoMeagher Playerprofile.htm.

12. Fitsell, *Hockey's Captains, Colonels, and Kings*, 31–39; Earl Zukerman, "McGill University: The Missing Link to the Birthplace of Hockey," in *Total Hockey*, 2nd ed., ed. Dan Diamond et al. (Toronto: Sport Media, 2003), 16–19; E. M. Orlick, "McGill Contributions to the Origin of Ice Hockey," *McGill News* (Winter 1943): 13–16; Michel Vigneault, "The Origins of Hockey, Montreal 1875–1885," unpublished paper

presented at the annual meeting of North American Society for Sport History, Saskatoon, Saskatchewan, May 1994.

13. Maclennan, *Shinty*, 29–73.

14. Stephen Hardy, "Memory, Performance, and History: The Making of American Ice Hockey at St. Paul's School, 1860–1915," *International Journal of the History of Sport* 14, no. 1 (1997): 114; John Arlott, *Oxford Companion to World Sports and Games* (New York: Oxford University Press, 1975), 484.

15. "Hockey on Ice," *Montreal Gazette*, February 27, 1877; Fitsell, *Hockey's Captains, Colonels, and Kings*, 38–39; Zukerman, "Missing Link," 18.

16. "Hockey on Ice."

17. Fitsell, *Hockey's Captains, Colonels, and Kings*, 40.

18. Metcalfe, *Canada Learns to Play*, 48.

19. *The Compact Edition of the Oxford English Dictionary* (New York: Oxford University Press, 1971), 2788.

20. Walter Prichard Eaton, "Shinny," *Outing* 63 (December 1913): 289.

21. Arthur Farrell, *Hockey: Canada's Royal Game* (Montreal: Cornell, 1899), 26, https://www.bac-lac.gc.ca.

22. Metcalfe, *Canada Learns to Play*, 135–36; Morrow et al., *Concise History of Sport in Canada*, 11–12.

23. Ibid.

Chapter 4. Global Capitalism and the World of Sport: 1877–1920

1. Arthur Farrell, comp., *Spalding Athletic Library: Ice Hockey and Ice Polo Guide* (New York: American Sports, 1901), 76, https://archive.org/details/officialrules for06newy.

2. Ibid., 97; Peter Levine, *A. G. Spalding and the Rise of Baseball: The Promise of American Sport* (New York: Oxford University Press, 1985), 71–96.

3. Levine, *A. G. Spalding and the Rise of Baseball*, 7; Arthur Farrell, *Hockey: Canada's Royal Winter Game* (Montreal: Corneil, 1899); Michel Vigneault, "Arthur Farrell," *Dictionary of Canadian Biography*, vol. 13, 1901–1910 (Toronto: University of Toronto Press, 1994), 333–34.

4. Richard Gruneau, *Class, Sport, and Social Development* (1983, repr. Champaign, Ill.: Human Kinetics, 1999).

5. Jeffry Frieden, *Global Capitalism: Its Fall and Rise in the Twentieth Century* (New York: Norton, 2006), 16.

6. Frieden, *Global Capitalism*, 46; Kenneth Norrie and Douglas Owram, *A History of the Canadian Economy* (Toronto: Harcourt Brace Jovanovich, 1991).

7. J. M. Staudenmaier, "Rationality, Agency, Contingency: Recent Trends in the History of Technology," *Reviews in American History* 30 (2002): 168–81.

8. Stephen Hardy, "Sport in Urbanizing America," *Journal of Urban History* 23, no. 6 (September 1997): 675–708; Neil Tranter, *Sport, Economy and Society in Britain*

1750–1914 (Cambridge: Cambridge University Press, 1998); Frieden, *Global Capitalism*, 60, 63.

9. Tobias Stark, "Folkhemmet på is: Ishockey, modernisering och nationell identitet i Sverige 1920–1972" (The People's Home on Ice: Ice Hockey, Modernization and National Identity in Sweden 1920–1972), doctoral thesis, Linnéuniversitetet, 2010, OAI: DiVA.org:lnu-5606. Thanks to Professor Stark for sharing his insights here and elsewhere.

10. John Rickards Betts, "The Technological Revolution and the Rise of Sport, 1850–1900," *Mississippi Valley Historical Review* 40, 2 (1953): 231–56.

11. Michael Oriard, *Reading Football: How the Popular Press Created an American Spectacle* (Chapel Hill: University of North Carolina Press, 1995), 58, 64.

12. Joseph Schumpeter, *Business Cycles: A Theoretical, Historical, and Statistical Analysis of the Capitalist Process* (New York: McGraw-Hill, 1939), 1:243.

13. *Henley's Official Polo Guide* (Richmond, Ind.: Henley, 1885); J. A. Tuthill, ed. *Spalding Ice Hockey and Ice Polo Guide, 1898* (New York: American Sports, 1897).

14. John Chi-kit Wong, *Lords of the Rinks: The Emergence of the National Hockey League, 1875–1936* (Toronto: University of Toronto Press, 2005), 4.

15. Alexis de Tocqueville, *Democracy in America*, trans. George Lawrence, ed. J. P. Mayer (New York: Doubleday-Anchor, 1969), 2:513.

16. Louise McReynolds, *Russia at Play: Leisure Activities at the End of the Tsarist Era* (Ithaca, N.Y.: Cornell University Press, 2003), 92–93; James Riordan and Arnd Krüger, eds. *European Cultures in Sport* (Bristol, UK: Intellect, 2003), esp. 67–88; Alan Tomlinson and Christopher Young, "Toward a New Historiography of European Sports," *European Review* 19, no. 4 (2011), 487–507; Stefan Szymanski, "A Theory of the Evolution of Modern Sport," *Journal of Sport History* 35 (Spring 2008): 1–32.

17. Tony Mason, *Association Football and English Society, 1863–1915* (Sussex: Harvester, 1980), 21–68; Charles Korr, *West Ham United: The Making of a Football Club* (Urbana: University of Illinois Press, 1986).

18. Eric Hobsbawm, *The Age of Empire: 1875–1914* (New York: Vintage, 1989), 84–95, 142–83; David C. Young, "How the Amateurs Won the Olympics," in *The Archeology of the Olympics*, ed. Wendy J. Raschke (Madison: University of Wisconsin Press, 1988), 55–75; S. W. Pope, "Amateurism and American Sports Culture: The Invention of an Athletic Tradition in the Unites States, 1870–1900," *International Journal of the History of Sport* 13, no. 3 (December 1996), 290–309; Nancy B. Bouchier, *For the Love of the Game: Amateur Sport in Small-Town Ontario, 1838–1895* (Kingston: McGill-Queen's University Press, 2003).

19. Adrian Harvey, *The Beginnings of a Commercial Sporting Culture in Britain, 1793–1850* (Hants, UK: Ashgate, 2004); Ted Vincent, *Mudville's Revenge: The Rise and Fall of American Sport* (New York: Seaview, 1981).

20. Melvin Adelman, *A Sporting Time: New York City and the Rise of Modern Athletics, 1820–70* (Urbana: University of Illinois Press, 1986).

21. Whitney in David C. Young, "How the Amateurs Won the Olympics," in *The*

Archeology of the Olympics: The Olympics and Other Festivals in Antiquity, ed. Wendy J. Raschke (Madison: University of Wisconsin Press, 1988), 57, 59; *Spirit of the Times*, April 7, 1888; S. W. Pope, "Amateurism and American Sports Culture: The Invention of an Athletic Tradition in the United States, 1870–1900," *International Journal of the History of Sport* 13, no. 3 (December 1996): 290–309; Bouchier, *For the Love of the Game*.

22. Benjamin G. Rader, *Baseball: A History of America's Game* (Urbana: University of Illinois Press, 2008).

23. Wray Vamplew, *Pay Up and Play the Game: Professional Sport in Britain, 1875–1914* (Cambridge: Cambridge University Press, 1988); Korr, *West Ham United Football Club*.

24. Nathan O. Hatch, ed. *The Professions in American History* (South Bend, Ind.: University of Notre Dame Press, 1988); Andrew C. Holman, *A Sense of Their Duty: Middle-Class Formation in Victorian Ontario Towns* (Kingston: McGill-Queen's University Press, 2000), ch. 2.

Chapter 5. Breakout in Canada: 1877–1900

1. Fanny E. Coe, *Our American Neighbors* (New York: Silver, Burdett, 1891), 50; Sylvie Dufresne, "Le Carnaval d'hiver de Montréal, 1803–1889," *Urban History Review* 11, no. 3 (February 1983): 25–45; Don Morrow, "Frozen Festivals: Ceremony and *Carnaval* in the Montreal Winter Carnivals, 1883–1889," *Sport History Review* 27 (1996): 173–90.

2. Arthur Farrell, *Hockey: Canada's Royal Winter Game* (Montreal: Corneil, 1899); J. Macdonald Oxley, *My Strange Rescue and Other Stories of Sport and Adventure in Canada* (London: Nelson, 1895), 340.

3. John Bale, "International Sports History as Innovation Diffusion," *Canadian Journal of History of Sport* 15, no. 1 (May 1984): 38.

4. Jason Kaufman and Orlando Patterson, "Cross-National Cultural Diffusion: The Global Spread of Cricket," *American Sociological Review* 70, no. 1 (February 2005): 82–110; Allen Guttmann, "'Our Former Colonial Masters': The Diffusion of Sports and the Question of Cultural Imperialism" *Stadion* 14, no. 1 (1988): 49–63; J. A. Mangan, *The Games Ethic and Imperialism: Aspects on the Diffusion of an Ideal* (New York: Viking, 1986); Bale, "International Sports History," 53–59.

5. M. Huggins, "The Spread of Association Football in North-East England, 1876–1900: The Pattern of Diffusion" *International Journal of the History of Sport* 6, 3 (1986): 299–318.

6. James Sutherland et al., "Origin of Hockey in Canada: Report submitted to the Canadian Amateur Hockey Association Annual Meeting, Royal York Hotel, Toronto, Ontario, April 1942," McGill University Archives.

7. Sources: J. W. Fitsell, *Captains, Colonels and Kings* (Erin, Ont.: Boston Mills, 1987); John Wong and Michel Vigneault, "An English Team in a French Environ-

ment: The Rise and Fall of Professional Hockey in Quebec City, 1911–1920" in *Putting It on Ice: Vol. 1, Hockey and Cultural Identities,* ed. Colin Howell (Halifax: Gorsebrook, 2001), 17; James M. Whalen, "Kings of the Ice" *Beaver* 74 (February 1, 1994); Morris Mott, "'An Immense Hold in the Public Estimation': The First Quarter Century of Hockey in Manitoba, 1886–1911," *Manitoba History* 43 (Spring/Summer 2002); Len Kotylo, "The History of Hockey in Toronto: From Granite Club to Air Canada Centre," in *Total Hockey*, 2nd ed., ed. Dan Diamond et al., (Kingston, N.Y.: Total Sports, 2000), 27; Fitsell, "The Rise and Fall of Ice Polo: The Roots of Hockey" in Diamond et al., *Total Hockey*; A. J. "Sandy" Young, *Beyond Heroes: A Sport History of Nova Scotia*, vol. 2 (Hantsport, N.S.: Lancelot, 1988); *Toronto Globe*, February 7, 1890; http://www.geocities.com/hamiltontigers/hhh.html; M. H. (Lefty) Reid, *Peterborough and the Ontario Hockey Association, 1891–1940: A Hockey Compendium* (Peterborough, Ont.: Transcontinental, 1997); Scott Young, *100 Years of Dropping the Puck: A History of the OHA* (Toronto: McClelland and Stewart, 1989); Gary W. Zeman, *Alberta on Ice* (Edmonton: GMS2, 1985) 2; Brenda Zeman et al., *Hockey Heritage: 88 Years of Puck-Chasing in Saskatchewan* (Regina: Saskatchewan Sports Hall of Fame, 1983) 4; Terence O'Riordan, "The 'Puck Eaters': Hockey as a Unifying Community Experience in Edmonton and Strathcona, 1894–1905," *Alberta History* 49, no. 2 (Spring 2001): 7; R. S. Lappage, "The Kenora Thistles' Stanley Cup Trail," *Canadian Journal of History of Sport* 19, no. 2 (December 1988): 79; Jim Roper, ed. *From Pond to Pro: A History of Hockey in the Moncton Region from 1894 to 1996* (Moncton, N.B.: Moncton Hockey History Committee, 1997); L. J. Roy Wilson, "Medicine Hat—'The Sporting Town,'" *Canadian Journal of History of Sport* 16, no. 2 (December 1985): 21; Ernie Fitzsimmons, *History of Hockey in Fredericton*, pt. 1 (Fredericton, N.B.: E. Fitzsimmons, [2003]); Craig H. Bowlsby, *The Knights of Winter: Hockey in British Columbia, 1895–1911* (Vancouver, B.C.: Bowlsby, 2006).

8. J. W. Fitsell, *Hockey's Captains, Colonels, and Kings,* 39.

9. Gillian Poulter, "Montreal and Its Environs: Imaging a National Landscape, ca. 1867–1885," *Journal of Canadian Studies* 38, no. 3 (Fall 2004): 85.

10. Ibid.; "Shoeshowing and Lacrosse: Canada's Nineteenth-Century 'National Games,'" in J. A. Mangan and Andrew Ritchie, eds. *Ethnicity, Sport, Identity: Struggles for Status* (London: Cass, 2004), 235–58.

11. *Montreal Daily Star*, Carnival Number 1887, repr. in Dufresne, "Le Carnaval d'hiver de Montréal," 31.

12. Dufresne, "Le Carnaval d'hiver de Montréal," 37. Authors' translation.

13. Earl Zukerman, "McGill University: The Missing Link to the Birthplace of Hockey," in Dan Diamond, ed. *Total Hockey*, 2nd ed. (Scarborough, Ont.: Total Sports, 2000), 18.

14. Morrow, "Frozen Festivals," 185, 187.

15. "New Rules for the Regulation of the Game," *Montreal Gazette*, January 8, 1886.

16. James M. Whalen, "Kings of the Ice."

17. Alan Metcalfe, *Canada Learns to Play: The Emergence of Organized Sport, 1807–1914* (Toronto: McClelland and Stewart, 1987), 64, 73; Mott, "An Immense Hold."

18. Mott, "An Immense Hold"; Vigneault, "La Diffusion," 65.

19. Farrell, *Hockey*, 29; *Constitution, By-Laws and Rules of the City Amateur Hockey League of St. John* (Saint John, N.B.: Paterson, 1895).

20. Qtd. in Farrell, *Hockey*, 20.

21. AHAC record housed in CHA-NHA Minute Books, a61, February 17, 1894, "Doc" Seaman Research Centre, Hockey Hall of Fame Archives, Toronto.

22. John Chi-Kit Wong, *Lords of the Rinks: The Emergence of the National Hockey League, 1875–1936* (Toronto: University of Toronto Press, 2005) 27, and chs. 2, 3.

23. Mott, "An Immense Hold."

24. Alan Metcalfe, "Power: A Case Study of the Ontario Hockey Association," *Journal of Sport History* 19, no. 1 (Spring 1992): 6–7; Young, *100 Years.*

25. Fitsell, *Hockey's Captains, Colonels and Kings*, 81.

26. Michael Robidoux, "Imagining a Canadian Identity through Sport: A Historical Interpretation of Lacrosse and Hockey," *Journal of American Folklore* 115, no. 456 (2002): 220–21.

27. Fitsell, *Hockey's Captains, Colonels and Kings*, 44–45, 47; "Low, Albert Peter," in *The Canadian Men and Women of the Time: A Handbook of Canadian Biography*, ed. Henry J. Morgan (Toronto: Briggs, 1898), 593.

28. W. A. H. Kerr, "Hockey in Ontario," *Dominion Illustrated Monthly* 2, no. 2 (March 1893): 99.

29. Fitsell, *Hockey's Captains, Colonels and Kings*, 59.

30. Leonard Kotylo, "The History of Hockey in Toronto: From Granite Club to Air Canada Centre," Dan Diamond et al., *Total Hockey*, 2nd ed. (Kingston, N.Y.: Total Sports, 2000), 27; Fitsell, *Hockey's Captains, Colonels and Kings*, 74–75, 78, 80.

31. *The Canadian Parliamentary Companion*, 1891 (Ottawa: Durie, 1891), 105.

32. Mott, "An Immense Hold."

33. Mott, "Flawed Games, Splendid Ceremonies: The Hockey Matches of the Winnipeg Vics, 1890–1903," *Prairie Forum* 10, no. 1 (1985): 169.

34. Brenda Zeman, *Hockey Heritage*, 3.

35. Fitsell, *Hockey's Captains, Colonels and Kings*, ch. 6; A. J. "Sandy" Young, *Beyond Heroes: A Sport History of Nova Scotia*, vol. 2 (Hantsport, N.S.: Lancelot, 1998), 12–21.

36. Whalen, "Kings of the Ice."

37. Andrew C. Holman, *A Sense of Their Duty: Middle-Class Formation in Victorian Ontario Towns* (Kingston, Ont.: McGill-Queen's University Press, 2000); Robert A. J. McDonald, *Making Vancouver: Class, Status and Social Boundaries, 1863–1913* (Vancouver: University of British Columbia Press, 1996).

38. Colin D. Howell, *Blood, Sweat, and Cheers: Sport and the Making of Modern Canada* (Toronto: University of Toronto Press, 2001) 45; Peter Fortna, "'A Firm Referee that Will Make Both Sides Adhere by the Rules': Gentlemanly Status and Hockey Referees in Edmonton, Alberta, 1893–1907," *Past Imperfect* 12 (2006): 1–26.

39. Farrell, *Hockey*, 35.

40. James Hedley, "The Toronto Granite Club," *Outing* 15, no. 1 (1889): 39.

41. Kotylo, "The History of Hockey in Toronto," 27; Stephen J. Harper, *A Great Game: The Forgotten Leafs and the Rise of Professional Hockey* (Toronto: Simon and Schuster, 2013).

42. Metcalfe, "Power," 5–25.

43. Farrell, *Hockey*, 20; Fitsell, *Hockey's Captains, Colonels and Kings*, 73, 77.

44. O'Riordan, "The 'Puck Eaters'," 5, 4.

45. M. Gertrude Cundill, "A Hockey Match," *Outing* 33 (1899): 334–40; "Very Rev. Alexander John Doull," in *British Columbia from the Earliest Times to the Present*, ed. E. O. S. Scholefield and F. W. Howay (Vancouver, B.C.: Clarke, 1914), 3:961.

46. Ken Cruikshank, *Close Ties: Railways, Government, and the Board of Railway Commissioners, 1851–1933* (Kingston, Ont.: McGill-Queen's University Press, 1991), 8.

47. George Ham, qtd. in Daniel Francis, *National Dreams: Myth, Memory and Canadian History* (Vancouver, B.C.: Arsenal Pulp, 1997) 21.

48. Pierre Berton, *The National Dream: The Great Railway, 1871–81* (Toronto: Anchor Canada, 1970); Pierre Berton, *The Last Spike: The Great Railway, 1881–1885* (Toronto: Anchor Canada, 1971); Francis, *National Dreams*, ch. 1; W. K. Lamb, *A History of the Canadian Pacific Railway* (New York: Macmillan, 1977).

49. N. J. Woodside, "Hockey in the Canadian North-West," *Canadian Magazine*, January 1896, 244; Wayne Simpson, "Hockey," in *The Concise History of Sport in Canada*, ed. Don Morrow et al. (Toronto: Oxford University Press, 1989), 176.

50. Zeman et al., *Hockey Heritage*, 2; Zeman, *Alberta on Ice*, 9.

51. Andrew C. Holman, "Playing in the Neutral Zone: Meanings and Uses of Ice Hockey in the Canada-U.S. Borderlands, 1895–1915," *American Review of Canadian Studies* 34, no. 1 (Spring 2004): 41.

52. Metcalfe, *Canada Learns to Play*, 145; "Ice Hockey: King of Winter Sports," *Philadelphia Inquirer*, January 7, 1894.

53. Paul Kitchen, "The Dey Brothers' Rinks: Home to the Senators," *Hockey Research Journal* 2, no. 2 (1994): 23–28.

54. Kitchen, "Dey Brothers' Rinks," 25–26. Metcalfe, *Canada Learns to Play*, 64, 67.

55. Arthur Farrell, *How to Play Ice Hockey* (New York: American Sports, 1910), 8, 11.

56. Maarten Van Bottenburg, *Global Games* (Urbana: University of Illinois Press, 2001), 42, 44.

57. Farrell, *Hockey*, 17.

58. Howell, *Blood, Sweat, and Cheers*, 144–45.

59. "A Famous Victory: The Stalwart Sons of the Prairie Capital Show Easterners How to Play Hockey," *Manitoba Free Press* [Winnipeg], February 14, 1896.

Chapter 6. Alternative Games: 1880–1900

1. Dave Bidini, *Tropic of Hockey: My Search for the Game in Unlikely Places* (Guilford, Conn.: Lyons, 2000).

2. Carl Giden, Patrick Houda, and Jean-Patrice Martel, *On the Origin of Hockey* (Stockholm: Hockey Origin, 2014).

3. *Horae Scholasticae* 11 (November 29, 1877); *Rural Record* [the school journal], January 11, 1876, St. Paul's School (SPS) Archives, Concord, N.H.; *Rural Record*, December 5, 1876; Stephen Hardy, "Performance, Memory, and History: The Making of American Ice Hockey at St. Paul's School, 1860–1915," *International Journal of History of Sport* 14, no. 1 (April 1997): 97–115.

4. Arthur Stanwood Pier, *St. Paul's School 1855–1934* (New York: Scribner's, 1934), 200–201; James P. Conover, *Personality in Education* (New York: Moffat, Yard, 1908), 104–17.

5. *Horae Scholasticae* 17 (November 29, 1883).

6. Ibid., 17 (December 19, 1883); 18 (December 17, 1884, March 14, 1885); 19 (December 17, 1885); 21 (December 17, 1887); 22 (October 10, 1888, December 19, 1888); *Record*, December 2, 1887; December 7, 1888; December 8, 1888; issue of the *Rural Record*, 1881–1889.

7. Photo in SPS Archives. *Horae Scholasticae* 18 (October 8, 1884; November 27, 1884; December 17, 1884).

8. *Rural Record*, December 5, 1874; November 14, 16 and 28, 1874; December 9, 1876; *Horae Scholasticae* 1 (January 1862).

9. *Horae Scholasticae* 3 (December 1867, December 1868); 17 (November 29, 1883); 21 (November 24, 1887).

10. *Rural Record* (1890), 3; (1891), 38, 41–43.

11. S. King Farlow, "Bandy, or Ice Hockey," in *The Isthmian Library: Ice Sports*, ed. Theodore Andrea et al. (London: Ward Lock, 1901): 199, 200.

12. C. G. Tebbutt, "Bandy," in *Skating*, ed. J. M. Heathcote and C. G. Tebbutt (London: Longmans, Green, 1894), 434–40.

13. Tebbutt, "Bandy," 440–41; Farlow, "Bandy, or Ice Hockey," 210–12. Thanks to Michael Talbot for sending us the National Skating Association Rules in pamphlet, February 27, 2009.

14. Tebbutt, "Bandy," 438–39, 442; Bill Sund, "The Origins of Bandy and Hockey in Sweden," in *Putting It on Ice: Vol 2, Internationalizing "Canada's Game,"* ed. Colin Howell (Halifax, N.S.: Gorsebrook, 2002), 16.

15. Sund, "Origins," 17.

16. Robert Edelman, *Serious Fun: A History of Spectator Sports in the USSR* (New York: Oxford University Press, 1993), 28, 32; Sund, "Origins," 15; James Riordan, *Sport in Soviet Society* (Cambridge: Cambridge University Press, 1977), 10, 13; Louise McReynolds, *Russia at Play: Leisure Activities at the End of the Tsarist Era* (Ithaca, N.Y.: Cornell University Press, 2003).

17. Sund, "Origins," 17.

18. Igor Kuperman, "From Andora to Yugoslavia: The History of Hockey and Its Structure Today in Each IIHF Nation," in *Total Hockey*, ed. Dan Diamond et al. (New York: Total Sports, 1998), 445, 450.

19. This section is adapted from Stephen Hardy, "'Polo at the Rinks': Shaping Markets for Ice Hockey, 1880–1900," *Journal of Sport History* 33, no. 2 (Summer 2006): 401–17. See also Bill Fitsell, "The Rise and Fall of Ice Polo and Its Influence on Maritime Hockey," *Hockey Research Journal* 4 (Spring 1999): 11–17; Dwight Hoover, "Roller Skating toward Industrialism" in *Hard at Play: Leisure in America, 1840–1940*, ed. Kathryn Grover (Amherst, Mass. and Rochester, N.Y.: University of Massachusetts Press and Strong Museum, 1992), 61–76.

20. Foster Rhea Dulles, *A History of Recreation: America Learns to Play*, 2nd ed. (New York, 1965), 193–94, 241; *Henley's Official Polo Guide* (Richmond, Ind.: Henley, 1885), 5–6; *New York Times*, September 9, 1883; Roger Pout, *The Early Years of English Roller Hockey, 1885–1914* (self-published, 1993).

21. *Polo on Skates: American Skaters' Polo Rules*, pamphlet in Library of Congress (n.p., 1884).

22. Mark Pollack, *Sports Leagues and Teams: An Encyclopedia*, 1876–1996 (Jefferson, N.C.: McFarland, 1998) 359–420; Fitsell, "Rise and Fall of Ice Polo," 6; Connie Julien, "Copper County Hockey History," www.cchockeyhistory.org; Pout, *Early Years*, 6.

23. *Pioneer Press*, February 22, 1885, qtd. in George Hage, "Games People Played: Sports in Minnesota's Daily Newspapers, 1860–1890," *Minnesota History* (Winter 1981): 327; *Muncie Daily News* qtd. in Dwight Hoover, "Roller Skating toward Industrialism," 70; *Boston Herald*, November 28, 1883.

24. Hoover, "Roller Skating," 73; *Boston Herald*, November 28, 1883.

25. *Henley's Official Polo Guide*, 8–14, 62–63; *Boston Herald*, December 2, 1883; December 9, 1883; December 23, 1883; January 4, 1885; January 6, 1885; January 14, 1885; December 23, 1894; Bob Cubie, "Slap Shot on Wheels," *Brockton Enterprise*, May 23, 1993, 25, 29.

26. Promotion qtd. in Robert Weir, "Take Me Out to the Brawl Game: Sports and Workers in Gilded Age Massachusetts," in *Sports in Massachusetts: Historical Essays*, ed. Ronald Story (Westfield, Mass.: Institute for Massachusetts Studies, 1991), 21; Cubie, "Slap Shot on Wheels," 25; *Boston Herald*, January 5, 1896.

27. Lynne Marks, *Revivals and Roller Rinks: Religion, Leisure, and Identity in Late Nineteenth-Century Small-Town Ontario* (Toronto: University of Toronto Press, 1996).

28. *St. Paul Globe*, January 24, 1886; February 9, 1886; January 23, 1887; *Pioneer Press* [St. Paul and Minneapolis], January 6, 1887, 5, 9; Donald M. Clark, "Ice Polo in Minnesota," unpublished manuscript, n.d., in authors' possession; Fitsell, "Rise and Fall of Ice Polo," in Diamond et al., *Total Hockey*, 5–6; Alexander Meiklejohn, "Hockey Pioneers," *Brown Alumni Monthly* 51 (April 1951): 5–6. Thanks to Chris Hardy for securing the Meiklejohn memoir.

29. Fitsell, "Rise and Fall of Ice Polo," 5–6; "Roller Hockey," *Vancouver Province*, January 7, 1903. Thanks to John Wong for sending us the Vancouver article.

30. *Pioneer Press*, March 16, 1885; *Boston Herald*, January 9, 1885, and January 10, 1885; Hoover, "Roller Skating toward Industrialism," 66; Roger Pout, *Early Years*, 96–98; *New York Times*, December 9, 1939.

31. Fitsell, *Hockey's Captains, Colonels and Kings*, 99; Paul Kitchen, "The Early Goal Net: Hockey Innovation and the Sporting Page, 1896–1912," in *Putting It on Ice: Vol 1, Hockey and Cultural Identities*, ed. Colin Howell (Halifax, N.S.: Gorsebrook, 2002), 35–46.

Chapter 7. Forecheck into America: 1890–1920

1. Beverley Bogert, "Ice Hockey," *Outing*, 21 (January 1893), 252–56.

2. Paul Kitchen, "Hockey on the Lake: The First International Tournament," in *Total Hockey: The Official Encyclopedia of the National Hockey League*, ed. Dan Diamond (Kansas City: Andrews McNeel, 1998), 20.

3. Andrew C. Holman, "Playing in the Neutral Zone: Meanings and Uses of Ice Hockey in the Canada-U.S. Borderlands, 1895–1915," *American Review of Canadian Studies* 34, no. 1 (Spring 2004): 33–57.

4. "Ready for the Carnival," *Plattsburgh Sentinel*, January 17, 1902; "Plattsburgh Wins," *Plattsburgh Sentinel*, January 24, 1902.

5. "Buffalo's Chance for a Hockey Game," *Toronto Evening News*, December 15, 1898.

6. Daniel Mason and Barbara Schrodt, "Hockey's First Professional Team: The Portage Lakes Hockey Club of Houghton, Michigan," *Sport History Review* 27 (1996): 56; Bill Sproule, "Houghton: The Birthplace of Professional Hockey," *Hockey Research Journal* 8 (Fall 2004): 1–4; www.cchockeyhistory.org/CCIceRinks.htm.

7. William Julison Files; Vera McIntosh, typescript with inserted notes for "Hannah 1896–1996: 100 Years" (Hannah Centennial Book Committee, 1996) found in Elwyn B. Robinson Department of Special Collections, Chester Fritz Library, University of North Dakota; "Hockey League" Hannah, *Moon*, January 19, 1906; "Hockey" Hannah, *Moon*, February 7, 1908.

8. Holman, "Neutral Zone," 45–49.

9. "Moyie Hockey Match," *Nelson Weekly News*, February 19, 1910.

10. William McLennan, "Hockey in Canada," *Harper's Weekly* 39 (January 12,

1895): 45–46. This section adapted from Stephen Hardy, "'Polo at the Rinks': Shaping Markets for Ice Hockey, 1880–1900," *Journal of Sport History* 33, no. 2, (Spring 2006): 156–74.

11. Alexander Meiklejohn, "Hockey Pioneers," *Brown Alumni Monthly* 51 (April 1951); *Toronto Globe*, December 24, 1894; *New York Times*, December 28, 1894; J. W. Fitsell, *Hockey's Captains, Colonels and Kings* (Erin, Ont.: Boston Mills) 99–101.

12. *Toronto Globe*, December 27, 1894; December 29, 1894; December 31, 1894; January 1, 1895; January 2, 1895; January 3, 1895; January 4, 1895; *Toronto Evening Star*, December 27, 1894; *New York Times*, December 29, 1894; December 31, 1894; January 2, 1895. *Toronto Mail* quotation in Fitsell, *Hockey's Captains, Colonels and Kings*, 100–101.

13. Fitsell, *Hockey's Captains, Colonels and Kings*, 101. Meiklejohn qtd. in "Hockey Pioneers," 6.

14. "Rain Made Skaters Slurry," *Boston Herald*, January 2, 1893; John Blanchard Adams, *H Book of Harvard Athletics* (Cambridge, Mass.: Harvard Varsity Club, 1923), 555–56.

15. Donald Clark, "Early Artificial Ice," in *Total Hockey: The Official Encyclopedia of the National Hockey League*, vol. 2., ed. Dan Diamond and James Duplacey (New York: Total Sports, 2000), 564–65; *Illustrated London News*, May 13, 1876; *Washington Post*, January 15, 1878; September 8, 1889; Paul DeLoca, "The Ice and the Eagle: Skating's Shift from Saint to Show and from Chaos to Science, 1380–1915," unpublished manuscript.

16. "Skating on Artificial Ice," *Scientific American* 7 (January 1893): 11.

17. J. A. Tuthill, ed., *Spalding's Ice Hockey and Ice Polo Guide, 1898* (New York: American Sports, 1897), 36; Arthur Farrell, *Hockey: Canada's Royal Winter Game* (Montreal: Corneil, 1899), 32.

18. Fitsell, *Hockey's Captains, Colonels and Kings*, 102; *Baltimore Sun*, February 3, 1896; *New York Times*, December 20, 1894; Judith Ann Schiff, "History on Ice," *Yale Alumni Magazine*, February 2003, http://archives.yalealumnimagazine.com/issues/03_02/old_yale.html.

19. Tuthill, *Spalding's*, 36–40.

20. *Washington Post*, January 7, 1896; January 16, 1896; *Scientific American*, March 21, 1896, 74.

21. "Hockey at the Ice Palace; Canada's Champion Team Will Play the Baltimore Boys To-night," *Washington Post*, January 9, 1896; "Hockey at the Ice Palace: A Washington Team Organized to Beat the Baltimoreans," *Washington Post*, January 26, 1896; "How to Play Hockey: Rules of the Game According to the Canadian Association," *Washington Post*, January 29, 1896.

22. "An Artificial Ice Rink," *Scientific American*, January 4, 1896, 11; *New York Times*, November 20, 1895; November 29, 1895.

23. *New York Times*, March 3, 1896; March 9, 1896.

24. *New York Times*, March 7, 1896.

25. *Montreal Daily Herald*, February 29, 1896; *New York Times*, March 2, 1896; *New York Times*, March 8, 1896.

26. *New York Times*, March 11, 1896; *New York Times*, March 12, 1896.

27. "Another Skating Rink," *New York Times,* November 20, 1895.

28. *New York Times*, March 12, 1896; March 24, 1896; March 26, 1896.

29. *New York Times,* March 29, 1896; April 2, 1896; April 4, 1896; April 5, 1896; J. Parmly Paret, "Ice Hockey," *Outing* 31 (January 1898): 372.

30. *Pioneer Press*, February 17, 1895, and February 19, 1895, qtd. in S. Kip Farrington, *Skates, Sticks and Men: The Story of Amateur Hockey in the United States* (New York: McKay, 1972), 117, 118; Fitsell, *Hockey's Captains, Colonels and Kings*, 102.

31. Roger Godin, *Before the Stars: Early Major League Hockey and the St. Paul Athletic Club* (St. Paul: Minnesota Historical Society, 2005), 7–8; M. B. Palmer, "Hockey in the St. Paul District," *Official Ice Hockey Guide 1912* (New York: American Sports, 1912), 23–35.

32. Godin, *Before the Stars*, 11; Donald Clark, "History of Indoor Ice Rinks in Minnesota," unpublished manuscript, 2.

33. Donald Clark, "Eveleth Hockey, First Fifty Years, 1903–1952," unpublished manuscript, 1–2; [n. a.], "Eveleth: The Hockey Capital of the USA," and G. P. Finnegan, "The Eveleth Hockey Story," in *Missabe Iron Ranger*, December 1952, 5, 7, 11, 15, 16–17, 31, 49, "Eveleth" folder, US Hockey Hall of Fame Archives, Eveleth, Minn. Thanks to USHHF Curator Tom Sersha for providing these materials.

34. Edward Thierry, "Hockey in the Pittsburgh District," in *Spalding Ice Hockey and Ice Polo Guide*, comp. Arthur Farrell (New York: American Sports, 1908), 41–42; Robert G. Carroon, "A Century of Ice Hockey in Milwaukee," *Milwaukee History* 10 (Spring 1987): 19–20; Rockwell Hinkley, "Ice Hockey in Milwaukee," *Official Ice Hockey Guide 1916* (New York: American Sports, 1915), 45; W. H. McAvoy, "Hockey in Cleveland," in *Official Ice Hockey Guide 1909*, ed. Frederick Toombs (New York: American Sports, 1908), 53–57; Leslie Scully, "Cleveland Athletic Club," in *Official Ice Hockey Guide 1915* (New York: American Sports, 1914), 31–33.

35. Harry Stiles, "Hockey in Boston and Vicinity," *Official Ice Hockey Guide 1909* (New York: American Sports, 1908), 59–63; Fred Hoey, "Hockey through the Years," *Boston Garden Sports News* 18, no. 5 (Winter 1945–46): 4.

36. Stephen Hardy, "Long before Orr: Placing Hockey in Boston, 1897–1929," in *The Rock, the Curse, and the Hub: Random Histories of Boston Sports*, ed. Randy Roberts (Cambridge, Mass.: Harvard University Press, 2005), 245–89; Edwin Teale, "Science Turns Ice Hockey into Big Business," *Popular Science Monthly*, February 1935, 109.

37. "The Story of the Boston Arena," n. p., n. d., 5, 7; Henry R. Ilsley, "Boston's New Ice Rink Will Boom Skating," *Baseball Magazine* (January 1910): 33–35. Thanks to Jack Grinold of Northeastern University for copies of these articles.

38. "Automobile Promises to Be the Fad of the New Era," *Brooklyn Eagle*, December 30, 1900.

39. W. A. Kearns, "Amateur Hockey in Oregon," *Official Ice Hockey Guide 1916* (New York: American Sports, 1915), 51.

40. Gordon Reed, "High School Hockey in the Central West," *Official Ice Hockey Guide, 1918* (New York: American Sports, 1917, 40; *San Diego Sun*, June 17, 1916, 3; Kearns, "Amateur Hockey in Oregon," 49–51.

41. Thierry, "Hockey in the Pittsburgh District," 41–42; "Short Jabs at All 'Round Sports," *Wilkes-Barre Times*, October 9, 1914; Dan Mason, "The International Hockey League and the Professionalization of Ice Hockey, 1904–07," *Journal of Sport History* 25 (Spring 1998): 1–17.

42. *Spalding Guide 1898*, 44–46; "Interscholastic Ice Hockey League," *Official Ice Hockey Guide 1911* (New York: American Sports, 1910), 35–39; Palmer, "Hockey in the St. Paul District," 33; "All Stars in Boston," *Boston Herald*, February 26, 1912; *Boston Post*, December 11, 1910; Reed, "High School Hockey in the Central West," 40.

43. *Spalding Guide 1898*, 35; David Tirrell, "Early Days of Collegiate Hockey," *Official NCAA Ice Hockey Guide, 1955* (New York: National Collegiate Athletic Bureau, 1955), 12.

44. *Spalding Guide 1898*, 23–33; *Spalding Ice Hockey and Ice Polo Guide 1905* (New York: American Sports, 1905), 97–101; Paret, "Ice Hockey," 529.

45. Godin, *Before the Stars*; "Ice Hockey in San Francisco," *Official Ice Hockey Guide 1918* (New York: American Sports, 1917), 49.

46. Andrew C. Holman, "Frank Merriwell on Skates: Heroes, Villains, Canadians and Other Others in American Juvenile Sporting Fiction, 1890–1940," in *Now is the Winter: Thinking about Hockey*, ed. Jamie Dopp and Richard Harrison (Hamilton, Ont.: Wolsak and Wynn, 2009), 53–67; Ralph Henry Barbour, *The Crimson Sweater* (New York: Century, 1905); Ralph Henry Barbour, *Guarding His Goal* (New York: Appleton, 1919); Arthur Stanwood Pier, *Boys of St. Timothy's* (New York: Scribner's, 1904); *Harding of St. Timothy's* (Boston: Houghton Mifflin, 1906); Graham B. Forbes, *The Boys of Columbia High on the Ice* (New York: Grosset and Dunlap, 1911); Edward Stratemeyer, *Dave Porter and His Rivals* (Boston: Lothrop, Lee, and Shepard, 1911).

47. Godin, *Before the Stars*, 59; Roger Godin, "Facing the Falcons: The 1920 United States Olympic Team," *Hockey Research Journal* 6 (Fall 2002): 23–31; William Haddock, "Hockey in the United States," *Official Ice Hockey Guide 1921* (New York: American Sport, 1921), 5–6; *New York Times*, May 3, 1920.

Chapter 8. What Game? Forging a Distinct Product: 1890–1920

1. "Ottawa Defeats Tigers at Hockey," *New York Times*, January 6, 1914; "Ottawa College Beat Princeton," *Toronto Globe*, January 6, 1914; "Hockey Results," *Toronto Globe*, January 8, 1914; "'Bad Joe' Hall Fought with 'Newsy' Lalonde," *Toronto Globe*, December 31, 1914; "Torontos Doubled Score on Quebec," *Toronto Globe*, January 2, 1914; "Joe Hall," http://www.hhof.com/html/legendsplayer.shtml.

2. *Boston Herald*, February 12, 1908; *New York Times*, December 18, 1908.

3. *Boston Herald*, February 26, 1912; *Boston Journal*, February 5, 1913; Herbert Reed, "Building Up American Hockey," *Country Life in America*, 31, no. 2 (December 1916): 59. Thanks to Eddie Doyle for sharing the *Country Life* article.

4. *Boston Herald*, January 21, 1912; John Davies, *The Legend of Hobey Baker* (Boston: Little, Brown, 1966), 47, 73; Emil R. Salvini, *Hobey Baker: American Legend* (St. Paul, Minn.: Hobey Baker Memorial Foundation, 2005).

5. Davies, *Legend of Hobey Baker*, 96.

6. G. T. Gurnee, "On the Sidelines," *Lexington Herald*, November 16, 1919; *New York Globe* quote cited in *Literary Digest*, January 18, 1918; Ron Fimrite, "A Flame That Burned Too Brightly," *Sports Illustrated*, March 18, 1991, 78–90; Salvini, *Hobey Baker*, 117–21.

7. George Frazier, "Homage to Hobey," *Boston Herald*, March 9, 1962.

8. Michael McKinley, *Putting a Roof on Winter: Hockey's Rise from Sport to Spectacle* (Vancouver: Greystone, 2000), 71.

9. Stan and Shirley Fischler, "Cyclone Taylor," *Heroes and History: Voices from the NHL's Past* (Toronto: Hill-Ryerson, 1994), 4–5.

10. Ibid.; Stan Fischler with Tom Sarro, *Metro Ice: A Century of Hockey in Greater New York* (New York: H and M, 1999), 19.

11. Eric Whitehead, *Cyclone Taylor: A Hockey Legend* (New York: Doubleday, 1977); John Chi-Kit Wong, "Boomtown Hockey: The Vancouver Millionaires," in *Coast to Coast: Hockey in Canada to the Second World War*, ed. John Chi-Kit Wong (Toronto: University of Toronto Press, 2009), 223–58; Craig H. Bowlsby, *Empire of Ice: The Rise and Fall of the Pacific Coast Hockey Association* (n. p.: Author, 2012); Eric Whitehead, *The Patricks: Hockey's Royal Family* (Toronto: Doubleday, 1980), 93.

12. *Renfrew Mercury* quoted in Whitehead, *The Patricks*, 78–79; "Joe Hall Fined $100," *Toronto Globe*, February 3, 1910.

13. Fischler, "Cyclone Taylor," 6.

14. Morris Mott, "Flawed Games, Splendid Ceremonies: The Hockey Matches of the Winnipeg Vics, 1890–1903," *Prairie Forum* 10, no. 1 (1985): 167–87; Alfred "Ralph" Winsor in John Blanchard Adams, ed., *The H Book of Harvard Athletics, 1852–1922* (Cambridge, Mass.: Harvard Varsity Club, 1923), 565.

15. *Victoria (BC) Times*, January 3, 1912, cited in Ron Boileau and Philip Wolf, "The Pacific Coast Hockey Association," in Dan Diamond et al. *Total Hockey*, 2nd ed. (Kingston, N.Y.: Total Sports, 2000), 51.

16. H. Reed, "Speeding It Up on the Ice," *Harper's Weekly* 60 (January 9, 1915): 41; E. B. Moss, "King of Winter Sports," *Harper's Weekly* 56 (February 10, 1912), 15; H. Reed, "Genius in Hockey," *Harper's Weekly* 60 (January 16, 1915), 62; R. F. Kelley, "Fastest Game on Two Feet," *Outing* 77 (December 1920): 132–33.

17. *Montreal Star*, January 26, 1907; *Montreal Herald*, January 26, 1907, qtd. in Mike Aiken, *Kenora Thistles: Our Hockey Heritage*, (Kenora, Ont.: Bowes, 2006), 45–46.

18. See Mott, "Flawed Games"; Arthur Farrell, *Hockey: Canada's Royal Game* (Montreal: Corneil, 1899), 95.

19. Farrell, *Hockey*, 80.

20. Michael Oriard, *Reading Football: How the Popular Press Created an American Spectacle* (Chapel Hill: University of North Carolina Press, 1993), 39.

21. National Hockey Association Minutebook, vol. 5, November 25, 1912, "Doc" Seaman Research Centre, Hockey Hall of Fame Archives, Toronto.

22. Morey Holzman and Joseph Nieforth, *Deceptions and Doublecross: How the NHL Conquered Hockey* (Toronto: Dundurn, 2002), 41; National Hockey Association Minutebook, vol. 5, December 31, 1912; February 12, 1913; American Amateur Hockey League rulebook, found in Frederic Dare Huntington Papers (1889–1940), box 98, folder 27, Amherst College Archives, Amherst, Mass.; Boileau and Wolf, "Pacific Coast Hockey Association," 53.

23. Hicks, *How to Play Ice Hockey*, 6.

24. "Hockey Requires Quick Thinking, Says Winsor," *Boston Herald*, January 20, 1918.

25. "The Latest Style of Play," *Toronto Globe*, February 5, 1895; Aiken, *Kenora Thistles*, 20.

26. Fred J. Hoey, "American Hockey Is Superior to Canadian," *Boston Herald*, January 7, 1918.

27. Thomas Howard, "Hockey in the United States," in Arthur Farrell, comp., *Ice Hockey and Polo Guide* [Spalding Athletic Library] 1905 (New York: American Sports, 1905), 89; Oriard, *Reading Football*, 35–56.

28. Emphasis added. Farrell, *Hockey*, ch. 4; Hicks, *How to Play Ice Hockey*, 12.

29. On "The Wizard," see Huntington Papers, box 98, folder 27; Hicks, *How to Play Ice Hockey*, 15.

30. Hoey, "American Hockey."

31. Ibid.

32. Stacy L. Lorenz and Geraint B. Osborne, "'Talk About Strenuous Hockey': Violence, Manhood, and the 1907 Ottawa Silver Seven-Montreal Wanderer Rivalry," *Journal of Canadian Studies* 40, no. 1 (Winter 2006): 131–32; Alan Metcalfe, *Canada Learns to Play: The Emergence of Organized Sport, 1807–1914* (Toronto: McClelland and Stewart, 1987), 69–71; Richard Gruneau and David Whitson, *Hockey Night in Canada: Sport, Identity and Cultural Politics* (Toronto: Garamond, 1993), ch. 8; Oriard, *Reading Football*, 191.

33. Howard, "Hockey in the United States," in Farrell, *Ice Hockey and Polo Guide*, 89.

34. Farrell, *Hockey*, 79.

35. *Spalding Ice Hockey Guide 1911* (New York: American Sports, 1910), 21.

36. Lorenz and Osborne, "Talk about Strenuous Hockey."

37. Caspar Whitney, "Hoodlumism in Hockey" *Outing* 41, no. 5 (1903): 641.

38. *Ottawa Journal*, March 8, 1907; *Spalding Ice Hockey Guide 1911*, 20–21.

39. Frederick R. Toombs, ed., *Official Ice Hockey Guide 1915* (New York: American Sports, 1914), 41 (AAHL), 55 (OHA).

40. Arthur Farrell, *Hockey*, 54.

41. Brian Cuthbertson, "The Starr Manufacturing Company: Skate Exporter to the World," *Journal of the Royal Nova Scotia Historical Society* 8 (2005): 58–60.

42. *Harper's New Monthly Magazine* 95, no. 570 (November 1897): 1086.

43. *Globe*, February 4, 1895.

44. Cuthbertson, "Starr Manufacturing Company," 64–65.

45. *Spalding Ice Hockey and Ice Polo Guide 1904* (New York: American Sports, 1904), 77; Stephen Hardy, "Sporting Goods and the Shaping of Leisure: 1800–1990," in *For Fun and Profit: The Transformation of Leisure into Consumption*, ed. Richard Butsch (Philadelphia: Temple University Press, 1990), 71–104.

46. *Spalding Ice Hockey and Ice Polo Guide 1904*, 88; *Spalding Ice Hockey and Ice Polo Guide 1905* (New York: American Sports, 1905), n. p.

47. Cuthbertson, "Starr Manufacturing Company," 66; Advertisement for "Spalding Tubular Hockey Skates," *Official Ice Hockey Guide 1912* [Spalding Athletic Library] (New York: American Sports, 1912) n. p.

48. Cuthbertson, "Starr Manufacturing Company," 60–63; Bruce Dowbiggin, *The Stick: A History, a Celebration, an Elegy* (Toronto: Macfarlane, Walter and Ross, 2002); Toombs, *Spalding Official Ice Hockey Guide 1915*, 70.

49. Farrell, *Hockey*, 54–55; Toombs, *Spalding Official Ice Hockey Guide 1915*, 72.

50. Oriard, *Reading Football*, ch. 2.

51. Stacy Lorenz, "'In the Field of Sport at Home and Abroad': Sports Coverage in Canadian Daily Newspapers, 1850–1914," *Sport History Review* 34, no. 2 (2003): 133–67; Stacy Lorenz, "'Bowing Down to Babe Ruth': Major League Baseball and Canadian Popular Culture, 1920–1929," *Canadian Journal of History of Sport* 26, no. 1 (1995): 22–39.

52. F. C. Lane, "Hockey—The Baseball of Winter," *Baseball Magazine* 8, no. 5 (March 1912): 18.

53. Lorenz, "In the Field," 140; Oriard, *Reading Football*, 70–71.

54. *Toronto Globe*, February 7, 1920.

55. *Toronto Globe*, February 3–8, 1890; February 4–9, 1895; February 5–10, 1900; January 30–February 4, 1905; January 31–February 5, 1910; February 1–6, 1915; February 2–7, 1920.

56. "Paris Makes a Clean Score," *Toronto Globe*, February 4, 1895.

57. "St. Pats Beaten by Fleet French," *Toronto Globe*, February 5, 1920; "Argos Confident of Beating St. Michael's," February 2, 1915.

Chapter 9. Whose Game? Class, Language, Race, Sex, and Nation

1. Frederic Dare Huntington Papers, folder 26: Hockey Correspondence (1915–16), Amherst College Archives, Amherst, Mass; Fred Hoey, "Hockey through the Years," *Boston Garden Sports News* 18, no. 6 (1945–46): 6–7; Stephen Hardy, "Long before Orr: Placing Hockey in Boston, 1897–1929," in *The Rock, the Curse and the Hub: A Random History of Boston Sports*, ed. Randy Roberts (Cambridge, Mass.: Harvard University Press, 2005), 255–56.

2. Mary Louise Adams, "The Game of Whose Lives? Gender, Race, and Entitlement in Canada's National Game," in *Artificial Ice: Hockey, Culture and Commerce*, ed. David Whitson and Richard Gruneau (Peterborough, Ont.: Broadview, 2006), 71–84.

3. Arthur Farrell, *Hockey: Canada's Royal Winter Game* (Montreal: Corneil, 1899), 35.

4. Nancy B. Bouchier, *For the Love of the Game: Amateur Sport in Small-Town Ontario, 1838–1895* (Montreal: McGill-Queen's University Press, 2003); Colin D. Howell, *Blood, Sweat and Cheers: Sport and the Making of Modern Canada* (Toronto: University of Toronto Press, 2001), ch. 2; S. R. Pope, "Amateurism and American Sports Culture: The Invention of an Athletic Tradition in the United States, 1870–1900," *International Journal of the History of Sport* 13, no. 3 (1996): 290–309.

5. John Chi-Kit Wong, *Lords of the Rinks: The Emergence of the National Hockey League, 1875–1936* (Toronto: University of Toronto Press, 2005), 23.

6. J. Parmly Paret, "Ice Hockey," *Outing* 31 (January 1898); 373–74.

7. Alan Metcalfe, *Canada Learns to Play: The Emergence of Organized Sport, 1807–1914* (Toronto: McClelland and Stewart, 1987), 69.

8. Daniel S. Mason and Gregory H. Duquette, "Newspaper Coverage of Early Professional Ice Hockey: The Discourses of Class and Control," *Media History* 10, no. 3 (2004): 169; Peter Fortna, "'A Firm Referee that Will Make Both Sides Adhere by the Rules': Gentlemanly Status and Hockey Referees in Edmonton, Alberta, 1893–1907," *Past Imperfect* 12 (2006): 1–26.

9. A. J. "Sandy" Young, *Beyond Heroes: A Sport History of Nova Scotia*, vol. 2 (Hantsport, N.S.: Lancelot, 1988), 23.

10. John Davies, *The Legend of Hobey Baker* (Boston: Little, Brown, 1966), xii, 50, 82, 55.

11. Morey Holzman and Joseph Nieforth, *Deceptions and Doublecross: How the NHL Conquered Hockey* (Toronto: Dundurn, 2002), 28.

12. Holzman and Nieforth, *Deceptions and Doublecross*, 302, 53.

13. Bill Sproule, "The MacNaughton Cup: One of Hockey's Oldest Active Trophies," *Hockey Research Journal*, 8 (Fall 2004): 19–22.

14. Hugh MacLennan, *Two Solitudes* (New York: Collins, 1945).

15. Jean Harvey, "Whose Sweater Is This? The Changing Meanings of Hockey in Quebec," in Whitson and Gruneau, *Artificial Ice*, 32.

16. Michel Vigneault, "Montreal's Francophone Hockey Beginnings, 1895–1910," in *The Same but Different: Hockey in Quebec*, ed. Jason Blake and Andrew C. Holman (Montreal: McGill-Queen's University Press, 2017), 36–61.

17. Harvey, "Whose Sweater Is This?," 34; John Wong and Michel Vigneault, "An English Team in a French Environment: The Rise and Fall of Professional Hockey in Quebec City" in *Putting It On Ice, Vol. 1, Hockey and Cultural Identities*, ed. Colin Howell (Halifax: Gorsebrook, 2002), 17–24; Blake and Holman, *Same but Different*.

18. Sucheng Chan, ed. *Entry Denied: Exclusion and the Chinese Community in America, 1882–1943* (Philadelphia: Temple University Press, 1990); Hugh J. M.

Johnston, *The Voyage of the Komagata Maru: The Sikh Challenge to Canada's Colour Bar* (Delhi: Oxford University Press, 1979); J. R. Miller, *Skyscrapers Hide the Heavens: A History of Indian-White Relations in Canada* (Toronto: University of Toronto Press, 1989); John Higham, *Strangers in the Land; Patterns of American Nativism, 1865–1926* (New York: Atheneum, 1963).

19. Gerald R. Gems, "The Construction, Negotiation, and Transformation of Racial Identity in American Football: A Study of Native and African Americans," *American Indian Culture and Research Journal* 22, no. 2 (1998): 131–50; Randy Roberts, *Papa Jack: Jack Johnson and the Era of White Hopes* (New York: Free Press, 1983); and Bruce Kidd, "In Defence of Tom Longboat," *Canadian Journal of History of Sport* 14, no. 1 (1983): 34–63.

20. Michael Robidoux, "Imagining a Canadian Identity through Sport: A Historical Interpretation of Lacrosse and Hockey," *Journal of American Folklore* 115, no. 456 (Spring 2002): 220.

21. Gillian Poulter, "Montreal and Its Environs: Imagining a National Landscape c. 1867–1885," *Journal of Canadian Studies* 38, no. 3 (Fall 2004): 72.

22. *Minneapolis Journal*, January 26, 1907, cited in Steve R. Hoffbeck, "Bobby Marshall: Pioneering African American Athlete," *Minnesota History* 59, no. 4 (2004): 168.

23. Frank Cosentino, *Afros, Aboriginals and Amateur Sport in Pre World War One Canada*, Canadian Historical Association (Canadian Ethnic Group Series) Booklet No. 26 (Ottawa: CHA, 1998), 9.

24. Sheldon Gillis, "Putting It on Ice: A Social History of Hockey in the Maritimes, 1890–1914," M.A. thesis, St. Mary's University, 1994; George Fosty and Darril Fosty, *Black Ice: The Lost History of the Colored Hockey League of the Maritimes, 1895–1925* (New York, Stryker-Indigo, 2004).

25. *Acadian Recorder*, February 20, 1904; *Sydney Post*, March 9, 1904, qtd. in Fosty and Fosty, *Black Ice*, 46–49, 75–76, 105, 111.

26. Garth Vaughan, "The 'Colored' Hockey Championship of the Maritimes," in Howell, *Putting It on Ice*, 1:25–27.

27. *Acadian Recorder*, January 28, 1904, and February 24, 1904, qtd. in Fosty and Fosty, *Black Ice*, 104, 108.

28. Fosty and Fosty, *Black Ice*, 118.

29. James Milks, "Was NHL History Made in 1918?," SIHR *Hockey Research Journal* (2003), 3–4.

30. Gary Zeman, *Alberta on Ice* (Edmonton: Westweb, 1985), 9; Robidoux, "The Subaltern Framework of Aboriginal Hockey: Gnoseology and Thinking along the Borders," in Howell, *Putting It on Ice*, 1:29–34.

31. Robidoux, "The Subaltern Framework"; Robert Pitter, "Racialization and Hockey in Canada: From Personal Troubles to a Canadian Challenge," in Whitson and Gruneau, *Artificial Ice*, 123–39; W. P. Kinsella, "Truth," in *The Fencepost Chronicles* (Don Mills, Ont.: Totem, 1986), 1–12.

32. Brian McFarlane, *Proud Past, Bright Future: One Hundred Years of Canadian Women's Hockey* (Toronto: Stoddart, 1994), ch. 2.

33. Margaret Marsh, "Suburban Men and Masculine Domesticity, 1870–1915," *American Quarterly* 40, no. 2 (1988): 165–86.

34. McFarlane, *Proud Past, Bright Future*, ch. 1; and M. Ann Hall, *The Girl and the Game: A History of Women's Sport in Canada* (Peterborough, Ont.: Broadview, 2002), 37.

35. See McFarlane, *Proud Past, Bright Future*, chs. 1 and 2; Joanna Avery and Julie Stevens, *Too Many Men on the Ice: Women's Hockey in North America* (Victoria, B.C.: Polestar, 1997), chs. 2, 3; Metcalfe, *Canada Learns to Play*, 67.

36. Maxwell L. Howell and Reet A. Howell, *History of Sport in Canada* (Champaign, Ill.: Stipes, 1985), 219.

37. Andrew C. Holman, "Stops and Starts: Ideology, Commercialism and the Fall of American Women's Hockey in the 1920s," *Journal of Sport History* 32, no. 3 (Fall 2005): 328–50.

38. *Boston Herald*, March 23, 1917.

39. See Carly Adams, "Troubling Bodies: 'The Canadian Girl,' the Ice Rink, and the Banff Winter Carnival," *Journal of Canadian Studies* 48, no. 3 (Fall 2014): 200–220.

40. Avery and Stevens, *Too Many Men on the Ice*, 62–63.

41. Holman, "Stops and Starts"; Carly Adams, "Organizing Hockey for Women: The Ladies Ontario Hockey Association and the Fight for Legitimacy, 1922–1940," in *Coast to Coast: Hockey in Canada to the Second World War*, ed. John Chi-Kit Wong (Toronto: University of Toronto Press, 2009), 132–59.

42. McFarlane, *Proud Past, Bright Future*, 29.

43. Wayne Simpson, "Hockey," in *A Concise History of Sport in Canada*, ed. Don Morrow et al. (New York: Oxford University Press, 1990), 176.

44. Nancy Theberge, "Gender and Sport," in *Handbook of Sports Studies*, ed. Jay Coakley and Eric Dunning (London: Sage, 2000), 325.

45. "Hannah, ND Hens" Hockey Team 1907–08." Photograph and accompanying manuscript commentary, Elwyn B. Robinson Department of Special Collections, Chester Fritz Library, University of North Dakota, Grand Forks.

46. Morrow and Wamsley, *Sport in Canada*, 202–3. Emphasis added.

47. W. G. Beers, *Lacrosse: The National Game of Canada* (Montreal: Dawson, 1869).

48. Carl Berger, *The Sense of Power: Studies in the Ideas of Canadian Imperialism, 1867–1914* (Toronto: University of Toronto Press, 1914); Goldwin Smith, *Canada and the Canadian Question* [1891] (Toronto: University of Toronto Press, 1971).

49. Robidoux, "Imagining a Canadian Identity through Sport," 220.

50. J. Macdonald Oxley, *My Strange Rescue and Other Stories of Sport and Adventure in Canada* (New York: Nelson, 1895); "Oxley, James Macdonald," *Canadian Men and Women of the Time: A Handbook of Canadian Biography*, ed. Henry J. Morgan (Toronto: Briggs, 1898), 792–93.

51. J. Parmly Paret, *Outing* (May 1899): 208–9; Paret, "Ice Hockey," 375.

52. Paret, "Ice Hockey," 374.

53. *Spalding Ice Hockey Guide 1911* (New York: American Sports, 1911) 20.

54. Fred J. Hoey, "American Hockey Is Superior to Canadian," *Boston Herald*, January 7, 1918; "Hockey Requires Quick Thinking, Says Winsor," *Boston Herald*, January 20, 1918; Hardy, "Long before Orr."

Chapter 10. Across the Ponds: 1895–1920

1. Arthur Farrell, *Hockey: Canada's Royal Winter Game Handbook* (Montreal: Corneil, 1899), 17; Kevin Shea and John Jason Wilson, *Lord Stanley: The Man behind the Cup* (Bolton, Ont.: Fenn, 2007), 316.

2. "Hockey on Ice in Europe," *Brooklyn Eagle*, December 13, 1896.

3. George Meagher, *Lessons in Skating—With Suggestions Respecting Hockey, Its Laws, and American Hockey Rules* (New York: Dodd, Mead, 1900), 82, 84.

4. Birger Nordmark, "Les Avants and the Bohemians: The Birth of International Hockey," in *World of Hockey: Celebrating a Century of the IIHF, 1908–2008*, ed. Szymon Szemberg and Andrew Podnieks (Bolton, Ont.: Fenn, 2007), 2–3.

5. The *Times* report of January 9, 1864, is quoted in the *Brooklyn Eagle*, January 28, 1864; Shea and Wilson, *Lord Stanley*, esp. 348–86, 410–15.

6. Peter Patton, *Ice-Hockey* (London: Routledge, 1936), 4–5; Phil Drackett, *Flashing Blades: The Story of British Ice Hockey* (Ramsbury: Crowood, 1987), 29–33.

7. Martin C. Harris, "Bethune Minet 'Peter' Patton," *Hockey Research Journal* 6, no.1 (2002): 31; William S. Marshall, *Frozen in Time: The Lost History of Scottish Ice Hockey, 1895–1940* (Kilkerran, Scot.: Grimsay, 2014), 2–3; Daryl Leeworthy, "Skating on the Border: Hockey, Class, and Commercialism in Interwar Britain," *Histoire Sociale/Social History* 48 (May 2015): 199–200.

8. Robert Giddens, *Ice Hockey: The International Game* [Foyles Handbooks] (London: Baylis, 1950), 24–25.

9. Marshall, *Frozen in Time*, 7, 10–14.

10. J. R. Gilmour, "Scottish Ice-Hockey" in Patton, *Ice-Hockey*, 22–23; Marshall, *Frozen in Time*, 21–26, corrects Gilmour on several important points.

11. Giddens, *Ice Hockey*, 36. Some of Giddens's observations contradict the Australian sources. See "New South Wales Ice Hockey," http://www.nswicehockey.com.au/history.aspx. On the *USS Baltimore*, see http://www.spanamwar.com/baltimor.htm.

12. Frank Grace, "Record" [1907–1953], 35–36. Ontario Lacrosse Hall of Fame, St. Catharines, Ontario.

13. Giddens, *Ice Hockey*, 33; "New South Wales Ice Hockey."

14. Giddens, *Ice Hockey*, 33; "New South Wales Ice Hockey."

15. Giddens, *Ice Hockey*, 42–43.

16. Igor Kuperman, "From Andora to Yugoslavia: The History of Hockey and Its Structure Today in Each IIHF Nation," *Total Hockey*, 1st ed. (New York: Total Sports, 1998), 457.

17. Horst Eckert and Ernst Martini, *90: IIHF 90th Anniversary, 1908–1998* (Zurich: International Ice Hockey Federation, 1998), 93; "Hockey in Berlin," http://de.wikipedia.org/wiki/Eishockey_in_Berlin.

18. "A Big Honor for a Brantford Boy, 12 March 1906 news story; Charles G. Hartley, D.D.S.," *Minneapolis Dental Society Program Number*, October 1921; "Ice Emissaries from the Sunny South," *Globe and Mail*, December 15, 1938, clippings in Dr. Charles G. Hartley Scrapbook, pp. 1, 3, 16, property of Dr. Jillian Hartley. Thanks to Jillian for providing copies. On Hartley, see also Patrick Houda, Carl Gidén, Birger Nordmark, "Charles Hartley, a Famous Dentist Who Developed European Ice Hockey," http://w1.871.comhem.se/~u87152366/CharlesHartleybiography.htm.

19. Maxwell Stiles, "Dr. Hartley Master Hockey Teacher," news clipping, March 19, 1932, Hartley Scrapbook, 13; Houda, Gidén, and Nordmark, "Charles Hartley."

20. Kuperman, "From Andora to Yugoslavia," 447; Andrew Podnieks et al., *Kings of the Ice: A History of World Hockey* (Richmond Hill, Ont.: NDE, 2002), 155; Sparta Praha Hockey Club History, http://www.hcsparta.cz/eng.

21. Jan Velinger and Katrin Bock, "A Brief History of Czech Ice Hockey," http://www.radio.cz/print/en/53259; Podnieks, et al., *Kings of the Ice*, 156.

22. Kuperman, "From Andora to Yugoslavia," 445, 450.

23. Ibid., 448, 499.

24. Email communication from Tobias Stark, March 25, 2013; Stark, "Folkhemmet på is: Ishockey, modernisering och nationell identitet i Sverige 1920–1972," PhD diss., Linnéuniversitetet, 2010; Tobias Stark, "Ice Hockey, Europe," in *Sports around the World: History, Culture, Practice*, ed. John Nauright and Charles Parrish (Santa Barbara, Calif.: ABC-Clio, 2012), 343–48.

25. Bill Sund, "The Origins of Bandy and Hockey in Sweden," in *Putting It on Ice: Vol. 2, Internationalizing "Canada's Game,"* ed. Colin Howell (Halifax, N.S.: Gorsebrook, 2002), 17; email communication from Tobias Stark, March 25, 2013; Keith Hansen, "The Birth of Swedish Ice Hockey: Antwerp, 1920," in *Citius, Altius, Fortius: The Official Publication of the International Society of Olympic Historians* 4, no. 2 (1996): 5–27.

26. Sund, "Origins," 19; Swedish newspapers qtd. in Hansen, "Birth of Swedish Ice Hockey," 7, 8; Stark "Ice Hockey, Europe," 348.

27. Stark, "Ice Hockey, Europe," 348; Sund, "Origins," 19; Hansen, "Birth of Swedish Ice Hockey," 26.

28. Kuperman, "From Andora to Yugoslavia," 449; "Le Club des Patineurs de Paris" at http://www.hockeyarchives.info/archives.htm#a1969; Nordmark, "Les Avants and the Bohemians," 4.

29. Allen Guttmann, *The Olympics: A History of the Modern Games* (Urbana: University of Illinois Press, 2002).

30. Prochazka qtd. in Podnieks, et al. *Kings of the Ice*, 155; http://www.iihf.com/iihf-home/the-iihf/100-year-anniversary/100-top-stories/story-50; "Club des Patineurs de Paris"; Nordmark, "Les Avants and the Bohemians," 6.

31. Eckert and Martini, *90,* 48, 74; Harris, "Bethune Minet 'Peter' Patton," 31; http://www.hockeyarchives.info/amical1904.htm.

32. Martin C. Harris, "The Original Oxford Canadians," *Hockey Research Journal* 6, no.1 (2002): 29–30; Michael Talbot, "The Oxford Canadians," http://oxfordice-hockey.com.

33. Lanctôt qtd. in Nordmark, "Les Avants and the Bohemians," 4; *Deutscher Wintersport*, January 3, 1913, qtd. in Harris, "Original Oxford Canadians," 29.

34. Guttmann, *Olympics*, 39; Roger Godin, *Before the Stars: Early Major League Hockey and the St. Paul Athletic Club Team* (St. Paul: Minnesota Historical Society Press, 2005) 58; Roland Renson, "Why Winter Sports at the Antwerp Olympic Games 1920," in *Winter Games, Warm Traditions: Selected Papers from the 2nd ISHPES Symposium, Lillehammer*, ed. Matti Goksøyr, Gerd von der Lippe, Kristen Mo (Sankt Augustin: Academia, 1996), 141–53.

35. Paul Loicq biographies, http://www.hhof.com/html/legends.shtml and http://www.iihf.com/iihf-home/history/the-iihf/iihf-hall-of-fame; Szymon Szemberg, "The Longest-Serving President," in *World of Hockey*, 5.

36. Hewitt qtd. in Hansen, "Birth of Swedish Ice Hockey," 14; Sweden-Czech game quote in Renson, "Why Winter Sports," 148.

37. Swedish quotes in Hansen, "Birth of Swedish Ice Hockey," 9–10; Belgian quote in Renson, "Why Winter Sports," 148.

38. Hansen, "Birth of Swedish Ice Hockey," 10; Godin, *Before the Stars*, 66–67.

39. "FIB History," http://www.worldbandy.com/about_fib.html.

40. Email from Tobias Stark, March 25, 2013; "1908–1913 Ligue Internationale De Hockey Sur Glace," IIHF History, http://www.iihf.com/iihf-home/history/the-iihf/epochs/1908–1913; Hansen, "Birth of Swedish Hockey," 26.

41. Carl Gidén, Patrick Houda, and Jean-Patrice Martel, *On the Origin of Hockey* (Stockholm: Hockey Origin, 2014).

42. "Irwin Has a New Game," *Washington Post*, October 23, 1899.

43. Andreii S. Markovits and Steven L. Hellerman, *Offside: Soccer and American Exceptionalism* (Princeton, N.J.: Princeton University Press, 2001), 15; Maarten Van Bottenburg, "Thrown for a Loss? (American) Football and the European Sport Space," *American Behavioral Scientist* 46, no. 11 (July 2003): 1550–62; J. Parmly Paret, "Ice Hockey," *Outing*, 31 (January 1898): 372.

44. "Ice Hockey," *Philadelphia Inquirer,* January 7, 1894; "Shut Out at hockey," *Washington Post*, January 28, 1897; Paret, "Ice Hockey," 372.

45. Al Ries and Laura Ries, *The 22 Immutable Laws of Branding* (New York: Harper Business, 1998), 39–48.

Chapter 11. Hot Wars, Cold Wars, and Brand Wars

1. "Premiere in a Snow-Storm," *Literary Digest*, February 15, 1936, 37; "Olympics: Germany Plays Host for Fourth Winter Sports," *News-Week*, February 8, 1936, 24.

2. David Clay Large, *Nazi Games: The Olympics of 1936* (New York: Norton, 2007), 114.

3. "Olympics: Germany Plays Host," 24; "Premiere in a Snow-Storm," 38; "Olympics: IVth Winter Sports Wind Up a Norwegian Triumph," *News-Week*, February 22, 1936, 33; Large, *Nazi Games*, 122–44.

4. "Games at Garmisch," *Time*, February 17, 1936, 37; Large, *Nazi Games*, 119–22.

5. "Olympics: Germany Plays Host," 24; "Olympics: IVth Winter Sports," 33.

6. Associated Press (AP), "U.S. Sextet Upset in Rough Contest," *New York Times*, February 9, 1936; Albion Ross, "German Girl Wins in Olympic Skiing; U.S. Six Is Beaten," *New York Times*, February 9, 1936; "Olympics: IVth Winter Sports," 33; Frederick Birchall, "Cold Snap at Garmisch," *New York Times*, February 11, 1936; Large, *Nazi Games*, 128.

7. Seamus O'Coughlin, *Squaw Valley Gold: American Hockey's Olympic Odyssey* (San Jose, Calif.: Writer's Showcase, 2001), 95–96; Phil Drackett, "The 1936 British Olympic Team," in *Total Hockey: The Official Encyclopedia of the National Hockey League*, ed. Dan Diamond, Igor Kuperman, and James Duplacey (New York: Total Sports, 1998), 459–61.

8. AP, "Three Fail to Vote," *New York Times*, February 6, 1936; Albion Ross, "Authorities Will Investigate Credentials of Hockey Players," *New York Times*, February 5, 1936; AP, "Polish Team Routed," *New York Times*, February 7, 1936; AP, "Canadian Team Gains," *New York Times*, February 8, 1936.

9. Canada lost the World Championship to the United States in 1933. AP, "Fight Is Renewed in Olympic Hockey," *New York Times*, February 10, 1936; "Tribute to Canadian Six," *New York Times*, February 18, 1936; AP, "Hockey Draw Is Made," *New York Times*, February 11, 1936; Albion Ross, "Spectacular Victory Is Scored," *New York Times*, February 11, 1936; AP, "U.S. Six Wins, 2–1, to Gain Olympic Finals," *New York Times*, February 14, 1936; Drackett, "1936 British Olympic Team," 459–61.

10. Interview with Franklin Farrell III, May 22, 1995, by Jacqueline Baker, 1932 Olympic Winter Games Oral History Collection, 1932 and 1980 Lake Placid Winter Olympics Museum Archives, Lake Placid, N.Y.; Birchall, "Cold Snap at Garmisch."

11. John Wong, "Sport Networks on Ice: The Canadian Experience at the 1936 Olympic Hockey Tournament," *Sport History Review* 34 (November 2003): 196; Ken Dryden, *The Game: A Thoughtful and Provocative Look at a Life in Hockey* (Toronto: Macmillan of Canada, 1983), 231.

12. Finnish and Swedish quotes in Markku Jokisipilä, "Maple Leaf, Hammer, and Sickle: International Ice Hockey during the Cold War," *Sport History Review* 37, no. 1 (2006): 47.

13. Barbara J. Keys, *Globalizing Sport: National Rivalry and International Community in the 1930s* (Cambridge, Mass.: Harvard University Press, 2006), 9, 39.

14. Arthur J. Daley, "An Athlete May Go Far," *New York Times*, May 17, 1936; Daniel Gorman, "Amateurism, Imperialism, Internationalism and the First British Empire Games," *International Journal of the History of Sport* 27, no. 4, (March 2010): 611–34;

Akira Iriye, *Global Community: The Role of International Organizations in the Making of the Contemporary World* (Berkeley: University of California Press, 2002).

15. Carl Lotus Becker, *The History of Political Parties in the Province of New York, 1760–1776* (Madison: Bulletin of the University of Wisconsin, 1909), 22; Julie Stevens, "The Development of the Canadian Hockey System: A Process of Institutional Divergence and Convergence," in *Putting It on Ice: Vol. 2, Internationalizing "Canada's Game,"* ed. Colin D. Howell (Halifax, N.S.: Gorsebrook, 2001), 53.

16. Tony Judt, *Postwar: A History of Europe since 1945* (New York: Penguin, 2005), 4; Thomas K. McCraw, *Prophet of Innovation: Joseph Schumpeter and Creative Destruction* (Cambridge, Mass.: Harvard University Press, 2007), 111, 281.

17. Jeffry Frieden, *Global Capitalism: Its Fall and Rise in the Twentieth Century* (New York: Norton, 2006), 191; Keys, *Globalizing Sport*, 188; Keynes quote in Frieden, *Global Capitalism*, 189; Grant Jarvie, "Internationalism and Sport in the Making of Nations," *Identities: Global Studies in Culture and Power* 10, no. 4 (2003): 541.

18. Keys, *Globalizing Sport*, 188; Mark Dyreson, *Making the American Team: Sport, Culture, and The Olympic Experience* (Urbana: University of Illinois Press, 1998); James Riordan and Arnd Kruger, eds. *European Cultures in Sport* (Bristol, UK: Intellect, 2003); "Forum: Sport in Modern Europe," *Journal of Sport History* 37, no. 1 (Spring 2010): 1–98.

19. Mike Huggins and Mike O'Mahony, "Prologue: Extending Study of the Visual in the History of Sport," *International Journal of the History of Sport* 28, nos. 8–9 (2011): 1089–104; Michael Oriard, *King Football: Sport and Spectacle in the Golden Age of Radio and Newsreels, Movies and Magazines, the Weekly and the Daily Press* (Chapel Hill: University of North Carolina Press, 2001).

20. "Television," *News-Week*, February 15, 1936; "Telephoto: Wide World Will Send News Photos by Telephone," *News-Week*, February 29, 1936, 20.

21. Bernat López, "Sport, Media, Politics and Nationalism on the Eve of the Spanish Civil War: The First Vuelta Ciclista a Espan (1935)" *International Journal of the History of Sport* 27, no. 4 (March 2010): 635–57.

22. Stephen Hardy, Brian Norman, and Sarah Sceery, "Theorizing the History of Sport Branding," *Journal of Historical Research in Marketing* 4, no. 4 (November 2012): 482–509.

23. David Goldblatt, *The Ball Is Round: A Global History of Soccer* (New York: Riverhead, 2008), 161, 169–70, 203–4; Mélanie Bernard-Béziade and Michaël Attali, "Football: A History of Semantic and Cultural Borrowing," *International Journal of the History of Sport* 26, no. 15 (December 2009): 2219–35.

24. Goldblatt, *Ball Is Round*, 215, 338–39; Victoria de Grazia, "Mass Culture and Sovereignty: The American Challenge to European Cinemas, 1920–1960," *Journal of Modern History* 61, no. 1 (March 1989): 53–87.

25. Goldblatt, *Ball Is Round*, 267; Eduardo Archetti, "In Search of National Identity: Argentinian Football and Europe," in *Tribal Identities: Nationalism, Europe, and Sport*, ed. J. A. Mangan (London: Cass, 1996), 201–19.

26. Jokisipilä, "Maple Leaf, Hammer, and Sickle," 39.

27. Beverley Bogert, "Ice Hockey," *Outing* 21 (January 1893): 252–56; "Ice Hockey," *Philadelphia Inquirer*, January 7, 1894; J. A. Tuthill, ed., *Spalding's Ice Hockey and Ice Polo Guide*, 1898 (New York: American Sports, 1897), 61–70.

28. Mark Savoie, "Broken Time and Broken Hearts: The Maritimes and the Selection of Canada's 1936 Olympic Hockey Team," *Sport History Review* 31 (2000): 120–38; Greg Gillespie, "Big Liners and Beer Gardens: The Port Arthur Bearcats, Shamateurism, and the Selection Controversy Surrounding Canada's 1936 Olympic Hockey Team," in *Canada's Game: Hockey and Identity*, ed. Andrew C. Holman (Kingston: McGill-Queen's University Press, 2009), 11–25; Wong, "Sport Networks," 190–212.

29. "Foreword," "Rules Changes for 1928–1929," "Uniformity of Amateur Rules Desirable," and "Unnecessary Rough Play," in *NCAA Ice Hockey Rules and Official Ice Hockey Guide, 1928–29*, ed. Rufus James Trimble (New York: American Sports, 1928), 27, 29, 31; David A. Tirrell, "The Ice Hockey Rules Committee," *Official Ice Hockey Guide 1947* (New York: Barnes, 1946), 15.

30. Carly Adams, "'Queens of the Ice Lanes': The Preston Rivulettes and Women's Hockey in Canada, 1931–40," *Sport History Review*, 39 (May 2008): 12.

31. Bruce Kidd and John Macfarlane, *The Death of Hockey* (Toronto: New Press, 1972), 104, and Bruce Kidd, *The Struggle for Canadian Sport* (Toronto: University of Toronto Press, 1996).

32. Richard Gruneau and David Whitson, *Hockey Night in Canada: Sport, Identities and Cultural Politics* (Toronto: Garamond, 1993), 27. James Andrew Ross, "Hockey Capital: Commerce, Culture, and the National Hockey League, 1917–1967," PhD diss., University of Western Ontario, 2008, rev. and pub. as *Joining the Clubs: The Business of the National Hockey League to 1945* (Syracuse University Press, 2015).

33. Stephen Hardy and Andrew Holman, "Hockey Towns: The Making of Special Places in America and Canada," paper presented at "Constructing the Hockey Family: Home, Community, Bureaucracy, and Marketplace" Conference, July 12–14, 2012, Halifax, Nova Scotia, available at http://www.smu.ca/webfiles/4HardyHolman.pdf; John Bale, *Landscapes of Modern Sport* (Leicester: University of Leicester, 1994); Blake Gumprecht, "Stadium Culture: College Athletics and the Making of Place in the American College Town," *Southeastern Geographer* 33, no. 1 (May 2003): 28–53.

Chapter 12. North American Core Brands: 1920–1945

1. G. P. Finnegan, "The Eveleth Hockey Story," *Missabe Iron Ranger* [magazine of the Duluth, Missabe, and Iron Range Railway], December 1952, 16–18, 31; Donald M. Clark, "Eveleth Hockey: First Fifty Years, 1903–1952," unpub. ms., "Eveleth" folder, US Hockey Hall of Fame, Eveleth, Minnesota (hereafter US HHoF).

2. "United States Amateur Hockey Association," *Official Ice Hockey Guide 1924* (New York: American Sports, 1924), 5, 77–78; "Alliance Agreement," ibid., 85–87.

3. "Cup Regulations," *Official Ice Hockey Guide 1924* (New York: American Sports, 1924), 80, 82–83.

4. Eveleth Hockey Association, Financial Report, 1923–24 Season, March 31, 1924; Eveleth Hockey Association, Operating Statement, 1924–25 Season; Arrowhead Hockey Association, Statement of Receipts and Disbursements, March 29, 1926; Walter Percy Galbraith, NHL Players Contract, 1924–25 Season; Norbert Steele Contract 1941–42—all in "Eveleth" folder, US HHoF.

5. Stacy L. Lorenz, "Bowing Down to Babe Ruth: Major League Baseball and Canadian Popular Culture, 1920–29," *Canadian Journal of History of Sport* 26, no. 1 (May 1995): 22–39; Don Morrow, "Lionel Pretoria Conacher," *Journal of Sport History* 6, no. 1 (Spring 1979): 5–37.

6. John Kieran, "George Owen Takes the Ice," *New York Times*, January 11, 1929; Kieran, "The College Products," *New York Times*, February 2, 1929; "George Owen," Hockey Hall of Fame website, http://www.legendsofhockey.net/LegendsOfHockey/jsp/SearchPlayer.jsp?player=13907.

7. Frank Cosentino, *The Renfrew Millionaires: The Valley Boys of Winter, 1910* (Burnstown, Ont.: General Store, 1990), 17–19; Dan Diamond et al., *Total Hockey: The Official Encyclopedia of the National Hockey League* (Total Sports, 1998), 1798.

8. "Graduates Win the S.P.A. Title . . . Trottier the Star," *Toronto Daily Star*, December 2, 1927.

9. "Wings Take Dave Trottier Out of Unemployed Ranks," *Toronto Globe and Mail*, December 14, 1938; "Dave Trottier," Hockey Hall of Fame website, http://www.legendsofhockey.net/LegendsOfHockey/jsp/SearchPlayer.jsp?player=14574.

10. Kieran, "George Owen Coming," *New York Times*, January 18, 1927.

11. "Hugh John Plaxton," Hockey Hall of Fame website, http://www.hhof.com/LegendsOfHockey/jsp/SearchPlayer.jsp?player=13998.

12. Frederick Wilson, "What Grads for Pro Hockey?" *Toronto Globe*, February 28, 1928.

13. "Ottawa and Trottier Affair," *Toronto Globe*, October 9, 1928.

14. Frederick Wilson, "Trottier Selects His Club," *Toronto Globe*, November 28, 1928.

15. Frederick Wilson, "Worters Scores against Pirates and the N.H.L," *Toronto Globe*, November 29, 1928.

16. Ralph Allen, "Mostly Incidental," *Toronto Globe and Mail*, February 6, 1941.

17. See Frederick Wilson, "O.H.A. Maintains Its Traditions," *Toronto Globe*, December 7, 1925; "O.H.A. Adds to Record of Progress," *Toronto Globe*, November 19, 1928.

18. "Founding of an Association," *ODHA Newsletter* (Special 75th Anniversary Edition, June 1995), http://www.hockeyeasternontario.ca/pages/about/history.htm.

19. Harold L. Post, "History of the New Brunswick Amateur Hockey Association," Hockey New Brunswick, at http://www.hnb.ca/en/hnb/about-hnb/history.

20. Hockey Canada, http://www.hockeycanada.ca.

21. "Organize for Bigger Season, Ladies Hockey," *Lethbridge Herald*, November 13, 1925; "Invasion of Pros Fails to Diminish Ranks of Amateurs," *Toronto Globe*, March 31, 1931.

22. "'Break' Now Appears Imminent between C.A.H.A. and A.A.U.," *Ottawa Citizen*, November 30, 1936.

23. "New Leaders for Quebec Hockey," *Toronto Star*, April 20, 1931; "Quebec Amateur Hockey Association Returns Entire Board to Office," *Montreal Gazette*, May 1, 1939.

24. "Nearly 4,000 Players in Three O.H.A. Series," *Toronto Star*, December 5, 1925; "Large Entry Shown in Executive Report," *Toronto Star*, November 28, 1936.

25. "Juvenile Midget Hockey Organized," *Ottawa Citizen*, November 19, 1937.

26. "See Bigger Junior Series as Promise for Future," *Toronto Star*, November 21, 1931.

27. Alan Metcalfe, "Power: A Case Study of the Ontario Hockey Association, 1890–1936," *Journal of Sport History* 19, no. 1 (Spring 1992): 18.

28. Ibid., 10.

29. "Probe Demanded by Boston Club: Westminster Officials Resent Canadian-Made Charge that City Is "Tourist" Mecca," *Manitoba Free Press*, November 18, 1921; "O.H.A. to Hear Cases of Hockey Itinerants To-morrow," *Toronto Star*, November 23, 1933.

30. "Form Intermediate Hockey League," *Lethbridge Herald*, November 2, 1920; Robert Kossuth, "Chinook Country Hockey: The Emergence of Hockey in Pre–Second World War Southern Alberta," in *Coast to Coast: Hockey in Canada to the Second World War*, ed. John Chi-Kit Wong (Toronto: University of Toronto Press, 2009), 210; "Several Alberta Pros Reinstated," *Manitoba Free Press*, November 24, 1919.

31. "O.H.A. Adds to Record of Progress," *Toronto Globe*, November 19, 1928.

32. http://www.bchockey.net/About/HistoryDetails.aspx?id=1.

33. *New York Times*, October 19, 1937; *Official Ice Hockey Guide 1924* (New York: American Sports, 1924), 5.

34. *Boston Evening Transcript*, March 18, 1922, qtd. in Godin, *Before the Stars*, 103.

35. "Constitution of the United States Amateur Hockey Association," *Official Ice Hockey Guide 1924* (New York: American Sports Publishing Co., 1924), 80–81; Roger Godin, *Before the Stars: Early Major League Hockey and the St. Paul Athletic Club Team* (Minnesota Historical Society Press, 2005), 123–24.

36. *Boston Herald*, February 16, 1924; *Boston Herald*, December 21, 1924; McGeehan quoted in James Andrew Ross, "Hockey Capital: Commerce, Culture, and the National Hockey League, 1917–1967," PhD diss., University of Western Ontario, 2008, 94.

37. Bruce Kidd, *The Struggle for Canadian Sport* (Toronto: University of Toronto Press, 1995), 79.

38. "History—1930s and 40s," BC Hockey, http://www.bchockey.net/About/HistoryDetails.aspx?id=2.

39. "O.H.A. Yells for Red Ink: Down $5,862 on Season," *Toronto Star*, November 28, 1936.

40. Metcalfe, "Power," 13; M. J. Rodden, "Which Professionals Will Seek Amateur Cards?" *Toronto Globe*, November 25, 1933; "Pros Must Stay Out a Year—Reinstatement after That," *Toronto Globe and Mail*, April 24, 1940.

41. Kidd, *Struggle for Canadian Sport*, 86–87; Scott Young, *100 Years of Dropping the Puck: A History of the Ontario Hockey Association* (Toronto: McClelland and Stewart, 1989), 189–90.

42. John Chi-Kit Wong, *Lords of the Rinks: The Emergence of the National Hockey League, 1875–1936* (Toronto: University of Toronto Press, 2005), 148.

43. Kidd, *Struggle for Canadian Sport*, 185.

44. Wong, "Boomtown Hockey: The Vancouver Millionaires," in *Coast to Coast*, 223–57; Craig Bowlsby, *Empire of Ice: The Rise and Fall of the Pacific Coast Hockey Association* (self-published, 2012).

45. Lynn Dumenil, *The Modern Temper: American Culture and Society in the 1920s* (New York: Hill and Wang, 1995); 56–97; Michael E. Parrish, *Anxious Decade: America in Prosperity and Depression* (New York: Norton, 1992), 7–51.

46. Grantland Rice, "Boxing for a Million Dollars," *American Review of Reviews* 74 (October 1926): 416–20; Steven A. Riess, *City Games: The Evolution of American Urban Society and the Rise of Sports* (Urbana: University of Illinois Press, 1989), 172–79, 203–9; Guy Lewis, "World War I and the Emergence of Sport for the Masses," *Maryland Historian* 4 (Fall 1973): 109–23.

47. Bruce Kuklick, *To Everything a Season: Shibe Park and Urban Philadelphia, 1909–1976* (Princeton, N.J.: Princeton University Press, 1991), 191–93.

48. Russell Field, "Passive Participation: The Selling of Spectacle and the Construction of Maple Leaf Gardens," *Sport History Review* 33, no. 1 (2002): 42.

49. Ross, "Hockey Capital," 55–56, 76–106; *Joining the Clubs: The Business of the National Hockey League to 1945* (Syracuse University Press, 2014), 103–17; Wong, *Lords of the Rinks*, 82–106; Kidd, *Struggle for Canadian Sport*, 184–231.

50. Jack Kofoed, "The Master of Ballyhoo," *North American Review* 227 (March 1929): 282–286; Chad Seidfried and Ari de Wilde, "Building the Garden and Making Arena Sports Big Time: 'Tex' Rickard and His Legacy in Sport Marketing," *Journal of Macromarketing* 34, no. 4 (2014): 452–70.

51. Ross, "Hockey Capital," 103–4; *Joining the Clubs*, 111–13.

52. *New York Times*, November 6, 1926; *Chicago Daily News*, April 17, 1926; Ross, "Hockey Capital," 137.

53. David Cruise and Alison Griffiths, *Net Worth: Exploding the Myths of Pro Hockey* (New York: Penguin, 1992), 26–55; Wong, *Lords of the Rinks*, 133–42.

54. See also Willie Runquist, *Hockey Night in Hollywood: A History of Hockey in Los Angeles, 1925–1966* (Union Bay, B.C: n. p., 1995).

55. "Minor Pro Hockey Leagues Caused by Artificial Ice," *London Free Press*, February 15, 1928; "Minutes of the Canadian Professional Hockey League," "Doc" Seamans Research Centre, Hockey Hall of Fame, Toronto.

56. Handley Cross, "How Hockey Is Organized," *Sport Story* 14, no. 4 (January 22, 1927): 140.

57. Holzman and Nieforth, *Deceptions and Doublecross*, 259–69, 274–94.

58. Wong, *Lords of the Rinks*, 119.

59. "Farm System in Hockey Has Borne Fruit this Season," *Montreal Gazette*, December 24, 1936.

60. "Patrick Cuts Loose Blast on Amateur Hockey Body," *Toronto Daily Star*, October 19, 1939.

61. Charles Edwards, "Gigantic Farm System Would Make N.H.L. Boss of Amateur Hockey," *Ottawa Citizen*, June 22, 1943.

62. Kidd, *Struggle for Canadian Sport*, 226.

63. "Patrick Fingers in Hockey Pie," *Literary Digest*, January 18, 1936, 36.

64. M. A. Blanchard, "Advertising Photography," in *History of the Mass Media in the United States: An Encyclopedia*, ed. M. A. Blanchard (Chicago: Fitzroy Dearborn, 1998), 56–57.

65. Conn Smythe (with Scott Young), *If You Can't Beat 'Em in the Alley: The Memoirs of the Late Conn Smythe* (Toronto: McClelland and Stewart, 1981), 113; Kidd, *Struggle*, 222–23, 254–61; Ross, "Hockey Capital," 188–90, 200, 232; Field, "Passive Participation," 40; Fred Hoey, "Hockey through the Years," *Boston Garden Sports News* 18, no. 7 (1945–46): 7; *Boston Herald* radio columns January 5, 6, 9, and 12, 1926.

66. *Boston Herald*, December 8, 1924; December 9, 1924.

67. Walter Trumbull, "Hockey Fans Are Demanding More Scoring in Contests," *Boston Globe*, February 1, 1929; Charles L. Coleman, *The Trail of the Stanley Cup*, vol. 2 (Montreal: NHL, 1966), 87; E. A. Batchelor, "Detroit Gets 'Big League' Hockey," *Detroiter* 18 (December 13, 1926).

68. "Patrick Would Change Rule: Plan to Lessen Offsides," *Toronto Globe and Mail*, December 28, 1939.

69. *Boston Herald*, November 27, 1924; *Boston Herald*, December 22, 1924; *Chicago Defender*, November 20, 1926, pt. 2; December 4, 1926, pt. 2.

70. "Why Stitches Decorate the Hockey Player's Dome," *Literary Digest*, February 12, 1927, 75; Morry Stiles, "If You Want to Try a Fast Game—Try Hockey," *Arena and Strength* 18, no. 10 (January 1934): 31; Robert F. Kelley, "Ice Hockey—A Game, or Assault and Battery?" *Sportsman* 1, no. 2 (February 1927): 36–37.

71. "Thrills and Spills in the Hockey Rink," *Literary Digest*, January 12, 1929, 56.

Chapter 13. Diverging North American Brands: 1920–1945

1. Fred Kerner, "Quebec Amateur Hockey Body Reaches Quarter-Century Mark," *Montreal Gazette*, January 19, 1944.

2. John Meisel and Vincent Lemieux, *Ethnic Relations in Canadian Voluntary Organizations*, Documents of the Royal Commission on Bilingualism and Biculturalism 13 (Ottawa: Information Canada, 1972), quoted in Jean Harvey, "Sport and the Quebec Clergy, 1930–1960," in *Not Just a Game: Essays in Canadian Sport Sociology*, ed. Jean Harvey and Hart Cantelon (Ottawa: University of Ottawa Press, 1988), 85.

3. James Andrew Ross, "Hockey Capital: Commerce, Culture, and the National Hockey League, 1917–1967," PhD diss., University of Western Ontario, 2008, rev. and pub. as *Joining the Clubs: The Business of the National Hockey League to 1945* (Syracuse University Press, 2015), 139; Ross, *Joining the Clubs*, 141.

4. "Quebec Amateur Hockey Association Returns Entire Board to Office," *Montreal Gazette*, May 1, 1939.

5. "Lengthy Meeting of QAHA Held in Metropolis" and "Changes in Hockey Rules," *Quebec Chronicle Telegraph*, December 1, 1922.

6. See "Hockey Players on the Railway," http://www.freewebs.com/hockeyrailroader/railwaytelephoneleague.htm; "President Suspends 22 Players," *Toronto Star*, January 30, 1934.

7. "Favor Lifting Hockey Ban," *New York Times*, October 6, 1933.

8. "Bossing the Bosses of Hockey," *Toronto Globe*, October 22, 1925.

9. "Quebec Seeks Redmen Ages," *Toronto Globe and Mail*, April 1, 1937.

10. "Cy Allen and Don Willson Are Given Permission to Play in Montreal," *Toronto Globe and Mail*, December 9, 1937.

11. "Quebec Decides to Ignore C.A.H.A. and Their Rulings," *Toronto Star*, December 9, 1937.

12. "Duncan Suspends Q.A.H.A. Plans Commission," *Toronto Star*, December 9, 1937.

13. "Allow Quebec Teams in C.A.H.A. Playdowns," *Toronto Globe and Mail*, January 24, 1938; "Quebec Teams Again Eligible for Playdowns," *Globe and Mail*, February 3, 1938.

14. "Duncan Steps Out as C.A.H.A. President," *Toronto Globe and Mail*, April 14, 1938.

15. Steve Knowles, "Canadian University Hockey," in Dan Diamond et al., *Total Hockey*, 2nd ed. (Total Sports, 2000), 71–72.

16. Qtd. in Scott Young, *100 Years of Dropping the Puck: A History of the OHA* (Toronto: McClelland and Stewart, 1989), 163.

17. Knowles, "Canadian University Hockey," 71.

18. Hardy went on to become president of the CAHA in 1938–39, and president of the International Ice Hockey Federation from 1948 to 1951.

19. Bruce Kidd, *The Struggle for Canadian Sport* (Toronto: University of Toronto Press, 1995), 87–88; Young, *100 Years*, 189–90; W. G. Hardy, "Should We Revise Our Amateur Laws? Yes." *Maclean's*, November 1, 1936.

20. "Alcide Gagnon Has Sense of Humor," *Toronto Globe and Mail*, March 15, 1934, 14.

21. "Duncan Denies Puck Break with Union," *Toronto Star*, December 9, 1936.

22. "Hockey Opener Listed," *New York Times*, November 17, 1936; "Hockey Dates Set in College League," *New York Times*, December 1, 1936; "Noted on the Sports Horizon," *Toronto Globe*, March 2, 1936; Mike Rodden, "On the Highways of Sport," *Toronto Globe*, December 17, 1936; Thomas A. Reed, *The Blue and White: A Record of Fifty Years of Athletic Endeavour at the University of Toronto* (Toronto: University of Toronto Press, 1944), 201–10.

23. Knowles, "Canadian University Hockey," 71.

24. Ronald A. Smith, *Pay for Play: A History of Big-Time College Athletics* (Urbana: University of Illinois Press, 2010).

25. "Texas Ice Hockey," in *NCAA Ice Hockey Rules and Official Ice Hockey Guide, 1930–31*, ed. Rufus James Trimble (New York: American Sports, 1930), 62; Iowa and San Francisco club reports, ibid., 149, 151.

26. "Olympic Games," ibid., 47, 49.

27. Frederick Rubien, "AAU National Ice Hockey Championships," in *NCAA Ice Hockey Rules and Official Ice Hockey Guide, 1935–36*, ed. Louis Keller (New York: American Sports, 1935), 63–64.

28. "Hockey's Blast and 'Caesar's Wife,'" *Literary Digest*, February 29, 1936, 38; Pleban qtd. in Seamus O'Coughlin, *Squaw Valley Gold: American Hockey's Olympic Odyssey* (San Jose, Calif.: Writer's Showcase, 2001), 92.

29. "Intercollegiate Ice Hockey League," *Official Ice Hockey Guide and Winter Sports Almanac 1921*, ed. Tom Howard (New York: American Sports, 1921), 13.

30. David Aaker, *Building Strong Brands* (New York: Free Press, 1996), 68–69; "Foreword," "Rules Changes for 1928–1929," "Uniformity of Amateur Rules Desirable," and "Unnecessary Rough Play," in *NCAA Ice Hockey Rules and Official Ice Hockey Guide, 1928–29*, ed. Rufus James Trimble (New York: American Sports, 1928), 29.

31. *Official Ice Hockey Rules of the NCAA, 1928–29*, ed. Rufus James Trimble (New York: American Sports Publishing Co., 1928), 25–27, 29.

32. "Professional Rules Changes," in *NCAA Ice Hockey Rules and Official Ice Hockey Guide, 1929–30* (New York: American Sports, 1929), 43–45 (emphasis in the original).

33. "Laws of Hockey as Compiled by the National Professional Hockey League," in *Official Ice Hockey Guide and Winter Sports Almanac 1921*, ed. Tom Howard (New York: American Sports, 1921), 63; *Official Ice Hockey Rules of the NCAA, 1928–29*, ed. Rufus Trimble (New York: American Sports, 1928), 19.

34. "Hockey on Ice," *Montreal Gazette*, February 27, 1877, 4, rules repr. in John Chi-Kit Wong, *Lords of the Rinks: The Emergence of the National Hockey League,*

1875–1936 (Toronto: University of Toronto Press, 2005), 157; "CAHA Rules," in *Official Ice Hockey Guide and Winter Sports Almanac 1921*, ed. Tom Howard (New York: American Sports, 1921), 68; "Playing Rules of the United States Amateur Hockey Association," *in Official Ice Hockey Guide 1924*, ed. Tom Howard (New York: American Sports, 1924), 92; "Laws of Hockey as Compiled by the National Professional Hockey League," in *Official Ice Hockey Guide and Winter Sports Almanac 1921*, ed. Tom Howard (New York: American Sports, 1921), 63.

35. NCAA Ice Hockey Rules Committee Minutes, June 1933, 2, in NCAA collection, MC 206, box 1, folder 1, Charles Holt Archives of American Hockey, Dimond Library, University of New Hampshire; *Official Rules for Ice Hockey 1926–27* (n. p.: National Collegiate Athletic Association, 1926), 18; *Official Ice Hockey Rules of the NCAA, 1928–29*, ed. Rufus Trimble (New York: American Sports, 1928); "National Hockey League Laws of Hockey (Professional)," in *Official Rules for Ice Hockey, Speed Skating, Figure Skating, and Curling* (New York: American Sports, 1930), 11.

36. "Yale Coach Believes Pro Hockey of Benefit to College Game," *Boston Evening Globe*, March 4, 1929.

37. "Dartmouth College Pentagonal League Champions," *Official NCAA Ice Hockey Guide 1943* (New York: Barnes, 1942), 15; "Western Intercollegiate Conference," in *Official Ice Hockey Rules of the NCAA, 1928–29*, ed. Rufus Trimble (New York: American Sports, 1928), 35.

38. *NCAA Ice Hockey Rules and Official Ice Hockey Guide, 1929–30*, ed. Rufus Trimble (New York: American Sports, 1929), 56; "University of Southern California," *NCAA Ice Hockey Rules and Official Ice Hockey Guide, 1933–34*, ed. Louis Keller (New York: American Sports, 1933), 53; "University of California," *NCAA Ice Hockey Rules and Official Ice Hockey Guide, 1937–38*, ed. Louis Keller (New York: American Sports, 1938), 51; "Gonzaga, Loyola, University of California, University of California at Los Angeles," *NCAA Ice Hockey Rules and Official Ice Hockey Guide, 1938–39*, ed. Louis Keller (New York: American Sports, 1938), 48, 49, 51; "College Hockey in the Far West," in *Official NCAA Ice Hockey Guide 1950*, ed. David Tirrell (New York: Barnes, 1949), 151.

39. "Bay State Interscholastic Ice Hockey League," *NCAA Ice Hockey Rules and Official Ice Hockey Guide*, 1937–38, ed. Louis Keller (New York: American Sports, 1938), 61; "Bay State League," *NCAA Ice Hockey Rules and Official Ice Hockey Guide, 1938–39*, ed. Louis Keller (New York: American Sports, 1938), 67; "Scholastic," *Official Ice Hockey Guide 1924*, ed. Tom Howard (New York: American Sports, 1924), 37.

40. "College, High School and Amateur Hockey Clubs," *NCAA Ice Hockey Rules and Official Ice Hockey Guide, 1938–39*, ed. Louis Keller (New York: American Sports, 1938), 82–85.

41. Stan Fischler with Tom Sarro, *Metro Ice: A Center of Hockey in Greater New York City* (Flushing, N.Y.: H and M, 1999), 78–79.

42. Thomas Deegan, "Amateur Circuit to Remain Intact," *New York Times*, March 3, 1937.

43. Ibid.; "AAU Declares Orioles Are Out," *Boston Daily Globe*, March 2, 1937; Thomas Deegan, "Amateur Sextets Form New League," *New York Times*, March 4, 1937; "AAU Warns Hockey Clubs Not to Play Eastern Leaguers," *Boston Daily Globe*, December 15, 1937.

44. W. A. Whitcomb, "Follows in His Dad's Footsteps," *Boston Daily Globe*, October 28, 1937.

45. "Amateur Teams Out for Title," *Boston Daily Globe,* March 8, 1940; "'97' Club Wins First U.S. Amateur Hockey Championship," *Boston Daily Globe*, March 10, 1940.

46. *1948 Official Hockey Guide of the Amateur Hockey Association of the USA* (n.p., n.d.), 6–7; *1949 Official Hockey Guide of the Amateur Hockey Association of the USA*, (n.p., n.d.), 7–9, accessed at USA Hockey offices, Colorado Springs, Colo., May 2007; "New York Wins Amateur Title," *Boston Daily Globe*, April 4, 1942; "Pics Beat Falcons, 5–2," *Boston Daily Globe*, April 1, 1945.

47. John Cranfield, Kris Inwood, and J. Andrew Ross, "The Borders of Size: Height, Weight and Body Mass Index of Major League Hockey Players, 1876–1990," unpublished paper presented at the "Hockey on the Border" scholarly conference, Buffalo, N.Y., June 2010.

48. Lloyd Percival, *The Hockey Handbook* (Toronto: Copp Clark, 1951), vii.

49. Lester Patrick, "Foreword" to Richard F. Vaughan and Holcomb York, *Hockey for Spectator, Coach and Player* (New York: McGraw-Hill, 1939), xii; "How Canadian Boys Learn Hockey," *Sport Story* 33, no. 1 (October 11, 1931): 94.

50. Thomas K. Fisher, *Ice Hockey: A Manual for Player and Coach* (New York: Scribner's, 1926); "Hockey," in *Intimate Talks with Great Coaches*. Wingate Memorial Lectures 1929–30, ed. E. Dana Caulkins (New York: Wingate Memorial Fund), 193–244; Alexander Sayles and Gerard Hallock, *Ice Hockey: How to Play and Understand the Game* (New York: Barnes, 1931).

51. Mervyn Dutton, *Hockey: The Fastest Game on Earth* (New York: Funk and Wagnalls, 1938); Vaughan and York, *Hockey, for Spectator, Coach and Player.*

52. Patrick, "Foreword," in Vaughan and York, *Hockey*, xii.

53. Vaughan and York, *Hockey*, 42.

54. Handley Cross, "Speed Plus Teamwork Wins in Hockey," *Sport Story* 14, no. 3 (January 8, 1927): 94.

55. Fisher, *Ice Hockey*, 83; "Pro Hockey Here More Systematic," *London Free Press*, January 27, 1928; Burt Perry, "An Outburst of Scoring in Canadian League," *Toronto Globe*, February 15, 1929.

56. Charlie Querrie, "25 Years in Sport," *Toronto Star*, February 24, 1930.

57. "You Have to Be Fit to Play Hockey," *Sport Story* 63, no. 2 (April 2, 1939): 94.

58. Handley Cross, "The Fastest Game in the World," *Sport Story* 10, no. 4 (January 22, 1926): 96.

59. Vaughan and York, *Hockey*, 264; W. T. Munns, "Maroon Can 'Forecheck' as Well as the Hawks Did," *Toronto Globe*, January 2, 1935.

60. Dutton, *Hockey*, 72.

61. Edward Hagerman, *The American Civil War and the Origins of Modern Warfare* (Bloomington: Indiana University Press, 1988).

62. Dutton, *Hockey*, 78, 79; Vaughan and York, *Hockey*, 168.

63. Andy Lytle, "Leafs Illustrate Values of Defenders that Rush," *Toronto Star*, January 21, 1935; Tommy Munns, "'Play Wide-Open Hockey' Will Be Leafs' Slogan," *Toronto Globe*, October 20, 1936; Munns, "Game with Maroons Will Test Leafs' New System," *Toronto Globe and Mail*, March 4, 1938.

64. Bert Perry, "It's Enough to Make Frank Nighbor Weep," *Toronto Globe*, January 12, 1929; Perry, "Detours through the Sport Maze," *Toronto Globe*, December 22, 1930; Vaughan and York, *Hockey*, 41.

Chapter 14. Teams and Leagues of Their Own: 1920–1945

1. *Brantford Expositor*, March 6, 1928, 10; "Marlboro Juniors Beat Sault Ste. Marie 5 to 0," *Winnipeg Free Press*, March 10, 1928.

2. "Lank" Leonard, "Sammy Rothschild of N.Y. Americans is Outstanding Jewish Hockey Star," *New Haven Journal-Courier*, February 10, 1928.

3. *Globe*, February 28, 1933; John Kieran, "Taking a Turn on the Ice," *New York Times*, December 7, 1933.

4. "Sports in the Colleges, North," *Baltimore Afro-American*, April 4, 1931. On Johnson, see Jackie MacMullan, "Cold Comfort: Black Hockey Players of Past Generations Played for Love of the Game," *Boston Globe*, February 28, 2006.

5. "Sports in the Colleges, North."

6. "Maracle Scores Six for Haileybury H.S.," *Toronto Globe*, February 8, 1922.

7. "North Bay Gets Maracle," *Sudbury Star*, May 22, 1923.

8. "Murdoch, Ching Johnson, Chabot, Gray and White with N.Y. Team," *Winnipeg Free Press*, August 23, 1926.

9. "New York Rangers Start Ice Training: Sixteen Signed Players Report to Coach Connie Smythe on Toronto Surface," *New York Times*, October 20, 1926.

10. "Rangers Recall Buddy Maracle from Springfield," *Winnipeg Free Press*, February 13, 1931; "Rangers Secure Maracle in Exchange for Carrigan," *Toronto Globe*, February 13, 1931.

11. "Much Activity in Pro Hockey Loops: Rangers Turn Over Regan and Maracle to Bronx Team—Trottier Signs," *Toronto Star*, November 3, 1931; "Heximer Stars as New Haven Wins, 4–2," *Winnipeg Free Press*, January 5, 1934; "The Veteran Elmer ("Buddy") Maracle . . ." *Syracuse Herald*, November 2, 1934; "Tulsa Beats Wichita," *Winnipeg Free Press*, March 6, 1936,; "Tulsa Icers to Play Saturday," *Miami (Oklahoma) News-Record*, December 24, 1936; "Pontiac Warriors Sink Holzbaugh Puck Squad," *Toronto Star*, February 28, 1939; "Sports Take Hockey Game: Charleston Downs Toledo, 4–2," *Charleston (West Virginia) Daily Mail*, January 21, 1940.

12. Springfield Beaten at Philadelphia, 3–0," *Boston Globe*, December 29, 1927; "Indians to Meet Eagles Tomorrow," *Bridgeport Telegram*, February 4, 1928; "Toronto

Pucksters Are Released from Rangers' Payroll," *Lethbridge Herald*, November 3, 1931.

13. John J. Hallahan, "Unbeaten Tigers All Set for Indians," *Boston Globe*, December 3, 1927.

14. John J. Hallahan, "Tigers Blanked by Springfield Indians," *Boston Globe*, December 4, 1927; "New Haven Eagles to Invade Boston Garden," *Christian Science Monitor*, November 29, 1933.

15. "Redskin Icer," *Olean (New York) Evening Times*, March 5, 1931.

16. Jim Mancuso, *Hockey in Springfield* (Charleston, S.C.: Arcadia, 2005); Hallahan, "Unbeaten Tigers."

17. "Real Indians Play Here Sunday," *New Haven Journal-Courier*, February 8, 1928.

18. "Springfield Took Rough Play-Down: Beat Quebec, 1–0, in First Game of Canadian-American Series; Riot Came Early," *Montreal Gazette*, March 23, 1927.

19. "Hockey Title Won by Springfield Six . . . Maracle Scores in First," *New York Times*, April 8, 1928.

20. "Bud Elmer Maracle," NHL Player Search, Hockey Hall of Fame website, http://www.legendsofhockey.net.

21. W. T. Munns, "Play Up, Play Up, and Play and Game," *Toronto Globe*, January 19, 1929.

22. Bruce Kidd, "In Search of Tom Longboat," *Canadian Journal of History of Sport* 14, no. 1 (1983): 34–63; Janice Forsyth, "Fred Simpson Is No Tom Longboat: Public Memory and the Construction of Historical Knowledge," *Sport History Review* 45, no. 1 (2014): 37–58; "Unexpected Death of Louis Sockalexis," *Bangor Daily News*, December 25, 1913, in Ed Rice, *Baseball's First Indian* (Windsor, Conn.: Tide-mark, 2008).

23. "Boston Tigers Tie at Springfield, 1–1 . . . Police Stop Fight Between Maracle and Redding," *Boston Globe*, February 20, 1927.

24. "Maracle Back to Indians," *Christian Science Monitor*, December 15, 1931.

25. "Hockey Team to Tour Country: Is Seeking Players," *Chicago Defender*, June 16, 1934.

26. "Negro Teams to Play Here," *Niagara Falls Evening Review*, March 20, 1937; "Colored Teams to Play Tonight," *Niagara Falls (New York) Gazette*, March 22, 1937; "Falls Beat Orioles," *Niagara Falls Gazette*, March 23, 1937; Bill Sootheran, "Off the Cuff," *Niagara Falls Evening Review*, January 27, 1938; "With the Puck Chasers," *Niagara Falls Evening Review*, March 21, 1938; John Rowland, "Negro Puck Club," *Toronto Daily Star*, undated clipping, likely February 17, 1937, found in St. Catharines Museum collection.

27. John Schudlo, "Hockey Team Endured Racism," *St. Catharines Standard*, February 22, 2007; William Humber, *A Sporting Chance: Achievements of African-Canadian Athletes* (East York, Ont.: Natural Heritage/Natural History, 2004), 103–5; Sue Ferguson, "Hockey's Blacked-Out History," *Maclean's*, May 22, 2000, 8; Jack

Gatecliff, "Canada's Only All-Black Hockey Team Based Here," *St. Catharines Standard*, April 11, 1977.

28. "Organize First Hockey Team in Niagara Falls," *Afro-American*, March 20, 1937.

29. Sheldon Gillis, "Putting It on Ice: A Social History of Hockey in the Maritimes," master's thesis, Saint Mary's University, 1994, ch. 3; George Fosty and Darrell Fosty, *Black Ice: The Lost History of the Colored Hockey League of the Maritimes, 1895–1925* (Halifax, N.S.: Nimbus, 2008).

30. "Canada's Only All-Colored Team—St. Kitts Orioles," *St. Catharines Standard*, February 19, 1937.

31. "Colored Squad Enters League," *St. Catharines Standard*, February 16, 1937.

32. Fred McNabb, ed., *Sports History of St. Catharines: The Sports Capital of Canada* (St. Catharines: Advance, 1969), 27, 43, 85; "Canuck Boxers Now under Ban," *St. Catharines Standard*, February 8, 1937; "'Touch' Woods 1938 President," *St. Catharines Standard*, March 10, 1938.

33. "St. Catharines Man Honored: H.G. (Touch) Woods Appointed to Canadian Olympic Committee," *St. Catharines Standard*, March 7, 1939; Bill Gaynon, "Sport Desk," *Niagara Falls Evening Review*, March 4, 1939.

34. "Amateur Fight Card Monday," *Toronto Globe and Mail*, January 11, 1940.

35. "Harold G. Woods Is Widely Mourned," *St. Catharines Standard*, January 21, 1941; Clayton Browne, "In Memoriam," in "Sport Done Browne," *St. Catharines Standard*, January 21, 1941; "High Tribute Paid Late St. Catharines Sports Executive," *St. Catharines Standard*, January 24, 1941; "Sportdom Pays Rich Tribute to Memory of 'Touch' Woods," *St. Catharines Standard*, February 25, 1941.

36. McNabb, *Sports History of St. Catharines*, 132.

37. Tommy Munns, "Scanning the Sports Field," *Toronto Globe and Mail*, October 20, 1937; McNabb, *Sports History of St. Catharines*, 147–48.

38. "Prominent Sports Figures Join in Luncheon Sendoff for Toronto Leafs Hockey Club," *Toronto Globe and Mail*, October 16, 1940.

39. "'Touch' Woods," the *St. Catharines Standard* declared, "believes in hot-stove publicity." *St. Catharines Standard*, February 3, 1938.

40. Tommy Munns, "Scanning the Sport Field," *Toronto Globe and Mail*, February 17, 1937; Rowland, "Negro Puck Club."

41. "Duskies vs. Falls," *Niagara Falls Gazette*, March 11, 1937; "Duskies Defeated," *Niagara Falls Gazette*, March 12, 1937.

42. Tommy Munns, "Scanning the Sport Field," *Toronto Globe and Mail*, February 17, 1937.

43. "Colored Team Visits Guelph Tuesday Night," *Guelph Mercury*, March 14, 1938; Bill Coulter, "Sports Slants from All Angles," *Guelph Mercury*, March 15, 1938; "Canada's Only All-Colored Hockey Team Plays Guelph All-Stars Here," *Guelph Mercury*, March 15, 1938.

44. "Guelph Stars Defeat Orioles in Loose Game," *Guelph Mercury*, March 16, 1938.

45. "Orioles Drop Hockey Debut," *St. Catharines Standard*, March 1, 1937; Clayton Browne, "Sport Done Browne," *St. Catharines Standard*, March 1, 1937.

46. "Colored Transports Lose to Guelph, 17–7," *St. Catharines Standard*, March 16, 1938; Rowland, "Negro Puck Club."

47. "Orioles Drop Hockey Debut," *St. Catharines Standard*, March 1, 1937.

48. Browne, "Sport Done Browne."

49. "Orioles Lose to Arena Squad," *St. Catharines Standard*, March 11, 1937.

50. Patricia Jasen, "Native People and the Tourist Industry in Nineteenth-Century Ontario," *Journal of Canadian Studies* 28, no. 4 (1993–94): 21; Bruce W. Hodgins and Jamie Benedickson, *The Temagami Experience, Recreation, Resources, and Aboriginal Rights in the Northern Ontario Wilderness* (Toronto: University of Toronto Press 1989), 116–18; "Indian Hockey Stars Who Will Flash on Elysium Ice Tonight," *Cleveland Plain Dealer*, January 28, 1928.

51. Philip J. Deloria, *Playing Indian* (New Haven, Conn.: Yale University Press, 1998); Alan Trachtenberg, *Shades of Hiawatha: Staging Indians, Making Americans, 1880–1930* (New York: Hill and Wang, 2004).

52. "Indians Arrive," *Pittsburgh Post-Gazette*, January 30, 1928; *New Haven Journal-Courier*, February 13, 1928; "Indian Hockey Teams Turn Deaf Ear to Pro Offers," *Providence Journal*, February 14, 1928; "Redskins Provide an Interesting Puck Exhibition at Arena," *Springfield Union*, February 24, 1928; "Crees, Seemingly Beaten, Rise and Defeat Ojibways," *Philadelphia Inquirer*, February 5, 1928.

53. "Indian 'Pow Wow' . . . Y.M.C.A. Was Scene of a Big Gathering Last Evening," *Brantford Expositor*, January 17, 1928; "The Indian Pow-Wow," *Orillia Packet and Times*, January 12, 1928; "Indian Hockey Teams Play Here Thursday," *Springfield Republican*, February 21, 1928.

54. *Toronto Globe*, January 13, 1928; "Ingersoll Ties Indian Sextet," *London Free Press*, January 20, 1928.

55. "Cree Hockey Team Coming: Redskin Braves Play Chicks Here at Arena," *Border Cities (Windsor) Star*, January 19, 1928; "Indians Arrive," *Pittsburgh Post-Gazette*, January 30, 1928.

56. Stan Baumgartner, "Crees, Seemingly Beaten, Rise and Defeat Ojibways," *Philadelphia Inquirer*, February 5, 1928.

57. "Where It's All Ice and Indians," copy from the *Cleveland News*, reprinted in the *Toronto Globe*, January 31, 1928.

58. "Crees Go on Rampage; Defeat Ojibways, 12–4," *Toronto Globe*, January 13, 1928; "Indian Hockeyists Ready for Action," *Providence Journal*, February 17, 1928; "Maracle Will Handle Ojibways-Crees Game," *Springfield Republican*, February 20, 1928.

59. "Indian Hockeyists Ready for Action," *Providence Journal*, February 17, 1928; "Real Indians Will Play Here Sunday," *New Haven Journal-Courier*, February 8, 1928; "Indian Icers Play to Large Crowd," *Cleveland Plain Dealer*, January 29, 1928.

60. "Locals Win Fast Game from Indian Team . . . Indians Play in Old Style," *Woodstock Sentinel Review*, January 19, 1928.

61. "Indian Icers Play to Large Crowd," *Cleveland Plain Dealer*, January 29, 1928; "Chicks Drub Indians, 7–1: Crees Lack System and Punch of Locals," *Border Cities (Windsor) Star*, January 24, 1928.

62. "Ingersoll Ties Indian Sextet," *London Free Press*, January 20, 1928; "Indians to Stage Title Game Here," *Providence Journal*, February 16, 1928.

63. Michael Oriard, *King Football: Sport and Spectacle in the Golden Age of Radio and Newsreels, Movies and Magazines, the Weekly and the Daily Press* (Chapel Hill: University of North Carolina Press, 2001), ch. 9.

64. ". . . and Sex Is Everything," from Richard Harrison, "Rhéaume," *Hero of the Play* (Hamilton, Ont.: Wolsak and Wynn, 1994), 51; *Judge*, February 18, 1922, cover.

65. Dorothy M. Brown, *Setting a Course: American Women in the 1920s* (Boston: Twayne, 1987); Margaret A. Lowe, *Looking Good: College Women and Body Image, 1875–1930* (Baltimore: Johns Hopkins University Press, 2003), ch. 5; Paula Fass, *The Damned and the Beautiful: American Youth in the 1920s* (New York: Oxford University Press, 1977), 23–25, 280–83, 306–10.

66. Andrew C. Holman, "Stops and Starts: Ideology, Commercialism and the Fall of American Women's Hockey in the 1920s," *Journal of Sport History* 32, no. 3 (Fall 2005): 328–50.

67. Elizabeth Stevenson, *Babbitts and Bohemians from the Great War to the Great Depression* (New York: Macmillan, 1967), 139.

68. Allen Guttmann, *Women's Sports: A History* (New York: Columbia University Press, 1991), 146; Brown, *Setting a Course*, 42–47.

69. John R. Tunis, "The Business of Sport," *Harper's* 159 (July 1929): 212, 221.

70. Women's Athletic Editorial Committee of the APEA, *Winter Activities in Snow and Ice 1931–32* (New York: American Sports, 1931), 6; Gay Ingham Berlage, "The Development of Intercollegiate Women's Ice Hockey in the United States," *Colby Quarterly* 32 (March 1996): 62.

71. *Winter Activities in Snow and Ice 1931–32*, 10.

72. M. Ann Hall, *The Girl and the Game: A History of Women's Sport in Canada* (Peterborough, Ont.: Broadview), 57.

73. Hall, *Girl and the Game*, 57.

74. "Women Plan Ice Hockey League," *New York Times*, December 17, 1920; "Women Ice Hockey League," *Philadelphia Inquirer*, December 17, 1920.

75. "Women's Hockey Teams Have Hot Struggle," *Boston Globe*, January 28, 1921.

76. Wayne Norton, "'Fair Manipulators of the Twisted Hickory': Women's Hockey in Fernie, 1919–1926," in *The Forgotten Side of the Border*, ed. Norton Miller and Naomi Miller (Kamloops: Plateau, 1998), 206–16; Carly Adams, "Troubling Bodies: 'The Canadian Girl,' the Ice Rink, and the Banff Winter Carnival," *Journal of Canadian Studies*, 48, no. 3 (Fall 2014): 200–220.

77. "Ladies' Hockey at Banff," *Boston Globe*, January 9, 1921.

78. Hall, *Girl and the Game*, 58.

79. "Hockey Title to Aura Lee Girls," *New York Times*, April 4, 1928.

80. "Montreal Enters Finals for Allan Cup," *New York Times*, April 11, 1939.

81. Myrtle Cook's *Montreal Star* clippings collected in Helen Nicholson Collection, "Doc" Seaman Resource Centre, Hockey Hall of Fame, Toronto.

82. Carly Adams, "Organizing Hockey for Women: The Ladies Ontario Hockey Association and the Fight for Legitimacy, 1922–1940," in *Coast to Coast: Hockey in Canada to the Second World War*, ed. John Chi-Kit Wong (Toronto: University of Toronto Press, 2009), 146; Carly Adams, "'Queens of the Ice Lanes': The Preston Rivulettes and Women's Hockey in Canada, 1931–1940," *Sport History Review* 39 (2008): 1–29; "Preston Women Keep Title, *New York Times*, March 29, 1936.

83. "Miss Seamans Challenges for the U.S. Skating Championship," *Boston Globe*, March 22, 1917.

84. William T. Tilden II, *The Art of Lawn Tennis* (New York: Doren, 1921), ch. 17.

85. Jonathan Struthers, "Elsie Muller McLave: World-Class Speedskater," *Hastings Historian* 21, no. 1 (Winter 1992): 10–12; "Miss Muller New York Captain," *Philadelphia Inquirer*, December 27, 1920; "Skaters Prepare for Title Events," *Philadelphia Inquirer*, December 24, 1920.

86. Brian McFarlane, *Proud Past, Bright Future: One Hundred Years of Canadian Women's Hockey* (Toronto: Stoddart, 1994), 55–56.

87. "Best in Canada," *St. Catharines Standard*, February 1, 1940.

88. Adams, "Organizing Hockey for Women," 147–49.

89. Kidd, *Struggle for Canadian Sport*, 102–3.

90. Hall, *Girl and the Game*, 3.

91. Hall, *Girl and the Game*, 45.

92. Holman, "Stops and Starts."

93. Northern Girls Win for Met: Hockey Trophy," *Montreal Herald*, March 2, 1928; "At the Metropolitan League Play-Off," *Montreal Herald*, March 2, 1928.

94. Hall, *Girl and the Game*, 97.

95. Adams, "Organizing Hockey for Women," 133.

96. Nancy Theberge, "Gender and Sport," in *Handbook of Sports Studies*, ed. Jay Coakley and Eric Dunning (London: Sage, 2000), 325; Theberge, *Higher Goals: Women's Ice Hockey and The Politics of Gender* (Albany: State University of New York Press, 2000), intro.

Chapter 15. Europe, the LIHG, and Olympic Hockey: 1920–1945

1. Karel Wendl, "The Olympic Oath: A Brief History," *Citius, Altius, Fortius: Journal of Olympic History* 3 (Winter 1995): 4; Allen Guttmann, *The Olympics: A History of the Modern Games* (Urbana: University of Illinois Press, 1992), 38–39.

2. Niall Ferguson, *The War of the World: Twentieth-Century Conflict and the Descent of the West* (New York: Penguin, 2006), 73.

3. IIHF website, "1914–1933," http://www.iihf.com/iihf-home/history/the-iihf/epochs/1914–1933.

4. Coubertin quote in Roland Renson and Marijke den Hollander, "Sport and Business in the City: The Antwerp Olympic Games of 1920 and the Urban Elite," *Olympika* 6 (1997): 81.

5. Robert F. Wheeler, "Organized Sport and Organized Labour: The Worker's Sports Movement," *Journal of Contemporary History* 13 (April 1978): 201.

6. David Imhoof, "The Game of Political Change: Sports in Göttingen during the Weimar and Nazi Eras," *German History* 27, no. 3 (2009): 374–94; Barbara Keys, "Soviet Sport and Transnational Mass Culture in the 1930s," *Journal of Contemporary History*, 38 (July 2003): 413–34.

7. Victoria de Grazia, "Mass Culture and Sovereignty: The American Challenge to European Cinemas, 1920–1960," *Journal of Modern History* 61, no. 1 (March 1989): 53–87; Barbara Keys, "Spreading Peace, Democracy, and Coca-Cola: Sport and American Cultural Expansion in the 1930s," *Diplomatic History* 28 (April 2004): 165–96.

8. Robert Giddens, *Ice Hockey: The International Game,* Foyles Handbooks (London: Baylis, 1950); Geoffrey H. Movius, ed., *The Second H-Book of Harvard Athletics, 1923–1963* (Cambridge, Mass.: Harvard Varsity Club, 1964), 277–82, 897; "R. G. 'Bobby' Giddens," at British Ice Hockey Hall of Fame, Ice Hockey Journalists UK website, http://www.ihjuk.co.uk/halloffame/rGiddens.html.

9. Stephen Hardy, "Long before Orr: Placing Hockey in Boston, 1897–1929," in *The Rock, the Curse, and the Hub: Random Histories of Boston Sports*, ed., Randy Roberts (Cambridge, Mass.: Harvard University Press, 2005), 245–89.

10. Giddens, *Ice Hockey*, 2, 22–27; Phil Drackett, *Flashing Blades: The Story of British Ice Hockey* (Ramsbury: Crowood, 1987), 58–59; Daryl Leeworthy, "Skating on the Border: Hockey, Class, and Commercialism in Interwar Britain," *Histoire sociale/Social History* 48 (May 2015): 208–12.

11. Martin C. Harris, *Homes of British Ice Hockey* (Stroud: Stadia, 2005), 152–56.

12. Giddens, *Ice Hockey*, 7–8; Harris, *Homes*, 46, 118, 123.

13. Drackett, *Flashing Blades*, 72, 75; Giddens, *Ice Hockey*, 26; Martin C. Harris, "Crossing the Link: The NHL and the British Hockey Leagues, 1935–1960," *Hockey Research Journal* 3, no. 3 (1997): 29–33.

14. "John Francis 'Bunny' Ahearne," British Ice Hockey Journalists UK website, http://www.ihjuk.co.uk. Martin C. Harris indicates Ahearne's birth date as 1900: see *The British Ice Hockey Hall of Fame* (Stroud, Gloucestershire: Stadia, 2007), 22–23.

15. Seamus O'Coughlin, *Squaw Valley Gold: American Hockey's Olympic Odyssey* (San Jose, Calif.: Writer's Showcase, 2001), 85; Harris, *British Ice Hockey Hall of Fame*, 22.

16. O'Coughlin, *Squaw Valley Gold,* 90.

17. http://www.ihjuk.co.uk/halloffame/jAhearne.html; Drackett qtd. in O'Coughlin, *Squaw Valley Gold*, 80–81.

18. O'Coughlin, *Squaw Valley Gold*, 214.

19. David Cruise and Alison Griffiths, *Net Worth: Exploding the Myths of Pro*

Hockey (Toronto: Penguin, 1992), 215; Murray Williamson, *The Great American Hockey Dilemma* (Wayzata, Minn.: Turtinen, 1978), 37.

20. Kraatz quote in Harris, *British Ice Hockey Hall of Fame*, 25; Scott Young, *War on Ice: Canada in International Hockey* (Toronto: McClelland and Stewart, 1976), 73.

21. Drackett, *Flashing Blades*, 58.

22. "I'm off to South Africa," *Ice Hockey World Annual*, 1953–54, 8, US Hockey Hall of Fame, Eveleth, Minnesota; Andrew Podnieks, "Last Days of Canada's World Dominance, 1947–1953," in Szymon Szemberg and Andrew Podnieks, eds. *World of Hockey: Celebrating a Century of the IIHF* (Bolton, Ont.: Fenn, 2007), 30; Andrew Podnieks et al., *Kings of the Ice: A History of World Hockey* (Richmond Hill, Ont.: NDE, 2002), 157; Igor Kuperman, "From Andora to Yugoslavia: The History of Hockey and its Structure Today in Each IIHF Nation," in *Total Hockey*, ed. Dan Diamond (New York: Total Sports, 1998), 451, 454.

23. Kuperman, "From Andora to Yugoslavia," 447; Walter Brown, "Hockey in Europe," in *NCAA Ice Hockey Rules and Official Ice Hockey Guide, 1935–36*, ed. Louis Keller (New York: American Sports, 1935), 77.

24. Podnieks et al., *Kings of the* Ice, 177; Patrick Houda, "Josef Maleček," Swedish Ice Hockey Historical and Statistical Society (hereafter SIHSS), http://www.sihss.se/josefmalecek.html.

25. Houda, "Josef Maleček"; Jan Velinger and Katrin Bock, "A Brief History of Czech Ice Hockey," http://www.radio.cz/print/en/53259; Sparta Praha Hockey Club History, http://en.hcsparta.cz/zobraz.asp?t=history; "Olympic, World, and European Championships," in Diamond, *Total Hockey*, 500.

26. Brown, "Hockey in Europe," 77; Giddens, *Ice Hockey*, 43; Kuperman, "From Andora to Yugoslavia," 457; "Olympic, World, and European Championships," 500.

27. "History," Spengler Cup Official website, https://www.spenglercup.ch/en/hall-of-fame/history; "Carl Spengler," *Whonamedit: A Dictionary of Medical Eponyms*, http://www.whonamedit.com/doctor.cfm/2212.html; Giddens, *Ice Hockey*, 47; David Goldblatt, *The Ball Is Round: A Global History of Soccer* (New York: Riverhead, 2008), 241.

28. Kuperman, "From Andora to Yugoslavia," 449; "Olympic, World, and European Championships," 513.

29. Quote in Marshall Jon Fisher, *A Terrible Splendor: Three Extraordinary Men, a World Poised for War, and the Greatest Tennis Match Ever Played* (New York: Crown, 2009), 167; Stephan Müller, "Gustav Jaenecke," SIHSS, http://www.sihss.se/GustavJaeneckebiography.htm; Birger Nordmark and Patrick Houda, "Rudi Ball," SIHSS, http://www.sihss.se/RudiBallbiography.htm.

30. *Der Sturmer* quote in William J. Baker, *Sports in the Western World* (Totowa, N.J.: Rowman and Littlefield, 1982), 247; Birger Nordmark and Patrick Houda, "Rudi Ball."

31. Bill Sund, "The Origins of Bandy and Hockey in Sweden," in *Putting It on Ice: Vol 2: Internationalizing "Canada's Game,"* ed. Colin Howell (Halifax: Gorsebrook,

2002), 18; "Olympic, World, and European Championships," 499; Niels Kayser Nielsen and John Bale, "The Contribution of Sport to the Nordic Third Way," *Journal of Sport History* 38 (Summer 2011): 223–36.

32. Sund, "Origins of Bandy and Hockey," 18–19; Kuperman, "From Andora to Yugoslavia," 456; Tobias Stark, "Ice Hockey, Europe," in *Sports around the World: History, Culture, Practice*, ed. John Nauright and Charles Parrish (Santa Barbara, Calif.: ABC-Clio, 2012), 343–48.

33. Kuperman, "From Andora to Yugoslavia," 448.

34. Robert Edelman, *Serious Fun: A History of Spectator Sports in the USSR* (New York: Oxford University Press, 1993), 33–34.

35. *Krasny Sport* quote in James Riordan, *Sport in Soviet Society* (Cambridge: Cambridge University Press, 1980), 133; Edelman, *Serious Fun*, Stalin quote at 57, 74.

36. Barbara Keys, "Sport and Transnational Mass Culture in the 1930s," *Journal of Contemporary History* 38 (July 2003): 420; Edelman, *Serious Fun*, 75.

37. *Soviet Fizkultura i Sport* magazine quoted in Kuperman, "From Andora to Yugoslavia," 454; Edelman, *Serious Fun*, 75; Hart Cantelon, "Revisiting the Introduction of Ice Hockey into the Former Soviet Union," in *Putting it on Ice: Vol. 2, Internationalizing "Canada's Game,"* ed. Colin D. Howell (Halifax, N.S.: Gorsebrook, 2002), 30.

38. Kuperman, "From Andora to Yugoslavia," 454; Edelman, *Serious Fun*, 75.

39. Edelman, *Serious Fun*, 75.

40. Christopher Young, Anke Hilbrenner, and Alan Tomlinson, "European Sport Historiography: Challenges and Opportunities," *Journal of Sport History* 38 (Summer 2011): 181–88.

41. Gigliola Gori, "Italy: Mussolini's Boys at Hitler's Olympics," in Kruger and Murray, *Nazi Olympics,* 119.

42. To add insult to injury, Canada beat Britain 3–0. Giddens, *Ice Hockey*, 66.

43. "Olympic, World and European Championships," 501–2; Giddens, *Ice Hockey*, 68.

44. Rufus J. Trimble, "Olympic Ice Hockey," in *NCAA Ice Hockey Rules and Official Ice Hockey Guide, 1932–33*, ed. Rufus James Trimble (New York: American Sports, 1932), 40–43; IIHF, "History, 1914–33" at http://www.iihf.com/iihf-home/history/the-iihf/epochs/1914–1933; "Olympic, World, and European Championships," 500.

45. Trimble, "Olympic Ice Hockey," 43.

46. "Rules of the Ligue Internationale de Hockey sur Glace," Rule V,B, articles 99–106 in *NCAA Ice Hockey Rules and Official Ice Hockey Guide, 1931–32*, ed. Rufus James Trimble (New York: American Sports, 1931), 65, 74, 53.

47. "Olympic, World, and European Championships," 500; LIHG 1931 Rule V, E, "Charging and Rough Play," articles 111–13, "Rules of the Ligue Internationale de Hockey sur Glace," in *NCAA Ice Hockey Rules and Official Ice Hockey Guide, 1931–32*, ed. Rufus James Trimble (New York: American Sports, 1931), 76.

48. Giddens, *Ice Hockey,* 44, 46.

Chapter 16. Strength Down Center—North American Brands: 1945–1971

1. *Here's Hockey!* (Ottawa: National Film Board of Canada, 1953); Karen Skinazi, "The Mystery of a Canadian Father of Hockey Stories: Leslie McFarlane's Break Away from the Hardy Boys," in *Canada's Game: Hockey and Identity*, ed. Andrew C. Holman (Kingston: McGill-Queen's University Press, 2009), 98–125.

2. The Boston Bruins, Chicago Black Hawks, Detroit Red Wings, Montreal Canadiens, New York Rangers, and Toronto Maple Leafs.

3. The added franchises were, in 1967, California Seals, Los Angeles Kings, Minnesota North Stars, Philadelphia Flyers, Pittsburgh Penguins, and St. Louis Blues; in 1970, Vancouver Canucks and Buffalo Sabres; in 1971, Atlanta Flames and New York Islanders.

4. Sam Goldaper, "Clarence Campbell Is Dead at 78: President of N.H.L. for 31 Years," *New York Times*, June 25, 1984; J. Andrew Ross, *Joining the Clubs: The Business of the National Hockey League to 1945* (Syracuse, N.Y.: Syracuse University Press, 2015), 1–2, 4–5; "Clarence Campbell," Honoured Members (Builders Category), Hockey Hall of Fame, http://www.hhof.com.

5. Benoît Melançon, *The Rocket: A Cultural History of Maurice Richard* (Vancouver, B.C.: Greystone, 2009), 123–29; Sidney Katz, "The Strange Forces behind the Richard Hockey Riot," *Maclean's*, September 17, 1955.

6. "The 'Richard Riot,'" CBC Digital Archives, http://www.cbc.ca/archives/entry/the-richard-riot1.

7. Stan Fischler and Shirley Fischler, *Who's Who in Hockey* (Riverside, N.J.: Andrews McMeel, 2003), 58.

8. "Campbell, Clarence Sutherland," in *Saskatchewan Sports: Lives Past and Present*, ed. Brian Mlazgar and Holden Stoffel (Regina, Sask.: Canadian Plains Research Centre, 2007), 20.

9. Todd Denault, *Jacques Plante: The Man Who Changed the Face of Hockey* (Toronto: McClelland and Stewart, 2009), 129.

10. Ross, "Hockey Capital: Commerce, Culture, and the National Hockey League, 1917–1967," PhD diss., University of Western Ontario, 2008, 597.

11. Ross, "Hockey Capital," 597.

12. Ross, "Hockey Capital," 387, 471–73, 531, 563.

13. See Michael McKinley, *Putting a Roof on Winter* (Vancouver, B.C.: Greystone, 2000), 142–66.

14. Norris to Conn Smythe, October 18, 1971, quoted in Ross, "Hockey Capital," 577n15.

15. Joseph C. Nichols, "Ex-Pros Skating as Amateurs Now," *New York Times*, March 7, 1958.

16. Ross, "Hockey Capital," 329; Donald R. Ellis, "Waivers, Drafts, and the Sponsorship List," in *Years of Glory, 1942–1967: The National Hockey League's Official Book of the Six-Team Era*, ed. Dan Diamond (Toronto: McClelland and Stewart, 1994).

17. Milt Dunnell, "Gordon Left Out the Punch Lines," *Toronto Star*, February 15, 1966.

18. Ross, "Hockey Capital," 492.

19. See Ross, "Hockey Capital," 458; Mark Parsons, "The Sponsorship System—The Pre-Expansion NHL's Monopsony on Players," in Historical Hockey Stats and Trivia, http://historicalhockey.blogspot.com/2012/12/the-sponsorship-system-pre-expansion.html.

20. "Lewicki Case Starts C Clause Talk Anew," *Winnipeg Free Press*, April 7, 1949.

21. C. N. Butler, Regina, SK, to Ken Reardon, Club de Hockey Canadien, August 1, 1960, Canadian Amateur Hockey Association fonds, MG28, series I-15, vol. 53, E7, Library and Archives of Canada.

22. "Don't Sign Pro, Coaches Tell Players," *Toronto Globe and Mail*, May 4, 1961.

23. "Young Players Exploited," *Winnipeg Free Press*, April 20, 1949.

24. See Louis J. Fusk, "What Gives on Sports" and "Pro Hockey's Threat to Civil Liberties," undated clippings in Charles Mayer fonds, "Hockey Amateur" file, Library and Archives of Canada, Ottawa.

25. "Copie de la déclaration de l'honorable Maurice L. Duplessis" and "Statement by R.L. Seaborn, Anglican Dean, Quebec," Charles Mayer fonds, "Hockey Amateur" file, Library and Archives of Canada, Ottawa; "Exploitation of Pucksters Condemned," *Winnipeg Free Press*, March 15, 1952.

26. "Hockey Strikes Back at Scathing Attack," *Winnipeg Free Press*, April 20, 1949.

27. "Smythe Defends Hockey's C Form," *Lethbridge Herald*, April 26, 1949.

28. Clarence Campbell, Testimony before the Subcommittee on Antitrust and Monopoly of the Committee of the Judiciary (Kefauver Committee 1958), United States Senate, S. Res. 231 on H.R. 10378 . . . (Washington, DC: GPO, 1958), 508.

29. "Clash of NHL, Sport Task Force Expected over Reserve Clause," *Toronto Star*, May 12, 1969.

30. Milt Dunnell, "This Peonage Is Not Penury," *Toronto Star*, December 31, 1969.

31. See Red Burnett, "Decision of Leaf Players on Labor Bargaining Agent Is Association's Big Test," *Toronto Star*, November 5, 1957; "Drop All Hockey Litigation: Better Pension Is Biggest Gain of Player Group," *Toronto Star*, February 5, 1958.

32. David Cruise and Alison Griffiths, *Net Worth: Exploding the Myths of Pro Hockey* (Toronto: Penguin, 1992); Russ Conway, *Game Misconduct: Alan Eagleson and the Corruption of Hockey* (Toronto: Macfarlane, Walter and Ross, 1995).

33. Canadian Amateur Hockey Association Fonds, Library and Archives of Canada, Ottawa.

34. See "Canadian Ice Group in Break with U.S.," *New York Times*, January 15, 1961.

35. Hart Cantelon, "Have Skates, Will Travel: Canada, International Hockey, and the Changing Hockey Labour Market," in *Artificial Ice: Hockey, Commerce and Culture*, eds. David Whitson and Richard Gruneau (Toronto: University of Toronto Press, 2006), 231; Bruce Kidd and John Macfarlane, *The Death of Hockey* (Toronto: New Press, 1972), 79.

36. "Committee Named to 'Sell' Hockey," *Winnipeg Free Press*, June 4, 1949; "CAHA Registers 85,000 Players," *Winnipeg Free Press*, May 30, 1957; "Will Recommend Not to Send Puck Team to Winter Olympics," *Lethbridge Herald*, May 22, 1962; "CMJHL Back with CAHA," *Medicine Hat News*, May 23, 1967; "CAHA against State Control," *Toronto Star*, May 23, 1972.

37. Ed Fitkin, *Maurice Richard: Hockey's Rocket* (Toronto: Baxter, 1951); Hugh Hood, *Strength Down Centre: The Jean Béliveau Story* (Scarborough, Ont.: Prentice-Hall, 1970); Jim Hunt, *Bobby Hull* (Toronto: McGraw-Hill Ryerson, 1971); Jim Vipond, *Gordie Howe, Number 9* (Toronto: McGraw-Hill Ryerson, 1971); Hal Bock, *Dynamite on Ice: The Bobby Orr Story* (New York: Scholastic, 1972); Scott Young, *Scrubs on Skates* (Boston: Little, Brown, 1952), *Boy on Defense* (Boston: Little, Brown, 1953), *A Boy at the Leafs' Camp* (Boston: Little, Brown, 1963).

38. See "The History of the Hockey Hall of Fame," http://www.hhof.com/html GeneralInfo/gi20300.shtml#Birth.

39. Ryan Edwardson, "'Kicking Uncle Sam out of the Peaceable Kingdom': English-Canadian 'New Nationalism' and Americanization," *Journal of Canadian Studies* 37, no. 4 (Winter 2003–04): 131–50; J. L. Granatstein, *Yankee Go Home? Canadians and Anti-Americanism* (Toronto: Harper Collins, 1996), chs. 5, 6, 9.

40. M. J. Caveney, "NHL Moneybags in US Enslave Canadian Hockey Players," *Toronto Star*, April 15, 1966.

41. Bob Bossin, "What This Country Needs . . ." *Maclean's* 83 (July 1970): 13–14.

42. Gary Mossman, *Lloyd Percival: Coach and Visionary* (Woodstock, Ont.: Seraphim, 2013), 22–28.

43. Ibid., 33, 35; Reid Forsee, "CBC Sports College," *CBC Times* 1, no. 4 (July 16, 1948): 1, 8.

44. Lloyd (Ace) Percival, "Hints for Goalkeepers," in *Official NCAA Ice Hockey Guide 1950*, ed. David Tirrell (New York: Barnes, 1949), 12–13; Lloyd Percival, *The Hockey Handbook* (New York: Barnes, 1960 [1951]), vii.

45. Mossman, *Lloyd Percival*, 54–68, 75–78.

46. Percival, *Hockey Handbook*, 260; Douglas M. Fisher, "Head Coach Lloyd Percival," *Canadian Forum* (June 1953), 61; Mossman, *Lloyd Percival*, 52.

47. Seamus O'Coughlin, *Squaw Valley Gold: American Hockey's Olympic Odyssey* (San Jose, Calif.: Writer's Showcase, 2001), 125.

48. "Olympic Hockey War Flares Anew!" *Boston Daily Globe*, September 6, 1947; Gordon MacDonald, "A Colossal Embroglio: Control of Amateur Ice Hockey in the United States and the 1948 Olympic Winter Games," *Olympika: The International Journal of Olympic Studies* 7 (1998): 43–60.

49. O'Coughlin, *Squaw Valley Gold*, 125.

50. *1948 Official Hockey Guide of the AHAUSA* (n. p., n. d.), 7–15, quote at 7, USA Hockey Archives, Colorado Springs (hereafter USAHA).

51. "Berlin, N.H., Another Great Hockey Town," *United States Amateur Hockey* 2, no. 3 (April–May 1960): 5, 6, 30, Art Berglund Collection, USAHA; Larz Anderson,

NEAHA "Senior N.E. Championship," in *1948 Official Hockey Guide of the AHAUSA* (n. p., n. d.), 144, USAHA; O'Coughlin, *Squaw Valley Gold*, 29.

52. "The Fabulous Warroad Story," *United States Amateur Hockey* 1, no. 2 (November 1959): 10–13, Art Berglund Collection, USAHA; Warren Strandell, *Cal and the Lakers: Winning under Two Flags* (Steinbach, Man.: Derksen, [1997]).

53. O'Coughlin, *Squaw Valley* Gold, 24.

54. IHL Constitution, memo, and salary figures in "IHL, 1959–60" folder, Benjamin N. Berger Papers, Minnesota Historical Society, St. Paul, Minn. (hereafter Berger Papers).

55. O'Coughlin, *Squaw Valley Gold*, 30.

56. The 2 percent figure appears in a letter from P. E. M. Thompson, AHAUS secretary, to Lowell Kaplan, Minneapolis, December 2, 1961, Berger Papers, box 19, folder "IHL 1961"; Bulletin 158 of the Amateur Hockey Association of the United States, August 20, 1960, in Berger Papers, box 20, "Hockey Associations" folder; AHAUS Statement of Receipts and Disbursements General Account, Fiscal Year Ending April 30, 1963, Berger Papers, box 20, "IHL May 1963" folder.

57. Dr. F. Kraatz, "I See a Great Future in Ice Hockey," *Ice Hockey World Annual, 1953–54*, 23.

58. O'Coughlin, *Squaw Valley Gold*, 32–33.

59. *United States Amateur Hockey* 1, no. 1 (September–October 1959): 2, Art Berglund Collection, USAHA.

60. "Special Team Insurance," *United States Amateur Hockey* 3, no. 4 (November 1961): 16, 17; "Each Team Should Belong," *Hockey* 5, no. 1 (January 1963): 4, 5, Art Berglund Collection, USAHA.

61. "A Substantial Difference," *United States Amateur Hockey* 3, no. 2 (February–March 1961): 3, Art Berglund Collection, USAHA.

62. Ronald A. Smith, *Sports and Freedom: The Rise of Big-time College Athletics* (New York: Oxford University Press, 1988); Michael Oriard, *Reading Football: How the Popular Press Created an American Spectacle* (Chapel Hill: University of North Carolina Press, 1998).

63. "Pete Dawkins: Black Knight on Ice," *United States Amateur Hockey* 1, no. 1 (September–October 1959): 18–20, Art Berglund Collection, USAHA.

64. Harry Cleverly, "Looking Ahead," *United States Amateur Hockey* 2, no. 3 (April–May 1960): 30, Art Berglund Collection, USAHA; William Rothwell, "The Life of Victor Heyliger and His Contributions in the Establishment and Development of Intercollegiate Hockey in the United States," PhD diss., Ohio State University, 1977, 112–14.

65. Theodore A. Briedenthal, "Golden Moments: Ice Hockey Championship Celebrates 50th Anniversary," *NCAA News*, December 2, 1997, 8; Rothwell, "Life of Victor Heyliger," 110; *NCAA National Championship Hockey Tournament Official Program 1953* (Colorado Springs: Broadmoor Ice Palace, 1953), US Hockey Hall of Fame, Eveleth, Minn. (hereafter USHHoF).

66. Louis F. Keller, "History of Ice Hockey Rules," *NCAA Ice Hockey Guide 1951* (New York: National Collegiate Athletic Bureau, 1950), 18–20.

67. Percy C. Rogers, "How to Form an Officials' Association," *NCAA Ice Hockey Guide 1951* (New York: National Collegiate Athletic Bureau, 1950), 84–85.

68. "A College Profile/Bowdoin College, Brunswick Maine," *United States Amateur Hockey* (February–March 1961): 18–19, Art Berglund Collection, USA Hockey.

69. Sid Watson, interview with Stephen Hardy, September 11, 2000, in box 1, MC 213, Charles E. Holt Archives of American Hockey, Milne Special Collections, Dimond Library, University of New Hampshire (hereafter Holt Archives).

70. John Neihart, "Minnesota College Conference," *NCAA Ice Hockey Guide 1951* (New York: National Collegiate Athletic Bureau, 1950), 44; Roland A. Vandall, "Minnesota State College Conference," ibid., 45.

71. Don Clark, "Brief History"; Rothwell, "Life of Victor Heyliger," 118–126.

72. Bernard M. Corbett, *The Beanpot: Fifty Years of Thrills, Spills, and Chills* (Boston: Northeastern University Press, 2002), 115.

73. Murray Murdoch, "The Eastern Championship Selections," *Official Ice Hockey NCAA Guide 1955* (New York: National Collegiate Athletic Bureau, 1954), 13; Leonard M. Fowle, James H. Fullerton, and R. B. Priestley, "The East," in *NCAA Ice Hockey Guide 1962* (New York: National Collegiate Athletic Bureau, 1961), 11; Art Dunphy, "Eastern College Athletic Conference Tournament," in *NCAA Ice Hockey Guide 1963* (New York: National Collegiate Athletic Bureau, 1962), 11.

74. Program, Eleventh Annual Lawrenceville School Invitation Hockey Tournament, 1958, 2; uncatalogued program in "High School" box, USHHoF.

75. "16th New England interscholastic hockey tournament," *United States Amateur Hockey* 1, no. 3 (December 1959), 7–9, Art Berglund Collection, USAHA.

76. Don Riley, "Prep Hockey Ducats Go on Sale Monday," 1948–49 folder, Harding High School Scrapbooks, Minnesota Historical Society; Gary L. Philips, *Skate for Goal: Highlights from Minnesota's State Hockey Tournament* (Afton, Minn.: Afton, 1982), 4.

77. Program, Eighteenth Annual Minnesota State High School Hockey Tournament, St. Paul Auditorium, February 22–24, 1962, uncatalogued program in "High School" box, USHHoF, 2, 6; "Fifty-Fifth State Tournament Played in 2003," official program, 2004 Minnesota State Boys Hockey Tournament, 7, uncatalogued program in "School" box, USHHoF.

78. "We Said It Before, And We Will Say It Again," *Hockey* 4, no. 2 (September–October 1962), 4, Art Berglund Collection, USAHA.

Chapter 17. Cold Wars and International Ice: 1945–1971

1. Tony Judt, *Postwar: A History of Europe since 1945* (New York: Penguin, 2005), 13–40, 86–134; Anne Applebaum, *Iron Curtain: The Crushing of Eastern Europe, 1944–1956* (New York: Doubleday, 2012), 3–22; Keith Lowe, *Savage Continent: Europe in the Aftermath of World War II* (New York: St. Martin's, 2012).

2. "The Life and Times of Hubert Brooks M.C. C.D.: A Canadian Hero," digitized diary at: http://hubertbrooks.com/9_3HubertBrooks_Games.html.

3. Ibid.

4. "The English Set-Up," *Ice Hockey World Annual*, 1952–53, 7.

5. "Big Six," "Directory of British Ice Rinks," in *Ice Hockey World Annual*, 1952–53, 37, 109–11.

6. Quotes in Giddens, "This I Believe," *Ice Hockey World Annual*, 1953–54, 3. See also Giddens, Editor's Preface, *Ice Hockey World Annual*, 1951–52, 159.

7. "What It Costs to Run a Team," *Ice Hockey World Annual*, 1954–55, 35. Recollections in Phil Drackett, *Flashing Blades: The Story of British Ice Hockey* (Ramsbury, UK: Crowood, 1987), 133; Stephen Hardy, telephone interview with Ken Johannson, October 14, 2014. Our thanks to Dave Ogrean for setting up the interview.

8. Drackett, *Flashing Blades*, 140, 142.

9. Judt, *Postwar*, 8, 28, and 357–58 for the mid-1950s deteriorating economic conditions in Britain.

10. John F. Ahearne, "The Championships," Official Program, World and European Ice Hockey Championships, Harringay Arena, March 15, 1950, 4–5.

11. Kraatz, "I See a Great Future in Ice Hockey," *Ice Hockey World Annual*, 1953–54, 22–23.

12. Giddens, *Ice Hockey*, 49, 51.

13. Giddens, *Ice Hockey*, 52; Andrew Podnieks et al., "Arne Stromberg," *Kings of the Ice: A History of World Hockey* (Richmond Hill, Ont.: NDE, 2002), 419–20.

14. Giddens, *Ice Hockey*, 52.

15. "The Ahearne Trophy," *Ice Hockey World Annual*, 1952–53, 84–85.

16. *Ice Hockey World Annual*, 1954–55, 21.

17. "'A 10-Years Explosion': Ice Hockey in Sweden," in official bulletin, World Championship Ice Hockey Tournament, Stockholm, March 15–30, 1969 (Stockholm: Organizing Committee of the 1969 Games, 1969), 6–7; Tobias Stark, "Ice Hockey, Europe," in *Sports around the World: History, Culture, Practice*, ed. John Nauright and Charles Parrish (Santa Barbara: ABC-Clio, 2012), 348; Sterner, Bjorn, and Stolz, see Podnieks et al., *Kings of the Ice*, 291, 319, 325–26, 342, 388; V. Viktorov, *Wizard of Ice Hockey*, trans. D. Svirsky (Moscow: Foreign Languages Pub., 1957), 15; Tobias Stark, "The Pioneer, the Pal, and the Poet: Masculinities and National Identities in Canadian, Swedish, and Soviet-Russian Ice Hockey during the Cold War," in *Putting It on Ice: Vol 2, Internationalizing "Canada's Game,"* ed. Colin D. Howell (Halifax, N.S.: Gorsebrook, 2002), 39–44.

18. Tobias Stark, "How Swede It Is: Börje Salming and the Migration of Swedish Ice Hockey Players to the NHL, 1957–2012," paper presented at the International Hockey Conference "Constructing the Hockey Family: Home, Community, Bureaucracy and Marketplace," St. Mary's University, Halifax, N.S., July 12–14, 2012, 2–3.

19. Jani Mesikämmen, "From Part-Time Passion to Big-Time Business: The Professionalization of Finnish Ice Hockey," in *Putting It on Ice*, 2:22.

20. Osmo Kivinen et al., "A Case Study in Cultural Diffusion: British Ice Hockey and American Influences in Europe," *Culture, Sport, Society* 4, no. 1 (Spring 2001):

57–58; Igor Kuperman, "From Andora to Yugoslavia: The History of Hockey and is Structure Today in Each IIHF Nation," in *Total Hockey*, vol.1, ed. Dan Diamond (New York: Total Sports, 1998), 448.

21. Giddens, *Ice Hockey*, 48; Igor Kuperman, "The Fall of the Maple Leaf and the Rise of the Star, 1954–62, in *World of Hockey: Celebrating a Century of the IIHF, 1908–2008*, ed. Szymon Szemberg and Andrew Podnieks (Bolton, Ont.: Fenn, 2007), 47–48.

22. Stan Obodiac, "Canadian Coaches in Switzerland," *Ice Hockey World Annual*, 1953–54, 99; M. Thoma, "Genuine Amateurs Make It Difficult to Compete," *Ice Hockey World Annual*, 1954–55, 99; Donna Spencer, "Canada Loses to Switzerland 3–2 in a Shootout at World Hockey Championship," *Toronto Globe and Mail*, May 5, 2013.

23. "Germany Enters Two Teams," *Ice Hockey World and Ice Hockey Review*, February 26, 1955, U.S. Hockey Hall of Fame (hereafter USHHoF); Kuperman, "From Andora to Yugoslavia," 449.

24. Arnd Kruger, "Germany," in *European Cultures in Sport*, ed. James Riordan and Arnd Kruger, (Bristol, UK: Intellect, 2003), 81, 83.

25. Judt, *Postwar*, 117; Central Committee quote in James Riordan and Hart Cantelon, "The Soviet Union and Eastern Europe," in Riordan and Kruger, *European Cultures in Sport*, 97.

26. Podnieks et al., *Kings of the Ice*, 318, 321, 324, 534.

27. Viktorov, *Wizard of Ice Hockey*, 3, 5–6; Lawrence Martin, *The Red Machine: The Soviet Quest to Dominate Canada's Game* (Toronto: Doubleday Canada, 1990), 36–49.

28. Quotes in Robert Edelman, *Serious Fun: A History of Spectator Sports in the USSR* (New York: Oxford University Press, 1993), 111–12.

29. Igor Kuperman, "Tarasov's Unstoppable Dynasty, 1963–1971," in *World of Hockey*, 51; Bubnik quote in Kuperman, "Fall of the Maple Leaf," 36; Edelman, *Serious Fun*, 115; Lev Filatov, *Hockey* (Moscow: Novosti, 1966), 19–22.

30. Murray Williamson, *The Great American Hockey Dilemma* (Wayzata, Minn.: Turtinen, 1978), 88–89; Anatoli Tarasov, *Road to Olympus* (Toronto: Griffin House, 1969), 108–10; Interview with Anatoly Firsov, http://www.pbs.org/redfiles/sports/deep/interv/s_int_anatoly_firsov.htm.

31. Kraatz, "I See a Great Future in Ice Hockey," 23; Filatev, *Hockey*, 9; Kuperman, "Fall of the Maple Leaf," 43; "Russians Teach Canadians Lesson in Stickhandling," *Ottawa Journal*, March 8, 1954; "Meet the Champions," *Ice Hockey World and Ice Hockey Review*, February 26, 1955, 8; "World Champions," *Ice Hockey World Annual*, 1954–55, 51.

32. "A Sliver of Shame," *Ice Hockey World Annual*, 1954–55, 52–53.

33. Wolfgang Keller, "The World Series," *Ice Hockey World and Ice Hockey Review*, February 26, 1955, 5.

34. "We Couldn't Have It Both Ways," *Ice Hockey World Annual*, 1955–56, 43; "Quotes on the Vital Game," *Ice Hockey World Annual*, 1955–56, 45; Kuperman,

"Fall of the Maple Leaf," 47; Dan MacKinnon, "Myth, Memory, and the Kitchener-Waterloo Dutchmen in Canadian International Hockey," *Sport History Review* 31 (May 2000): 1–2.

35. Podnieks et al., *Kings of the Ice,* 287–88.

36. Judt, *Postwar*, 139.

37. John B. Garrison, "Winter Olympic Games of 1948," in *1949 Official Ice Hockey Guide of the Amateur Hockey Association of the United States* (New York: AHAUS, 1948), 267; a biography of Masaryk can be found at http://en.wikipedia.org/wiki/Jan_Masaryk.

38. "Josef Malecek," in Podnieks et al., *Kings of the Ice*, 177–78; Patrick Houda, "Josef Malecek," http://www.sihss.se/josefmalecek.html.

39. Harry Missildine, "The Call Came from Prague to Trail," *Spokane Spokesman Review*, January 16, 1958.

40. Anne Applebaum, *Iron Curtain: The Crushing of Eastern Europe, 1944–1956* (New York: Doubleday, 2012), xxiv; David Goldblatt, *The Ball Is Round: A Global History of Soccer* (New York: Riverhead, 2008), 338; http://www.hcsparta.cz/zobraz.asp?t=historie; http://en.wikipedia.org/wiki/HC_Sparta_Praha.

41. Judt, *Postwar*, 177–78.

42. Jan Velinger and Katrin Bock, "A Brief History of Czech Ice Hockey," at http://www.radio.cz/en/section/czechs/a-brief-history-of-czech-ice-hockey; http://en.wikipedia.org/wiki/HC_Sparta_Praha; "Olympic, World, and European Championships," in *Total Hockey,* ed. Dan Diamond et al. (New York: Total Sports, 1998) 503; "Story #48: Czechoslovakian Team Jailed for Treason: Entire Generation Lost," March 11, 1950, http://www.iihf.com/sk/iihf-home/the-iihf/100-year-anniversary/100-top-stories/story-48.html.

43. Kraatz, "I See a Great Future," 23; "Vlastimil Bubnik" and "Karel Gut," Podnieks et al., *Kings of the Ice*, 307–8, 322–23.

44. "Jaroslav Jirik," "Jan Suchy," and "Jiri Holik," *Kings of the Ice*, 393–94, 426–28, 429.

45. Judt, *Postwar*, 176.

46. Quotes in Szymon Szemberg, "Two Games Czechoslovakia Simply Couldn't Lose," in *World of Hockey,* 59; Podnieks et al. *Kings of the Ice*, 354; Joe Pelletier, "Where Were You in '69? Czech Victory Surpasses 1972 Dramatics," *Hockey Research Journal* 6 (2002), http://www.sihrhockey.org/public_journals.cfm.

Chapter 18. Postwar Brand Wars: 1945–1971

1. "Wins Olympics," *Ice Hockey World Annual,* 1952–53, 81; "Canada Ponders Abandoning of Olympic Hockey," *Boston Daily Globe*, March 6, 1952.

2. "Television," *News-Week*, February 15, 1936, n. p.

3. V. Viktorov, *Wizard of Ice Hockey*, trans. D. Svirsky (Moscow: Foreign Languages Pub., 1957), 24, 44, 47.

4. Scott Young, *War on Ice: Canada in International Hockey* (Toronto: McClelland

and Stewart, 1976), 8, 10; "World Championship Rules," official program, World and European Ice Hockey Championships, Harringay Arena, March 15, 1950, 11.

5. Tony Judt, *Postwar: A History of Europe since 1945* (New York: Penguin, 2005), 197–225.

6. 1954 quote in Scott Young, *War on Ice*, 10; Anatoly Tarasov, *Tarasov: The Father of Russian Hockey*, trans. Svetlana Kokhanovskaya (Glendale, Calif.: Griffith, 1997), 3–12; Robert Baumann, "The Central Red Army Sports Club (TsSKA): Forging a Military Tradition in Soviet Ice Hockey," *Journal of Sport History* 15, no. 2 (Summer, 1988): 151–66.

7. Anatoli Vladimirovich Tarasov, *Road to Olympus* (Toronto: Griffin House, 1969), 49; Gary Mossman, *Lloyd Percival: Coach and Visionary* (Niagara Falls, Ont.: Seraphim, 2013), 305; Lloyd Percival, *The Hockey Handbook*, rev. ed. (South Brunswick, N.J.: Barnes, 1960 [1951]), vii, 9, 48–52.

8. Bill Cleary interview with Stephen Hardy, January 9, 2012, transcript in author's possession. Tarasov's criticisms in Robert Edelman, *Serious Fun: A History of Spectator Sports in the USSR* (New York: Oxford University Press, 1993), 114.

9. Gladwin Hill, "Russian Tip Helps U.S. Win Olympic Hockey," *New York Times*, Feb. 29, 1960; William Leggett, "Our Never-Say-Die Hockeymen," *Sports Illustrated*, March 7, 1960, 22–23; "Understanding and Sportsmanship," interview with Anatoli Tarasov, *United States Amateur Hockey*, April–May 1960, 12, 13, 15.

10. John Soares, "Boycotts, Brotherhood, and More: International Hockey from Moscow to Colorado Springs via Squaw Valley (1957–1962)," in *Now Is the Winter: Thinking about Hockey*, ed. Jamie Dopp and Richard Harrison (Hamilton, Ont.: Wolsak and Wynn, 2009), 97–111.

11. Bill Cleary interview with Stephen Hardy, January 9, 2012; Tarasov, *Road to Olympus*, 51. On Khomenkov, see Jon Sanful, "The Reign of the Red: 1963–1971 Soviet National Team," in *Total Hockey*, ed. Dan Diamond et al. (New York: Total Sports, 1998), 465–68.

12. Tarasov, *Road to Olympus*, 4–5.

13. Ibid., 8, 17; Vladislav Tretiak, *Tretiak: The Legend*, trans. Sam Budman and Maria Budman (Edmonton: Plains, 1987), 14.

14. Eddie Jeremiah, *Ice Hockey* (New York: Barnes, 1942), 21; Percival, *Hockey Handbook*; Cantelon, "Revisiting the Introduction of Ice Hockey into the Former Soviet Union," in *Putting It on Ice: Vol. 2, Internationalizing "Canada's Game,"* ed. Colin Howell (Halifax, N.S.: Gorsebrook, 2001), 32.

15. Tretiak, *Tretiak: The Legend*; Edelman, *Serious Fun*, 94; Yuri Brokhin, *The Big Red Machine: The Rise and Fall of Soviet Champions* (New York: Random House, 1977), 174.

16. Andrew C. Holman, "The Canadian Hockey Player Problem: Cultural Reckoning and National Identities in American Collegiate Sport, 1947–80," *Canadian Historical Review* 88, no. 3 (September 2007): 439–68.

17. *The Official National Collegiate Athletic Association Ice Hockey Guide 1947*, ed. David A. Tirrell (New York: Barnes, 1946), 31–33; *The Official National Collegiate*

Athletic Association Ice Hockey Guide 1956, ed. David A. Tirrell ([New York]: National Collegiate Athletic Bureau, 1955), 16–19; *The Official National Collegiate Athletic Association Ice Hockey Guide 1966*, ed. John S. Rossi (New York: National Collegiate Athletic Bureau, 1965), 17–19; *The Official National Collegiate Athletic Association Ice Hockey Guide 1976*, ed. John S. Rossi (Shawnee Mission, Kan.: NCAA Publishing Service, 1975), 33–39.

18. John U. Bacon, *Blue Ice: The Story of Michigan Hockey* (Ann Arbor: University of Michigan Press, 2001), 150; Keith Magnuson, *None Against!* (New York: Dodd Mead, 1973), 79–80.

19. Whitney Tower, "U.S. Colleges Take to the Ice," *Sports Illustrated*, February 21, 1955, 8, 10; "400 Canadians playing in U.S. College Hockey," *Toronto Globe and Mail*, March 2, 1967.

20. "Imported Canadian Club," *Time*, January 6, 1961, 55.

21. Dean McGowen, "College Hockey, with Canadian Flavor, Fast-Moving Sport in United States," *New York Times*, December 5, 1971.

22. Tower, "U.S. Colleges Take to the Ice," *Sports Illustrated*, February 21, 1955, 10.

23. Ibid., 9; John B. Garrison, Lincoln, Mass. to William J. Cleary, Harvard University, Cambridge, Mass., November 30, 1979, Paul Duffy Collection, Holt Hockey Archives, Dimond Library, University of New Hampshire (hereafter HHA).

24. "Blair Wants Colleges to Produce Pros," *Toronto Globe and Mail*, December 3, 1969; "MacMillan Says College Hockey Was Hindrance," *Toronto Globe and Mail*, September 19, 1963.

25. Magnuson, *None Against!*, 90.

26. Minutes of the Annual Meeting of the NCAA Ice Hockey Rules Committee, 1967, HHA, series V: NCAA box 1, folder 4; Annual Report of the President of the NHL to the Board of Governors, "Doc" Seaman Research Centre, Hockey Hall of Fame, Toronto, 1966–67, 10–11. Thanks to Andrew Ross for this source.

27. Holman, "Canadian Hockey Player Problem," 461–65; "N.C.A.A. Proposes to Limit Players," *New York Times*, December 5, 1969; "Minutes of the 1973 Annual Meeting of the NCAA Ice Hockey Rules and Tournament Committee," Duffy Collection, HHA; "Play, Johnny, Play: But Not Too Hard," *NCAA Ice Hockey Championship Program 1971*, 29, Duffy Collection, HHA.

28. Jenifer Parks, "Verbal Gymnastics: Sports, Bureaucracy, and the Soviet Union's Entrance into the Olympic Games, 1946–52," in *East Plays West: Sport and the Cold War*, ed. Stephen Wagg and David Andrews (New York: Routledge, 2007), 30; James Riordan, *Sport in Soviet Society* (Cambridge: Cambridge University Press, 1977), 80.

29. Charles W. Thayer, "A Question of the Soul," *Sports Illustrated*, August 15, 1960.

30. Dr. F. Kraatz, "I See a Great Future in Ice Hockey," *Ice Hockey World Annual*, 1953–54, 23.

31. Allen Guttmann, *The Games Must Go On: Avery Brundage and the Olympic Movement* (New York: Columbia University Press, 1984), 128.

32. *IIHF Statutes and By-Laws* (London: Empire House, 1963), 17–18; Young, *War on Ice*, 95, 98.

33. Jani Mesikämmen, "From Part-Time Passion to Big-Time Business: The Professionalization of Finnish Ice Hockey," in *Putting It on Ice*, 2:25.

34. Godfrey Wood, "Pro-Amateur Hockey Situation in U.S. Should Be Clarified," *Boston Globe*, February 13, 1966, 52; Murray Williamson, *The Great American Hockey Dilemma* (Wayzata, Minn.: Turtinen, 1978), 43–44, 47, 98.

35. Tarasov, *Road to Olympus*, 169.

36. Lynda Baril, *Nos Glorieuses: Plus de Cent Ans de Hockey Féminin au Québec* (Montréal: Les Éditions La Presse, 2013), 91.

37. See Brian McFarlane, *Proud Past, Bright Future: One Hundred Years of Canadian Women's Hockey* (Toronto: Stoddart, 1994), chs. 4 and 5; Joanna Avery and Julie Stevens, *Too Many Men on the Ice: Women's Hockey in North America* (Victoria, B.C.: Polestar, 1997), chs. 2 and 3.

38. "Blue and White," *Toronto Globe and Mail*, February 18, 1950; "Reeve Hangs in Lobby during Charity Night," *Toronto Globe and Mail*, February 19, 1955; "Pulford, Brewer Coach Girls at UCC Old Boys' Night," *Toronto Globe and Mail*, January 20, 1961.

39. McFarlane, *Proud Past*, 109. A search for girls' and women's hockey coverage in in the 1940s and 1950s in Toronto's *Globe and Mail* turns up a total of five stories.

40. Baril, *Nos Glorieuses*, 105–21.

41. Avery and Stevens, *Too Many*, 78; Dan Proudfoot, "Of Bobby Pins, Hair Brushes and Grandmothers," *Toronto Globe and Mail*, April 27, 1970.

42. "Blue and White," *Toronto Globe and Mail*, February 18, 1950.

43. Baril, *Nos Glorieuses*, 113.

44. Scott Young, "Has Your Sweetie a Charley Horse?" *Toronto Globe and Mail*, January 16, 1962.

45. Scott Young, "Hayman Says It's News to Him," *Toronto Globe and Mail*, January 23, 1962.

46. Martha Guran, "Boroughs Offering Skating Classes," *Toronto Star*, January 9, 1971; "Ruth E. Smith," *Toronto Star*, July 12, 1975; "Hockey Finals Regent Park Show," *Toronto Star*, March 8, 1971; "History," Ringette Canada, http://www.ringette.ca/our-sport/history-of-ringette.

47. "Ice Hockey at the London Rinks," *London Daily Mail*, December 17, 1930.

48. "Sport d'Hiver a Chamonix," *Le Figaro*, January 31, 1932, "Le Hockey sur Glace au Palais des Sports," *Le Figaro*, February 12, 1933; "Sports et Sportifs. Le Hockey sur Glace," *Dimanche-Illustré*, December 9, 1934.

49. "6-ft. WOMAN ICE Player: In England Team to Meet France," *London Daily*

Mirror, March 11, 1936; *London Daily Mirror*, March 1, 1934; W. F. Sanderson, "The Ice Lambs: Women's Thrilling Hockey Gambols," *London Daily Mail*, March 3, 1932.

50. Authors' translation and emphasis. "Racines" [Roots] *La Ligne Bleue* (December 2010), Fédération Française de Hockey sur Glace, http://www.hockeyfrance.com/upload/archives-newsletters/files/662/673.html.

51. "Racines" and Simon Barnes, "Sporting Diary . . . Jolly Hockey," *London Times*, March 23, 1985. On Australia, see http://icelegendsaustralia.com/1stIceChampions-whockey.html.

52. On CCM, see John A. McKenty, *Canada Cycle and Motor: The CCM Story, 1899–1983* (Belleville, Ont.: Epic, 2011).

53. Gilles Pelchat, *Sher-Wood et son batisseur Léopold Drolet* (Sherbrooke, Que.: GGC, 2000), 37, 75.

54. Warren Strandell, "The Christian Story," pamphlet published by Christian Brothers, 1994. On Northland, see "What Makes a Good Stick?" *United States Amateur Hockey* 1, no. 3 (December 1959): 15–17.

55. "The Ice Age: Will the Echo Generation Swap Their Toys for Hockey Sticks?" *Canadian Business* 76, no. 9 (May 12, 2003): 18; "From the Archives of *Sporting Goods Dealer*—October '74," in *SGB's Inside Sporting Goods*, vol. 15, no. 37 (October 8, 2004), n.p.

56. "Ice Hockey and TV," *Ice Hockey World Annual*, 1954–55, 5.

57. Drake McFeely, email communication with Stephen Hardy, October 10, 2014; "A Review of the Summer Schools," *United States Amateur Hockey* 1, no. 3 (December 1959): 10–11.

58. Jim Kernaghan, "They Pokecheck Summer Away," *Toronto Star*, July 23, 1966; Jim Kernaghan, "NHL Stars Cash In on Their Names," *Toronto Star*, July 5, 1969.

59. Herb Ralby, "Summer Hockey: A Boom in Schools for Young Blades," *Boston Globe*, August 28, 1966.

60. Marcel Pronovost, "Effective Defensive Play," *United States Amateur Hockey* 3, no. 2 (February–March 1961): 22.

Chapter 19. The Old Order Disrupted: 1972

1. Tom Dowling, "The Orr Effect," *Atlantic Monthly* 227 (April 1971): 63.

2. Ibid., 65–67; Bobby Orr, *Orr: My Story* (New York: Putnam's, 2013), 92; Alan Eagleson, with Scott Young, *Hockey Czar* (Toronto: McClelland and Stewart, 1991), 59.

3. Dowling, "Orr Effect," 65, 67.

4. Neil Earle, "The Global Game: The Internationalization of Professional Hockey and Technological Modernism," *Studies in Popular Culture* 21, no. 1 (October 1998): 58–72.

5. "Story #19: IIHF Allows Bodychecking in All Three Zones," http://www.iihf

.com/sk/iihf-home/the-iihf/100-year-anniversary/100-top-stories; John B. Garrison, "Winter Olympic Games of 1948," in *1949 Official Ice Hockey Guide of the Amateur Hockey Association of the United States* (New York: AHAUS, 1948), 268–69.

6. "Annual Report of the President of the NHL to the Board of Governors, Hockey Hall of Fame and Museum: 1968–69," 6; Igor Kuperman, "Tarasov's Unstoppable Dynasty, 1963–1971," in *World of Hockey: Celebrating a Century of the IIHF, 1908–2008*, ed. Szymon Szemberg and Andrew Podnieks (Bolton, Ont.: Fenn, 2007), 55; Scott Young, *War on Ice: Canada in International Hockey* (Toronto: McClelland and Stewart, 1976), 147–50.

7. Anatoli Tarasov, *Tarasov: The Father of Russian Hockey*, trans. Svetlana Kokhanovskaya (Glendale, Calif.: Griffith, 1997), 31; "Story #19: IIHF Allows Bodychecking."

8. Kuperman, "Tarasov's Unstoppable Dynasty," 55, 59; "Pros Will Play in World Hockey," *New York Times*, July 9, 1969; Young, *War on Ice*, 148.

9. Young, *War on Ice*, 151–58; Kuperman, "Tarasov's Unstoppable Dynasty," 60; "Olympic, World, and European Championships," in *Total Hockey*, ed. Dan Diamond (New York: Total Sports, 1998), 505.

10. Tarasov, *Road to Olympus*, 169; Roy MacSkimming, *Cold War: The Amazing Canada-Soviet Hockey Series of 1972* (Vancouver: Greystone, 1996), 5–9; "Anatoli Tarasov," in Andrew Podnieks et al., *Kings of the Ice: A History of World Hockey* (Richmond Hill, Ont.: NDE, 2002), 357.

11. Ken Dryden with Mark Mulvoy, *Face-Off at the Summit* (Boston: Little, Brown, 1973), 45–46; Jay Scherer, Gregory H. Duquette, and Daniel S. Mason, "The Cold War and the (Re)articulation of Canadian National Identity: The 1972 Canada-USSR Summit Series," in *East Plays West: Sport and the Cold War*, ed. Stephen Wagg and David Andrews (New York: Routledge, 2007), 173–74.

12. Pierson's unforgettable line recalled by author Hardy, who watched the original broadcast.

13. Harry Sinden, *Hockey Showdown: Canada–Russia Hockey Series* (Toronto, Ont.: Doubleday Canada, 1972), 9; Vladislav Tretiak, *Tretiak: The Legend*, trans. Sam Budman and Maria Budman, (Edmonton, Alb.: Plains, 1987), 55.

14. Sinden, *Hockey Showdown*, preface.

15. Dryden, *The Game: A Thoughtful and Provocative Look at a Life in Hockey* (New York: Times, 1983), 275, 277–79.

16. Gerald Eskenazi, "Campbell Defends NHL Ban of Hull from Canada Team for Soviet Series," *New York Times*, July 22, 1972; Dryden with Mulvoy, *Face-Off at the Summit*, 4; Alan Eagleson with Scott Young, *Power Play: The Memoirs of Hockey Czar Alan Eagleson* (Toronto: McClelland and Stewart, 1991), 87.

17. Ed Willes, *The Rebel League: The Short and Unruly Life of the World Hockey Association* (Toronto: McClelland and Stewart, 2004), 8–9; Gary Davidson with Bill Libby, *Breaking the Game Wide Open* (New York: Atheneum, 1974), 3.

18. Peter L. de Rosa, "The World Hockey Association and the Economics of Rival Leagues," paper presented at "Canada's Game? Critical Perspectives on Ice Hockey

and Identity," Plymouth, Mass., April 14–16, 2005, 4; Willes, *Rebel League*, 17; *1972–73 World Hockey Association Action Annual* (Santa Ana, Calif.: WHA, 1972), 1.

19. Willes, *Rebel League*, 29.

20. Gerald Eskenazi, "Bobby Hull Shifts Hockey Leagues for $2.5 Million," *New York Times*, June 28, 1972; Gerald Eskenazi, "After All These Years, N.H.L. Thinks It Has Found a Way to Stop Bobby," *New York Times*, June 29, 1972, 149.

21. Davidson, *Breaking the Game*, 145.

22. Gerald Eskenazi, "Temporary Injunction against NHL Frees Hull and Others to Play in WHA," *New York Times*, November 9, 1972; "Reserve Clause in Hockey Shattered: May Affect Flood," *Jet* 43, no. 10 (November 30, 1972): 51; Charles P. Korr, *The End of Baseball as We Knew It: The Player's Union* (Urbana: University of Illinois Press, 2002).

23. Dave Anderson, "Hull's Conflict of Interest," *New York Times,* July 2, 1972.

24. Minutes of the Annual Meeting of the NCAA Ice Hockey Rules Committee, 1967, Charles Holt Archives of American Hockey (hereafter cited as HHA), series V: NCAA box 1, folder 4, Dimond Library, University of New Hampshire.

25. Minutes of the Annual Meeting of the NCAA Ice Hockey Rules Committee, 1968, 1971,1972, series V: NCAA box 1, folders 4, 5, HHA. *Official NCAA Ice Hockey Guide 1973* (Phoenix: College Athletics, 1972), IH-3.

26. Bob Monahan, "College Hockey Gets Pro Look as NCAA Alters Checking Rule," *Boston Globe*, March 22, 1972.

27. Joe Concannon, "College Ice Hockey Enters New Era—Greater Scope, Exposure Than Before," *Official NCAA Ice Hockey Guide 1973* (Phoenix, Ariz.: College Athletics, 1972), 5.

28. Julie Stevens and Anna H. Lathrop, "Boom or Bust: The Impact of the 1972 Summit Series on the Development of Women's Hockey in Canada," in *Coming Down the Mountain: Rethinking the 1972 Summit Series*, ed. Brian Kennedy (Hamilton, Ont.: Wolsak and Wynn, 2014), 143–59.

29. Ying Wushanley, *Playing Nice and Losing: The Struggle for Control of Women's Intercollegiate Athletics, 1960–2000* (Syracuse, N.Y.: Syracuse University Press, 2004); "Woman Recalls How Five Words Led to Creation of Title IX," *NCAA News*, July 21, 1997, 5; Amanda Ross Edwards, "Why Sport? The Development of Sport as a Policy Issue in Title IX of the Education Amendments of 1972," *Journal of Policy History* 22, no. 3 (2010): 300–36.

30. Bill Gilbert and Nancy Williamson, "Sport Is Unfair to Women," *Sports Illustrated*, May 28, 1973, 91; Bill Gilbert and Nancy Williamson, "Are You Being Two-Faced?" *Sports Illustrated*, June 4, 1973, 44–54; Bill Gilbert and Nancy Williamson, "Programmed to Be Losers," *Sports Illustrated*, June 11, 1973, 62.

31. Project on the Status and Education of Women, "What Constitutes Equality for Women in Sport?" (Washington, DC: Association of American Colleges, 1974); Bill Gilbert and Nancy Williamson, "Women in Sport: A Progress Report," *Sports Illustrated*, July 24, 1974, 26–30.

32. Bruce Kidd and John Macfarlane, *The Death of Hockey* (Toronto: New Press, 1972), 104–9.

33. Bruce Kidd, *The Struggle for Canadian Sport* (Toronto: University of Toronto Press, 1996).

34. John Nelson Washburn, "Soviet Hockey Gets Start in Kindergarten," *New York Times*, September 17, 1972.

35. Dryden with Mulvoy, *Face-Off at the Summit*, 113.

36. Julie Stevens, "The Development of the Canadian Hockey System: A Process of Institutional Divergence and Convergence," in *Putting It on Ice: Vol. 2, Internationalizing "Canada's Game,"* ed. Colin D. Howell (Halifax, N.S.: Gorsebrook, 2001), 59; Donald Macintosh and David Whitson, *The Game Planners: Transforming Canada's Sport System* (Kingston: McGill-Queen's University Press, 1990).

37. Frieden, *Global Capitalism*, 398, 416–17; Joyce Appleby, *The Relentless Revolution: A History of Capitalism* (New York: Norton, 2010), 334.

38. Vladislav Tretiak, *Tretiak: The Legend*, trans. Sam Budman and Maria Budman (Edmonton: Plains, 1987), 57; Bruce Levett, "Canadians in Moscow for Series Don't Have Tickets for Games," *Simcoe (Ontario) Reformer*, September 22, 1972, http://www.1972summitseries.com/SimcoeReformer/newspaperclippings.html.

39. David J. Whalen, "Communications Satellites: Making the Global Village Possible," http://www.hq.nasa.gov/office/pao/History/satcomhistory.html.

40. Judt, *Postwar*, 345–46; Stefan Szymanski, "'Jeux avec Frontières': Television Markets and European Sport," in *Sport and the Transformation of Modern Europe: States, Media and Markets 1950–2010*, ed. Alan Tomlinson, Christopher Young, and Richard Holt (London: Routledge, 2011), 112–27.

41. Brian Winston, *Media Technology and Society: A History from the Telegraph to the Internet* (London: Routledge, 1998), 311–16; Patrick Parsons, "The Evolution of the Cable-Satellite Distribution System," *Journal of Broadcasting and Electronic Media* 47, no. 1 (2003): 1–17.

42. Hockey Night in Boston Hockey 1982, Summer Tourney Program, 15, 21. Hockey Night in Boston, 8th Annual High School Preview Magazine, 1982–83, 2, 5, 23, 27. Uncatalogued programs in High School box, US Hockey Hall of Fame, Eveleth, Minn.

43. John Sinclair, Elizabeth Jacka, and Stuart Cunningham, eds., *New Patterns in Global Television: Peripheral Vision* (New York: Oxford University Press, 1996).

Chapter 20. Restructuring North America: 1972–1988

1. Robert McFadden, "Cheers Resound across Nation," *New York Times*, February 23, 1980; Craig Nickerson, "Red Dawn in Lake Placid: The Semi-Final Hockey Game at the Winter Olympics as Cold War Background," *Canadian Journal of History of Sport* 26 (1995): 73, 75; Steven R. Weisman, "Olympians, Received by Carter, Offer Petition Opposing Boycott," *New York Times*, February 26, 1980.

2. See "Story #1: Miracle on Ice," http://www.iihf.com/sk/iihf-home/the-iihf/100-year-anniversary/100-top-stories; Tim Wendell, *Going for the Gold: How the U.S. Won at Lake Placid, 1980* (Westport, Conn.: Lawrence Hill, 1980); Wayne Coffey, *The Boys of Winter: The Untold Story of a Coach, a Dream, and the 1980 U.S. Olympic Hockey Team* (New York: Crown, 2005).

3. John Gilbert, *Herb Brooks: The Inside Story of a Hockey Mastermind* (Minneapolis: Voyageur, 2008), 32.

4. "Forging the Team," *Newsweek*, March 3, 1980, 85; Gilbert, *Herb Brooks*, 24.

5. Murray Williamson, *The Great American Hockey Dilemma* (Wayzata, Minn.: Turtinen, 1978), 88–89; Tom Caraccioli and Jerry Caraccioli, *Striking Silver: The Untold Story of America's Forgotten Hockey Team* (Champaign, Ill.: Sports Publishing, 2006).

6. Gilbert, *Herb Brooks*, 217; Caraccioli and Caraccioli, *Striking Silver*, 95–98; Kevin Allen, *Star-Spangled Hockey: Celebrating 75 Years of USA Hockey* (Chicago: Triumph, 2011), 78–79.

7. Neil Amdur, "Thaw in Cold War," *New York Times*, December 10, 1983; Jeff Z. Klein, "Coach Helped Hockey Flourish beyond Asphalt," *New York Times*, December 3, 2014.

8. "An International Hockey Event—USSR vs. NHL," special edition of *Goal Magazine*, December 1975, 10, 41–42.

9. Wendell, *Going for the Gold*, 7, and William Oscar Johnson, "Of Gold and Gophers," *Sports Illustrated*, December 10, 1979, 60.

10. John Powers, "Easy Money," *Boston Globe*, March 28, 1980; Gilbert, *Herb Brooks*, 133–34, 158, 233; John Powers and Arthur C. Kaminsky, *One Goal: A Chronicle of the 1980 US Olympic Hockey Team* (New York: Harper and Row, 1984), 27–29.

11. "Names: Brooks Mulling Offer," *Boston Globe*, May 27, 1980; Carlos V. Ortiz, "Sports Log: Brooks Rejects Rockies," *Boston Globe*, May 31, 1980.

12. Peter L. de Rosa, "The World Hockey Association and the Economics of Rival Leagues," paper presented at "Canada's Game? Critical Perspectives on Ice Hockey and Identity," Plymouth, Mass., April 2005, 8; Stephen Laroche, *Changing the Game: A History of NHL Expansion* (Toronto: ECW, 2014).

13. Gary Davidson with Bill Libby, *Breaking the Game Wide Open* (New York: Atheneum, 1974), 176, 179; Ed Willes, *The Rebel League: The Short and Unruly Life of the World Hockey Association* (Toronto: McClelland and Stewart, 2004), 36–37.

14. de Rosa, "World Hockey Association," 10–11; Davidson, *Breaking the Game*, 212–13; Shirley Fischler, "The World Hockey Association," in *Total Hockey*, ed. Dan Diamond, (New York: Total Sports, 1998), 1:374–75.

15. See "List of National Hockey League Arenas," https://en.wikipedia.org/wiki/List_of_National_Hockey_League_arenas.

16. http://en.wikipedia.org/wiki/North_American_Hockey_League_%281973%E2%80%9377%29; http://en.wikipedia.org/wiki/Southern_Hockey_League_%281973%E2%80%9377%29; and Jim Mancuso, "The ACHL: The Incredible Shrinking League," *SIHR Journal of Hockey Research* 16 (2012–13): 159–72.

17. Scott Young, *The Boys of Saturday Night: Inside Hockey Night in Canada* (Toronto: Macmillan, 1990), 212.

18. On NHL TV in the United States and Peter Puck, see https://en.wikipedia.org/wiki/History_of_the_National_Hockey_League_on_United_States_television; https://en.wikipedia.org/wiki/Peter_Puck.

19. Marvin Miller, *A Whole Different Ball Game: The Sport and Business of Baseball* (New York: Birch Lane, 1991), 214; Charles Korr, *The End of Baseball As We Knew It* (Urbana: University of Illinois Press, 2002).

20. David Cruise and Alison Griffiths, *Net Worth: Exploding the Myths of Pro Hockey* (New York: Penguin, 1992), 157; Bobby Orr, *Orr: My Story* (New York: Putnam's, 2013), 191.

21. Cruise and Griffiths, *Net Worth*, 193–225, Smythe quote at 207; Alan Eagleson, *Power Play: The Memoirs of Alan Eagleson*, with Scott Young (Toronto: McClelland and Stewart, 1991).

22. Cruise and Griffiths, *Net Worth*, 255–320.

23. Orr, *Orr*, 189. Russell Conway, *Game Misconduct: Alan Eagleson and the Corruption of Hockey* (Toronto: Macfarlane Walter and Ross, 1995).

24. Sources: *Official NCAA Ice Hockey Guide 1956*, ed. David Tirrell (New York: National Collegiate Athletic Bureau, 1955), 16–19; *Official Collegiate-Scholastic Ice Hockey Guide 1966*, ed. John S. Rossi (New York: National Collegiate Athletic Bureau, 1965), 17–19; *Official Collegiate-Scholastic Ice Hockey Guide 1976* (Shawnee Mission, Kan.: NCAA Publishing, 1975), 33–39; *1982 NCAA Ice Hockey* (Shawnee Mission, Kan.: NCAA Publishing, 1981), 12–20.

25. Dave Phillips, "New Collegiate Ice League Gets Name: Hockey East," *Providence Journal*, January 19, 1984; Rick Pearl, "Hockey East's New Executive Director," *Eastern College Hockey* 3, no. 2 (November 1987): 12–13.

26. Joe Concannon, "College Ice Hockey Enters New Era: Greater Scope, Exposure than Before," *NCAA Guidebook 1973*, 5.

27. J. R. McKenzie, "How to Beat the Saturday Blahs," *Hockey*, January 1978, 14–17; Ernie Roberts, "ECAC Hockey Tournament Belongs in Garden—But Will It Stay?" *Boston Globe*, March 14, 1979; Jack Craig, "Reagan's Reminiscences Charmed Viewers," *Boston Globe*, November 30, 1980.

28. Joe Concannon, "Judge Sides with BU Hockey Pair in NCAA Eligibility Dispute," *Boston Globe*, November 13, 1973; "BU Players Eligible: Judge Scores NCAA Rules," *Boston Globe*, November 28, 1973; "Buckton, Marzo: Now Gets Off the Ice, and into the Courtroom," *Boston Globe*, March 17, 1974; "Buckton, Marzo Reinstated by ECAC," *Boston Globe*, June 20, 1974.

29. "College Hockey: Buckton Cleared, Three Suspended," *Boston Globe*, November 17, 1974; "NCAA Eases Hockey Rules," *Boston Globe*, October 25, 1974; William E. Stedman Jr, "NCAA Hockey Ban Menaces Six from Harvard," *Harvard Crimson*, November 12, 1974.

30. Art Kaminsky, "Western Colleges Hold Balance of Power after a Short-Lived

Eastern Resurgence," *1977 Official Collegiate-Scholastic Ice Hockey Guide* (Shawnee Mission, Kan.: NCAA Pub., 1976), 6.

31. "Ontario Juniors Get Open Invitation to Join West Revolt," *Toronto Star*, June 10, 1968; "CAHA Decides Not to Buck NHL on Junior Age," *Toronto Star*, May 23, 1969.

32. Arlie Keller, "Junior A Hockey Goes National," *Toronto Star*, June 5, 1974.

33. For league numbers, see http://www.hockeydb.com/ihdb/stats/leagues.html.

34. Scott Young, *100 Years of Dropping the Puck: A History of the OHA* (Toronto: McClelland and Stewart, 1989), 292.

35. "Junior Hockey May Sign TV Deal," *Toronto Star*, October 28, 1982; "Junior Hockey Game of the Week to be Televised," *Toronto Star*, December 9, 1982.

36. Frank Orr, "Crucible for NHL Stars," *Toronto Star*, January 23, 1971.

37. Young, *100 Years*, 294.

38. "CAHA Expands Titles to Include Juveniles in National Playoffs," *Toronto Star*, May 20, 1980.

39. National Arena Census May 2005–December 2005, Canadian Recreation Facilities Council (Ottawa 2006).

40. "CAHA Against State Control," *Toronto Star*, May 23, 1972.

41. "CAHA Expands Titles."

42. "Hockey in Deep Trouble Government Report Says," *Toronto Star*, May 9, 1979.

43. Robert Pitter, "Racialization and Hockey in Canada: From Personal Troubles to a Canadian Challenge," in *Artificial Ice: Hockey, Culture and Commerce*, ed. David Whitson and Richard Gruneau (Peterborough, Ont.: Broadview, 2006), 123–39.

44. See Peter Gossage and Jack Little, *An Illustrated History of Quebec* (Oxford University Press, 2013), ch. 11.

45. Jason Blake and Andrew C. Holman, eds. *The Same but Different: Hockey in Quebec* (Kingston: McGill-Queen's University Press, 2017); Jean Harvey, "Whose Sweater Is This? The Changing Meanings of Hockey in Quebec," in *Artificial Ice*, 29–52.

46. See Gary McCarthy, "Quebec PeeWee Hockey 'Dream' Now Rich Reality," *Montreal Gazette*, February 7, 1970. See "Histoire," Tournoi international de hockey Pee-Wee de Quebec, http://www.tournoipee-wee.qc.ca/en/index.html.

47. "History," Tournoi international de midget de Drummondville, http://www.hockeymidgetdrummond.com/en/index.php/history.

48. "Équipe-Quebec est lancée!" *Montreal La Presse*, August 19, 1981; "Guy Lafleur donne un coup de pouce," *Montreal La Presse*, July 30, 1981; Réjean Tremblay, "Le projet d'Équipe-Québec: Bertrand s'est bien repris," *Montreal La Presse,* August 20, 1981.

49. Guy Robillard, "La LNH néglige les talents francophones: L'idée d'une équipe québécoise internationale refait surface," *Montreal La Presse*, August 8, 1986.

50. "University Hockey Can Learn from U.S. Game," *Toronto Star*, March 25, 1988.

51. Grant Kerr, "Canadian Universities Take Back Seat," *Brandon Sun*, October 25, 1985.

52. Neil Singelais, "What's Happened to Hockey," *Boston Globe*, October 19, 1979.

53. Jim Kaplan, "A Wintry Heritage," *Sports Illustrated*, February 9, 1976; "Fifty-Fifth State Tournament Played in 2003," official program, 2004 Minnesota State Boys Hockey Tournament, 7, 17, United States Hockey Hall of Fame Archives, Eveleth Minn.; Gary L. Philips, *Skate for Goal: Highlights from Minnesota's State Hockey Tournament* (Afton, Minn.: Afton, 1982), ix.

54. Kaplan, "A Wintry Heritage"; Wendell, *Going for the Gold*, 54.

55. Norm MacLean, "Oh, Junior," *Hockey* 5 (October 1979): 48–50; Gilbert, *Herb Brooks*, 43.

56. Allen, *Star-Spangled Hockey*, 111; "Hal Trumble," *USA Hockey 75th Anniversary Commemorative Program* (Minneapolis: USA Hockey and Touchpoint Media, 2012), 48.

57. "The Hockey Interview: Hal Trumble," *Hockey* 5 (October 1979): 18, 20; "Through the Pages of Time," *USA Hockey 75th Anniversary Commemorative Program*, 60–61.

58. Steve Newman, "First Goal," *Coaching Review* 5 (May–June 1982): 14–15, quote at 15; Orr, *Orr*, 222–25.

Chapter 21. Global Visions of Open Ice: 1972–1988

1. Borje Salming with Gerhard Karlsson, *Blood, Sweat and Hockey: 17 Years in the NHL* (Toronto: HarperCollins, 1991), 40; Tobias Stark, "From Sweden with Love: The Summit Series and the Notion of the Contemporary Canadian Hockey Player in Sweden," in *Coming Down the Mountain: Rethinking the 1972 Summit Series*, ed. Brian Kennedy (Hamilton, Ont.: Wolsak and Wynn, 2014), 165–74.

2. "The European Icehockey League," http://www.angelfire.com/space/u_line/esl73.htm; Phil Drackett, *Flashing Blades: The Story of British Ice Hockey* (Ramsbury, UK: Crowood, 1987), 149–51.

3. Horst Eckert and Ernst Martini, *90: IIHF 90th Anniversary, 1908–1998* (Zurich: IIHF, 1998), 22–23; Martin C. Harris, *The British Ice Hockey Hall of Fame* (Stroud, Gloucestershire: Stadia, 2007), 25; Robert K. Barney, Stephen R. Wenn, and Scott G. Martyn, *Selling the Five Rings: The International Olympic Committee and the Rise of Olympic Commercialism* (Salt Lake City: University of Utah Press, 2002), 85.

4. Allen Guttmann, *The Olympics: A History of the Modern Games* (Urbana: University of Illinois Press, 1992), 142–43, 166; Lincoln Allison, *Amateurism in Sport: An Analysis and a Defense* (London: Frank Cass, 2001), 168–69.

5. Gunther Sabetzki, "Summary of the Four-Year Period 1978–82," *International Ice Hockey Guide 1982–1983*, ed. Tom Ratscunas (Tampere, Fin.: FIHL, 1982) 7; Eckert and Martini, *90*, 23–24.

6. Salming with Karlsson, *Blood, Sweat and Hockey*, 13–14, 29, 53.

7. Tobias Stark, "How Swede It Is: Börje Salming and the Migration of Swedish Ice Hockey Players to the NHL, 1957–2012," paper presented at the International Hockey Conference, "Constructing the Hockey Family: Home, Community, Bureaucracy and Marketplace," St. Mary's University, Halifax, N.S., July 12–14, 2012, 3–4, 8, 16; Stark, "Ice Hockey, Europe," in *Sports around the World: History, Culture, Practice*, ed. John Nauright and Charles Parrish (Santa Barbara, Calif.: ABC-Clio, 2012), 348.

8. Stark, "How Swede It Is," 13–15; Salming, *Blood, Sweat and Hockey*, 163–67. The quote on Volvo Cup is in Bo Carlsson and Jyri Backman, "The Blend of Normative Uncertainty and Commercial Immaturity in Swedish Ice Hockey," *Sport in Society: Cultures, Commerce, Media, Politics* 18, no. 3 (2014): 5.

9. Jani Mesikämmen, "From Part-Time Passion to Big-Time Business: The Professionalization of Finnish Ice Hockey," in *Putting It on Ice: Vol. 2, Internationalizing "Canada's Game,"* ed. Colin D. Howell (Halifax, N.S.: Gorsebrook, 2002), 25.

10. Ibid., 23, 25.

11. Mark Mulvoy, "Boris and His Boys Prepare for a Few Friendlies," *Sports Illustrated*, January 5, 1976, 24; Lawrence Martin, *The Red Machine: The Soviet Quest to Dominate Canada's Game* (Toronto: Doubleday Canada, 1990), 7–8.

12. Ibid.

13. Robert Edelman, *Serious Fun: A History of Spectator Sports in the USSR* (New York: Oxford University Press, 1993), 168; Edelman "Sport on Soviet Television," in *Sport and the Transformation of Modern Europe: States, Media and Markets 1950–2010*, ed. Alan Tomlinson, Christopher Young and Richard Holt (London: Routledge, 2011), 100–112.

14. Robert Baumann, "The Central Red Army Sports Club (TsSKA): Forging a Military Tradition in Soviet Ice Hockey," *Journal of Sport History* 15, no. 2 (1988): 151–66; Edelman, *Serious Fun*, 163.

15. Martin, *Red Machine*, 170, 174, 196, 226; Vsevolod Kukushin, "Interview with Viktor Tikhonov," in *World of Hockey: Celebrating a Century of the IIHF, 1908–2008*, ed. Szymon Szemberg and Andrew Podnieks (Bolton, Ont.: Fenn, 2007), 61; Malcolm Dixelius, Bengt Löfgren, *CCCP-Hockey*, first aired in 2004 on SVT1, Housebars Produktion. See http://www.housebars.com/?p=62.

16. Baumann, "Central Red Army," 164; Edelman, *Serious Fun*, 163; Jim Riordan, "Rewriting Soviet Sports History," *Journal of Sport History* 20 (Winter 1993), 254; Philip Taubman, "Hockey Rivals May Be Catching Up to Soviet," *New York Times*, December 23, 1987.

17. Tony Judt, *Postwar: A History of Europe since 1945* (New York: Penguin, 2005), 594, 597, 599.

18. Jim Riordan, "Playing to New Rules: Soviet Sport and Perestroika," *Soviet Studies* 42, no. 1 (January 1990): 137–38; Edelman, *Serious Fun*, 221.

19. Ken Dryden and Roy MacGregor, *Home Game: Hockey and Life in Canada* (Toronto: McClelland and Stewart, 1989), 234.

20. Tal Pinchevsky, *Breakaway: From behind the Iron Curtain to the NHL: The Untold Story of Hockey's Great Escapes* (Mississauga, Ont.: Wiley Canada, 2012), 7; Tony Judt, *Postwar*, 616; Dan Diamond, *Total Hockey* (New York: Total Sports, 1998), 510–16.

21. Vic Duke, "Perestroika in Progress? The Case of Spectator Sports in Czechoslovakia," *British Journal of Sociology* 41, no. 2 (June 1990): 150–51; Podnieks et al., *Kings of the Ice: A History of World Hockey* (Richmond Hill, Ont.: NDE, 2002), 288–89.

22. Mark *Mulvoy*, "Check and Double-Czech," *Sports Illustrated* 41, no. 5 (July 29, 1974), 52; Pinchevsky, *Breakaway*, 9–28; Podnieks et al., *Kings of the Ice*, 420–22.

23. E. M. Swift, "Don't Call Us, We'll Call You: Two Czech Stars Got on the Phone to Quebec, and Came in from the Cold," *Sports Illustrated* 53, no. 21 (November 17, 1980): 84; Podnieks et al., *Kings of the Ice*, 645; Pinchevsky, *Breakaway*, 39–61.

24. Pinchevsky, *Breakaway*, 18, 60.

25. Duke, "Perestroika in Progress," 150–53.

26. Alice O'Brien, *Rinks and Arenas: Ten Years of British Ice Hockey* (Nottingham, UK: Castle, 1998), vii, 3; Phil Drackett, *Flashing Blades*, 153, 168.

27. Klaus Zaugg, "New World Order: The End of Hockey's Old Power Balance," in *World of Hockey*, 98; Joe Bertagna, "A Yankee Tours Europe Playing Post-Grad Hockey," *Hockey* 2, no. 6 (December 1976): 46, 47.

28. *International Ice Hockey Guide, 1980–81* (Toronto: Hockey News, 1980), 9.

29. Horst Eckert, ed. *Eishockey Almanack: International IIHF Yearbook, 1987–88* (Konigsbrunn, Ger.: Henry, 1987), 8, 143; Eckert, ed. *Eishockey Almanack 1991: International IIHF Yearbook, 1990–91* (Munich: CoPress Verlag GmbH, 1990), 126.

30. *International Hockey Guide 1979* (Tampere, Fin.: SM-Liga, 1979), 3, 8, USA Hockey Archives, Colorado Springs (hereafter cited as USAHA); John Ziegler, "Message from the President," *International Ice Hockey Guide, 1980–81* (Toronto: Hockey News, 1980), 22, 11, USAHA.

31. Elizabeth Etue and Megan K. Williams, *On the Edge: Women Making Hockey History* (Toronto: Second Story, 1996), 103; Joanna Avery and Julie Stevens, *Too Many Men on the Ice: Women's Hockey in North America* (Vancouver: Polestar, 1997); Brian McFarlane, *Proud Past, Bright Future: One Hundred Years of Canadian Women's Hockey* (Toronto: Stoddart, 1994), chs. 5, 6.

32. Lynda Baril, *Nos Glorieuses: Plus de Cent Ans de Hockey Féminin au Québec* (Montréal: Les Éditions La Presse, 2013), 128–29.

33. See Bob Koep, "Mississauga Tops in Women's Hockey," *Toronto Star*, April 21, 1975; "This Game's for Girls Only," *Lethbridge Herald*, December 7, 1982; Avery and Stevens, *Too Many Men*; Etue and Williams, *On the Edge*, chs. 3, 4, 5; McFarlane, *Proud Past, Bright Future*, chs. 5–6; Baril, *Nos Glorieuses*, 128–29.

34. Lois Kalchman, "Hockey Group Acts to Solve a Parent Problem at Meeting," *Toronto Star*, May 24, 1988; Etue and Williams, *On the Edge*, 70–82.

35. "Sexually Integrated Hockey Still a Problem for CAHA," *Toronto Star*, May 27, 1981.

36. Baril, *Nos Glorieuses*, 132–33.

37. "Toronto Girl Fails in Bid to Change Rules of CAHA," *Toronto Star*, May 25, 1972; "Last Season for 'Mike' McKay Because Boy Is Really a Girl," *Toronto Star*, February 28, 1974; M. Ann Hall, *The Girl and the Game: A History of Women's Sport in Canada* (Peterborough, Ont.: Broadview Press, 2002), 180–82.

38. Gwen Brodsky, "Justine Blainey and the Ontario Hockey Association: An Overview," *CAAWS Newsletter* (1987), 17; CAAWS HerStory, http://www.caaws.ca/about-caaws/caaws-herstory.

39. John Roberston, "Blainey Ruling Risky Business for Girls," *Toronto Star*, April 28, 1988.

40. "Locker Room Lib," *Time*, March 11, 1974, 73; Nathaniel Sheppard, "Women's Ice Hockey is Enjoying Surge but Not without Resistance," *New York Times*, March 12, 1978; Gai Berlage, "The Development of Intercollegiate Women's Ice Hockey in the United States," *Colby Quarterly* 32, no. 1 (March 1996): 58–71.

41. Letter, Richard Stevens to Mike O'Neil, October 28, 1974; Memorandum, O'Neil to Alan Tuveson, November 4, 1974; Memorandum, Tuveson to O'Neil, November 5, 1974; Memorandum, Tuveson to Lynn Heyliger, November 14, 1974, all in box 1, folder 1, Friends of UNH Women's Hockey Files, 1975–2002, University Archives, Milne Special Collections and Archives, Dimond Library, University of New Hampshire; Gerry Miles, "Icewomen Begin 77–78 Season," *The New Hampshire*, December 2, 1977, 21, 24; Lesley Visser, "They Finish 15-0, but No Place to Go," *Boston Globe*, March 7, 1978.

42. Colleen Coyne, "A Chronological Account of the Growth of Women's Collegiate Hockey in the U.S.," unpublished paper, 2000, in author Hardy's possession.

43. Lesley Visser, "Well, Why Not?" *Hockey* 13 (December 1977): 40–43; Scott A. Dahl, "Sun, Surf and Slap Shots in L.A.," *Hockey* 2, no. 2 (March 1976): 32; 1981 U.S. National Invitational Girls Hockey Tournament, printed program, United States Hockey Hall of Fame, Eveleth, Minn.

44. "Women's Ice Hockey on the Attack," in *Eishockey Almanack 1989*, 181–86, quote at 181.

45. Ibid., 184–86.

46. Ibid., 182.

Chapter 22. The Game on the Ice: 1972–1988

1. *Slap Shot* (dir. George Roy Hill, Universal Pictures, 1977); Jim Naughton, "Bruins Win, Then Battle with Fans at Garden," *New York Times*, December 24, 1979.

2. Stephen Smith, *Puckstruck: Distracted, Delighted and Distressed by Canada's Hockey Obsession* (Vancouver, B.C.: Greystone, 2014), 13.

3. Scott Morrison, "Taking Fighting out of Hockey Would be Wrong," CBC News, March 24, 2007. By 2000–2001, fights per game in the NHL had declined to 0.56, and by 2014–15 to 0.32. See "NHL Fight Stats" at http://hockeyfights.com/stats.

4. Scott Surgent, *The Complete Historical and Statistical Reference to the World Hockey Association, 1972–1979* (Tempe, Ariz: Xaler, 1995), 9.

5. "Shack Says Hockey Not So Rough," *Winnipeg Free Press*, October 31, 1975; "Tell Hull to Relax, Says the Old Master," *Winnipeg Free Press*, October 27, 1975; "Good, Bad, Undecided on Hull's Decision," *Winnipeg Free Press*, October 25, 1975.

6. "North Star Injury: Was It a Crime?" *Toronto Star*, January 9, 1975; "Maloney First to Test McMurtry's Purge," *Ottawa Citizen*, November 7, 1975; Robert McKenzie, "Hockey Violence: Life Ban Demanded for Calgary Player," *Toronto Star*, April 13, 1976; "Ted Lindsay Backs Off but Paiement Suspended," *Toronto Star*, October 28, 1978; "Ciccarelli Cited for Assault," *New York Times*, August 25, 1988; "Hockey Violence Causes Dilemma," *Medicine Hat News*, February 19, 1982.

7. Lawrence Scanlan, *Grace under Fire: The State of Our Sweet and Savage Game* (Toronto: Penguin Canada, 2002), ch. 8; Bobby Orr, *Orr: My Story* (New York: Putnam's, 2013), 248–54.

8. See "National Hockey League History and Statistics," at http://www.hockeydb.com/ihdb/stats/leagues/141.html.

9. See "Philadelphia Flyers Statistics and History," http://www.hockeydb.com/stte/philadelphia-flyers-7439.html.

10. Punch Imlach, "Pray that Orr Misses the Plane," in Gary Ronberg, *The Ice Men: The Violent World of Professional Hockey* (New York: Crown, 1973), 104.

11. "Violence, Spearing Incident Dearly Costs Mets' Lecuyer," *Brandon Sun*, October 20, 1976.

12. "School Hockey: It's Growing into a Violent Beast," *Boston Globe*, February 27, 1977; "How Do You Feel about Excessive Violence in Hockey?" *Hockey* 2, no. 5 (November 1976): 16–17.

13. "Hockey Violence: Assault on Ice," *Canada and the World* 41, no. 5 (January 1976): 3; J. D. Reed, "Week of Disgrace on the Ice," *Sports Illustrated* 44, no. 17 (April 26, 1976): 22–25; "Violence—A Cancer at Hockey's Throat," *Maclean's* 92, no. 9 (February 26, 1979): 40–41; and Joyce Randolph, "Another Black Eye for Hockey's Image," *Maclean's* 95, no. 35 (August 30, 1982): 40–41.

14. Michael D. Smith, "The Legitimation of Violence: Hockey Players' Perceptions of their Reference Groups' Sanctions for Assault," *Canadian Journal of Sociology and Anthropology* 12 (1975): 72–80; Smith, "Hockey Violence," *Canadian Dimension* 13 (1979): 42–45; Smith, "Toward an Explanation of Hockey Violence," *Canadian Journal of Sociology* 4 (1979): 105–24; Jack C. Horn, "Sir Lancelot of the Rink: The Ritual of Hockey Fights," *Psychology Today* 15, no. 2 (February 1981): 15–16.

15. Ray Kennedy, "Wanted: An End to the Mayhem," *Sports Illustrated*, November 17, 1975, 18.

16. G. Néron, "Rapport Final du Comité d'Étude sur la Violence au Hockey Amateur au Québec," Quebec: Gouvernement du Québec, Haut-Commisariat a la Jeunesse, aux Loisirs et aux Sports, 1977.

17. United States Congressional Hearings, "Excessive Violence in Professional

Sports: Hearings before the Subcommittee on Crime of the Committee on the Judiciary," House of Representatives, Ninety-Sixth Congress, Second Session, on H.R. 7903, September 30 and November 19, 1980.

18. William R. McMurtry, "Investigation and Inquiry into Violence in Amateur Hockey," report submitted to the Minister of Community and Social Services, Government of Ontario, August 1974, 36.

19. Scott Young, *100 Years of Dropping the Puck: A History of the OHA* (Toronto: McClelland and Stewart, 1989), 286–87.

20. "Lois Kalchman, "Rear Checking Ban Urged," *Toronto Star*, April 28, 1984; Scott Taylor, "MAHA Tackles Hockey Violence," *Winnipeg Free Press*, May 4, 1987.

21. Young, *100 Years*, 288–89; "Police Seek Policy on Hockey Violence," *Winnipeg Free Press*, February 18, 1982; "Baetz Says Government No Threat to Hockey," *Toronto Star*, March 28, 1980.

22. "CAHA Criticizes NHL for Game's Poor Image," *Winnipeg Free Press*, May 20, 1987; "Jelinek 'Not Satisfied,'" *Toronto Star*, May 21, 1987.

23. Gare Joyce, *When the Lights Went Out: How One Brawl Ended Hockey's Cold War and Changed the Game* (Toronto: Anchor Canada, 2007), 11–12.

24. Brian Kennedy, "Confronting a Compelling Other," in *Canada's Game: Hockey and Identity*, ed. Andrew Holman (Kingston: McGill-Queen's University Press, 2009), 44–61.

25. Peter Mathias, *The First Industrial Nation: The Economic History of Britain 1700–1914*, 2nd edition (London: Routledge, 2013).

26. See Edward Hagerman, *The American Civil War and the Origins of Modern Warfare: Ideas, Organization, and Field Command* (Bloomington: Indiana University Press, 1992).

27. Stan Fischler, *Slashing! A Tough Look at Hockey from a Writer Who Loves the Game* (New York: Crowell, 1974), 146–47.

28. Vladimír Kostka, "Tactical Aspects in Hockey," in *International Symposium on Research and Development in Ice Hockey*, ed. Fernand Landry and William A. R. Orban (Miami: Symposia Specialists, 1978), 16.

29. Imlach, "Pray that Orr," 70; Harry Neale and Roger Neilson, "The Changing Modern Game," in *Total Hockey*, 2nd edition, ed. Dan Diamond (Kingston, N.Y.: Total Sports, 2000), 376.

30. Neale in Neale and Neilson, "Changing Modern Game," 376.

31. "N.Y. Hockey Has a Colorful History," *Montreal Gazette*, May 7, 1986.

32. Imlach, "Pray that Orr," 74.

33. Phil Esposito and Peter Golenbock, *Thunder and Lightning: A No-B.S. Memoir* (Chicago: Triumph, 2003), 130.

34. Neilson in Neale and Neilson, "Changing Modern Game," 381.

35. Shero in John Brogan, "The Russian Connection," An International Hockey Event—USSR vs. NHL, special edition of *Goal Magazine*, December 1975, 41–42; Neale in Neale and Neilson, "Changing Modern Game," 386.

36. Kearney in Fischler, *Slashing!*, 144.

37. Jay Scherer and Hart Cantelon, "1974 WHA All-Stars vs. the Soviet National Team: Franchise Recognition and Foreign Diplomacy in the 'Forgotten Series,'" *Journal of Canadian Studies* 47, no. 2 (Spring 2013): 29–59.

38. Todd Denault, *The Greatest Game: The Montreal Canadiens, the Red Army, and the Night that Saved Hockey* (Toronto: McClelland and Stewart, 2011).

39. Peter L. de Rosa, "The World Hockey Association and the Economics of Rival Leagues," paper presented at "Canada's Game? Critical Perspectives on Ice Hockey and Identity," Plymouth, Mass., April 14–16, 2005, 9.

40. Vladislav Tretiak, *Tretiak: The Legend*, trans. Sam and Maria Budman (Edmonton: Plains, 1987), 70.

41. Fred Shero, "The Top Man Tells Why the Flyers Beat the Russians," *New York Times*, March 14, 1976, sec. 5, 2; Imlach, "Pray that Orr," 66.

42. Surgent, *Complete Historical and Statistical*, 8; Ed Willes, *The Rebel League: The Short and Unruly Life of the World Hockey Association* (Toronto: McClelland and Stewart, 2004), 227.

43. Andrew Podnieks et al., *Kings of the Ice: A History of World Hockey* (Richmond Hill, Ont.: NDE, 2002), 541–740.

44. Willes, *Rebel League*, 174–75.

45. An International Hockey Event—USSR vs. NHL, special edition of *Goal Magazine* (December 1975), 10.

46. "Proceedings, 1977 National Coaches Certification Program: Level V Seminar" (Canadian Amateur Hockey Association, 1977); "Proceedings, 1978 National Coaches Certification Program: Level 5 Seminar" (Canadian Amateur Hockey Association).

47. Lois Kalchman, "Minor Clubs Ready for Year of Change," *Toronto Star*, September 5, 1980.

48. Peter Krivel, "Soviet Skating Coach Toronto Bound," *Toronto Star*, July 15, 1974; "Up-and-Coming Skaters, Hockey Players to Benefit from Soviet Expert's Teaching," *Winnipeg Free Press*, October 4, 1975; Ken McKee, "Hula Hoops, Volleyballs Are Skating Coach's Props," *Toronto Star*, November 15, 1975; "Soviet Teacher Emphasizes Skating," *Toronto Star*, March 2, 1979.

49. Jim Proudfoot, "Speed's Not Vital for Valiquette, a Veteran at 20," *Toronto Star*, December 29, 1976; "Toronto Maple Leafs Statistics and History," at http://www.hockeydb.com/stte/toronto-maple-leafs-8490.html.

50. "George Kingston," in Mike Johnston and Ryan Walter, *Simply the Best: Insights and Strategies from Great Hockey Coaches* (Surrey, B.C.: Heritage House, 2004), 154.

51. "Kingston Would Love to Go Out a Winner," *Brandon Sun*, March 1, 1974.

52. Jim Proudfoot and Frank Orr, "Canada Cup Notes: Perreault's Back as a Fan," *Toronto Star*, September 9, 1981.

53. "AAH Event Underway," *Lethbridge Herald*, June 21, 1974; Jim Proudfoot, "Soviet Leaders Are Still Seeking a New Tretiak," *Toronto Star*, July 10, 1984.

54. "Skaters Start on Snowy Grass," *Winnipeg Free Press*, November 27, 1975.

55. "George Kingston," 171–72.

56. "USA Selects Takes Final," *New York Times*, January 1, 1989.

57. John Soares, "East Beats West: Ice Hockey and the Cold War," in *Sport and the Transformation of Modern Europe: States, Media and Markets 1950–2010*, ed. Alan Tomlinson, Christopher Young, and Richard Holt (London: Routledge, 2011), 35–49.

58. "Swedish Nationals Sign Billy Harris," *Toronto Star*, June 4, 1971; "Len Melvin Lunde," Hockey Hall of Fame Legends of Hockey, http://www.legendsofhockey.net.

59. On Ruhnke, see "Money Talks in Pro Hockey but Not Always," *Toronto Star*, December 30, 1980. On Stewart, see "The History of EVZ," http://www.evz.ch/en/about-us/history; and "Hockey," *Montreal Gazette*, December 4, 1984.

60. Renaud Tschoumy, "Paul-André Cadieux stoppe ses activités d'entraineur" *Lausanne Le Matin*, March 18, 2014, http://www.lematin.ch/sports/hockey/Paul Andre-Cadieux-stoppe-ses-activites-d-entraineur/story/24103243.

61. "Brooks: No Regrets on Coaching Move," *New York Times*, January 4, 1981.

62. Robert Sarner, "Canada Returns the Favor," in "Today," *Lethbridge Herald*, May 17, 1980.

63. "Canadian Hockey Players in Europe Spearhead Teams to National Titles," *Toronto Star*, February 19, 1979.

64. "European Sports with Bob Koep," *Toronto Star*, January 4, 1972; "Ex-NHLer Finds Going Rough: Swiss Hockey Club Officials Criticize His Lack of Offence," *Toronto Star*, October 4, 1983; "Swiss Not Impressed with Ex-Leaf Derlago," *Toronto Star*, November 9, 1987.

65. One website described him thus: "Gary teaches mainly the North American style of hockey." See "Gary Prior" at http://www.okanaganhockey.eu.

66. "George Galbraith" at http://www.hockeydb.com.

67. "Upper Canada College Beats Bunny Ahearne Joining Swedish Group," *Toronto Star*, January 7, 1975.

68. "St. Andrews Wins," *Toronto Star*, March 26, 1982. See also "U.C.C. Minor Bantams Off to Helsinki," *Toronto Star*, November 28, 1985.

69. "Coach Leads Fight for Better Refs," *Toronto Star*, January 21, 1975.

70. George Gross, "The Father of Soviet Hockey," in "An International Hockey Event—USSR vs. NHL," special edition of *Goal Magazine* (December 1975), 16.

71. "Soviets Play Rough in a Tight Battle," *Toronto Star*, February 8, 1977.

72. Reyn Davis, "Latest Jets Coup: A 'Dashing' Swede Is Lars-Erik," *Winnipeg Free Press*, May 24, 1974; "According to Poll, Canadians Want Less of NHL," *Brandon Sun*, January 31, 1987.

73. Dan Synovec, "Ex-Boston U. Hockey Player Signs with Bremerhaven German Team," *European Stars and Stripes* [Darmstadt, Hesse, Germany], May 9, 1978.

74. Tobias Stark, "The Pioneer, the Pal, and the Poet: Masculinities and National Identities in Canadian, Swedish, and Soviet-Russian Ice Hockey during the Cold War," In *Putting It on Ice: Vol. 2, Internationalizing "Canada's Game,"* ed. Colin D. Howell (Halifax, N.S.: Gorsebrook, 2002), 42.

Chapter 23. From Calgary to the KHL: 1989–2010

1. Alan Adams, "Cup Receives Lukewarm Reception: Chilly Weather, Lack of Publicity Keep Red Square Crowd Down," *Toronto Star*, August 18, 1997; Marina Lakhman, "Stanley Cup Goes for a Jaunt In Red Square," *New York Times*, August 18, 1997; Bob Wojnowski, "Native Wings' Red Square Visit Laden with Symbolism," *USA Today*, August 19, 1997.

2. Fred Weir, "Russian Red Wings Bring Home Stanley Cup," *Toronto Globe and Mail*, August 18, 1997; Wojnowski, "Native Wings' Red Square Visit."

3. "Of Miracles and Men," ESPN Films *30 for 30*, prod. Philip Aromando and Alex Evans, Hock Films and Maggievision Productions, 2015.

4. "Viacheslav Fetisov," in *Kings of the Ice: A History of World Hockey*, ed. Andrew Podnieks et al. (Richmond Hill: Ont.: NDE, 2002), 651; Lawrence Martin, *The Red Machine: The Soviet Quest to Dominate Canada's Game* (Toronto: Doubleday Canada, 1990), 178, 202.

5. Martin, *Red Machine*, 219, 251–52; "Of Miracles and Men"; "Igor Larionov Openly Revolts against Coach, System, October 1988," http://www.iihf.com/sk/iihf-home/the-iihf/100-year-anniversary/100-top-stories/story-65.html; Tal Pinchevsky, *Breakaway: From behind the Iron Curtain to the NHL; The Untold Story of Hockey's Great Escapes* (Mississauga, Ont.: Wiley Canada, 2012), 161–62, 176–86.

6. Robert Edelman, *Serious Fun: A History of Spectator Sports in the USSR* (New York: Oxford University Press, 1993), 202, 208, 225, 230–31; "Of Miracles and Men"; Pinchevsky, *Breakaway*, 186.

7. Vassili Ossipov, "'Russian Five' Changed Hockey's Fabric Forever," *NHL Insider*, NHL.com, October 27, 2015, http://www.nhl.com/ice/news.htm?id=784942.

8. Joe Lapointe, "Play Hockey! Settlement Ends 10-Day Strike," *New York Times*, April 11, 1992.

9. Sean McIndoe, "The Often Forgotten 1994 NHL Lockout," *Grantland*, September 3, 2014, available at http://grantland.com/the-triangle/the-often-forgotten-1994-nhl-lockout.

10. Dupont, "Lost Season Is Players' Fault," *Boston Globe*, February 17, 2005; "A Look at the Deal," *Boston Globe*, July 22, 2005; "Goodenow Resigns as Head of NHL Players' Association," *Street and Smith's SportsBusiness Journal*, August 1, 2005, 8.

11. Kevin Allen, "League Balance, Livelier Offense Power Resurgence," *USA Today*, June 28, 2006; "NHL Ticket Sales," *Street and Smith's Sports Business Journal*, January 29, 2007, 9; "Bettman, Collins Outline Growth Strategy," *Street and Smith's Sports-Business Journal*, October 1, 2007, 24; Michael Farber, "The Lord of the Lockout," *Sports Illustrated*, March 11, 2013, 52–57.

12. Tripp Mickle, "Sun Belt Hot and Cold for NHL," *Street and Smith's Sports-Business Journal*, October 5–11, 2009, 22; Bernard J. Mullin, Stephen Hardy, and William A. Sutton, *Sport Marketing*, 4th edition (Champaign, Ill.: Human Kinetics, 2014), 31–32; Kevin Allen, *Star-Spangled Hockey: Celebrating 75 Years of USA Hockey* (Chicago: Triumph, 2011), 105–6.

13. L. J. Wertheim, "Hot Prospects in Cold Places," *Sports Illustrated*, June 21, 2004, 62–66; Zaugg, "New World Order," in *World of Hockey: Celebrating a Century of the IIHF*, ed. Szymon Szemberg and Andrew Podnieks (Bolton, Ont.: Fenn, 2007), 100, 104–5.

14. Szymon Szemberg, "Research on Europeans Playing in North America," 1, IIHF study, http://www.iihf.com/fileadmin/user_upload/PDF/Study_summary.pdf.

15. Osmo Kivinen, Jani Mesikämmen, and Timo Metsä-Tokila, "A Case Study in Cultural Diffusion: British Ice Hockey and American Influences in Europe," *Culture Sport, Society* 4, no. 1 (Spring 2001): 49–62.

16. Zaugg, "New World Order," 101, 104; Tobias Stark, "Ice Hockey, Europe" in *Sports around the World: History, Culture, Practice*, ed. John Nauright and Charles Parrish (Santa Barbara, Calif.: ABC-Clio, 2012), 345.

17. Kivinen, Mesikämmen, and Metsä-Tokila, "Case Study," 59; Gerhard Karlsson, "Swedish Hockey," in Börje Salming with Gerhard Karlsson, *Blood, Sweat and Hockey: 17 Years in the NHL* (Toronto: HarperCollins, 1991), 169–73; Tobias Stark, "Ice Hockey, Europe," 347–48.

18. Tony Judt, *Postwar: A History of Europe since 1945* (New York: Penguin, 2005), 657, 688.

19. James Riordan, "Sport after the Cold War: Implications for Russia and Eastern Europe," in *East Plays West: Sport and the Cold War*, ed. Stephen Wagg and David Andrews (London: Routledge, 2007), 283.

20. Michael Schwirtz, "Russia Is Luring Back N.H.L. Stars," *New York Times*, February 29, 2008.

21. Michael Schwirtz, "A Return, Not to Glory," *New York Times*, October 16, 2011.

22. "Note from Rene Fasel," *Eishockey Almanach 95: International IIHF Yearbook 1994–95*, ed. Horst Eckert (Munich: Copress Verlag GmbH, 1994), 4.

23. Dennis Gibbons, "The International Ice Hockey Federation," in *Total Hockey*, ed. Dan Diamond, (New York: Total Sports, 1998), 442–44. "2010 IIHF World Championship: A television success story," http://www.infrontsports.com.

24. EHL information in *Eishockey Almanach 98: International IIHF Yearbook 1997–98*, ed. Horst Eckert (Munich: Copress Verlag GmbH, 1997), 80–81; *Millenium Skoda Auto European Hockey League 1999–2000 Yearbook*, 2–3, 78, 286–92,

306–15; *Eishockey Almanach 2000: International IIHF Yearbook 1999–2000*, ed. Horst Eckert (Munich: Copress Verlag GmbH, 1999), 7–8; Horst Eckert and Ernst Martini, *90—IIHF 90th Anniversary, 1908–1998* (Zurich: IIHF, 1998), 29–30.

25. Kevin Paul Dupont, "US Power Players Lacked Passion and Purpose," *Boston Globe*, February 24, 2006.

26. Brad Evenson, "Giving Hockey More 'Swoosh,'" *Hamilton Spectator*, September 11, 1996; Viv Bernstein, "Fedorov Will Just Do It: Wing Unveils New Nike Skate at All-Star Game," *Montreal Gazette*, January 20, 1996; "Nike Aims to Ice a Winner: Athletic Shoe Giant Failed in Bid to Score Big With Hockey Skates," *Hamilton Spectator*, September 29, 1999; Ian Austen, "Hockey Fan, and Investor, Buys Bauer from Nike," *New York Times*, February 22, 2008.

27. Stephen Hardy, "Where Did You Go, Jackie Robinson? or, The End of History and the Age of Sport Infrastructure," *Sporting Traditions* 16 (November 1999): 85–100; E. M. Swift, "Big Shots," *Sports Illustrated*, October 11, 1993, 90–94.

28. See "Odyssey Trust," http://www.theodyssey.co.uk; Alan Bairner, "On Thin Ice? The Odyssey, the Giants, and the Sporting Transformation of Belfast," *American Behavioral Scientist* 46, no. 11 (July 2003): 1519–32; Michael Farber, "Peace, Love, and Hockey in Belfast," *Sports Illustrated*, March 21, 2011, 98–104.

29. Nicholas Kulish, "Ice Hockey Helps Tear Down a Berlin Wall in the Mind," *NY Sunday Times*, November 14, 2008, 6.

30. "2004–2005 NCAA Men's and Women's Hockey Players: Breakdown of Where ALL VARSITY Players Come From," *Stops and Starts* [AHCA Newsletter], May–June 2005, 19.

31. Ty Halpin, "Frozen Bracket: Profit, Parity Drive Desire to Expand Men's Ice Hockey Field for First Time since 1988," *NCAA News*, December 6, 1999, 10; Halpin, "Frozen Game Is Red Hot," *NCAA News*, February 18, 2002, 7; Beth Rosenburg, "New and Improved," *NCAA News*, February 16, 2004, 5.

32. Benjamin Jennings, "A 'Miracle' of Hockey Growth in the U.S.," NHL.com, February 25, 2000, available at http://www.1972summitseries.com/Globe/1980%20Olympics%200004.html.

33. AHCA brochure, 1997, in authors' possession.

34. "Remarks by Paul Kelly, Executive Director, College Hockey, Inc.," *Stops and Starts*, January 2010, 8; Roy MacGregor, "New Thrust in U.S. Promotes College Hockey over Major Junior," *Toronto Globe and Mail*, January 4, 2010.

35. "Junior Hockey Players Hit Books, Too," *Ottawa Citizen*, August 2, 2010.

36. Bruce Luebke, "Ex-Wheat King Sets Good Example for WHL," *Brandon Sun*, January 21, 2010.

37. John Lewandoski, "Danton Accepted to Play University Hockey at Saint Mary's," *Toronto Star*, January 14, 2010; Allan Maki, "How Can the CIS Stem the Flow of Top Players?" *Toronto Globe and Mail*, January 7, 2010.

38. See "Olympians Play Tonight at Varsity," *Toronto Star*, February 2, 1987.

39. Rachel Lenzi, "The Path of Dreams: Junior Hockey Provides a Route to

College, but Is It Always Worth the Price?" *Portland Press Herald*, March 28, 2006; Nate Crossman, "Juniors at a Glance" and "Junior Hockey: Big Dreams Not Always Fulfilled," *Quincy (Mass.) Patriot Ledger*, February 24, 2006.

40. Andy Prest, "The Meat Market: The Dark Side of Canada's Junior Hockey System," *Vancouver (B.C.) Sun*, September 1, 2006; David Naylor, "Franchise Values a Good Indication of a Rosy Future," *Toronto Globe and Mail*, May 20, 2005; "Junior Hockey Gets a Facelift: Officials Approve Sweeping Changes 'In the Best Interest of Our Players,'" *Hamilton Spectator*, May 24, 2005.

41. Michael Farber, "Soul on Ice," *Sports Illustrated*, October 4, 1999, 63–96; Devon O'Neil, "Lofty Goal," *Boston Globe Magazine*, December 9, 2007, 31–42; Roy MacGregor, "Persevering Ted Nolan Is Making a Difference," *Toronto Globe and Mail*, December 8, 2007.

42. "History of Sled Hockey,": http://olympics.usahockey.com/page/show/1117297-sled-hockey-history.

43. Gary Kingston, "Sledge Hockey Players Chase the 2010 Golden Trifecta," *Vancouver Sun*, March 12, 2010; Canadian Press, "Hockey Gold for Canada!—Sledge, That Is," *Vancouver Province*, March 19, 2006; Lisa Burke, "Silver for Sledge Hockey Team," *Ottawa Citizen*, March 15, 1998.

44. Nicholas Brown, "Upward Slide," *Athletic Business*, May 2009, 44–45; Fred Mason, "Athletic, but Ambivalent and in Brief: Canadian Newspaper Coverage of Sledge Hockey Prior to Vancouver 2010," *Sport in Society: Cultures, Commerce, Media, Politics* 16, no. 3 (2013): 310–26.

45. Douglas Lederman, "Colgate U. Becomes a Battleground over Equity in College Athletics," *Chronicle of Higher Education*, February 17, 1993, A27–28.

46. John Vellante, "Wildcats Get First Dibs on Title," *Boston Globe*, March 22, 1998.

47. Lois Kalchman, "Youngster Seeks Help at the Top," *Toronto Star*, March 15, 1988; Lois Kalchman, "Girl, 11, Lobbies for Women's Hockey," *Toronto Star*, January 25, 1989.

48. Walter Bush Jr., telephone interview with Stephen Hardy, October 9, 2014. Allen, *Star-Spangled*, 154.

49. Brian McFarlane, *Proud Past, Bright Future: One Hundred Years of Canadian Women's Hockey* (Toronto: Stoddart, 1994), 154–56; Bush telephone interview; Aykroyd, "Women's Hockey Goes Global," in *World of Hockey*, 108–25.

50. Jim Reid, "She Shoots, She Scores," *Toronto Star*, March 18, 1993; Mark Clayton, "In Canada, Women's Hockey Rises Unchecked," *Christian Science Monitor*, February 4, 1994.

51. Hockey Canada, "Female Hockey: Statistics and History," http://www.hockeycanada.ca/en-ca/Hockey-Programs/Female/Statistics-History.aspx; Michael Popke, "Double Hat Trick: Girls' Ice Hockey Skates Ahead in a Half-Dozen States," *Athletic Business*, November 2002, 38, 40, 42.

52. Allan Maki, "The Fight that Changed Hockey," *Toronto Globe and Mail*, May 12, 2012; Joe Lapointe, "Some Players Revert to Tactics of Ice Age," *New York Times*,

March 28, 1997; Tracey Tyler, "Criminal Probe Justified in Beating, Lawyers Say," *Toronto Star,* March 10, 2004.

53. Rodney J. Paul, "Variations in NHL Attendance: The Impact of Violence, Scoring, and Regional Rivalries" *American Journal of Economics and Sociology* 62, no. 2 (April 2003): 345–64; Kostya Kennedy, "Twilight of the Goons," *Sports Illustrated*, March 8, 1999, 29.

54. "Hockey Fights a Concern," *New York Times*, February 20, 1992.

55. Nejlepší česká hokejová bitka - PSG Zlín, HC Sparta Praha, https://www.youtube.com/watch?v=oH8t5yixWLI; Dan Treadway, "Evgeny Tsaregorodtsev Loses It" *Huffington Post*, August 14, 2011.

56. "Jonathan Roy Suspended Seven Games, Patrick Roy Five," *Hockey News*, March 25, 2008.

57. Larry Brooks, "Sanderson Death Must Change Hockey Culture," *New York Post*, January 11, 2009.

58. Charlie Gillis, "Can We Please Now Ban Fighting in Hockey?" *Maclean's*, February 3, 2009.

59. Ken Campbell, "NHL Takes Another Crack at It," *Toronto Star*, September 11, 2002; "Clutch and Grab" *Toronto Star*, January 17, 1994; "Slowed to Crawl, NHL Considers New Rules," *Washington Post*, March 4, 1995; Paul Hunter, "All Holds Barred as NHL Season Opens," *Toronto Star*, October 6, 1995.

60. Pavel Barta, "Nagano, the Czechs, the Slovaks: A Dynasty and a Seventh Superpower," in *World of Hockey*, 128.

61. John Kreiser, "Boring Is Beautiful," *Hockey Digest* 32, no. 1 (November 2003): 22.

62. For another version, see Tim Panaccio, "Murray Seeking Key to Left Wing Lock," *Philadelphia Inquirer*, May 29, 1997.

63. Jim Hynes, "Research and Discovery: The Science of Hockey," *McGill Reporter* 40, no. 13 (March 6, 2008).

64. Bob Calandra, "Hockey2000: Head to Toe Hockey," *Sporting Goods Business* 33, no. 14 (September 15, 2000): 24.

65. Michael Farber, "Why So Many Players are Picking Up High-Tech Sticks," *Sports Illustrated*, December 23, 2002; J. T. Worobets et al., "The Influence of Shaft Stiffness on Potential Energy and Puck Speed During Wrist and Slap Shots in Ice Hockey," *Sports Engineering* 9 (2006): 191–200.

66. Lawrence Scanlan, *Grace under Fire: The State of Our Sweet and Savage Game* (Toronto: Penguin Canada), 63.

67. N. Biasca et al., "The Avoidability of Head and Neck Injuries in Ice Hockey: An Historical Review," *British Journal of Sports Medicine* 36 (2002): 423.

68. Travis Roy and E. M. Swift, *Eleven Seconds: A Story of Tragedy, Courage and Triumph* (New York: Warner, 1998).

69. Lois Kalchman, "NHL's Rules a Risk for Youth? Hockey Canada to Consider Changes," *Toronto Star*, May 16, 2006.

70. Edward Swift, "Facing Up to the Face Mask," *Hockey* 2, no. 5 (November 1976): 13–15; Lois Kalchman, "Minor Clubs Ready for Year of Change," *Toronto Star*, September 5, 1980.

71. See Frank Orr, "Mask or Macho?" *Toronto Star*, January 11, 1986; Kevin Paul Dupont, "Fully Equipped . . . Still at Risk," *Boston Globe*, October 31, 1995; Al Strachan, "Point/Counterpoint: To Wear a Helmet; Risks Versus Rewards," *Toronto Globe and Mail*, August 27, 1992.

72. Katie Carrera, "NHL Closer to Making Visors Mandatory," *Washington Post*, June 5, 2013.

73. Mary Caton, "Windsor Minor Hockey Coach Who Pioneered STOP Program Dies," *Windsor Star*, February 23, 2016.

74. John Branch, "For Canada's Faithful, a Gold That Means Most," *New York Times*, March 1, 2010; Cam Cole, "Canada Takes Gold, but Future's in Doubt," *Ottawa* Citizen, February 26, 2010; Gary Kingston, "Sledge Hockey Players Chase the 2010 Golden Trifecta," *Vancouver Sun*, March 12, 2010.

75. Randy Boswell, "Historic Olympics a Nation-Building Milestone for Canada," *Edmonton Journal*, March 1, 2010; Doug Ward, "Black Bloc Taints Anti-Olympic Movement," *Vancouver Sun*, February 27, 2010; Rod Mickleburgh, "Canada Reels, Japan Goes Wild—and Sledge Hockey Makes It to the Big Time," *Toronto Globe and Mail*, March 19, 2010.

76. Cole, "Canada Takes Gold."

77. Michael Russo, "Not Just Fun and Games for the NHL and IOC," *Minneapolis Star Tribune*, February 28, 2010.

78. Simon Houpt and Andrew Willis, "Companies Fight for Their Share of Olympic Glory," *Toronto Globe and Mail*, February 27, 2010.

79. Quotes in Simon Shuster, "Russia's Olympic Flop Sparks Soviet Nostalgia," *Foster's Sunday Citizen*, March 7, 2010.

80. "Ice Hockey Legend Fetisov: 'We Didn't Learn Any Lessons from Vancouver,'" *RT Sport*, December 29, 2010, available at https://www.youtube.com/watch?v=8GnABxwv_9A.

Epilogue: Back to the Future?

1. Alessa Johns, ed. *Dreadful Visitations: Confronting Natural Catastrophe in the Age of Enlightenment* (London: Routledge, 1999).

2. Sarah Skidmore Sell, "Going for Gold Is Costly Experience," *Halifax Chronicle Herald*, August 2, 2016.

3. Fluto Shinzawa, "It's Not Frozen in Time: Tourney's Tradition Endures and Evolves," *Boston Sunday Globe*, February 6, 2005.

4. Kevin Paul Dupont, "Frozen Solid: The Portable Venue for the Winter Classic Is a Marvel of Modern Engineering," *Boston Globe*, December 31, 2015.

5. "U.S. Pond Hockey Championships," http://www.uspondhockey.com; "World Pond Hockey Championship," http://worldpondhockey.ca/en/home,.

6. Robert D. Putnam, *Bowling Alone: The Collapse and Revival of American Community* (New York: Simon and Schuster, 2000), 19; IIHF, "Survey of Players" for 2010 and 2015, http://www.iihf.com/iihf-home/the-iihf/survey-of-players.html.

7. Seth Berkman, "With Contract Fight Over, Hard Work Begins for Women's Team," *New York Times*, April 2, 2017; *IIHF, "Survey of Players."*

8. Kelley Steadman, blog at http://hockeylife9.blogspot.ca,; Shira Springer, "Breaking the ice: The Boston Pride of the Fledgling NWHL Hope to Find Their Niche in a Crowded Sports Landscape," *Boston Globe*, December 24, 2015; Michael Drapack, "China's Kunlun Red Star Officially Joins CWHL," http://www.cbc.ca/sports/hockey/cwhl-china-hc-red-star-kunlun-join-1.4147421.

9. Nicole Kwan, "Paralyzed Marine Turns to Growing Sport of Sled Hockey for Rehabilitation, Community," FoxNews.com, December 22, 2015; Tara Deschamps, "Punjabi Hockey Broadcasts Bring Families Together," TheStar.com, February 20, 2015.

10. http://www.gayhockey.org/groups/gforce/; http://www.gayhockey.org/groups/stockholm; Chicago Gay Hockey Association, "Other Gay Hockey Teams," http://chicagogayhockey.org/links/other-gay-hockey-teams; "Toronto Gay Hockey Association," http://outsporttoronto.org/organisations/toronto-gay-hockey-association; Stephen McElroy, "Camaraderie on Ice," *New York Times*, October 14, 2010.

11. On First Nations hockey in Canada, see Michael A. Robidoux, *Stickhandling through the Margins: First Nations Hockey in Canada* (Toronto: University of Toronto Press, 2012).

12. See Jeff Hale, "Backtalk; Worrying about Hockey Is Canada's National Sport," *New York Times*, February 10, 2002.

13. "Hockey, Canada's Game, Not Its Most Popular: Hockey by the Numbers," CBC News, September 30, 2013, http://www.cbc.ca/news2/interactives/sports-junior.

14. "No Canada! All Seven Teams Miss Playoffs for the First Time since 1970," *Toronto Globe and Mail*, March 31, 2016; "Woe Canada: How We Got to an NHL Playoffs without Canadian Teams," *Toronto Globe and Mail*, April 8, 2016; Murat Yukselir and James Mirtle, "No Teams from Canada, but Nearly Half of the Players in NHL Playoffs Are Canadian," *Toronto Globe and Mail*, April 15, 2016; "Mismanagement and a Lack of Vision Plague Canada's NHL Teams," *Toronto Globe and Mail*, June 30, 2016; "The NHL Takes Canadians for Granted," *Toronto Globe and Mail*, June 1, 2016.

15. "Hockey in Canada—More than Just a Game," Canadian Museum of Civilization, http://www.historymuseum.ca/event/hockey-in-canada-more-than-just-a-game.

16. Lawrence Martin, "'We the North': How Canada's Preoccupation with Hockey Has Changed," *Toronto Globe and Mail*, May 2, 2016.

17. Richard Harrison, *Hero of the Play* (Toronto: Wolsak and Wynn, 2004 [1994]).

18. "Will Speed Demon Penguins Spawn a Legion of NHL Copycats?" *Hockey News*, June 13, 2016; Michael Traikos, "Questionable Signings around the NHL When Speed, Skill Were Key Ingredients for Penguins," *Toronto Sun*, July 2, 2016.

19. Doug Lunney, "No Check, Please: A3 Bantam Hockey Won't Have Contact This Season," *Winnipeg Sun*, September 20, 2015; Harry Thompson, "USA Hockey 20/20: The Future of Youth Hockey; As We Look to the Future, How Will Today's Programs Impact How The Game Is Played Tomorrow?" *USA Hockey Magazine* (January 2013), http://www.usahockeymagazine.com/article/2013–01/usa-hockey-2020-future-youth-hockey; Emily Mertz, "Hockey Edmonton Bans Body Checking at Many Levels of Bantam and Midget Hockey," April 20, 2016, http://globalnews.ca/news/2651002/hockey-edmonton-bans-body-checking-in-house-league; "Greater Toronto Hockey League Bans Body-Checking for Bantam As," CBC News Toronto, March 7, 2015, http://www.cbc.ca/news/canada/toronto/greater-toronto-hockey-league-bans-body-checking-for-bantam-as-1.2985904.

20. USA Hockey, "ATO, December 29, 2014," http://www.usahockey.com/news_article/show/460237?referrer_id=1369225.

21. "CAHA Rule Discourages Slapshot Use," *Toronto Star*, July 29, 1977.

22. See for example, South Colchester [N.S.] Minor Hockey Association, "HHS Introduces Pilot 3 on 3 League," October 1, 2012, http://scmha.goalline.ca/news.php?news_id=516987; Richard Bercuson, "De[f]lections: No More Slapshots . . . But Why?" *Hockey Now*, November 24, 2015, http://hockeynow.ca/blog/delections-no-more-slapshots-but-why-part-1.

23. "Cross Ice Passes the Test: Hockey Eastern Ontario Pilot Project," Hockey Canada, October 22, 2015, https://www.hockeycanada.ca/en-ca/news/2015-cross-ice-passes-the-test.

24. IIHF, "Survey of Players," http://www.iihf.com/iihf-home/the-iihf/survey-of-players; "Modest Trade Recovery to Continue in 2015 and 2016 Following Three Years of Weak Expansion," WTO: 2015 press releases, Press/739, April 14, 2015, https://www.wto.org/english/news_e/pres15_e/pr739_e.htm.

25. James Mirtle, "How Auston Matthews Became Hockey's Hottest Prospect," *Toronto Globe and Mail*, June 20, 2016; Seth Berkman, "Honing Skills in U.S., a Group of Teenagers Is Fueling China's Hockey Shift," *New York Times*, January 30, 2016.

26. Jeffry Frieden, *Global Capitalism: Its Rise and Fall in the Twentieth Century* (New York: Norton, 2006), 467; Grant Jarvie, "Internationalism and Sport in the Making of Nations." *Identities: Global Studies in Culture and Power* 10 (2003): 537–51; "Local Heroes: Sporting Labour Markets Are Becoming Global; But What about Sports Themselves?" *The Economist*, July 31, 2008.

27. Michael Ignatieff, "The New World Disorder," *New York Review of Books*, September 25, 2014, 30.

28. Ian Thomas, "League Raises Bar, Targets $4.5B in Revenue," *Street and Smith's Sports Business Journal*, September 21, 2015, 18; Ian Thomas, "NHL, Union

Link World Cup, European Appeal," *Street and Smith's Sports Business Journal*, March 2, 2015, 5.

29. Ben Shpigel, "N.H.L. Says Its Players Will Not Participate in 2018 Winter Olympics," *New York Times*, April 3, 2017.

30. Jyri Backman, "Jokerit to the KHL—Season 2014," presentation at Hockey Conference, University of New Brunswick, Fredericton, N.B., July 7, 2016; J. J. Regan, "KHL Receives Permission to Explore Expansion to London," July 16, 2016, http://www.csnmidatlantic.com/washington-capitals/khl-receives-permission-explore-expansion-london.

31. Marissa Payne, "Slava Fetisov Suggests Banning Russian Players from NHL until Age 28," *Washington Post*, May 23, 2015, http://www.washingtonpost.com/blogs/early-lead/wp/2015/05/23/slava-fetisov-suggests-banning-russian-players-from-nhl-until-age-28.

32. Tobias Stark, "Ice Hockey, Europe," in *Sports around the World: History, Culture, Practice*, ed. John Nauright and Charles Parrish (Santa Barbara, Calif.: ABC-Clio, 2012), 346; Backman, "Jokerit to the KHL."

33. Adam Steiss, "IIHF, NHL Officials Meet in Zurich: Player Safety, Sochi Preparations Discussed at Seminar," IIHF, Home of Hockey News, August 20, 2011, http://www.iihf.com/home-of-hockey/news.

34. David Northrup, "Globalization and the Great Convergence: Rethinking World History in the Long Run," *Journal of World History* 16, no. 3 (2005): 266; Arthur Farrell, *Hockey: Canada's Royal Game* (Montreal: Cornell, 1899), 26.

INDEX

STEPHEN HARDY is a retired professor of kinesiology and affiliate professor of history at the University of New Hampshire. His publications include *Sport Marketing*, Fourth Edition and *How Boston Played: Sport, Recreation, and Community*.

ANDREW C. HOLMAN is a professor of history and the director of Canadian studies at Bridgewater State University. His publications include *Canada's Game: Hockey and Identity* and *The Same but Different: Hockey in Quebec*.

SPORT AND SOCIETY

A Sporting Time: New York City and the Rise of Modern Athletics, 1820–70
Melvin L. Adelman
Sandlot Seasons: Sport in Black Pittsburgh *Rob Ruck*
West Ham United: The Making of a Football Club *Charles Korr*
Beyond the Ring: The Role of Boxing in American Society *Jeffrey T. Sammons*
John L. Sullivan and His America *Michael T. Isenberg*
Television and National Sport: The United States and Britain *Joan M. Chandler*
The Creation of American Team Sports: Baseball and Cricket, 1838–72
George B. Kirsch
City Games: The Evolution of American Urban Society and the Rise of Sports
Steven A. Riess
The Brawn Drain: Foreign Student-Athletes in American Universities *John Bale*
The Business of Professional Sports *Edited by Paul D. Staudohar and James A. Mangan*
Fritz Pollard: Pioneer in Racial Advancement *John M. Carroll*
A View from the Bench: The Story of an Ordinary Player on a Big-Time Football Team (*formerly* Go Big Red! The Story of a Nebraska Football Player)
George Mills
Sport and Exercise Science: Essays in the History of Sports Medicine
Edited by Jack W. Berryman and Roberta J. Park
Minor League Baseball and Local Economic Development *Arthur T. Johnson*
Harry Hooper: An American Baseball Life *Paul J. Zingg*
Cowgirls of the Rodeo: Pioneer Professional Athletes *Mary Lou LeCompte*
Sandow the Magnificent: Eugen Sandow and the Beginnings of Bodybuilding
David Chapman
Big-Time Football at Harvard, 1905: The Diary of Coach Bill Reid
Edited by Ronald A. Smith
Leftist Theories of Sport: A Critique and Reconstruction *William J. Morgan*
Babe: The Life and Legend of Babe Didrikson Zaharias *Susan E. Cayleff*
Stagg's University: The Rise, Decline, and Fall of Big-Time Football at Chicago
Robin Lester
Muhammad Ali, the People's Champ *Edited by Elliott J. Gorn*
People of Prowess: Sport, Leisure, and Labor in Early Anglo-America
Nancy L. Struna
The New American Sport History: Recent Approaches and Perspectives
Edited by S. W. Pope
Making the Team: The Cultural Work of Baseball Fiction *Timothy Morris*
Making the American Team: Sport, Culture, and the Olympic Experience
Mark Dyreson

Viva Baseball! Latin Major Leaguers and Their Special Hunger *Samuel O. Regalado*

Touching Base: Professional Baseball and American Culture in the Progressive Era (rev. ed.) *Steven A. Riess*

Red Grange and the Rise of Modern Football *John M. Carroll*

Golf and the American Country Club *Richard J. Moss*

Extra Innings: Writing on Baseball *Richard Peterson*

Global Games *Maarten Van Bottenburg*

The Sporting World of the Modern South *Edited by Patrick B. Miller*

Female Gladiators: Gender, Law, and Contact Sport in America *Sarah K. Fields*

The End of Baseball As We Knew It: The Players Union, 1960–81 *Charles P. Korr*

Rocky Marciano: The Rock of His Times *Russell Sullivan*

Saying It's So: A Cultural History of the Black Sox Scandal *Daniel A. Nathan*

The Nazi Olympics: Sport, Politics, and Appeasement in the 1930s *Edited by Arnd Krüger and William Murray*

The Unlevel Playing Field: A Documentary History of the African American Experience in Sport *David K. Wiggins and Patrick B. Miller*

Sports in Zion: Mormon Recreation, 1890–1940 *Richard Ian Kimball*

Sweet William: The Life of Billy Conn *Andrew O'Toole*

Sports in Chicago *Edited by Elliot J. Gorn*

The Chicago Sports Reader *Edited by Steven A. Riess and Gerald R. Gems*

College Football and American Culture in the Cold War Era *Kurt Edward Kemper*

The End of Amateurism in American Track and Field *Joseph M. Turrini*

Benching Jim Crow: The Rise and Fall of the Color Line in Southern College Sports, 1890–1980 *Charles H. Martin*

Pay for Play: A History of Big-Time College Athletic Reform *Ronald A. Smith*

Globetrotting: African American Athletes and Cold War Politics *Damion L. Thomas*

Cheating the Spread: Gamblers, Point Shavers, and Game Fixers in College Football and Basketball *Albert J. Figone*

The Sons of Westwood: John Wooden, UCLA, and the Dynasty That Changed College Basketball *John Matthew Smith*

Qualifying Times: Points of Change in U.S. Women's Sport *Jaime Schultz*

NFL Football: A History of America's New National Pastime *Richard C. Crepeau*

Marvin Miller, Baseball Revolutionary *Robert F. Burk*

I Wore Babe Ruth's Hat: Field Notes from a Life in Sports *David W. Zang*

Changing the Playbook: How Power, Profit, and Politics Transformed College Sports *Howard P. Chudacoff*

Team Chemistry: The History of Drugs and Alcohol in Major League Baseball *Nathan Michael Corzine*

Wounded Lions: Joe Paterno, Jerry Sandusky, and the Crises in Penn State Athletics *Ronald A. Smith*
Sex Testing: Gender Policing in Women's Sports *Lindsay Parks Pieper*
Cold War Games: Propaganda, the Olympics, and U.S. Foreign Policy *Toby C. Rider*
Game Faces: Sport Celebrity and the Laws of Reputation *Sarah K. Fields*
The Rise and Fall of Olympic Amateurism *Matthew P. Llewellyn and John Gleaves*
Bloomer Girls: Women Baseball Pioneers *Debra A. Shattuck*
I Fight for a Living: Boxing and the Battle for Black Manhood, 1880–1915 *Louis Moore*
The Revolt of the Black Athlete: 50th Anniversary Edition *Harry Edwards*
Pigskin Nation: How the NFL Remade American Politics *Jesse Berrett*
Hockey: A Global History *Stephen Hardy and Andrew C. Holman*

REPRINT EDITIONS
The Nazi Olympics *Richard D. Mandell*
Sports in the Western World (2d ed.) *William J. Baker*
Jesse Owens: An American Life *William J. Baker*

The University of Illinois Press
is a founding member of the
Association of American University Presses.

Designed by Jim Proefrock
Composed in 10.8/14 Scala Sans
with Trade Gothic display
at the University of Illinois Press
Cover designed by Jason Gabbert
Cover image: Puck image ©iStock.com/Garrett Aitken;
background image ©iStock.com/StockFinland.
Manufactured by Sheridan Books, Inc.

University of Illinois Press
1325 South Oak Street
Champaign, IL 61820-6903
www.press.uillinois.edu